Writing & Literacy in Early China

Writing & Literacy in Early China

Studies from the Columbia Early China Seminar

Edited by
Li Feng and David Prager Branner

University of Washington Press
Seattle & London

This project was supported by the Columbia University Seminars and the Chiang Ching-Kuo Foundation Inter-University Center for Sinology at Harvard University.

© 2011 Feng Li and David Prager Branner
Printed in the United States of America
Design and composition by Li Feng and David Prager Branner
16 15 14 13 12   5 4 3 2 1

All rights reserved. No part of this publication may be reproduced or transmitted in any form or by any means, electronic or mechanical, including photocopy, recording, or any information storage or retrieval system, without permission in writing from the publisher.

University of Washington Press
P.O. Box 50096, Seattle, WA 98145 U.S.A.
www.washington.edu/uwpress

Library of Congress Cataloging-in-Publication Data

Writing & literacy in early China : studies from the Columbia early China seminar / edited by Li Feng and David Prager Branner.
   p. cm.
   Includes bibliographical references and index.
   ISBN 978-0-295-99152-8 (hardback : alk. paper)
1. Chinese language—to 600. 2. Literacy—China—History.
3. Books and reading—China—History. I. Li, Feng, 1962–
II. Branner, David Prager.
PL1077.W65 2011
302.2'2440931—dc23   2011017770

The paper used in this publication is acid-free and meets the minimum requirements of American National Standard for Information Sciences—Permanence of Paper for Printed Library Materials, ANSI Z39.48-1984.∞

Contents

Acknowledgments	vii
Early China Chronology	viii
Map of Important Archaeological Sites	ix

Introduction: Writing as a Phenomenon of Literacy   3
   Li Feng and David Prager Branner

PART I: ORIGINS AND THE LINGUISTIC DIMENSION

Chapter 1. Getting "Right" with Heaven and the Origins of Writing in China   19
   David W. Pankenier

Chapter 2. Literacy and the Emergence of Writing in China   51
   William G. Boltz

Chapter 3. Phonology in the Chinese Script and Its Relationship to Early Chinese Literacy   85
   David Prager Branner

PART II: SCRIBAL TRAINING AND PRACTICE

Chapter 4. Literacy to the South and the East of Anyang in Shang China: Zhengzhou and Daxinzhuang   141
   Ken-ichi Takashima

Chapter 5. The Evidence for Scribal Training at Anyang   173
   Adam Smith

Chapter 6. Textual Identity and the Role of Literacy in the Transmission of Early Chinese Literature   206
   Matthias L. Richter

PART III: LITERACY AND SOCIAL CONTEXTS

Chapter 7. The Royal Audience and Its Reflections in Western
    Zhou Bronze Inscriptions   239
    Lothar von Falkenhausen

Chapter 8. Literacy and the Social Contexts of Writing in the
    Western Zhou   271
    Li Feng

Chapter 9. Education and the Way of the Former Kings   302
    Constance A. Cook

PART IV: THE EXTENT OF LITERACY IN THE EARLY EMPIRE

Chapter 10. Soldiers, Scribes, and Women: Literacy among the
    Lower Orders in Early China   339
    Robin D. S. Yates

Chapter 11. Craftsman's Literacy: Uses of Writing by Male and
    Female Artisans in Qin and Han China   370
    Anthony J. Barbieri-Low

Abbreviations   401
Bibliography   404
Contributors   443
Index   452

Acknowledgments

The editors express their deep appreciation to the Leonard Hastings Schoff Fund, University Seminars, Columbia University, for its help with this publication. The ideas presented have benefited from discussions in the Early China Seminar. We thank the Chiang Ching-Kuo Foundation for International Scholarly Exchange for its generous award of an additional publication subsidy to support this volume.

We are most grateful to the Chiang Ching-Kuo Foundation Inter-University Center for Sinology at Harvard University (formerly the Chiang Ching-Kuo Foundation Center for Chinese Cultural and Intellectual History at Columbia University) and to its director, David Der-Wei Wang, for having supported the Early China Seminar ever since its first days of life as well as this volume and the conference that preceded it.

We are also most indebted to our rapporteurs, Mr. Han-Peng Ho and Mr. Nicholas Vogt, and to the tireless staff of the University Seminars office at Columbia University. We thank particularly Nicholas Vogt for his assistance in the editing and publication of this book. Many members of the Early China Seminar have taken part in the discussions that led to this book. There are too many to name individually, but Martin Kern and Thomas H. C. Lee deserve special mention, for they both delivered papers on literacy at our meetings but were unable to continue as contributors to this book. We thank Jeremiah Trinidad-Christensen for providing us with the fine map included in this volume.

Lastly, we are grateful to Lorri Hagman, executive editor at the University of Washington Press, and Marilyn Trueblood, our managing editor, who have both enthusiastically supported this book and overseen its publication. We are also grateful to the mother of one of us, Shirley Prager Branner, who has devoted some five months of her time to compile the index. We thank, too, the individuals who provided illustrations for this book.

Li Feng and David Prager Branner
November 15, 2010
New York City

Early China Chronology

	Archaeological	Dynastic	
5000 B.C.E.	Yangshao 仰韶		
3000 B.C.E.			
	Longshan 龍山		2000 B.C.E.
1900 B.C.E.		Xia (?)	
	Erlitou 二里頭		1554 B.C.E.
1500 B.C.E.	Erligang 二里崗		
1300 B.C.E.		Shang	
1200 B.C.E.	Huanbei 洹北		
	Anyang 安陽		
1045 B.C.E.	Zhangjiapo 張家坡	Western Zhou	1045 B.C.E.
771 B.C.E.			771 B.C.E.
	Zhongzhoulu 中州路	Spring and Autumn	481 B.C.E.
		Warring States	
221 B.C.E.		Qin	221 B.C.E.
		Western Han	206 B.C.E.
		Eastern Han	25 C.E.
			220 C.E.

Map of Important Archaeological Sites

Writing & Literacy in Early China

Introduction: Writing as a Phenomenon of Literacy

Li Feng and David Prager Branner

From the very beginning, the contributors to this volume were thoroughly aware of the challenge it presents: in a time considered the formative stage of a certain civilization, when the population figure is largely unknown, it is difficult if not impossible to measure the level of literacy quantitatively. For instance, in the study of literacy in the Classical West, scholars have often had to find satisfaction in hazy terms such as "minimal," "tolerable," "widespread," "high," "remarkably high."[1] Only certain social institutions such as the Greek practice of ostracism and the Roman ballot law, which were by no means universal and which mandated the collective expression of political wills by a citizenry employing writing, offer some concrete ground for establishing an estimated percentage.[2] But even in modern times, the accuracy with which we estimate the literacy rate of a people or a region is often a matter of controversy, depending on which modern government we consider entitled to conduct a thorough survey, and perhaps even more on the definition by which literacy is measured.[3]

---

1. See, e.g., William V. Harris, *Ancient Literacy* (Cambridge, Mass.: Harvard University Press, 1989), 7, 94, 139, 151, 169, and 173.
2. The Athenian practice of ostracism, which required citizens to cast a written vote, allows modern historians to estimate the rate of literacy among the population of Attica at between 5 percent and 10 percent during the fifth and fourth centuries B.C.E., and the use of written ballots in Rome allows an estimate of the literacy level in the Roman Republic near but not exceeding 10 percent in the second and early first centuries B.C.E. Harris, *Ancient Literacy*, 114, 167–73.
3. For instance, in 1958, the United Nations Educational, Scientific, and Cultural Organization (UNESCO) defined an illiterate person as someone "who cannot with understanding both read and write a short simple statement of his everyday life"; Harris, *Ancient Literacy*, 3. In 1950, the People's Congress in China defined literacy as the ability to read and use 1,000 characters, and the standard was raised to 1,500 later; see Evelyn Sakakida Rawski, *Education and Popular Literacy in Ch'ing China* (Ann Arbor: University of Michigan Press, 1979), 3. Further, "Ordinances for Eliminating Illiteracy" issued by the Ministry of Education in the People's Republic of China (PRC)

Fortunately, numerical estimation is not the only method by which to assay human life. There are other social and cultural dimensions along which we can assess the extent of literacy in a particular given time in history. The most obvious way is to look at literacy's hold on different social groups that were either ranked by their wealth and social influence or arranged in accordance with their occupational roles. This is because, historically, literacy tended to develop first at the higher strata of a society and among groups that were closer to the center of power, discerning literacy's extension to the socially peripheral and less significant groups provides a concrete sense of its prevalence in a society. Literacy may also be measured in terms of its "strength" in penetrating cultural borders (even language barriers) — a point that is particularly relevant to the study of literacy in the Bronze Age, in a setting in which interlays between different cultures were routine.[4] Similarly, literacy can be measured by its expansion over geographic space, often stretching from the center of a literate society to more distant localities. Within a society that had developed a certain level of literacy, however, different spheres of social activity constitute another important scale along which to assess the extent of literacy. Surely, too, the degree of literacy in a society may be evaluated with regard to the range of literary works it produced and the level of literary excellence such works achieved. All of these dimensions of literacy need extensive research in order to illuminate their specific historical and regional contexts. This volume offers a series of such concrete and original efforts in the context of Early China, which we date from the Neolithic to 220 C.E.

Writing as Literacy

Therefore, our most urgent concern is not what percentage of the population in any period of Early China could read and write — although that is certainly also within the purview of this volume — but specifically

---

    in 1988 (revised in 1993) determined the standard of individual literacy to be the ability to read, for peasants, 1,500 characters or, for workers and city-town residents, 2,000 characters; to read with comprehension newspapers and magazines in plain language; to make simple accounting records; and to perform simple business writing. http://www.moe.edu.cn/edoas/website18/15/info3915.htm (accessed 5 January 2010).

4. See, e.g., Li Feng, "Literacy Crossing Cultural Borders: Evidence from the Bronze Inscriptions of the Western Zhou Period (1045–771 B.C.)," *Bulletin of the Museum of Far Eastern Antiquity* 74 (2002): 210–42.

who actually read and wrote, where and under what conditions they did so, what it was they read and wrote, and how well or poorly they read. The casting of this broad line of research is largely in agreement with the concept of literacy adopted in many recent studies of literacies in Western contexts, which tend to redefine it as "an activity embedded in cultural and social practice" and "something to be employed, and employed in diverse ways for activities which are meaningful in some way for individuals and communities."[5] Therefore, literacy is understood here, not merely as the "skill" of writing and reading, but as a phenomenon possessing multiple social extensions and serving multiple contexts within which it is meaningful and by which it can be measured. The extent of literacy, understood in this way, would refer to the range of literary activities across variously demarcated social and cultural distinctions.

Writing is the foundation of literacy, because essentially everything that is written is intended to be read. Although all scholars can agree that writing and reading are two inseparable processes in the acquisition of literacy, the relationship between them is not entirely straightforward or immune to debate. William Boltz suggests that in a developmental process some kind of literacy can arise even before writing emerges, relating to a preexisting graphic notation system; in this sense, literacy of some kind is even necessary for the rise of true writing.[6] For historical linguists, literacy may mean reading alone, without the action of writing, or (even more narrowly) the process of recognizing and making use of the written script as a form of phonetic transcription.[7] Indeed, studies show that many societies have achieved a much higher level of ability in reading than in writing, and there are examples of non-writing readers in many cultures that have developed a basic level of literacy.[8] On the one hand, literacy certainly has an oral element when reading is directed to an audience that needs to hear the content of the written words. On the other hand, reading does not necessarily require pronouncing aloud; it can be a silent process in which the reader makes purely mental connections between the written

---

5. Rosalind Thomas, "Writing, Reading, Public and Private 'Literacies': Functional Literacy and Democratic Literacy," in *Ancient Literacies: The Culture of Reading in Greece and Rome*, ed. William A. Johnson and Holt N. Parker (Oxford: Oxford University Press, 2009), 13.
6. See William G. Boltz, "Literacy and the Emergence of Writing in China," chapter 2 in this volume, 51-84.
7. See David Prager Branner, "Phonology in the Chinese Script and Its Relationship to Early Chinese Literacy," chapter 3 in this volume, 85-137.
8. Harris, *Ancient Literacy*, 4–5.

script and the required sounds that he or she does read aloud at some other time. However, no matter in what manner one is supposed to read, there can be no reading without the written word as basis. Therefore, reading and literacy defined broadly can be regarded as essentially "text-oriented events,"[9] which emerge from direct connections with the written word.

This point is very important and indeed less problematic in the study of early literacy than in study of the more developed stage. With absolutely no chance to observe how the ancients actually read and pronounced words, we have recourse only to the extant written forms if we are to know how they were read or were intended to be read. Written documents from Early China are therefore the foundation of this study of literacy in Early China and are examined with methodologies appropriate to different disciplines.

The Purpose of This Book

It is an embarrassment that so little study has been undertaken of the development of literacy in a civilization such as China's, supremely devoted as it is to the values of writing and reading. The only Western book that systematically discusses literacy in traditional China is Evelyn Rawski's 1979 study of the Qing period (1644–1911).[10] There is nothing on the topic for any time earlier than the late empire, although in the past fifty years, substantial interest has developed in the area of the study of writing, primarily in pre-imperial China, and education, focused largely on imperial China. Research on the latter aspect has been conducted mainly in the discipline of history or intellectual history,[11] while research on the

---

9. See William A. Johnson and Holt N. Parker, eds., *Ancient Literacies: The Culture of Reading in Greece and Rome* (Oxford: Oxford University Press, 2009), 3.
10. Rawski estimated on the basis of her extensive research that male literacy under the Qing empire had achieved a level of 30–45 percent, and female literacy was 2–10 percent. So an average figure of 16–27.5 percent can be deduced for the literacy rate of the whole population; Rawski, *Education and Popular Literacy*, 22–23, 140. In comparison, in preindustrial England, the adult literacy level during the period of 1580–1700 was nowhere higher than 20 percent; Harris, *Ancient Literacy*, 22.
11. By way of just a few examples, see William Theodore de Bary and John W. Chaffee, eds., *Neo-Confucian Education: The Formative Stage* (Berkeley: University of California Press, 1989); Benjamin A. Elman and Alexander Woodside, eds., *Education and Society in Late Imperial China, 1600–1900* (Berkeley: University of California Press, 1994). See also Thomas H.C. Lee, *Education in Traditional China: A History* (Leiden: Brill, 2000).

former aspect has involved much broad and multidisciplinary effort. Historians and philologists make up the two largest groups of scholars who are concerned with the development of the writing system and its cultural-historical roles in Early China. Combining disciplinary training in both history and philology, the subject of writing has also been explored, often more intensively, in the subfield of paleography. Since most of the sources of writing as paleography emerged from the archaeological context, archaeologists also play a constructive role in the study of the writing system, particularly on the issue of the writing's origin. Furthermore, because a large quantity of written materials in the form of text-manuscript (some of which have transmitted counterparts) have been excavated from Warring States tombs in the last thirty years, research interest has also taken hold among scholars of literature and philosophy who wish to explore the role of writing in the transmission of the various philosophical and literary texts from pre-imperial to early imperial times.

In this volume, scholars with substantial research experience in the various disciplines mentioned above explore the problem of literacy in Early China from the unique perspectives of their individual fields. Operating with a broad concept of literacy as a cultural phenomenon that is based on writing and has the multiple social extensions enumerated above, our general goal is to offer the first coordinated multidisciplinary understanding of the rise, condition, extent, and expansion of literacy in Early China. In support of this general goal, we ask a wide range of specific and often interrelated questions that fall largely into the following four categories: (1) the circumstances that gave rise to literacy and the possible stages in the invention of the Chinese writing system; (2) the methods and ways by which literacy was acquired in Early China and factors that influenced the learning process; (3) the qualification of our current evidence for literacy and the multiple social spheres it represents; and (4) the extent of literacy across regions, classes, genders, and professional social groups.

It is not our purpose, however, to produce a unified interpretation of literacy in Early China; on the contrary, we fully understand the need to preserve the fresh, distinct voices that have gone into a collaborative project. The project was carried out within an institutional structure, the Columbia University Seminar on Early China that gave rise to this book. Standing at the beginning of a very promising field of research, we hope that the preliminary conclusions presented here will open up new topics and raise new questions for deeper exploration in the future.

The Early China Seminar and the Literacy Project

The Early China Seminar is one of ninety University Seminars currently meeting on the Columbia campus. Outwardly, they appear to be the same as any other academic lecture series, but they are not a lecture series, nor are they "seminars" in the sense of research colloquia. Strictly speaking, they are part of an intellectual movement with a "missionary" element.[12] The University Seminars were founded after World War II, not limited to the Academy and not for students but intended to foster interaction between faculty and the larger world. They were brought into being by the historian and sociologist Frank Tannenbaum (1893–1969), who said that he wanted to add "to the ancient and honorable house of learning . . . a fourth dimension: . . . [to] accumulate, preserve, transmit, and focus knowledge upon some specific issue."[13]

In a word, University Seminars are intended to foster wide-ranging synthesis. Tannenbaum's biographer, Joseph Maier, describes their principles in the early decades this way:

> The "seminar" technique was a way favored by Tannenbaum in looking at a problem. As he defined it, it had to be a multi-disciplinary and Socratic analysis. One found one's ignorance by putting oneself and one's colleagues "on the rack." One arrived at understanding of a problem, not its solution, by seeing it from different angles of vision. . . . The technique in each of the seminars was to pose a problem, for example, political stability, economic advancement, the impact of United States diplomacy, or the role of the soldier, and to discuss it with students and non-students of different backgrounds.[14]

---

12. The Seminars are missionary in the same way that Columbia's renowned Contemporary Civilization curriculum for undergraduate discussion of "great books" is missionary. Contemporary Civilization was created in the sober aftermath of World War I, in the words of John Coss, to "introduce the students to the insistent problems of to-day through acquainting them with the materials of their situation: nature's resources and human nature and its recent history"; it became the model for similar programs at countless other colleges in the decades that followed. See John J. Coss, "The New Freshman Course in Columbia College," *Columbia University Quarterly* 21 (1919): 248; cited in Timothy P. Cross, *An Oasis of Order: The Core Curriculum at Columbia College* (New York: Columbia University, Columbia College, 1995), 12.
13. Frank Tannenbaum, "Origin, Growth, and Theory of the University Seminar Movement," in *Community of Scholars: The University Seminars at Columbia*, ed. Frank Tannenbaum (New York: Praeger, 1965), 3–45, esp. 6. This entire book documents the idealistic (and missionary) intellectual atmosphere at Columbia in the two decades after World War II.
14. Joseph Maier, *Frank Tannenbaum: A Biographical Essay* (New York: University

At its founding, the Early China Seminar had no such clearly defined problem. In late February 2002, Li Feng, a historian and archaeologist newly hired at the Department of East Asian Languages and Cultures, persuaded Robert L. Belknap, director of the University Seminars, of the urgency of creating a scholarly forum within the University Seminar structure, in order to bring archaeological discoveries in China to the Columbia campus and to discuss the problems they raise on a continuing basis.[15] Its inaugural meeting was held on September 21, 2002, and its founding members included six New York–area scholars associated in one way or another with Columbia and representing a diverse range of disciplines, with various interests in history, archaeology, art history, literature and language, religion and philosophy: Moss Roberts, Elizabeth Childs-Johnson, John Major, Gopal Sukhu, Li Feng, and David Prager Branner. All of the members were discontented with the fact that American sinology had become dominated by attention to later periods, and all believed that the study of Early China should have a strong position in our academic inquiry. With the generous support of the Chiang Ching-Kuo Foundation Center for Chinese Cultural and Intellectual History at Columbia (since fall 2005, the Chiang Ching-Kuo Foundation Inter-University Center for Sinology at Harvard) and the University Seminars Office of Columbia University, it quickly became the main forum for discussion of Early China scholarship on the East Coast. Sinologists and archaeologists from all over the world discussed their research — some dozen each year — with growing emphasis on new archaeological discoveries and their implications. But there was still no central "problem."

The idea that literacy could serve as a suitable focus of the Seminar's attention first arose on 3 December 2005 over lunch at Ollie's Noodle Shop and Grill before a presentation on the *Huainanzi* by John Major (chair in 2002–3). Constance A. Cook and Sarah Allan were parties to the conversation, along with Major, Li, and Branner. In spring 2006, Li and Branner, then co-chairs of the Seminar, mapped out a three-year project on

---

Seminars, Columbia University, 1974), 37.
15. Before that, a small Early China study group met once in late 2001, hosted by Elizabeth Childs-Johnson in her apartment on the West Side in New York, and another time in February 2002, hosted by Li Feng in Kent Hall, Columbia University. These activities gave rise to the idea of establishing a long-term seminar, but at that time, it was not clear whether institutional support could be found for it.

the subject and began to solicit papers from members on any aspect of literacy in Early China, to be delivered and discussed over the next two years. This plan resulted in a series of ten presentations in the Seminar between September 2006 and May 2008, under the general project title "Literacy and Social Uses of Writing in Early China." Most of those papers, together with some new ones, were then substantially revised in light of the Seminar's discussions and presented at the project's concluding conference on 7–8 February 2009. After that, the papers were revised once more as a result of the conference discussions and an intensive process of collegial review and criticism.

The volume you see before you is the result of this long and carefully executed project. Or, it would be better to say, this volume is the culmination of our discussions so far, conducted in the hope of achieving the first multifaceted assessment of the condition of literacy in pre-imperial and early imperial China.

The Specific Contributions of This Book

This book's specific contributions lie in the following areas: the invention of writing, the relationship between language and writing, the practice of literacy among the elites, the extension of literacy into the rest of society, and issues connected with scribes and scribal training.

Two chapters deal with the ultimate origins of writing and literacy, a highly contentious issue in the study of early civilizations. David W. Pankenier, in chapter 1, "Getting 'Right' with Heaven and the Origins of Writing in China," studies archaeological examples such as the recently discovered Taosi 陶寺 Neolithic astronomical "observatory," seeking the origins of Chinese writing in a calendrical notational system somewhat like the *khipu* used by Inka astrologers.[16] He argues that such a system of notation must have been indispensable to the operation of the observatory and identifies remnants of graphic signs that possibly were once used in the Shang oracle bone inscriptions. He also proposes that the *gānzhī* 干支 dating system shows evidence of having once been a mnemonic rhyme, oral in nature, and that the form of the heavenly stem *dīng* 丁 originated in the shape of a constellation that was once of vital importance to

---

16. "Inka" and "*khipu*" are the preferred Aymara and Quechua spellings of these words. Other spellings commonly seen include "Inca" and "*Quipu*."

astronomical timekeeping. Pankenier notes further the recently reported finding of Neolithic signs from Shuangdun 雙墩 in Anhui that might have belonged to a certain sign system adopted by more than one site in the region.[17] In chapter 2, "Literacy and the Emergence of Writing in China," William G. Boltz, drawing on Middle Eastern examples, seeks a preexisting notational system that determined the semantic values of signs in that system. According to this theory, the moment of writing arrived when certain signs in the system began to gain phonetic values. Boltz sees indexicality as the key to the development of writing systems and suggests that two kinds of literacy should be defined: one associated with a "prewriting notational system" and the other with "true glottographic writing." Boltz, analyzing examples from the Shang oracle bone inscriptions, offers evidence of very early "polyphonic" signs (one graph representing more than one word) or "indexical" signs (application of an existing graph to another word suggested by the graph's form) such as the graph 禾, used to represent both the usual word *hé* 'grain' and *nián* 年 'harvest', and 卜, used to represent both *bǔ* 'to practice bone-divination' and *wài* 外 'outer'. For Boltz, this polyphony implies that the Shang script was "close structurally, and perhaps also temporally, to the formative stage of the writing system overall."

Linguistic evidence for the spread of literacy is treated in two chapters. In chapter 3, "Phonology in the Chinese Script and Its Relationship to Early Chinese Literacy," David Prager Branner examines two modern theories about the role of phonological content in the structure of the

---

17. Previously, two Neolithic pottery shards were known to carry multiple incised signs. The first was found in a Longshan period center at Dinggong 丁公 in Shandong, and it renders eleven graphs in five columns; the second, from Longqiuzhuang 龍虬莊, a Liangzhu culture site in Jiangsu, has four rows, each clearly depicting a certain animal preceded by a graphic sign ahead (left) of it. While their relations to a possible Neolithic writing system or systems in China are hotly debated, future analysis of such materials will benefit from the contributions of Boltz and Pankenier here. For published views on the two shards, see Qiu Xigui 裘錫圭, "Jiujing shibushi wenzi: Tantan woguo xin shiqi shidai shiyong de fuhao" 究竟是不是文字 — 談談我國新石器時代使用的符號, *Wenwu tiandi* 1993.2, 26–30; Feng Shi 馮時, "Shandong Dinggong Longshan shidai wenzi jiedu" 山東丁公龍山時代文字解讀, *Kaogu* 1994.1, 37–54; Matsumaru Michio 松丸道雄, "Kanji kigen mondai no shintenkai: Santō shō Suihei ken shutsudo no 'Teikō tōhen' o megutte" 漢字起源問題の新展開 — 山東省鄒平縣出土の「丁公陶片」をめぐって, in *Chūgoku kodai no moji to bunka* 中國古代の文字と文化 (Tokyo: Kyūko Shoin 汲古書院, 1999), 3–29.

Chinese script: the "crypto-phonogram" hypothesis, which holds that every compound character must have some component that is ultimately phonetic in nature, and the "protoform" hypothesis, which seeks to decipher ancient graphs as known words in the Chinese language of recent times. Both are difficult to falsify, but both support the idea that the phonological system embodied in the early script is far less finely specified and more simply functional than has previously been believed. Branner maintains that such a rough system of phonological representation would have aided the spread of literacy in Early China's linguistically diverse world, across which any notion of a standard spoken language would have been difficult to promulgate. In chapter 3, "Literacy to the South and East of Anyang in Shang China," Ken-ichi Takashima examines oracle bone inscriptions from Zhengzhou 鄭州 and Daxinzhuang 大辛莊, situated at a distance from Anyang 安陽, the dominant center of inscriptions in the Shang. He concludes that scribes in both places had traditions of literacy separate from that of Anyang although perhaps originally related to it at an earlier period. In addition to the early geographic transmission of literacy, Takashima also documents in Anyang inscriptions some evidence for the influence of non-Anyang local dialects that might have been spoken by diviners from different regions.

Six chapters of the book demonstrate the process of literacy's expansion in Early China after the initial invention of the Chinese writing system. On one hand, Adam Smith, in chapter 5, "The Evidence for Scribal Training at Anyang," offers examples of "practice engraving" on bones, which, he argues, was done by people who were learning to write for the first time rather than by literate people learning to carve for the first time — a conclusion he feels is compatible with the supposition that literacy was socially quite restricted during the late Shang. On the other hand, Takashima's chapter shows that, geographically, literacy was not limited to Anyang even if, socially, it may have been quite restricted. The Western Zhou, however, was certainly a critical time for the spread of literacy, as modern excavation has unearthed bronzes from that period with longer inscriptions and from a much larger geographic space in northern China than from earlier eras. Chapter 8, "Literacy and the Social Contexts of Writing in the Western Zhou," by Li Feng, shows that literacy had penetrated various social spheres by then and was by no means restricted to religious use. It had clearly begun playing an indispensable role in the management of the Western Zhou state and social life. Li's chapter suggests that, in contrast to the restriction of literacy to professional scribal groups as in Shang, a much wider readership existed among the Western Zhou elites who needed to use and appreciated the art of writing. By the Eastern Zhou period, as Constance A. Cook demonstrates in chapter 9, "Education and the Way of the Former Kings," literacy combined with the ritual culture of the royal Zhou had become an essential basis of learning for elite youth even in formerly peripheral areas such as the lower and middle Yangzi regions. Further expansion of literacy to the lower classes under the early empires is substantially discussed in chapter 10, "Soldiers, Scribes, and Women," by Robin D. S. Yates and chapter 11, "Craftsman's Literacy," by Anthony Barbieri-Low.

In this regard, a number of conceptual tools have been discussed in this book as ways of characterizing literacy of different magnitudes or at different levels, although we are aware that at present, such quantitative measurement is impossible for Early China. These conceptual tools include scribal literacy, elite literacy, craftsman's literacy, functional literacy, professional literacy, and mass literacy. Mass literacy was never achieved anywhere in the ancient world, but functional literacy is now shown to have been far more widespread in China than has been previously believed — at the latest, by the time of the early empire. In chapter 10, Yates reviews evidence from a variety of recently excavated bamboo manuscripts and shows that at least some ordinary people, including soldiers and their families, merchants, and women as well as men, were functionally literate in the Qin and Han periods. He further shows that as the state bureaucracy required the population to be semi-literate in order to better control and exploit them, people soon found ways of manipulating the skill to their advantage and even used it as a node of resistance by which to "subvert the aims of the state." In chapter 11, Anthony Barbieri-Low reviews the evidence that some female and male craftsmen were able to write and inscribe their names and even short sentences on the products they produced in the Qin and Han. He argues that artisans in early imperial China were compelled by the state to become functionally literate through regulations and processes similar to those described by Yates for soldiers and heads of households. He further asserts that most of the 130,285 officials employed by the Han government in 5 B.C.E. may safely be assumed to have been functionally or fully literate.

The expression of literacy in both oral and written forms and the interplay between the two entities are fully discussed in a number of chapters. Lothar von Falkenhausen, in chapter 7, "The Royal Audience and Its Reflection in Western Zhou Bronze Inscriptions," proposes that certain long bronze inscriptions transcribe actual dialogues, possibly in a highly formal register, between the person responsible for casting the bronze and his royal patron. Through identifying the originally "oral" segments in the inscriptions, Falkenhausen offers a new way of reconstructing the process by which the inscription texts were produced. For Cook, the process of learning literacy was originally inseparable from the physical or even oral imitation of the so-called awesome decorum of the formal kings. In a slightly different way, Li offers a concrete example of a document with judicial power originally read and signed by officials during an inter-polity conference that was afterward cast onto a bronze that still presents the signature line of the original document.

Scribal training and its importance for transmitted written documents is another important issue discussed in the volume. The contributions of Takashima and Smith have already been mentioned above. Matthias L. Richter reviews the material features of two manuscripts from Mawangdui 馬王堆 in chapter 6, "Textual Identity and the Role of Literacy in the Transmission of Early Chinese Literature," and concludes that Manuscript A was intended for actual reading, while Manuscript B was meant primarily to be beautiful. Both functions, Richter suggests, could have played roles in the transmission of the text. Identifying certain reading marks in the manuscripts, he calls for patience in recovering the actual practice of "reading competence," which, he contends, is best pursued through the study of individual manuscripts.

To recapitulate, it is the consensus of all contributors to this book that, although it remained the preserve of a privileged few over most of the period, literacy expanded continuously in Early China. In particular, functional literacy is now shown to have been far more widespread in Early China than had been believed. It existed among the working classes during the Han and was present even during the Western Zhou in the entire, diverse social context of the bronzes. In its earliest stages, Chinese writing may have been connected with astronomical observation, but by the late Shang, literacy does not seem to have been restricted to Anyang even as it remained restricted socially. The distinctive structure of the Chinese script itself seems to have favored its use across a range of linguistically diverse communities. The spread of literacy seems to have gone in two directions: both outward from the political center beginning in the Shang and gaining speed in the Western Zhou and downward from those who were close to power to those who were exploited by them.

INTRODUCTION 15

In spite of the many conclusions this book suggests or demonstrates, it is not a summary of the nature of literacy in Early China, sealed, final, and ready to be entombed. It is, we hope, the first of a series of probes into the darkness.

PART I

Origins and the Linguistic Dimension

CHAPTER 1

Getting "Right" with Heaven and the Origins of Writing in China

David W. Pankenier

It has long been recognized that the *tiāngān dìzhī* 天干地支, or "heavenly stems" and "earthly branches," may provide a clue to the origins of the Chinese writing system. Indeed, it is probable that the ten stems and twelve branches are the most archaic remnant of a very early stage of written Chinese.[1] Even though some appear originally to have had concrete referents or to bear a resemblance to Shang graphs whose meaning is known, the one and only application of the binary *gānzhī* 干支 combinations is as ordinals and, uniquely in the case of the ten stems, as cultic appellations for the royal ancestors. As Edwin G. Pulleyblank remarked:

> The curious thing about these twenty-two signs is that neither the graphs nor the names attached to them have any separate meaning. Their meaning is simply the order in which they occur in the series to which they belong. It is true that a few of the characters are also used to write other homophonous words, but these are a small minority and such words have no apparent relation to the cyclical signs as such.[2]

---

1. Recent studies of the origins of writing in East Asia include Robert Bagley, "Anyang Writing and the Origin of the Chinese Writing System," in *The First Writing: Script Invention as History and Process*, ed. Stephen D. Houston (Cambridge: Cambridge University Press, 2008), 190–249; William G. Boltz, *The Origin and Early Development of the Chinese Writing System* (New Haven, Conn.: American Oriental Society, 1994); Victor H. Mair, "Language and Script: Biology, Archaeology, and (Pre)history," *International Review of Chinese Linguistics* 1.1 (1996), 33b of 31a–41b.
2. Edwin G. Pulleyblank, "The *Ganzhi* as Phonograms and Their Application to the Calendar," *Early China* 16 (1991), 39–80. See also Mikhail Kryukov, "K probleme

These unique characteristics suggest that by the Yinxu 殷墟 period in late Shang (late thirteenth–mid-eleventh century B.C.E.), any semantic origins of these cyclical signs were obscure. Indeed, if traditional historiography is any guide, the ten stems were already being used as (posthumous?) royal appellations by the rulers of Xia 夏. This would mean that their invention predates the appearance in the archaeological record of the oracle bone script by several hundred years.

The Cyclical Signs and the Early Calendar

It has been suggested that the origin of the stems and branches may be traced to their use in the late Shang ancestral cult, but this is a minority opinion.[3] The calendrical use of the cyclical signs is considerably more archaic and may have originated in a pre-Shang culture. Moreover, it is difficult to understand why, given an imperative to devise ordinal designations for the deceased ancestors, signs lacking separate meanings like the ten stems would have been adopted *unless* they possessed a special significance by virtue of their very archaism, or because of their supposed numinous origins or connection with temporal power and authority (viz., the calendar).[4] Arbitrariness in the initial choice of signs to represent numbers is well documented (e.g., in cuneiform) and illustrates the

---

tsiklicheskikh znakov v Drevnem Kitae," in *Drevnye sistemy pis'ma—etnicheskaja semiotika,* ed. Ju.V. Knorozov (Moscow: Nauka, 1986), 107–113.

3. Cf. Nicholas Postgate, Tao Wang, and Toby Wilkinson, "The Evidence for Early Writing: Utilitarian or Ceremonial?" *Antiquity* 69 (1995): 463. In William G. Boltz's view, "We cannot assume writing to have arisen in an exclusively religious context"; "Language and Writing," in *The Cambridge History of Ancient China: From the Origins of Civilization to 221 b.c.,* ed. Michael Loewe and Edward L. Shaughnessy (Cambridge: Cambridge University Press, 1999), 108. Cf. David N. Keightley, "The Origins of Writing in China: Scripts and Cultural Contexts," in *The Origins of Writing,* ed. W. M. Senner (Lincoln: University of Nebraska Press, 1989), 197. After critical review of such proposals, Robert W. Bagley concludes: "The idea that writing in China was confined to the ritual context in which we first encounter it, though firmly embedded in the literature, has no basis"; Bagley, "Anyang Writing," 226.
4. On this point, David N. Keightley says: "The Shang ritualists were . . . certainly calendar, day, and sun watchers, whose temporal and jurisdictional concerns were sanctified by profound religious assumptions." See David N. Keightley, *The Ancestral Landscape: Time, Space, and Community in Late Shang China (ca. 1200–1045 B.C.)* (Berkeley, Calif.: Institute of East Asian Studies, 2000), 51. The conventional interpretation of the ten stems as denoting the mythical solar progenitors of royal Shang clans elides the question of their origin as written signs.

essential independence of writing in being able to represent ideas directly — ideographic writing was not initially a "graphic echo of speech."[5] There is still no scholarly consensus on how the Shang kings' temple names were chosen or why they were selectively adopted, though perhaps the original ordinal significance of the signs was being invoked in some way, even if the information thus encoded is now obscure.[6] It is also true that some stems were thought more auspicious than others, which was certainly the case later.[7]

Calendrical Notation as a Cultural Imperative

Figure 1.1 shows the layout of the solar observation platform attached to the southeast wall of the middle period city recently excavated at Xiangfen 襄汾, Taosi 陶寺, in Shanxi. This unprecedented discovery dates from around 2100 B.C.E. and is both the earliest and the most elaborate Neolithic or Bronze Age structure ever discovered in China that was unequivocally dedicated to astronomical observation. The structure outlined in the drawing originally consisted of a curved rammed-earth wall, facing east-southeast, perched atop three concentric rammed-earth terraces.

---

5. "Writing was, after all, an attempt to represent the message visually, not the sounds associated with a narrative version of the same message." See Merlin Donald, *The Origins of the Modern Mind: Three Stages in the Evolution of Culture and Cognition* (Cambridge, Mass.: Harvard University Press, 1991), 294. My intentional use of the disputed term "ideograph" is informed by Merlin Donald's discussion of the neuropsychological evidence for the independence of visual and phonological reading; ibid., 300ff.
6. Kwang-chih Chang's analysis ruled out the possibility that the heavenly stems in posthumous royal appellations were assigned on the basis of birth or death dates, because the sequence of posthumous temple names is anything but random. Instead, Chang proposed, "the Shang royal lineages were organized into ten ritual units, named after the ten *gān*-signs (day-signs). Kings were selected from various units and were named posthumously according to their day-sign units, which also regulated the rituals performed to them." See K.C. Chang, *Shang Civilization* (New Haven, Conn.: Yale University Press, 1980), 169, 172. David N. Keightley has offered an alternative conjecture in *The Ancestral Landscape*, 35.
7. Keightley, *The Ancestral Landscape*, 33. K.C. Chang's tabulation of 1,295 bronze inscriptions with ancestral names containing heavenly stems showed that the even-numbered stems (*yǐ* 乙, *dīng* 丁, *jǐ* 己, *xīn* 辛, *guǐ* 癸) were far and away the more preferred, and of these, the first two outstripped the others in frequency by a wide margin; see Chang, *Shang Civilization*, 169–70.

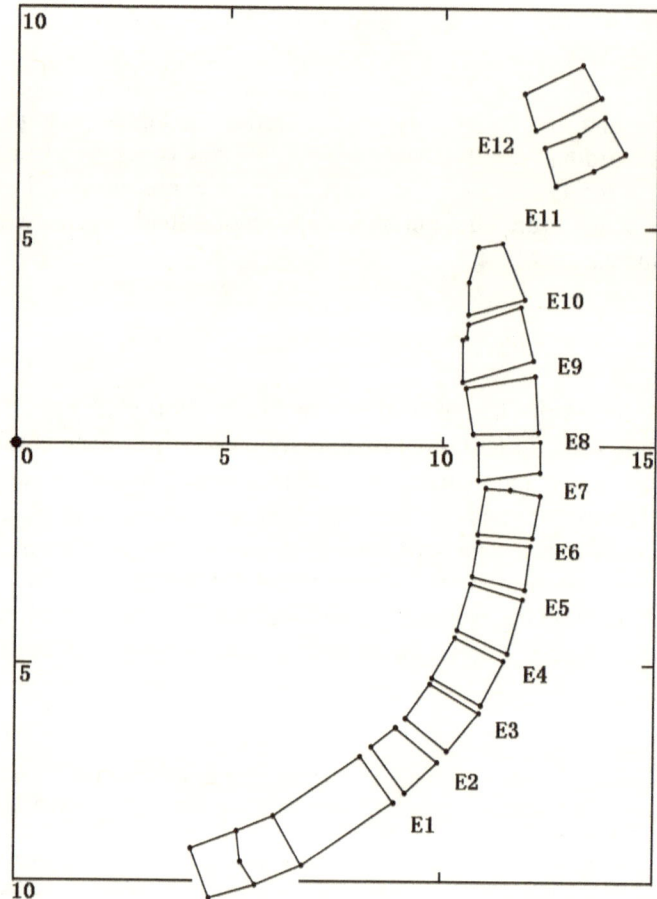

Figure 1.1. Scale drawing of the Taosi solar-observing apertures and observation point "0" (scale is in meters). After Pankenier et al., "The Xiangfen, Taosi Site: A Chinese Neolithic Observatory?" Drawing courtesy of Liu Ciyuan.

The curved wall was perforated by narrow slits, forming an array of twelve pillars. The spot marked by the dot on the left edge of the drawing is about ten meters from the wall. The spot marks the location of a small, round, rammed-earth pedestal from which observations were intended to be made through slits in the wall opposite as the sun rose above the mountain ridge to the east. Analysis has shown that this structure would have permitted its users to devise a calendar based on the movements of the rising sun along

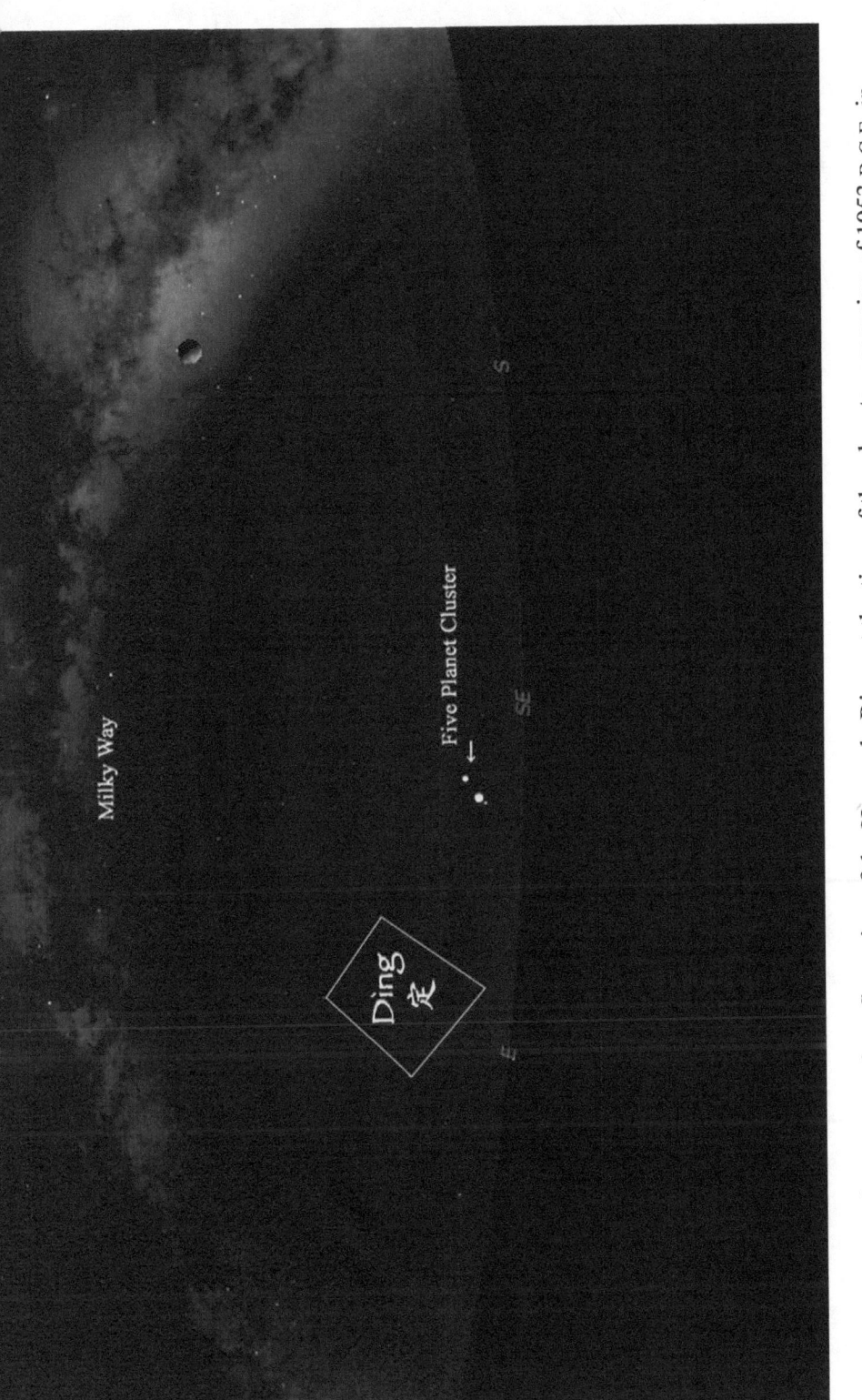

Plate 1 The unique seasonal configuration of the Heavenly River at the time of the planetary massing of 1953 B.C.E. in Ding, the Celestial Temple. Starry Night Pro 5.

Plate 2 Rejoined plastron from Daxinzhuang (T2302⑤B:1). Scanned image of original photograph courtesy of the Institute of Eastern Archaeology, Shandong University.

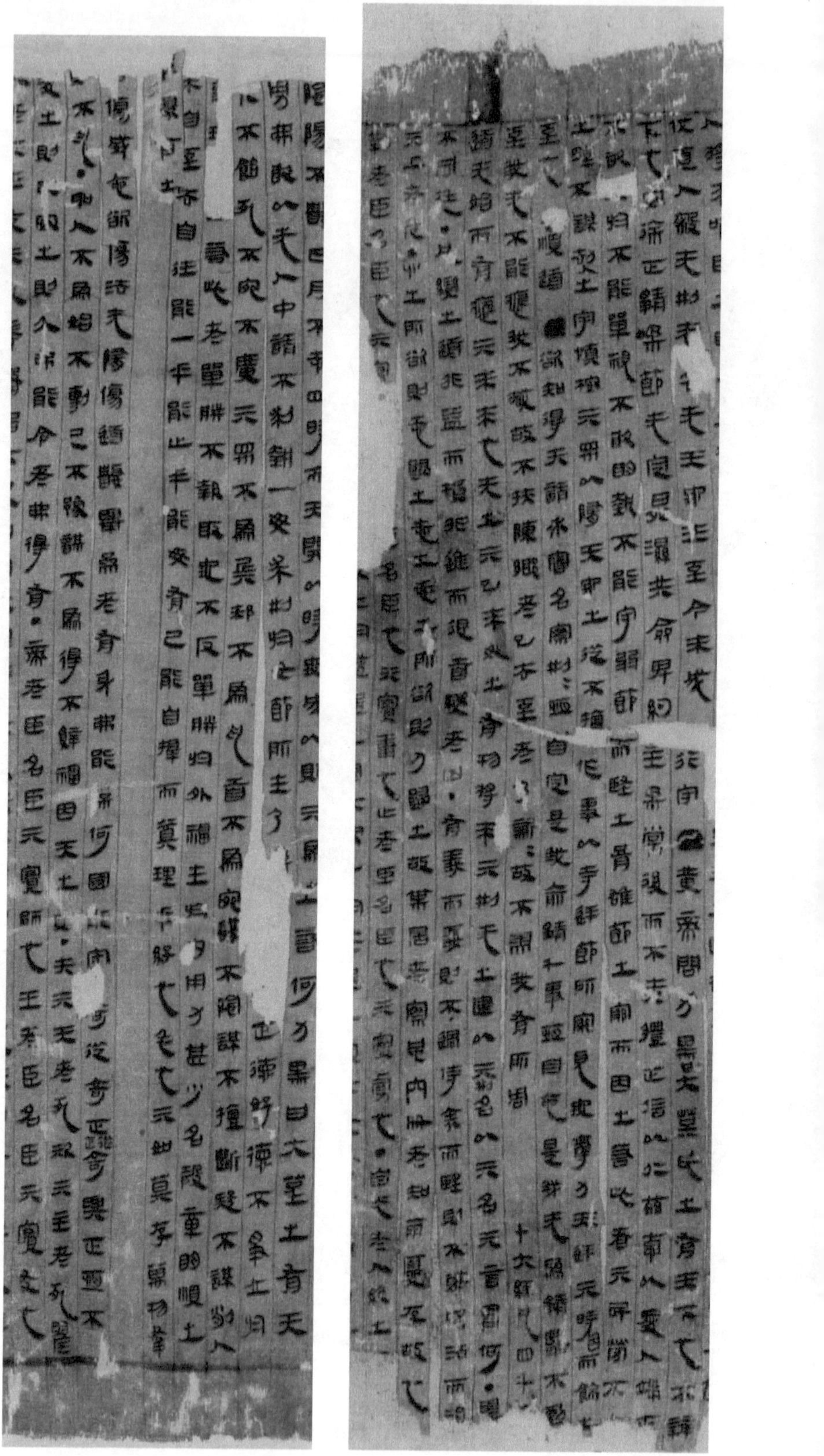

Plate 4 Fragments of Manuscript B (upper half of column to the right, lower half to the left)

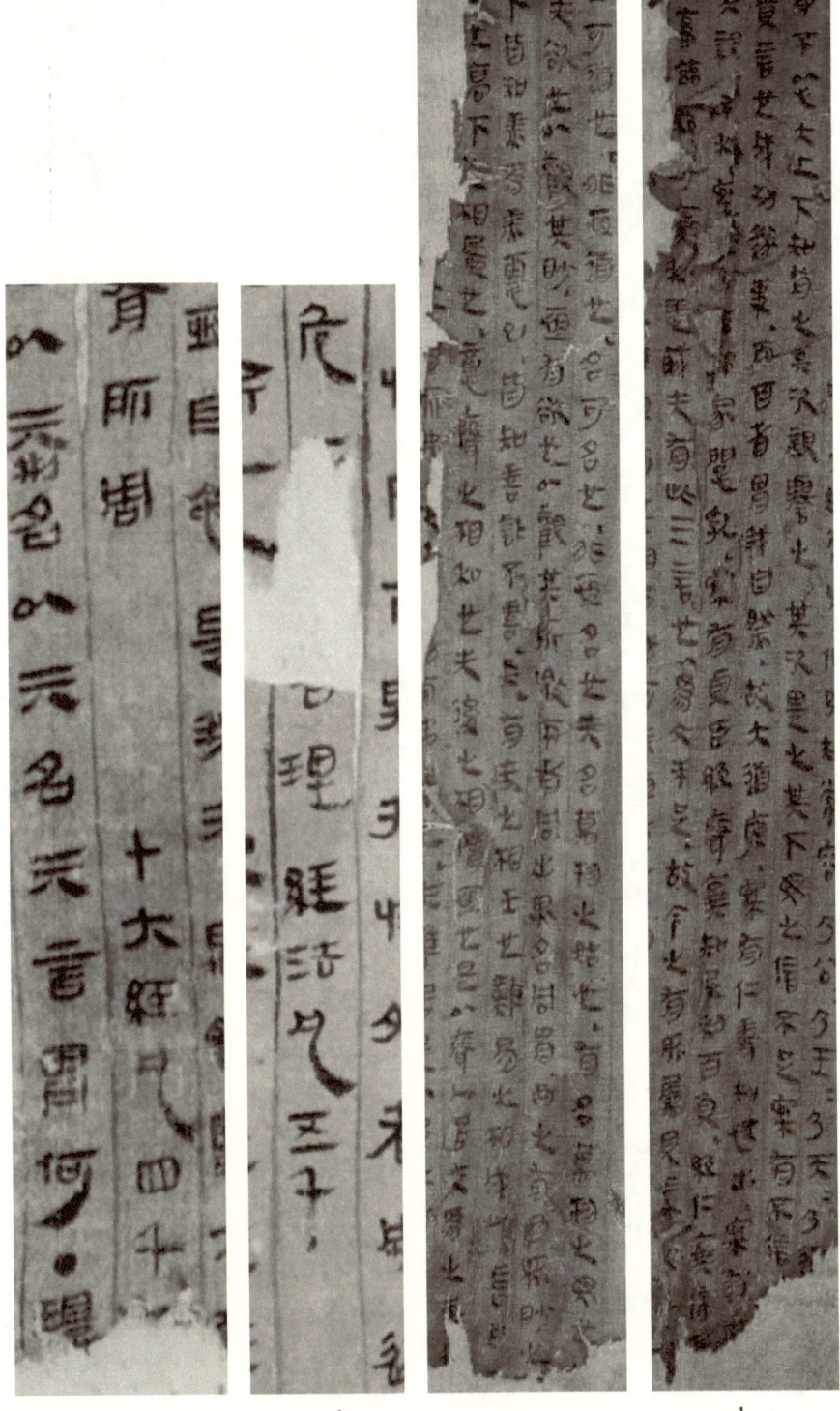

Plate 5 Details of Manuscript A and Manuscript B. (a) MS.B, col. 124a, end of text 2 [*Shiliu jing*]; (b) MS.B, col. 77b, end of text 1 [*Jing fa*]; (c) MS.A, cols. 93–96; (d) MS.A, cols. 124–27.

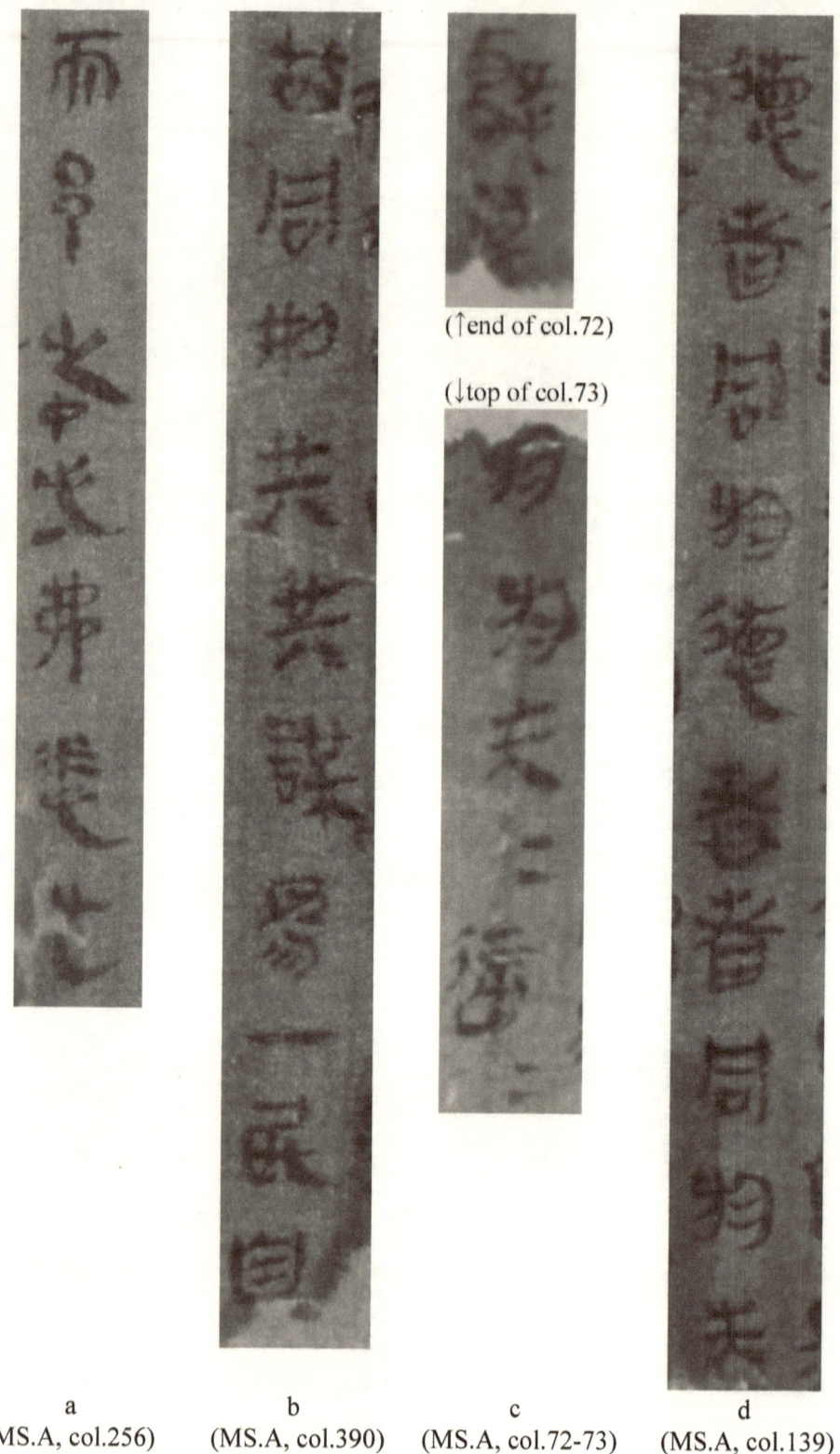

Plate 6 Errors and corrections in Manuscript A.

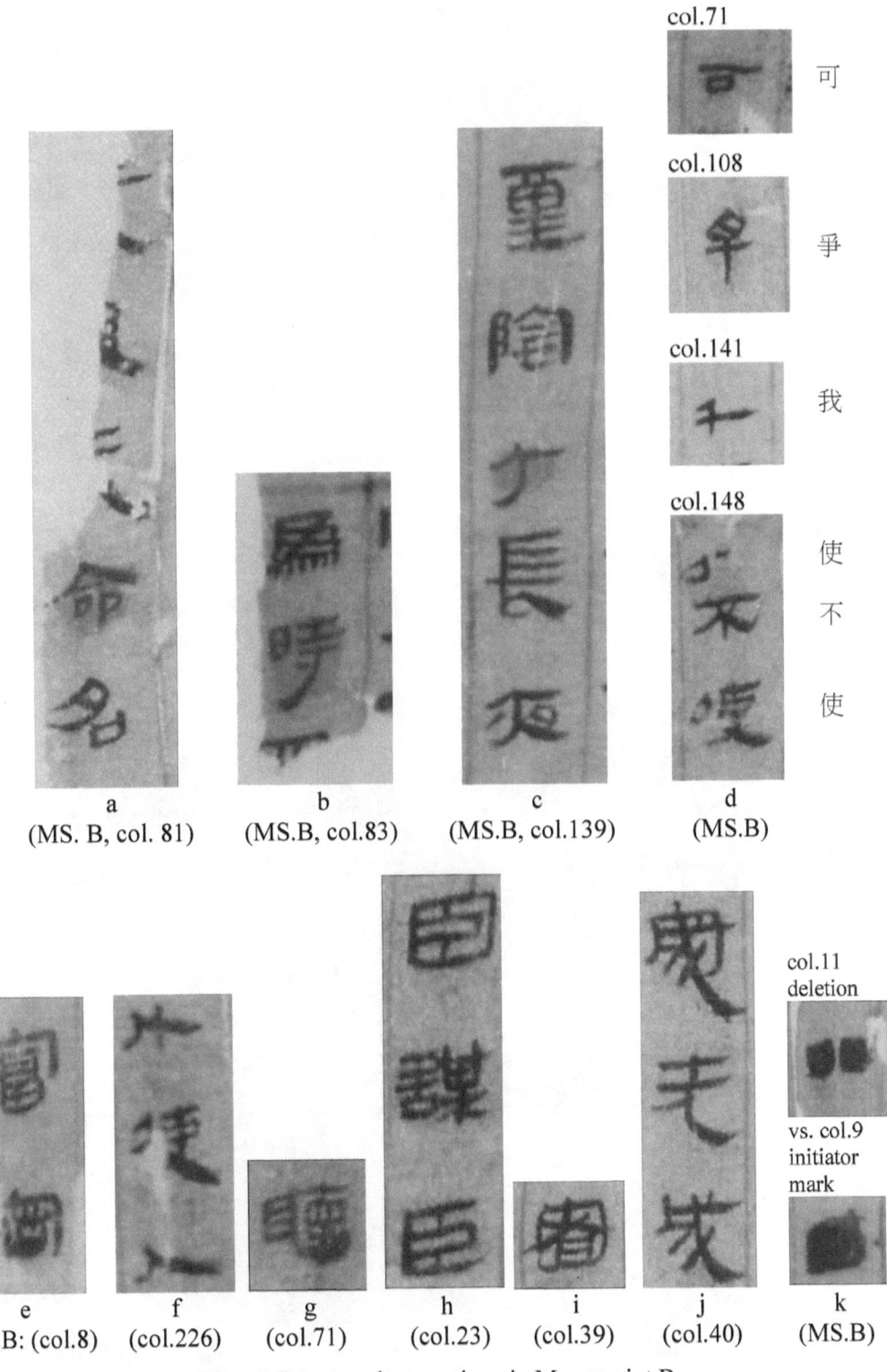

Plate 7 Errors and corrections in Manuscript B.

Plate 8 Inscribed artisan names of Qin period (221–207 B.C.E.). (a) Terra-cotta figure (inscribed "Yi of Xianyang City"), Museum of the Qin Emperor's Terra-cotta Warriors and Horses, Lintong County, Shaanxi. Photo courtesy of Cultural Relics Publishing House. (b) Shallow bowl (inscribed "Woman Ao of Huan Village"), painted lacquer over wooden core, diam. 18 cm, Hubei Provincial Museum. Photo courtesy of Hubei Provincial Museum.

the horizon as it oscillated between the solstitial extremes (observing slits E2 and E12).[8] Such a horizonal calendar could have yielded an approximation of the length of the solar year, perhaps to within a week or so. This degree of attention paid to the solar year clearly shows that Taosi's designers were interested in correlating the tropical year with the lunar months, an effort that would eventuate in a luni-solar calendar of the type that became conventional by late Shang (at least in the context of the oracle bone divinations), as demonstrated by the Shang use of an intercalary thirteenth month to maintain synchronization between solar and lunar cycles. Some have even suggested, based on the number of viewing apertures at Taosi, that the observing platform represents an early effort to create a fortnightly scheme of twenty-four solar periods (*jiéqì* 節氣) like that familiar to us from much later times, though this suggestion is problematic.[9] It is immediately apparent from the design and layout of the viewing platform that those early calendar priests (and priest-astronomers they most certainly would have been, judging from the elite burials adjacent to the platform) must have possessed a number of crucial concepts and related terminology. Whether in the construction or the use of the facility, those concepts and terms ought to have included sun, moon,

---

8. David W. Pankenier, Liu Ciyuan, and Salvo de Meis, "The Xiangfen, Taosi Site: A Chinese Neolithic 'Observatory'?" in *Archaeologia Baltica: Astronomy and Cosmology in Folk Traditions and Cultural Heritage* (Klaipeda, Lithuania: University of Klaipeda Press, 2008), 141–48; cf. Liu Ciyuan et al., "A Chinese Observatory Site of 4,000 Year [sic] Ago," *Journal of Astronomical History and Heritage* 8.2 (2005): 129–30; Wu Jiabi 武家璧, Chen Meidong 陳美東, and Liu Ciyuan 劉次沅, "Taosi guanxiangtai yizhi de tianwen gongneng yu niandai" 陶寺觀象台遺址的天文功能與年代, *Science in China* (G: Physics and astronomy issue) 38.9 (2008): 1265–72.
9. The twelve observing slits are evenly spaced. However, the sun takes only six months to travel from one extreme to the other, and near the equinoxes the sun moves six times as fast along the horizon as around the solstices, so wall segments of similar size necessarily partition the year into unequal intervals, varying between about eight days or so near the equinoxes and over a month near the solstices. (The location of moonrise on the horizon would have been too irregular and difficult to pin down by means of such viewing apertures.) A similar scheme described in the "Dahuang jing" 大荒經 section of the *Shanhaijing* 山海經 may be a throwback to the archaic Taosi model; see Hwang Ming-chorng 黃明崇, "Ming-tang: Cosmology, Political Order and Monuments in Early China" (PhD diss., Harvard University, 1996), 596. The "Tianwen" 天文 chapter of the *Huainanzi* 淮南子 describes a horizontal solar calendar comprising seven *shè* 舍 'lodgings, habitations' arrayed along the eastern horizon from winter solstice to summer solstice. See John S. Major, *Heaven and Earth in Early Han Thought* (Albany: State University of New York Press, 1993), 87.

stars, horizon, sight line, direction, location, elevation, aperture, diameter, curve, straight line, to measure, unit of measure (Neolithic yard?), and so forth. More apropos in terms of the present discussion, their technical vocabulary must also have included such temporal concepts as day, night, month, sunrise, moonrise, solstice (and possibly achronical and heliacal rising in reference to the stars). The implications of this are momentous. It was Otto Neugebauer who called astronomy the first of the exact sciences, and as Merlin Donald has said:

> The earliest evidence of an elementary form of theory formation is found in ancient astronomy. Astronomical knowledge, like writing, was a powerful device of social control; the measurement of time in terms of astronomical cycles was probably the ultimate controlling activity in early agricultural societies, setting dates for planting, harvesting, storage, and distribution of grain for religious observations, as well as a number of cyclical social functions. . . . Quite early in the history of visuographic symbolism, analog devices were invented that served both a measurement and predictive function in representing time. These devices eventually allowed humans to track celestial events, construct accurate calendars, and keep time on a daily basis.[10]

There is no doubt that, whatever other cultic or ritual purpose Taosi might have served, the observing platform was certainly an analog device for measuring and predicting time in the form of the sun's progress along the horizon. Traditional accounts confirm that other analog methods, presumably inspired by the art of weaving, relied on knotting cords to record information. As the "Appended Commentary" (Xici zhuan 繫辭傳) of the *Book of Changes* (Yijing 易經) says: "In high antiquity they knotted strings and brought order; the Sages of later generations switched to writing with inscribed graphs" (上古結繩而治，後世聖人易之以書契). No examples of such "tools of governance" have survived in China — the invention of writing is too ancient for that — but analogous devices have appeared elsewhere, for example, in the form of the Inka *khipu*.[11] Many of these survived the holocaust of the Spanish Conquest, though examples of calendar *khipu* are extremely rare.[12] Maintained by specialists who were

---

10. Donald, *The Origins of the Modern Mind*, 335.
11. "Inka" and "*khipu*" are the preferred Aymara and Quechua spellings of these words. Other spellings commonly seen include "Inca" and "*Quipu*."
12. For an interpretation of the code employed in the *khipu*, see Gary Urton, *Signs of the Inka Khipu* (Austin: University of Texas Press, 2003); also Charles C. Mann, "Cracking

the schedulers of the religious rites of the Inka and guardians of their cultural astronomy and cosmology, these devices were zealously sought out by the Spanish missionaries as repositories of "pagan devil worship" and consigned to the bonfires of pre-Columbian cultural artifacts.

A remarkable example of such a calendar *khipu* for the year 1532 has survived in the form of a reproduction in a seventeenth-century Spanish text, however (fig. 1.2, a), and it is well worth examining in some detail for what it reveals about this method of recordkeeping in preliterate societies.[13] The thirteen square cartouches arrayed along the top cord are ideograms representing the noteworthy agricultural activities or ceremonials for which each month of the year was named or with which it was identified.[14] Suspended from these are cord pendants on which groups of red and yellow knots mark the days. The knots are separated into continuous ten-day weeks by allowing space between the groups. Tags attached to particular days signify events of note, including astronomical phenomena of importance: full moons, the Pleiades rising, eclipses, and so forth. Seven long months of thirty days and five short months of twenty-nine days occur in irregular sequence, and a thirteenth month is appended that contains ten epagomenal days, bringing the total number of days represented to 365, matching the number of days in the solar year.

Contemporaneous accounts of Inka *khipu* and their use as external recording devices in conjunction with counting pebbles attest to their impressive capacity to preserve complex information, including periodic tribute, barter and exchange agreements, and even narratives, which information was read out as required by elite officials known as "knot-readers" (*khipukamayuq*) (fig. 1.2, b).[15] This is an example of a

---

the *Khipu* Code," *Science* 300 (13 June 2003): 1650–51.

13. See Laura Laurencich Minelli and Giulio Magli, "A Calendar *Quipu* of the Early 17th Century and Its Relationship with the Inca Astronomy," *History of Physics* 801 (*ArXiv e-prints*, January 2008; arXiv:0801.1577v1, Web version).

14. The cartouche images resembling Bactrian camel humps are *sucancas*, or the pairs of pillars bracketing crucial astronomical rising or setting points on the high mountain ridges around Cuzco.

15. Gary Urton, "From Knots to Narratives: Reconstructing the Art of Historical Record Keeping in the Andes from Spanish Transcriptions of Inka *Khipus*," *Ethnohistory* 45.3 (1998): 409–38. Accounts of the process indicate that the *khipu* reader "parsed the knots by inspecting them visually, and by running their fingers along them Braille-style, sometimes accompanying this by manipulating stones"; Mann, "Cracking the *Khipu* Code," 1650.

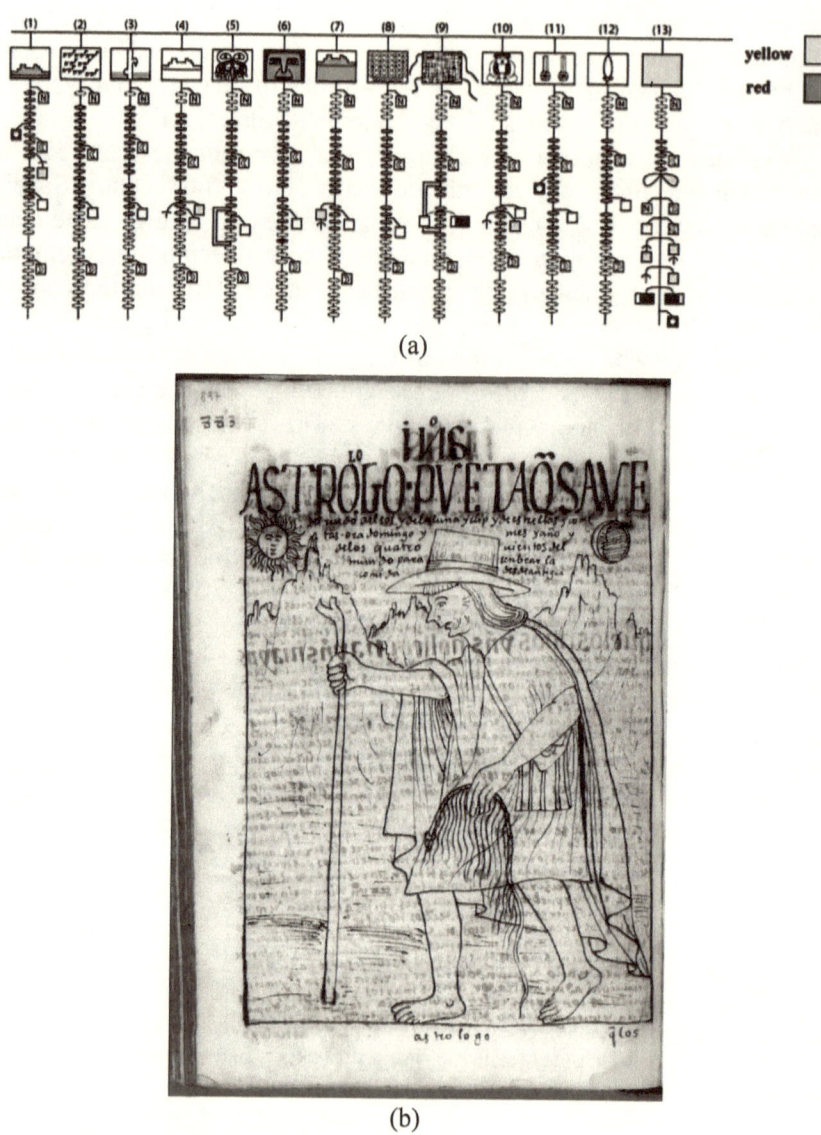

Figure 1.2. Inka calendar *khipu* (a) and Inka "knot-reader" (astrologer) (b), carrying in his right hand a forked astronomical sighting rod and in his left a *khipu*. Top: from Laurencich Minelli and Magli, "A Calendar Quipu of the Early 17th Century"; (b): from Felipe Guaman Poma de Ayala, *El primer nueva corónica y buen gobierno* (1615/1616) (Copenhagen: Det Kongelige Bibliotek, GKS 2232 4°). Reproduced with permission.

kind of analog device from another context that would have preceded the invention of writing (in contrast to the mercantile tokens familiar from the Mesopotamian context). It illustrates the kinds of information that ultimately had to be converted into written form — a number set to count the days, the ten-day week, terms for the phases of the moon, various celestial bodies, names of the months, colors, rituals, agricultural products, tribute items, seasons, a variety of action verbs, and so on, analogous in many respects to the technical vocabulary that would have been employed by the designers of the Taosi "observatory."

In other words, once the mental leap was made from the ideographic representation of a *khipu*-like device to zodiographs,[16] a substantial repertoire of contextually related signs would have to have been invented (or appropriated from existing religious symbolism, textile motifs, and other visuographic symbols or "iconic images" [*xiàng* 象] such as those abundantly documented from the Chinese Neolithic) in order to accomplish the transition to a written calendar. The application of writing in this specialized way could have come about in short order. If it were to be functional, such a written calendar, once conceived, would need to embody from the outset the kinds of elements and concepts itemized above. Short of pointing to the corresponding *khipu* cartouche, an ideograph for "corn-planting month," say, would have to be named to be spoken of, and all that is required to produce a zodiograph is for the spoken word to stick to the conventional graphic representation. In the case of the depictions of *sucancas* (pillars on the horizon marking the sun's location on critical dates) in cartouches 1, 4, and 7, for example, because of their similarity, the reading of each would have to have been distinctive and quite specific. The *khipu* cartouches may have already been more than merely incipient zodiographs.

It is not so difficult to imagine how the non-glottographic representation of a concept, for example, the graphic for "corn-planting month," could imperceptibly be transformed in conventional usage into the glottographic denotation of that month. Once the technique of representing words graphically emerged, as it independently did in different contexts and cultures, the conversion of a notational system into writing and the

---

16. In terms of the developmental stages of writing: "When a graph is primarily a depictive representation of a thing, it is a *pictograph* and is not writing. When the same graph, or a modified version of it, represents primarily the name of the thing, that is, the word for the thing, and stands for the thing itself only as information conveyed by the word, we call it a *zodiograph* and define it as writing"; see Boltz, "Language and Writing," 110.

spread of the process to other contexts *could* occur quite suddenly, yet it *need* not. Whether such a development was imminent in the Inka context is unknown.

Calendrical Use of the Cyclical Signs

Visual symbols had immediate advantages over speech. Lists of transactions and numbers were much better expressed in writing than in speech. Lists of genealogies, and other historical sequences, were also much clearer in written form, and *devices such as astronomical almanacs . . . simply could not be formulated or expressed in spoken language.*[17]

For the purposes of counting the days between full moons at Taosi, not to mention solstices, harvest festivals, and so on, a primitive number system (e.g., 1, 2, 3, many) and reliance on memory alone would simply not do. At a minimum, one either devised a scheme to represent "1, 2, 3 . . . 10, 20, 30 . . .," or maintaining a horizon calendar over time would have been impossible. A rudimentary number set consisting of "1, 2, 3, many" coupled with an oral narrative listing regularly observed astronomical or meteorological events such as full moons would certainly be inadequate to the task — biological memory is far too limited.[18] Given their conceptual toolkit, the elite users of the Taosi observing platform must have possessed an external recording device like a *khipu*, if not a system of written signs, and this some eight centuries before Shang king Wu Ding 武丁. This chapter puts forward the hypothesis that the set of cyclical signs was a mental tool initially devised in response to the conceptual demands outlined above, that their origin is crucially related to the origin of the

---

17. Donald, *The Origins of the Modern Mind*, 290 (emphasis mine).
18. On the advantages of writing in particular, Merlin Donald writes: "Part of the gain was in the transportability and permanence of records; but another important part was in the ability to arrange virtually endless lists of items. The *list* is a peculiarly visual institution. The usefulness of oral listing is very limited, owing to memory limitations; orally memorized lists tend to tie up working memory, preventing further processing of the list. In contrast, visual lists can be arranged in various ways, and juxtaposed to simplify the later treatment of the information they contain. List arrangement can facilitate the sorting, summarizing, and classifying of items and can reveal patterns otherwise not discernible. With the invention of visual lists, the newly created state could acquire, analyze, and digest the information it needed to function." See Donald, *The Origins of the Modern Mind*, 288.

calendar, and that it was calendrical astronomy that lent impetus to the invention of writing in China.[19]

Calendar tables from the Shang inscriptional materials provide useful information. They are clearly not divination texts, nor do they all represent calligraphy "practice."[20] The two examples described below were analyzed in 1929 by Guo Moruo 郭沫若 in his pioneering monograph on the origins of the cyclical signs, "Shi zhigan" 釋支干 [sic].[21] Guo points out that examples that repeat only the first three ten-day weeks (xún 旬) several times in succession are actually about as numerous as those that reproduce the whole series of sixty cyclical signs. He inferred that these thirty-day tables are an indication that the Shang months originally comprised three xún of thirty days, which means that every month would have begun with jiǎzǐ 甲子 (day 1) and ended with guǐsì 癸巳 (day 30). This is an entirely reasonable proposition, since alternation of long and short months must have appeared as a corrective some considerable time after the invention of the twelve-month calendar, when it was realized that

---

19. Stephen D. Houston makes the point that "writing is a sequence of step-like inventions" and that "most early script did not expand to fulfill every conceivable function — an anachronistic fallacy — but served, at least initially, very limited needs;" Stephen D. Houston, "Overture to the First Writing," in *The First Writing: Script Invention as History and Process* (Cambridge: Cambridge University Press, 2008), 11–12.

20. In contrast, an example of a practice inscription is HJ: 18946, on which essentially the same sequence of fewer than ten characters is repeated in five separate lines. A number of such tables of cyclical signs may be found following HJ: 38044. For practice inscriptions as an index of literacy in late Shang, see Adam Smith, "The Evidence for Scribal Training at Anyang," chapter 5 in this volume. David N. Keightley concluded that many examples such as those identified by Guo are, in fact, written calendars used for reference; Keightley, *The Ancestral Landscape*, 39. In a similar context, Qiu Xigui 裘錫圭 cites the Xiaochen Qiang 小臣牆 bone, one side of which recorded events in what is the longest non-oracular Shang inscription so far discovered, while the reverse displays a table of cyclical signs, suggesting a connection between historical record and reference calendar; Qiu Xigui 裘錫圭, *Wenzixue gaiyao* 文字學概要 (Beijing: Shangwu Yinshuguan, 1996 [1988]), 41, fig. 6 (reprinted in *Chinese Writing*, trans. Gilbert L. Mattos and Jerry Norman [Berkeley, Calif.: Society for the Study of Early China, 2000], 62, fig. 6).

21. See Guo Moruo, "Shi zhigan" 釋支干, in *Guo Moruo quanji* 郭沫若全集 (Beijing: Kexue Chubanshe, 1982), 1:155–340. This is not the place for an analysis of Guo's hypothesis concerning the astral correlates of the stems and branches and their supposed Babylonian origins. Many of his philological analyses have not stood the test of time; for a recent critique, see Wang Ning 王寧, "Shi zhigan bianbu" 釋支干辨補, *Zhongguo xian Qin shi* 中國先秦史 (30 July 2006), http://www.zgxqs.cn/article/2006/0730/article_905.html (accessed 2 April 2009).

twelve months of 30 days are actually some 5 days longer than twelve lunations of 354 days.

The arrangement of some of the tabulations Guo cites proves that they are calendars. In one (HJ: 21783), the cyclical signs from *jiǎzǐ* (day 1) through *guǐhài* (day 60) are arranged in four registers, the first two registers together comprising twenty-nine days and the second two comprising thirty-one days. Furthermore, the distribution of the days among the four registers is 14-15-17-14, reproducing a count of days for two successive months, the first short and the second long, divided at the full moon. This arrangement could hardly be accidental, nor could this be intended as a tabulation of cyclical signs designed purely for reference or scribal practice, since the irregular layout and the month of thirty-one days are both highly unusual. Conclusively, however, in figure 1.3 (HJ: 24440), transcribed as table 1.1, a scribe has again reproduced the sequences of *gānzhī*, but in this unique inscription, the names of the months are supplied — "Month 1 Regular is called 'Eat Wheat'" 月一正曰食麥 and "Second month Father X" 二月父X. In addition to showing that this table is indisputably a fragment of a calendar, the thirty days of two successive long months are enumerated using the cyclical signs 1 through 60, with one fortnight per column. (Since adequate space was available, it is curious that the scribe felt no compunction in splitting *jǐsì* 己巳 [day 6] at the bottom of column 1 and *gēngxū* 庚戌 [day 47] at the bottom of column 6, for no apparent reason.) Remarkably, the inscription records what must have been the conventional names for the first two months of the year, the first of which, "Eat Wheat" (*Shímài* 食麥), is corroborated by later textual evidence, for example, from the "Monthly Ordinances" (Yueling 月令) chapter of the *Yi Zhou shu* 逸周書.[22] Guo Moruo called this inscription "China's earliest calendar."[23] It certainly is the earliest

---

22. The activities prescribed in the "Monthly Ordinances" for the first month of spring, "when the sun is in Yingshi," include the admonition to "eat wheat and mutton." Winter wheat is harvested in late spring, so some have argued on this basis that if the Shang month was named for the first fruits of that harvest, the first month should have fallen near the summer solstice. See Yang Shengnan 楊升南, *Shangdai jingji shi* 商代經濟史 (Guiyang: Guizhou Renmin Chunbanshe, 1992), 121. For the same reason, the association of wheat and mutton with the first month of spring in the Monthly Ordinances seems incongruous.

23. The oracle bone inscription (OBI) graph for *shi* 食 is not immediately recognizable on the rubbing, as strokes have been omitted; for analysis, see Guo Moruo, "Shi zhigan," 161. See also Yang Shengnan, *Shangdai jingji shi*, 121.

Figure 1.3. Two-month calendar table from HJ: 24440 showing successive thirty-day months beginning the year.

Table 1.1. Transcription of HJ: 24440 rubbing in Figure 1.3.

【月】	巳	戊	丁	【㐅】	壬	戌	己
【一】	庚	寅	亥	甲	寅	辛	未
【正】	午	己	戊	午	癸	亥	庚
【日】	辛	卯	子	乙	卯	壬	申
【食】	未	庚	己	未	甲	子	辛
【麥】	壬	辰	丑	丙	辰	癸	酉
	申	辛	庚	申	乙	丑	壬
	癸	巳	寅	丁	巳	甲	戌
	酉	壬	辛	酉	丙	寅	癸
	甲	午	卯	戊	午	乙	【亥】
	戌	癸	壬	戌	丁	卯	
	乙	【未】	辰	己	未	丙	
	亥	甲	癸	亥	戊	辰	
	丙	申	巳	庚	申	丁	
	子	乙	【二】	子	己	巳	
	丁	酉	【月】	辛	酉	戊	
	丑	丙	【夕】	丑	庚	午	

discovered to date. It must reflect early calendrical usage, since, with the exception of "Month One Regular" (*yuè yī zhèng* 月一正), none of the noteworthy features of this calendar are used in the dating formulas of the actual Shang divination texts, which typically alternate twenty-nine and thirty-day months and invariably enumerate the months rather than naming them.[24]

---

24. Cf. David N. Keightley's observation: "I suspect, in fact, that 'the start of the year' could have involved more than one kind of year. The Shang diviners might have pegged the first moon of their luni-solar calendar to the first lunation after the winter solstice, while the peasants might have tied their agricultural calendar to the observation of stars and constellations. It would have been the first, liturgical system,

The reconstructed readings of the twenty-two signs reveal the patterns that might emerge from different arrangements. Table 1.2 reproduces the Old Chinese reconstructions of the cyclical signs. To the right of these reconstructions, the rhymes are labeled D, A, B, C, a, and X (X signifying no obvious rhyme with the other signs in the set or with each other).[25]

Several features are immediately apparent in the earthly branches, the second element in each pair of cyclical signs, which one would expect to have occupied the stressed, rhyming position when the series was recited. First, apart from *wǔ* 午 and *xū* 戌, the other ten signs all share four rhymes, perhaps about 12 percent of those available, one of which, "a," is in assonance with "A." Second, the "A" rhymes divide the twelve signs roughly in two. Third, remarkably, among the codas there are no labials, only a single nasal, and no velars (excluding the seemingly overrepresented *-q*, a glottal stop). Compare these features with those of the ten stems. Rhyme pairs are almost entirely lacking, but the stems display a full range of codas. The contrasting features of the twelve earthly branches are certainly eye-catching and appear prima facie to suggest that, by comparison with the ten stems, some deliberate process of selection must have been operative at the time the twelve branches were created. In other words, the choice of rhymes and perhaps even the sequence of signs may not be random.[26]

---

not the second, agricultural system, that gave rise to the numbered moons recorded in the divination inscriptions"; see Keightley, *The Ancestral Landscape*, 44.

25. I am grateful to Paul R. Goldin, Wolfgang Behr, and David Prager Branner for comments and corrections with regard to Old Chinese rhyming and phonetics. The reconstruction given here (the "Baxter-Sagart" system, before its last revision), is that presented in Robert H. Gassmann and Wolfgang Behr, *Antikchinesisch — Ein Lehrbuch in drei Teilen*, Teil 1 (Bern: Peter Lang, 2005): *-q* represents glottal stop in final suffixal position; doubled initials represent "type A" syllables.

26. Having said that, I am not persuaded by Pulleyblank's thesis about the deliberate selection of the twenty-two stems and branches to serve as phonograms as early as the second millennium B.C.E. This strikes me as too self-conscious and sophisticated a linguistic analysis to impute to such an early stage in the development of Chinese writing. See Pulleyblank, "The *Ganzhi* as Phonograms," 39–80.

Table 1.2. Old Chinese phonetic reconstructions of the *gānzhī*

	天干		OC	Rhyme
1.	甲	[八部]	*kkrap	
2.	乙	[十二部]	*qrik	
3.	丙	[十部]	*prang	D
4.	丁	[十一部]	*tteng	
5.	戊	[三部]	*mu-s	
6.	己	[一部]	*kə-q	
7.	庚	[十部]	*kkrang	D
8.	辛	[十三部]	*sing	
9.	壬	[七部]	*nəm	
10.	癸	[十五部]	*k^Wij-q	

	地支		OC	Rhyme
1.	子	[一部]	*tsə-q	A
2.	丑	[三部]	*hnru-q	B
3.	寅	[十二部]	*lin	C
4.	卯	[三部]	*mmru-q	B
5.	辰	[十三部]	*dər	a
6.	巳	[一部]	*s-lə-q	A
7.	午	[五部]	*ngnga-q	X
8.	未	[十五部]	*mət-s	a
9.	申	[十二部]	*hlin	C
10.	酉	[三部]	*lu-q	B
11.	戌	[十二部]	*s-mit	X
12.	亥	[一部]	*ggə-q	A

The implications of this become apparent when we examine a thirty-day tabulation of *gānzhī*, considering only the rhyme of the second element in each binary combination:

First column:	A	B	C,	B	a	A,	x	a	C,	B
Second column:	x	A|	A	B	C,	B	a	A,	x	a
Third column:	C,	B	x	A|	A	B	C,	B	a	A

Vertical slashes show where the sequence begins to repeat, so that there are two and one-half repetitions of a sequence of twelve ordinals, with alternation between two rhymes in third position as in xxC/xxA/xxC/xxA. Even without speculating about sources of uncertainty in the reconstructions, the features of the earthly branches suggest that a pattern such as this, even if based only on vocalic assonance or generic rhyming, may have played a role in the arrangement.

To this, some might object that the recursive pattern is merely an artifact of the pairing of twelve branches with ten stems that produced the cycle of sixty signs, since a pattern must necessarily emerge. This is true, of course, but one cannot ignore the stark contrast between the two sets of terms — the ten stems with their random selection of rhymes and finals and the twelve branches with their prominent rhymes and series of codas that conspicuously avoids labials and velars (except for the special case of coda *-q).[27] Some will object that extrapolating Old Chinese reconstructions back a thousand years before the *Book of Poetry* (Shijing 詩經) is a risky proposition, but while the criticism may apply to the precise details of the reconstructed Old Chinese pronunciation, phonetic change does follow more or less regular patterns, so that the same rules should apply to all members of a given set of words. Thus, it is probable that, while the phonological complexion of the individual members of the two sets of stems and branches in the early to mid-second millennium B.C.E. may not have been exactly as represented, the fundamental *contrast* between the linguistic features of the two sets is unlikely to have changed that much. A further objection might be that there is no unequivocal evidence of rhyming of any kind earlier than the Western Zhou bronze inscriptions. This is also true, but here, however, the argument is for

---

27. This latter feature was called to my attention by Paul R. Goldin (personal exchange), who stressed the unlikelihood of this being a random occurrence. By contrast, fully half the ten stems have labial or velar finals, and nasals are well represented, too.

self-conscious use of rhyme not as literary embellishment but merely as a simple device that may have been useful in remembering the repetitive sequence of binary cyclical signs whose recitation would naturally have tended to be rhythmic.

Keeping in mind the likely calendrical origin of the ten stems, perhaps one might infer that the two series were created at different times. Initially, the ten stems were invented to enumerate the days of the ten-day week, and only later were they complemented by the twelve branches that may have once denoted the months.[28] Originally, the days would have been named using just the ten stems, an arbitrary set of signs easily committed to memory, but this meant that each stem had to repeat three times a month, once each week. At some point, possibly to help resolve ambiguity in dating events, the series of twelve branches was paired with the ten stems in sequential fashion by matching successive branches with each of the ten stems. Proceeding in this fashion for six ten-day weeks until the first pair — *jiǎzǐ* — reappeared produced the familiar series of sixty unique signs (in fact, only half the 120 possible combinations). But now each combination of signs would repeat only six times a year, in different months sixty days apart, in contrast to thirty-six appearances spaced ten days apart for the unpaired stems. This meant that the number of unique combinations requiring memorization would have increased by a factor of six, so that at this point, rhythmic repetition and rhyming might conceivably have been called upon as an aid to memory. The sequence of rhymes illustrated above — minimally xxC/xxA/xxC/xxA — would repeat five times within

---

28. The twelve earthly branches are generally thought to derive from a different source than the ten stems, about which there has been much speculation, including their putative origin, in Guo Moruo's view, as astronyms derived from Babylonian astronomy. Richard S. Cook makes a case for an early representational and etymological connection between *chén* (a conventional designation for lunar lodges 4-6 Fang 房, Xin 心, Wei 尾), and a scorpion, while leaving the identification with the dragon unexplained; see "The Etymology of Chinese 辰 *Chén*," *Linguistics of the Tibeto-Burman Area* 18.2 (1995). Some of Cook's claims about the connections between *Chén* 辰 and a scorpion, as well as other aspects of his astronomical analysis, are based on mistranslation of the "Treatise on the Celestial Offices" (Tianguan shu 天官書) in the *Records of the Grand Scribe* (Shiji 史記) and oracle bone inscriptions; see David W. Pankenier, *Bringing Heaven down to Earth: Astrological and Cosmological Foundations of Chinese Civilization* (New York: Cambridge University Press) forthcoming. Guo's, Cook's, and others' claims of the likely diffusion of astronomical concepts from Mesopotamia to China do not bear scrutiny from the perspective of the history of Chinese astronomy; see Jiang Xiaoyuan 江曉原, *Tianxue zhenyuan* 天學真原 (Shenyang: Liaoning Jiaoyu Chubanshe, 1991; rev. ed., 2004), 276–94.

the sequence of sixty cyclical signs, perhaps providing basic rhythmic cues.

It may be, therefore, that two sets of cyclical signs, stems and branches, were initially devised to respond to the conceptual and recordkeeping demands of the calendar, and the origins of the two are crucially related. It is likely that calendrical astronomy lent impetus to the development of writing in China and prefigured its application to other forms of recordkeeping that emerged later, including the Shang divinations, in which we see a mature written language fully formed. Rhyme may have provided a crucial connection between orality and functional notation, linking the practical use of the two sets of ideographs and the *idea* of writing words. In other words, rhyming may have served as the notional stimulus prompting the realization that the sounds of individual spoken words could be attached to specific conventional graphic signs and thus serve as analogs of speech, in effect inventing a new medium — true writing. This is conjectural, of course, so it remains for us to establish if possible a *direct* connection between the early calendar, astronomy, and the inspiration leading to the invention of the cyclical signs.

Finding Inspiration in the Sky

Study of the cosmological significance of the North Pole in ancient Chinese thought suggests that ritual specialists in Bronze Age China, like their earlier counterparts in ancient Egypt, used the circumpolar stars to find true north, a task complicated during the last two millennia B.C.E. by the absence of a comparatively bright star near the Pole.[29] Similarly, archaeological discoveries from the Xia, Shang, and Zhou periods show

---

29. See David W. Pankenier, "A Brief History of *Beiji* 北極 (Northern Culmen), with an Excursus on the Origin of the Character *di* 帝," *Journal of the American Oriental Society* 124.2 (2004), 211–36; and, especially, Ban Dawei (David W. Pankenier), "Zai tan beiji jianshi yu di zi de qiyuan" 再談北極簡史與「帝」字的起源, in *Xi fang Zhongguo shi yanjiu luncong* 西方中國史研究論叢, vol. 1: *Gudai shi yanjiu* 古代史研究, ed. Chen Zhi (Shanghai: Shanghai Guji Chubanshe, in press); Noemi Miranda et al. offer persuasive evidence of the use of a hand-held standard to align with stars in the bowl of the Dipper and the Pole; "Uncovering Seshat: New Insights at the Stretching of the Cord Ceremony," in *Archaeologia Baltica: Astronomy and Cosmology in Folk Traditions and Cultural Heritage* (Klaipeda, Lithuania: University of Klaipeda, 2008), 57–61. Figure 1.2 above shows a more primitive, but conceptually analogous implement.

that it had become crucially important to achieve a cardinal orientation of the built environment — walls, palaces, temples, tombs, common burials, and even storage pits give evidence of a preoccupation with N-S axial alignment.[30] There are nearly ubiquitous methods for achieving cardinality involving observations of the sun's shadow using a gnomon, but what follows is a brief description of a quite original solution to the problem that makes use of the stars. Until now, scholars have overlooked this method, one that underscores the distinctive polar-equatorial focus of Chinese astronomy and also links astronomy with the origin of the ten stems.

Evidence for this indirect technique designed to achieve precise alignment on the north celestial Pole is provided by the ode "Dìng zhi fang zhong" 定之方中 (no. 50) in the "Airs of Yong" (Yong feng 鄘風) section of the *Book of Poetry*:[31]

定之方中，作於楚宮；揆之以日，作於楚室。[32]

When [the asterism] Dìng just culminated, he started work on the *Chu Palace*; When he had measured it by the sun, he started work on the *Chu Hall*.

Determining the correct orientation in the landscape of the main ancestral hall takes pride of place among the activities described. Commentators all agree that the time to commence work, "just when Dìng was centered" (Dìng zhi fang zhong 定之方中), refers to the moment when the asterism Dìng transited the local meridian due south in the evening. A previous study demonstrated that the asterism Dìng is none other than the combination of Yingshi 營室, lunar lodge 13, and Dongbi 東壁, lunar lodge 14, immediately to the east.[33] The two bright stars of Yingshi form

---

30. Keightley, *The Ancestral Landscape*, 82.
31. The ode celebrates the restoration of Duke Wen 文 of Wey 衛 at Chuqiu 楚丘 in 658 B.C.E. (Duke Min 閔 of Lu 魯, second year) after Wey had been destroyed by an invasion of the Di 狄. Resettlement of Duke Wen and the remnant population of Wey was brought about through the intervention of Duke Huan 桓 of Qi 齊, who drove the Di out of the area.
32. Bernhard Karlgren, *The Book of Odes* (Stockholm: Museum of Far Eastern Antiquities, 1950), 33 (modified).
33. Before the fifth century B.C.E., Yingshi and Dongbi formed a single asterism Dìng, which continued to be graphically represented as a square in Han dynasty tomb murals. See Ban Dawei (David W. Pankenier), "Beiji de faxian yu yingyong," 北極的發現與應用, *Ziran kexueshi yanjiu* 自然科學史研究, 27.3 (2008): 281–300. *Erya* 爾雅

the western side of the prominent asterism known to us as the Great Square of Pegasus, which forms the torso of the celestial winged horse.

The Alignment Function of Asterism Dìng

If one looks at the longitudinal meridian lines on the star chart in figure 1.4, which depicts the situation in 650 B.C.E., one can see that the Eastern and Western Walls of Dìng (i.e., Yingshi and Dongbi) align with the meridians converging on the Pole to the north. Therefore, by early Zhou at the latest, the Chinese possessed a technique capable of precisely locating true north in the absence of a bright star at the Pole. Now, the large distance from Yingshi-Dongbi to the Pole means that it was not possible to observe the circumpolar sky in the north and the Dìng asterism in the south at the same time. In addition, the diurnal and annual revolutions of Pegasus also mean that Yingshi-Dongbi would have been useful only for the purpose of aligning on the pole at a singular time — on transiting the meridian in the evening when the two parallel sides of Dìng would have been perpendicular to the horizon and pointing overhead through the zenith to the Pole. At other times of the year when Dìng was either invisible or oriented at some oblique angle to the horizon, it could not have served the stated purpose. Here, then, is the meaning of Mao Heng's commentary:

> Dìng is Yingshi; *fāng zhōng* [means] at dusk to rectify (*zhèng* 正) the four directions. . . . Watching to the south [he] observes Dìng, and to the north he aligns on the Pole, in order to rectify (正) south and north.[34]

Investigation reveals that the best time for such alignment observations in late Shang and Western Zhou would have been in early evening in late autumn, when Dìng would have been optimally positioned right after sunset. Various sources confirm that it was in late autumn, after the end of the agricultural season, that this "aligning by the stars" would have taken

---

("Shitian" 釋天) says, "Yingshi is called Dìng" 營室謂之定. Guo Pu's 郭璞 (276–324) comment reads: "Dìng is *zhèng* (正). In building temples and halls all take Yingshi's culmination [on the meridian] to be straight and true" (定，正也。作宮室皆以營室中为正). See *Shisanjing zhushu* 十三經注疏, ed. Ruan Yuan 阮元 (Beijing: Zhonghua Shuju, 1980), 6:2609 (number before colon corresponds to traditional division of chapters in a particular text). My rendering of *zhèng* as "true" here means "exact, accurate, precise; correct" as in "straight and true."

34. See *Shisanjing zhushu*, 2:2609.

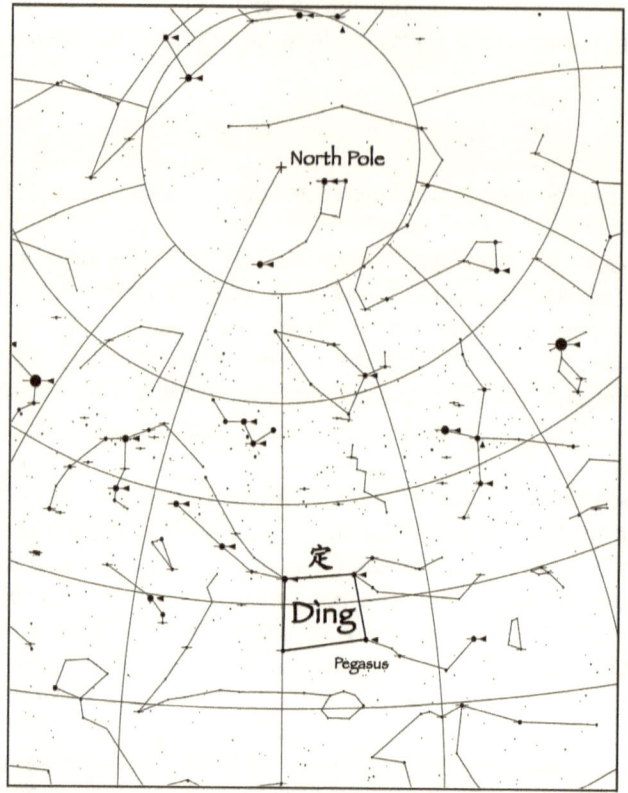

Figure 1.4. Dìng, the Great Square, due south on the local meridian, 10 November 650 B.C.E. Note the exact alignment of the meridian and Dongbi, the Eastern Wall, defined by the two stars at the corners of the left side of the square. Viewing from Luoyang, China. Longitude: 112° 27′ 06″ Latitude: 34° 40′ 11″. 650 BC/11/10 8:16:09 PM (Local). Chart center (J2000): RA: 23h 29.215m Dec: 48° 9.427′. Altitude: 89° 56.562′. Azimuth: 179° 57.558′ (south). FOV: 126°. Limiting magnitude: 5.8. Starry Night Pro 5, Imaginova Canada Ltd.

place. In the "Zhouyu" 周語 section of *Tales of the States* (Guoyu 國語), it says, "When Ying Palace is centered [on the meridian], the work of building begins" (營宮其中，土功其始).[35] *Zuozhuan* 左傳 (Duke Zhuang 莊公, twenty-ninth year) says:

---

35. See *Guoyu* 國語, *Sibu beiyao* ed. (repr., Taipei: Taiwan Zhonghua Shuju, 1975), 2.9b.

凡土功，龍見而畢務，戒事也。火見而致用，水昏正而栽，日至而畢。[36]

As to the work of building, when the Dragon [asterism] appears, [farming] labors end, for [the Dragon] alerts to the undertakings [to come]. When the Fire Star (Antares in Scorpius) appears, [the laborers] are put to work. When "Water" (Yingshi) culminates at dusk, the foundations are built; at winter solstice, [the work is] finished.

Similarly, the "Monthly Ordinances" chapter of the *Lüshi chunqiu* 呂氏春秋, concerning the activities appropriate to mid-autumn, says that this is the time to construct walls and build capitals and cities.[37] Implicit in the reference to the culmination of Dìng ("Ying Palace" in *Tales of the States*) is that asterism's identity as the prototypical Celestial Temple and its specialized function as an accurate guide for aligning symbolic structures on the Pole. Thus, Dìng's evening culmination precisely marks the season reserved for laying out walls and temples whose construction is to follow.

Dìng "Right and True"

The "Inward Training" (Neiye 內業) chapter of *Guanzi* 管子 says:

天主正，地主平，人主靜 ... 能正能靜，然後能定。[38]

For the heavens, the ruling principle is to be *regular* 正. For the earth, the ruling principle is to be level. For human beings, the ruling principle is to be tranquil. . . . If you can be regular and tranquil, only then can you be *stable* 定.

In all references to these alignment procedures above, the word *zhèng* 正 (**tengs*) 'correct~regular' characterizes the observations integral to, as well as the outcome of, the specific alignment procedures. Similarly, *jīng*

---

36. See *Shisanjing zhushu*, 2:1782; see especially Kong Yingda's 孔穎達 (574–648) *Zhengyi* 正義 commentary. "Water" here refers to Yingshi.
37. See *Lüshi chunqiu xin jiaozheng* 呂氏春秋新校正, *Xinbian zhuzi jicheng* 新編諸子集成 ed (Taipei: Shijie Shuju, 1974), 7:76.
38. See *Guanzi* 管子, *Ershi'er zi* ed. (Shanghai: Shanghai Guji Chubanshe, 1986) 16, pp. 155; Harold Roth, Original *Tao: Inward training (Nei-yeh) and the Foundations of Taoist Mysticism* (New York: Columbia University Press, 1999), 58–61. For the significance of *zhèng* 正 'to square up ~ center ~ align' in the "Inward Training" chapter, see Roth, *Original Tao*, 109.

經 (*keng) 'arrange in order' and yíng 營 (*weng) 'delimit ~ delineate ~ lay out', in the "Luogao" 洛誥 and "Shaogao" 召誥 chapters in the *Book of Documents* (Shangshu 尚書) refer to the large-scale arrangement of walled settlements or temple compounds and the "four quarters" of the kingdom. All three words share a common rhyme as well as a close semantic relationship, "be or make straight ~ be or make right ~ put in order." More than that, however, they share a rime with the name of the asterism actually used to accomplish the task, "Dìng" 定.[39] It seems clear that dìng 定 (*ttengs) and zhèng 正 are essentially the same word in such contexts, so that alignment procedures like those described draw on the root meaning of "right ~ straight ~ correct ~ regular" (zhèng).[40] That dìng 定 and zhèng 正 seem to be interchangeable is borne out by the fact that zhèng 正 (*tengs) is simply the B-syllable version of dìng 定 (*ttengs). What the A/B-syllable distinction represents, both phonologically and semantically, is still a matter of debate; however, it is clear that such words must be cognate. This phonophoric series also includes the cognate zhēn 貞 (*treng) used to introduce the charge to the bone in the Shang divinations.[41]

---

39. When, therefore, the "Shaogao" chapter represents King Cheng 成王 as saying, "when the Duke had fixed the site" 公既定宅, dìng zhái may mean more than merely to "settle on" a location. It could actually connote making the layout conform to the celestial standard using the Dìng asterism.
40. Yu Xingwu 于省吾, *Jiagu wenzi gulin* 甲骨文詁林 (Beijing: Zhonghua Shuju, 1996), 1:790. See also Sergey Starostin's compilation of cognate words in Sino-Tibetan; Starostin, "The Tower of Babel Project: Evolution of Human Language Project; Sino-Tibetan Etymology" (Internet version http://starling.rinet.ru/babel.php?lan=en, accessed 4 October 2009). In the specialized language of the epigram above taken from the "Inward Training" chapter, the practice of zhèng 'aligning' means "adjusting or lining up something with an existing pattern or form," where the focus is the physical alignment of the body. See Roth, *Original Tao*, 109. This also calls to mind that it was said of the Sage in the "Xiang dang" 鄉黨 chapter of the *Analects* (Lunyu 論語): *Xi bùzhèng bùzuò* 席不正不坐, "if the mat was not straight, he did not sit"; see *Shisanjing zhushu*, 10:2495. Perhaps there was more to Confucius' fastidiousness than previously suspected.
41. Dǐng 鼎 (*tteng-q) 'cauldron' is used interchangeably with zhēn in the oracle bone divinations, in some instances even in the same inscription; see Yu Xingwu, *Jiagu wenzi gulin*, 3:2718ff. Cf. William G. Boltz, "Three Footnotes on the *Ting* 鼎 'Tripod'," *Journal of the American Oriental Society* 110.1 (1990): 1–8, and Ken-ichi Takashima, "Settling the Cauldron in the Right Place: A Study of 鼎 in the Bone Inscriptions," in *Wang Li Memorial Volumes* (English volume) (Hong Kong: Joint Publishing Company, 1987), 408–9.

A politico-religious imperative lay behind the impulse to correctly align sacred precincts and structures on the Pole using the circumpolar stars or asterisms: "At a time when the Lord-on-High's intentions vis-à-vis the Shang state were very much a national security concern, 'taking direction' *literally* from the ultimate source of supernatural power, may well have called for a more direct 'polar' method."[42] As discussed above, the method attested in the ode "Dìng zhi fang zhong" could have produced accurate alignment on the Pole throughout Shang and Zhou, and possibly earlier. More important, the intentionality this technique discloses is surely revealing. Given the clear connection between the concrete meaning of "fix ~ true up ~ make straight ~ rectify" at the root of the *dìng* 定 – *zhèng* 正 series, to which *zhēn* 貞 – *dǐng* 鼎 'establish ~ fix ~ settle' also belong, then one can discern in the use of *zhēn* 貞 – *dǐng* 鼎 in the oracle bones the analogous noetic impulse to "verify congruence with" the supernatural forces, which lies at the heart of the divination phenomenon.[43] In other words, "making right" (*dìng* 定 – *zhèng* 正) the delimiting of physical space by aligning on the locus of celestial power has its psychological counterpart in the exercise in mental space of establishing the correctness of a proposition through oracular communication *zhēn* 貞 with those supernatural entities.

The Very Image of the Written Word

The imperative to conform precisely to Heaven from the earliest times made it essential to devise practical methods of achieving that objective. The practice of divination is one modality that exemplifies this impulse. Devising a calendar is another. The symbolic design of ritual precincts is another. The accumulation of knowledge about the celestial "landscape" and its application to the orientation of sacred space on the ground is still another. Transcending in importance its figurative role in the eponymous

---

42. Pankenier, "A Brief History of *Beiji*," 229.
43. Cf. David S. Nivison's gloss of *zhēn* 貞 in the oracle bone inscriptions, "Officially verify the correctness of the results of a divination about"; see Nivison, "The 'Question' Question," *Early China* 14 (1989): 125. This interpretation agrees with the earlier analysis of Paul L.-M. Serruys, for which see the discussion in Ken-ichi Takashima, "Introduction," *English Translation of Fascicle Three of Inscriptions from the Yin Ruins*, vol. 1 (Taipei: Institute of History and Philology, Academia Sinica, forthcoming).

ode, insight into the ancient method of aligning on the Pole using Dìng, together with the nexus of phonetic and semantic linkages within the *dìng* 定 – *zhèng* 正 – *zhēn* 貞 – *dǐng* 鼎 word family, reveals this to have been the "right and true" method, designed, literally, to bring the normative celestial images *xiàng* 象 down to earth.[44] The alignment method described above, making use of the Celestial Temple asterism Dìng's precise alignment on due north, is abundantly well documented beginning in mid-Zhou dynasty, though it could potentially have been exploited centuries earlier. A final question to consider, therefore, is, how early can we trace this focus on asterism Dìng, the Great Square of Pegasus, and its special attributes?

Earlier, reference was made to the passage in *Tales of the States* in which the Yingshi is mentioned. There, the calendrical function of the Farmer's Auspice (Nóngxiáng 農祥; lunar lodge Fang Chamber in Scorpius) was described: "When Farmer's Auspice is 'right' on the meridian at dawn, the sun and moon are in the Celestial Temple" (農祥晨正, 日月底於天廟). Wei Zhao's commentary explains:

> 農祥，房星也。晨正，謂立春之日，晨中於午也。農時之候，故曰農祥也。底，至也。天廟，營室也。孟春之月，日月皆在營室也。
>
> Farmer's Auspice is asterism Fang. "Right" at dawn means to say, on the day "Spring Begins," at dawn [Fang] is on the meridian. [Fang] is the harbinger of the agricultural season, so it is called "Farmer's Auspice." Dǐ is "to reach." "Celestial Temple" is Yingshi (Align the Hall). In the first month of spring, sun and moon are both in Yingshi.[45]

---

44. Among the earliest and most striking Neolithic pictographs so far unearthed are those discovered in 1992 at a site near the village of Shuangdun 雙墩 in Bengbu 蚌埠, Anhui 安徽, dating from 7330 to 6900 B.P. Numerous depictions of fish, deer, and pigs as well as stilt-huts, suns, woven patterns, and the like were found inscribed on the bases of clay pots, and this three millennia before Taosi; see Xu Dali 徐大立, "Bangbu, Shuangdun yizhi kehua fuhao jianshu" 蚌埠雙墩遺址刻畫符號簡述, *Zhongyuan kaogu* 中原考古 3 (2008): 75–79. What is particularly interesting is that the same symbols are reported to have been found at another site some sixty kilometers from Shuangdun. It is hardly a stretch to imagine that during the many centuries between Shuangdun and Taosi those early peoples came to identify distinctive stellar patterns with depictions of the domesticated and wild animals on which their lives depended; hence the later designation of such images as *xiàng* 象 — itself originally a pictograph of an elephant.

45. See *Guoyu, Sibu beiyao* ed. (Taipei: Taiwan Zhonghua Shuju, 1975), 1.6b–7a.

Not only is the astronomy in *Tales of the States* technically correct; the application of this calendrical maxim in Warring States times is confirmed by the inscription on a lacquer box from the tomb of Marquis Yi of Zeng 曾侯乙 (circa 433 B.C.E.), the same tomb that yielded the famous lacquer hamper with a depiction of the entire scheme of twenty-eight lunar lodges written on its lid. This second box bears the inscription: "It is Fang to which the people sacrifice; when the syzygy (alt. 'sun's chronogram') is at the (intercardinal) node, the 'Heavenly Quadriga' begins the year" (民祀唯房，日辰於維，興歲之駟). "Heavenly Quadriga" is another name for the array of four stars composing lunar lodge Fang.[46] The meridian passage near dawn of Farmer's Auspice or Heavenly Quadriga (and by implication, the new moon marking the Beginning of Spring in the Celestial Temple) would have been serviceable as a harbinger of the arrival of spring throughout the Xia, Shang, and Zhou dynasties. In view of our earlier discussion of calendrical astronomy, this allusion to the location of the sun in Dìng (Yingshi-Dongbi) in the "regulation" (*zhèng* 正) month that begins the year has special significance.

Ancient Chinese calendar priests from Taosi in Shanxi were observing sunrise daily at least as early as 2100 B.C.E.[47] Needless to say, those calendar priests and their successors would also have paid attention to the regular sequence of asterisms rising in succession just before sunrise and after sunset during each month of the year. It is worth noting here that in February 2100 B.C.E., the first month of the year, when the sun was in

---

46. In an article discussing the imagery on the front of the famous lunar lodge hamper from the tomb, Wu Jiabi 武家璧 identified the asterism depicted as lodge Fang in its guise as Heavenly Quadriga. Wu further conjectured that the hamper and inscribed box were both originally used in the very Farmer's Auspice ritual alluded to in *Tales of the States* and documented in the inscription on the second box; see Wu Jiabi, "Zeng Hou Yi mu qixiang fang xing tukao" 曾侯乙墓漆箱房星圖考," *Ziran kexue shi yanjiu* 20.1 (2001): 90–94. This function of Fang underscores the error of Richard S. Cook's identification of Fang and Tiansi, "Heavenly Quadriga," with the Great Square of Pegasus; see "The Etymology of Chinese *Chén*," 23–29.
47. Cf. Liu Ciyuan et al., "A Chinese Observatory Site of 4,000 Year [sic] Ago," 129–30; He Nu 何駑, "Taosi zhongqi xiaocheng daxing jianzhu jizhi IIFJT1 shidi moni guanxiang baogao"陶寺中期小城大形建築基址II FJT1實地模擬觀象報告, *Gudai wenming yanjiu tongxun* 古代文明研究通訊 [Ancient Civilizations Review] 29 (2006): 3–14; Wu Jiabi and He Nu, "A Preliminary Study about the Astronomical Date of the Large Building IIFJT1 at Taosi," *Gudai wenming yanjiu tongxun* 古代文明研究通訊 8 (2005): 50–55; Wu Jiabi, Chen Meidong, and Liu Ciyuan, "Taosi guanxiangtai yizhi de tianwen gongneng yu niandai."

Yingshi, the leading or "determinative" star of Yingshi, Markab (Alpha Peg), would have risen on the mountain ridge east of Taosi at azimuth 95.5°, precisely in the aperture marked E7 in figure 1.1. They would have observed the correlation of the Dragon constellation (and lunar lodge Fang near its center) with the arrival of spring and the all-important initiation of farming activity. No doubt this is a principal reason the Dragon came to figure so prominently in myth and iconography and as a seasonal indicator in popular astral lore (including the line texts of hexagram *Qián* 乾 in the *Book of Changes*).[48] Ancient skywatchers awaiting sunrise in the twentieth century B.C.E. also could not have failed to notice still another dawn phenomenon. An impressive massing of all five visible planets occurred in late February 1953 B.C.E. in the longitude of the star Alpha Peg (fig. 1.5), the earliest such phenomenon alluded to in the early texts.[49]

The star Alpha Peg is none other than Markab, the determinative star of lunar lodge Yingshi — the Celestial Temple. Clearly, we have here a persuasive explanation for why the ancients' attention might have been powerfully drawn to asterism Dìng as early as the twentieth century B.C.E. This sanctioning by means of a spectacular celestial phenomenon, together with Dìng's unique polar alignment, could well explain that asterism's later function as the standard in architectural, calendrical, and ritual

---

48. Léopold de Saussure was the first sinologist to discuss the correlation between the Dragon asterism's appearance as it seasonally rose and traversed the sky with hexagram *Qián*'s 乾 description of the dragon's behavior in the *Book of Changes*; see de Saussure, "Les origines de l'astronomie Chinoise: La règle des cho-ti," in *Les origines de l'astronomie Chinoise* (Paris: Maisonneuve, 1930), 378. See also Feng Shi 馮時, *Zhongguo tianwen kaoguxue* 中國天文考古學 (Beijing: Zhongguo Shehui Kexue Chubanshe, 2007), 416–17. Edward L. Shaughnessy illustrates the correlations between the hexagrams' line statements and the Dragon constellation's appearance; see "The Composition of 'Qian' and 'Kun' Hexagrams," in *Before Confucius: Studies in the Creation of the Chinese Classics* (Albany: State University of New York Press, 1997), 197–219. In fact, the Dragon constellation was an accurate seasonal indicator throughout both summer and winter, and the connection with hexagram *qian* was never very obscure. In glossing "dragon" *lóng* 龍, for example, *Shuowen jiezi* 說文解字 explains: ". . . It climbs into the sky at the vernal equinox and hides in the abyss at autumnal equinox" (春分而登天, 秋分而潛淵). See *Shuowen jiezi* (Beijing: Zhonghua Shuju, 1963; repr., 1979), 245. Even today, there is the popular saying, "On the second of the second month, the dragon lifts its head" (*èr yuè èr, lóng tái tóu* 二月二龍抬頭).
49. David W. Pankenier, "The Cosmo-Political Background of Heaven's Mandate," *Early China* 20 (1995): 123.

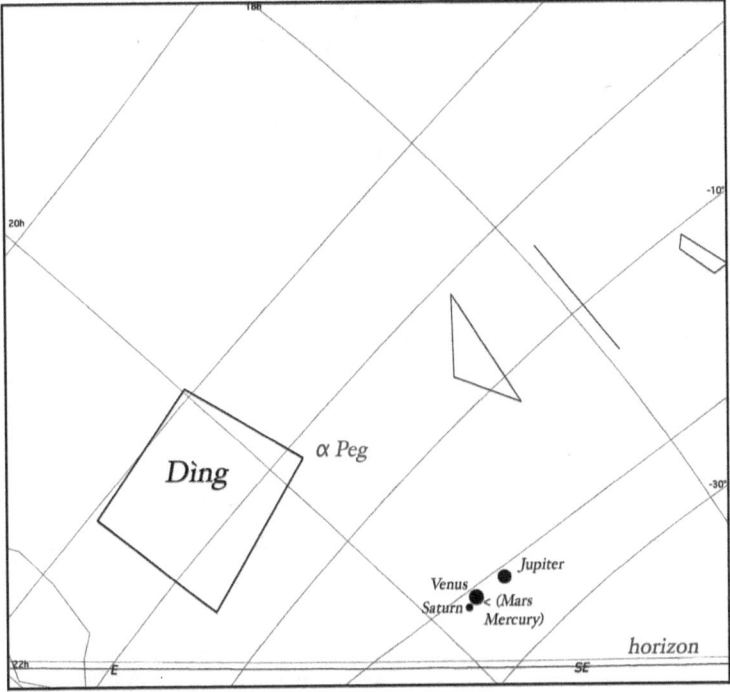

Figure 1.5. The cluster of the five planets in Yingshi at dawn on 26 February 1953 B.C.E. Mars and Mercury are both obscured by the disk of Venus in this view. Starry Night Pro 5, Imaginova Canada Ltd.

contexts.[50] If we now include in the above phonophoric series the fourth heavenly stem *dīng* 丁 (**tteng*), then the celestial inspiration for the "exchanging of knotted cords for written signs" alluded to in the passage from the "Appended Commentary" quoted above comes into sharper focus

---

50. The nexus I am attempting to describe signals the formulation of a new theoretic culture, whose manifestation in the advent of urban planning is described by Xu Hong 許宏, "Erlitou yizhi kaogu xin faxian de xueshu yiyi" 二里頭遺址考古新發現的學術意義, *Zhongguo wenwu bao* 中國文物報 (17 September 2004); rpt., http://www.kaogu.cn/cn/detail.asp?ProductID=8497 (2007-12-19) (accessed 2 April 2009). As Merlin Donald put it: "The critical innovation underlying theoretic culture is visuographic invention, or the symbolic use of graphic devices"; see Donald, *The Origins of the Modern Mind*, 275.

— asterism Dìng (*ttengs) is the celestial square or Temple, and in its earliest form, dīng 丁 (*tteng) is written □, a square.⁵¹

Conclusion

Two sets of cyclical signs, stems and branches, were initially devised to respond to the conceptual and recordkeeping demands of the calendar; the origins of the two are crucially related. Calendrical astronomy lent impetus to the development of writing in China and prefigured its application to other forms of recordkeeping that emerged later, including the Shang divinations, in which we see a mature written language fully formed and capable of expressing virtually anything.⁵² Rhyme may have provided a link between orality and functional notation, serving as a notional connection between the practical use of a set of notational ideographs and the *idea* of glottographic writing. In other words, rhyming may have served as a stimulus prompting the realization that the sounds of spoken words could be attached to conventional graphic signs and serve as analogs of speech.

A prominent example of just such a transformational sign is *dīng* 丁, which demonstrates the connection between the early calendar, astronomy, and the inspiration leading to the adoption of that stem-sign. This one

---

51. See the rubbing of HJ: 24440 reproduced in figure 1.3. In *zhèng* 正 ᙢ (*tengs) 'right ~ correct ~ upright', this same element □ evidently combines both phonophoric and semantic roles. Bagley provides further examples from the oracle bone inscriptions and Shang bronzes; "Anyang Writing," 203–4. One example showing the character *zhēng* 征 (fig. 7.6c, 203) represents □ with rounded corners. In other bronze inscriptions, □ may be rendered as either a solid or an open circle, a stylistic variation permitted by the plastic medium — curvilinear graphs done with a stylus in the still moist clay mold. By this time, the connection between the graph *dīng* □ and its precursor square in the sky may already have been obscure, at least for members of the artisanal class, such as scribes.
52. On this point, Bagley comments, "without the pressure of new needs, or the lure of new possibilities, full writing would never have come into being. Comparison with these well-charted developments in the Near East argues that the writing system we encounter in the Wu Ding oracle texts is the end product of a gradual spread to a broad range of applications." See Bagley, "Anyang Writing," 225. William G. Boltz maintains, based on comparisons with Egyptian and Mesopotamian evidence, that "glottographic writing is likelier to have emerged as a development from pre-existing non-glottographic notational systems than entirely *ex nihilo*." See Boltz, "Literacy and the Emergence of Writing in China," chapter 2 in this volume.

graph may now be seen to provide a crucial link between the abode of the Celestial Thearch above, time management in the form of the first or *zhèng* 正 month of the calendar, the idea of a supernaturally revealed standard of what is "right" and "true" both spatially and conceptually, and, it could be argued, *the realization that the nexus of these several meanings could be represented graphically as a square.* That is to say, the phoneticization of an ideograph derived from the shape of an asterism produced the glottographic manifestation in writing of *dīng* □. *Dīng/dìng*, therefore, is none other than the grapheme in the pre-Shang language for "a square; be straight ~ be square; make straight ~ square up" and, no doubt, "four ~ the fourth."[53]

The profoundly important cultural innovation of writing was acknowledged in the canonical tradition to have been Heaven bestowed. If the *Yi Zhou shu* can still preserve from more than a thousand years earlier a reference to the common name for the first month of the Shang calendar, "Eat Wheat," and if the "Lesser Annuary of Xia" (Xia xiaozheng 夏小正) and the "Canon of Yao" (Yaodian 堯典) can still preserve the seasonal stellar correlations of a calendar from the second millennium B.C.E., then perhaps it is not merely a rhetorical flourish when the "Appended Commentary" of the *Book of Changes* asserts that Heaven suspended images in the heavens for the Sages to "make of themselves their semblance" and the text says that a "River Diagram" mysteriously emerged from the Yellow River. These are explicit claims about the celestial origins of writing and the supernatural sanction for the

---

53. John C. Didier, in "In and Outside the Square: The Sky and the Power of Belief in Ancient China and the World of 4500-100 bc," *Sino-Platonic Papers* 192 (2009), offers an interpretation of the cross-cultural significance of a gigantic square constellation, improperly incorporating stars in the handle of the Big Dipper, which he imagines to have boxed in the celestial Pole. Didier takes up the significance of stem *dīng* 丁 in the Shang divination inscriptions, finding in its shape support for the centrality of his imagined polar asterism, based largely on questionable readings of sacrifices to royal *dīng* 丁-ancestors (or the four quarters) as sacrifices to his polar "square" qua locus of Shang spiritual power. Only after my formal presentation of an earlier version of the present paper to the Columbia Early China Seminar in February 2009 did Didier (by his own admission, vol. 2, 235), add an appendix to "In and Outside the Square" vigorously attacking my identification of Dìng 定 with the Square of Pegasus. Prior to my formal presentation in 2009, Didier had never discussed the Ode "Dìng zhi fang zhong" or stem sign *dīng* 丁 in connection with asterism Dìng 定, nor did he analyze the *dìng* 定 ~ *zhèng* 正 ~ *zhēn* 貞 ~ *dǐng* 鼎 ~ *dīng* 丁 word family.

"impersonation" of such patterns, an account that appears to have a historical basis.

Yingshi or Dìng is strategically located just south of the Milky Way and is reached from the circumpolar region via the asterism Gedao 閣道 (Cassiopeia) "stepped passageway" spanning that Heavenly River.[54] This special configuration had its terrestrial analog in the actual layout of the Qin 秦 capital of Xianyang 咸陽, according to the "Basic Annals of Qin."[55] Just at the time of the planetary massing of 1953 B.C.E. in Yingshi, the Heavenly River or Milky Way would also have been on brilliant display, arching across the sky from northeast to southwest just above Dìng, the Celestial Temple, and midway between it and the Celestial Thearch's abode at the pole (plate 1).[56] This archetypal alignment of the Milky Way may explain why the Qin began the year with the tenth month, when the northeast-to-southwest orientation of both celestial and terrestrial rivers exactly mirrored each other — precisely also when Dìng, the Great Square, was "right" on the meridian. It is just possible, therefore, that the "diagram" that emerged "out of the River" was none other than the Great Square or Dìng 定 ≈ dīng 丁, with the five unblinking planets spectacularly clustered beside it. The well-known representations of the River Diagram as a "magic square" with the number five at its center, the latter conventionally represented by the dots and bars configuration so familiar from the asterisms on traditional star charts, appear quite late. Nevertheless, the two key elements — geometric shape and the number five — figure most prominently, suggesting the persistence of these elements in cultural memory over the centuries as well. As in many other cultures around the world, a kernel of astronomical truth may lie at the heart of several ancient Chinese foundational myths.

---

54. This special configuration was invoked in the actual layout of the Qin 秦 capital Xianyang 咸陽. See Ban Dawei (David W. Pankenier), "Beiji de faxian yu yìngyong," 284.
55. See "Beiji de faxian yu yingyong," 284.
56. For the Milky Way as the celestial analog of the Yellow River in Warring States "field allocation" astrology, see David W. Pankenier, "Characteristics of Field Allocation (fēnyě 分野) Astrology in Early China," in *Current Studies in Archaeoastronomy: Conversations across Time and Space*, ed. J.W. Fountain & Rolf M. Sinclair (Durham: Carolina Academic Press, 2005), 499-513.

CHAPTER 2

Literacy and the Emergence of Writing in China

William G. Boltz

How the notion of literacy should properly be defined is a challenging question that often confounds studies attempting to assess the extent to which a particular society or culture may be called "literate." Does literacy entail knowing only how to read or how to both read and write? And to read what and to write what? Is the ability to recognize one's own name, and perhaps to write it, sufficient to deem one literate? Or should a literate person be expected to be able to read *Ulysses* and to write like Bertrand Russell? Or does a reasonable definition of literacy fall somewhere in between these extremes? In all likelihood the answer will depend on the specific framework and purposes of the investigation in question and will thus vary from study to study. When the focus is on the question of how and when writing per se first came about, the problem of delimiting the scope of literacy would seem to be very simple. Literacy is indicated by the emergence of writing itself. The fact of graphs appearing and functioning as writing presupposes the existence of someone who can both produce and use those graphs.[1] It also presupposes, according to the

---

I am grateful to Viviane Alleton and Wolfgang Behr for their thoughtful comments, suggestions, and corrections to earlier drafts of this paper and to Yang Li 楊莉 for her research assistance with Shang inscription material.

1. In the case specifically of Shang China the ability to produce characters is probably not by itself sufficient to define literacy in a meaningful sense, since it seems that at least in some cases the scribes who were responsible for incising on bones and shells the texts of divinatory proceedings did so in a very mechanical way, cutting all of the vertical and sloping "strokes" of a large number of characters at once and then apparently turning the bone or shell 90 degrees and similarly cutting all of what would become the horizontal "strokes" to complete the characters and finish the job. This suggests that the technical aspect of incising characters was different from what we would normally think of as the literate exercise of writing a text, and to have such a technical skill was

implications of recent investigations into the emergence of writing in Mesopotamia and Egypt, precursor graphic notational systems, and these in turn entail their own kind of literacy. At the formative stage of a writing system the inventors and users of the script constitute the literate population. When a writing system itself has not moved beyond an initial "first use" stage, there can be no question of extent in connection with defining literacy as conventionally understood, since there is nothing beyond the first use in which to be literate. Our problem instead is to identify and explain the nature and scope of that first use. Ideally, the archaeological record would provide direct testimony of the first use and the first users of writing, but in fact such an archaeological record has not yet been uncovered. We must redirect our investigation to focus on what we might call the "first attested use" and on the structure of the writing system found there. Whatever we are able to say about the nature and extent of literacy will have to be qualified as pertaining only to the "first attested use" of the script. If, as seems likely, writing systems that appear to have emerged de novo in fact arose from preexisting graphic notational systems, we can then speak of two kinds of literacy: (1) the ability to construct and use a pre-writing graphic notational system and (2) the comparable ability to use "writing proper." The emergence of "writing proper" out of a precursor graphic notational system then becomes a matter of accounting for a development from one kind of literacy to another. For China, the archaeological record at present tells us very little about the circumstances of such a possibility.

Definition of Writing

The challenge in probing the origin of writing lies first in the definition of writing itself, not of literacy. In talking about the origin of writing we frequently encounter an implied assumption, if not an explicit claim, that writing consists of graphs and signs of whatever semantic import regardless of whether or not they actually represent language. This constitutes a kind of "broad view" of writing. By the same token we see an equally common preference for a "narrow-view" alternative that would

---

distinct from knowing how to "read and write." This does not prove that the scribes were not literate, but it certainly allows for that possibility. See David N. Keightley, *Sources of Shang History: The Oracle-Bone Inscriptions of Bronze Age China* (Berkeley: University of California Press, 1978), 49. See also in this regard "The Evidence for Scribal Training at Anyang," by Adam Smith, chapter 5 in this volume.

restrict the term "writing" to those graphs and signs that represent *spoken language* at some level in some way (or "writing proper"). In the first case, for example, the graph 🚭 constitutes writing because it has a meaning and conveys a message, precisely the central function of language, even though the graph 🚭 itself does not stand conventionally for any specific word or phrase in any given language.[2] Proponents of the former view rightly contend that signs used to convey meaning are communicative devices and, to the extent that language is the communicative device of humans par excellence, such signs should naturally be seen as reflective of language and should therefore be considered a form of writing. Advocates of the second, more limited view point out that there is a world of meaningful signs around us that communicate something, but many of them we would be reluctant to call "writing" in any intuitively natural or acceptable sense. Writing, however broadly or narrowly prescribed, must serve to communicate, in the words of Elizabeth Hill Boone, "relatively specific ideas in a conventional manner by means of permanent, visible marks."[3] The criterion "permanent" in Boone's definition is relative, and the criterion "conventional" is crucial to the definition. To be effective as a part of a notational sign system, a graph must be perceived and understood consistently in the same way by all members of the sign-using community, that is, the literate population in question. For a sign that functions as "writing proper," this means that it must be *readable,* that is, it must evoke the same speech response among all members of the sign-using community. A sign becomes "writing" at the moment when "it changes from being non-phonetic to phonetic," and the change has to be "permanent and conventional."[4] The "visible marks" that serve as the

---

2. We can assign a reading to the graph, such as "no cell phones," and if all of the speakers of the language community in question accept this reading, and no other, then the graph 🚭 would indeed constitute writing proper, that is, writing in the "narrow sense." But as it stands, we might easily find some "readers" reading it as "no cell phones," while others read it as "cell phones off," or "cell phones not allowed," or "cell phones prohibited," or "cell phones barred," or still something else. All of these alternative "readings" make good sense and are entirely reasonable cognitive and linguistic responses to the graph 🚭. When a graph clearly conveys a meaning, as this one does, and is easily "verbalizable" but has no single, unambiguous, conventionally associated reading, it is "writing" in the broad, first sense mentioned here but not in the second, narrow sense.
3. Elizabeth Hill Boone, "Beyond Writing," in *The First Writing*, ed. Stephen D. Houston (Cambridge: Cambridge University Press, 2004), 313.
4. William G. Boltz, *The Origin and Early Development*, 51. The sign is, as Elizabeth

tangible signs of writing, whether in the broad or the narrow sense, in Elizabeth Boone's definition we shall call "graphs," abbreviated **G**.

In order to avoid having to choose between the broad and narrow views of writing, each of which has a measure of validity and usefulness, or having to debate the definition every time we want to talk about writing, we can distinguish, within the confines of the notion of a graph as set out above, between *glottographic* and *non-glottographic* writing. When we wish to indicate writing explicitly in the narrow sense, as graphs that represent spoken language, we refer specifically to glottographic writing.[5] Writing in the broader, more liberal sense is, by contrast, called non-glottographic writing.[6] Any graph **G** that functions as writing, whether glottographic or non-glottographic, will have by definition some conventionally understood semantic import; in other words, it has a semantic value. We will formally designate this feature of **G** as {+S}. A graph that does not convey any conventionally understood meaning (i.e.,

---

Boone has emphasized, a visual graph, but once "phoneticized," it has become invested with a phonetic value (i.e., a sound value) with which it is from then on conventionally associated. See Boone, "Beyond Writing," 313. The sign now evokes a predictable, conventional verbal response in a reader. The "permanent" and "conventional" criteria apply to the use of a sign in any graphic system, whether a non-writing notational system or a writing system. If we assume that the graphs of an embryonic writing system have devolved from the graphs of a precursor non-writing notational system, then the difference between the two is that in the latter, the sign has acquired a "sound value," that is, it has changed from being non-phonetic to phonetic. Exactly how this change comes about remains still unclear for all early writing systems, but the change itself as a defining feature of the emergence of writing should present no puzzle.

5. Malcolm Hyman, "Of Glyphs and Glottography," *Language & Communication* 26 (2006): 233–34. For an earlier use of the term "glottographic," see Geoffrey Sampson, *Writing Systems* (Stanford, Calif.: Stanford University Press, 1985), 29. The salient point, rarely discussed prior to Hyman's paper, is that, as the apparent "natural" counterparts to "glottograph" and "glottography," the terms "semasiograph" and "semasiography" are too general and vague to bring the complexity of the problem adequately into focus. Sampson expressly contrasts semasiographic systems with glottographic systems, failing to notice the imprecision of the former label; see Sampson, *Writing Systems*, 29.

6. The interplay between non-glottographic and glottographic writing can be usefully exploited to focus attention on the social and functional context in which a script operates and may have implications for how notational uses that did not have clear phonetic values might have interacted systematically with newly emergent glottographic signs. This is how John Baines seems to take advantage of the distinction in his survey of early Egyptian writing. See John Baines, "The Earliest Egyptian Writing," in *The First Writing*, ed. Stephen D. Houston (Cambridge: Cambridge University Press, 2004), 150–51; John Baines, *Visual and Written Culture in Ancient Egypt* (Oxford: Oxford University Press, 2007).

that has no semantic value) is thus {–S} and is unlikely to constitute an element in any kind of notational system. There is thus a formal difference between "semantic value" and "meaning" in relation to graphs of a writing system and to visual objects in general. The former is a distinctive feature that depends on an agreed-upon conventional understanding of a graph **G** within a notational system, while the latter is an individually perceived or subjectively determined quality of any visual object ad hoc.

In addition to whether or not a graph has a semantic value, it also may or may not have a phonetic value. The two features operate independently of each other. When a graph does have a phonetic value we mark it as {+**P**}; when it does not we mark it as {-**P**}. The linguistic level of the {**P**} value in this formulation is irrelevant to the definition; the pronunciation of the graph can be at the level of the single sound (<**b**> = /b/, as in *buffalo*), the syllable (<**b**> = /bij/, as in *bar-b-que*), the morpheme (<**b**> = /bi-/, as in *b4* 'before'), or the word (<**b**> = 'bee' as in *b hive*). The salient point is to distinguish between graphs that have some conventionally associated phonetic value {**P**} and those that do not, between, in other words, what are here called *glottographic writing* and *non-glottographic writing*, irrespective of the level at which the glottographic element is operating.

Logically we ought to recognize that "glottographic" writing is by definition the same thing as "phonetic" writing, but the latter term has largely come to refer only to writing in which the individual graphs stand for sound at a level *below* the morphemic or lexical, at a level where no graphic component is simultaneously {+**P**} and {+**S**}. Modern Chinese writing, for example, is often contrasted with "phonetic" writing, implying that it is somehow "non-phonetic," in spite of the obvious fact that every Chinese character has a specific, concrete, recognized pronunciation (i.e., a {**P**} value) just as graphs in alphabetic scripts do, and that every literate Chinese speaker can read it (i.e., can give phonetic values to it), just as literate speakers of languages written with alphabets do. There is no objective reason for restricting the term "phonetic writing" to scripts in which the individual graphs are {-**S**}. Doing so mistakenly implies that a graph that is both {+**P**} and {+**S**} is somehow "not phonetic," when in fact such a graph is clearly "phonetic" and perfectly natural.[7]

---

7. The equally illogical corollary to this is to use the technical terms "logogram" and "phonogram" (or "-graph") as complementary with respect to each other, the former designating a {+**P**, +**S**} graph and the latter a {+**P**, -**S**} graph, whereas logically a phonogram is any {+**P**} graph, regardless of its **S** value.

The features {S} and {P} thus constitute two independent binary variables that, taken together, describe a graph **G** with respect to both meaning and pronunciation. This gives a four-way set of distinctions:

1. **G** : {-P, -S}, non-writing
2. **G** : {-P, +S}, non-glottographic writing
3. **G** : {+P, +S}, glottographic writing type I (morphemic or logographic)
4. **G** : {+P, -S}, glottographic writing type II (syllabic or alphabetic)

Of the four possible types of **G**, three can be considered writing; of these three, the last two constitute glottographic writing. The discussion here of the origin of the Chinese writing system concerns glottographic writing, though non-glottographic sign systems likely played an important role in the eventual emergence of glottographic writing.

The Structure of the Chinese Writing System

When discussing the Chinese script we shall use the word *graph* as an equivalent of what is commonly called a "character" (漢字: Japanese *kanji*, Korean *hanja*, Chinese *hànzì*; in cuneiform studies, graphs are typically called "signs"). The "rule" of Chinese orthography from the earliest time we know and continuing to the present has been that graphs will always be {+P, +S}.[8] This fact alone accounts for the chief difference between the

---

8. This generalization has to be qualified slightly by recognizing a comparatively small number of characters that seem to write only syllabic parts of what linguistically are clearly bisyllabic words. The matter is complicated by the nature of the Chinese writing system. Such seemingly {-S} characters are all the same written typically with constituent graphic components that imply a semantic value and that are the basis of a semantic classification scheme in traditional dictionaries. Consider, for example, the modern (somewhat literary) Chinese word *xīshuài* 'cricket', written 蟋蟀. The Chinese word and the English word both consist of two syllables, neither of which has any meaning except in combination with the other. No one would think of entering *cric* in an English-language dictionary, with a separate entry for *ket* later on, each "defined" as 'cricket'. But this is exactly what happens mutatis mutandis in traditional Chinese-language dictionaries for *xīshuài* 蟋蟀 and for many similar bisyllabic words. We find the single character 蟋 entered as 蟋蟀也 (*xī* means *xīshuài*, i.e.,"*cric* means 'cricket' ") and the second character, 蟀, entered separately with the same definition, 蟋蟀也 (*shuài* means *xīshuài* = "*ket* means 'cricket'.") Beyond this, the two characters both have the 虫 "zoa-entomoid" semantic component, suggesting that even if 蟋 *xī-*

Chinese script and all other scripts in the world, both diachronically and synchronically. Graphs, as they occur and function in the Chinese script, past and present, can be either simple or compound. A simple graph consists of a single graphic element, unanalyzable into any smaller constituent parts save individual strokes. Such a graph is called a *unit character*. Conversely, a character that can be analyzed into two or more constituent parts (i.e., that consists of two or more graphic components) is called a *compound character* (see table 2.1).

Table 2.1 Unit and Compound Characters

Unit characters	犬	石	日	之	月	工	又	五	口	子
Compound characters										
two-part:	吠	岩	明	芝	朔	左	友	吾	名	好
three-part:	然	鮑	盟	尉	蒴	佐	受	語	銘	孺
four-part:	燃	勢	激	犟	疑	隋	授			學
five-part:					凝	隨				
six-part						髓				

With few exceptions, the constituent parts of compound characters are, or at least once were, graphs that serve or served independently as viable unit characters.[9] Writing systems, like spoken languages, are characterized

---

and 蟀 -*shuài* are not "real words" by themselves, each is nonetheless a graph with a fixed pronunciation and a meaning that has something to do with "bugs," thus, {+P, +S}. This results in the syllable *xī*- in *xīshuài* being perceived as "distinct" from the syllable *xī* - with exactly the same pronunciation in other bisyllabic words, for example, in *xīyì* 'lizard' (written 蜥蜴). Except for the effect of the writing system, such a perception about the individual syllables of bisyllabic words such as *xīshuài* is unlikely to have arisen. See George A. Kennedy, "The Monosyllabic Myth," *Journal of the American Oriental Society* 71.3 (1951): 161–66; George A. Kennedy, "The Butterfly Case (part I)," *Wenti* 8 (1955): 1–25.

9. As can be seen from the examples here, the constituent parts of compound graphs are typically identifiable by simple inspection. In a few cases, an analysis based on graphic history is required to understand the componential structure of a character. Some components that have come to function in the received orthography as unit characters (e.g., 骨) are historically in fact compound characters of more than one part. Conversely, a few graphs that are historically unit characters may appear to be analyzable into constituent parts, for example, the character 犬 in the chart given here. This character is in fact not historically derived from the character 大 plus a "dot," in spite of its modern appearance. Such analyses are ahistorical and fortuitous, though

structurally by what is called a "duality of patterning," often called simply *duality*. The French linguist André Martinet first described duality of patterning for spoken language, calling it *double articulation*.[10] In general terms this refers to a scheme in which a small number of meaningless, but individually distinctive items or signs can be combined in various ways to make a large number of meaningful items or signs. In the case specifically of language, the small number of meaningless items will typically be a language's inventory of phonemes and the large number of meaningful groupings is then the language's words, which are combinations of those phonemes.[11] Words are *sense-determinative*, that is, each one has an associated meaning that distinguishes it from all others. Phonemes are *sense-discriminative*, but not sense-determinative, because they distinguish one word from another but do not carry any intrinsic meaning themselves. In English, for example, /k/ and /r/ are phonemes and thus sense-discriminative, because they distinguish, for example, the words /kajt/ 'kite' and /rajt/ 'right' from each other, but neither /k/ nor /r/ is in itself sense-determinative, that is, neither carries any meaning in its own right. The /k/ discriminates /kajt/ from all other /consonant + ajt/ possibilities, but beyond that there is nothing about the sound /k/ itself that has to do with the meaning "kite."[12]

In order to have anything in a writing system that comes close to functioning in a way comparable to double articulation in language, the script must possess two sets of items, a set of sense-discriminators and a set of sense-determiners, related hierarchically one to the other.[13] Items of

---

they may well figure quite legitimately in a strictly synchronic analysis of the modern script.

10. See André Martinet, *Elements of General Linguistics*, trans. Elisabeth Palmer (Chicago: University of Chicago Press, 1964), 22–28.
11. Technically, "words and morphemes."
12. The notion of double articulation, or more generally, duality, as sketched here is applicable to any number of things besides language and writing. Most recently, scientists at the Fred Hutchinson Cancer Research Center in Seattle have been able to explain how the human sense of smell works such that we have the capacity to recognize up to 100,000 different smells with only 350 different odor receptor cells. They have found that it is just this kind of combining of "sense discriminator cells" into groups that become then "sense determiners," sense in this case being "smell." Dr. Linda Buck explains it as analogous to "the use of letters to form different words . . . you put letters of the alphabet together in different combinations and you have different words. Similarly, you can put these different receptors together and get different smells." *Seattle Times*, 5 October 2004.
13. Holenstein defines double articulation thus: "[a] system of signs is called doubly articulated when it consists of two levels of organization, a first level of signs with a

the second set generally will be composed of items from the first set. This is the normal relation between the two sets that is found in alphabetically constituted orthographies. In English and other languages written with alphabets, a compound graph is merely a string of letters that constitutes a word. In such orthographies, there is typically a close (but not perfect) match between the sense-discriminating items of the script and the same items of the language. That is to say, the letters of alphabetic scripts typically map in an approximately one-to-one correspondence onto the phonemes of the spoken form of the language written, and therefore the set of sense-discriminators in the written language is a close isomorphism of the set of sense-discriminators of the spoken language. Thus, /l, i, n, g, u, s, and t/ are sense-discriminators, that is, phonemes in English, and /linguist/ is a sense-determiner, that is, a word, constituted of those phonemes.[14] The orthographic counterpart is exactly the same: < l, i, n, g, u, s, and t > are sense-discriminators in the writing system, and < linguist > is a sense-determiner.[15]

On analogy with a Chinese character, here called a *graph*, abbreviated **G**, a single alphabetically written word, such as <linguist>, should also be called a "graph."[16] By the same token, on analogy with "phoneme" a single graphic constituent part of a graph should be called a *grapheme*, which we might abbreviate **g**. Thus, < l, i, n, g, u, s, and t > are graphemes and < linguist > is a graph. The extent to which the match between the phonemes of a spoken language and the graphemes of its written form approaches a perfect one-to-one "fit" varies from language to language. English and French, for example, are generally rather imperfect, but Spanish, German, and Hungarian come closer to an ideal one-to-one match.[17] No everyday script achieves a perfect, unambiguous one-to-one

---

sense-determinative function (morphemes, words, sentences) and a second level with a *sense-discriminative* function (distinctive features, phonemes, syllables)" (emphases in original). See Elmar Holenstein, "Double Articulation in Writing," in *Writing in Focus*, ed. Florian Coulmas and Konrad Ehlich (Berlin: Mouton, 1983), 45.

14. The /n/ here is realized phonetically as [ŋ].
15. Slash marks are conventionally used to mark phonemes. Angle brackets are used to mark graphs or graphemes.
16. It is well known that whole words typically are apprehended and perceived as single graphic units rather than consciously as composites of segmentable graphemic constituents. For a discussion of how this may bear on the early evolution of the Chinese writing system, see Adam Smith, "Writing at Anyang: The Role of the Divination Record in the Emergence of Chinese Literacy" (PhD diss., University of California, Los Angeles, 2008), 86–126 (sec. 1.6).
17. Allowing for the frequent use of two-letter "digraphs" in Hungarian for single

correspondence between its individual graphemes and the phonemes of the language that it is used to write. Exactly comparable to double articulation in language is the capacity to use a limited number of established graphemes within a script as combining elements with which to produce a potentially unlimited number of compound graphs. This allows the script to represent the entire scope of the language in question without an unmanageably large number of different graphemes.[18] This structural basis of writing systems applies to the Chinese writing system as much as to alphabetic writing systems.

In the Chinese script, most unit characters are also found as constituent parts of compound characters; that is, they function in the writing system as both sense-determiners and sense-discriminators, as both graphs and graphemes. Conversely, most if not all graphemes are in origin, if not in the modern writing system, unit characters, that is, graphs. This relation between graphs and graphemes in the Chinese script is fundamentally different from the relation between graphs and graphemes in alphabetic scripts. In the Chinese script the sense-discriminators (i.e., the graphemes) are for the most part entirely unrelated to the set of phonemes in the spoken language and are instead vestiges of the early development of the writing system itself. For example, the modern script includes many sets of characters structured like those in table 2.2 below.[19]

As can readily be seen, all of these characters have the grapheme <古> as the common, recurring component in their structure, and all have a pronunciation similar to, but not necessarily identical with, the reading of that common component when it is used as an independent graph to write the word *gǔ* < *kka-q 'antiquity'.[20] If the unit graph *gǔ* 古 always stood

---

segmental sounds.

18. Bruce Trigger observes: "[w]riting, like languages and symbolic systems generally, requires an inner ordering to be effective. In a fully developed writing system, a finite, and hence learnable, set of symbols must be capable of recording an unlimited variety of utterances." See Bruce Trigger, "Writing Systems: A Case Study in Cultural Evolution," in *The First Writing*, ed. Stephen D. Houston (Cambridge: Cambridge University Press, 2004), 39.

19. Old Chinese forms are given according to the scheme set out in Robert H. Gassmann and Wolfgang Behr, *Antikchinesisch*, but with occasional modifications that are not necessarily accommodated in their proposals.

20. Note that when the character 古 is used to write the word *gǔ* < *kka-q 'antiquity', it is a graph, but when it occurs as a component in compound graphs, such as in numbers 2 through 12 of the list, it is a grapheme. There is nothing unusual about this (cf. English < a > in < graph >, where it is a grapheme, versus in < a graph >, where on its first occurrence it is a graph).

Table 2.2 古 Phonophoric series

	Graphs	Modern Chinese		Old Chinese	Definition
1.	古	gǔ	<	*kka-q	'antiquity'
2.	罟	gǔ	<	*kka-q	'net'
3.	姑	gū	<	*kka	'aunt'
4.	沽	gū	<	*kka	(river name)
5.	故	gù	<	*kka-s	'past'
6.	固	gù	<	*kka-s	'firm(ly)'
7.	胡	hú	<	*N-kka	'dewlap'
8.	枯	kū	<	*kkha	'withered'
9.	苦	kǔ	<	*kkha-q	'bitter'
10.	居	jū	<	*ka	'dwell'
11.	祜	hù	<	*N-kka-q	'blessing'
12.	怙	hù	<	*N-kka-q	'rely on'

for the exact pronunciation gǔ < *kka-q, it would be called a "syllabograph," but as can be seen from the list, the actual pronunciations vary. The phonetic variation falls within a narrow range, to be sure, but nevertheless the pronunciations vary unpredictably. It is therefore not possible to regard the graph gǔ 古 as a syllabograph in any precise sense.[21] All the same, there is an undeniable sense in which the character 古, with the pronunciation gǔ < *kka-q, serves as the defining graphic and phonetic feature of this set of characters. All of the characters in the set are graphically constituted of gǔ 古 plus an additional graphic component, and all of the pronunciations are similar to gǔ < *kka-q. We therefore infer a cause-and-effect relation between the two, and we generalize this with respect to the writing system as a whole such that we call any set of characters that shows this kind of cause-and-effect relation a "phonophoric series."[22]

---

21. On this point, see Ignatius G. Mattingly and Pai-ling Hsiao, "Are Phonetic Elements in Chinese Characters Drawn from a Syllabary?" *Psychologia* 42.4 (December 1999): 281–89.
22. More commonly, such a series is often called a "phonetic series." The Chinese term is

The great majority of Chinese characters in the transmitted writing system have graphic structures based on a phonophoric series. In such a series the common graphic element is called the *primary* grapheme; this is the component around which the series is formed (*gǔ* 古 in the example here). Each graph in the series, apart from the primary unit graph itself, includes at least one additional graphic element, also properly called a *grapheme*, that distinguishes it from all of the rest. This is the stereotypical pattern upon which the Chinese writing system is built.[23] The salient difference between Chinese characters and the written words of a Western alphabetic script is that with alphabets, the letters that make up a written word approximate the set of phonemes that constitute the spoken word, whereas the pronunciation of a compound Chinese character is not reducible to combinations of individual sounds that correspond in any way to the character's constituent parts.

In theory, each of the compound graphs in a phonophoric series arose as a consequence of the primary unit character having been used at one time or another during the formative period of the script to write all of those different words that are now seen in the series. We can call the use of a single character to write additional words, based on phonetic similarity, such as in the *gu* 古 series illustrated here, *phonetically based extended use* (or, for convenience, simply "extended use").[24] According to the

---

xiéshēng 諧聲 or *xíngshēng* 形聲 series, and an individual character in such a series is called a *xiéshēng* or *xíngshēngzì* 形聲字.

23. The idea of analyzing the Chinese writing system in terms corresponding to linguistic double articulation was first broached, to my knowledge, by the late John DeFrancis in his book *Visible Speech: The Diverse Oneness of Writing Systems* (Honolulu: University of Hawai'i Press, 1989), 253–62.

24. In traditional descriptions of how the Chinese writing system is presumed to have developed, the extended use of a primary unit graph to write any number of homophonous or near homophonous words beyond the one with which it is fundamentally associated is called "loan-graph" (*jiǎjiè* 假借) usage, and a character so used is called a "loan graph" (*jiǎjièzì* 假借字). This orthographic phenomenon is often called in somewhat more technical terminology *paronomasia*, a term that in its precise classical Hellenistic sense refers to the practice of juxtaposing one word with a second word for literary or rhetorical effect, where the second word shows a slight, non-morphological phonetic difference from the first. The amusing effect of the "punning" feature often associated with paronomastic usages in English is secondary in the classical Greek (and Chinese) setting.

The extended use of a graph, as described here, is also often called a "rebus usage." The term "rebus," literally "by [pictures of] things," ought strictly to be limited to such writing as the 🐝 + 🍃 = 'belief' or 👁 = 'I' kind, in which actual pictures

traditional understanding of the formation of such sets of characters, this kind of extended usage was possible because of the similar pronunciations of the words that were to be so written.²⁵ In order to manage the heavy burden of semantic ambiguity that such widespread extended usages would entail, for each additional use of a given graph, a secondary grapheme was added to the original character based on the meaning of the word in question, to disambiguate its written form from all others. This secondary grapheme is called a *semantic determinative* because its disambiguating function is based on meaning. Thus, the word *hú* < *N-kka 'dewlap', for example, was in theory once written with 古 alone, based on the similarity of the pronunciation *gŭ* < *kka-q 'antiquity', the word that 古 conventionally stands for, with the pronunciation of the word *hú* < *N-kka for 'dewlap'. The presumed next step was to write *hú* < *N-kka 'dewlap' with a character that consisted of the primary graph for the series augmented by a secondary graphic component that would distinguish the character for this word from all other extended usages of *gŭ* 古. This is the

---

of things are used to write the syllables of phonetically identical but semantically unrelated words. Because rebus usages are widely presumed to have played a fundamental role in the origin of all writing systems, being generally responsible for a greatly increased capacity for graphs with iconic origins to be used to write additional words based solely on phonetic identity or similarity, the term has continued to be used to refer to the graphic phenomenon that is functionally comparable to the original, literal "writing by pictures" sense of the term "rebus," even after the graphs themselves have lost all iconic or "pictographic" quality.

25. The variation we see in the modern Chinese pronunciations of the characters in a phonophoric series is due in part to sound changes that have occurred in the individual words in the more than two millennia since the characters were created, making the modern pronunciations of words look more different from one another than they actually were when the characters arose as a result of extended usage. The practice of extended usage itself and the rebus principle that underlies it historically sensu stricto require an unchanging {P} value, allowing the {S} value to vary freely, but as can be seen in the example given here, the requirement in the Chinese case seems to have allowed for near-homophony as well as perfect homophony, and this accounts for the variation in pronunciation that cannot be ascribed to diachronic sound changes. How different two pronunciations can be from each other while still qualifying as "near-homophony" for extended use, and consequently for *xiéshēng* purposes, remains a difficult question to answer. Recent work has attempted to account for many of these kinds of sound variations within a phonophoric series as the result of an unvarying word "root" affected by various affixes, sometimes morphologically identifiable, sometimes not. As successful as this has been in explaining a comparatively few cases of morphologically based lexical derivation, it does not yet provide a motivated explanation for the great number of Chinese characters with phonophoric-series structure.

theoretical origin of the character 胡, standing for the word *hú* < *N-kka 'dewlap'. It consists of the original 古 augmented by the graph 月 (<肉), which stands independently for the word *ròu* 'meat' but here serves as a semantic determinative for 'flesh'. It is unlikely in fact that every one of the characters in a phonophoric series arose through an actual extended usage of the primary graph. It seems likelier that the structure of the writing system had become well enough established and rule-governed that the early scribes were able to create an appropriate compound graph at the outset, *as if* in response to a genuine extended usage with its attendant ambiguity.

The conventions that governed the development of the Chinese script allowed already-compound graphs to be used still again in an extended fashion, which then allowed for the addition of another graphic component serving as a new semantic determinative. The process of extended usage was, in other words, recursive, in the end yielding graphs of three, four, or even five or more components (see table 2.1), though the number of actual characters in regular use with four or more components is markedly low. Among the members of the 古 *xiéshēng* series, for example, are three-part characters such as the following: [26]

湖, 楛 and 胡, all *hú* < *N-kka

菇 and 嫴, both *gū* < *kka

堌, 稒, 涸, 痼 and 棝, all *gù* < *kka-s

鋸 and 倨, both *jù* < *ka-s

腒 *qú* < *N-ka

鶋 *jū* < *ka

In each case, the constituent parts can readily be identified; every character consists of the base *gǔ* 古 augmented by secondary components used as semantic determinatives. The character *hú* 胡, for example, is itself used to write the homophonous word *hú* < *N-kka 'lake' and then comes to be

---

26. Shen Jianshi 沈兼士 lists no characters of four or more parts in this *xiéshēng* series. Some of these three-part characters stand for free words, some only for syllables in bisyllabic words and some are distinctly uncommon. None of that affects the fact of their graphic structure or history. See Shen Jianshi, *Guangyun shengxi* 廣韻聲系 (Taipei: Zhonghua Shuju, 1969), 91–96.

augmented with the "water" semantic determinative 氵 (the usual combining form of *shuǐ* 水) and written *hú* 湖. In principle there seems to have been no limit to the number of "extended use recyclings" a character might have been subject to, each time acquiring another secondary (relative to the immediately preceding form) component, but in practice there are very few characters with more than four or five components, suggesting that practical considerations and common sense imposed a check on this aspect of the script's productivity. The end result is a Chinese character structure in which all of the graphemes apart from the primary one have been added on the basis of meaning, not sound, so that there is no relation between the phonemes of the language and the graphemes of the script. All the same, the role of the original primary grapheme is phonetic, and hence all derivative characters within a *xiéshēng* series can correctly be described as phonetically motivated.

The inventory of characters available for use as semantic determinatives seems, at least in theory, to have consisted of the set of all existing unit graphs in the writing system. For practical reasons, such as ease of execution, or for aesthetic reasons, for example, calligraphic appeal, some graphs might have been deemed more suitable than others for such secondary use, but there seems in principle to have been no barrier to the use of any existing unit graph within the writing system as a component in a larger compound graph. By the same token the presumption is that every grapheme used as a combining element in a compound graph had at some point in its history a viable usage as an independent graph within the writing system, although documentary evidence of this in the form of attested usages in extant texts is sometimes wanting.

The Origin of Chinese Writing

The inscription texts from Anyang, dating from the last century and a half of the Shang period (circa 1200–1050 B.C.E.), are the earliest unambiguous attestations of Chinese writing presently known. These consist primarily of divinatory inscriptions on ox scapulas or turtle plastrons and secondarily of bronze inscriptions. A great variety of pottery marks, sometimes "pictographic" signs of varying degrees of realism, more often geometrically very simple, rudimentary marks of only two or three strokes each, appear on pre–Anyang period objects, mostly pottery shards, found all over north and central China. These kinds of markings date from as early as the late Neolithic period, three or more millennia earlier than the

Anyang inscriptions, down to the finds from the Dawenkou sites of circa 2000 B.C.E.[27] Traditional approaches to the question of the origin of Chinese writing have often tried to match the graphs of the Anyang inscription texts with various examples of these diverse kinds of earlier, Neolithic or early Bronze Age marks. The assumption seems to be that showing graphic similarities, if not identities, between the pre-Anyang marks and the Shang inscription forms of characters is sufficient to establish developmental connections between them, even though the ostensible connections are based on nothing more than similarity of graphic shape alone.[28]

It is highly doubtful that any of these scattered late Neolithic marks could have anything to do with the origin of the Chinese writing system that we know.[29] The function of these marks is entirely unknown; they are graphically rudimentary and apparently without any analyzable internal structure, and they date in most cases from times and places far removed from Anyang. The language or words they might have written are unknown, nor is it certain that they represent words or language at all. They are not used in any way that suggests a system, nor do they show any

---

27. For representative examples, see Qiu Xigui, *Chinese Writing*, trans. Gilbert L. Mattos and Jerry Norman (Berkeley: Society for the Study of Early China and Institute of East Asian Studies, University of California, 2000), 29–44; the Mattos and Norman translation takes two different editions of Qiu Xigui's book as its basis, which means that it is not always possible to match a given part of the English-language translation with a specific section of a particular Chinese version. For this reason, all citations hereafter will be to the translation.

28. Qiu Xigui expresses considerable skepticism about the possibility that any of these early marks are direct precursors to the Chinese script. He acknowledges that this represents in part a shift from his earlier view that there might have been some link between the Dawenkou pictographs and Shang writing. See Qiu Xigui, *Chinese Writing*, 38. I explored briefly the possibility that the Dawenkou signs might have a functional link to the late Shang *zúmíng* 族名 'lineage signs' found on numerous bronze vessels and might in that context have something to do with the shift from non-phonetic to phoneticized graphs. See Boltz, *The Origin and Early Development*, 44–51. Bagley claims that I "favored Dawenkou emblems as the likely starting point" for Chinese writing. See Bagley, "Anyang Writing," 249 n. 91. In fact I neither "favored" them nor said that they were a "likely" starting point. My discussion was couched in strictly hypothetical terms, precisely to allow for consideration of a remote possibility in the absence of any more obvious alternatives. I concluded by proposing a "possible, if speculative, link" between the Dawenkou signs and the Shang "lineage signs," a proposal intended to provoke further research, not a claim to be accepted as a conclusion. This remains something that I would continue to think "possible, if speculative."

29. Boltz, *The Origin and Early Development*, 34–44.

internal structure suggestive of anything other than that they are individual, isolated marks. If we are so much in the dark about the inherent function and nature of these early marks themselves, there is little to gain from matching them with much later forms based on nothing more than a fortuitous coincidence of graphic shape. To see them, either in part or in the whole, as somehow constituting a genuine source or early developmental stage for the Anyang writing system is, in the absence of any tangible, objectively documentable links, an untenable thesis.

The circumstances surrounding Chinese writing at Anyang are well known. Writing in China is first unambiguously attested in the bronze inscriptions and bone and shell divinatory inscriptions from the time of the reign of King Wu Ding of the late Shang state, at the capital Anyang, roughly around 1200 B.C.E. Both the bronze inscriptions and the divinatory inscriptions alike seem to be specialized uses of writing related in one way or another to ancestral sacrifices, ceremonies, and rituals and pertaining exclusively to the ruling elite.[30] The writing system found in both these inscription texts does not appear to differ significantly in its structural features from the modern Chinese script. It is, of course, outwardly very different in appearance and in its inventory of individual characters, but these are secondary considerations. In the principles of its orthographic structure, it is in most respects fundamentally the same as the modern Chinese script. This suggests to most people that the Shang inscriptions, whether bronze or bone, are not anything that could be thought of as the starting point or origin of Chinese writing; there must have been some precursor form or stage of which there is so far no direct record or hard archaeological testimony. What was the nature of that precursor stage or those precursor forms? How "pre" were they? More important than knowing what the earlier written graphs looked like is determining what the function of that "pre–fully formed" writing was and how it came to reshape itself into what we recognize as Chinese writing.[31]

---

30. "Sacrifices to ancestors are the dominant theme of Yin dynasty inscriptions." This is the sentence with which Itō Michiharu opens his recent treatise on Shang religion and society. See Itō Michiharu and Takashima Ken-ichi, *Studies in Early Chinese Civilization: Religion, Society, Language and Palaeography* (Osaka: Kansai Gaidai University, 1996), 3.
31. A substantial new corpus of divination texts was discovered in 1991 in a locale within the Anyang area, east of the village of Huayuanzhuang 花園莊 and therefore known as the Huayuanzhuang Dongdi 東地 corpus. The material is contemporaneous with the well-known Anyang inscription texts and is of great interest for what it can contribute to the overall picture of late Shang divination practices and by extension of

In his 2004 essay on Anyang writing, Robert W. Bagley takes the position that because the writing found at Anyang is fully developed, and because the known texts consist only of hard, durable media and reflect only a very specialized use, this cannot be a representative sample of either the uses or the extent of Shang (or earlier) Chinese writing but is instead merely an accident of an imperfect archaeological record; writing on durable materials survived and writing on perishable materials, such as bamboo strips, did not.[32] He emphasizes that the Anyang corpus cannot be assumed to represent either the place or the time of the script's invention, or to represent the full range of functions that writing served, nor can it be expected to reveal the circumstances that at some earlier time led to the invention of writing in China.

To be sure, we should not *assume* that Anyang writing tells us anything about the origin of the Chinese script. By the same token, neither should we *assume* that it doesn't. The question remains open. There are in fact several different questions in this regard, and the significance of the archaeological record varies with each. Certainly it is natural to recognize that texts written on durable materials survive and those on perishable materials do not. In this respect what the archaeological record preserves of Shang texts is probably not representative. But varying durability of the physical medium does not automatically equal variation of content or difference in time. However skewed the archaeological record may be with respect to the physical nature of what is preserved, it does not necessarily follow that the lost textual materials would have been either significantly earlier than or markedly different in content or kind from the extant inscriptional materials. The crucial point is to guard against prematurely dismissing all aspects of the extant late Shang corpus as no more than an aberrancy of an accidental and imperfect archaeological record and thereby to overlook something that might throw some light on the origin of the Chinese writing system. Whatever might have been the nature and duration of the precursor period leading up to the writing we know from

---

the social, religious, and political structure of the late Shang state. Early research into the linguistic and paleographic aspects of the new inscription material does not seem to suggest the need for any major revisions in how the language and writing system should be understood. For a comprehensive introduction to the paleographic aspect of these materials, see Yao Xuan 姚萱, *Yinxu Huayuanzhuang dongdi jiagu buci de chubu yanjiu* 殷墟花園莊東地甲骨卜辭的初步研究 (Beijing: Xianzhuang Shuju, 2006). To date, the best English-language study of this find is Smith, "Writing at Anyang," 174–302, esp. ch. 3.

32. Bagley, "Anyang Writing," 190.

the Shang inscriptions, there is at present no tenable basis for assuming that it is necessarily so far removed from the Wu Ding period as to render the moment of the script's invention utterly divorced from the time and circumstances of its first known use. There is at least the suggestive circumstantial observation that even with all of the extensive archaeological activity of the last several decades in China, over a wide area, not a single credible piece of evidence has thus far been unearthed attesting to Chinese writing anywhere other than at Anyang for any time significantly earlier than the time of Wu Ding.[33]

Writing arose de novo, or, we might say, from scratch, four times in antiquity: in Mesopotamia, in Egypt, in China, and in Mesoamerica.[34] For both Mesopotamian cuneiform and Egyptian hieroglyphic writing, scholars now have a substantial fund of archaeological material that, when fully analyzed and understood, may yield some answers to the question of origins. The Mesopotamian material consists of a large number of seemingly pictographic inscription tablets from the Uruk IV and III periods, as early as 3400 B.C.E., called generally "proto-cuneiform" texts because the graphs have not yet assumed the distinctive wedge-shaped ductus that is the basis for calling them "cuneiform" (fig. 2.1).

There is no complete agreement on whether the writing of these tablets actually represents spoken language fully, partially, or not at all. What is agreed upon is that they are meaningful written records involving commodities (grain, oil, beer, livestock, etc.), indicating quantities, giving proper names, and specifying various kinds of dispersals. The constituent graphs of the tablets are therefore surely invested with meaning (i.e., are {+S}) whether or not they have associated conventional sound values. There are three kinds of graphs in the proto-cuneiform inscription texts: some look like they were iconic in origin and represent, presumably, the

---

33. For a discussion and analysis of the most significant evidence in this regard, see "Literacy to the South and the East of Anyang in Shang China: Zhengzhou and Daxinzhuang," by Ken-ichi Takashima, chapter 4 in this volume, 141-72.
34. Mesopotamianists and Egyptologists alike generally acknowledge the possibility, if not the probability, that in some way not yet clear the "idea" of writing was passed between Mesopotamia and Egypt at the time of the first appearance of writing in those two areas, around 3400 B.C.E. From which place to which place is uncertain, and there is no evidence of any identifiable graphic influence of either on the other in the actual writing systems that emerged. Beyond this, apart from the vague notion of "stimulus diffusion," there is nothing that would suggest any link or influence of any one of these ancient scripts on any other.

Figure 2.1 Mesopotamian proto-cuneiform tablets, Uruk IV, circa 3400 B.C.E. From Nissen, Damerow, and Englund, *Archaic Bookkeeping*, 33, 37. Copyright University of Chicago; reproduced with permission.

thing that they were created to depict; some look iconic but represent names or seem to have meanings different from what their iconicity would suggest directly; and some are abstract, that is, symbolic, and have been shown to represent numbers or quantities. There are no graphs that look like they represent anything that can be identified as grammatical features of a language or functional "particles" as opposed to "full words." Given this lack of any clear reflection of the grammar, whether morphology or syntax, and the generally uncertain glottographic function of the graphs, these texts have been described as only "weakly" related to language.[35]

The earliest pertinent Egyptian material seems to be a similar kind of thing, though much more recently discovered and much less well understood than the proto-cuneiform material. These are the pottery marks and the bone and ivory "tags" from tomb U-j in Abydos, in upper Egypt.[36]

---

35. See Hans J. Nissen, Peter Damerow, and Robert K. Englund, *Archaic Bookkeeping: Writing and Techniques of Economic Administration in the Ancient Near East* (Chicago: University of Chicago Press, 1993), 116–24; Peter Damerow, "The Origins of Writing as a Problem of Historical Epistemology," *Cuneiform Digital Library Journal* 1 (2006): 1. For a very detailed analytical study of the writing system of the Uruk proto-cuneiform tablets and its relation to language, see Robert K. Englund, "Texts from the Late Uruk Period," in *Mesopotamien: Späturuk-Zeit und Frühdynastische Zeit*, ed. Josef Bauer, Robert K. Englund, and Manfred Krebernik (Freiburg, Germany: Universitätsverlag, 1998), 65–82.
36. See Günter Dreyer, *Umm el-Qaab I: Das prädynastische Königsgrab U-j und seine frühen Schriftzeugnisse* (Mainz: Phillipp von Zabern, 1998).

  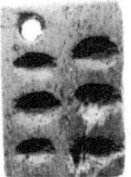

Figure 2.2 Egyptian proto-hieroglyphic signs, Abydos, tomb U-j, circa 3400 B.C.E. From Dreyer, *Umm el-Qaab*, tables 14, 27, and 33. Copyright DAIK; reproduced with permission.

This corpus of materials seems, as with the proto-cuneiform texts, to include iconic graphs that may represent things or names and abstract, symbolic graphs that likely represent numbers. Unlike the proto-cuneiform texts, the two kinds of graphs in the Egyptian materials almost never co-occur on the same tag or pot. The iconic graphs are impressionistically suggestive of later hieroglyphs, but in only a few cases are they formally identifiable with specific hieroglyphs of the established writing system, and in these few cases the apparent relation may be fortuitous. These pottery and tag materials, on analogy with the proto-cuneiform texts, may be called *proto-hieroglyphic* texts.

The Egyptian case again presents inscription material that seems to have only a weak relation to language, and again the obvious question arises: Is this, or any part of this, writing?[37] John Baines says that, taken

---

37. The late Malcolm Hyman suggested that we may constrain our options too narrowly by thinking only of a binary scheme in which something is either writing or not-writing and that we may need to recognize hybrid systems in which some parts of the text are writing according to the narrow definition and some parts are non-writing but functionally convey information that can be verbalized all the same. See Hyman, "Of Glyphs and Glottography," 241. Looking at the proto-cuneiform tablets as in some sense "transitional" is one way of allowing for this hybrid structure, and the philologist's task is to determine what parts of the text are writing, if any, and what parts are verbalizable non-writing, and how the balance shifts over time. The same approach would seem to apply to analyzing the proto-hieroglyphic materials from

as a whole, these "proto-hieroglyphic" materials may be thought of as constituting "writing" under a broad, functional definition but that the extent to which they can be said to record "language" remains uncertain.[38] The way Baines has phrased his discussion, straddling the fence between "writing" broadly defined by function (non-glottographic) and narrowly understood as recording language (glottographic), reflects a perception of the same "weak relation" to language that Damerow observes for the proto-cuneiform tablets and shows the same measure of glottographic ambiguity and uncertainty that attends the proto-cuneiform materials. This is just what we would expect if these were "transitional" materials, reflecting in some way the context in which the shift from {-P, +S} graphs (non-glottographic writing) to {+P, +S} graphs (glottographic writing) took place. As with the proto-cuneiform texts, the answer is not yet clear. What is assumed, though, is that both are instances of inscription material that has some kind of notational or accountancy significance, that serves some kind of record-keeping function, and that seems to constitute a system designed to keep track of commodities, quantities, names of owners, producers, buyers, sellers, or recipients (including temple beneficiaries, in the case of the proto-cuneiform texts).[39] The current hypothesis among Egyptologists is that the U-j material represents a notational system that, however it worked, led one way or another to the invention of writing, but at present it is not clear how.

The evidence for notational precursors to both Mesopotamian and Egyptian writing has led to a hypothesis that writing systems in general, rather than emerging out of thin air as entirely new inventions, have arisen

---

Abydos, as John Baines's discussion would suggest, but in this case, the basic understanding of the texts is still very uncertain. See Baines, "The Earliest Egyptian Writing" and *Visual and Written Culture*.

38. See Baines, "The Earliest Egyptian Writing," 161, 165, 171, et passim; the scare quotes with "writing" and "language" are his, but the wording here is mine. See also John Baines, "Birth of Writing and Kingship-Introduction," in *Egypt at Its Origins 2*, ed. B. Midant-Reynes and Y. Tristant (Louvain, Belgium: Peters, 2008), 842–49; Ilona Regulski, "The Origin of Writing in Relation to the Emergence of the Egyptian State," in *Egypt at Its Origins 2*, ed. B. Midant-Reynes and Y. Tristant (Louvain, Belgium: Peters, 2008), 985–1009. I am grateful to Robert W. Bagley for drawing my attention to these last two articles.

39. The supposition that a graph serves a "practical" notational function, whether as a part of a system or in isolation, should not be allowed automatically to preclude seeing it also as having a "ceremonial" or "ritual" function or status. The two are not necessarily mutually exclusive. See David Wengrow, "Limits of Decipherment: Object Biographies and the Invention of Writing," in *Egypt at Its Origins 2*, 1021–32.

as adaptations of preexisting graphic notational systems of the kind that the Uruk and Abydos archaeological material may represent. The first emergence of a writing system might then best be explained by determining how it could have arisen as a development from a preexisting graphic notational system. What needs of its users did the new writing system meet that had not been met by notational systems already in place?[40] Writing arose in response to what new demands on the pre-writing notational system, and what is the nature of the transition from the stage of pre- or proto-writing to the moment of the first appearance of true writing? Once writing appears, the question of its development quickly becomes a linguistic and orthographic problem. But the question of the first emergence of anything that can properly be identified as writing is an epistemological issue of function.

When we consider this hypothesis in connection with literacy, it is clear that any community of users of a non-glottographic notational system will by definition be literate with respect to the notational system in question. It seems reasonable to suppose that the same basic cognitive and psychological aspects of literacy that pertain to writing systems proper will pertain equally to pre-writing graphic notational systems. In both cases, literacy means knowing how to operate and interpret the graphic system in question according to whatever set of rules governs the structure and functioning of the system and how this represents information or knowledge. Literacy, in other words, as a mark of human society precedes the invention and use of true writing and, in fact, is likely to have been a cognitive prerequisite to the emergence of glottographic writing. Seen this way, the problem then becomes one of determining how one kind of literacy evolved into the other. The archaeological record in China as presently understood is largely mute with respect to such a phenomenon.[41]

---

40. See Damerow, "The Origins of Writing as a Problem of Historical Epistemology," 8.
41. At the Columbia University Early China Seminar (January 2006), I speculated about the possibility that the *tiāngān dìzhī* 天干地支 cyclical counting system might constitute such a phenomenon, ultimately having an origin in such a pre-glottographic notational system that led somehow to the emergence of Chinese writing, though hard archaeological evidence for such a proposal was, as far as I was aware, entirely wanting. David Pankenier, in his "Getting 'Right' with Heaven and the Origins of Writing in China," chapter 2 in this volume, has given tantalizing shape to that earlier speculative proposal. Many scholars, Chinese and Western both, for many decades have sought to find some kind of link between the set of twenty-two *tiāngān dìzhī* signs and the origin of the Chinese writing system. (See references in chapter 2 in this volume.) With a few exceptions, these efforts generally have centered on finding a non-Chinese "outside" source or influence to account for the *tiāngān dìzhī* set and have proved largely

Our best recourse in the absence of archaeological evidence is to analyze the script in the first attested use of Chinese writing and on that basis to infer backwards, to discern what formative processes might have led to the script as found in Shang inscriptions.

If we accept the hypothesis, implicit in recent studies of the earliest inscription materials from both Mesopotamia and Egypt, that glottographic writing is likelier to have arisen from a preexisting non-glottographic notational system than entirely ex nihilo, we can then define the emergence of writing as follows. Glottographic writing arises, by definition, when a {+S} sign or mark that had not been associated conventionally with any specific pronunciation, takes on a fixed phonetic value, that is, becomes {+P}. The precise sense in which we can speak of the *origin* of writing, then, is to say that for any set of functionally meaningful graphs, that is, {+S} graphs, when each graph **G** becomes conventionally associated with a distinct pronunciation {P}, we have writing. The number of graphs in the set may be small; in principle it need be no more than a single graph. In practice it is likely to have involved more than just one or two; the "systematic" part of the notion of a "writing system" presupposes that there are enough {+P} graphs in the set to be used contrastively or combined meaningfully with one another according to some set of rules to allow for the written representation of more than just a few names or words without any context. Nowhere does the archaeological evidence show us unambiguously this emergent step for any writing system. All the same, the earliest evidence for glottographic writing wherever it was invented independently of any influence or effect of preexisting writing systems tends to show {+P, +S} graphs, that is, graphs that have semantic values as well as phonetic ones. This follows logically if glottographic writing did indeed arise from a non-glottographic precursor notational system.

Conventional accounts typically suggest that writing arose in two initial steps: first with "pictographs" that were based on a realistic depiction of the thing that the word they wrote referred to, and second with the rebus usage of those "pictographs" variously for homophonous or nearly

---

inconclusive. The proposal referred to in passing here, and that Pankenier has elaborated with a specific hypothesis about one part of the *tiāngān dìzhī* set, differs fundamentally from earlier work in that the goal here is to identify an indigenous non-glottographic notational context within the Chinese archaeological domain proper that might have served as the locus (or one of several loci) for the genesis of Chinese glottographic writing.

homophonous words whose meanings were not easily depictable directly. While this "two-step" sketch significantly misrepresents and oversimplifies the facts, it also contains a germ of accuracy. Pictographs ought to be defined precisely as graphs that are direct depictions of things, not words. To the extent that writing developed out of non-glottographic notational systems, whatever role pictographs played would have been determined at least in part by their role in the precursor notational system. But the word "pictograph" itself can be a misleading term. When a graph conveys meaning by virtue of its depictive realism within a notational system, we shall call it an *icon*, or *iconograph*. This is functionally and conceptually different from a "pictograph" as defined above, which is simply a graph depicting a thing. The means by which an iconic graph functioning within a notational system conveys its meaning includes not just its realistic depictive quality but also its meaning as an element that contrasts with other elements within a system. Its meaning is in part, in other words, determined by what graph it is not, that is, by what meanings are excluded by virtue of the meanings of the other graphs within the system with which the graph in question contrasts functionally. A second occurrence of a pictograph is simply a new picture of the thing in question, but a second occurrence of an iconograph is a second token of a single sign-type.[42] This means that when "pictographs" (properly, iconographic signs) become phoneticized and serve as graphs in a glottographic writing system, both their semantic aspect and their function will likely have already been predetermined to some extent by their use in a precursor notational system. They are in effect "preconditioned" to convey meaning by virtue of standing for a word, that is, as logographs. As a consequence, once a graph has become phoneticized, the semantic burden carried by its iconicity diminishes and its depictive realism often tends quickly to fade. This in turn strengthens the graph's glottographic quality.

In discussing the *gŭ* 古 phonophoric series above (pages 60-65), we set out the basic process whereby such a graphic series arises through the extended use of a primary graph supplemented by a variety of semantic determinatives according to the meaning of the word written in each instance. This recourse is the predominant means by which the number of Chinese characters has increased over time. It is moreover a means for producing new characters that works at any time in the history of the

---

42. See Boltz, "Pictographic Myths," *Bochumer Jahrbuch zur Ostasienforschung* Bd. 30 (2006): 46; Hyman, "Of Glyphs and Glottography," 240–41.

language, simply because it depends on nothing more than phonetic similarity between two words, one of which has an established written form. Formally, this means that a graph **G** : {+**P**, +**S₁**} is used to write a second word that is {+**P**, +**S₂**}, in which the pronunciation feature has been held constant (within the bounds of permissible near-homophony) and the semantic value allowed to vary. The next orthographic step is to add a secondary grapheme, serving as a semantic determinative, to **G** for either {+**P**, +**S₁**} or {+**P**, +**S₂**}, or for both, to determine the meaning in question unambiguously. Because the process is recursive, it allows in principle for the unlimited proliferation of characters, each of which will be {+**P**, +**S**} and have one more graphic component than its immediate predecessor.

There is an early counterpart to the extended use pattern, less widely recognized than that phonetically-based practice, but fundamental all the same, that entails the use of a graph **G**, already established to write a given word A, to write a second word B that is *semantically* akin to the first but with an unrelated pronunciation. This is tantamount to maintaining a stable **S** value while letting the **P** value vary; in formal terms, a graph **G** stands for either {+**P₁**, +**S**} or {+**P₂**, +**S**}. This is just the complement to extended usage based on phonetic similarity. Such a usage is typically called *polyphony* because the graph has two distinct and presumably unrelated **P** values, **P₁** and **P₂**, but a stable **S** value.[43] Polyphony of graphs is a well-known orthographic phenomenon in cuneiform studies, somewhat less widely recognized in Egyptian and Maya but still identifiable in those orthographic contexts all the same. In the tradition of Chinese paleographic studies, it tends generally to be overlooked. One important exception is Shen Jianshi 沈兼士 (1887–1947), who noticed that the use of the character 月, conventionally standing for the word *yuè* 'moon', occurs in the *Spring and Autumn Annals* (Chunqiu jing 春秋經), appearing to stand for the word *shuò* 'first day of the new month', written normally in the received orthography as 朔. From this, together with his understanding of how the Chinese script seems to have taken shape in general, he speculated that in origin the single graph 月 stood equally for two semantically akin but phonetically distinct words, *yuè* 'moon' and *shuò* 'first day of the new month'.[44]

---

43. On analogy, we could call the consequence of the extended use of a given graph based on phonetic similarity *polysemy*.
44. See William G. Boltz, "Notes on *Shuoh*," in *Dem Text ein Freund: Erkundungen des chinesischen Altertums, Robert H. Gassmann gewidmet*, ed. Roland Altenburger, Martin Lehnert, and Andrea Riemenschnitter (Bern: Peter Lang 2009), 47–49.

The claim of a stable semantic feature in this case entails accepting the premise that the graph 月 can write the word for "moon" on the one hand and equally effectively the word for "first day of the new moon/month" on the other. The graph itself in its earliest form would have been iconically representative of the first meaning and directly suggestive of the second, the dual usage being in both cases non-arbitrarily motivated by the graph's iconicity. In the course of its transmission, when the character 月 was used to write the word *shuò* (Old Chinese *sŋŋrak), it acquired the secondary graphic component 屰 (*zŋak), serving as a phonetic determinative to specify unambiguously that reading as opposed to *yuè* (*ŋʷat), which reading for its part became conventionally associated with the unaugmented graph 月.[45] The occurrence of 月 standing for the word *shuò* in the *Spring and Autumn Annals* is an unexpected vestige in a transmitted text of this early graphic usage. Typically, textual evidence of polyphony is found only in very early excavated materials, chiefly the late Shang divinatory inscriptions. Notice, for example, the graph 禾, used primarily to write the word *hé* < *ggoj 'grain, millet' but also used to write the word *nián* < *znnin 'harvest' in Shang texts.[46] Just as the graph 月 acquired a phonetic determinative to specify the pronunciation *shuò*, so the graph 禾 was augmented with the graph 人 *rén* < *znin ['person'] to serve as a phonetic determinative to specify the reading *nián* < *znnin 'harvest', thus 秂 (> 年), subsequently with a semantic shift to 'year'. The orthographic principle is the same as for the graph 月: in both usages, 禾 writing *hé* 'grain, millet' or writing *nián* 'harvest', the graph itself is in its earliest form iconically representative of the first meaning and directly suggestive of the second. The dual usage is non-arbitrarily motivated by the graph's iconicity.

Consider the graph 卜, conventionally standing for the word *bǔ* 'prognosticate by cracking', attested in thousands of occurrences in extant Shang divinatory inscription texts. Clearly, as can be seen in the illustration, the graph is an iconic representation of a ritually induced

---

45. The function and purpose of phonetic determinatives are analogous to the use of semantic determinatives to specify meanings in cases of phonetically based extended usages.
46. See Matsumaru Michio 松丸道雄 and Takashima Kenichi 高嶋謙一, *Kōkotsu moji jishaku sōran* 甲骨文字字釋綜覽 (Tokyo: Tōkyō Daigaku, 1993), no. 0871.

Figure 2.3 Shang inscription example of 卜 *bǔ* 'prognosticate by cracking' (BB: 104). (From Zhang Bingquan, *Xiaotun* 2: *Yinxu wenzi bingbian*, [Taipei: Zhongyang Yanjiuyuan Lishi Yuyan Yanjiusuo 中央研究院歷史語言研究所, 1965–72], part 1, no. 2, 96).

"divination crack." The same graph 卜 is also attested in the Shang inscription corpus standing for the word *wài* 'outside, outer' (conventionally written 外), for example, in royal ancestor names found in Shang sacrifice inscriptions. The name Wai Bing 外丙, according to *Mencius* 5A.6 the son of Da Ding 大丁,[47] is written 卜丙 (fig. 2.4, upper row). Similarly, the name Wai Ren 外任, the son of Da Wu 大戊 and brother of Zhong Ding 中丁, is written 卜壬 (fig. 2.4, lower row).

In addition to these occurrences in proper names, the same graph 卜 is attested used for the common word *wài* 'outside, outer' in Yinxu and Huayuanzhuang inscriptions alike (fig. 2.5).

---

47. But, according to the *Records of the Grand Scribe* (Shiji 史記), the younger brother of Da Ding. See *Shiji* (Beijing: Zhonghua Shuju, 1959), 98.

LITERACY AND THE EMERGENCE OF WRITING 79

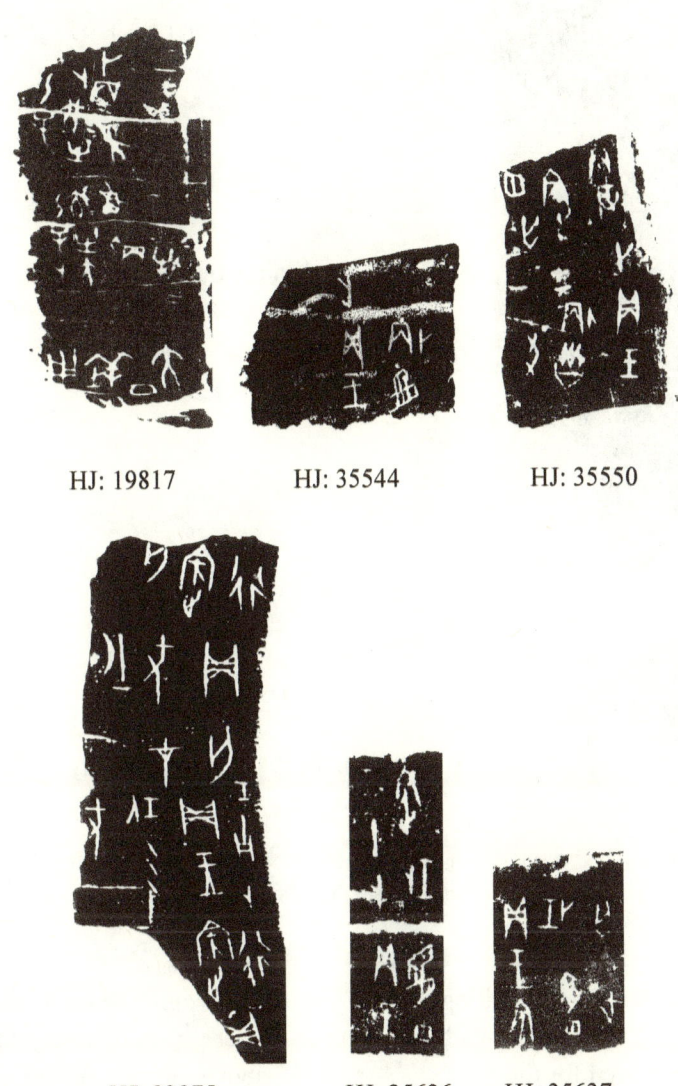

Figure 2.4 Shang inscription examples of 外丙 Wai Bing (HJ: 19817, 35544, 35550) and 外壬 Wai Ren (HJ: 22875, 35636, 35637). (From Zhongguo Shehui Kexueyuan Lishi Yanjiusuo, *Jiaguwen heji*, 7:2579; 8:2964; 12:4448–49, 4457).

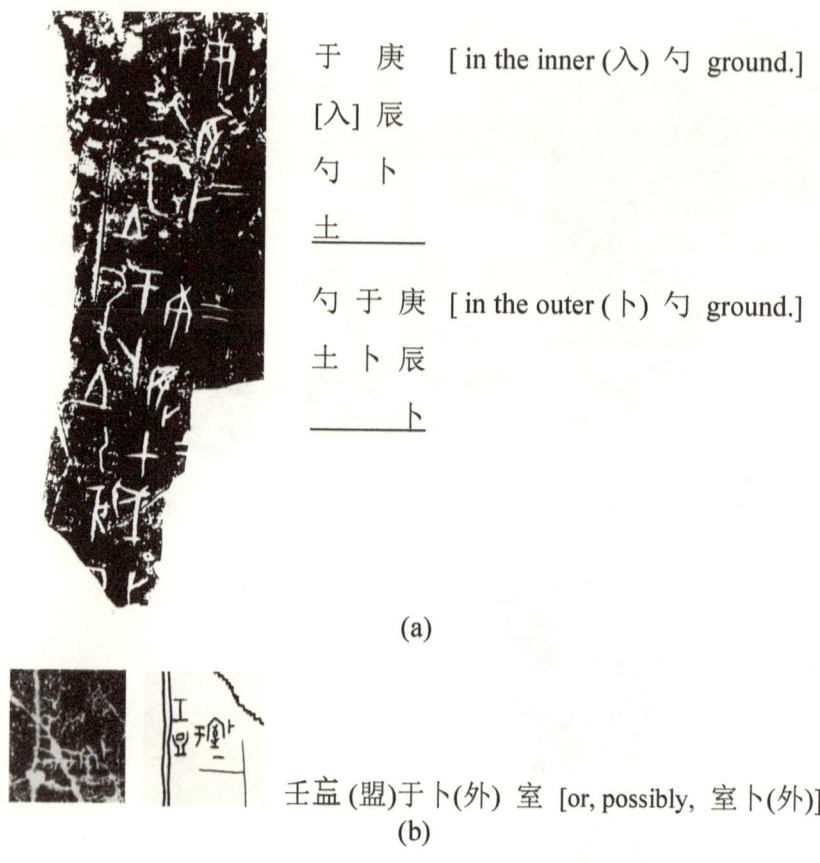

Figure 2.5 Shang inscription examples of 卜 *wài* 'outer, external'. (a: HJ: 34189; b: HD: 236, and see Yao Xuan, *Yinxu Huayuanzhuang dongdi*, 120–23)

The motivation for writing the two words *bǔ* 'prognosticate by cracking' and *wài* 'outside, outer' with the same character 卜 is precisely the same as that proposed for the graphs 月 and 禾 above, namely, the graph itself in its earliest form would have been iconically indicative of the first meaning, 'crack' > 'prognosticate from reading the cracks' and directly suggestive of the second, 'crack' > 'separation' > 'separated from, apart' > 'external, outside, outer'. Just as the *shuò* < *sŋrak reading of 月 was augmented by the phonetic determinative 屰 < *zŋak, and the *nián* <

*znnin reading of 禾 was augmented by the phonetic determinative 人 rén < *znin, so here the wài < *ŋŋʷats reading of 卜 was augmented by the phonetic determinative 夕 (月) yuè < *ŋʷat, yielding the compound character 外.

These three examples illustrate the fundamental, but still largely unrecognized, feature of the formative stage of the script we called "polyphony." What Shen Jianshi recognized about the early usage of the character 月, and the comparable use that we have been able to show for 禾 and 卜, is what the nineteenth-century American philosopher Charles Sanders Peirce (1839–1914) identifed as the twin functional semiotic features of iconicity and indexicality. This distinction constituted a central part of Peirce's formal theory of signs consisting of the trichotomy of *icon*, *index*, and *symbol*, summarized as follows:[48]

• An "icon" is a graphic sign that refers to the object that it denotes by virtue of directly reproducing the physical or visual appearance of the object itself. An iconic graph, in other words, conveys meaning by looking like the thing it stands for.
• An "index" is a graphic sign that refers to the object that it denotes by virtue of a direct concrete or tangible suggestiveness or effect that is non-arbitrarily related to the object in question. An indexical graph conveys its meaning by looking like something associated with or suggestive of the thing it stands for but does not depict the thing itself.
• A "symbol" is a graphic sign that refers to the object that it denotes by virtue of a law that operates so as to cause the symbol to be interpreted as referring to that object. A symbolic graph conveys its meaning by arbitrary, conventional agreement alone and does not look like anything having to do with the thing in question.

Irrespective of their degree of iconicity in origin, all graphs in any established glottographic writing system are technically symbols, because they represent sounds of the spoken language at some level. Sounds, whether single phonemes, syllables, or words, have no direct visual substance, and therefore any graphic representation of them must be by definition governed by an arbitrary convention, thus symbolic.[49] How

---

48. See Boltz, "Pictographic Myths," 47; Boltz, "Notes on *Shuoh*," 49–52.
49. There is a sense in which certain features of spoken language, and their corresponding reflections in what is still fundamentally a symbolic glottographic writing system, can be called "iconic." Notice, for example, that in English the addition of a segmental sound to a noun to form a plural (e.g., 'beer' / 'beers') can be seen as iconic, that is, non-arbitrary, to the extent that it is a tangible increase in the word's phonetic

graphs arose and came to function in a glottographic script can, and typically does, involve both iconic and indexical uses. For 月, 禾, and 卜, the first of the meanings conveyed is what underlies the presumed iconic origin of the graphs themselves, what in Peircean terms constitutes an *iconic* use. The second is not directly represented by the graph's iconicity but is closely enough associated with that feature of the graph to be effectively indicated all the same; this is what Peirce called an *indexical* use. It is precisely the relation between iconic uses and indexical uses of the same sign that defines what we mean by "maintaining a stable **S**" and that underlies what in glottographic terms we call "polyphony."

The phonetically-based extended use of a graph **G** means that the **P** value is held constant while the **S** value is allowed to vary. The polyphonic use of a graph is just the reverse; the **P** value varies while the (underlying) **S** value remains the same. Thus, in both cases, the usage is *motivated*, that is, it is not arbitrary. To this extent the two graphic usages are complementary, and taken together they show the multivalent potential for any graph. But there are two important differences between phonetically-based extended usage and polyphonic usage. Because the phonetic value of a {+**P**} graph can always be associated with the graph separately from the word that the graph conventionally writes, extended usage is an available option at every stage of the written language. In the examples of 月, 禾, and 卜, by contrast, polyphonic usage, requiring a stable semantic identity, depends on the original iconicity of the graph to maintain the **S** value when the **P** value is allowed to vary. Apart from its original iconic quality, there is no aspect of a graph **G** with which a semantic value can be non-lexically associated when it is used to write a word different from the one that it primarily writes. Therefore, the polyphonic use of a graph **G** is limited to the formative period of the writing system, when, presumably, the original iconicity of **G** was still identifiable and viable. Secondly, because the basis of extended usage is a constant **P** value, that possibility exists only for graphs within a

---

substance corresponding to a concrete, physical increase in the word's referent, to wit, from a singular beer to a plurality of beers. When a writing system reflects this directly, as in the case of the suffix-*s* for many English plurals, the same claim of iconicity may obtain. See Roman Jakobson, "Quest for the Essence of Language," in *On Language*, ed. Linda R. Waugh and Monique Monville-Burston (Cambridge, Mass.: Harvard University Press, 1990), 407–21. For a recent comprehensive survey of the question of iconicity in language, see Klaas Willems and Ludovic De Cuypere, eds., *Naturalness and Iconicity in Language* (Amsterdam: John Benjamins, 2008).

glottographic writing system. Polyphony, on the other hand, depends on a stable S value for its effect and therefore can function in a non-glottographic notational system just as effectively as in a glottographic writing system.[50] These two differences taken together suggest that polyphony is developmentally earlier and more fundamental to the formation of a writing system than extended usage based on phonetic similarity. By the same token, it disappears as a viable option for graphic usage early in the history of the script. This means that any writing system that shows evidence of operative polyphony, indicated by identifiable indexical usages of graphs, is likely to be not far removed from the context of its initial formation.[51] To the extent that this applies to the script of the Shang inscription texts, we have a basis for regarding that script as close structurally, and perhaps also temporally, to the formative stage of the writing system overall.[52] Notice that the iconicity of the graph ⼘, the basis for the indexical use that we have tried to identify as "external, outer," reflects not just "crack" generically but clearly indicates the crack shape that specifically characterizes plastron and scapula pyromancy. This would suggest, at least for this one character, that the Shang divination inscription corpus is in fact the context for the graph's origin. The fact that the indexical use of signs is a graphic device equally well suited to non-glottographic and glottographic writing systems alike may provide a focus for investigating the mechanisms leading to the

---

50. When this graphic recourse occurs in a non-glottographic context, the term "polyphony" would not at first glance seem to be apt. But, non-glottographic does not mean non-verbalizable; graphs even in such notational systems can naturally be associated with words, and the possibility of "polyphonic" uses is therefore not excluded.
51. The example that Shen Jianshi noted in the *Spring and Autumn Annals* text, discussed above, is in that literary context far removed from the formative period of the writing system and is not evidence that polyphony or the indexical usage of graphs was an operative part of the writing system at such a late date. It is instead, clearly, a singularly unexpected ossified vestige, preserved in a transmitted Classical text, of the much earlier graphic phenomenon of indexical usage, and it raises interesting questions about the textual history of the *Spring and Autumn Annals* itself, quite apart from the early history of the script.
52. Examples of polyphony, or what now might better be called indexicality, in the early Chinese script have been identified in the scholarly literature many times. See, for examples and discussion, Peter A. Boodberg, "Some Proleptical Remarks on the Evolution of Archaic Chinese," *Harvard Journal of Asiatic Studies* 2 (1937): 330–45 et passim; Ken-ichi Takashima, "The Graph ⊟ for the Word 'Time' in Shang Oracle-Bone Inscriptions," *Bulletin of Chinese Linguistics* 1.1 (2006): 61–79; Boltz, *Origin and Early Development*, 62–72 and 102–26; William G. Boltz, "Three Footnotes," (1990): 1–8.

eventual phoneticization of the former resulting in the latter, in a way that a rebus usage at the earliest stage of the formation of the script or phonetically-based extended usages later do not, and in a way that has yet to be fully explored for the Chinese script.

CHAPTER 3

Phonology in the Chinese Script and Its Relationship to Early Chinese Literacy

David Prager Branner

On first consideration, the tantalizing subject of literacy in Early China might seem beyond our reach to discuss intelligently. For all that written Chinese is documented continuously back to the second millennium B.C.E., we see nothing concrete in the way of reflection on that tradition or on the systematization of it until the very end of the early period, in the first century.

No discussions of the practice of reading and writing or the relationship between the sound and the recorded form of language have survived into the received pre-Han canon. Received tools for classifying characters by shape are not seen until the *Shuowen jiezi* 說文解字 (hereafter, *Shuowen*) of the late first century (and the redaction of it dates from the tenth century).[1] Received tools for determining systematically how characters

---

This chapter is dedicated to the memory of Gilbert L. Mattos (1939–2002). Most of this chapter was originally read as "Crypto-phonograms in Chinese and the Ideography Debate," at the 213th Annual Meeting of the American Oriental Society, 4 April 2003, Nashville, in memory of Mattos; the sections "Continuity of Literacy" and "Functional Homophony" were presented as "Loan-graphs and the Sound of Written Chinese," at the 218th Annual Meeting of the American Oriental Society, Chicago, 15 March 2008; and the content of the section "Initial Types for *Xiéshēng* Groups" is adapted from an unpublished manuscript on the *xiéshēng* series. I am indebted to Mark Asselin, Jakob Dempsey, and Zev Handel for discussions about some of these matters during our student years in the 1990s and to eleven years' worth of my own students at the University of Minnesota, National Chengchi University, and the University of Maryland, where I have taught using William Boltz's *The Origin and Early Development*. I am grateful to a number of members of the Early China Seminar, who gave the chapter very close reading in 2009 — particularly Peter Daniels, William Boltz, Ken-ichi Takashima, and Matthias Richter. Thanks also to Keith Cunningham,

are read date from the sixth century, and their most unsystematic origins do not seem to date back more than a few hundred years. Expositions relating sound to form in the early script begin in the early nineteenth century. The oldest known Chinese glossary, the *Erya* 爾雅, says nothing about written form and seems to have been constructed without taking into consideration the obvious fact (obvious to us) that some characters represent more than one word with more than one pronunciation and meaning.[2]

People who wrote and read Chinese in early times must have thought critically about what they were doing from the beginning, but whatever they thought does not seem to have made its way into the received tradition until rather late.

Actually, complete silence on the subject would be strange if literacy really was common in Early China; we would expect to hear about it from some source or other and perhaps we will soon, through excavated texts. But for now, let us put our doubts aside and consider the evidence we can find in the explicit phonological content of the ancient script. Explicit phonological content is mainly found in the type of compound character known as the *xíngshēngzì* 形聲字, or "phonogram," to use the translation adopted by Gilbert Mattos and Jerry Norman.[3]

Phonology is the study of relationships among the sounds of a language. Chinese historical phonology, in spite of appearances, is not mainly concerned with the reconstructed pronunciations of old words; it is concerned with the systematic relationships among and within Chinese speech sounds at points in the past and over time. In order to study the gross phonological freight of the script for the question of literacy, the motivating premise here is a major modern hypothesis about the historical structure of the Chinese writing system. The hypothesis is controversial and serves as an aid to discussing the phonological content of Chinese writing and considering what that implies about literacy in Early China. Note that this chapter restricts itself to the more passive aspect of literacy,

---

who in 2004 helped me collate a bibliography on experimental studies of reading and related issues. And thanks to one of the anonymous prepublication reviewers of this book, who made extensive suggestions and caught many errors.

1. The *Shuowen* is an inventory of characters, organized by structure and containing sporadic discussion of the relationship between structure, sound, and meaning. There is some question as to whether it should be described as a "dictionary."
2. David Prager Branner, "On Early Chinese Morphology and Its Intellectual History," *Journal of the Royal Asiatic Society*, ser. 3, 15.1 (2003): 60.
3. Qiu Xigui, *Chinese Writing*.

the process of reading.

The argument in this chapter is divided into six parts, each discussed and then summarized in its own section.

The Crypto-phonogram Theory of Chinese Character Structure

The modern hypothesis under consideration in this chapter is what may be called the "crypto-phonogram theory" of Chinese character structure. No other name exists for it now. In the words of William G. Boltz, it states that "there is no way a character can be 'invented' by putting together constituent elements none of which is intended to have any phonetic function" and that "many . . . characters constituted of two or more elements allegedly based only on the meaning of the elements, not the sound, are after careful analysis explicable as phonetic compounds."[4] Boltz's phrasing here is unequivocal. The originator of the theory, Peter A. Boodberg (1903–1972), in his last published statement on the subject, described purely semantic compounds as "a relatively small but exceedingly important class of graphs."[5] Boltz's stronger formulation, however, is more useful for discussion.

As an example, consider table 3.1, showing the graph *xìn* 信, composed of two elements, one of which serves as the "phonetic component" (or "phonetic" or "phonophore") — the element that indicates the sound of the word the character is intended to represent — and the other as the "semantic component" or "signific," a determinative token that disambiguates graphs for different words represented by the same phonetic. Here, *rén* 人 is the phonetic element in *xìn* 信 and, according to the theory, 言 serves to disambiguate 人 from other uses, such as those disambiguated as 仁 'kernel', 千 'thousand' (historically 人 with a mark, i.e., 犭). A "reading" of {N-in (真)} for the graph 人 is adequate to show that it serves as the phonetic element in 信 {N-in (真)}.[6]

---

4. See William G. Boltz, *The Origin and Early Development*, 72.
5. Peter A. Boodberg, "The Chinese Script: An Essay on Nomenclature (the First Hecaton)," *Zhongyang yanjiuyuan lishi yuyan yanjiusuo jikan* 中央研究院歷史語言研究所集刊 29.1 (1957): 118.
6. A note on the early Chinese readings used here: Early Chinese phonology is known to us only in outline; although some highly detailed reconstructions have been published, most of that detail cannot be fully confirmed or in many cases even tested. Regrettable though it is, that is the nature of the subject. But two elements are essential for

Table 3.1 *Xìn* 信 as an example of a phonogram

	Component elements		Compound graph
Modern graph	人	言	信
Meaning	person	to say; words	trust
Readings	{N-in (真)}	{NG-an (元)}	{N-in (真)}
	Phonetic element	Semantic component	

Although this example seems simple enough, *xìn* 信 may be considered a "crypto-phonogram" because in the mainstream Chinese tradition, the phonetic function of *rén* 人 was not understood until very late. Instead, *xìn* was described in the *Shuowen* as having *huìyì* 會意 'combined meanings' structure — in other words, as being a purely semantic compound.

As it happens, *xìn* 信 seems to be a relatively late graph; it is not attested in oracle bones or bronze inscriptions, although there are plenty of Qin and Han examples of it. In the received corpus, it appears in the *Book of Poetry* (Shijing 詩經), the *Zuozhuan* 左傳, and the *Erya*, and it is the given name of two important military figures who died at the beginning of the Han; it is often used interchangeably in early records with 申 and 伸 {L-in (真)} and, to a lesser degree, with 新 and 親 {S-in (真)} and with 身 {L-in (真)}. So it is an important word. It is curious and worth noting that although modern scholars see the graph to be a phonogram, *Shuowen*, compiled at the end of the Han, considers it a semantic compound. (And it

---

explaining the behavior of *xiéshēng* 諧聲 contact in phonetic compound characters: the place (but not usually the manner) of articulation of the syllable-initial, and the syllable-final or "rime category," which is typically named with an exemplary Chinese character. In order to represent this information as a "reading," I am using a set of ten capital letters representing the main initial types together with William Baxter's 1992 reconstruction of the Old Chinese rime categories. "Baxter's 1992 reconstruction" refers throughout this chapter to the system published as William H. Baxter, *A Handbook of Old Chinese Phonology* (Berlin and New York: Mouton de Gruyter, 1992). Although Baxter, working with Laurent Sagart and other collaborators, has greatly revised his reconstruction, at present the 1992 version is the most complete in print, and that is the version cited here. See the section "Initial Types for *Xiéshēng* Groups" at the end of the chapter for a list of the initial types and what they correspond to in terms of fuller phonological systems.

may be significant that the reading {N-in (真)} is at variance with the readings {S-in (真)} and {L-in (真)}.)

Boodberg's theory was not merely that the compilation had missed some of the phonetic elements in its explanations but that many early Chinese graphs were polyphonous" — having more than one reading — and that sometimes an otherwise unknown reading has served as the phonetic element in a compound graph. It is because that phonetic function is claimed to have been unknown that the special term "crypto-phonogram" is needed; as explained below, it seems important that some phonetic elements have been well known through history and others unknown. The term "crypto-phonetic" is used here to mean the historically unrecognized phonetic element of a crypto-phonogram.

A well-known example of a polyphonous graph is that of *shān* 彡 'hair', which has a usual reading of {L-om (侵)}. Boodberg proposed that it once had a second reading with a labial initial, {P-iw (幽)}, as evidenced by the pair of crypto-phonograms shown in table 3.2.[7] But note that *biāo* 髟 has a second reading in medieval sources, equivalent to *shān* 衫 and *shān* 彡; Boodberg's first example of 彡 being read {P-iw (幽)} is thus not strictly necessary.

Table 3.2 *Biāo* 髟 and *biāo* 彪 as crypto-phonograms

	Component elements		Compound graph
Modern graph	彡	長	髟
Meaning	hair	long	long hair
Readings	*{P-iw (幽)}	{T-ang (陽)}	{P-iw (幽)}
	Crypto-phonetic	Semantic component	

	Component elements		Compound graph
Modern graph	彡	虎	彪
Meaning	hair	tiger	tiger's stripes
Readings	*{P-iw (幽)}	{K-a (魚)}	{P-iw (幽)}
	Crypto-phonetic	Semantic component	

---

7. See Boodberg, "Some Proleptical Remarks," 329–72.

An even more celebrated case is that of the graph *xì~xī* 夕 'night' (shown in table 3.3), which has an early Chinese reading of {L-Ak (鐸)} but which Boodberg proposed once had a second reading identical to 冥 'night' {M-ing (耕)}.[8] Boodberg argued that *kǒu* 口 'mouth', too, had a reading presumably of {M-ing (耕)} (see table 3.4).[9]

Table 3.3 *Míng* 名 as a crypto-phonogram

	Component elements		Compound graph
Modern graph	夕 standing for what is now written 冥	口	名
Meaning	night	mouth	name
Readings	*{M-ing (耕)}	{K-o (侯)}	{M-ing (耕)}
	Crypto-phonetic	Semantic component	

Table 3.4 *Míng* 鳴 and *mìng* 命 as crypto-phonograms

	Component elements		Compound graph
Modern graph	口	鳥	鳴
Meaning	mouth	bird	to sing, sound
Readings	*{M-ing (耕)}	{T-iw (幽)}	{M-ing (耕)}
	Crypto-phonetic	Semantic component	

	Component elements		Compound graph
Modern graph	口	令	命
Meaning	mouth	command	command
Readings	*{M-ing (耕)}	{L-ing (耕)}	{M-ing (耕)}
	Crypto-phonetic	Semantic component	

Boodberg's original statement of this theory was elaborated in two rejoinders to articles by Herrlee Creel;[10] it was eventually codified with

---

8. Boodberg, "Some Proleptical Remarks," 342; cf. Boltz, *The Origin and Early Development*, 63, 103–5.
9. Boodberg, "Some Proleptical Remarks," 342.
10. Boodberg, "Some Proleptical Remarks"; Peter A. Boodberg, "'Ideography' or

far more substantial support and more careful argument by William Boltz.[11] At the outset, Boodberg seems to have been elaborating an original hypothesis, although he sounds as though he is stating established fact.[12] Of Boltz's many contributions to the hypothesis, his most important has been to introduce the theory of word families as a way of justifying otherwise irretrievable readings.

Reactions to the crypto-phonogram theory among sinologists and Asianists are mixed but rarely neutral. One active school of thought, represented by John DeFrancis (1911–2009) and J. Marshall Unger, opposes the notion of purely semantic compounds without explicit phonological content, known by the popular terms "ideogram" and "ideograph."[13] In his influential study of writing systems, Ignace Gelb mentions Boodberg's opposition to Creel's use of the term "ideography," adding (without judgment) that it had remained in common use in Egyptology and cuneiform studies.[14] Today, the situation in those fields remains as it was in Gelb's day, but resistance to these terms seems to be quite pronounced among some sinologists.[15]

Iconolatry?" *T'oung pao* 35 (1940): 266–88; Herrlee G. Creel, "On the Nature of Chinese Ideography," *T'oung pao* 32 (1936): 85–161; Herrlee G. Creel, "On the Ideographic Element in Ancient Chinese," *T'oung pao* 34 (1938): 265–94.

11. Boltz, *The Origin and Early Development*.
12. David Lurie has described Boodberg's papers as exhibiting a more developed sense of sinological "disciplinarity" than Creel's; David B. Lurie "Language, Writing, and Disciplinarity in the Critique of the 'Ideographic Myth': Some Proleptical Remarks," Language & Communication 26 (2006): 250–69, 254–55. That may be a gentle way of criticizing Boodberg's austere academic tone, since Creel seems to have been rather more familiar than Boodberg with the early script as attested in bronze inscriptions; see Herrlee G. Creel, "Bronze Inscriptions of the Western Chou Dynasty as Historical Documents," Journal of the American Oriental Society 56.3 (1936): 335–49. It does not appear that Boodberg took much time to look at excavated materials.
13. John DeFrancis, *The Chinese Language: Fact and Fantasy* (Honolulu: University of Hawai'i Press, 1984); J. Marshall Unger and John DeFrancis, "Logographic and Semasiographic Writing Systems: A Critique of Sampson's Classification," in *Scripts and Literacy*, ed. I. Taylor and D. R. Olson (Dordrecht, Netherlands: Kluwer Academic Publishers, 1995), 45–58; J. Marshall Unger, *Ideogram: Chinese Characters and the Myth of Disembodied Meaning* (Honolulu: University of Hawai'i Press, 2004).
14. Ignace J. Gelb, *A Study of Writing: The Foundations of Grammatology* (Chicago: University of Chicago Press, 1952), 107; Ignace J. Gelb, *A Study of Writing* (Chicago: University of Chicago Press, 1963), 107.
15. In 2002 and 2003, I learned from conversations with the Egyptologist James P. Allen and cuneiform authorities Gene Gragg and Craig Melchert that it is generally accepted in their fields that some graphs are composites of semantic elements only. I wish to

The positing of such a "concept script" is a Neo-Platonist idea with a long history in Europe; in antiquity, it was the mystical lens through which Egyptian hieroglyphics were viewed, and in the Renaissance, it found its way into discussions of Chinese. On the one hand, some modern opponents of ideography indulge in polemics, as perhaps befits a response to mysticism intruding into objective philology. In that respect, they recall Peter Duponceau (1760–1844), whose assertion that Chinese writing represented spoken language rather than pure ideas is considered correct and inspired, even though he lacked the evidence to make a clear, accurate, and self-contained case.[16]

On the other hand, most native speakers as well as many sinologists and Asianists reject the categorical way in which the universality of the phonetic principle is sometimes asserted by its supporters. Articulate expression of this rejection has been made by Françoise Bottéro, who has published the most spirited of the responses to Boltz. One of her main points is that Chinese has many compound graphs, attested from an early period, in which neither element appears to be phonetic.[17] As an example, she cites 武, analyzed in an early native text as 止 'foot; to stop', combined with 戈 'halberd', shown in table 3.5.[18] Neither 止 nor 戈 has received readings with any phonetic likeness to that of the compound graph 武.[19] We could make quite a list of such characters, clearly

---

acknowledge their help and also that of the scholar of Persian and Sogdian David A. Utz, grammatologist Peter T. Daniels, and the scholar of Canaanite Eva von Dassow.

16. Y. R. Chao commented, "With such poor language equipment, it is all the more remarkable that Du Ponceau had such a sound and penetrating view of Chinese writing"; see Yuen Ren Chao, "A Note on an Early Logographic Theory of Chinese Writing," *Harvard Journal of Asiatic Studies* 5.2 (1940): 189–91, 190.

17. Françoise Bottéro, "Review of Boltz, *The Origin and Early Development of the Chinese Writing System*," *Journal of the American Oriental Society* 116.3 (1996): 574–77; Françoise Bottéro, "Writing on Shell and Bone in Shang China," in *The First Writing: Script Invention as History and Process*, ed. Stephen D. Houston (Cambridge: Cambridge University Press, 2004), 252–54.

18. Bottéro, "Review of Boltz," 576.

19. After completing this chapter, I learned of Boltz's 2006 paper, which proposes that 止 had a second reading {M-a (魚)}, allowing it to serve as the phonetic in *wǔ* 武; Boltz notes that 武 is attested in the meaning "footstep" and that the reading {M-a (魚)} is more commonly associated with the graph *bù* 步 {P-a (魚)} 'footstep, pace'. William G. Boltz, "Phonographic Motivation in the Formation of Compound Chinese Characters: The Case of *Wǔ* 武," in *Écriture chinoise: Données, usages et représentations*, ed. Françoise Bottéro and Redouane Djamouri (Paris: École des Hautes Études en Sciences Sociales, Centre de Recherches Linguistiques sur l'Asie

containing two elements yet with no obvious phonophore.[20] But even if adduced in great number, they cannot disprove the crypto-phonogram hypothesis, for a simple reason: although we need ancient readings in order to illustrate the phonetic structure of every compound graph, the hypothesis does not claim that all such readings survive or are even deducible.

Table 3.5 Is *wǔ* 武 a phonogram?

	Component elements		Compound graph
	OBI HJ: 20197 Bronze JC: 4292	OBI HJ: 3335 Bronze JC: 11117	OBI HJ: 36080 Bronze JC: 2523
Graph	止	戈	武
Meaning	foot; to stop	halberd	war; martial
Readings	{T-ɨ (之)}	{K-aj (歌)}	{M-a (魚)}

Note: Oracle bone inscription (OBI) graphs are cited by HJ numbers, from *Jiaguwen heji*; bronze graphs are cited by JC numbers, from *Yin Zhou jinwen jicheng*.)

As a theory, the crypto-phonogram hypothesis is weak because it is not strictly falsifiable at all. Indeed, neither Boodberg nor Creel was offering falsifiable explanations of graphic structure; it is difficult to frame either one in predictive terms that could be disproved conclusively. Creel's method is completely passive: he simply combines the meanings of the component elements in whatever way is necessary to produce the known meaning of the compound. It is a beautiful example of tautology. By comparison, the crypto-phonogram theory is stronger in two respects. First, it can at least be rephrased as a sort of long-term pseudo-prediction: in what appear to be purely semantic compounds, at least one element will eventually prove to have a reading that makes it plausible as a phonetic element. In the shorter term, Boodberg's method could also perhaps be

---

Orientale, 2006), 55–73.
20. See Bottéro, "Writing on Shell and Bone," 252–54, for more recent comments. The example she gives of *qǔ* 齲/𪘏 'tooth decay' as a composite of 齒/牙 in combination with "worm" is treated in table 3.10, below.

subjected to statistical analysis, although no one has attempted it to date; statistical analysis could be used to justify or attack the significance of the number of attested crypto-phonograms. Those two facts make crypto-phonogram hypothesis at least potentially superior to Creel's method.

To summarize, neither the crypto-phonogram hypothesis nor the "ideographic" principle of pure semantic compounding is falsifiable, although in formal terms, the former is somewhat stronger. It goes without saying that this whole question is modern. Today we follow Duan Yucai's 段玉裁 (1735–1815) dictum that "[characters] sharing a phonophore are always in the same rhyming group" (*tōngshēng bì tóngbù* 同聲必同部).[21] But phonology never seems to have been understood as the organizing principle of the script until Duan's time. It is one thing for us to posit models to explain the past and confirm their plausibility; but of course that does not mean that the models themselves were also known in antiquity.[22]

Complex Pictographs and Analytical Composite Graphs

If the crypto-phonogram and ideographic approaches appear irreconcilable, they are not. Both are concerned with explaining the origins of compound characters as composites of two or more known simpler characters — as if the reader were consciously assembling whole words out of their component parts, just as the writer does. That, however, is a clear anachronism. Neither is a true analytical composite of the kind that developed later. Chinese characters are read, not deciphered.[23]

---

21. "The original sounds are transformed, so that even when [graphs] share a phonophore, they are scattered through different rimes and rhyming groups. [. . . The patterns] are irregular and the tradition of scholarship has often doubted them. But if we seek their origins, [graphs] with the same phonophore must have been in the same rhyming group" (自音有變轉，同一聲而分散於各部各韻 … 參錯不齊，承學多疑之，要其始，則同諧聲者必同部也); Duan Yucai 段玉裁, "Gu shiqibu xiesheng biao 古十七部諧聲表," *Liushu yinyun biao* 六書音韻表, 2.1A, in *Shuowen jiezi zhu* 說文解字注 (Jingyun Lou cangban 經均樓藏版, repr. Shanghai: Shanghai Guji Chubanshe, 1986 [1981]), 818.
22. A parallel case is that of derivational morphology in early Chinese. The history of our slow awakening to the plausibility of early morphology is narrated in Branner, "On Early Chinese Morphology".
23. Since presenting this paper in 2003, I have become aware of the important work of Galambos (2006), discussing the history of structural variation in the early Chinese

Many compound graphs seem to have originated as what may be called "complex pictographs": they contain two or more recognizable elements interacting in some way. Through the process of normalization, at some point those elements came to be written as discrete characters, and in time the whole characters were analyzed as compounds. Complex pictographs in their original forms are considered here as indivisible units and not necessarily as the juxtaposition of independent characters into which the whole is supposed to be divided analytically.

Take as an example the graph depicting an arrow in a bow. Oracle bone inscription (OBI) forms such as 😀 (HJ: 29355) and 😀 (HJ: 28392) are common and quite typical; a minority of similar forms (e.g., 😀 JC: 2559) and a majority with a hand added next to the line depicting the bowstring 😀 (JC: 2784) are seen in bronze. This graph is well established as the antecedent of modern *shè* 射 'to shoot' {L-ak (釋)}. The original is not simply one pictograph juxtaposed to another — *shǐ* 矢 'arrow' {L-ij (脂)} plus *gōng* 弓 {KW-ing (蒸)} — but actually a single unit in which the relative positions of the elements are part of the depiction. It is a whole depiction. The original OBI form could perhaps have been normalized as 弢 but is instead 射, which is structurally opaque, seeming to consist of *shēn* 身 'body' and *cùn* 寸 'inch' (in addition, there is a received variant 躲). *Shè* 射 in its original form was a complex pictograph, but it has been normalized as a false compound graph; the original pictograph is now represented as what appears to be 身, historically a different graph and word.[24]

---

script. His discussion of "the myth of an ideal structure" in the period leading up to *Shuowen* is especially interesting. See Imre Galambos, *Orthography of Early Chinese Writing: Evidence from Newly Excavated Manuscripts* (Budapest: Department of East Asian Studies, Eötvös Loránd University, 2006), esp. 66–77.

24. The received tradition retains another graph *shǐ* 弰 and its variant 矧, which *Shuowen* describes as "To get the point of what is being said, [as quickly as] the firing of an arrow" (取詞之所之如矢也) and glossed elsewhere in received scholia as "the gums"; its most common use is as a loangraph for a grammar particle meaning "no less; how much more so." See Ding Fubao, *Shuowen jiezi gulin* 說文解字詁林 (Shanghai: Yixue Shuju, 1930), no. 3297. The sense of "drawing back" implied by the components 弓 and 引 is better suggested by the usage "to bare the gums": "[During mourning], laughter/smiling does not reach the point of baring the gums and anger does not reach the point of revilement" (笑不至矧, 怒不至詈); see *Shisanjing zhushu* (Qu li 曲禮 2 of *Liji* 禮記, 2:1243–44. Assuming 引 is phonetic in 矧, this graph would be read

The process of normalization was not at first an act of standardization, because it neither was planned nor involved consistent application of principles. It continued over a very long time; the medieval rime books of the fifth to seventh centuries must be considered an important part of the process at a late stage, since they promulgated not only standard *kǎishū* 楷書 (square script) forms but also standard readings and equivalences between characters and, beyond that, a model of phonology vastly more detailed than the explicit phonology of the script.[25] It is evident that as time passed, the principle of phonetic compounding was accepted and phonograms made up the great majority of standard characters. Many phonograms were produced by adding semantic determinatives to simpler graphs, but the marketplace of normalization sometimes also allowed competing phonograms and unrelated pictographs (simple or complex) for the same word to coexist in the rime books (table 3.6).

In the received tradition, there are few clear examples of characters normalized as composites of two whole written words until rather late. The earliest examples are scribal ligatures. These are seen in Warring States–Han bamboo manuscripts, usually with what is traditionally called a "doubling mark" (*chóngwén hào* 重文號) under the two characters, to show that they are written in the space of one.[26] In Western Zhou bronze inscriptions, this mark usually seems to mean that the character is to be read twice, but by the time of the bamboo manuscripts, what is apparently the same sign is being used to mark ligatures (granted, not strictly "doubling" in the original sense). A ligature in Chinese usually consists of two characters fused into the space of one and sharing some graphic element; this hybrid character has the mark under it, indicating that two words are meant. Usually a ligature replaces a recognized compound, such as *jūnzǐ* 君子 'person of breeding'; the bottom part of 君 is made to

---

{L-in (真)}, which is equivalent to 身. So perhaps the normalization of 𠂤 as 身 is not entirely arbitrary, although even with the reading {L-in (真)}, 身 is not a plausible crypto-phonetic in 射 {L-ak (鐸)}.

25. "Rime book" is the translation of the Chinese term *yùnshū* 韻書: these are not books of rhyme-words for poetry but philological dictionaries organized by "rime" (syllable-final category). Hence the special spelling "rime," distinct from "rhyme."

26. Matthias Richter has given considerable thought to distinguishing the functions of the different marks found in the bamboo manuscripts; see his "Textual Identity and the Role of Literacy in the Transmission of Early Chinese Literature," chapter 6 in this volume.

Table 3.6 Redundant pictographs and phonograms in the medieval phonological sources

Meaning	Pictograph (simple or compound)	Phonogram	Reading
ceremonial covering for the knees	市	韍	P-ot (月)
to discern, make out	釆	辨	P-an (元)
lovely	美	嫩	M-ij (微)
quiver (for arrows)	葡	箙	P-ik (職)
large tripod for cooking	鬲	鑂	L-eik (錫)
insects	蚰	蜫	K-un (文)
flame	焱	焰	L-am (談)? L-om (侵)?
to look to either side	䀠	眴	KW?- L?- + -a (魚)? KW?- L?- + -o (侯)?
to demote, devalue	㝡	貶	P-am (談)? P-em (侵)?

double as the top part of 子, as illustrated in the Guodian forms shown in figure 3.1.

Figure 3.1 A normal ligature from the Guodian manuscripts. (From *Jianbo shufa xuan* bianji zu, *Guodian Chu mu zhujian: Tang Yu zhi dao*, 16, and ibid., *Xing zi ming chu*, 20, 56).

With regard to the difference between compound and composite characters, ligatures are significant in that they are clearly made of two word-characters, not just two elements. Perhaps some of them represented actual contractions in speech or reading. For instance, a number of these ligatures in the bamboo manuscripts stand for multiples of ten, three of which survived as graphs into the rime book tradition and as oral contractions into modern times, as shown in table 3.7.[27]

Table 3.7 Numeric ligatures representing oral contractions, a type of composite graph

Ligature in the rime books	Contraction of	Baxter's 1992 reconstructions of uncontracted numbers	Presumed reading of ligature in Baxter's 1992 reconstruction	Modern Mandarin character readings	Modern Taiwanese
卄	二十 'twenty'	*njijs + *gjip	*njip	niàn	jī chảp > jiáp
卅	三十 'thirty'	*sum + *gjip	*sup	sà	saⁿ chảp > siap
卌	四十 'forty'	*s(p)jij/ts + *gjip	*sjip	xì	*sì chảp > *siap

---

27. In Taiwanese, the expected reading for "forty" would be homophonous with "thirty," which perhaps explains why it is not attested. Note that the Taiwanese pronunciations are true contractions of the current colloquial names of the numerals, not reflexes of the early Chinese or medieval readings. Taiwanese forms are from William Campbell, *A Dictionary of the Amoy Vernacular* (Tainan, Taiwan: Ho Tai Hong Print, 1913), 276, 618. The Mandarin dictionary readings *sà* 卅 and *xì* 卌 match the medieval readings and are never used in speech. The Mandarin reading *niàn* 卄 is both a dictionary reading and phonologically irregular, and there is an interesting problem connected with it. *Niàn* is homophonous with *niàn* 念, and the same homophony is attested in a significant number of Wu dialects, in which 卄 represents a common colloquial word for "twenty" (personal communication, Richard VanNess Simmons). That reading, though incompatible with the *Guangyun* 廣韻, is attested as far back as the eleventh century: Gu Yanwu 顧炎武 (1613–1682) writes, "On the back of the stele it says, '. . . written on the 念-fifth day of the tenth month of 1091'; the practice of writing 卄 as 念 is first attested here" (碑陰 . . . 有曰, . . . 元祐辛未陽月念五日題, 以卄為念, 始見於此); see Gu Yanwu 顧炎武, *Jinshi wenzi ji* 金石文字記, in *Zhihai congshu* 指海叢書 (*Congshu jicheng chubian* 叢書集成初編 edition, vols. 1517–18) (Shanghai: Shangwu Yinshuguan, 1935–40; repr., Beijing: Zhonghua Shuju, 1991), 3.173–14. It is unclear why the standard Chinese and Wu pronunciation of *niàn* 卄 has a nasal coda, with *-m changing to -n in standard Chinese and to vowel-nasalization in conservative Wu; Shanghai has [ɲiɛ₁₃]; see Xu Baohua 許寶華 and Tao Huan 陶寰, *Shanghai fangyan cidian* 上海方言詞典 (Nanjing: Jiangsu Jiaoyu Chubanshe, 1997), 14, 96. Is the *-m coda perhaps an early attempt to preserve the original *-p ending? Or was there another word for "ten" in Chinese, now lost to memory?

Contractions represented as ligatures are a very clear case of composite graphs that are intended to be read analytically. We may assume that *niàn* 廿 and *sà* 卅, at least, were being read as single syllables in the second century B.C.E., because in the metrically regular stele inscriptions of the first Qin emperor, they occupy the space of a single character and syllable; two of these inscriptions survived in physical form late enough to be attested in partial rubbings, so we can be reasonably confident that their received texts in the *Records of the Grand Scribe* (Shiji 史記) are not middle period fabrications.[28]

And the bamboo manuscripts contain another sort of ligature that is even clearer — this kind seems to be a graphic pun. A recognized character appears with the "doubling" mark under it. There is no reason to think that these graphs represent oral contractions or rhyming binoms or the traditional repetition of a whole word. Contextually, we grasp that two characters are meant: the character we see, and also a second character whose form is entirely contained within the strokes of the recognized character. A few examples are shown in table 3.8.

It is as though today we were to write "立々" to represent "並立," "夫々" to represent "大夫," and so on.[29] What is significant about these ligatures is the sense of play that seems to have been responsible for their creation. Play is surely a sign of considerable comfort with the rules of writing; it may be said to be a sign of the maturity of a writing system.

In the received tradition, there is no such clear evidence of play with the structure of characters until much later. Though there are a few dubious early cases of "portmanteau" graphs — whole characters combined playfully as whole words (e.g., *liè* 劣 and *fěi* 朏/ *pò* 咄 and a few others) — this type of structure is not discussed in *Shuowen*, and records of definite cases do not appear until well into the medieval period. Table 3.9 shows some representative examples. Portmanteaux constitute a graphic game of a kind that is still enjoyed today in the Chinese-literate world.[30]

---

28. For texts, see the critical translations in Martin Kern, *The Stele Inscriptions of Ch'in Shih-huang: Text and Ritual in Early Chinese Imperial Representation* (New Haven: American Oriental Society, 2000). *Niàn* 廿 appears on page 12, text 1 line 10; page 18, text 2 line 4; page 25, text 3 line 1; page 35, text 4 line 1; page 38, text 5 line 1. *Sà* 卅 appears at page 44, text 7 line 4.
29. 々 is one of the "ditto marks" in handwritten Chinese, normally representing a repetition of the previous character.
30. For detailed discussion of these and other examples, see David Prager Branner,

Table 3.8 Guodian "punning" ligatures, a type of composite graph.

	Ligature	Combines these two graphs		Meaning
Manuscript graph	[graph]	[graph]	[graph]	to stand side by side
Modern normalization		並(竝)	立	
Manuscript graph	[graph]	[graph]	[graph]	grandee ("great man")
Modern normalization		大	夫	
Manuscript graph	[graph]	[graph]	[graph]	to be in dire straits ("one's self is used up")
Modern normalization		身	窮	
Manuscript graph	[graph]	[graph]	[graph]	land
Modern normalization		土	地	

Note: Examples from the Guodian manuscripts. See Zhang Shouzhong, Sun Xiaocang, and Hao Jianwen, *Guodian Chu jian wenzibian* (Beijing: Wenwu Chubanshe, 2000).

Table 3.9 Medieval portmanteau graphs, a type of composite graph

Character	Presumably to be interpreted analytically as	Representing this word and conventional graph	When attested
䛒	qiǎoyán 巧言 'facile words'	biàn 辯 'to argue'	6th century
㤣	bǎiniàn 百念 'one hundred concerns'	yōu 憂 'worry'	6th century
曌	míngkōng 明空 'to brighten the void'	zhào 照 'to shine on'	7th century
迯	wàizǒu 外走 'run away'	táo 逃 'to flee'	8th century

"Portmanteau Characters in Chinese," to appear in the *Journal of the American Oriental Society* 131.1 (2012): 73-82.

What is significant is how late these true composite graphs are attested in Chinese history, probably not much before the middle of the sixth century. Even counting the earlier manuscript ligatures, the first clear examples of analytically composite graphs — two whole graphs being combined in such a way that their meanings are seen to combine, *as words* — come very late in the history of written Chinese. Both ligatures and portmanteaux, in any case, are varieties of explicitly analytic character structure, since the components represent whole words rather than meanings independent of their vocalized form.[31]

Now compare those analytic composite graphs with this chapter's so-called complex pictographs in table 3.10.[32] These graphs may be explained as either crypto-phonograms or semantic compounds; indeed, they may not be complex pictographs at all and may have been created as compounds to begin with. But it is not necessary to analyze them in pieces as is done with ligatures and portmanteau words; they can and should be recognized as units. That is to say, no matter whether they can be analyzed phonogrammatically or not, they are fundamentally logographs: whole symbols for whole words. Asserting that Chinese characters are logographs is a matter not of philosophical viewpoint but of reproducible measurement: a fluent reader's brain recognizes them as whole words or whole morphemes.

Long after Boodberg's time, it was demonstrated empirically that there is a "word superiority effect" in the reading of Chinese characters and Japanese *kanji*, just as in the reading of alphabetic and even patently phonetic scripts — meaning that it is measurably more efficient for the brain to recognize whole and meaningful written words than to piece those words together analytically out of their components. Fluent readers of Chinese tend to recognize whole characters rather than analyzing them by

---

31. It may be objected that a portmanteau character involves elements that can actually be vocalized as words while a putative ideograph or pure semantic compound involves non-vocalized elements, and that these are two different things. But the experimental evidence for logography means that all elements with meaning must function essentially as though vocalized. Though there is no explicit support for this particular image from the Chinese linguistic world, one may recall Ezra Pound's ideographic explanation of *xìn* 信 'sincere' as "man standing by his word"; Ezra Pound, Appendix to *The Chinese Written Character as a Medium for Poetry*, by Ernest Francisco Fenollosa (San Francisco: City Lights Books, 1936), 41.
32. For the example of 毓, see Boltz, *The Origin and Early Development*, 110–13; for 鯀, see ibid., 123–25.

Table 3.10 "Complex pictographs," perhaps not composite

Ancient graphs	As complex pictograph, apparently represents	Modern graph seems to be composite of	Reading and gloss of recognized word	Crypto-phonetic explanations?
OBI HJ: 27145 Bronze JC: 5396	parturition: woman giving birth to child	毓(育): 每 + 㐬; not obvious as modern graphs	L-uk (育): to give birth, rear	㐬 = inverted 子 'child', i.e., 子: related to 孝 {L-uk (育)}
Bronze JC: 2200	fish on a line	鰥: 魚 'fish' + 系 'thread'	KW-in (鰥): fish, big fish	系 = 幺: related to 玄 {KW-in (鰥)}
OBI HJ: 13662	rot in the teeth	齲/䶕: 牙 or 齒 'tooth' + 禹 'bug, beast' (*Shuōwén*)	KW-a (齲): rotten tooth	(*Shuōwén* says 禹 is phonetic)
Bronze JC: 4315	rice bent over with full ear	穆: 禾 'rice' + 㣎 'fine markings' (*Shuōwén*)	L-iwk (穆): fine-looking rice	(*Shuōwén* says 㣎 is phonetic, but it is unattested before *Shuōwén*)

decomposition as do non-fluent native and foreign learners.[33] Even multicharacter words seem to be processed as whole words rather than character by character.[34] It has been suggested that the brain must have an

---

33. Hiroyuki Kaiho and Hirofumi Saito, "Measuring Various Aspects of Kanji (Chinese Characters) and Its Psychological Implications," *Quantitative Linguistics* 39 (1989): 151–63; Fook Kee Chua, "Visual Perception of the Chinese Character: Configural or Separable Processing?" *Psychologia* 42.4 (1999): 209–21; Xiangzhi Meng, Hua Shu, and Xiaolin Zhou, "Children's Chinese Characters Structure Awareness in Character Output," *Psychological Science* (China) 23.3 (2000): 260–64.
34. Naoko Sakuma, Itoh Motonobu, Sasanuma Sumiko, "Recognition Units of Kanji Words: Priming Effects on Kanji Recognition," *Shinrigaku kenkyū* 心理学研究 (The Japanese journal of psychology) 60.1 (1989): 1–8; Ignatius G. Mattingly and Yi Xu, "Word Superiority in Chinese," *Haskins Laboratories Status Report on Speech Research* 113 (1993): 145–51.

"orthographic processing system" for indivisible character components, but the exact positioning and complexity of those components seem to be essential to that system; components are not recombined freely before the whole character is recognized.[35]

Still more significantly, a long series of experiments since the 1980s has shown that recognizing a Chinese character or Japanese kanji has an immediate phonological implication in the brain.[36] Whether or not it has an explicit phonogram structure, every character has a phonological value for the brain as soon as it is recognized. For fluent readers, there is no lag between recognition of a character — due to graphic, analytic, or other processes — and assignment of its phonological value.

It may, of course, be argued that all these experiments have been conducted on people who are already familiar with explicitly phonetic writing, in the form of *zhùyīn fúhào* 注音符號, pinyin, or *kana* 仮名, and that these findings do not explain decisively how people read characters in the days before phonetic scripts were widespread. But for the foreseeable future, experiments such as these will be the only measurements that can be brought to the study of this problem. The neural basis of modern

---

35. Marcus Taft and Xiaoping Zhu, "Submorphemic Processing in Reading Chinese," *Journal of Experimental Psychology: Learning, Memory, and Cognition* 23.3 (1997): 761–75; Guosheng Ding, Danling Peng, and Marcus Taft, "The Nature of the Mental Representation of Radicals in Chinese: A Priming Study," *Journal of Experimental Psychology: Learning, Memory, and Cognition* 30.2 (2004): 530–39. It is regrettable that both phonetic and semantic components are usually called "radicals" by experimental researchers, confusing *bùshǒu* 部首 'dictionary section-heads' with *bùjiàn* 部件 'component parts' or 'elements'. Some authors do, however, explain which sense they mean. It would be better if experimenters followed normal sinological usage.

36. A major review of the literature may be found in Li-hai Tan and Charles A. Perfetti, "Phonological Codes as Early Sources of Constraint in Chinese Word Identification: A Review of Current Discoveries and Theoretical Accounts," *Reading and Writing* 10.3-5 (1998): 165–200. See also Lien-chong Mou and Nancy S. Anderson, "Graphemic and Phonemic Codings of Chinese Characters in Short-term Retention," *Bulletin of the Psychonomic Society* 17.6 (1981): 255–58; Connie Suk-Han Ho and Peter Bryant, "Learning to Read Chinese beyond the Logographic Phase," *Reading Research Quarterly* 32.3 (1997): 276–89; Connie Suk-Han Ho, "The Importance of Phonological Awareness and Verbal Short-term Memory to Children's Success in Learning to Read Chinese," *Psychologia* 40.4 (1997): 211–19; Chih-Wei Hue and James R. Erickson, "Short-term Memory for Chinese Characters and Radicals," *Memory & Cognition* 16.3 (1988): 196–205; Sumiko Sasanuma, Sakuma Naoko, and Kitano Kunitaka, "Reading Kanji without Semantics: Evidence from a Longitudinal Study of Dementia," *Cognitive Neuropsychology* (United Kingdom) 9.6 (1992): 465–86.

reading was not necessarily "prefigured" in the historical evolution of the script, but it is axiomatic that writing systems evolve through a process of optimization, which includes cognitive optimization as well as societal pressures and surely imponderables now unknown to us.

Thus there is no reason to assume that a compound character lacking an obvious phonetic is meant to be analyzed semantically. The brain recognizes it today as a whole graph, and in the absence of other evidence, it is reasonable to assume that this has always been the case. Such a graph may be characterized as a complex but unitary pictograph.

The Value of Phoneticism

If all characters, regardless of their structure, are read as logographs, then what is the significance of phonogram structure, whether patent or concealed? Experimental research has been inconclusive to date. In the 1980s, a number of studies suggested that the presence of a phonophore facilitates recognition of low-frequency but not high-frequency characters.[37] More recent studies suggest that reading high-frequency characters, too, is facilitated by phonophores,[38] but others suggest facilitation by non-phonetic components as well.[39] It seems that the most important point of disagreement is the mechanism by which "recognition" is facilitated. It is experimentally clear, however, that the presence of a phonetic speeds recognition.

In the absence of a settled experimental explanation, let us approach phoneticism by returning to another point made by Bottéro, involving variant graphs. She cites *shǐ* 豕 'pig', which has a likely reading of {L?-ij (脂)} but which in *zhú* 逐 'to chase' she suggests might have the reading

---

37. See the review in Li-hai Tan et al., "Phonological Codes," 191–94.
38. Alexander Pollatsek et al., "The Role of Phonological Codes in Integrating Information across Saccadic Eye Movements in Chinese Character Identification," *Journal of Experimental Psychology: Human Perception and Performance* 26/2 (2000): 607–33; Jie-Li Tsai et al., "Use of Phonological Codes for Chinese Characters: Evidence from Processing of Parafoveal Preview When Reading Sentences," *Brain and Language* 91/2 (2004): 235–44.
39. Xiaolin Zhou et al., "Is There Phonologically Mediated Access to Lexical Semantics in Reading Chinese?" in *Reading Chinese Script: A Cognitive Analysis*, ed. Jian Wang et al. (Mahwah, NJ: Lawrence Erlbaum Associates, 1999), 135–71; Xiaolin Zhou et al., "The Relative Time Course of Semantic and Phonological Activation in Reading Chinese," *Journal of Experimental Psychology: Learning, Memory, and Cognition* 26/5 (2000): 1245–65; Ding, "The Nature of the Mental Representation," 530–39.

later written *zhū* 豬 'pig' {T-a (魚)}.[40] She notes that in early inscriptions, the same word is written with what is plainly an antlered deer in place of the pig and observes that, under the circumstances, an element that is replaced in variant forms of the compound graph cannot be claimed as phonophore.

There are two answers to this. The first is that *lù* 鹿 'deer' is more plausible than either *shǐ* 豕 or *zhū* 豬 as the phonetic element of *zhú* 逐, since both initial and rime are much closer, as shown in table 3.11. The reader who has entered into the spirit of crypto-phonogrammism may

Table 3.11 Is *zhú* 逐 a phonogram?

	Component elements		Compound graph
Ancient graph	OBI [graph] HJ: 20197	OBI [graph] HJ: 28334	OBI [graph] HJ: 10654
Modern graph	止	鹿	逐
Meaning	foot; to stop	deer	to chase
Readings	{T-i (之)}	{L-uk (屋)}	{L-iwk (覺)}
	Semantic component	Crypto-phonetic?	

	Component elements		Compound graph
Ancient graph	OBI [graph] HJ: 20197	OBI [graph] HJ: 10307	OBI [graph] HJ: 35263
Modern graph	止	豕	逐
Meaning	foot; to stop	pig	to chase
Readings	{T-i (之)}	{L?-ij (脂)}, based on received *shǐ* or *{T-a (魚)}, standing for the word *zhū* now written 豬	{L-iwk (覺)}
	Semantic component	Crypto-phonetic?	

---

40. The status of the early Chinese initial of *shǐ* 豕 is uncertain, hence I have marked it with a question mark. The likeness of the Mandarin readings *zhū* and *zhú* is wholly fortuitous.

wonder, first, whether 逐 is not merely a variant of the true phonogram 㲋 rather than the other way around and, second, whether *zhǐ* 止 does not have a second reading that could be phonetic in *zhú* 逐.⁴¹

But turning Bottéro's objection around offers a second answer, an answer to what she is really asking: If 㲋 and 逐 represent the same word, how can the part that varies be the phonophore? The answer is another question: How do we actually know that 㲋 and 逐 represent the same word in the first place?

A historical phonologist relies wholly on specialists for the identification and normalization of ancient graphs. The process of identification consists of a series of guesses that are concealed by the final equation of an ancient graph X with a specific modern word Y, and that process has been carried out for the most part by people who are traditionally trained and believe in the validity of semantic compounds. Crypto-phoneticism was first proposed only seventy years ago in the West and remains very poorly known among Chinese scholars. Sun Haibo 孫海波 (1909–1972) and the other specialists who compiled and revised *Jiaguwen bian* 甲骨文編 surely never considered that 鹿 might be phonetic in 逐, just as the *Shuowen* identifies the phonogram *xìn* 信 as a semantic compound.

The main pieces of information that equated 㲋 and 𡳿 were surely graphic parallelism as well as usage in context. The equation itself is not in doubt. But without the modern graph 逐 and its association with the word *zhú* to equate with 𡳿, and without the context of OBI sentences in which

---

41. *Zhǐ* 止 is widely seen in early graphs, in places where it has been replaced (as here, by *chuò* 辵/辶) or omitted in the process of normalization. Too little is known about the phonological value of *chuò* {apparently T? N? L?-ak (鐸)} to hazard a guess as to whether it might be the phonetic in *zhú* 逐, although on the basis of the apparent rime group, that seems unlikely.

it appears to be used as a verb describing an action followed by the capture of an animal, how would we know that "foot" was combined with "pig" to mean "to chase" in the first place? Why not "to track or follow (prey)," "to approach (prey) in stealth," "to harry (prey)," "to run (said of prey)," "to walk (a stud boar)" instead?

Outside of contextual usage, there is no obvious heuristic for choosing which word is meant by a semantic compound graph. To decode it analytically inevitably risks arbitrariness on one side and circular reasoning on the other.

In contrast, explicitly phonetic writing makes readers much more certain about the word they are reading. It lets them identify the word from the sound, assuming they actually know the word (surely a necessary precondition of literacy). Systematically speaking, a phonetic compound represents a specific word more parsimoniously than does a semantic compound, and the larger the number of explicit phonograms in the inventory of graphs, the more efficiently that inventory can be learned.

Another advantage is that unfamiliar characters can be assigned a reading instantly; whether correctly or not is secondary to the issue of speed. Anecdotally, it is common to encounter phonograms pronounced not according to their dictionary definitions but using the isolation reading of one of the phonetic elements. The examples in table 3.12 use the names of edible plants.[42] This has been a very common process in Chinese: the

Table 3.12 Phonograms popularly assigned the modern reading of the historical phonophore

Standard name in dictionaries	Name commonly heard	Characters	Meaning	Graphic substitution implied in the name commonly heard
gǒuqǐzi	gǒujǐzi	枸杞子	wolfberry fruit	qǐ 杞 read as jǐ 己
qiánmá	xúnmá	蕁麻	nettle	qián 蕁 read as xún 尋
jìcài	qícài	薺菜	shepherd's purse	jì 薺 read as qí 齊
piělan (in Běijīng dialect, the traditional name is piěla)	pīlan	苤藍	kohlrabi	piě 苤 read as pī 丕

---

42. These examples were collected in ongoing interviews with literate native speakers of accented Mandarin in New York City, beginning in May, 2004.

imposition on speech of the phonology embodied in the script, without a direct phonetic intermediary.

In sum, the significance of phonetic components in the script is the economy they bring about. Any such economy streamlines the process of reading.

Continuity of Literacy

So the systematic value of phoneticism is not in doubt. What then are the implications of the crypto-phonogram hypothesis for literacy?

A key idea of the hypothesis is that phonetic information originally used in the construction of some characters has been lost. Evidently, at some point in the past, such information was not recoded by the normalization of older graphs as new phonograms. This suggests that literacy (in the sense chiefly of reading rather than writing) was not a continuous tradition in Early China, quite a surprising idea, considering the efficiencies that phoneticism bestows on learning and reading a script. The notion that Chinese written and spoken languages are of separate origin has been alive in the West since the time of Étienne Fourmont (1683–1745) and should not be dismissed out of hand, but there are other explanations — for instance, that some of the spoken words or readings necessary to interpret characters phonogrammatically became extinct early in the process of communication.

If modern views are correct about the genetic relationship between Chinese and Tibeto-Burman, then there must have been a significant shift in the typology of spoken Chinese, perhaps through creolization and presumably due to language contact brought about by colonization and migration.[43] But literacy must have been a continuous tradition on the whole. The primary reason is the apparent integrity of the *xiéshēng* series, the gross inventory of phonetic elements in the set of all phonograms.

As an example, take the phonophore 爿. It is not identified in *Shuowen* and does not seem to have been distinguished anciently from what is now written 片: the elements 爿 and 爿 are apparently interchangeable in OBI and bronze script. Xu Kai 徐鍇, in the tenth century, equates it with *chuáng* 牀 'bed, frame for supporting something' and also apparently

---

43. David Prager Branner, *Problems in Comparative Chinese Dialectology: The Classification of Miin and Hakka*, Trends in Linguistics series, no. 123 (Berlin: Mouton de Gruyter, 2000), 160–66.

with *chuáng* 疒 'sickness; sick abed'. The ancient graph identified as its antecedent is a complex pictograph that appears to depict a person on a bed in the presence of particles or drops. Zheng Qiao 鄭樵, in the twelfth century, considers it homophonous with *qiáng* 牆 'wall' and glosses it 'to kill; also, a split piece of wood' (殳也、亦判木也).[44] Its early Chinese reading, based on either modern word, is {S-ang (陽)}. Table 3.13 shows 爿 appearing as a phonetic element in a number of ancient graphs that, if identified correctly, remain known today but share no obvious etymological content.

Being able to identify correspondence sets like this one — a list of phonograms sharing a phonetic element and with attested medieval readings that allow for reconstruction of an early Chinese reading — is a statement about the linguistic identity of the graphs but not necessarily about the cognatehood of the words they represent.[45] Continuity between the ancient graphs and the medieval readings of their normalized forms implies continuity between the language connected with the ancient script and the medieval language that by definition is Chinese as we now know it. Even if the *xiéshēng* series should turn out to have been borrowed whole from somewhere else, the fact that it appears to correspond regularly to later phonology means that there is continuity from at least the time of the borrowing until the era of the later phonology.

It is difficult to test assumptions about such continuity, because continuity is routinely taken for granted in identifying characters. Consider the principle of the *chūwén* 初文 or "protoform" (as Mattos and Norman translate it). An ancient graph X is identified as representing not the morpheme with which it is associated in later records, but some other (and semantically more basic) morpheme that is usually also attested today, written with a different graph Y. The morpheme with which X is usually associated in later records is assumed to be a loan usage. Phonetic loaning is thought to be the same process that underlies the *xiéshēng* series, but in the case of protoforms, both the sound and meaning of a modern word (usually in rime-book phonology) is involved.

---

44. Zheng Qiao 鄭樵, *Tongzhi* 通志 ("Liushu lüe 六書略"). Wang Shumin 王樹民 (Beijing: Zhonghua Shuju, 1995), 1.254.
45. On the nature and meaning of correspondence sets, see Branner, *Problems in Comparative Chinese Dialectology*, 24–37.

Table 3.13 Words and graphs in the *chuáng* 爿 *xiéshēng* series

Ancient graph	Modern normalization	Gloss	Medieval reading	Baxter 1992 reconstruction
OBI ⋯ HJ: 13753	爿 = 牀	bed, frame for supporting something	{dzrang$_3$}	*dzrjang
	疒	sickness, sick abed		
OBI ⋯ HJ: 35301	戕	to kill brutally	{tsang$_1$}	*tsang
OBI ⋯ HJ: 5652	妝	to adorn	{tsrang$_3$}	*tsrjang
Bronze ⋯ JC: 2840.2	壯	robust	{tsrangH$_3$}	*tsrjangs
Bronze ⋯ JC: 154	牆 (=醬)	meat sauce	{tsangH$_3$}	*tsjangs
Bronze ⋯ JC: 100	臧	good	{tsang$_1$}	*tsang
Bronze ⋯ JC: 10175	牆	wall	{dzang$_3$}	*dzjang
Bronze ⋯ JC: 2588	獎 (=莊)	impressive	{tsrang$_3$}	*tsrjang
Bronze ⋯ JC: 118	斨	axe-head	{tshang$_3$}	*tshjang

Note: For an explanation of the transcription of medieval phonology, please see the tables in David Prager Branner, "Appendix II: Comparative Transcriptions of Rime Table Phonology," in *The Chinese Rime-tables: Linguistic Philosophy and Historical-comparative Phonology* (Amsterdam: John Benjamins, 2006), 265–302.

A classic application of the protoform principle is to explain the original graph *yǒng* 永 as meaning not "eternally" but "to swim" (table 3.14).

Table 3.14 *Yǒng* 永 as protoform of *yǒng* 泳 'to swim'

	Ancient graphs	Normalized modern graphs	Gloss	Reading
Graphs	OBI 〔graph〕 HJ: 25759	永	eternally	{KW-ang (陽)}
	Bronze 〔graph〕 JC: 2829	辰 (=派)	tributary	{P-e (支)}
Possible protoform of		泳	to swim	{KW-ang (陽)}

In other words, *yǒng* 永 in the modern sense "eternally" is a phonetic loan, and the graph 〔graph〕/〔graph〕 was originally created to write *yǒng* 'to swim', now written 泳. This 〔graph〕/〔graph〕 appears to be a complex pictograph, consisting of the figure of a person surrounded by lines suggesting water. Table 3.15 shows another example.

Table 3.15 *Yě* 也 / *tā* 它 as protoform of *shé* 蛇 'snake'

	Ancient graphs	Normalized modern graphs	Gloss	Reading
Graphs	OBI 〔graph〕 HJ: 22296	也	[particle]	{L-aj (歌)}
	Bronze 〔graph〕 JC: 10243	它	other	{L-aj (歌)}
Possible protoform of		蛇	snake	{L-aj (歌)}

Yě 也 (particle) and *tā* 它 'other' as read today are phonetic loans and (according to this theory, for there are others) 〔graph〕/〔graph〕 were originally created as pictographs to write *shé* 'snake', now 蛇. In table 3.16, two modern words are possible sources of the basic graph.

The modern particle *qiě* and an obsolete word *jū* 'good' are loangraphs, and the form 且 is a pictograph depicting some sort of board, perhaps a chopping block (modern *zǔ* 俎) or ancestral tablet (modern *zǔ* 祖, now 'ancestor'), or perhaps they were the same word. (Competing explanations, for instance, that the original graph represents a word for "penis," are not supported by protoform evidence.)

Table 3.16 *Qiě~jū* 且 as protoform of *zǔ* 祖 'ancestor' and *zǔ* 俎 'butcher block'

	Ancient graphs	Normalized modern graphs	Gloss	Reading
Graphs	OBI HJ: 1714 Bronze JC: 2818	且	[particle] good/[particle]	{S-a (魚)} {S-a (魚)}
Possible protoform of	OBI HJ: 22999 Bronze JC: 271	祖	ancestor	{S-a (魚)}
	OBI HJ: 18604 Bronze JC: 9727	俎	butcher block	{S-a (魚)}

Another example is shown in table 3.17.

Table 3.17 *Yì* 亦 as protoform of *yè~yì* 腋 'armpit'

	Ancient graphs	Normalized modern graphs	Gloss	Reading
Graphs	OBI HJ: 36511 Bronze JC: 2833	亦	[particle]	{K-ak (鐸)}
Possible protoform of		腋	armpit	{K-ak (鐸)}

Yì 亦 is seen as a loangraph when it represents the grammar particle; its original meaning would be the word *yè~yì* 'armpit', now written 腋.⁴⁶ Such examples typically involve the same sound-bearing element in the two characters; since they are part of the same phonetic series, no revision of the phonological interpretation is needed.

Table 3.18 illustrates another protoform relationship.

---

46. The Mandarin pronunciation *yì* is consistent with medieval records; *yè* appears to be a case of adopting the reading of the phonetic component, mentioned on p. 107.

Table 3.18 *Yōu* 攸 as protoform of *dí* 滌 'to rinse'

	Ancient graphs	Normalized modern graphs	Gloss	Reading
Graphs	OBI HJ: 39515 Bronze JC: 4344	攸	smoothly and swiftly (of movement); [particle]	{L-iw (幽)}
Possible protoform of		滌	to wash, rinse	{L-iwk (覺)}

The ancient forms of *yōu* 攸 seem to be complex pictographs depicting a hand applying an object to a person; the bronze includes dots, which are found in a great many graphs and often are interpreted as particles or drops of liquid. This suggests that the protoform of *yōu* 攸 is likely the word *dí* 'to wash or rinse', now written 滌. Phonologically, it is a good match; whether this equivalence is supported in actual usage is a separate question.

Table 3.19 shows another relationship that has not yet been published.

Table 3.19 *Wéi* 為 as protoform of *huī* 撝 or *huī* 麾 'to lead'

	Ancient graphs	Normalized modern graphs	Gloss	Reading
Graphs	OBI HJ: 40482 Bronze JC: 226	為	to take as, for the purpose of, because of	{M-aj (歌)}
Possible protoform of		撝	to lead, direct	{M-aj (歌)}
		麾	to lead, direct	{M-aj (歌)}

Ancient forms of present-day *wéi~wèi* 為/爲 appear to be complex pictographs depicting a hand near the head of an elephant, protoforms of *huī* 撝 and *huī* 麾, both 'to lead or direct'. They are homophones in medieval phonology as in Mandarin; Baxter's reconstructions differ slightly, 撝 *hw(r)jaj*, 麾 *hm(r)jaj*, because of their different graphic structures, but phonologically, both relationships appear to be regular.[47]

In all six examples above, the ability to propose protoform relationships depends on assuming continuity between the language of antiquity and the medieval compendia of character readings. So, naturally, protoform relationships cannot also be used as evidence of such continuity, which would be circular reasoning. A premise can be falsified by showing that its logical implications are false, but it cannot be shown to be true using those implications. The premise may indeed be true, but if the evidence is circular, the truth of the premise cannot actually be known, even if we believe it is true.

Taking this a step further, let us admit that the protoform principle is inherently circular, because we can propose the relationship only if the modern word or a word family exists. And because of that circularity, protoforms are sometimes proposed in ways that actually seem to undermine the whole conception of phonological continuity between the period of ancient characters and medieval phonology.

Table 3.20 shows an example of undermined continuity; it is well attested but phonologically less straightforward than the examples in tables 3.14–3.19.

Table 3.20 *Zì* 自 as protoform of *bí* 鼻 'nose'

	Ancient graphs	Normalized modern graphs	Gloss	Reading
Graphs	HJ: 3449 JC: 3618	自	oneself	{S-it (質)}
Possible protoform of		鼻	nose	{P-it (質)}

---

47. In a competing, crypto-phonetic explanation, Jerry Norman has observed that the Vietnamese word for "elephant," *voi*, could conceivably be phonetic in 𧰼 (personal communication, 1991). He has also suggested that Vietnamese words for "mouth" *miệng* and "mouthful" *miếng* could account for the crypto-phonetic reading of 口 in 名 and 鳴; see Boltz, *The Origin and Early Development*, 63 n. 14. Vietnamese forms are from Nguyễn Đình-Hoà, *Essential English-Vietnamese Dictionary* (Boston: Tuttle Publishing, 1983).

This relationship is often interpreted as evidence of polyphony.[48] 自, now read zì {S-it (質)}, is presumably the protoform of the modern word bí {P-it (質)} 'nose', now written 鼻, which includes a phonetic. But the fact that the rimes are the same suggests to some that a phonetic, bí 畀, loan was intended. If that is so, this relationship violates the basic principle we now impute to all phonetic loans: that of consonantal homorganicity, first detailed in modern linguistic terms by Li Fang Kuei.[49]

The protoform relationship is evidence of the linguistic continuity that is routinely taken for granted in identifying characters. In practice, however, many protoforms seem to be suggested on graphic grounds alone and make no sense phonologically. Table 3.21 shows the first of three widely seen examples.

Table 3.21 *Xiǎo* 小 and *shǎo~shào* 少 as protoforms of *shā* 沙 'sand'

	Ancient graphs		Normalized modern graphs	Gloss	Reading
Graphs	OBI	HJ: 40314	小	small	{S-ew (宵)} or {L?-ew (宵)}
	Bronze	JC: 2678			
	OBI	HJ: 20960	少	few	{L?-ew (宵)}
	Bronze	JC: 2782			
Possible protoform of	Bronze	JC: 4321	沙	sand	{L? P? K?-aj (歌)}

By no stretch of the usual phonological correspondences can a word in rime {-ew (宵)} serve as phonophore for one in rime {-aj (歌)}. Either there is another reading missing somewhere or the word *shā* 'sand' has nothing to do with the ancient graphs for words meaning "small" and "few."[50]

Table 3.22 shows another example.

---

48. See Qiu, *Chinese Writing*, 9–10.
49. Boodberg, however, reconstructed a cluster initial "BS-"; Boodberg "Some Proleptical Remarks," 340–42.
50. Somewhat less improbable is the idea that 水 'water' {L?-uj (微)} is phonetic in 沙 'sand' {L? P? K?-aj (歌)}.

Table 3.22 *Bù~pǐ~fǒu* 不~否 as protoforms of *fū* 柎 'drum-stand, calyx'

	Ancient graphs	Normalized modern graphs	Gloss	Reading
Graphs	OBI HJ: 14762 Bronze JC: 2810	不~否	[particles]	{P-i (之)}
Protoform of		柎	legged drum-stand, calyx of a flower	{P-o (侯)}

Xiéshēng contact between the early Chinese rime groups {-i (之)} and {-o (侯)} is known, although less common than {-i (之)} contact with {-ɨ (之)}. If we say that the ancient graph for 不 actually depicts the object named by the word *fū* 'drum-stand with legs', we are saying we can accept protoform relationships that are not close homophones.

Table 3.23 presents one more such case.

Table 3.23 *Fán* 凡 as protoform of *pán* 盤 'platter'

	Ancient graphs	Normalized modern graphs	Gloss	Reading
Graphs	OBI HJ: 33146 Bronze JC: 2838	凡	[particle]	{P-om (侵)}
Protoform of	OBI HJ: 2205 Bronze JC: 10137	盤	platter	{P-on? (元)} {P-an? (元)}

This, too, is a widely seen explanation but is phonologically irregular. We are asked to accept that a word with a reading {P-on (元)} has been borrowed to write one read {P-om (侵)}. Under the principle of homorganicity, that would be considered a long shot, especially because a number of words that are read {P-i/um (侵)} and written with 凡 as the phonetic (such as 風, 芃, and 鳳) are found in medieval sources to have merged with words that are read {P-ing (蒸)} (e.g., 馮, 夢) and {P-ong (東)} (e.g., 豐). Contact between {-on (元)} and {-om (侵)} is considered rare.

The best kind of evidence for continuity in the tradition of early Chinese literacy is that which connects the early script to mainstream Chinese words in later periods. The best example is the extant *xiéshēng* series. The practice of identifying ancient graphs as the protoforms of later words also assumes such continuity, although it flirts with circular logic and is sometimes carried out in ways that violate the usual rules of sound correspondence between early and medieval Chinese phonology, which by implication denies the continuity of the *xiéshēng* series.

Or could there be something wrong with those rules of sound correspondence?

Functional Homophony in an Underspecified Phonological Representation

Let us admit that the finely detailed early Chinese reconstructions of the Karlgren model must be regarded as fictions.[51] The Karlgren model takes the precise rhyming distinctions of the late fifth and sixth centuries, when for a brief century or two it was the fashion to observe such distinctions minutely, and imposes that precision on the early period, whose chief form of phonological expression was the phonophore. Surely no reconstruction should be more precise than its sources are accurate. But what notion of phonology underlies the *xiéshēng* series and loangraphs? Simply to say that Chinese phonophores are logographs is too weak; that would be the situation for native Japanese words (*kun* 訓-readings) written with the phonophores of the 月 series shown on page 109 (readings from Morohashi) (see table 3.24).[52]

---

51. Surely the starting point for all such discussions should be Jerry Norman and W. South Coblin, "A New Approach to Chinese Historical Linguistics," *Journal of the American Oriental Society* 115.4 (1995): 576–84. But even that paper fails to address the idea that traditional Chinese expressions of phonology (in both the rime books and the *xiéshēng* series) are themselves formal representations, to whatever extent they were intended to be prescriptive.
52. Morohashi Tetsuji 諸橋轍次, *Dai Kan-Wa jiten* 大漢和辭典 (Tokyo: Taishūkan Shoten, 1955–60).

Table 3.24 *Kun* 訓-readings (native Japanese words) associated with graphs in the *chuáng* 爿 *xiéshēng* series

Character	Medieval Chinese reading	Common Japanese *on*-readings	Variety of attested Japanese *kun*-readings	Meaning
爿	{dzrang₃}	—	nedai	sleeping platform
牀	{dzrang₃}	sō, shō	toko	bed
			yuka	floor
			nedai	sleeping platform
			koshikake	seat
			sunoko	indoor platform
壯	{tsrangH₃}	sō	sakan	vigorous
			isamashī	courageous
醬	{tsangH₃}	shō	hishio	salted meat
臧	{tsang₁}	zō	yoi	good
			atsui	thick
牆	{dzang₃}	shō	kaki	fence
妝	{tsrang₃}	sō	yosō	style of dress
莊	{tsrang₃}	sō, shō	ogosoka	solemn
			tsutsushimu	discreet
戕	{tsang₁}	zō	koroso	to kill
			sokonau	to harm

In contrast, the Chinese script is attempting a degree of phonological representation not possible in Japanese. We can call the Japanese case (i.e., *kun* readings) pure logography because it represents whole words without considering their sounds at all, but the Chinese script is more properly "defective," in the technical, linguistic sense of the word: it attempts to represent phonology but does so without full precision.

What notion of phonology underlies the *xiéshēng* series and loangraphs? In order to answer that question, let us consider the implications of saying that 凡 is the protoform of 盤 {P-on? -an? (元)} and was later borrowed to write an unrelated particle, read {P-om (侵)}. How common are such irregular relationships? Is it possible that early users of the script did not consider *-om* and *-on* to be different sounds?

Generally speaking, labial and dental sounds are very well segregated by the phonological sources of the medieval period, but it is possible that this is the result of normalization. In the *xiéshēng* series, there are two important examples of the conflation of {-p} and {-t} (table 3.25).[53]

Table 3.25 P/t contact in the larger *rù* 入 *xiéshēng* series

*-t			*-p			
Graph	Meaning	Baxter 1992 reconstruction	Graph	Meaning	Baxter 1992 reconstruction	Rime group
內	within	*nuts	入	to enter	*njup	物部
世	generation	*hljats	葉	leaf	*ljap	月部

Li Fang Kuei believed that 內 and 入 represented cognate words and resolved the apparent problem by proposing that the *-t* coda had assimilated from an earlier *-p*, in contact with *-s* representing proto-*qùshēng*: 內 *nuts < **nups. Baxter resolved the problem of the second pair of words the same way: 世 *hljats < 葉 **hljaps.

In fact, these are not two isolated pairs of cognates; there are sets of common words in both phonetic series — that is, a larger phonological relationship encompassing several different words. Table 3.26 shows the 內/入 series.

For 訥, Baxter has proposed *nut (perhaps < **nuts < **nups). For the sense "to go/send in," the graphs 內 and 納 did not begin to be distinguished until the period of standardization. If we believe that the *xiéshēng* series does not distinguish labial and dental codas, we are saying that {N-ut} and {N-up} actually represent one and not two syllables within the precision of the representation.

Similarly, for the 世/葉 series, we are saying that {L-at} and {L-ap} represent one and not two distinct syllables within the limit of tolerance (table 3.27).

---

53. Baxter's full 1992 reconstructions are used in the discussion that follows, because the traditional early Chinese rime groups do not distinguish {-p} and {-t} codas in the rimes concerned. Since the rime groups themselves do not distinguish these two codas, they cannot be used to definitively construct reading-tokens (of the kind used elsewhere in this chapter) with labial-stop finals in the system of Baxter 1992.

Table 3.26 Other examples of p/t contact in the larger *rù* 入 *xiéshēng* series

*-t			*-p		
Graph	Meaning	Baxter 1992 reconstruction	Graph	Meaning	Baxter 1992 reconstruction
內	within	*nuts	入	to enter	*njup
訥	halting of speech	*nut	納	to go in, send in	*nup
吶	halting of speech	*nrjot	軜	inward-facing halter for outer horses on a team	*nup
炳	to burn (熱)	*njot			

Table 3.27 P/t contact in the larger *shì* 世 *xiéshēng* series

*-t			*-p		
Graph	Meaning	Baxter 1992 reconstruction	Graph	Meaning	Baxter 1992 reconstruction
世	generation	*hljats	枼/葉	leaf	*ljap
泄	to spread, leak	*sljat	蝶	butterfly	*lep
(Same)	garrulous	*ljats	韘	archer's thumb-ring	*hljap

There is also a common word that seems to confuse *-m* and *-n*: 稹 'spear handle', read {K-in (真)}; it has an ancient variant 矜, with 今 {K-im (侵)} suggesting *-m* coda. This example seems weak — it is isolated and depends on a variant graph.

There are, however, several cases of initials *m-/*n-* being conflated within a phonetic series in common words such as those shown in table 3.28.

To summarize, if we suppose that *xiéshēng* series were only a rough way of representing relationships in sound, then we can find a number of common words in which labial and dental codas and also nasal initials do not appear to be distinguished. It is not that there was no distinction between them in speech or reading aloud but that the script treats them as functionally homophonous — sufficiently congruent for the purpose of written representation.

Table 3.28 Examples of m/n contact in the *xiéshēng* series

*n-			*m-		
Graph	Meaning	Baxter 1992 reconstruction	Graph	Meaning	Baxter 1992 reconstruction
柔	pliable	*nju*	矛	spear	*m(r)ju*
耳	ear	*nji?*	弭	tip of a bow	*mje?*
爾	many (flowers)	*njaj?; njij?*	彌	to end; distant	*mjej?*

Perhaps even what we think of as polyphony may originally have been a kind of lax but functional homophony, within the limits of tolerance of the early users of this script. Here are two more pairs of words whose early graphs are considered "cognate" by many — that is, originally a single polyphonous form, later differentiated — and whose reconstructed pronunciations might be considered crudely alike if labial and dental nasals are allowed to be congruent for the purposes of the writing system. The first involves initials (table 3.29).

Table 3.29 A dubious example of m/n contact in the *xiéshēng* series

	*n-			*m-		
Ancient graphs	Modern graph	Meaning	Baxter 1992 reconstruction	Modern graph	Meaning	Baxter 1992 reconstruction
	女	woman	*n(r)ja?*	母	mother	*m(r)o/i?*

The second involves codas (table 3.30).

Granted, this last example is extreme, but Chinese paleography has already accustomed itself to this degree of phonological laxness. After all, consider how few distinctions there are among the early Chinese rime categories in their traditional twentieth-century paradigm, as used by Li Fang Kuei (table 3.31).

Table 3.30 A dubious example of m/n contact in the *xiéshēng* series

	*-n			*-m		
Ancient graphs	Modern graph	Meaning	Baxter 1992 reconstruction	Modern graph	Meaning	Baxter 1992 reconstruction
𠒤 𠒥	言	to speak	*ngjan	音	to make music	*ʔ(r)jim

Table 3.31 The Old Chinese rime reconstructions of Li Fang Kuei (1971)

Number	"Open" coda	Li 1971 reconstruction	Stop coda	Li 1971 reconstruction	Nasal coda	Li 1971 reconstruction
1	之部	*-əg	職部	*-ək	蒸部	*-əng
2	幽部	*-əgw	覺部	*-əkw	冬部	*-əngw
3	宵部	*-agw	藥部	*-akw	—	
4	侯部	*-ug	屋部	*-uk	東部	*-ung
5	魚部	*-ag	鐸部	*-ak	陽部	*-ang
6	支部	*-eg	錫部	*-ek	耕部	*-eng
7	歌部	*-ar	月部	*-at	元部	*-an
		*-ad				
8	脂部	*-id	質部	*-it	真部	*-in
9	微部	*-əd	物部	*-ət	文部	*-ən
10		—	緝部	*-əp	侵部	*-əm
11		—	葉部	*-ap	談部	*-am

Li uses a total of thirty-one rime categories. (Tonal distinctions are generally ignored in *xiéshēng* contact.) It is usual for words with open, stop, and nasal codas to be allowed to be in contact (*duìzhuǎn* 對轉 'contact between corresponding codas'), bringing the effective number of discrete rime categories down to eleven (the numbered rows of table 3.31), without even mentioning the tendency of allowing contact between separate rimes (*xiéyùn* 叶韻, such as between 之部 and 幽部).

Among initials, the system used in this chapter reduces the fifty-five simple and complex initials of Baxter's 1992 system to ten basic types, representing each of them using only its core consonant. It appears that this principle is a reasonably accurate model of *xiéshēng* initial-contact.

A system of ten initials and eleven rimes, without tones or medials, can distinguish only 110 syllables, a clear case of phonological underspecification. Quite possibly even 110 distinct syllables are more than the *xiéshēng* system is meant to represent, but suppose there were meant to be even twice or three times that many. (Since there are plenty of examples of loangraph contact between different *xiéshēng* elements after standardization, it seems unlikely that each element was intended to serve as a distinct unit of phonology.) Compare an inventory of two hundred or three hundred rough syllable types with the fine distinctions made in Karlgren's Chinois archaïque and its successor reconstructions, built on the model of the *Qièyùn* 切韻. How much more is lost by allowing 月部 to be merged with 葉部, and 物部 with 緝部? To look at early Chinese phonology this way goes against the philosophy of all reconstructive work since Karlgren's time and of the late fifth-century philosophy of euphony that led to the *Qièyùn*. But it follows the practice of the most eminent modern paleographers of Chinese and may represent the actual phonological system of the *xiéshēng* series.

If *xiéshēng* relationships are based on very crude distinctions, plausible crypto-phonetic explanations should be easy to find, leaving aside the more difficult question of whether they are historically valid.

Literacy and Diglossia

What does such a crude system of phonological representation suggest about early Chinese literacy?

The answer depends on how we imagine the system coming into being. William Boltz has proposed that after a period of rapid advance around the third century B.C.E., true phoneticism was arrested by conflict with what he calls "the inherited orthodox world-view," which favored the semantic explicitness of phonograms.[54] Imre Galambos considers that preference for phonograms to have been motivated by the adoption of the script by colonized peoples who would have used different spoken languages.[55]

---

54. Boltz, *The Origin and Early Development*, 168–77.
55. Galambos, *Orthography of Early Chinese Writing*, 146–50. An even more extreme statement of this idea is contained in Jerry Norman's suggestion about Vietnamese words being at the bottom of some "Chinese" cryptophonograms, mentioned in note 47.

These views are compatible in that both see the dramatic growth of phonograms as part of a new process of normalization brought on by pressure for political unity around the time of Qin and early Han.

Assuming that to be so, any phonological relationships we can extract from the *xiéshēng* series must effectively date from around the time of the normalization, regardless of their prior lineage. Normalization was a watershed in the history of phonology because it introduced a systematic set of phonophores. Earlier graphic forms (such as most of those cited in this chapter) should therefore be kept strictly out of the study of *xiéshēng* phonology, though they remain of great interest for what may be called the prehistory of the phonology. As to the question of the continuity of literacy suggested by the integrity of correspondences between *xiéshēng* and later phonology, it, too, can only be claimed to go back to Qin–Han normalization. To ask (remembering Fourmont) whether the script was native or borrowed before that time is meaningless, because with normalization, it has become in effect a fresh system. And the crypto-phonogram hypothesis, which by definition asserts that vital phonological information has been omitted from normalized phonograms and lost to the heritage of literacy, also becomes a matter only of prehistory. That would explain the lack of continuity discussed above and also the presence of a residue of phonetically opaque non-phonograms within an increasingly phonogrammatic system.

What then is the relationship of the written phonological system to the rest of the language and to literacy? Of course, *xiéshēng* was cruder than the diverse distinctions of any real language — any hope of realistic phonetic representation was lost. But what was gained? It seems that diglossia was reduced, and that seems to have opened the door to a flowering of narrative and exegesis, sure evidence of self-conscious literacy.

Diglossia, the "caste system" of language, is suggested by the views of Boltz and Galambos quoted above, although neither author addresses it directly. In various forms, the basic idea is popularly expressed in the English saying "Never use a shilling word when a sixpenny one will do," the idea being that some words are of higher "price" or "value" than others, or that socially they are more elevated.[56] More technically, the canonical

---

56. Apparently first attested in George Johnson, "Place-names," in *The Educational Review Supplementary Readings*, ed. George Hay (Saint John, N[ew] B[runswick], Canada: Barnes & Co., 1900), 1898.4: 87–94, 88.

modern definition is that of Charles A. Ferguson (1921–1998): [57]

> Diglossia is a relatively stable language situation in which, in addition to the primary dialects of the language (which may include a standard or regional standards), there is a very divergent, highly codified (often grammatically more complex) superposed variety, the vehicle of a large and respected body of written literature, either of an earlier period or in another speech community, which is learned largely by formal education and is used for most written and formal spoken purposes but is not used by any section of the community for ordinary conversation.

There is textual evidence for pre-Qin diglossia in the form of a passage in the *Analects* in which the term *yǎyán* 雅言 'elegant language' appears, surely referring to high-register language. It can be punctuated two different ways:

子所雅言，詩書執禮，皆雅言也。[58] (as traditionally punctuated)
Where the Master spoke elegantly: the *Shi* and *Shu* and the practice of ritual; in each of these he used elegant language.

子所雅言詩書，執禮皆雅言也。
Where the Master used [or What the Master considered] elegant language was the *Shi* and *Shu*; in carrying out ritual, he always spoke elegantly.

Some recent readers have conceived "elegant language" to mean a putative standard language, but it more likely refers to a high diglossic register, thought fitting for use with the most elevated texts and in ritual.[59]

Why should *yǎyán* not be "standard language"? Actually, there are terms for something like standard language from the second half of the

---

57. Charles A. Ferguson, "Diglossia," *Word* 15 (1959): 325–40, esp. 335. "Diglossia" is first attested in Karl Krumbacher, *Das Problem der neugriechischen Schriftsprache* (Munich: Königliche Bayerische Akademie, 1902); I am grateful to the late Alan Kaye (1944–2007) for supplying this reference (personal communication, 2004). For a review of developments in the application and philosophy of diglossia since the Ferguson article, see Harold F. Schiffman, "Diglossia as a Sociolinguistic Situation," in *The Handbook of Sociolinguistics*, ed. Florian Coulmas (London: Basil Blackwell, 1997).
58. *Lunyu* 論語 ("Shu er" 述而), *Shisanjing zhushu*, 7:2482.
59. David Prager Branner, " 'Red Cliffs' in Taiwanese *Hànbûn*," *CHINOPERL Papers* 24 (2002): 67–100, esp. 91–95.

Han. The principal one is *tōngyǔ* 通語 'common language', which appears in the Fangyan 方言. The *Fangyan* lists these words, arranged topically, and then sometimes cites a "common language" equivalent for them, as in the following examples:

> 頷、頤，頜也，南楚謂之頷。秦晉謂之頜。頤，其通語也。[60]
>
> *Hàn* 頷 and *yí* 頤 mean *hàn* 頜 'lower half of the face'. In Southern Chu it is called *hàn* 頷. In Qin and Jin it is called *hàn* 頜. *Yí* 頤 is the common term for these words.
>
> 瓬、瓭、甒、䍃、㽀、甇、甀、瓮、瓿甊、㽉，甖。靈桂之郊謂之瓬，其小者謂之瓭。周魏之間謂之甒。秦之舊都謂之㽀。淮汝之間謂之䍃。江湘之間謂之甇。自關而西、晉之舊都河汾之間、其大者謂之甀，其中者謂之瓿甊。自關而東，趙魏之郊謂之瓮，或謂之甖。東齊海岱之間謂之㽉。甖，其通語也。[61]
>
> *Gāng* 瓬, *dǎn* 瓭, *wǔ* 甒, *yóu* 䍃, *zhèng* 㽀, *chóng* 甇, *zhuì* 甀, *wèng* 瓮, *bùlǒu* 瓿甊, and *yì* 㽉 mean *yīng* 甖 'pitcher'. In the outskirts of Ling and Gui it is called *gāng* 瓬, and the small variety is called *dǎn* 瓭. Around Zhou Wei it is called *wǔ* 甒. In the old capital of Qin it is called *zhèng* 㽀. Between the Huai and Ru Rivers it is called *yóu* 䍃. Between the Yangzi and Xiang Rivers it is called *chóng* 甇. West of the Pass, in the old capital of Jìn and between the Yellow and Fen Rivers, the large variety is called *zhuì* 甀 and the medium-size variety *bùlǒu* 瓿甊. East of the Pass, in the outskirts of Zhao Wei, it is called *wèng* 瓮. In the eastern part of Qi and the Bohai-Dai region it is called *yì* 㽉. *Yīng* 甖 is the common term for this thing.

Tōngyǔ is very clearly being used in contrast to regional language and must mean some kind of *koinē*. (It could not truly have been a "standard" unless promulgated as such by some authority.) In contrast, teaching "the *Shi* and *Shu* and the practice of ritual" are exactly the sorts of formal contexts in which by definition we would expect to encounter high diglossic language. So it seems that the notion of diglossia was already in existence before the normalization of the script.

There is also linguistic evidence for the early existence of diglossia in

---

60. Standard Chinese readings following Zhou Zumo 周祖謨, *Fangyan jiaojian* 方言校箋 (Beijing: Kexue Chubanshe, 1950 [1956]; repr., 1993), 10:35, 66.

61. Zhou Zumo, *Fangyan jiaojian* 5.10, 33–34.

the typological conflict between ancient writing and highly conservative modern dialects.[62] Characters in the era before normalization would have had a set of readings not necessarily even close to spoken language — similar to the diversity of Japanese *on-* and *kun*-readings or some of the examples from the *Fangyan*. Standardization of the script with phonograms eventually made it much easier for the script to influence spoken language.

We must not think of the received Chinese phonological tradition as descended directly from the high-register inventory of readings, which are abstract and not whole syllables. Rather, the laxity of the writing system's phonological structure enabled the development of the received tradition. Then where did the Han exegetic tradition and its elaborate medieval systematization come from? Presumably, they were the reconstruction of an imagined earlier reading tradition — perhaps influenced by a reaction against or even a hyper-correct Xianbei 鮮卑 vision of such an imagined tradition — but not the faithful preservation of that tradition. The spread of a standard writing system with built-in phonology implies the spread of that phonology, as the basis of a high diglossic register shared by all. It is paradoxical that the representation of phonology may be essentially artificial and even strange to most speakers, but if it is shared by all, it will eventually influence all spoken languages. Written forms, especially those that embody explicit phonological relationships, tend to trickle down into lower-register language. Though not the ancestor of the spoken languages, over the long run the high-register form has the ability to encroach constantly on the low because it embodies a stable set of phonological relationships (though not absolute phonetic detail) that can constantly affect spoken language. And so, whatever the situation in earlier times, diglossia must ultimately have narrowed as a result of the normalization of written Chinese and the increase of phonograms in the Qin-Han.

How do script and speech interact? No one disputes that the Chinese script masks both the phonological detail and the variation of spoken language. A logographic script tends to conceal detail and variation by ignoring or lexicalizing it. Evidently, there is no means of observing or reconstituting colloquial language of the Han, but unexpected variation persists even now in China (although it is rarely remarked upon), as shown in one or two examples from modern times.

---

62. David Prager Branner, "Common Chinese and Early Chinese Morphology," *Journal of the American Oriental Society*, 122.4 (2002): 706–21, 717–19.

Consider a major regional language that is virtually never committed to writing in the normal course of things. In spoken Taiwanese, linguistically a variety of the large and far-flung Minnan dialect group, a number of common morphemes belong to upper-register tone-categories and have aspiration where it is not expected on historical or comparative grounds. The examples in table 3.32 are in the Church romanization system widely used in Taiwan.[63]

The uncanonical aspiration in these words may be a relic of some systematic sound change, or some lost phonological or morphological feature, or possibly a reduction of homophone pressure by morphemes moving to less densely occupied phonological spaces. Those are precisely the sorts of things one could also propose to explain the diversity of word families in early Chinese or the irregularity of correspondence sets in Sino-Tibetan, explanations that would apply to lower-register language masked by a logographic script.

There are many more such examples among the character readings in Campbell's dictionary, but table 3.32 illustrates ten that survive in speech, as documented in the descriptive lexicons of Russell Sprinkle and Bernard L. M. Embree. All of these are attested in the speech of older people now living, and some (such as *kho*, *khia*, and *thióng*) are still the usual ways to say these things, even for young speakers. Others have been replaced in common usage by the expected forms — *piau-chún* replacing *phiau-chún*, *kuí-tō* replacing *khuí-tō*, and so on — which more closely match Mandarin phonology (though not phonetics). It is as if a group of Mandarin speakers said *qūliú* for *jūliú* 拘留, *chǎnkai* for *zhǎnkai* 展開, and so forth. If those people came to feel pressure to adjust their pronunciation to match everyone else's, *qūliú* and *chǎnkai* would soon disappear. Phonological

---

63. Campbell, *A Dictionary of the Amoy Vernacular*; Russell Sprinkle et al., *Amoy-English Dictionary* (Taichung: Maryknoll Fathers, 1976); Bernard L. M. Embree et al., *A Dictionary of Southern Min* (Taipei: Taipei Language Institute, 1984). I have chosen aspirated stops in upper-register tones because they seems to be special to Southern Min. Distinctive patterns of aspiration in lower-register tones and in syllables with affricate sibilant initials are much more widely distributed in Min and Hakka; for discussion and references to Jerry Norman's seminal works, see Branner, *Problems in Comparative Chinese Dialectology*, 63–67, 109–13. For correspondence sets illustrating the regularity of the rime of *khia* 奇, see David Prager Branner, "A Gutyan Jongbao Dialect Notebook," *The Yuen Ren Society Treasury of Chinese Dialect Data I* (March 1995): 243–338. All examples given in this table happen to be in the *píng* and *shǎng* tones; *rù*-tone examples are also known, but for some reason *qùshēng* examples are vanishingly rare. I have intentionally supplied examples with initials from the three main places of articulation.

representation in the Chinese script is too rough to distinguish aspirated and unaspirated initials, and there would be nothing but oral tradition to preserve them.

Table 3.32 Rogue aspiration in upper-register Taiwanese words

Medieval reading	Taiwanese			
Character and phonological value	Expected reading	Attested character reading	Example in a living word	Sources
標 {pau_{3y}}	*piau	phiau	phiau-chún 標準 'standard'	Campbell 1913:578; Sprinkle et al. 1976:617; Embree et al. 1984:215
奔 {pen_1}	*pun	phun	phun-cháu 奔走 'to hasten, hurry'	Campbell 1913:578; Sprinkle et al. 1976:628; Embree et al. 1984:218
波 {pe_1}	*po	pho	pho-lōng 波浪 'wave'	Campbell 1913:580; Sprinkle et al. 1976:620; Embree et al. 1984:216
展 {$tranQ_{3b}$}	*tián	thián	thián=khui 展開 'to unroll, open up, develop'	Campbell 1913:1067; Sprinkle et al. 1976:829; Embree et al. 1984:283; no sandhi on first syllable
冢 {$trungQ_{3c}$}	*tióng	thióng	thióng 冢 'tomb, grave'	Campbell 1913:753; Sprinkle et al. 1976:833; Embree et al. 1984:285
刁 {tau_4}	*tiau	thiau	thiau-bân 刁蠻 'clever but obstinate'	Campbell 1913:751; Embree et al. 1984:284, second syllable miswritten 難
奇 {ki_{3bx}}	*kia	khia	khia-sò 奇數 'odd number'	Campbell 1913:388; Sprinkle et al. 1976:399; Embree et al. 1984:146
拘 {kuo_{3c}}	*ku	khu	khu-liû 拘留 'to detain'	Campbell 1913:401; Sprinkle et al. 1976:419; Embree et al. 1984:161
軌 {$kwiQ_{3cx}$}	*kuí	khui	khui-tō 軌道 'track, path'	Campbell 1913:413; Sprinkle et al. 1976:421; Embree et al. 1984:162
箍 {kuo_1}	*ko͘	kho͘	kho͘-tháng 箍桶 'to coop a barrel'	Campbell 1913:401; Embree et al. 1984:128; Sprinkle et al. 1976:409

So much for an unwritten language. But in a spoken language that has a normal written form, it is natural for even highly colloquial expressions to appear in print. Consider Northern Chinese, the regional language on which standard Mandarin is based, promoted as a vehicle for colloquial writing since the May Fourth movement. Colloquial Northern Chinese furnishes plenty of examples of irregular tone change in recent usage, many of which, unlike unexpected aspiration in Taiwanese, have made their way into print (table 3.33).[64]

The point is that not only does the tone of one morpheme vary, but the written form varies with it. The logographic script can be made to express variation by lexicalizing it. In other words, literate speakers are interpreting competing pronunciations as having different literal meanings and are varying the way they are written accordingly, reinforcing those competing pronunciations by formalizing them in print.[65] Because Mandarin became closely linked to the written language during the twentieth century, and because during that time writers have been swept by an ideology prescribing lower-register writing, it is not surprising to see the script mirroring the vernacular differences in pronunciation and understanding.

The advantage of expanding the inventory of phonograms in the Qin-Han was not just that a normalizing written language became semantically more stable and more flexible for use by colonized people because it was divorced from phonetics. A larger inventory also made possible a much closer relationship between high- and low-register language than had existed before, by virtue of the phonology that was now

---

64. Not all such changes make their way into print. In mid-twentieth-century Beijing, the colloquial word for "harelip" (both the person and the condition) was *tùchǔnr*; the standard Chinese word was *tùchún* 兔唇. For the second syllable of the colloquial word to be in the third tone violates the rules of regular correspondence, and I suggested to my informant that it was the intrusion of *chǔn* 蠢 'stupid', to add pejorative sense. (Pejoration is common in regional words for physical handicaps: in Taiwanese, for instance, to be unable to speak is expressed as to be *é-káu* 啞狗 'mute-dog'; "deaf" is *chhàu hīⁿ lâng* 臭耳聾 'stinky deaf'.) She insisted that it was an irregular change of tone, without any negative sense. But 蠢 is the only character at all common enough to represent the syllable *chǔn* in print, and indeed I can find no evidence at all of this word ever having been lexicalized; evidently there has been no temptation to write 兔蠢兒. For the informant's background, please see David Prager Branner, "The Linguistic Ideas of Edward Harper Parker," *Journal of the American Oriental Society* 119.1 (1999): 12–34.
65. All of these examples can be found in current or recent use on the Internet (October 2008) as well as in Chinese dictionaries from the 1980s onward. *Niù píqi* 拗脾氣 is the only form I have not found in a dictionary. *Shùnkǒu liù*, with 溜 read *liù*, is now occasionally seen as 順口六 '"six" easily out of the mouth'.

Table 3.33 Lexicalized but irregular tone change in Northern Chinese lexicon

Standard form	… seems to have this literal meaning	Also pronounced and written	… seems to have this literal meaning	… and actually has this idiomatic meaning
niú píqi 牛脾氣	the temper of an ox	niù píqi 拗脾氣	contrary temper	stubbornness; (as verb) to be stubborn
wūyǎn jī 烏眼雞	[to give someone the] "black-eyed chicken" look	wǔyǎn jī 五眼雞	[to give someone the] "five-eyed chicken" look	to look at angrily; (as noun) sworn enemies
jiáoguǒ(r) 嚼裹(兒)	chew-bundle	jiāoguǒ(r) 澆裹(兒), jiǎoguǒ(r) 繳裹(兒)	plant-watering bundle, pay-bundle	living expenses
shuǎi liǎnzi 甩臉子	to throw off one's facial expression	shuāi liǎnzi 摔臉子	to throw down one's facial expression	to show one's displeasure without regard for how it makes one look
qiào biànzi 翹辮子	to have one's braid stick up straight	qiāo biànzi 蹺辮子	to lift one's braid	to die (informal)
tǒng lóuzi 捅樓子, 捅婁子	to poke the building, to poke and create a problem	tǒng lòuzi 捅漏子	to poke the funnel (? or '… a leak'?)	to start an argument or make a mess of things
wōli fǎn 窩裡反	rebellion in the nest	wōlǐ fān 窩裡翻	upset in the nest	infighting
dǒu wēifēng 抖威風	to shake one's awesome aura around	dōu wēifēng 兜威風	to move one's awesome aura around	to throw one's weight around
xiànshì bào 現世報	retribution in one's present life	xiànshí bào 現時報	retribution at the present moment	short-term karmic retribution
shùnkǒu liū 順口溜 (-liù also attested)	[thing that] slides easily out of the mouth	shùnkǒu liú 順口流	[thing that] flows easily out of the mouth	doggerel or other rhymed saying
dà sāshǒu 大撒手	to use one's big scattering hand	dǎ sāshǒu 打撒手	to do the scattering-hand thing	to give up and let the situation take care of itself
méi diānsān 沒掂三	to lack "three on tiptoe" (?)	méi diànsān 沒店三	to lack "three in the store" (?)	to lack careful forethought
dǎ bāopiào 打包票	to do the contract-ticket thing	dǎ bǎopiào 打保票	to do the guaranteed-ticket thing	to give a guarantee
yìnbàzi 印把子	seal-handle	yìnbǎzi 印靶子	seal-target	official seal

systematic and explicit in the script. By being written down in Chinese and having a reading associated with it, every word could actually take on a high-register form, even if it had originally been low register. With the process of normalization, every character whose phonological structure was transparent could influence the spoken language. In the long run, the script became a force for phonological unity among the spoken Han languages and for reduced diglossic distance between high and low registers.

Although the gap between Chinese writing and speech seems huge to us today, the two are probably far closer than they were before the script was standardized. Literacy in antiquity surely required a larger inventory of graphs than literacy today does, because in antiquity a far higher proportion of words were monosyllabic and had to be distinguished. So far from being an obstacle to literacy because of its low level of phonetic explicitness, Chinese writing made widespread literacy possible because it adopted a very lax representation of phonological relationships, unencumbered by phonetic detail. Viewed in the large, the history of Chinese phonology has been a long contest between the defectiveness of the *xiéshēng*-based script and the excessive distinctions of the *Qieyun* tradition. The *Qieyun* tradition is the product of an ideology espousing fine phonetic precision, and that ideology has also profoundly affected modern reconstructional thinking about both the middle and early periods of the language. But the creators of the early script do not seem to have believed in phonetic precision. In the absence of a truly standardized spoken language, underspecification has done more to make literacy possible than has the phonological tradition of the medieval period, to which honor is usually shown although it is rarely adhered to in actual usage.

In sum, the defectiveness of the early script would have aided social forces in spreading literacy, while phoneticism (even imperfect phoneticism) would have aided cognitive factors. With the beginning of true standardization of spoken Chinese in the past century and the falling away of characters that are polyphonic or character-readings for graphs with irregular phonophores, we may finally be approaching a time when a phonetic script is feasible for the majority of Chinese speakers.

Supplement: Initial Types for *Xiéshēng* Groups

Since the time of Joseph Edkins (1823–1905), the study of the early period of Chinese phonology by Westerners has tended toward reconstruction —

the recovery of speech sounds either in actual phonetics or in some more abstract form. Chinese reconstructions are usually built on a number of kinds of evidence, but for the pre-Han period, the primary one is systematic medieval phonology, which provides a clear starting point for every one of the tens of thousands of characters known in the seventh through eleventh centuries. Medieval phonology is combined with information about rhyming and *xiéshēng* 諧聲 character structure and many lesser details, to manufacture what we know as Old Chinese (OC) reconstructions. Recent unpublished work by Laurent Sagart and William Baxter has also incorporated modern ideas about lost inflectional morphology, a two-way ("A/B") distinction in initial-type, an additional type of initial category, and other ideas. In this volume, chapter 1, by David W. Pankenier, and chapter 2, by William G. Boltz, use a reconstruction of Gassmann and Behr and similar to Sagart and Baxter's.

This chapter, however, presents the phonology embodied in the Chinese script as something intrinsically different from the diverse oral languages of the early Chinese world. This "orthographic phonology" of Chinese may be represented using a system of rough transcription for characters. It is not a reconstruction of any sort: it is not intended to represent actual speech sounds of any time or place in history, however abstractly. Rather, it is meant to encapsulate compactly what is known about significant categories of sound, encompassing medieval phonology, rhyming, and *xiéshēng* relationships in the script. For representing the phonological freight of the Chinese script in a phonetically suggestive form, it seems much better than a reconstruction because it is less explicit in matters with which phonetic realism is not to be trusted.

In this system, only the initial and "rime" (syllable-final) categories are represented, as those are the elements having the greatest bearing on the *xiéshēng* series. Tone categories (beyond those built into the rime categories themselves), reconstructed morphology, medial semivowels, and the A/B distinction are all excluded.

Rimes are represented directly by those proposed in Baxter's 1992 reconstruction, which remain largely unchanged in his and Sagart's latest work. Initials are represented as ten large, catch-all categories, each built around a single core consonant that appears in Baxter's reconstruction and is symbolized by a single Roman letter consonant. OC reconstructed initials feature a significant number of initial clusters (something almost always lacking in reconstructions of medieval phonology); the single "core" consonant of such a cluster is always the one isolated as representative.

The ten initial categories symbolize the actual units of *xiéshēng* 諧聲 contact; finer distinctions among medieval or reconstructed early Chinese initial categories are more precise than is needed for an accurate representation of *xiéshēng* contact.

Table 3.34 shows the ten initial categories and the corresponding medieval initial categories they encompass. For details of the reasoning underlying the reconstruction of various initial clusters, consult the appropriate sections of Baxter 1992, which are listed in the right-most column of the tables. Corresponding medieval categories are transcribed following Branner 2006. The notation "(合)" is used to include contrastively *hékǒu* 合口 syllables and those syllables that *bùfēn kāihé* 不分開合, for example, those with rounded vowels in the rime, in *shè* 攝 such as *tōng* 通, *liú* 流, and so on, for which *kāihé* 開合 is not contrastive.

By way of example, category {P} encompasses six distinct reconstructed OC initials: *p-, *ph-, *b-, *Np-, *b-r-, and *sp-. What the six have in common is that a labial stop *p* or *b* is thought to be the principal element of each in the OC materials. These six reconstructed initials correspond to medieval initial categories 幫 p, 滂 {ph}, 並 {b}, 明 {m}, 來 {l}, and 生 {sr} in certain environments; note that the medieval initials are not necessarily labial in articulation.

Category {M} encompasses five OC initials, with *m* or *w* as the principal element of each, and corresponding to six medieval initials.

Category {T} encompasses five OC initials, with *t* or *d* the principal element. Category {N} encompasses five initials, all based on *n*; category {L} encompasses eight initials, all based on *l* or *r*; and category {S} encompasses seven initials, all based on *s* or *z*.

Category {K} encompasses ten initials; category {KW}, six; category {NG}, three; and category {NGW}, two. It is well established that some sort of rounding contrast is meaningful only among initials of the velar and laryngeal types in Old Chinese.

Table 3.34 Correspondence of Baxter OC to medieval Chinese initials

Initial groups	Medieval initial category, after Branner 2006			Baxter's reconstructed "OC" (early Chinese) initial categories	
	一四等	三等		Baxter 1992	Where cited in Baxter 1992
		back vowel or *-rj- in Baxter	front vowel in Baxter	二三等 if different from regular 三等	
P	幫 p	幫 p	—	*p	6.1.1, 6.1.3.2 (*pr)
	滂 ph	滂 ph	—	*ph	6.1.1
	並 b	並 b	—	*b	6.1.1, 6.1.3.2 (*br)
	明 m	明 m	—	*Np	6.2.2
	來 l	來 l	—	*b-r	6.1.3.2
	—	生 sr	—	*sp	6.2.3.2
M	明 m	明 m	—	*m	6.1.1
	心 s	心 s	—	*sm	6.2.3.1
T	端 t	章 tsy	知 tr	*t	6.1.2.1, 2, 3, 6.1.3.1
	透 th	昌 tshy	徹 thr	*th	6.1.2.1, 2, 3
	定 d	禪 dzy	澄 dr	*d	6.1.2.1, 2, ·3
	泥 n	泥 n	—	*Nt	6.2.2
	—	書 sy	—	*st	6.2.3.2
N	泥 n	日 ny	(娘>)泥 n	*n	6.1.2.1, 2, 3
	透 th	書 sy	徹 thr	*hn	6.1.2.1, 2, 3
	清 tsh	心 s	清 tsh	*sn	6.2.3.1

Table 3.34 (*Continued*)

L	定 d	羊 y	—	*l	6.1.3.1
	—	邪 z	—	*zl	6.1.3.1
	—	船 zy	—	*L	6.1.3.1
	透 th	書 sy	—	*hl	6.1.3.1
	心 s	心 s	—	*sl	6.2.3.1, 2 (LFK's *st-)
	—	羊 y	—	*r	6.1.3.2
	透 th	徹 thr	—	*hr	6.1.3.2
	—	生 sr	清 tsh	*sr	6.2.3.1 (*srj > sr)
S	精 ts	精 ts	莊 tsr	*ts	6.1.4
	清 tsh	清 tsh	初 tshr	*tsh	6.1.4
	清 tsh	生 sr	—	*sr	6.1.4
	心 s	心 s	—	*s	6.1.4
	從 dz	從 dz	崇 dzr	*dz	6.1.4
	—	邪 z	俟(=崇 dzr)	*z	6.1.4
	—	邪 z	—	*zl	6.1.3.1
K	見 k	見 k	章 tsy	*k	6.1.5.1, 2
	溪 kh	溪 kh	昌 tshy	*kh	6.1.5.1, 2; 6.1.3.2 (*kr)
	匣 gh	群 g	禪 dzy	匣 gh	*g	6.1.5.1, 2; 6.1.3.2 (*gr)
	疑 ng	疑 ng	—	*Nk	6.2.2
	—	生 sr	—	*sk	6.2.3.2
	影 [0]	影 [0]	—	*?	6.1.5.1
	曉 h	曉 h	書 sy	*x	6.1.5.1, 2
	來 l	來 l	—	*g-r	6.1.3.2
	—	羊 y	—	*j	6.1.3.3
	—	書 sy	—	*hj	6.1.3.3

Table 3.34 (*Continued*)

KW	見(合) kw	見(合) kw	—	*kʷ	6.1.6
	溪(合) khw	溪(合) khw	—	*khʷ	6.1.6
	匣(合) ghw	匣(合) ghw	—	*gʷ	6.1.6
	—	禪 dzy	—	*sgʷ	6.2.3.2
	疑(合) ngw	疑(合) ngw	—	*Nkʷ	6.2.2 (implied)
	影(合) w	影(合) w	—	*ʔʷ	6.1.6
	匣(合) ghw	匣(合) ghw 羊(合) yw	—	*w	6.1.6
	曉(合) hw	曉(合) hw	—	*hw	6.1.6
	心(合) sw	心(合) sw	—	*sw	6.2.3.1
NG	疑 ng	疑 ng	日 ny	—	*ng	6.1.5.1, 2
	心 s	心 s		—	*sng	6.2.3.1
	曉 h	曉 h	書 sy	—	*hng	6.1.5.1, 2
NGW	疑(合) ngw	疑(合) ngw	—	*ngʷ	6.1.6
	曉(合) hw	曉(合) hw	—	*hngʷ	6.1.6

PART II

Scribal Training and Practice

CHAPTER 4

Literacy to the South and the East of Anyang in Shang China: Zhengzhou and Daxinzhuang

Ken-ichi Takashima

The paleographic sources of Shang China are in the form of inscriptions or writing on such materials as bone,[1] bronze, pottery, and stone (including jade). An intensive examination of the bone inscriptions suggests exploratory conclusions that may later be compared with a more comprehensive treatment of literacy using the other sources. This study is applicable to a small segment of the society in which literacy facilitated communication.

There are four main places supplying Shang osteopaleographic sources for investigation: Anyang 安陽, Zhengzhou 鄭州, Daxinzhuang 大辛莊, and Zhouyuan 周原.[2] The Anyang sources are by far the greatest in

---

The first part of this chapter was presented at the Conference Commemorating the Eightieth Anniversary of the Scientific Archaeological Excavation in Yinxu, held in Anyang (30 October–2 November 2008). Readers of earlier versions offered me valuable comments and criticisms, and I am grateful to them.

1. Anatomically, turtle shells and plastrons are considered to be bones just as much as cattle bones are; see Bernard G. Sarnat, "Gross Growth and Regrowth of Sutures: Reflections on Some Personal Research," *Journal of Craniofacial Surgery* 2003.14 (4): 438.
2. A preliminary investigation of the inscribed bones found in a few places in Shaanxi, Shanxi, Beijing, and Hebei indicates the centrality of literacy in Zhouyuan 周原, Shaanxi, particularly as may be deduced from the 2003, 2004, and 2008 finds of the early Western Zhou bone inscriptions in Zhougongmiao 周公廟, Qishan 岐山, Shaanxi. These inscriptions seem somewhat later than those found in Fengchu 鳳雛 (H11 and H31), Qishan 岐山, and Qijia 齊家, Shaanxi, but some seem to be contemporary with Anyang inscriptions (Di Xin period). For example, HB: 1, 2, 12, 13, 15, and so on; see Wang Yuxin 王宇信, *Xi Zhou jiagu tanlun* 西周甲骨探論 (Beijing: Kexue Chubanshe, 1984), 41ff.; Xu Xitai 徐錫台, "Zhouyuan chutu de jiaguwen suojian renming,

quantity, with a reliable estimate of about 130,000 inscribed pieces.³ The great majority of them, save for occasional errors and the so-called practice inscriptions, are well executed in ways that generally show particular structures and styles characteristic of various diviner groups and categories.⁴ This implies that there were certain standards of calligraphy among the scribes, who went beyond the level of acquiring basic literacy. In short, a high degree of literacy is evident in Anyang writings. We also need to make such an inference even as an assumption for comparative and heuristic purposes.

It was very rare for one scribe to move from one particular diviner group to another. Such an utterance as "Today I work for diviner so-and-so" is unheard of throughout the five oracle bone inscription (OBI) periods of Late Shang (circa 1230–1046 B.C.E.).⁵

---

guanming, fangguo, diming qianshi" 周原出土的甲骨文所見人名, 官名, 方國, 地名淺釋, *Guwenzi yanjiu* 古文字研究 1 (1979): 186, 188, 192; Li Xueqin 李學勤 and Yuxin Wang 王宇信, "Zhouyuan buci xuanshi" 周原卜辭選釋, *Guwenzi yanjiu* 古文字研究 4 (1980): 247, 251, 252–53, 255.

3. Sun Yabing 孫亞冰, "Bainian lai jiaguwen cailiao zai tongji" 百年來甲骨文材料再統計, *Zhongguo wenwu bao* 中國文物報, 28 September 2003.

4. The Anyang OBI are classified as belonging to either the Royal OBI (*wáng bǔcí* 王卜辭) or the Non-Royal OBI (*fēi wáng bǔcí* 非王卜辭). The Royal OBI consists of as many as twenty-two "diviner groups"; Huang Tianshu 黃天樹, *Yinxu wangbuci de fenlei yu duandai* 殷墟王卜辭的分類與斷代 (Taipei: Wenjin Chubanshe 文津出版社, 1991), 1–3. The number differs depending on how finely different styles of writing are distinguished. According to my estimate, there are at least twenty scribes in Bin 賓 diviner group alone. The Anyang OBI are also classified into categories such as "Huadong Zi" 花東子 (abbrev. of Huayuanzhuang Dongdi Zi *zu* 花園莊東地子組), Funü *lei* 婦女類 'women category', Yuanti *lei* 圓體類 'roundish-script category', and Lieti *lei* 劣體類 'Cacoform category' separate from diviner-name groups such as Shi *zu* 師組, Li *zu* 歷組, Bin *zu* 賓組, and so on. For details, see Huang Tianshu, *Yinxu wangbuci de fenlei yu duandai*.

5. An exceptional case of mixing writing styles, by a Bin-group scribe and by another scribe belonging to Zi group, is seen on the single scapula HJ: 21784. The rubbing shows that there is a divinatory statement with the name of a well-known court diviner Zheng 爭 of the Bin group appearing on top of HJ: 21784 and also well-written calendrical notations by the hand of a scribe of the Zi group appearing at the bottom of the same piece. This shows that Bin and Zi groups are contemporaneous, datable to Period I. There is another piece, NH: 2.55 (obverse) and 2.56 (reverse), that has a divinatory statement by Nan (?) 殷 (aka Ke 殷, Que 殷, but these two are incorrect [cf. n. 34]) on the obverse and a brush writing in red by the hand of a Li-group scribe on the reverse. As for the late Shang dates, I have separately arrived at around 1230–1046 B.C.E. The exact year of the Zhou conquest of Shang, 1046 B.C.E., which I follow, is by

In the kind of background sketched above, there was intergroup contact and mutual influence through writing and literacy in Anyang, Zhengzhou, and Daxinzhuang, and, judging from the sheer number of inscriptions, Anyang played the dominant role. The number of inscriptions in the latter two places is still very small, and thus the mutual-influence hypothesis must be a qualified one. However, the examples analyzed in this chapter may perhaps be indicative. It would be procedurally practical to pay attention first to the features of the Zhengzhou and Daxinzhuang inscriptions and then to compare them with those comparable to or contrastive with Anyang OBI. This will be done in terms of three aspects: script, lexicon, and grammar and content.

Zhengzhou Inscriptions

Volume 4 of the *Hebu* inscriptional corpus contains three inscriptions from Zhengzhou: HB: 310, 311, and 312 (hand-copy). Volume 6 has "interpretive transcription" (*shìwén* 釋文). We can add one more inscription to the Zhengzhou corpus, following Chen Mengjia and Henan Sheng Wenwu Gongzuodui.[6] Since any hand-copy involves the copyist's interpretation,[7] rubbings or photographs should be used as much as possible.

HB: 310

In April 1953, when the Yellow River water-conservancy work was being conducted in Zhengzhou, a bulldozer scooped up piles of dirt from a depth of about 50 centimeters. No archaeological context is available, but the piles of dirt yielded a piece of cattle rib with inscriptions on it. The

---

David W. Pankenier, "The Cosmo-Political Background of Heaven's Mandate," *Early China* 7 (1995): 15–37; "Astronomical Dates in Shang and Western Zhou," *Early China* 20 (1995): 130. I have found one more piece (TN: 911), which is a Li-group inscription, but on its back (TN: 912) there is a marginal notation signed by Nan 歆.

6. Chen Mengjia 陳夢家, *Yinxu buci zongshu* 殷虛卜辭綜述 (Beijing: Kexue Chubanshe, 1956), 27; Henan Sheng Wenhuaju Wenwu Gongzuodui 河南省文化局文物工作隊, *Zhengzhou Erligang* 鄭州二里岡 (Beijing: Kexue Chubanshe, 1959), 38.
7. The hand-copy in *Zhengzhou Erligang*, 38, and in *Hebu* (HB: 310) show differences; observe, for instance, the second graph from the bottom.

archaeologist Xia Nai 夏鼐 (1910–1985) brought it to Beijing for Chen Mengjia 陳夢家 (1911–1966), a paleographer at the Institute of Archaeology, to examine. Chen recorded his findings on 8 May 1953, raising two points directly relevant to this piece: (1) it has ten graphs that Chen called "practice inscriptions," and (2) the inscriptions on this rib piece resemble those of the late Yin, possibly datable to the late Yin.[8] Apart from Li Xueqin,[9] scholars did not pay much attention to this piece until 1984, when Pei Mingxiang presented a paper at a conference on Shang history held in Anyang. He argued that the inscription on this piece is datable to the "Erligang period" and is "the earliest writing ever found" in China.[10] Without any reliable archaeological context, Pei's argument would inevitably invite different interpretations. However, Li Xueqin, influenced by Pei's view, also dated this piece to the Erligang period.[11] He said: "the inscribed bones should be dated earlier than the Shang Erligang period in Yinxu." The "Shang Erligang period in Yinxu" is not clear, as cultural remains of Erligang in Yinxu are sporadic,[12] but Li evidently considers this piece earlier than the Anyang inscriptions. Arguably, however, they do not predate Wu Ding (circa 1230–1170 B.C.E.). There is no solid archaeological evidence for Li's view; it seems to be more a matter of trust in the opinion of Pei, who had long been engaged in archaeological work in Zhengzhou. Pei said, "In the piles of scooped-up dirt there were many potsherds of Shang Erligang, Song ceramic sherds . . . absolutely no remains belonging to the Shang Renmin Gongyuan phase or the late Yinxu periods in Anyang."[13] This is the extent of the background

---

8. Chen's May 8 notes have seven points. In addition to the two here, I selectively mention two more: (1) one piece of rib with practice inscriptions was previously found in Xiaotun (more recently, a total of eleven pieces has been reported [cf. n. 41]), and (2) many uninscribed bones and a small number of practice pieces were found in the peripheries of Xiaotun; see Chen Mengjia, *Yinxu buci zongshu*, 27.
9. Li Xueqin 李學勤, "Tan Anyang Xiaotun yiwai chutu de youzi jiagu" 談安陽小屯以外出土的有字甲骨, *Wenwu cankao ziliao* 文物參考資料 1956.11: 17.
10. Pei Mingxiang 裴明相, "Lüe tan Zhengzhou Shangdai qianqi de gu kewenzi" 略談鄭州商代前期的骨刻文字, *Quanguo Shangshi xueshu taolunhui lunwenji* 全國商史學術討論會論文集, ed. by Hu Houxuan 胡厚宣 (*Yindu xuekan zengkan* 殷都學刊增刊) (Anyang, 1985), 251-253.
11. Li Xueqin 李學勤, "Zhengzhou Erligang zigu de yanjiu" 鄭州二里岡字骨的研究, *Zhongguo shehuikexueyuan lishi yanjiusuo xuekan* 中國社會科學院歷史研究所學刊 2001.1: 3.
12. Jing Zhichun 荊志淳, personal communication, 15 January 2009.
13. Pei Mingxiang, "Lüe tan Zhengzhou Shangdai qianqi de gu kewenzi," 251-253.

of HB: 310, but seeing as there has not been any finding from a controlled archaeological survey, the import of Pei's judgment is unclear.

Unfortunately, the original bone is lost, and, according to Chen and Xu, two photographs were taken, one before 1954 and another between 1954 and 1957.[14] Yang and Yuan have the latter photograph, which is somewhat clearer than the former[15] but which dates from after the bone piece was evidently "repaired."[16] We do not know what was repaired or how.

Figure 4.1 shows three versions of HB: 310, two "originals" (rubbing and photograph) and one hand-copy based on them, followed by an analysis of the inscriptions in terms of the three aspects mentioned earlier: script, lexicon, and grammar and content.

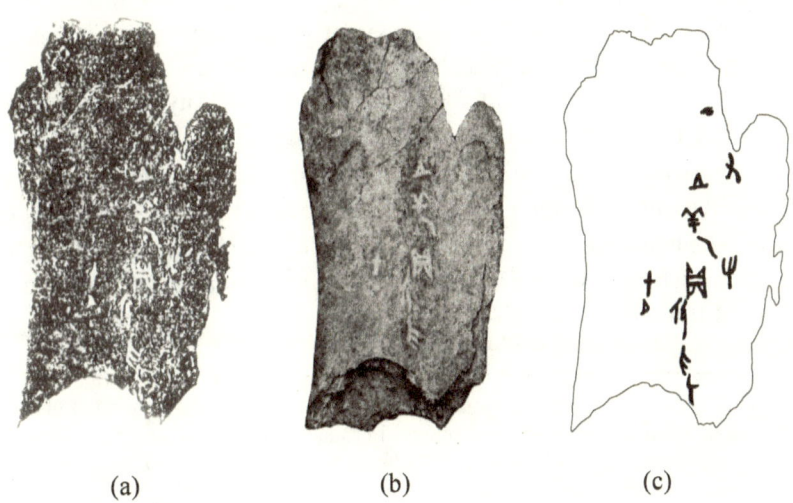

(a) (b) (c)

Figure 4.1 An oracle bone piece from Zhengzhou (HB: 310). (a) *Zhengzhou Erligang*, plate 30.24; (b) ibid., plate 16.3; (c) tracing by author, based on (a) while taking (b) into consideration.

---

14. Chen Xu 陳旭 and Xu Zhaofeng 徐昭峰, "Zhengzhou chutu Shangdai niu leigu keci shiwen louzi yuanyin tanjiu" 鄭州出土商代牛肋骨刻辭釋文漏字原因探究, *Zhongyuan wenwu* 中原文物 2006.3: 58–96.
15. Yang Yubin 楊育彬 and Yuan Guangkuo 袁廣濶, *20 shiji Henan kaogu faxian yu yanjiu* 20世紀河南考古發現與研究 (Zhengzhou: Zhongzhou Guji Chubanshe, 1997), unnumbered plate.
16. Chen Xu and Xu Zhaofeng, "Zhengzhou chutu Shangdai niu leigu," 58–59.

HB: 310 contains two sentences, one read in the top-down-left direction starting from the graph ⌐ in the mid line, and the other read from the top downward starting from 入:

(a) 乙丑貞及孚. 七月.

On the *yīchǒu* day, tested [the following proposition to gain sapience from the numen of the bone]:[17] (We will) get captives. Seventh month.

(b) □[18]又土羊.

(We should) make an offering of sheep (to) the spirit of the soil (土 = 社).

The first aspect to examine is script. The two photographs (fig. 4.1a, fig. 4.1b) show that the skill with which the graphs are inscribed — all seemingly by one hand — is apparently not very high. There are ten clearly recognizable graphs on this piece (table 4.1).

Although the graphs can all be identified with Anyang equivalents, the HB: 310 forms are distinctive. In the last column, 乙, 丑, 及, and 孚 are characterized as "unique." It is possible that 入 (又) should also be included. If so, five out of the ten graphs are distinctive. The expression "Bridging X Group" has been used as in 貞 (Shi-Li once), 七 (Li once), and 土 (Shi and Li each thrice).[19] Since Shi and Li are chronologically sequential in a short span of time, they can be subsumed under one period. In that event, at least

---

17. The square bracketed portion represents my most recent understanding of the term *zhēn* 貞, detailed in Ken-ichi Takashima, "Introduction," in *Studies of Fascicle Three of Inscriptions from the Yin Ruins*, Volume 1: *General Notes, Text and Translations* (Taipei: Institute of History and Philology, Academia Sinica, in press), D, 2.2. Henceforth I abbreviate this portion after *zhēn*. I follow Serruys's translation of *zhēn* as 'test'; see Paul L-M. Serruys, "Studies in the Language of the Shang Oracle Inscriptions," *T'oung Pao* 60.1-3 (1974): 22–23.
18. Li Weiming 李維明 takes the top white spot as ノ (= 乇) as a predecessor of 毫, for example, *bó*/**bak* (F.K. Li's Old Chinese [OC] reconstruction) 亳 in which 乇 is phonetic. He takes it as standing for the ancient capital Bo of the founder of Shang and wants to associate it with △ to read Boshe 亳社 'spirit of Bo altar'. Whether or not a graph existed in this spot is a very controversial issue that, in my view, cannot be resolved. If the spacing of 乙丑 is correct, the order ought to be ノ 入 △, rendering the "Boshe" reading irregular. Cf. Li Weiming, " 'Bo' bian" "亳" 辨, *Zhongyuan wenwu* 2006.6: 39–45.
19. The numbers given are only representative, not exhaustive. There are at least two scribal groups within the Li group. One of them writes the 土 graph with a triangular mound, △ (HJ: 34185), but another one writes it ◊ (HJ: 32119) or ◊ (HJ: 32675).

Table 4.1 The HB: 310 graphs in comparative perspectives

HB: 310	Inscription Number	Graphic components	Comparable Anyang forms	Diviner/Scribal group /period	Modern equivalent	Characterizing HB: 310 graph
⌐	(1)	(unigraph)	⌐ (HJ: 10366) ⌐ (HJ: 10403) ⌐ (HJ: 38025)	Bin/I Bin/I Huang/V	乙	Unique, though structure found in all diviner groups
ψ	(1)	(unigraph)	ψ (HJ: 35263)ᵃ	Shi-Li/I	丑	Unique
片	(1)	(unigraph)	片 (HJ: 33080) 片 (HJ: 22383) 片 (JB: 7)	Shi-Li/I Lieti/I Bin/I	貞	Bridging Shi-Li Related to Lieti Related to Bin
仈	(1)	亻 + 丨	亻 (HJ: 28085)	-Name/III-IV	及ᵇ	Unique
ᶜ	(1)	亻 + 亻	?	?	孚	Unique
十	(1)	(unigraph)	十 (HJ: 32331) 十 (HJ: 31085)	Li/I He/III-IV	七	Bridging Li Related to He
⌐	(1)	(unigraph)	⌐ (HJ: 38813) ⌐ (HJ: 38895) ⌐ (HJ: 32002)	Huang/V Huang/V Li/I	月	Related to Huang Related to Huang Bridging Li
入	(2)	(unigraph)	入 (HJ: 28238) 入 (HJ: 30391) 入 (HJ: 30321)	He/III -Name/III-IV He/III	又	Related to He Related to -Name Related to He
△ᵈ	(2)	― + △	△ (HJ: 21039) △ (HJ: 21106) △ (HJ: 21115) △ (HJ: 32012) △ (HJ: 32118) △ (HJ: 34185)	Shi/I Shi/I Shi/I Li/I Li/I Li/I	土	Bridging Shi Bridging Shi Bridging Shi Bridging Li Bridging Li Bridging Li
羊ᵉ	(2)	M + 羊	羊 (JB: 2185) 羊 (HJ: 37054) 羊 (HJ: 36090)	Huang/V Huang/V Huang/V	羊	Related to Huang Related to Huang Related to Huang

ᵃ This is the "closest" graph for *chǒu* I could find, one that, in my view, is classifiable to the Shi-Li transition group of Period I. No such a form as ψ is used in Anyang inscriptions.

ᵇ The transcription was first suggested by Chang Yuzhi 常玉芝 in her "Zhengzhou chutu de Shangdai niu leigu keci yu shesi yiji" 鄭州出土的商代牛肋骨刻辭與社祀遺蹟, *Zhongyuan wenwu* 2007.5: 99. However, there is simply no example of *jí* 及 written in this way. We might compare the form in HJ: 28085, but it is dissimilar. Yet *jí* 'get' makes far better sense than *cóng* 从 'follow' or *bǐ* 比 'compare, form an alliance with'. Cf. Li Xueqin, "Zhengzhou Erligang zigu," 3; Li Weiming, "Bobian," 40.

ᶜ The most common interpretation of this graph is *shòu* 受. Another candidate is the left side of the graph 𩰲 (XB: 5.8.1, Bin group), which stands for the word *fú* 俘 'captive'. The original form must have been like *𧾷, and this may be what the graph 𠂇 was intended to represent. The graphic component 𠂇 would then be an incompletely executed 孚 graph (Li Group as in HJ: 32979).

ᵈ While the typical Bin 賓 group scribes write it like ◯, the triangle shape is characteristic of Shi and Li Group scribes. It can also be seen in the Period III–IV Nameless Group (HJ: 28109–28111 and 28113), suggesting that the tradition of the Shi and Li scribes continued. Furthermore, judging from the way Period V Huang inscriptions in which the graph for sheep is written (see below), the tradition survived to Di Yi's time.

ᵉ This lower element is a schematic abbreviation of a sheep head (羊頭), rather than, in the view of *Shuowen* (...... 四足尾之形 'the form of four legs and a tail'; *Shuowen*, 4a/16a). A bronze form such as 羊 (JWB: 0615/4.261) shows the sheep's characteristic horns on top of its head, but the lower element of 羊 is written closer to the Huang Group forms.

four out of ten graphs (貞, 七, 土, 月) indicate that HB: 310 should be dated to the OBI Period I. "Related to Lieti" (劣體類 'cacoform category') should also be included here, as Lieti belongs to Period I (often in Shi Group). There are three examples (out of not many) comparable to He Group, Period III or Period III–IV: 七 (once) and 又 (twice), but since the above 𢆉 (HJ: 30391) belongs to the Nameless Group ("-Name" in the tables) of Period III–IV, the graph 𢆉, if comparable at all, has a late feature. However, since the same group writes it like 𢆉 (HJ: 26995o), 𢆉 cannot necessarily be judged as late. The typical Li Group form is 𢆉 (HJ: 32617), but it is hard to include 𢆉 in the Li Group by its own feature, particularly when other Li-group graphs are taken into account. As for 月 and 羊, they resemble the Huang Group of Period V. (This is hard to explain, but see at the end of note 23.)

Table 4.2 lists differences from Anyang graphs. It shows that the HB: 310 graphs on the whole are distinctive. It was much harder to find examples comparable to Anyang forms (see table 4.1) than those that are different from them (table 4.2). On the basis of the two tables and the foregoing analysis, the graphic features of HB: 310 can be said to form a class by themselves, but the graphs for 貞 and 土 show such early features as in the Shi, Shi-Li, and Li inscriptions. The graphs for 月 and 羊 show late features as well. If correct, there must be some historical reasons for them.

LITERACY TO THE SOUTH AND THE EAST OF ANYANG   149

Table 4.2 Uniqueness of the HB: 310 graphs

HB: 310/ Modern	Contrastive Anyang Forms	Diviner/ Scribal Group/ Period	HB: 310/ Modern	Contrastive Anyang Forms	Diviner/Scribal Group/Period
╲/乙	ʃ (HJ: 19771)	Shi/I		✝ (HJ: 36557)	Huang/V
	? (HJ: 33102)	Li/I	☽/月	((HJ: 20315)	Shi/I
	ʃ (HJ: 32625)	Li/I		ⅅ (HJ: 32014)	Li/I
	ζ (HJ: 6097)	Bin/I		) (HJ: 4611)	Bin/I
	ʃ (HJ: 5064)	Bin/I		) (HJ: 23395)	Chu/II
	ζ (HJ: 26975)	He/III		♪ (HJ: 31062)	-Name/III-IV
ψ/丑	ʄ (HJ: 19806)	Shi/I	ʎ/又	ʎ (HJ: 19838)*	Shi/I
	ʆ (HJ: 20017)	Shi/I		ʒ (HJ: 34309)	Li/I
	ʄ (HJ: 16736)	Li/I		ʎ (HJ: 2164)	Bin/I
	ʄ (HJ: 32320)	Li/I		ʎ (HJ: 21800)	Zi/I
	ʄ (HJ: 10405o)	Bin/I		ʎ (HJ: 22062)	Wu/I
	ʄ (HJ: 21546)	Zi/I		ʎ (HD: 27)	Huadong Zi/I
	ʆ (HJ: 22094)	Wu/I	*Graph almost identical in 24134.		Chu/II
	ʄ (HJ: 22258)	Funü/I	▲/土	◊ (HJ: 6406)	Bin/I
	ʄ (HD: 21)	Huadong Zi/I		'◊' (HJ: 6407)	Bin/I
貞/貞	⟦ (HJ: 28788)	Shi/I		◊ (HJ: 8490o)	Bin/I
	⟦ (HJ: 33615)	Li/I		⊥ (HJ: 22048)	Wu/I
	⟦ (HJ: 4317)	Bin/I		◊ (HD: 105)	Huadong Zi/I
	⟦ (HJ: 21811)	Zi/I		⊥ (HJ: 36975)	Huang/V
	⟦ (HJ: 22086)	Wu/I	⚹/羊	⚹ (HJ: 19943)	Shi/I
	⟦ (HJ: 22088)	Wu/I		⚹ (HJ: 21145)	Shi/I
	⟦ (HJ: 22231)	Yuanti/I		⚹ (HJ: 20523)	Shi-Li/I
	⟦ (HJ: 22259)	Funü/I		⚹ (HJ: 32623)	Li/I
	⟦ (HJ: 21413)	Funü/I		⚹ (HJ: 6483o)	Bin/I
	⟦ (HD: 3)	Huadong Zi/I		⚹ (HJ: 8812)	Bin/I
✝/七	+ (HJ: 10650)	Bin/I		⚹ (HD: 7)	Huadong Zi/I
	⊥ (HJ: 11503)	Bin/I		⚹ (HJ: 22853)	Chu/II
	+ (HJ: 13331)	Bin/I		⚹ (HJ: 27871)	He/III
/七(人)	+ (HJ: 6057)	Bin/I		⚹ (HJ: 29537)	-Name/III-IV

The second aspect we examine is lexicon. The shared vocabulary items would point to cultural contact and mutual intelligibility in writing. Four out of the ten items in the Zhengzhou inscriptions are used as time words (乙, 丑, 七, 月). If we adopt the notion of a common cognitive map in a community, time reckoning expressed in a certain specific way would tell us how the people organized their lives in that temporal frame. Literacy within the same language, including dialectal features, is a salient indicator of contact. On the basis of a shared cognitive map drawn from the common lexical items, we can speak of intergroup communication between scribal and diviner groups. That would be a synchronic interpretation, while it is equally possible that diachronically the Zhengzhou inscriptions had their own traditions, although their quantity does not at present allow for a more scrupulous investigation. Zhēn 貞, defined as 'test' (cf. note 17), is perhaps the most often used word in OBI and has a profound significance in understanding the nature of the divinatory language. If this chapter's reconstructed meaning for this word is correct, all things being equal, it must also have been understood similarly in the HB: 310 inscription.

The third aspect to be considered is grammar and meaning. Li Xueqin construed 又土羊 as 侑社羊 'offer a sheep to the spirit of the soil [shè 社].'[20] This is indeed possible. It has the structure $V_{of\ giving} + O_{indirect} + O_{direct}$ (abbreviated hereinafter as $V_g O_i O_d$). As opposed to this analysis, if 土羊 were taken as a noun phrase, 又土羊 would have a simpler structure: $V_g O_d$ 'make an offering of a ram', without specifying to whom the sacrificial object is to be offered. However, Li has a reason for his interpretation, which has to do with the nature of Zhengzhou as a city with its own shè 社.[21] This is a compelling idea, and it behooves us to examine the syntax of the verb yòu 又/侑 in particular reference to 土 and 羊.

First, however, none of the examples Li cites in support of the interpretation "offer a sheep to the spirit of the soil" has any bearing on it. Of his nine examples, eight have to do with liáo 燎 'to conduct a burnt sacrifice', not yòu 又 (侑) 'to offer'. Liáo (burnt) sacrifice is closely associated with shè.[22] Numerous examples, including those cited by Li,

---

20. Li Xueqin, "Tan Anyang Xiaotun," 35; "Zhengzhou Erligang zigu," 3.
21. "Any city of the Shang elite in residence had shè 社 'altar', and this rib inscription to mention sacrificing to shè agrees with the nature of Zhengzhou as a Shang city"; "Zhengzhou Erligang zigu," 5.
22. Sōrui: 172.3–173.1; Leizuan: 463.1–464.1.

show that it is an integral part of the sacrifice directed to *shè*. However, the *yòu*-offering is different. The only pertinent example that Li provided is:

...午卜方帝三豕山犬卯于土宰莽雨.(HJ: 12855 [Period I Bin group])
...*wǔ* day divined: (To) the (Powers in the four) quarters, (we) will perform the *dì*-binding sacrifice (帝=締) of three pigs and, in addition, a dog, and split open (卯=劉) a specially reared sheep to the spirit of the soil (in order to) pray for (莽=禱) rain.

In this example, 宰 is the direct object of the verb *liú* 劉. This shows that the diviner proposed to do the *dì*–binding sacrifice of three pigs and a dog as well as the *liú*-killing of 宰 directed to the spirit of the soil. The verb used in the former is *dì*, the latter *liú*. The recipient is 土 (=社), but the particle *yú* 于 is used to indicate to what these sacrificial victims are to be offered. Since there is no example of *yú* in the Zhengzhou inscriptions, we cannot be absolutely sure that 又土羊 is equivalent to *又于土羊. Admitting that it is, however, unwittingly involves us in the area of dialect grammar. That is, the meaning Li assigned to 又土羊 is indeed possible without the use of the particle *yú*, but by the word order.

There are two types of word order involving double objects in OBI: one has the structure $V_gO_iO_d$ and another has $V_gO_dO_i$. They express exactly the same meaning.[23] They are closely associated with particular diviners and, more generally (with some interesting exceptions), with some specific diviner groups to which they belong. For example, the former structure is observed in the inscriptions by diviner Zheng 爭, a member of the Bin group and a trusted diviner for King Wu Ding, whereas diviner Nan, even

---

23. This is similar to the double-object construction in Cantonese in which the $V_gO_dO_i$ order (Cant. 我畀[一]本書你 'I give [one] book you', equivalent to standard Chinese 我給你一本書 'I give you one-measure book') was predominant until recently, and still is, according to Lai Yin Yung 賴彥融 and Chin Chi On 錢志安, Cantonese speakers from Hong Kong (personal communications, 3 November 2008, 10 January 2009). Because of influences from standard Chinese and English, the traditional word order coexists with the new order, but the latter is more common with the younger, hip generations. This double-object construction is not limited to the language of OBI. Tan Buyun 譚步雲 provides three good examples from Shang bronze inscriptions datable to OBI Period V; see "Shangdai tongqi mingwen shidu de ruogan wenti" 商代銅器銘文釋讀的若干問題, *Zhongshan renwen xueshu luncong* 中山人文學術論叢 2005.5: 9–11. It is possible that Shi, Shi-Li, and Li group traditions survived to Period V, dovetailing with the Period V graph 𝍿, 𝍾, or 𝍽 in table 4.1.

though he belonged to the same Bin group, vacillates in his use of the two patterns, as in the following samples:

壬戌卜㱿貞㞢于祖[乙]. . . . make an offering to Zu (Yi). (HJ: 190[5])

㞢于<u>祖乙</u>五宰. offer five specially reared sheep to Zu Yi. (Ibid. [6])

三宰. Three specially reared sheep. (Ibid. [7])

㞢一<u>牛祖乙</u>. Offer one bovine to Zu Yi. (Ibid. [8])

宙伐彭于祖乙. It should be a human victim that (we) cut for Zu Yi. (Ibid. [9])

There is, however, other evidence that Nan is from a place different from Anyang,[24] and his dialect was different from that of Zheng, the king, and his entourage, whose language we assume to be standard,[25] that is, his place of origin used the latter word order as the predominant pattern.

Interestingly, the way in which Li Group and Shi-Li transition group use the transitive verb of "giving" entails this double-object construction. Out of a total of eighty-four samples of the verb *yòu* 又 (侑) 'to offer' (i.e.,

---

24. Lu Shixian 魯實先, "Buci xingshi tongshi zhi yi" 卜辭姓氏通釋之一, *Donghai xuebao* 東海學報 1.1 (1956): 8ff.; Li Xueshan 李雪山, "Zhenren wei fengguo shouling laichao zhizhang zhanbu jisi zhi guan" 貞人爲封國首領來朝職掌占卜祭祀之官, in Wang Yuxin, Song Zhenhao, and Meng, Xianwu, 286.

25. This sort of fluctuation is a clear sign of dialect or outside interference at work. Diviner Nan may have been trying to learn in the capital the standard language in which the word order involving Vg took the form of the Oi followed by Od, but had not yet quite mastered it; Ken-ichi Takashima and Anne O. Yue, "Evidence of Possible Dialect Mixture in Oracle-Bone Inscriptions," in *Memory of Professor Li Fang-Kuei: Essays of Linguistic Change and the Chinese Dialects*, ed. Ting Pang-Hsin and Anne O. Yue (Taipei: Institute of Linguistics, Academia Sinica, 2000), 31. Li Xueshan singled out ten diviners, claiming that their "original status" was vassalage and that they came from different areas to serve as diviners in the Shang court. Nan was one of them; see "Zhenren wei fengguo shouling," 285–86. (A few more examples: HJ: 13525–13527 and 13528.) Also, seven bronze "clan insignia" that look like 𠂤 (JL: 370) comparable to the OBI form 𠂤 have been found. In one case (JC: 9161), the graph appears inside the cartouche-like *yà* 亞 like 𠂤. This is significant because the epithet *yà* was for the elite. As for the location of Nan, I find it impossible to determine. Lu Shixian's argument that it should be identified with Gu 穀 as in Gubang 穀邦 'Gu state' at the time of Zhou Mu Wang 周穆王 is fraught with problems, the most fundamental being that the graph 𠂤 is unlikely to be 穀; cf. Lu Shixian, "Buci xingshi," 8ff.

V_g), for example, twenty-one have the order $yòuO_iO_d$ and sixty-three have $yòuO_dO_i$.[26] The key issue here is how to account for the competition between the two patterns, $yòuO_iO_d$ and $yòuO_dO_i$, to express the same meaning. To further illustrate the former word order, consider one of its twenty-one examples:

丙子貞丁丑又父丁伐三十羌歲三牢. (HJ: 32054 [Period I Li Group])

On the *bǐngzǐ* day, tested: On the *dīngchǒu* day (we should) offer *fá*-human victims numbering thirty Qiang and *guì*-cut three specially reared bovines (all) to Fu Ding.

Compare the above with the following, an example of the sixty-three cases of $yòuO_dO_i$:

又伐十五歲小宰上甲. (HJ: 32198 [Period I Li Group])

(We should) offer *fá*-human victims numbering fifteen and *guì*-cut (歲=劌) a small specially reared sheep to Shang Jia.

In the first example, the O_i is 父丁 following the verb *yòu* and O_d is 伐三十羌, while in the second, it is 伐 as O_d following the verb *yòu*, and O_i occurs after 小宰. Shen Pei went through the *Jiaguwen heji* ("HJ") and other collections and found a total of 439 examples of *yòu* used in the double-object construction in Anyang inscriptions, with 361 $yòuO_iO_d$ and 78 $yòuO_dO_i$.[27] The ratio is about 4.6 to 1. He did not classify the inscriptions into diviner groups as in the sampled statistics in this chapter. We can say that the Shang OBI in general have $yòuO_iO_d$ as the standard order, while the Li Group inscriptions, including several in the Shi-Li transition group, show the exact opposite: only twenty-one examples of $yòuO_iO_d$ and sixty-three examples of $yòuO_dO_i$, showing the ratio of 1 to 3. How should we interpret the significance of such a distribution?

Shen suggested that in the $yòuO_dO_i$ structure, O_d is "focused."[28]

---

26. The sampling was conducted by going through from HJ: 32050 to 32450, not the entire Li group inscriptions. In these 450 inscriptions, I limited the sample to the cases in which only the verb *yòu* 又 'to offer' is used with two objects, O_d and O_i, excluding incomplete inscriptions. Also, several examples may belong to the so-called Shi-Li transition group, such as 32072, 32213, 32214, and the like.
27. Shen Pei 沈培, *Yinxu jiagu buci yuxu yanjiu* 殷墟甲骨卜辭語序研究 (Taipei: Wenjin Chubanshe, 1992), 106–7.
28. Ibid., 117–18.

However, there are only two sets of examples he cited in the *Heji* that could support this interpretation, while a majority of the examples (see below) do not.[29] Thus, instead of looking for a criterion by which to choose one pattern over the other internally, we should remember that the Li and Shi-Li transition groups are special. They are special because the sixty-three, more than 80 percent, of the seventy-eight examples of *yòu*$O_d O_i$ belong to these groups, and there would undoubtedly be more if all the Li Group examples were examined (cf. note 26). Thus, one answer to the question posed at the end of the above paragraph is dialect mixture. This is an external reason in the sense that the question deals with outside influence from other dialects. If Shen's finding of 361 examples of *yòu*$O_i O_d$ in the Anyang corpus is used as a yardstick, 21 *yòu*$O_i O_d$ examples in the Li Group inscriptions indicate a change to conformity with the majority or something considered new (cf. Cantonese example, note 23). Some conservative diviners, usually of older generations, continue to use the *yòu*$O_d O_i$ order, while the younger, hip diviners began using the *yòu*$O_i O_d$ order like the rest of the diviners. This also has bearing on the question of dating HB: 310.

An earlier discussion about Nan vacillating in his use of the *yòu*$O_i O_d$ and *yòu*$O_d O_i$ orders suggested that because he came from a place other than Anyang he was trying to learn the standard language (*yòu*$O_i O_d$) but had not yet quite mastered it. If this is correct, where was his homeland? Given that the provenance of none of the seven bronzes with the Nan 戌 or Ya Nan 亞戌 emblem or of the three Shang bronze inscriptions with $V_g O_d O_i$ order that Tan pointed out (cf. note 23) can be established, Nan's homeland is unknown. Lu Shixian's interpretation that Nan is from Gubang 穀邦 'Gu state' is problematical (see note 25). Various diviners of the Li Group and Bin–Early Chu inscriptions have identical names. Qiu Xigui gave some fifty names occurring in the inscriptions of these groups,[30] but no example has been found to localize Nan.

Our script analysis of HB: 310 has indicated a resemblance with the Shi, Shi-Li transition, and Li Group inscriptions. The prefatory formula 乙丑貞 is very typical of Li Group. It would not be strange for Nan with a background in the Li Group to belong to the Bin group because of his

---

29. There are also examples that are neutral, that is, offering no evidence one way or the other. Note that the dialect-mixture theory can account for this.
30. Qiu Xigui 裘錫圭, "Lun Lizu buci de shidai" 論歷組卜辭的時代, *Guwenzi yanjiu* 古文字研究, 1981.6: 277–80.

prominence in divination,[31] tribute (HJ: 8797), warfare (HJ: 5447), and other matters of royal concern.[32] Qiu noticed HJ: 4284 (obverse), which has a divination by Nan, but on its reverse (reproduced separately in HJ: 35257), a Li Group scribe wrote in red "*guǐyǒu*" 癸酉 in typical Li Group fashion.[33] This is a prime example of Nan's association with a Li Group scribe. Thus the hypothesis that the place where Nan and Li Group scribes originally came from supplied scribes and diviners to Anyang is worth testing further. The dialect spoken in that area was evidently different from the standard language in Anyang. It had the double-object construction with the predominant $yòuO_dO_i$ order, and judging from the high ratio of three to one (sixty-three $yòuO_dO_i$ vs. twenty-one $yòuO_iO_d$), not only the scribes but also the diviners must have had ties to that area. Finally, the name Nan 毃 is written as 毃, 毃, 毃,[34] and although 毃 is a historically discontinuous character, the left element is clearly *nán* 南 'south'. It would be a kind of "default" hypothesis to infer that since Zhengzhou is a major Shang city south of Anyang, Diviner Nan might have adopted the name "South" metonymically. Out of other major civilizations south of Anyang (e.g., Wucheng 吳城, Niucheng 牛城, Sanxingdui 三星堆), however, Zhengzhou is the only place that has yielded a few inscriptions that form sentences, and so Zhengzhou is worth keeping in mind as a hypothesis until more pertinent evidence comes to light.

HB: 311 and 312

The original bones of both HB: 311 (89H1.1) and HB: 312 (H10.4) are now kept at the Zhengzhou Shang City work station of the Henan Institute

---

31. Of the seventeen diviners in the *Bingbian*, Nan divined more than any other diviners including Bin 賓 and Zheng 爭; Takashima Ken-ichi 高嶋謙一, *Yinxu wenzi bingbian tongjian* 殷虛文字丙編通檢 (Taipei: Institute of History and Philology, Academia Sinica, 1985), 439–68.
32. Li Xueshan ("Zhenren," 285–86) says that Nan's "leader" [why not Nan himself?] was given a fief and the title *yà* 亞. Li also states that Nan was an old diviner who served in the Shang court for a long time. See Li Xueshan, "Zhenren wei fengguo shouling," 285–86.
33. Qiu Xigui, "Lun Lizu buci de shidai," 270.
34. The left elements of 毃 and 毃 being no more than variants are shown in HJ: 1777, where the ancestral name Nan Geng 南庚 appears; 毃 is just an abbreviated way of writing 毃. The transcriptions *què* 殼 or *ké* 殼 are incorrect. Since the *shū* 殳 radical is used mostly as a signific in other graphs, I would read 毃 as *nán*.

of Cultural Relics and Archaeology. The former piece was unearthed at "about 400m from the southern wall, now under Zijingshan lu 紫荊山路, in November [December?] 1989," and the latter "in the mid layer of the eastern wall of the Shang City in early 1990."[35] Apart from a brief report of its finding by the Zhengzhou Water-Conservancy Works Office No. 1,[36] no archaeological context is available for HB: 311. For a report of HB: 312, see the discussion below.

A tracing of the printouts of the new color photographs of HB: 311 and 312 is shown in figure 4.2.

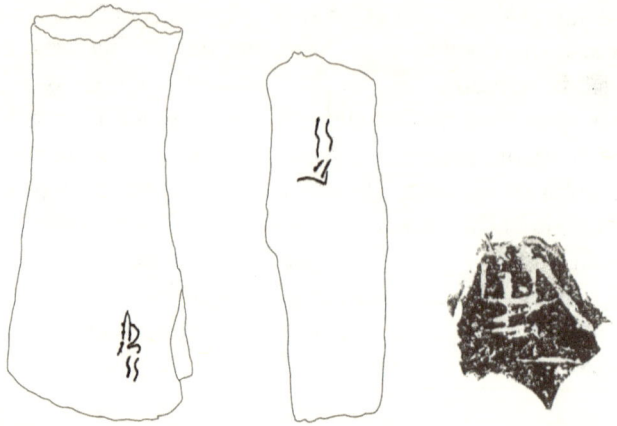

(a) HB: 311 (89H1.1)   (b) HB: 312 (H10.4)   (c) Single-graph piece

Figure 4.2 Oracle bone pieces from Zhengzhou. (a) and (b): Tracings of printouts of new photographs of HB: 311 and HB: 312 courtesy of Li Suting (n. 39); (c) Henan Sheng, *Zhengzhou Erligang*, 38.

---

35. Personal communication, 20 January 2009, with Li Suting 李素婷 of the said institute. The site is referred to as Zhengzhou Dianli Xuexiao 鄭州電力學校. For a brief description of the archaeological context of HB: 312, see the section "The Problem of Dating" below. I am much indebted to her for providing me with a set of new color photographs of the actual bones. On 25 August 2009, I went to Zhengzhou to examine the bones firsthand. The tracings are generally accurate, but the top portion of the first graph in HB: 312 may have two short lines extending in about 45 degrees. If so, the graph should be transcribed as the negative *wù* 勿, but since the engraving of the graph is so shallow, that was hard to discern.
36. Henan Sheng Wenwu Yanjiusuo 河南省文物研究所, "Zhengzhou Dianli Xuexiao kaogu fajue baogao" 鄭州電力學校考古發掘報告, in *Zhengzhou Shangcheng kaogu xinfaxian yu yanjiu* 鄭州商城考古新發現與研究 (Zhengzhou: Zhongzhou Guji Chubanshe, 1993), 183.

HB: 311: 🝆 �1 卪(?) 水   Perform the exorcism ritual [=御=禦] on (water:) [floods?].

HB: 312: 〔〕 _/ 水卪   (As for) water [floods?] perform the lustration ritual (?).

These are different from the hand-copy in HB: 311 (〔token〕, transcribed as 卪 勿) and HB: 312 (〔token〕, transcribed as 勿卪).

HB: 311 and HB: 312 appear to have been inscribed by two different hands. The skill with which 〔〕 and 〔〕 are written seems somewhat better than the HB: 310 graphs seen earlier. Both of them look like Period I Li Group inscriptions.[37] Since the left-side element of 🝆 is completely absent in Anyang graphs, the *yù* 卪 interpretation is uncertain. Assuming it is, however, HJ: 32042 (〔〕) and 32043 (〔〕), a couple of Li Group samples, show that the way the kneeling figure of a person is written is similar to that of HB: 311, but in HB: 312, it is executed in a "running" manner: _/. This is unique. We can perhaps interpret it as a "stroke extension" (*bǐshì* 筆勢) of 〔〕 (for a reason, see n. 38). These examples indicate that while the Zhengzhou scribes had their own style, they also had some connection with the Li Group in Anyang. In addition to the "running" manner, the second graph in HB: 312 is inscribed in an irregular way. Anyang OBI have a VO compound 卪水 (HJ: 10152) or 卪大水 (14407, source YZ 835), and this is the reason for interpreting the graph 〔〕 as 水 rather than *chuān* 川, which is typically written 〔〕 (HJ: 10161, Bin), 〔〕 (21661, Zi), 〔〕 (22098, Wu), and 〔〕 (29687, He).

As regards the lexical aspect of HB: 311 and 312, *yù* 卪 is found in Anyang OBI, suggesting intergroup communication. In terms of grammar, the VO order in HB: 311 conforms to the standard word order, but HB: 312 has the OV order. This may have been due not to any linguistic reason but to scribal reasons.[38]

---

37. Cf. HJ: 31969-35255, in particular 33355, 33356, 33357, and compare these with 33354. These are similar in kernel to 〔〕, 〔〕 (HJ: 33355, 33357; Li) and 〔〕 (HJ: 22288, a Shi inscription), that is, *shuǐ* 水 'water' (but without the dots on either side of 〔〕 and 〔〕). 水 is written 〔〕, 〔〕 (HJ: 14407, 10152, Bin inscriptions).
38. It is possible that one scribe wrote HB: 311 first, and another one saw it and "corrected" it by showing how to write these graphs separately for illustration purposes.

Single-Graph Piece

The last example from Zhengzhou, the single-graph piece in figure 4.2, is inscribed on a bovine elbow joint.[39]

The graph 山 is a typical Bin and Shi-Li writing of Period I. It cannot be considered Li Group writing because the Li Group scribes simply did not write *yòu* in this way; they wrote it 㞢 (又), more typically 㞢. This suggests that the graph 山 is not used here as a verb or a conjunction but as a proper noun. Li Xueqin identified this with You 山 in the inscription of an early Western Zhou bronze, Yongbo *ding* 雍伯鼎 (JC: 2531).[40] If we allow the possibility of interchange among those involved in scribal activities in Anyang and Zhengzhou, there must also have been contact between some non-Li scribes and the scribe who wrote this graph. It goes without saying that this is all based on the assumption that this piece, and indeed the three other pieces we have examined, were not brought to Zhengzhou from Anyang. The fact that all three pieces are bovine rib and one bovine elbow-joint piece suggests that they are of local origin.[41]

The Problem of Dating

The Zhengzhou inscriptions can be dated in the framework of relative dating developed for the Anyang inscriptions. HB: 310, 311, 312, and the single-graph piece in figure 4.2 suggest Period I. Archaeologically, there

---

39. Chen Mengjia, *Yinxu buci zongshu*, 27; Henan Sheng, *Zhengzhou Erligang*, 38.
40. Li Xueqin, "Zhengzhou Erligang zigu," 3. Li cites Chen Pan, who quotes Du Yu's 杜預 (222–284) commentary on the *Zuozhuan*: 雍國在河內山陽縣西 'State of Yong is in the Henei region, west of Anyang *xiàn*'. Chen Pan then says: 按山陽, 在懷州修武 'It is my view that Shanyang is in Xiuwu of Huaizhou'. Evidently, Shanyang is not too far from Zhengzhou; see Chen Pan 陳槃, *Chunqiu dashibiao lieguo juexing ji cunmiebiao zhuanyi* 春秋大事表列國爵姓及存滅表譔異, (Taipei: Institute of History and Philology, Academia Sinica, 1969), 4:327.
41. Anyang inscriptions rarely used bones other than turtle plastrons and bovine scapula. Liu Yiman 劉一曼 collected eleven inscribed rib pieces, all practice inscriptions, found in Anyang; see her "Yinxu shougu keci chutan" 殷墟獸骨刻辭初探, *Yinxu bowuyuan yuankan* 殷墟博物苑苑刊 (Chuangkan hao 創刊號) 1989:113. Out of the roughly 130,000 pieces of Anyang bones, these 11 pieces are only a minuscule proportion, whereas all 4 pieces from Zhengzhou are bovine rib and elbow joint. On the issue of learning to write and/or learning to engrave, see "The Evidence for Scribal Training at Anyang," by Adam Smith, chapter 5 in this volume.

are two Shang phases in Zhengzhou, Lower Erligang and Upper Erligang.[42] What is commonly referred to as Renmin Gongyuan 人民公園 (RG) phase is roughly coeval with Yinxu culture Period I or II.[43] There are two periods of RG culture, and although the latter overlies the former, the published sources say that there is a disjunction in ceramics. This would mean that there is a period or two missing between Upper Erligang II and RG I. The sources go on to say that based on similarities of ceramics, RG I is coeval with Yinxu Dasikongcun and Miaopu I, and RG II with Dasikongcun and Miaopu II, further equating them with the first part of the Yinxu period. In the case of HB: 310, the sources acknowledge having no layer information. As for the single-graph piece, it is said to have been unearthed in trench T30, which can be spotted on a map, but no archaeological layer is shown.[44]

Li Xueqin relies on Pei, who, as mentioned, asserted that HB: 310 and the single-graph piece should be dated "absolutely no later than the RG and late Yinxu periods," namely, "Erligang period." More definite information would have been required. This is simply not available, as the unearthing of HB: 310 and the single-graph piece was an accident during the Yellow River water-conservancy work, not a controlled archaeological excavation. In contrast, an archaeological report of 312 (H10.4) is found in Zhengzhou Erligang.[45] Four cultural layers were identified, and H10.4 was in the lower third/fourth Shang layer of the Erligang period. This corresponds to RG I or II, roughly coeval with Yinxu I or II just before Wu Ding, during Wu Ding and early Zu Geng.

Finally, the double-object construction $V_g O_i O_d$ in HB: 310 suggests that the diviner who used this pattern must have had a relationship with the majority of Anyang diviners — that is, this piece, too, should be dated as

---

42. Beijingdaxue Lishixi Kaogu Jiaoyanshi Shang Zhou Zu 北京大學歷史考古教研室商周組, *Shang Zhou kaogu* 商周考古 (Beijing: Wenwu Chubanshe, 1979), 30–37; Zhongguo Shehui Kexueyuan Kaogu Yanjiusuo 中國社會科學院考古研究所, *Xin Zhongguo de kaogu faxian yu yanjiu* 新中國的考古發現與研究 (Beijing: Wenwu Chubanshe, 1984), 219–20; *Zhongguo kaoguxue Xia Shang juan* 中國考古學夏商卷 (Beijing: Zhongguo Shehui Kexue Chubanshe, 2003), 164.
43. The correspondence of the four periods in Yinxu culture with the relative chronology of OBI is generally accepted as the following: Yinxu II = OBI Period I (King Wu Ding) and Period II (Kings Zu Geng and Zu Jia); Yinxu III = OBI Period III (Kings Lin Xin, Kang Ding) and IV (Kings Wu Yi, Wen Wu Ding); Yinxu IV = OBI Period V (Kings Di Yi, Di Xin).
44. See Henan Sheng, *Zhengzhou Erligang*, 7.
45. Ibid., 183, 162–65.

Period I. Also, the result of this chapter's graphic analysis of HB: 310 generally agrees with the features of HB: 311 and 312, that is, the Zhengzhou inscriptions date to early periods in terms of Anyang OBI chronology but not as early as pre–Wu Ding or as late as OBI Period III–IV.

Shandong Daxinzhuang Inscription

The most up-to-date and detailed archaeological study of Daxinzhuang 大辛莊 is that of Li Min, who includes his own firsthand experiences at that site.[46] It is far more substantial than the initial report in *Kaogu* (2003.6: 3–6).

In March 2003, an inscribed turtle plastron was found on the floor of a semi-subterranean house dated to a time from Yinxu II to early Yinxu III. Assuming that the dating applies to the inscribed plastron, it may be roughly contemporaneous with the Zhengzhou inscriptions. The plastron originally consisted of seven inscribed fragments, four of which were later rejoined by Fang Hui 方輝, a major participant in the dig (plate 2).

The order of reading in figure 4.3 and table 4.3 is shown by the numbers in parentheses; arrows indicate the direction of reading. Transcription of the inscriptions, English translation, and analysis in terms of script, lexicon, and grammar and content follow.

↓(1) 允徙.   (X) is surely to be relocated.[47]

↑(2) 不徙.   (X) is not to be relocated. (The arrow signs ↓ and ↑ taken together show that the inscriptions form a pair [*duìzhēn* 對貞].)

↓(3) 允徙.   (X) is surely to be relocated.

↑(4) 不徙.   (X) is not to be relocated.

↓(5) 徙.   (X) is to be relocated.

↑(6) 不徙.   (X) is not to be relocated.

---

46. See Li Min, Conquest, Concord, and Consumption: Becoming Shang in Eastern China (PhD diss., University of Michigan, 2008), 68–87.
47. See the discussion on lexicon, grammar, and content for what this passage may have actually meant.

↓(7) 允徙.   (X) is surely to be relocated.

↑(8) 不徙.   (X) is not to be relocated.

(9) 允徙.   (X) is surely to be relocated.

↓(10) 卸四女彘豕豕豕. (We) should perform the lustration ritual (=御=禦) (directed to) Four Mothers (with the offering of) (a specie porcine:) pig-kinds (consisting of) boar, hog, and pig.

↑(11) 勿卸.   (We) should not perform the lustration ritual.

↓(12) 卸.   (We should) perform the lustration ritual.

↑(13) 允.   (We should) surely [perform the lustration ritual].

↓(14) ...酉盪 (溫). ... *yǒu* (day) (we should) (heat up:) prepare (the pigs).

↑(15) 勿盪 (溫). (We) should not (heat up:) prepare (the pigs).

(16) 一   One [crack notation].

(17) 二   Two [crack notation].

(18) ... 女一.... Mother [with] one [sacrificial object].

Table 4.3 shows that the scribal tradition reflects a relationship with Anyang script, but it has its own distinctive features as seen in the graphs 允, 女, 彘, 豕, 豕, and 盪, that is, six out of the eleven graphs are distinctive. These graphs can also be related to Shi, Shi-Li transition, and Bin group inscriptions: the examples for the Shi, Shi-Li, and Li Group include 徙 (𣥐), 不 (𠀚), 卸 (𠂤, 𠂤, 𠂤), 勿 (𠃬, 𠃬), and 酉 (酉). The examples for the Funü category are 女 (𠨞) and 彘 (𠂤). On the assumption that the graphs traveled with the scribes, this relationship suggests an interchange between Daxinzhuang and Anyang. Here it is conceivable that Daxinzhuang supplied some of the diviners and scribes to Anyang. Some of them may have moved back to Daxinzhuang, where they developed their own way of writing. The other direction, from Anyang to Daxinzhuang, is also conceivable, but if so, it must have taken some time to develop such characteristics because Daxinzhuang graphs are distinctive. The feature "unique" entered in the last column of the table reflects such an inference. In terms of relative chronology worked out for the Anyang inscriptions, the Daxinzhuang graphs all belong to Period I (column 5).

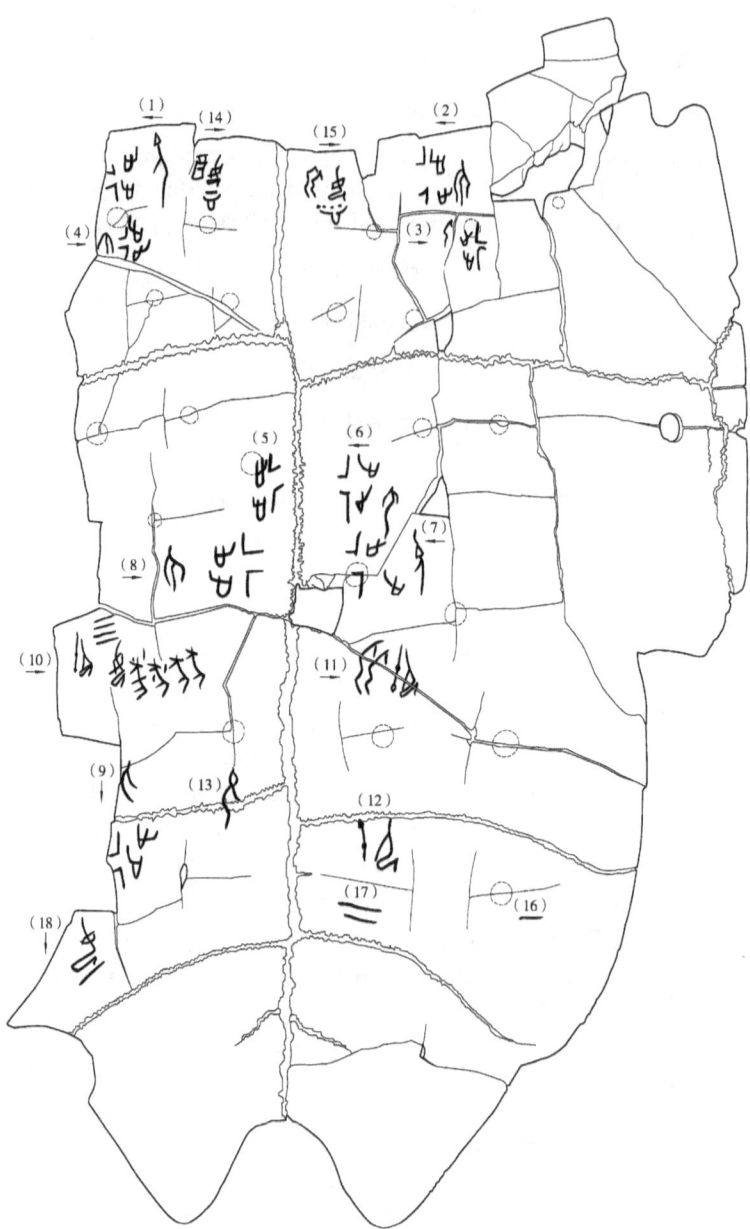

Figure 4.3 Tracing of Daxinzhuang: T2302⑤B:1 (by Li Miao)

Table 4.3 Script analysis of Daxinzhuang (DXZ) T2302⑤B:1 (numerals excluded).

DXZ graph	No. of occurrence/ inscription number	Graphic components	Comparable Anyang forms	Diviner group/ period	Modern equivalent	Characterizing DXZ graph
[graph][a]	5/(1), (3), (7), (9), (13)	𠂤 + 亻	Cp. (HJ: 1879)	Bin/I	允	Unique
[graph]	9/(1), (2), (3), ... (9)	彳 + 步	(HJ: 39987) (HJ: 20360)	Bin/I Shi-Li/I	彳 + 步 = 徏 = 徒	Bridging Shi-Li & Bin
[graph]	4/(2), (4), (6), (8)	(unigraph)	(Yibian 3400) (HJ: 117521) (HJ: 20939)	Bin/I Bin/I Shi-Li/I	不	Bridging Shi-Li & Bin
[graph]	3/(10), (11), (17)	亻 + 卩	(HJ: 20028) (HJ: 19809) (HJ: 34083)	Shi/I Shi/I Li/I	午 + 卩 = 卸	Bridging Shi & Li
[graph]	2/(10), (18)	(unigraph)	(HJ: 22259) cp.[b] (HJ: 21803) cf. (HJ: 22135)	Funü/I Zǐ/I Funü/I	女	Related to Funü
[graph]	1/(10)	豕 + — (= ↔)	(HJ: 22130) (HJ: 21289)	Funü/I Shi/I	豕+矢= 豤 = 豦	Related to Funü & Shi
[graph]	1/(10)	豕 + '	Rather remotely: (HB: 6886)	Shi-Li/I	豕+' =豕	Unique
[graph]	2/(10)	(unigraph)	?	?	豕	Unique
[graph]	2/(11), (15)	弓 + 弓	(HJ: 32812) (HJ: 34650) (HJ: 34555)	Shi-Li/I Li/I Li/I	弓+弓=弜 = 勿	Bridging Shi and Li
[graph]	1/(14)	(unigraph)	(HJ: 19946) (HJ: 32724)	Shi Shi-Li	酉	Bridging Shi and Li
[graph][c]	2/(14), (15)	母 + ... or ... + 皿	For 母, see above. (HJ: 19970) cf. (HJ: 22507)	Funü Shi Shi	女+水+皿 = 盥 = 溫	Unique

ᵃ Most Anyang forms abbreviate the shaft of a plow (*chūwén* 初文 of *sì* 耜). OBI scholars have paid attention to such common forms as 𠂉, 𠂉, and 𠂉, interpreting them, for instance, as "a person looking back" 象人回顧形 and the like, but none is correct; cf. *Gulin*, 39. *Shuowen* (8b/3b) gives: . . . 从儿㠯聲 '. . . a human figure signific and *yǐ* phonetic', which is the correct analysis because the small seal form (𠤎) continues the tradition of bronze forms like 𠂉 (Ban *gui* 班簋; JC: 4341), 𠂉 (Qingong *bo* 秦公鎛; JC: 268). Thus the Daxinzhuang form of *yǔn* is valuable in correctly identifying the element 𠂉 as 𠂉 (㠯). It also suggests the scribe had a tradition different from that of most Anyang scribes.

ᵇ The rubbing reproduced in HJ: 21803 is not very clear, but the original, YZ: 899, is much better. Note the lack of a characteristic curved body in 𠂉.

ᶜ The female grapheme is often interchangeable with the generic human one. The characteristic willowy body of 女, typical of the Funü category, is observed in the Daxinzhuang 𠂉.

The second aspect to be considered is lexicon. It has a symbiotic relationship with script, and the shared vocabulary items would also point to communication, specifically, mutual intelligibility in writing. All the lexical items mentioned are found in both Anyang and Daxinzhuang inscriptions, implying intergroup communication between the scribal and diviner groups at about the same time the inscriptions were made. This is a synchronic interpretation, while diachronically, the Daxinzhuang inscriptions had their own traditions. The fact that *zhēn* 貞, *bǔ* 卜, and the diviner's name are not even used in Daxinzhuang, while *zhēn* is used in Zhengzhou, will be significant only if more inscriptions are found. In other words, the nature of divination in the Daxinzhuang tradition may have been different from that of Anyang and Zhengzhou practices. But it is of interest that the positive-negative polarity in charging statements, *duìzhēn*, is the same as in the Anyang tradition. More important, however, the use of space, page design, the order and placement of inscriptions, and the preparation of the "hollows" are quite different from those seen in Anyang materials.[48] Regarding lexical items, this chapter focuses only on *xǐ* 徙, the words for "pigs" (*zhì* 彘, *chù* 豖, and *shǐ* 豕), and *wēn* (溫). It would be

---

48. Li Min, *Conquest, Concord, and Consumption*, 170–76, 179; Li Xueqin, "Daxinzhuang jiagu buci de chubu kaocha" 大辛莊甲骨卜辭的初步考察, *Wenshizhe* 文史哲 2003.4: 7.

more efficient to do so in conjunction with grammar and content.

Xǐ 徙:

Three different interpretations can be considered: (1) *xǐ*/*sjigx 徙 'move (to); relocate', (2) *bù*/*bagh 步 'walk, perambulate', and (3) *yán*/*ran 延 (延) 'to continue'. The first interpretation is preferable for the following reasons. *Leizuan* (860.3) gives only three examples for 徙, and although the *Leizuan* editors missed another example (HJ: 20360), the context is meager. One out of the four examples, however, has *qí* 其 before *xǐ* (HJ: 19276, poor quality); the Daxinzhuang examples themselves show that it is a verb, as it is negated by *bù* 不 and modified by an adverb *yǔn*. As for its meaning, we can perhaps do no better than follow Luo Zhenyu, who, in turn, relies on *Shuowen* (2b/4a): 延逻也 . . . 征徙或从彳 '*xǐ* means to move to . . . ; 征 is *xǐ* 徙 which otherwise consists of 彳'. *Yi* 逻 is defined immediately after this entry as "*yí* means *qiānxǐ*" (遷徙也 'relocate; move, migrate to'). Given the current state of knowledge, this is the likeliest gloss.

About half of the Daxinzhuang inscriptions concern the question of "doing or not doing *xǐ* 徙" (but see below). In the negative charge, *bù*/*pjəg 不 is used. This is significant because *bù* is used with the stative, aspectual, verbs of humanly uncontrollable action, while *fú* is used with the non-stative (action and process), punctual, verbs of humanly uncontrollable action.[49] It is in light of these features of the *p-type negatives that Sun's and Song's interpretation is attractive in that the subject of the verb *xǐ* is construed as referring not to the living but to some spirit.[50] They further suggest two interpretations for the meaning of 徙: one is "to move (to)" in the sense of "the spirit (moving to:) descending to this world to accept sacrifices" and another is in the (ultimate) sense of

---

49. Itō and Takashima, *Studies in Early Chinese Civilization*, 1:364–82.
50. Sun Yabing 孫亞冰 and Song Zhenhao 宋鎮豪, "Jinanshi Daxinzhuang yizhi xinchu jiagu buci tanxi" 濟南市大辛莊遺址新出甲骨卜辭探析), *Kaogu* 考古 2004.2: 72. I concur with their conclusion but modify it in the following way: first, the statement that "the use of *bù* and *fú* is close to each other" is acceptable if we define that the *p-type negatives, *bù* and *fú*, are for negating uncontrollable verbs, and their 事實 (fact) should be taken as negating the verbs in the past tense (often in the verifying statement); second, I would eliminate the contention that *bù xǐ* is in reference to the wishes of people. The *p-type negatives have the semantic feature [-will], so such negatives have nothing to do with human wishes in and of themselves. See Itō and Takashima, *Studies in Early Chinese Civilization*, 1:371–72, 382.

"the living relocating ancestral tablets." Their choice is the former, whereas in ours the latter is preferred, for both grammatical and religious reasons. Since this verb is negated with *bù*, it is stative, aspectual, and uncontrollable. In addition, *p-type negatives such as *bù* 不 are non-modal, as opposed to the modal *m-type negatives such as *wù* 毋. Sentence (1) has been translated in the passive as "(X) is surely to be relocated." The basic feature of the passive is a stative way of saying things, and here "(X) is to be relocated" can be contrasted with the active "(We) will relocate (X)." The stative here may also involve a sense of "imminence."[51] The verb is uncontrollable because the acceptability of relocation to an ancestral spirit is beyond the control of the living.[52] That is the raison d'être for the positive-negative antithetical charges from (1) to (9).

With regard to religious aspects, there are two cases that involve the manipulation of ancestral tablets. One has to do with the verb *bīn* 賓 'to treat . . . (some spirit) as a guest' and another has to do with the verb *zuò* 坐 'to (seat:) put . . . (some spirit) in situ (temple, bethel, shrine, and the like)'. Consider the following examples:

↓貞父乙(賓)于祖乙.   (HJ: 1657, obverse [3])

Tested: Fu Yi will be treated as a guest by Zu Yi.

↑父乙不賓于祖乙.   (Ibid. [4])

Fu Yi will not be treated as a guest by Zu Yi.

↓貞祖辛坐于父乙.   (HJ: 1779, obverse [1])

Tested: Zu Xin will (seated:) put at (the altar of) Fu Yi.

---

51. Ken-ichi Takashima, *Studies of Fascicle Three of Inscriptions from the Yin Ruins*, Volume 2: *New Palaeographical and Philological Commentaries* (Taipei: Institute of History and Philology, Academia Sinica, 2010), COM 1/7.
52. I used "the ancestral spirit be relocated from one place to another temporarily (遷徙 'relocate, migrate')" on the assumption that the ancestral tablets representing individual spirits — referred to as "Handle-shaped artifacts" (*bǐngxíngqì* 柄形器) with ancestral names brush-written in vermilion — were arranged hierarchically in the ancestral temples; for *bǐngxíngqì*, see Zhongguo Shehui Kexueyuan Kaogu Yanjiusuo 中國社會科學院考古研究所, *Anyang Yinxu faxian chutu yuqi* 安陽殷墟出土玉器 (Beijing: Science Press, 2005), 21–26. If so, we can interpret "the ancestral spirit/tablet be (relocated:) put from a lower to a higher place (or the other way round)" for sacrificial/ritual observances.

↑貞祖辛不坐于父乙.   (Ibid. [2])
Tested: Zu Xin will not be (seated:) put at (the altar of) Fu Yi.

In the first pair, Zu Yi (four generations before Wu Ding) is higher in the hierarchical order of ancestral spirits than Fu Yi (= Xiao Yi 小乙). It makes sense to think that Fu Yi's tablet was temporarily elevated to the level of Zu Yi. In the second pair, the verb *zuò* is used in the way opposite to *bīn*. That is, Fu Yi is lower in the hierarchical order than Zu Xin (three generations before Wu Ding). It seems that the living manipulated the ancestral tablets for the purpose of sacrifices and rituals (perhaps a prototype of *pèi jì/sì* 配祭/祀 'joint sacrifice/ritual' in Classical Chinese), but since they were unable to fathom the acceptability of joint sacrifice to ancestors, they appealed to divination, expressing the divinatory charges in the stative and passive.[53]

This chapter has devoted some space to the problem of the word *xǐ* 徙 in its lexical, grammatical, and cognitive-content analyses. It is necessary to relate all of these to the subject matter of this paper: how literacy played a role in the religious and ritual practices in Daxinzhuang and Anyang. If this reconstruction of the *xǐ* ritual activity in Daxinzhuang is correct, no exact counterpart existed in Anyang. But if the *bīn* and *zuò* rituals in the Anyang inscriptions are relevant to the *xǐ* ritual in the Daxinzhuang inscription, they might serve as a bridge by which to relate the two areas in terms of religious and ritual practices. The Daxinzhuang writings are related mainly to the Shi, Shi-Li transition, Li, and Funü group inscriptions. If so, there must have been contact between these groups and Daxinzhuang diviner(s) at some point in time.[54] The Anyang corpus is large, and a search for records about *xǐ* has identified only four occurrences in fragmentary texts, and they appear to be different from this Daxinzhuang context. In this single Daxinzhuang plastron, however, *xǐ* occurs nine times. If the reconstruction stated here is correct, they used a different expression for that sort of ritual observance, namely, *xǐ* rather than *bīn* and *zuò*.[55]

---

53. For more detail about the uncontrollable verb *bīn* 賓 'to treat . . . as a guest' (successful completion implied), see Takashima, *New Commentaries*, COM 39/2; for *zuò* 坐, see ibid., COM 225/1.
54. If the diviners and scribes served the elite, there must have been interchanges at the higher level of society as well.
55. There are descriptions about moving ancestral tablets from one niche to another in received Classical Chinese texts such as the *Zuozhuan* and *Tales of the States*, among others. The verb used for such ritual activity is none other than *xǐ* 徙. To cite only two

Zhì 豙, *chù* 豕, *shǐ* 豕, and *shǐ* 豕:

Although the three graphs do not have good matches in Anyang inscriptions, there is no problem in identifying these animals. Two issues, one grammatical and another archaeological, invite discussion.

Why did the diviner repeat the word *shǐ* 豕 'pig'? Sun and Song argued that Numeral$_1$ + Deity/Spirit constitute a unit.[56] According to them, when sacrifices are offered to such a unit, the pattern is Numeral$_2$ + Sacrificial victims, in which the Numeral$_2$ matches the Numeral$_1$ of the binomial unit. To cite one of their examples:

貞卯于三父三伐.　　　　　　　(HJ: 930 [Period I Bin group])
Tested: (We should) perform the lustration ritual directed to Three Fathers with three beheaded human victims.

When we apply this pattern to example (10), 卯四女豙豕豕豕, then the double use of 豕 could be explained as one pig offered to *each* of the Four Mothers because, even though *四豕 is not present, there are four pigs. The problem with this explanation is that the pattern is not necessarily maintained beyond the few examples provided by Sun and Song. For example:

丙戌卜二祖丁歲一牢.　　　　　(TN: 2364 [Period I Li Group])
Bǐngxū day divined: (To) Two Ancestors (we) will *guì*-cut [劌] one specially reared bovine.

---

examples here, we find in the eighteenth year of Duke Zhao in the *Zuozhuan*: "[Zi Chan 子產 made] Gongsun Deng move the great turtle; he made ritual officers *relocate* the main ancestral tablets [or cardinal stone niche] to the temple of Zhou [Li wang 厲王], [further] having made them announce [these deeds to the former rulers]" (. . . 使公孫登徙大龜, 使祝史徙主祏于周廟, 告于先君). Another example is from *Tales of the States*, which reads: "As for spirits, they are (solid:) stationary and are not to be *relocated* afar; if your (Majesty) look at it [= about the birth of Zhou Mu Wang 穆王] from this (standpoint), it should most certainly be the spirit of Dan Zhu (who was responsible for his birth)" (. . . 夫神壹, 不遠徙遷, 若由是觀之, 其丹朱之神乎); *Guoyu* (Zhouyu: 1). Wei Zhao 韋昭 (204–273) in his commentary to the above passage explains: "This is to say that the spirits are of singular mind, sticking with human, and not to be moved away afar" (言神壹心依憑於人, 不遠遷也). He interpreted the word *yī* 壹 as 壹心 (lit., "one mind"). But the word *yī* itself has a sense of "solid; unified," and because this is followed by 不遠徙遷, which is contrastive to *yī*, I took the liberty of interpreting the "solid" meaning as "stationary, not moving in its own right."

56. Sun Yabing and Song Zhenhao, "Jinanshi Daxinzhuang yizhi," 71.

Thus, the neat, corresponding pattern Sun and Song presented breaks down, and the enigmatic use of 豕豕 remains unexplained. Perhaps the second 豕 is an "echo noun/counter/classifier." Past studies suggest that the development of classifiers has its roots in Shang Chinese.[57] Chen Mengjia described a few expressions couched in the Noun + Numeral + Unit pattern as in 羌幾羌, 人幾人, 邕幾卣, 馬幾丙, and 貝幾朋.[58] Of these, the second noun after 幾 in 人幾人 and 羌幾羌 may be referred to as an "echo" noun. Counting is one of the basic functions of classifiers as developed later, and it is plausible that originally the classifiers began their lives as "clones" of the initial noun. The phrase 豩豕豕豕, then, is a kind of echo noun translatable to "(a specie porcine:) pig kinds consisting of boar, hog, and pig." Applying this explanation to the following example produces the following result:

卯祖癸豕祖乙豩祖戊豕豕. (TN-suppl. (附): 3 [Period I Li Group])

(We should) perform the lustration ritual (directed to or in the presence of) Zu Gui, Zu Yi, and Zu Wu with pig-kinds (consisting of) pig, hog, and pig.

There are other examples that belong to the Li Group inscriptions, yet another piece of evidence that the Daxinzhuang inscription is related to Li Group.

The archaeological problem of these inscriptions concerns the sacrificial use of pigs. Xu Hongxiu says there is a clear difference in the use of pigs in Daxinzhuang from that of cows and sheep as main sacrificial animals in Yinxu.[59] In regard to this, Okamura Hidenori has developed a theory on the link between kingship and the use of cattle for sacrificial purposes.[60] His view that the Shang rank-ordered their sacrificial animals, with bovines the highest and most coveted, followed by ovines and porcines, seems convincing.[61] Furthermore, such a ranking of the

---

57. Itō and Takashima, *Studies in Early Chinese Civilization*, 1:204–17.
58. Chen Mengjia, *Yinxu buci zongshu*, 94.
59. Xu Hongxiu 徐鴻修, "Daxinzhuang jiaguwen kaoshi" 大辛莊甲骨文考釋, *Wenshizhe* 文史哲 2003.3: 10.
60. Okamura Hidenori 岡村秀典, *Chūgoku kodai ōken to saishi* 中國古代王權と祭祀 (Tokyo: Gakuseisha, 2005), 117–20.
61. Okamura says that in transmitted texts *niú* 牛, *yáng* 羊, and *shǐ* 豕 are called *dàláo* 大牢, while *yáng* 羊 and *shǐ* 豕 are called *shàoláo* 少牢. This matches with *Da Dai Liji* 大戴禮記 (Zengzi tianyuan 曾子天圓) and Zheng Xuan's 鄭玄 (127–200) commentary

sacrificial animals is directly related to social class in that their consumption might have been state controlled. Of particular note are some 300,000 animal bones found in pit H27 of Huayuanzhuang locus south, and more than 98 percent of them are reported as bovine.[62] This area can be considered the domicile of a group of people close to the Shang royal house, and the closer to the royal palace, the more evidence there is of consumption of bovines.[63] In short, it would appear that the use of sacrificial animals depended not so much on the environment as on social, political, economic, and ritual factors, with the Shang court as the prevailing force. The relationship between all this and literacy is the question, and we can only imagine that some sort of state control, perhaps through writing and inventory, extended all the way to Daxinzhuang.

Wēn 溫 (溫):

There are two influential views about how to identify the graph with a known word: one is *wēn*/*ʔwən* 溫 'warm; heat up' (transitive) and the other is *yù*/*grjuk* 浴 'to bathe' (intransitive). The former is preferable for the following reasons. First, the *yù* interpretation is a typical "speculative etymology" (*wàngwén shēngyì* 望文生義) based on the graph 浴 in Shang

---

to *Yili* 儀禮 (Shaolao kuishili 少牢饋食禮). In his commentary to *Zhouli* 周禮 ("Tianguan" 天官, Zaifu 宰夫), however, Zheng Xuan says: "One *láo* is made up of three sacrificial animals, bovine, ovine, and porcine" (三牲牛羊豕具為一牢). Therefore, textual sources are fuzzy as to precise understanding of *dà* (or *tài* 太) *láo* and *shǎoláo*. Considering how the three animals are ranked in Shang, it would be safer to rely on the archaeological evidence as presented by Okamura; *Chūgoku kodai ōken*, 96.

62. Zhongguo Shehui Kexueyuan Kaogu Yanjiusuo Anyang Gongzuodui 中國社會科學院考古研究所安陽工作隊, "1986–1987 nian Anyang Huayuanzhuang nandi fajue baogao" 1986–1987年安陽花園莊南地發掘報告, *Kaogu xuebao* 考古學報 1992.1: 103.

63. A report of the animal bone remains at Huanbei Huayuanzhuang by Yuan and Tang shows that in a small area of 136 square meters, eleven different species of animal bones were found, of which pigs represent 60 percent, cattle 17 percent, sheep 10 percent, and wild animals 5 percent; Yuan Jing 袁靖 and Tang Jigen 唐際根, "Henan Anyang shi Huanbei Huayuanzhuang yizhi chutu dongwu guge yanjiu baogao" 河南安陽市洹北花園莊遺址出土動物骨骼研究報告, *Kaogu* 考古 2000.11: 75–81. This is in sharp contrast to the finds in the Huayuanzhuang locus south, on the other side of the Huan River, mentioned above. Okamura addresses this phenomenon and says that Huanbei Huayuanzhuang was inhabited by commoners or people of the lower aristocratic class; Okamura, *Chūgoku kodai ōken*, 119.

OBI. The graph is said to be a drawing of a person bathing in a water-filled basin. We cannot categorically reject any *wàngwén shēngyì* interpretation, but this Daxinzhuang graph is different from 浴. Also, the graph 浴 itself is subject to different interpretations. If the graph is interpreted as a pictograph of a person being boiled, equivalent to *zhǔ* 煮, how can it be evaluated objectively? Grammatically considered, because *wēn* is negated by the modal negative *wù*, *wēn* is an action-controllable verb, and its execution can be decided by human will. Thus, in sentence (15), it is stated in the negative with *wù* 勿. Contextually, it makes good sense to take *wēn* as meaning "heat up" (prepare, cook) the sacrificial victims mentioned in sentence (10). There is, then, contextual cohesion, while the "bathe" interpretation is unrelated to the rest of the inscriptions.

Conclusion

Examination of the Zhengzhou and Daxinzhuang inscriptions in terms of script, lexicon, and grammar and content shows that they are related to Anyang inscriptions but have their own distinctive, probably local, features. The typological classification of the Zhengzhou and Daxinzhuang graphs into diviner groups identifies diviner groups to which they may have been related. Both of these inscriptions — one from the south and the other from the east of Anyang — have affinities mainly with Shi, Li, and Funü group (only Daxinzhuang) inscriptions in Anyang. It is also possible, however, that they had their own traditions in literacy, though how far back in time the traditions might extend is difficult to discern. Because Shi and Li Group inscriptions are dated to Period I, it is likely that the contact was relatively early. Some of the scribes also appear to have gone to the capital to work for the Shang royal house. Others moved back to Zhengzhou or to Daxinzhuang, where they not only developed their own ways of writing but also used some sacrificial and ritual terms (*wēn* 'heat up' and *xǐ* 'relocate') in their own way. If this conclusion is correct, the process must have required a certain amount of time. In terms of script, the characterization "unique" entered in the last column of tables 4.1 and 4.3 reflects such an inference, although the uniqueness may have been the end product of the diviners and scribes originally sent from Anyang. Of particular interest in this sort of "literacy to the south" is Diviner Nan, who had a close relationship with a Li Group scribe and, moreover, spoke a dialect different from the standard language in the capital, although his place of origin could not be established. It is this sort of exchange backed by local traditions of writing that contributed to superior writing in general as witnessed in the Anyang inscriptions. As to why both Zhengzhou and Daxinzhuang inscriptions share the Shi Group and Li Group features, however, that is a question left open for further investigation.[64]

---

64. A possible avenue of research, for example, may be the issue of so-called "Erligang expansion" in the Yinxu I and II periods, including some pottery brush writings from Xiaoshuangqiao 小雙橋 near Zhengzhou of Middle Shang; Song Guoding 宋國定, "Zhengzhou Xiaoshuangqiao yizhi chutu taoqi shang de zhushu" 鄭州小雙橋遺址出土陶器上的朱書, *Wenwu* 2003.5: 35–44. Also, research by Jing Zhichun 荆志淳 (particularly using strontium analysis of human bones) concludes that "Erligang expansion" could explain a number of phenomena in such areas as Daxinzhuang and Anyang in early phases of Yinxu culture (personal communication, spring 2009).

CHAPTER 5

The Evidence for Scribal Training at Anyang

Adam Smith

Determining the functional, geographic and social range of literacy during the Anyang period (circa 1300–1050 B.C.E.) remains a difficult problem. The same could be said for literacy during the preceding five hundred years (if there was any at all) and subsequently during the Western Zhou and Spring and Autumn periods. Evidence for late-second-millennium Chinese literacy is overwhelmingly dominated, numerically speaking, by records of divination from inside the moated elite enclosure at the Late Shang site complex at Anyang. Does this salience of the divination record among attested text genres tell us something about the uses to which literacy was put? Or is it an accident of preservation and discovery?

Writing and Scribal Training at Anyang and Their Mesopotamian Parallels

There are many approaches to the question of literacy during the Anyang period, but one can simplify matters by considering where a particular theory of Shang literacy falls on a continuum between two imaginary extreme viewpoints. The first extreme conceives the Shang world having a population of more than a thousand literate individuals, deploying their skills not just at Anyang but also at relatively minor centers, managing the flow of raw materials, grain, and manufactured goods, communicating royal pronouncements, transmitting diplomatic correspondence to neighboring kingdoms, and registering the population of Henan, Hebei, and Shandong for the purposes of taxation, forced labor, and military service. The other extreme imagines a literate population of less than a dozen individuals, all in the immediate entourage of the Shang king and his family, based at Anyang but participating in excursions outside, and preoccupied with documenting divination, scheduling sacrifices, and occasionally labeling ritual implements and expensive gifts. In this chapter, these extremes will be referred to as the "maximal" and "minimal" hypotheses for late Shang literacy.

Drawing extensively on previously underexplored parallels with other early traditions of literacy, Robert Bagley has recently articulated an account of Chinese literacy in the second millennium that lies closer to the maximal extreme of literacy than to the minimal.[1] Although there is support for an alternative point of view lying closer to the extreme of minimal literacy,[2] the question is not at all close to being resolved. Exploring the detailed implications of the two competing hypotheses, and testing them against the evidence that is available, should continue to motivate research. The continued and growing preponderance of divination records on bone and shell is not, in itself, simple evidence one way or the other. Each hypothesis accounts for that preponderance in different ways. Instead, we need to seek out evidence that is accommodated and explained better by the implications of one hypothesis than by those of its competitor. The proposition here is that the evidence relevant to scribal training is more in keeping with the minimalist account. The evidence is also of considerable intrinsic interest and has previously attracted less attention than it deserves.

Bagley states that we lack "the smallest archaeological clue to how Wu Ding's diviners acquired their literacy."[3] This is to make an implicit claim about the nature of what are known in the Chinese-language literature as *xíkè bǔcí* 習刻卜辭 'practice-engraved divination records' that are

---

I would like to thank two anonymous reviewers, Lothar von Falkenhausen, Adam Schwartz, Ken-ichi Takashima, Crispin Williams, and the organizers of and participants in the Early China Seminar at Columbia University for their contributions to this chapter. Research was supported by the Cotsen Institute of Archaeology, University of California, Los Angeles, and a Henry Luce/ACLS East and Southeast Asian Archaeology and Early History Dissertation Fellowship (2006).

1. See Bagley, "Anyang Writing," 190–249.
2. See Smith, "Writing at Anyang."
3. See Bagley, "Anyang Writing," 221. Since diviner names occurring in divination records do not correlate one-to-one with the writing styles of the records, we know that it was not consistently the diviners (in the conventional sense of *zhēnrén* 貞人) who inscribed the records of their own divinations. See Keightley, *Sources of Shang History*, 48–49. Strictly speaking, we have no evidence that diviners (in general) were literate at all. In this chapter, however, I will make a tentative identification of a named diviner with a scribal trainee.

abundantly attested in the published corpora. We will assess this implicit claim below. "We depend on comparative evidence," Bagley continues, "to remind us that literacy is the result of schooling." The comparative evidence he adduces includes the curricular use of "myths, hymns to gods and kings, and dialogues" and accounts of Mesopotamian school life including Kramer's well-known "Schooldays" translation.[4] The claim, then, is that since the cuneiform tradition in Mesopotamia had schools (in the narrow sense of a building housing specialist instructors and offering a curriculum based around literary texts), so, too, did Anyang. According to Bagley, the absence of any remains of written exercises from such an institution is to be explained by — and indeed taken as evidence for — the massive failure of Anyang-period writing to be preserved on perishable media, as required by the maximal model of second-millennium Chinese literacy.[5]

The problem with this line of argument is that it compares evidence from very different points in the evolutionary history of the two literate traditions and so generates a potentially misleading comparative expectation. The depiction of the Mesopotamian "tablet-house" in "Schooldays," for instance, postdates the first attestation of cuneiform literacy by considerably more than a thousand years.[6] It thus invites comparison with the Han period rather than the Chinese second millennium. Exact parallels are readily found in the biographies of Han literati preserved in transmitted literature. See, for instance, the account of Wang Chong's education in the early first century.[7] At age eight, he joined more than a hundred other children in a local "writing hall" (shūguǎn 書館), where ugly writing "earned a whipping," before advancing to the study of difficult old literary texts and then an administrative career. Is there any good reason to think that the comparative parallel holds good for the earliest attested stage of Chinese literacy?

Sumerian literature, as Bagley notes, "has come down to us in the form

---

4. Samuel Noah Kramer, "Schooldays: A Sumerian Composition Relating to the Education of a Scribe," *Journal of the American Oriental Society* 69.4 (1949): 199–215.
5. Bagley, "Anyang Writing," 222.
6. Kramer, "Schooldays," 199, 213 n. 220.
7. See *Lunheng* 論衡, by Wang Chong 王充, *Sibu beiyao* edition (Taipei: Zhonghua Shuju, 1965), 30:1. For schools and the transmission of literacy during the Han period, see "Soldiers, Scribes, and Women: Literacy among the Lower Orders in Early China," by Robin D. S. Yates, chapter 10 in this volume.

of schoolboy exercises."[8] However, it has done so primarily as the debris of Old Babylonian (2000–1600 B.C.E.) scribal education,[9] and not from scribal training activities of the Late Uruk period (late fourth millennium), the period when cuneiform is first attested. Again, the Old Babylonian materials are a fruitful source of expectations about the developed state of literate and literary education during the Han period, expectations that are substantially fulfilled by what is known about the place of the *Book of Poetry* (Shijing), the *Book of Documents* (Shangshu), and Warring States literature in the higher scribal curriculum. But unless there is reason to think that the earliest literacy in China predates the Anyang period by close to a millennium, arguments about the form Anyang scribal training took that are based on Old Babylonian parallels should be regarded with suspicion.

If we were to take the evidence for scribal training from the Late Uruk period as our point of Mesopotamian comparison, we would derive a different set of expectations. The Late Uruk period provides no evidence for the existence of schools, in the sense of institutions where specialist instructors taught writing away from the context of its everyday use. Nor is there any sign of a curricular role for "myths, hymns to gods and kings, and dialogues." Rather, Late Uruk "school texts" (if we want to force that name on them) are very narrowly focused on the founding genre of the cuneiform tradition, namely, the administrative accounting text.

Englund describes several examples of practice accounting texts from Uruk.[10] The lexical lists are the most frequently discussed texts with a possible pedagogical function.[11] Although they are likely to have been elaborated beyond the needs of everyday administration as part of what Veldhuis refers to as their compilers' systematizing "drive to be complete,"[12] their categories — official titles, vessels and their contents, manufactured objects, livestock and other animals, and place-names — are

---

8. Bagley, "Anyang Writing," 221.
9. Niek Veldhuis, *Elementary Education at Nippur: The Lists of Trees and Wooden Objects* (PhD diss., University of Gröningen, 1997), sections 2.3-2.4:23–67.
10. Englund, "Texts from the Late Uruk Period," 106–10, 188–92.
11. Englund, "Texts from the Late Uruk Period," 82–110. For parallels between the Mesopotamian and later Chinese use of lexical lists, see Wang Haicheng, "Writing and the State in Early China in Comparative Perspective" (PhD diss., Princeton University, 2007), 328–36.
12. Niek Veldhuis, "How Did They Learn Cuneiform? 'Tribute/Word List C' as an Elementary Exercise," in *Approaches to Sumerian Literature in Honour of Stip (H.L.J. Vanstiphout)*, ed. Piotr Michalowski and Niek Veldhuis (Leiden: Brill, 2006), 189.

nevertheless those required for contemporary bookkeeping. Perhaps most remarkable is the so-called Word List C, of which fifty-six (fragmentary) witnesses survive from Uruk.[13] The text is organized around two verbatim presentations of a mundane list of quantified commodities: five units of salt, five ducks, one suckling calf, four metal knives, ten units of milk, and so forth. The habituating repetition of this text by trainee accountants propelled its conservative replication through the curricula of the Early Dynastic and Ur III periods, into the Old Babylonian, transforming the elementary scribal exercise into "a piece of venerated [and 'rather opaque'] traditional knowledge."[14]

If we were to assume that Anyang literacy, the earliest attested stage of Chinese writing, could be better approximated by the earliest attested stage of cuneiform literacy than by the activities of the Old Babylonian scribes, we would expect Anyang scribal training to be tightly focused on techniques for learning a narrow range of text genres around which the writing system first evolved. If Chinese literacy first emerged in the context of the routine performance by Shang kings of sacrifice, divination, and elite gift exchange, as the minimalist account of early Chinese literacy sketched above proposes, we would expect trainee scribes to concentrate on directly relevant text genres. It would be surprsing to find a curriculum with a free-floating scholastic rationale, dominated by literary texts.

Drawing a simple analogy between literacy at Anyang and the Late Uruk period is itself not unproblematic. In contrast to the case of proto-cuneiform, whose emergence from precursor non-literate accounting techniques can be traced with considerable chronological precision, it is not known exactly how long writing was in use prior to the reign of Wu Ding. The Anyang inscriptions' widespread use of phonetic determinatives in compound signs and complex natural-language syntax (both of which are absent from Late Uruk period proto-cuneiform) certainly suggest the possibility of development from a prior script stage. Nevertheless, the point here is to stress the inadequacies of an Old Babylonian model for literacy acquisition at Anyang. Selecting a different point of comparison within the cuneiform tradition generates very different expectations.

---

13. Of the thirteen multiply attested (i.e., standardized) lexical texts in proto-cuneiform, "Word List C" is third in frequency, after the "Professions" list (Lu A), and the "Vessels" list; see Veldhuis, "How Did They Learn Cuneiform?" 186.
14. Veldhuis, "How Did They Learn Cuneiform?" 196.

Anyang "Schools" and "Learning"

A number of recent works have summarized inscriptional evidence for the existence of "schools" at Anyang, sometimes suggesting that they may have been places for literacy training,[15] and it is useful to review the evidence and its interpretation here, since in several cases the summaries are inadequate and misleading.

The evidence concerns usage in the Anyang divination records of various graphs related to the received forms 學 and 教.[16] This range of graphic variation is not the issue here, so for typographical convenience, all graphs in this group will be written as 學. It is likely that many instances of these graphs are writing members of the word family that includes 學 *xué* ~ *xiào* 'to learn; to instruct'.

HJ: 8304 and HJ: 16406, a pair of small Wu Ding period plastron fragments with almost identical inscriptions in the same hand, are credibly taken as indicating that 學 can also write a noun, "school," possibly referring to the construction of one (*zuò xué* 作學). In isolation, this is exceedingly weak evidence for a place of literacy training. Several of the above-mentioned authors omit to mention the inscription on TN: 60, in which *dàxué* 大學 appears to be a candidate location for an obscure ritual procedure, as an alternative to other public structures.[17] Whatever the nature of this *dàxué*, there is a prima facie case for lexical and cultural continuity with the *xiǎoxué* 小學 and *tàixué* 大學 of much later received literature. Some further support is provided by two Western Zhou occurrences of *xiǎoxué*, possibly referring to a place of education or training (JC: 2837, JC: 4324-25). *Xué* 學 could possibly be a noun in HD: 181 (*wǎngxué* 往學 'to go to the *xué*') and in HD: 450 (*rùxué* 入學 'to enter the *xué*'), but these examples could equally be verbs (i.e., 'to go to learn,' 'to go in and learn'). That is the limit of the evidence from Anyang

---

15. Oliver Moore, *Chinese* (Berkeley: University of California Press, 2000), 25; Song Zhenhao 宋鎮豪, "Cong jiaguwen kaoshu Shangdai de xuexiao jiaoyu" 從甲骨文考述商代的學校教育, in Wang Yuxin et al., eds., 220–30; Wang, "Writing and the State," 322; Thomas H. C. Lee, *Education in Traditional China: A History* (Leiden: Brill, 2000), 41; Yang Kuan 楊寬, *Xi Zhou shi* 西周史 (Shanghai: Shanghai Renmin Chubanshe, 2003), 664.
16. To avoid lengthy paleographic descriptions of signs, I simply refer the reader to the literature collected in *Gulin*; see GL: 3230–3233.
17. For the procedure, see discussions under GL: 1036.

for the use of *xué* 學 as or in a nominal phrase referring to an educational institution.

We must also exclude HJ: 3250, which provides no support for the existence of institutionalized literacy training, despite its being often mentioned in discussions of the issue. The following is a loose transcription and partial translation of its divinatory proposition:

多子其延學疫，不遘大雨。

If the Many Children continue practicing X, they will not run into heavy rain.[18]

The only uncertain point of interpretation is the graph *yì* 疫, which is left untranslated.[19] There is no hint, however, that this inscription concerns literate education. Anyang diviners' concern with the prospects of rain is often connected with group activities performed in the open air, including rituals in ceremonial spaces. The concern in HJ: 3250 is probably whether rain will disrupt the practice of some such open-air activity.

This connection between the verb *xué* 'to practice' and group performances, specifically of dance or music, rather than literacy, is supported by records from Huayuanzhuang Dongdi (花園莊東地) of divination for a patron who was probably one of the Many Children.[20] For example, in five records (on HD: 487, HD: 336, and HD: 150), 學 writes a verb with *shāng* (?) 商 as its object. The meaning of this *shāng* is not known, but Song Zhenhao has plausibly argued that it refers to a dance or musical performance.[21] There are also divinations about "continuing to

---

18. "Many Children" is an indicator of kinship, not of age. It seems to include, but may not be limited to, offspring of the Shang king, who need not have been what we would think of as school-age children.
19. Adam Schwartz (personal communication) has cautioned against taking *yì* 疫 as the object of the verb *xué* 學 'to practice', on the basis of a comparison with HD: 181, in which the two words occur in a different syntactic relationship. He tentatively suggests that 疫 may instead be a verbal complement, to be rendered something like 'to practice to exhaustion'.
20. The patron is referred to as *zǐ* 子 'Child'. For the identity of the patron, and his ancestry, see the discussion in Yao Xuan, *Yinxu Huayuanzhuang dong di jiagu*, ch. 3; Chen Jian 陳劍, "Shuo Huayuanzhang Dongdi jiagu buci de 'ding' " 說花園莊東地甲骨卜辭的丁, *Gugong bowuyuan yuankan* 故宮博物院院刊 114 (2004.4): 51–63.
21. Song Zhenhao, "Cong jiaguwen kaoshu Shang dai," 224–25.

perform *shāng*" (*yán zòu shāng* 延奏商, on HD: 86, HD: 150, and HD: 382) and about "dancing *shāng*" (*wǔ shāng* 舞商, on HD: 130). At one point, an inspection of the Child's dance by Wu Ding is anticipated ("Ding will come to observe Child dancing" *Dīng lái shì Zǐ wǔ* 丁來視子舞, on HD: 183). The central theme of Song's article is appealing: the importance attached to learning ritual music and dance seen in inscriptions from Anyang and the descriptions of music and dance in elite education in early received literature represent a significant cultural continuity.

To summarize, the examples of *xué* 學 in the divination records, including HJ: 3250 translated above, are substantially focused on performance activities of that kind. A survey of Anyang inscriptions must firmly conclude that there is no evidence that the Shang elite received a literate "schooling" and that no association can be made between the abundant instances of the graph 學 and literacy acquisition.

The Xíkè Practice Inscriptions as Evidence for Scribal Training

The *xíkè* 習刻 (lit., "practice engraved") inscriptions are a large and well-known subset of the inscriptions on divination bones and shells from Anyang, characterized by varying degrees of incompetent writing or other features that suggest that the scribe is not recording divinations but rather learning or practicing the skills required to do so.[22] The questions are: Which skills are being practiced? Is literacy itself among them?

Date Tables

There is a strong association between incompetent *xíkè* handwriting and certain categories of text content, most prominently tables of *gānzhī* 干支 cyclical dates. Matsumaru Michio classified 156 occurrences of these date tables from *Heji* according to how competent or otherwise the writing on them appeared, ranging from the "extremely immature" (which he labeled

---

22. Wang Yuxin 王宇信 and Yang Shengnan 楊升南, eds., *Jiaguxue yi bai nian* 甲骨學一百年 (Beijing: Shehui Kexue Wenxian Chubanshe, 1999), 254–55; Keightley, *Sources of Shang History*, 47, nos. 99–100. A useful catalog of *xíkè* inscriptions from Xiaotun South is provided in Yao Xiaosui 姚孝遂 and Xiao Ding 肖丁, *Xiaotun nandi jiagu kaoshi* 小屯南地甲骨考釋 (Beijing: Zhonghua Shuju, 1985), 197–206.

type A), through relatively inferior (B), to "normal" competence (C).[23] For example, among 129 examples of Period V date tables in *Heji*, Matsumaru found thirty-six examples of type A hands, sixty-eight of type B, and thirty-one of type C (with several instances of hands of differing competence appearing on a single bone). He proposed that the type C date tables were model texts for sight copying by students, and that types A and B were student copies, but without making any claim as to whether the students were acquiring literacy or merely engraving skills.

Guo Moruo was probably the first to write about these practice inscriptions, in a 1937 annotated catalog. He described a *xíkè* date table in the following terms:[24]

> The content [of CB: 1468=HJ: 18946] consists of the *gānzhī* for days 1 to 10 engraved repeatedly. In the fourth line of text, the graphs are finely written and orderly, as though engraved by a teacher (*xiānshēng* 先生) to serve as a model (*fànběn* 範本). The rest are crooked and inferior, as though written by someone learning to engrave (*xuékè* 學刻). This is no different from the method by which today's children practice writing (*xízì* 習字). Shedding light on the educational circumstances of three thousand years ago, it is of the utmost interest. Furthermore, interspersed within the columns written by the trainee are finely written graphs identical to those of the model, where presumably the attendant teacher took up the knife. Examples include the 辰, 午, and 申 of the second line and the 卯, 己, and 辛 of the third.

There are two ways of interpreting this inscription, either as the remains of literacy acquisition (as arguably Guo seems to be doing) or as the remains of engraving practice by someone already literate. According to the first interpretation, the trainee was learning to write *gānzhī* dates. This would be a natural first exercise for a novice scribe. A *gānzhī* date is a standard component of a divination record and many other text-genres, and the various uses of the twenty-two *gānzhī* signs make up almost a quarter of the total graph-count of one corpus for which precise counts are

---

23. Matsumaru Michio 松丸道雄, "Jieshao yi pian sifang feng ming keci gu" 介紹一片四方風名刻辭骨, in Jinian *Yinxu jiaguwen faxian yibai zhou nian guoji xueshu yantaohui lunwenji* 紀念殷墟甲骨文發現一百周年國際學術研討會, ed. Wang Yuxin 王宇信 and Song Zhenhao 宋鎮豪 (Beijing: Shehui Kexue Wenxian Chubanshe, 2003), 83–87.
24. See CB: 1468.

readily available.[25] "Practicing one's *jiǎzǐ*" (*xí jiǎzǐ* 習甲子) remained a byword for acquiring the rudiments of literacy into the medieval period,[26] and *gānzhī* tables are among the most poorly executed examples of scribal training texts from the Han garrisons of the northwest frontier.[27] According to the second interpretation, the previously literate trainee already knew the *gānzhī* signs (as any literate person would) and was simply using them as a starting point for learning the engraving technique.

Both interpretations are possible, but the second has become the consensus. Consider, for example, Zhang Shichao's response to the remarks of Guo Moruo quoted above:[28]

> Prior to becoming engravers [of divination records], Shang people had to undergo a period of training. . . . the not inconsiderable number of practice inscriptions is proof of this. [Guo Moruo in his commentary on CB: 1468] did not distinguish learning to engrave from learning to write, and thereby invited misunderstanding. . . . the handwriting styles classified as practice inscriptions [*xíkè*] merely reflect the circumstances of learning to engrave. Those who were being trained to engrave would have previously mastered literacy skills.

No evidence or argument is offered for the final claim. One is left to fill in the reasoning that led to it, namely, that literacy during the Late Shang period was far more routinely performed on media other than those that are attested, that divination recording on bone and shell was an unusual specialization of literate practice that just happens to have been abundantly preserved, and hence that scribes would have first acquired the ability to

---

25. According to the electronic transcription of the Huayuanzhuang Dongdi corpus presented in Smith, "Writing at Anyang," appendix II, 4,014 graphs out of a total of 16,990 are written with signs from the *gānzhī* repertoire. This includes usages of the twenty-two signs other than for dates and day names (*rìming* 日名).
26. "Anyone who has ever recited the *Jíjiu* or practiced his *gānzhī* dates is wielding his writing brush and flourishing his literary talent, debating institutions and discoursing on the Way" (曾諷《急就》、習甲子者，皆奮筆揚文，議制論道). See *Jinshu* 晉書, "Xiahou Zhan liezhuan" 夏侯湛列傳, *Sibu beiyao* edition (Taipei: Zhonghua Shuju, 1965), 55:2.
27. See, e.g., Michael Loewe, *Records of Han Administration* (Cambridge: Cambridge University Press, 1967), 2:418–21; Gansu Sheng Wenwu Kaogu Yanjiusuo 甘肅省文物考古研究所, *Dunhuang Han jian* 敦煌漢簡 (Beijing: Zhonghua Shuju, 1991), item no. 841 (251, plate 80) and no. 1458 (274, plate 132).
28. Zhang Shichao 張世超, *Yinxu jiagu ziji yanjiu: Shizu buci pian* 殷墟甲骨字跡研究 — 師組卜辭篇 (Changchun: Dongbei Shifan Daxue Chubanshe, 2002), 27–28.

write on "everyday" media and subsequently retrained as engravers if called upon to specialize. A number of other scholars have recently reached similar conclusions.[29]

However, the learning-to-engrave interpretation leaves many questions unanswered that the learning-to-write interpretation has no difficulty dealing with. The date table is by no means the only category of trainee inscription, but why do trainees concentrate so much effort on producing this particular category of text?[30] If they were learning the script for the first time, we could point to the foundational role that this set of signs played in divination recordkeeping and literacy more generally. If they were already fully literate, should we not be surprised to see them spending so much time on just twenty-two signs from a repertoire of many hundreds, perhaps several thousand, that they had supposedly already acquired? Why do trainees always write out the cycle of sixty in (full or partial) tabular form, and why do the presumed instructors always model it that way? Under the learning-to-engrave interpretation, it would be sufficient for a model simply to list the twenty-two signs and for the trainee to copy individual signs repeatedly to fluency. Under the learning-to-write interpretation, the trainees are learning the sequence of sign pairs for the cycle of sixty for the first time and so need to be repeatedly exposed to its combinatorial structure.

The most important questions that the learning-to-engrave interpretation struggles to answer satisfactorily are: Why did the trainees seem to make errors that a previously literate person would be unlikely to make, and why did the least competent among them seem to have so little sense of how to arrange a line of text on a surface?

Consider HJ: 38058. The group of graphs discussed below is highlighted in figure 5.1. The accompanying table contrasts these with the more conventional forms that appear in adjacent columns. At least two and perhaps three levels of competence appear on this scapula, each writing ten-day weeks from the cycle of sixty in vertical columns. The least competent are the columns on the left, where, poor motor skills aside, the

---

29. Olivier Venture, Étude d'un emploi rituel de l'écrit dans la Chine archaïque (XIIIe–VIIIe siècle avant notre ère): Réflexion sur les matériaux épigraphiques des Shang et des Zhou occidentaux (PhD diss., Université Paris 7, 2002), 308; Wang, "Writing and the State," 326.
30. The 156 date tables discussed by Matsumaru are by no means all the examples known. He was simply surveying the cases conveniently gathered together in the organizational scheme of *Heji*.

scribe has (1) produced an unrecognizable *chǒu* 丑, (2) omitted the horizontal stroke in *bǐng* 丙 on its first appearance, and (3) rotated *yín* 寅 by 180 degrees.

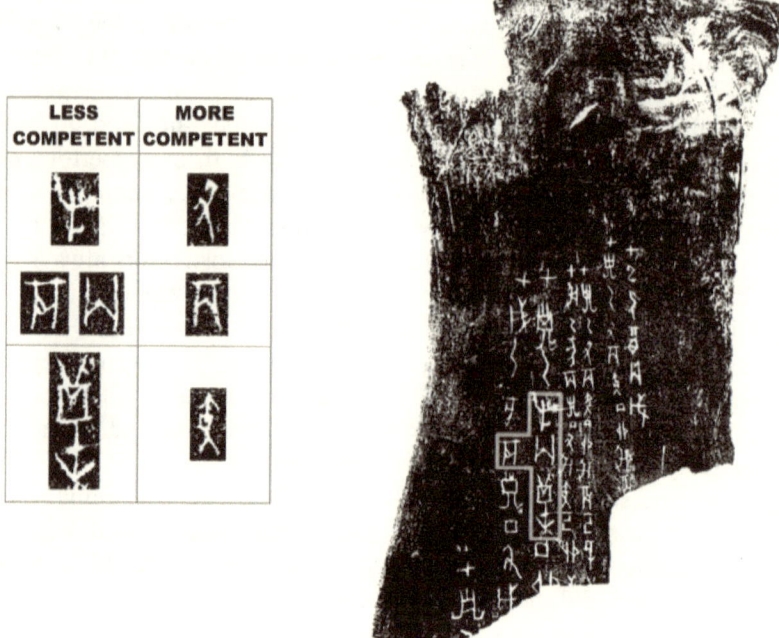

Figure 5.1 HJ: 38058, scapula fragment with date tables in trainee hands of varying competence. From HJ: 12:4736.

Some trainees who produced date tables also seem to have had great difficulty in keeping to the conventions for consistent graph size and placement that otherwise characterize the contemporary script, and with which any literate person could be presumed to be familiar. Their inscriptions often show no ability to anticipate the space required for an orderly arrangement of text.

HJ: 37995 (fig. 5.2b), for instance, besides being incompetently engraved, shows an uncontrolled variation in the space occupied by individual graphs, from the tiny fourth *gān*, *dīng* 丁, to the greatly elongated *zhī* signs *shēn* 申 and *yǒu* 酉. As a result, the tabular

EVIDENCE FOR SCRIBAL TRAINING 185

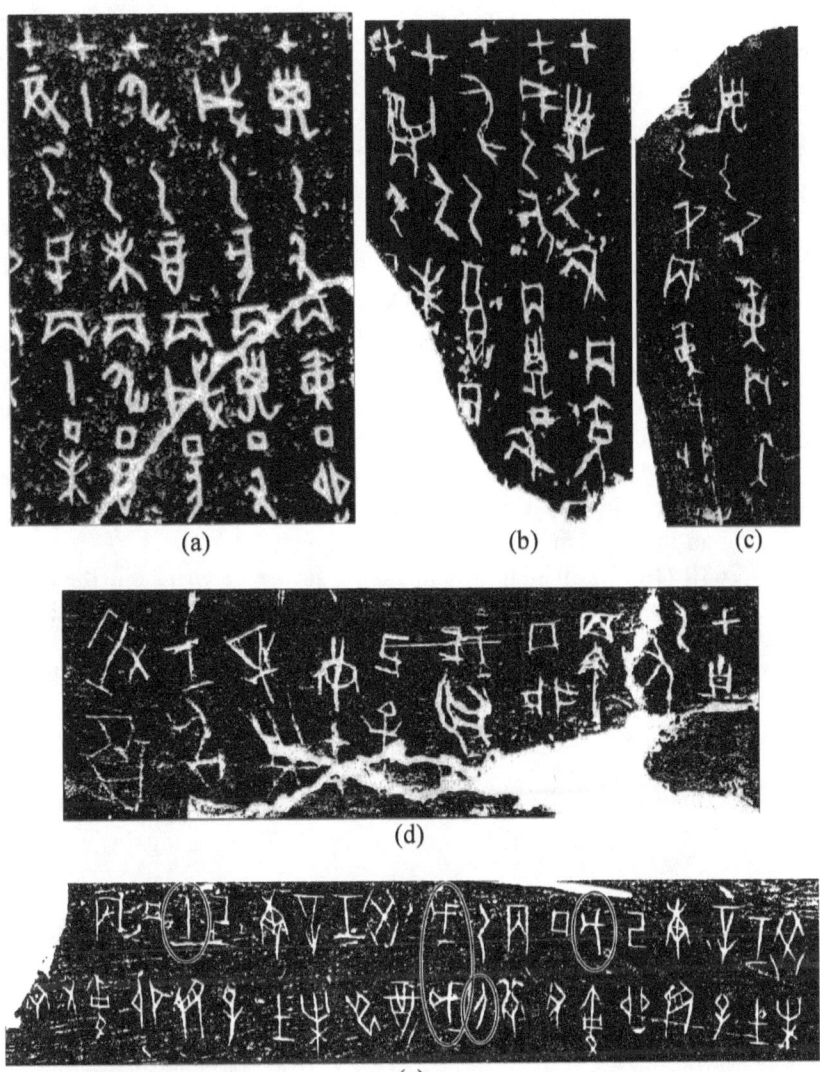

Figure 5.2 Date tables. Top row: model table on HJ: 37986 (a) contrasted with disorderly trainee tables on HJ: 37995 (b) and HJ: 38072 (c); middle row: egregiously incompetent graphs on TN: 2661 (d); bottom row: anomalies (circled in gray) on TN: 2630 (e). From HJ: 12:4718, 4720, 4739, and TN: 541, 574.

arrangement departs from the orderly arrangement of its contemporary models in the Huang Group (黃組), in which graphs occupy similar mounts of space and matching *gān* signs are aligned in horizontal rows (cf. fig. 5.2a and other examples in the range HJ: 37986–38114).

In HJ: 38072, (fig. 5.2c), in what appears to be the first attempt to write out the first few terms in the cycle of sixty (the column of graphs on the right), the scribe has (1) written *yǐ* 乙 not as a three-stroke s-curve but as an extended wiggle, (2) omitted one of the fingers of *chǒu* 丑, (3) incorrectly permuted the order of *bǐng* 丙 and *yín* 寅, and (4) attempted to repeat the *yín* 寅 before giving up and starting again.

TN: 2661 (fig. 5.2d) is engraved with the *gānzhī* for the first ten-day week. It is executed in a dramatically incompetent hand with the exception of the first pair of signs, on the left, neatly written one above the other, presumably by an instructor or more competent student. The first pair of signs by the student, for day 2, is not properly aligned, and the subsequent *gānzhī* pairs grow in size as the inscription proceeds from left-right to left, producing an impression of considerable naivety.

TN: 2630 (fig 5.2e) is an attempt by a scribe to write out the *gānzhī* terms for the first two ten-day weeks. Motor skills are fine, but (1) the first instance of *wù* 戊 is missing three strokes, appearing as [graph] instead of [graph], (2) *hài* 亥 for day 12 is missing its horizontal strokes, appearing as [graph] rather than the expected [graph], (3) day 11 (*jiǎxū* 甲戌) is written as day 35 (*wùxū* 戊戌), and (4) the *gān* for day 15 (*wù* 戊 again) is missing two strokes: [graph][31]

The concentrated occurrence on *gānzhī* date tables of errors of this kind, which are not easily explained under the learning-to-engrave interpretation, implies that the date tables are associated with the lowest rung of the ladder toward literacy.

An additional feature of trainee date tables, also discussed by Guo Moruo (see CB: 1467=HJ: 38076), is the occasional systematic absence of horizontal strokes from graphs. In addition to disorderly attempts at the cycle of sixty, Guo's example also has the *gānzhī* for days 1 to 4 in a

---

31. For a survey of similar errors, see Li Minling 李旼姈, *Jiagu wenli yanjiu* 甲骨文例研究 (Taipei: Taiwan Guji Chuban Youxian Gongsi, 2002), 107–14, 117–21.

secure-looking hand but with all horizontal strokes systematically omitted. This phenomenon has been discussed many times, and a variety of interpretations proposed.[32] The simplest way of accounting for the omission of horizontal strokes, though, would be as an attempt by the instructor to demonstrate the stroke order — verticals before horizontals — that constituted the de facto standard for his or her writing style and which presumably helped to minimize the rotation of surface or knife. This interpretation of the missing horizontals is compatible with both the learning-to-write and the learning-to-engrave account of the practice inscriptions. Nevertheless, it is a good illustration of the intimate pedagogical interaction between trainees and their instructors.

To summarize, the density of errors and incompetent text arrangement in the *xíkè* date tables provides a first line of evidence for interpreting visibly incompetent engraving in this category as the work of marginally literate individuals.

Simple Formulae and Sight-Copying of Divination Records

By learning only a small number of signs in addition to those in the *gānzhī* set, a trainee developed the ability to write out complete divination records of a simple, formulaic kind. There are many examples of insecure hands writing out versions of the *bǔxún* 卜旬 'divining for the week ahead' formula, which requires only five signs, all of high frequency, in addition to the *gānzhī*. Often, these are syntactically incomplete or jumbled in ways that would seem bizarre if the scribe were fully literate and merely learning to engrave.

TN: 1034 is a largely intact scapula on which the *bǔxún* formula has been repeated many times in an orderly but not fully fluent hand. On the far right-hand edge of the published reproduction, the formula appears garbled as 癸卜未貞旬亡禍, with the *bǔ* 卜 sign intruding between the date signs. The same error is repeated verbatim in the middle of the

---

32. For a comprehensive overview, see Li Minling, *Jiagu wenli yanjiu*, 122–48. Li's proposal that omitted strokes are "produced by negligence on the part of the scribe," though perhaps adequate to explain isolated instances in otherwise normal inscriptions, seems implausible as an account of the systematic, visually salient omission of most horizontal strokes from an entire inscription. The most impressive instance is the date table HJ: 24440 (see fig. 1.3 in "Getting 'Right' with Heaven and the Origins of Writing in China," by David W. Pankenier, chapter 1 in this volume), which must surely be connected with scribal training.

scapula. Perhaps the trainee is sight-copying his or her own inscriptions. The scapula had been prepared for and used in divination, and at least some of the trainee inscriptions are likely to be records of divinations actually performed on the bone.

An excellent example of an instructor and a trainee writing a set of *bŭxún* records together is provided by HJ: 34945 (=JB: 760) (fig. 5.3). *Bŭxún* formulae for days 40, 50, 60, 10, and 20 run in orderly sequence up the edge of this scapula fragment. They are records of divinations actually performed on the bone, as the presence of crack-numbering indicates. The earliest record, for day 40, is in a fluent and fully competent hand, while the subsequent records are evidently inferior.

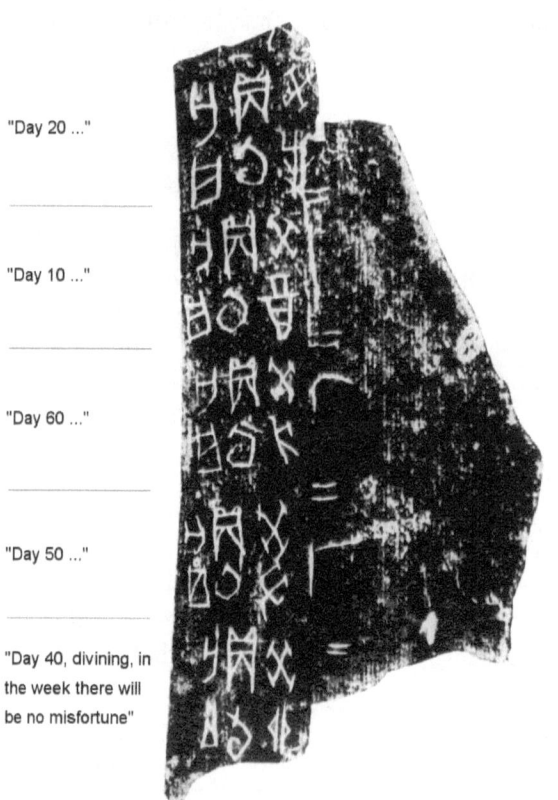

Figure 5.3 HJ: 34945, scapula with *bŭxún* 'divining for the week ahead' records, of which the earliest (day 40) is in a more competent hand than those that follow. From HJ: 11:4366.

Besides the *bǔxún* formula, simple and standardized hunting divinations were also features of the divination scribes' early training. The scapula HJ: 35261 appears not to have been used for actual divinations but is covered in more than a dozen repetitions of a simple hunting divination formula of which only the *gānzhī* date varies.

干支卜，逐麋，禽。
Day n cracking: If we pursue *mí*-deer, we will capture some.[33]

TN: 2693 has two versions of a hunting divination record, neither associated with any divinatory cracks on the scapula. The hand is far from secure. The naive arrangement of the graphs and the nonsensical anomalies (the "rain" 雨 sign is omitted in one case, and the "field" 田 sign, for "hunt," is omitted in the other) imply that this is less likely to be a previously literate individual learning to engrave than a novice scribe mechanically and inaccurately sight-copying a model.

辛未卜，王其[田?]，不雨。
Day 8 cracking: If the king [hunts?], it will not rain.

辛未卜，王其田，不[雨?]。
Day 8 cracking: If the king hunts, it will not [rain?].

The learning-to-engrave interpretation provides no explanation for why previously literate scribes would spend time concentrating on these formulaically trivial, high-frequency patterns, nor for their frequent errors.

Practice inscriptions often were not produced by individuals in isolation but involved interaction with more competent hands, presumably those of instructors. This visual dependence on an instructor's model, not just for engraving technique but also for sign forms and text content, is also hard to square with the learning-to-engrave interpretation. Trainees sight-copied models specially provided by instructors or simply copied actual divination records.

Consider, for example, the repeated attempts to get right the sign *yǎ* 亞, scattered with other practice graphs around the proximal end of scapula TN: 2174. The trainee was attempting to reproduce the sign that occurs in

---

33. Further fragments of a similar exercise, possibly in the same hand, are collected as HJ: 35262–35264.

a competently written divination record toward the distal end of this bone. A scribe who knew this sign would not need to practice it in this way and would not make such obvious errors in the geometry of the sign.

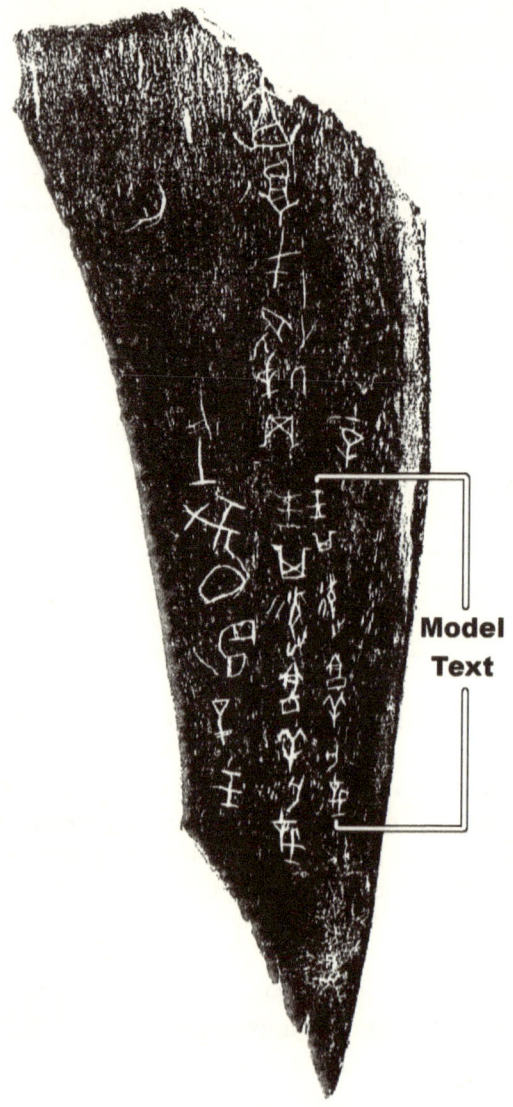

Figure 5.4 TN: 2731, competently written model text with multiple inferior copies. From TN: 587.

TN: 2731 (fig. 5.4) shows a trainee attempting to reproduce a divinatory proposition, graph for graph. There are no signs of divinatory cracks or crack-numbers associated with the model, suggesting that it was deliberately written out for the purpose. Though evidently less competent, the trainee approximates the model with an adjacent column of text and then rotates the bone 180 degrees for a second attempt (curiously reusing the now-inverted "king" 王 of the first copy as the first graph of the second copy). Graphs grow in size and become increasingly disorderly as the trainee appears to tire of the effort. There are two errors in the copy that show the trainee to be reproducing visually unfamiliar symbols. The commonly occurring "foot" 止 component in the third sign of the sequence has not been recognized and appears in the copy as a visually misunderstood jumble of strokes.[34] The fourth graph 羣, has been misconstrued as two separate signs, 言 and 羊, or at least is written as though that were the case. The same trainee's copies of the model continue on TN: 2737, another fragment from the same pit.

HJ: 27042 — A Complex Example of Student Copying

HJ: 27042 (fig. 5.5a) is the most complex of all the scribal training objects from Anyang and allows us to reconstruct the copying practices of scribal trainees in considerable detail.[35] The item is an almost complete scapula, densely inscribed on both faces. It is a join of two fragments (JB: 2692/2693 and JB: 2880/2881), both excavated in 1929 from an excavation unit known as the *dàliánkēng* 大連坑 (large joined trenches). The divination records on this bone are in a typical He Group II (何組二類) writing style.[36] The dating of this style is confirmed by the appearance of the appellation Father Jia (父甲)[37] in one of the practice inscriptions on this item. The inscriptions were thus produced in a workshop serving one

---

34. The sign in question is GL: 2307. For a clearer instance of the same sign in a similar inscription, see HJ: 28915 (=JB: 907).
35. For a fuller treatment of the object than can be provided here, including transcriptions and translations, see Smith, "Writing at Anyang," 320–42.
36. Li Xueqin 李學勤 and Peng Yushang 彭裕商, *Yinxu jiagu fenqi yanjiu* 殷墟甲骨分期研究 (Shanghai: Shanghai Guji Chubanshe, 1996), 139–73.
37. See K23 in Keightley's table of the royal genealogy, in Keightley, *Sources of Shang History*, 185–87.

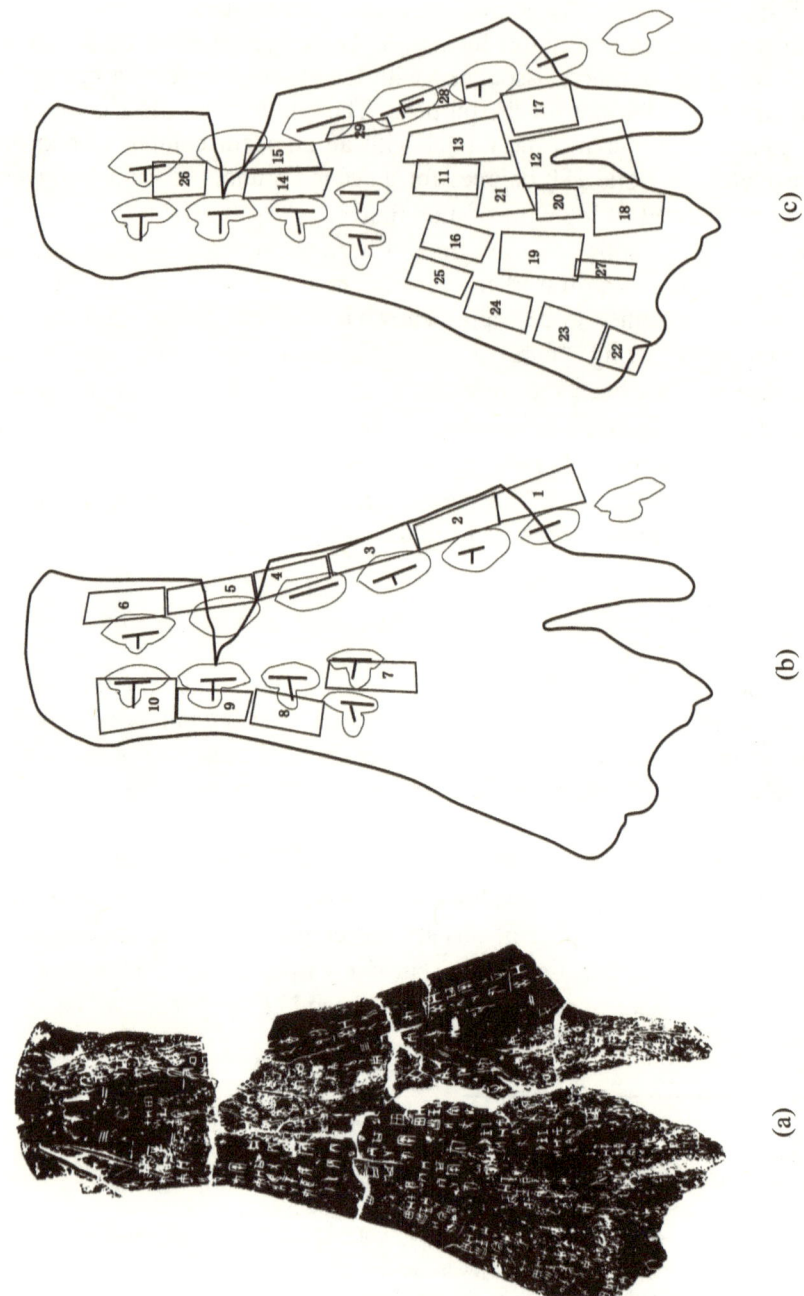

Figure 5.5 HJ: 27042, scapula (a) densely inscribed with a mixture of divination records (b) and trainee copies (c). From *Heji*, 9:3337.

of the royal patrons Kang Ding 康丁 or Lin Xin 廩辛.[38] The divinations actually carried out and recorded on the bone were performed by Diviner He 何. Some of the practice inscriptions are copies of records of divination performed by He's colleague, Diviner Zhu 宁, or the royal patron.

The scapula was first physically prepared for divination. The position of eleven hollows carved into the reverse can be clearly seen in the rubbing (HJ: 27042, reverse, not reproduced here). The six running along the left-hand side of the reverse are referred to here as Set 1, and the more centrally placed group of five as Set 2. The lowest hollow in Set 1 is only partially preserved, and it is almost certain from the crack-numbering that there was originally an additional seventh hollow below it that has been lost due to the break.

Figure 5.5b represents the positions of these hollows relative to the transcriptions, as if the bone were transparent. Superimposed over these are the positions of the divination cracks, to the extent to which they could be made out on the rubbing of the obverse. All eleven (originally twelve) hollows appear to have been cracked in divination events. These divinations are recorded on the obverse by inscriptions arranged in the standard manner adjacent to the resulting cracks. Figure 5.5b also shows the locations of the ten surviving records.

The inscriptions numbered 1–4 in figure 5.5b record a series of divinations performed by Diviner He on day 50 concerning sacrifice of livestock. The original first inscription in this set, like the corresponding hollow on the reverse, is missing. It would have specified the recipient of the sacrifice and was located below the surviving inscription 1. Inscription 17 (fig. 5.5c) may be a trainee copy of this missing record, allowing us to identify this set of divinations as concerning sacrifice to Father Jia on day 51, his name day.

Inscriptions 5–7, corresponding to the remaining two hollows in Set 1, plus one or both of the pair of hollows at the bottom of Set 2, record a further bout of divination by He on day 53 concerning sacrifice on day 54. The recipient would have been specified in the broken section of inscription 5, the first in the series. It is likely that the recipient was Wu Ding 武丁, grandfather of the two kings, the candidate patrons for this divination bone, who was being sacrificed to on his name day.

---

38. See K23a and K24 in Keightley's table, in Keightley, *Sources of Shang History*, 185–87.

Inscriptions 8–10 record divinations by He on day 57 concerning sacrifice to Female Ancestor Xin 妣辛 on her name day, day 58. The recipient is probably Fu Hao 婦好, wife of the previous recipient. The day 57 series of divinations exhausts the supply of hollows on the bone.

At this point, the scapula ceased to be a divinatory instrument and became a resource for scribal training, providing model texts (inscriptions 1–10) for copying and a surface on which to copy them. All inscriptions on this object other than the ten just discussed — nineteen inscriptions or parts thereof on the obverse of the bone (shown in fig. 5.5c), thirteen more on the reverse, and sundry isolated graphs — are trainees' copies or instructors' models (inscriptions 11 and 21). The grounds for this interpretation are as follows.

That the bone was used for practice of some kind is clear from the presence of the stray, obviously incompetent graphs labeled *xìkè* by the Moshi editors. Inscriptions 27–29 (discussed more fully below) also clearly could not be adequate records of divination. Discounting the stray graphs, all inscriptions on the scapula formally resemble divination records to some degree, but since the intact bone probably had only twelve hollows, they cannot possibly all be records of divinations performed on this bone.

The three series of divination records that can be matched to hollows (inscriptions 1–10) are grouped and arranged in a conventional, orderly manner by date, moving up through the two sets of hollows. The relationship between the dates and the relative positions of the remainder is haphazard, the result of filling in whatever space remained available. Inscriptions 14 and 15, for example, belong in the same group as inscriptions 12 and 13; inscription 26 belongs in the same group as 22–25; inscription 27 belongs in the same group as 28 and 29 (see fig. 5.5c). Given their placement, it is unlikely that these inscriptions could have been made sequentially on the days of the divinations they seemingly record.

Furthermore, the three series of actual divination records presented above do not contain any verbatim repetition of content: the first divination in each series proposes the date, the sacrifice, and the recipient, and the subsequent ones propose alternative details. In contrast, there is substantial repetition of redundant information among the other inscriptions, including exact repetition of content from inscriptions 1–10.

Finally and most importantly, all of the ten divination records (inscriptions 1–10) are written in a thoroughly competent hand. The other inscriptions, though approximating the same style, belong to an evidently less competent trainee hand. The only exceptions are inscriptions 11 and 21, which, as already mentioned, are likely to be instructor's models.

The training inscriptions on the obverse may be summarized as follows:

Inscriptions 11 and 21. These two adjacent inscriptions purport to be records of divinations carried out on day 59 and day 1 by He's colleague, Zhu. They are competently written in what appears to be the same hand as items 1–10. However, in neither case is an associated hollow present on the reverse of the bone, nor is any crack or crack-number visible on the obverse. They are not records of divinations performed on this scapula. Inscription 11 is copied verbatim five times in an inferior hand on the obverse (inscriptions 22–26) and three more times on the reverse. Inscription 21 is copied once immediately below (inscription 20) by an inferior hand.

Inscriptions 12–15. An inferior hand has produced verbatim copies from the set of records represented by inscriptions 1–4, including a probable copy of the missing first item in the set.

Inscription 16. This is a verbatim copy in an inferior hand of inscription 7.

Inscriptions 17–19. These appear to be student copies of records of divinations performed by Zhu on days 57 and 58. There is, however, no sign of the models, and it is possible that the trainee is copying from at least one other set of actual records besides those on HJ: 27042.

Inscription 20. As already noted, this is a copy of model 21.

Inscriptions 22–26. As already noted, these are verbatim copies of model 11.

Inscriptions 27–29. These fragmentary beginnings appear to be copies of a record for a divination by Zhu on day 7. The model is not present on HJ: 27042.

The thirteen more or less formulaically complete inscriptions on the reverse are almost all purported records of divinations by Zhu concerning the king's "hosting" (bīn 賓) of rituals to distant royal ancestors, and all are in a trainee hand. The models for these copies are not to be found on HJ: 27042, with the exception of inscription 11 on the obverse, discussed above. However, examples of records of precisely this kind of divination by Zhu, kept in the He Group II writing style, are plentiful among published corpora.[39] As with inscriptions 17–19 on the obverse, we can

---

39. Cf. HJ: 27086, 27177, 27508, 27645, 30548–30551, 30553–30558, 30572, and 30788.

assume that a suitable model would have been made available to the trainee.

Scribal Training within the He Group Divination Workshop

HJ: 27042 was discovered together with many other inscribed scapula and plastron fragments produced by the institution for which Diviners He and Zhu and the He Group II scribal hand(s) worked. The nature of these institutions remains rather obscure, but the term "divination workshop" reflects their best-attested sphere of activity. What we do know about these institutions comes primarily from the sophisticated typologies of divinatory inscriptions from Anyang that have been compiled by Chinese scholars.[40] These typologies and their supporting scholarship have shown that multiple such divination workshops could be in operation contemporaneously, each distinguished by its writing styles and documentary conventions, its set of named diviners, and its own locus of activity within the moated Xiaotun enclosure at the center of the Anyang site complex.

This is perhaps most readily illustrated by the divination workshops active during the reign of Wu Ding. For instance, during the latter half of that reign, the workshop responsible for the so-called Bin Group inscriptions (Bīnzǔ bǔcí 賓組卜辭) was active in the "palace area" north of Xiaotun village, the Li Group (Lìzǔ 歷組) workshop was active within and to the south of Xiaotun, and the recently excavated Huayuanzhuang East Group (Huādōngzǔ 花東組 or Huādōng zǐzǔ 花東子組) was being produced at a location on the very southern limit of the moated enclosure. The patron of the Li and Bin Group divinations was the Shang king, while one of his sons was the patron of the Huayuanzhuang East Group.[41]

The workshop that employed diviners He and Zhu, and the scribe(s) responsible for the He Group II style, whose respective roles in producing HJ: 27042 are discussed in the previous section, was active two generations later than Wu Ding.[42] As noted in the previous section, the

---

HJ: 30542 (and perhaps 30384 also) was produced, I suggest, by the same trainee who produced the inscriptions on HJ: 27042 that we are discussing, by copying the same kind of model; the bīn 賓 graph is diagnostic.

40. Li Xueqin and Peng Yushang, *Yinxu jiagu fenqi yanjiu*.
41. See above, note 21.
42. Li Xueqin and Peng Yushang, *Yinxu jiagu fenqi yanjiu*, 139–73.

pieces of HJ: 27042 were excavated from the so-called *dàliánkēng*, a group of excavators' trenches covering an area of about one hundred square meters.[43] The same season of excavations recovered large numbers of bones and shells produced by the same workshop,[44] inscribed in the He Group styles with records of divinations performed by He and fellow diviners, most frequently Peng 彭, Kou 口, and Da (?) 犾. The majority of these are records of entirely routine *bǔxún* 'divining for the week ahead' or *bǔxī* 卜夕 'divining for the night', with a minority of more complex records of sacrifice or hunting divinations. The majority of these records are competently, regularly, and fluently written.

However, HJ: 27042 is by no means the only remains of He Group scribal training activities from the *dàliánkēng*. The following examples are some of the more interesting and informative examples.

HJ: 26907 resembles HJ: 27042 in many respects. The obverse bears a mixture of real records of divination performed using the scapula and practice inscriptions by a trainee filling up the left-over space.[45] The real records consist of a set of five divinations about sacrifice to the Yellow River (Hé 河) and five more (possibly related) about numbers of sheep. All are written in a very neat hand, with the exception of the preface to the first record in the first set. A trainee has been allowed to write out the beginning of the record — "Day 6 cracking, Peng divined . . . 己巳卜彭貞 . . ." — before returning the record to the more competent scribe for completion. For reasons that will become clear, it may be that in this and the following examples, Diviner Peng was the trainee learning to write (and perhaps also learning to perform divination).

The remaining inscriptions on the obverse of HJ: 26907 are complex, fragmented, and disorderly, and none is associated with cracks, crack-numbers, or anything else to suggest that they are records of divinations performed on this bone. It is hard to be confident that they are

---

43. For the *dàliánkēng* excavation report, see Shi Zhangru 石璋如 and Gao Quxun 高去尋, *Jiagu kengceng zhi yi: Yi ci zhi jiu ci chutu jiagu* 甲骨坑層之一: 一次至九次出土甲骨 (Taipei: Zhongyang Yanjiuyuan Lishi Yuyan Yanjiusuo, 1985–86), 1:57–96.
44. The report states that 1,359 Period III inscribed fragments of bones and shells were recovered during the season that the *dàliánkēng* was excavated; the great majority of these were from the *dàliánkēng*, and for this context, "Period III" is equivalent to "He Group"; see Shi Zhangru and Gao Quxun, *Jiagu kengceng zhi yi*, 1:90.
45. HJ: 26907 is a complex join of multiple fragments, originally published as JB: 2471, 2491, 2492, 2501, 2605, and 2606.

all in a single hand, but the quality of the writing is consistently inferior to the neat calligraphy of the ten true divination records. Peng is named as diviner in two of these additional inscriptions.

The reverse of the scapula has a table of *gānzhī* in a student hand. Below that are what appear to be two records of "divining for the night" by the He Group diviner Da. Neither is a record of any divination performed on the bone, however, and scrutiny reveals that one is a model text and the other is an inferior sight-copy. The manner in which the two elements that make up the sign *jīn* 今 have been divorced from each other in the copy suggests that the copyist was not used to writing this everyday sign on any medium.

HJ: 26899 (JB: 2695) is again similar. Five true divination records in a competent hand survive on the right side of the scapula, including one that names the He Group diviner Kou. Attempts at copying signs from these records are interspersed within them. A sixth true record runs down the left edge of the scapula. It has been carefully but imperfectly copied alongside.[46] The remainder of the surface is again covered with complex but disorderly fragments. Some of the content (including a few low-frequency graphs) overlaps with that of HJ: 26907 discussed above, suggesting that the two items were produced as part of the same course of instruction.[47]

HJ: 27543 (JB: 2698) is covered with a disorderly jumble of divination records, each of which is written in two different hands. Each begins with the smaller, neater hand writing the usual preface, but on reaching the diviner name (Peng once again, note), a large and clumsy student hand takes over. There is no sign of cracks, crack-numbers, or the orderly arrangement one would expect from a real set of records.

On HJ: 31420 (JB: 2694), a competent hand has written a couple of prefaces for records of divination by He. Contrasting with these is a *bǔxún* formula for day 30 naming Diviner Peng in an evidently incompetent hand. There are no signs to indicate that the latter is a true divination record.

---

46. The copy is not dramatically incompetent, but there are revealing anomalies. Most obviously, the vertical column of text is disrupted, *jīn* 今 is written straddling a crack, and the final *yóu* 尤 is written incorrectly, to resemble *fù* 父. Perhaps responding to this error, one of the contributing scribes has written an otherwise out-of-context and difficult-to-explain *fù* 父 among the jumble of graphs up at the proximal end of the scapula.

47. Note in particular the large and pictographically rendered *shè* 射 'shoot' and deer signs that appear without meaningful context on both HJ: 26899 and HJ: 26907.

The following three items illustrate a single rather peculiar phenomenon. Each involves a *bǔxún* formula naming Peng as the diviner, written in an obviously immature hand and with the complete sequence of graphs permuted in bizarrely nonsensical ways. HJ: 27220 (JB: 2407) writes the *bǔxún* formula for day 40 precisely (and hence presumably deliberately) backward, that is, in ascending vertical columns. HJ: 27694 (JB: 2770) scrambles the formula for day 20 and writes *wèi* 未 incorrectly, to resemble 木. HJ: 28107 (JB: 2773) is another similar scrambling, though the date is not fully legible.

The evidence for scribal training from the *dàliánkēng*, of which the above is merely a selection, is interpreted here to indicate that the membership of the He Group included, alongside the diviners and scribes, at least one trainee who was learning to engrave and perhaps to divine but who was also certainly learning to write. Some of the more bizarrely anomalous (or perhaps playful?) behavior suggests a child. The repeated association of the diviner name Peng with these practice inscriptions suggests the possibility that Peng was the trainee.[48]

The many examples of records from the *dàliánkēng* that name Peng in the preface support that final contention. Unlike the examples we have just considered, the majority of these are cleanly and regularly written and appear to be records of divination actually carried out on the bone. In several instances, however, it seems that the single graph Peng 彭 is written in a different hand, inferior to the rest of the inscription, as though Peng were allowed to fill in his own name in a record made on his behalf by a more competent scribe. HJ: 31427 (JB: 2792) is one such example.

Model Texts and the Emergence of Textual Transmission

The examples of scribal training material discussed above include many instances of trainees copying texts written by competent scribes and several examples of competent scribes providing model texts for trainees. Recognizing the existence of these models and copies prompts several questions. Are there further examples of models or copies within the published corpus from Anyang that have gone unnoticed? Does the notion of an instructional model — a text deliberately composed for a student to copy — help explain features of inscriptions that hitherto have seemed

---

48. For Peng's career as a diviner, which spanned several reigns, see Li Xueqin and Peng Yushang, *Yinxu jiagu fenqi yanjiu*, 171–72.

puzzling? Did scribal training in the divination workshops at Anyang produce anything analogous to student texts from Uruk — such as the Professions List or Tribute/Word List C — which were faithfully copied over many generations for what became self-sustaining scholastic reasons, long after they had become obscure and their original function had been forgotten? This section tentatively offers affirmative answers to these three questions, drawing on a hypothesis put forward by Matsumaru Michio.

Figure 5.6 HJ: 33208, scapula with formulaically contrived practice text.

HJ: 33208 (JB: 622, fig. 5.6) is a largely intact scapula with what appear to be four divination records written on it. The writing is not obviously that of a novice hand. Nevertheless, the multiple, oddly oriented copies of the same quadruped pictogram that appear toward the distal end of the scapula are the first hint that this item is connected with scribal training. Four columns of text, ostensibly divination records, run down from the proximal end; however, their content is highly contrived. The prefaces date the records to days 1–4 of the sixty-day cycle, with one record for each day. The divinatory propositions all ask whether, if the king were to proceed in a particular direction, the Lord of Such-and-such would meet with a particular (probably violent) fate. The wording of the proposition is identical in the four versions, except for the direction of the king's motion, which cycles through the four cardinal directions: east, south, west, and north.

The permutation of preface dates and cardinal directions is entirely artificial, and the four records constitute a scribal exercise. The latter interpretation is supported by the fact that none of the four ostensible divination records has any associated cracks, crack-numbers, or hollows.[49]

A similarly artificial four-part text, cycling through the cardinal directions, appears on the well-known "Names of the Four Quarters and Winds" scapula, HJ: 14294. There are no signs of divination on the bone, and the columns of text are not even formally similar to divination records. They simply state what appear to be names for the four cardinal directions and their respective winds. The question of the purpose of this inscribed object naturally arises.

The names for the quarters and winds do appear embedded in actual divination records. There are eight examples, the most spectacular of which is the plastron HJ: 14295, excavated in 1936 from the Wu Ding period pit YH: 127 at Anyang.[50] Hu Houxuan pointed out that these

---

49. Wang Yuxin and Yang Shengnan interpret this as a *xíkè* inscription for similar reasons. See Wang Yuxin and Yang Shengnan, *Jiaguxue yibai nian*, 254–55. The absence of hollows from the reverse and from all the other relevant examples discussed here can be confirmed by consulting photographs of the previously undocumented reverse that have been made available online by the Institute of History and Philology, Academia Sinica; http://archeodata.sinica.edu.tw/ (accessed 7 April 2009).
50. For a recent Chinese-language study of the "Names of the Four Quarters and Winds" inscriptions, including a review of previous literature, see Zheng Huisheng 鄭慧生, "Shangdai buci sifang shenming fengming yu houshi chun xia qiu dong sishi zhi guanxi" 商代卜辭四方神名、風名與後世春夏秋冬四時之關係, *Shixue yuekan* 史學月刊 6 (1984): 7–12. For discussion, see Smith, "Writing at Anyang," 364–73.

names of the quarters and winds appear in later received literature, in obscure, textually corrupt contexts. The "Canon of Yao" (Yaodian 堯典) chapter of the *Book of Documents* preserves the names of the four quarters, in the guise of ethnonyms of peoples from the four cardinal directions. The *Shanhaijing* 山海經 preserves both quarter and wind names, sometimes using formulae reminiscent of HJ: 14294.[51] Although one is left with no doubt that these two texts do indeed preserve the same information as that contained in the text from Anyang, it is clear that a good number of "copying errors" had been introduced along the way and that the original role of the text had been entirely lost in transmission.

Matsumaru's contribution was to propose that HJ: 14294 had a function in scribal training. He was prompted toward this conclusion by a small, archaeologically unprovenanced scapula fragment that he also published.[52] The fragment bore partial remains of five inscriptions in a somewhat incompetent hand, three of which were ostensible divination records, one a *gānzhī* date table, and one a sequence of five graphs from the "Quarters and Winds" text. The latter, according to Matsumaru, was likely a reproduction of a model text like HJ: 14294. The evidence explored in this chapter, particularly the evidence for copying of model texts, suggests that Matsumaru is correct about the likely role of HJ: 14294 in scribal education. The replication of the "Quarters and Winds" text into received literature goes some way toward satisfying the comparative expectations generated by the Late Uruk student texts.

Conclusion

The characterization of practice inscriptions from Anyang as involving "meaningless repetitions of a graph" is misleading.[53] Rather, they are a complex source of information about how scribes were trained at Anyang. Wang Haicheng notes that student exercises may be expected to be done "on the cheapest and most readily available stationery" and that, cross-culturally, "student scribes used the same writing tools and surfaces

---

51. Hu Houxuan 胡厚宣, "Jiaguwen sifang fengming kao" 甲骨文四方风名考, in *Jiagu wenxian jicheng* 甲骨文獻集成, ed. Song Zhenhao 宋鎮豪 and Duan Zhihong 段志洪 (Chengdu: Sichuan Daxue Chubanshe, 2001), 21:287–90.
52. Matsumaru, "Jieshao yipian sifang feng ming keci gu," 83–87.
53. Bagley, "Anyang Writing," 244 n. 57. See also Wang, "Writing and the State," 326.

as those used for everyday writing."⁵⁴ He also implies that divination bones would have been an unlikely medium on which to practice literacy. In the Anyang divination workshops, however, the surface of bones and plastrons was an everyday writing surface, quite literally.⁵⁵ The divination record is the only text genre from the Chinese Bronze Age that we *know* was produced on a daily basis. Moreover, the reverse of a used scapula, or the uninscribed portion of the obverse, are by-products of the divination workshops' activities — they cost nothing at all — unlike bamboo slips, hair brushes, and ink, which require skill, effort, and materials to produce.⁵⁶ Used scapulae are an entirely natural choice for scribal training, especially if the scribe is being trained to keep divination records on that medium.

At least some of the practice inscriptions were produced by trainees who had no prior experience writing the Chinese script. They allow us to begin sketching the outlines of a curriculum that probably began with *gānzhī* date tables, moved on to simple formulae like the *bŭxún* records, which trainees could put to immediate use, and extended to copying a variety of more complex model texts, including actual divination records produced by practicing scribes as well as specially composed models.

The training seems to have involved intimate interaction with practicing scribes responsible for keeping divination records and learning through informal imitation. Scribal trainees seem for the most part to have imitated the writing style of the models they were copying. What we perceive now as considerable diversity among the styles used in contemporary divination workshops at Anyang may be a reflection of this "in-house" training. If the locations where trainee texts have been found are any guide to where they were produced, training took place at or in close proximity to places where divination was performed and recorded.⁵⁷ The exercise texts examined in this chapter are focused on the acquisition

---

54. Wang, "Writing and the State," 326.
55. See Yao Xuan's tables of synchronies for the Huayuanzhuang East inscriptions for evidence of the remarkable rate at which divinations documented in writing were being produced; see *Yinxu Huayuanzhuang dongdi jiagu*, appendix II. I have offered some reasons for modifying the estimate downward slightly but agree with the overall high-frequency picture; see Smith, "Writing at Anyang," 285–300.
56. Li Junming 李均明 and Liu Jun 劉軍, *Jiandu wenshu xue* 簡牘文書學 (Nanning: Guangxi Jiaoyu Chubanshe, 1999), 1–27.
57. I have reviewed only the evidence from the *dàliánkēng*. Similar arguments could be built around the abundant *xíkè* materials from Xiaotun South 小屯南地; see Yao Xiaosui and Xiao Ding, *Xiaotun nandi jiagu kaoshi*, 197–206.

of precisely the skills required to maintain divination records; there is no sign that the trainees were acquiring generalized literacy skills that could have been deployed to write a diversity of other genres.

What light is shed by the evidence for scribal training in the divination workshops on the choice to be made between the maximal and minimal hypotheses for late-second-millennium literacy? Most importantly, it weakens a prominent objection to the minimal hypothesis, an objection articulated best by Bagley,[58] that such a hypothesis would provide no mechanism for the intergenerational transmission of the script. The evidence presented in this chapter indicates that the divination workshops at Anyang would have been capable of sustaining transmission of the script between generations, whether or not there were any other frequent and routine uses of writing in the Late Shang world.

Nevertheless, the fact that *some* scribes seem to have been trained in the divination workshops does not by any means imply that *all* scribes were. The fact that they were trained to write divination records on bone does not mean that bone was the only text genre or medium they learned. We know that brush writing and some precursor to the "wood or bamboo documents" (*jiǎncè* 簡冊) of later periods existed, though we have little idea to what extent they were used. The best evidence for writing on *jiǎncè*, presumably with a brush, points toward their role in keeping track of livestock awaiting sacrifice.[59] The term "divination workshop" as used in this chapter is a convenient label for the institutions to which diviners and divination scribes belonged. However, it is likely that the institutions in question were the same ones that managed other aspects of the cult of sacrifice to the dead kings, and also perhaps ritual and ceremonial activities more generally, since that is what the written record of Shang divination is all about. To the extent that these other activities involved writing — livestock accounts, for instance, or labels on valuable objects — the same scribal trainees might be expected to have also been exposed to the relevant written genres.

---

58. Bagley, "Anyang Writing," 190–249.
59. Smith, "Writing at Anyang," 155–67. A second role for *jiǎncè* is attested by what could be called the "*chēngcè* 再冊 inscriptions," divination records in which that particular two-character phrase occurs. This appears to involve the presentation or exchange of an important document of some kind between individuals of high status; Qi Wenxin 齊文心, "Shi du 'Zhi Jia cheng ce' xiangguan buci" 釋讀 '沚戛再冊' 相關卜辭, in *2004 nian Anyang Yin-Shang wenming guoji xueshu yantaohui lunwenji*, ed. Wang Yuxin, Song Zhenhao, and Meng Xianwu, 251–60.

The minimal model for late-second-millennium Chinese literacy remains for the time being a creditable hypothesis, fully in keeping with what is known from existing evidence and what should be expected on comparative grounds about how writing may have functioned at its earliest period of attestation. The minimal hypothesis accounts well for the evidence of scribal training reviewed here and could comfortably accommodate the available evidence for writing on wood and bamboo as the product of activities by a handful of literate specialists supporting the ritual activities of the Shang king and his immediate family.

CHAPTER 6
Textual Identity and the Role of Literacy in the Transmission of Early Chinese Literature

Matthias L. Richter

Among the fundamental changes in the conditions for the study of early Chinese textual culture in the course of the twentieth century, the discovery of vast amounts of Warring States and early imperial manuscripts in the past three decades has been the most consequential. Not only have new texts been added to the corpus of transmitted literature and new versions of previously known texts emerged — the fact that we now have a substantial number of early Chinese texts (sometimes even in several versions) in the written form in which they existed at their time may be of even greater significance. What we know about early Chinese literature has hitherto relied almost exclusively on a corpus of literature established in the late first century B.C.E. in the course of the enormous project to re-create the literary heritage of the pre-imperial period, undertaken by a team of experts led by the imperial librarian Liu Xiang 劉向 (79–8 B.C.E.) and later by his son Liu Xin 劉歆 (46 B.C.E.–23 C.E.).[1] Of course, after having been established in the early Chinese empire, the texts underwent further changes in the subsequent two millennia of their transmission.

I wish to thank Anthony Barbieri-Low and Li Feng for their insightful comments and helpful criticism on an earlier draft of this chapter.

1. Cf. the "Bibliographic Treatise" (Yiwen zhi 藝文志) of the Han dynastic history as well as Liu Xiang's "Separate Records" (Bie lu 別錄) and Liu Xin's "Seven Summaries" (Qi lüe 七略). See *Hanshu* 漢書 (Beijing: Zhonghua Shuju, 1962), 30:1701-84. The transmitted fragments of these accounts, which father and son Liu gave of their work, were reconstructed by Yan Kejun 嚴可均 (1762–1843) and are included in his *Quan shanggu sandai Qin Han Sanguo Liuchao wen* 全上古三代秦漢三國六朝文 (Beijing: Zhonghua Shuju, 1958 [1836]), 38:336a–339b (*Bie lu*); 41:351b–353a (*Qi lüe*).

The excavated manuscripts now afford new insights both with regard to the identity of texts and to the role that literacy played in their transmission. Textual identity concerns questions such as: Where does a text begin and where does it end? Given the composite nature of most early Chinese texts, can we assume that the order of textual units was definite?[2] What was the precise wording within these textual units, and do the texts have titles? Finally, in the many cases of parallel texts, how do we decide whether to call two texts either different versions of one text or different texts with shared contents? To understand the role of literacy in textual transmission, we need to inquire into the modes of manuscript production, the purposes for which manuscripts were produced, and the ways in which they were actually used as well as the precise nature of literacy on the part of both the scribes and the readers.

This chapter reflects on the non-textual properties of what are usually chiefly considered textual sources. The *material* features of early Chinese manuscripts are a potential source of information about the role literacy actually played in the process of the formation, the presentation or performance, the reception, and finally the transmission of early Chinese texts. Since the concept of "material features" is often understood as everything *but* the writing on the manuscript, it needs to be pointed out that the writing in a manuscript is not the text itself but merely a visual representation of it. A manuscript text as such — just like any text, whether written or spoken or silent in a person's memory — is *immaterial*, whereas its visible instantiation in writing must be recognized as part of the materiality of a manuscript. This includes orthography and punctuation as well as spacing and more general layout features.

Manuscripts may contain traces showing, first, to which degree and in which sense the people who produced them were literate and, second, if and how the manuscripts were used. That is to ask: What were the strengths and shortcomings of whoever wrote the manuscripts? Were the manuscripts *intended* to be read? How well were they *suited* to be read, and do we have evidence showing that they were *actually* read? To which degree could they reliably transmit a particular text to someone entirely unacquainted with it? Or was this irrelevant, because they primarily served some other function?

---

2. For a study of this issue, see Boltz, "The Composite Nature of Early Chinese Texts," in *Text and Ritual in Early China*, ed. Martin Kern (Seattle: University of Washington Press, 2005), 50–78.

An inquiry like this must be made on a case-by-case basis, sometimes leading to fairly certain conclusions, sometimes merely indicating the more likely of several possible scenarios. In any case, the information gleaned from a particular manuscript must not be hastily generalized. The answers to the above questions will not be the same for all kinds of written texts. Indeed, the different kinds of texts will even require asking different questions, and there can be no general answer to any of these questions. Rather, we shall have to content ourselves with examining the available evidence item by item and patiently endeavor to add pieces to the puzzle so that, in the long term — over years and decades to come — a more complete and realistic picture of early Chinese textual culture may emerge.

This chapter focuses on texts that are likely to have been composed not just for one particular occasion but with a view to being transmitted over time[3] and examines (politico-philosophical) literary texts rather than technical ones. This is of fundamental importance for an examination of both the identity of texts and the role of scribal literacy, since we can assume with some confidence that the scribes who wrote transmission texts of a literary nature did not compose them.[4] A more refined classification of excavated manuscripts than the one presented here does not seem warranted for this study.[5]

---

3. Martin Kern has coined the term "texts with a history," in contradistinction to what he calls "occasional texts"; "Methodological Reflections on the Analysis of Textual Variants and the Modes of Manuscript Production in Early China," *Journal of East Asian Archaeology* 4.1–4 (2002): 145–48. I entirely concur with this distinction but suggest a slight change of terms to "tradition texts" versus "occasion texts," since "having a history" always depends upon a certain point in time from which the object is viewed, and it could be argued that administrative documents often have a history as well, even if their texts were not originally intended for transmission.
4. In his studies of a type of early and medieval Chinese technical manuscript texts that he terms "miscellanies," Donald Harper finds evidence of "the overlapping roles of compiler, copyist, and reader, and the practice of individuals producing manuscripts for personal use." In the same vein, he observes that, for "ancient and medieval manuscript miscellanies with occult content," "the roles of compiler, copyist, and reader for miscellanies must have been fluid, with instances of individuals who compiled and copied manuscripts for their own use as well as instances of readers who wanted to acquire the manuscripts" ("The Textual Form of Knowledge: Occult Miscellanies in Ancient and Medieval Chinese Manuscripts, Fourth Century b.c. to Tenth Century a.d.," unpublished draft of April 2008, written for *Looking at It from Asia: The Process That Shaped the Sources of History of Science*, ed. Florence Bretelle and Christine Proust).
5. Yuri Pines proposes a classification of "unearthed documents" (which he implicitly restricts to manuscripts unearthed from tombs), according to contents, "into four broad categories": (1) "inventories of funerary items," (2) "texts which contain useful

The Case of the Two Mawangdui "Laozi" Manuscripts

The two Mawangdui 馬王堆 silk manuscripts that each contain a counterpart of the *Laozi* are a particularly appropriate object for a discussion of textual identity and the role of literacy in textual transmission.[6] While it is usually difficult to decide whether the manuscripts found in a tomb were specially produced for the occasion of the burial, the manuscripts unearthed from Mawangdui tomb no. 3 in 1973 were very probably written over an extended period of time and would thus have served some purpose before the death of the tomb occupant. Also, silk lends itself well to examining the process of production of a manuscript, since scribal errors are better preserved on silk than they are in bamboo or wooden manuscripts.[7] Errors and corrections are, together with details of handwriting and graphic variation, the features of a manuscript that can give the most immediate information about both the actual writing

---

knowledge for everyday activities" in this world as well as in the afterlife, (3) texts "more explicitly connected with the mundane career of the deceased" that were to manifest the deceased's status in the afterlife, and (4) "philosophical, historical, and military writings," which were to demonstrate the deceased's prestige and textual expertise in the netherworld. Cf. Yuri Pines, "History as a Guide to the Netherworld: Rethinking the *Chunqiu Shiyu*," *Journal of Chinese Religions* 31 (2003): 118–20. This categorization relies heavily on rather speculatively assumed functions. Sound though most of these speculations are, it appears to me preferable not to apply such a pattern until the functions of tomb texts are better understood.

6. For detailed information on the tomb, see the excavation report in He Jiejun 何介鈞, ed., *Changsha Mawangdui er, san hao Han mu, 1* 長沙馬王堆二、三號漢墓, 第一卷 (Beijing: Wenwu Chubanshe, 2004). For concise information on the silk manuscripts, see Chen Songchang 陳松長, *Boshu shihua* 帛書史話 (Beijing: Zhongguo Dabaike Quanshu Chubanshe, 2000). The standard publication of these two manuscripts is still Guojia Wenwuju Gu Wenxian Yanjiushi 國家文物局古文獻研究室, ed., *Mawangdui Han mu boshu* 馬王堆漢墓帛書, vol. 1 (Beijing: Wenwu Chubanshe, 1980). A new edition with color reproductions is in preparation; its date of publication by Wenwu Press is uncertain as of this writing.

7. In silk manuscripts, scraping off an erroneous character — the most common form of correction in bamboo and wooden manuscripts — is extremely difficult, if not impossible, without damaging the fabric. In the few suspected cases of such corrections, it is still disputed whether the characters were removed by scraping or by another method (Chen Songchang 陳松長, personal communication, May 2007). Silk, unlike bamboo and wooden manuscripts, also does not offer the option of replacing an entire column of text. A great number of the manuscripts found so far were clearly bound *after* writing. Possibly this method was employed in part to allow corrections to be made without having to rebind the manuscript.

process and the skilfulness and competence of the scribe. Moreover, errors and corrections often provide traces of the actual use of a manuscript. Also, understanding the process of manuscript production requires a certain amount of text. Silk manuscripts can accommodate amounts of text that could not possibly be handled in one wooden or bamboo manuscript. Thus, a silk manuscript of some length provides a greater amount of text that we can be fairly sure was written within a short period of time, whereas in the case of several separate bamboo or wooden manuscripts, it is more difficult to decide whether or not they were written at different times. The two so-called Laozi manuscripts offer a considerable amount of text, each of them containing more characters than, for example, the entire cache of manuscripts unearthed from Guodian 郭店 tomb no. 1.[8] Another reason these two manuscripts are suited for the present study is that we have hard evidence for a transmission history of at least a century for a considerable portion of their text, namely, the parts titled by the editors of the manuscript *Laozi* and *Wu xing* 五行, which both have counterparts in the Guodian manuscripts of around 300 B.C.E. The fact that both Mawangdui *Laozi* manuscripts share the same mortuary context but differ in format and layout, assemblage of texts, style of script, and orthography and were most probably produced at different times makes them even more suited for the present study.

Manuscript Profiles as a Source of Information about Production and Use of Manuscripts

In order to understand how a manuscript was produced, it needs to be studied in its full complexity. Its different features must be related to one another, and the analysis of text and paratextual elements needs to take into account where in the manuscript a certain phenomenon occurs.[9] Such a method of description may be termed "manuscript profile."[10]

---

8. Cf. the publication of these manuscripts in Jingmen Shi Bowuguan 荊門市博物館, ed., Guodian Chu mu zhujian 郭店楚墓竹簡 (Beijing: Wenwu Chubanshe, 1998).
9. By "paratext," I refer only to the part that in Genette's terminology would strictly be called "peritext" (i.e., features like titles, word counts, and emendations) as opposed to "epitext" (the social context outside the actual written document itself). Cf. Gérard Genette, *Paratexts: Thresholds of Interpretation*, trans. Jane E. Lewin (Cambridge: Cambridge Uiversity Press, 1997), 1–5.
10. Cf. Matthias Richter, "Towards a Profile of Graphic Variation: On the Distribution of Graphic Variants within the Mawangdui *Laozi* Manuscripts," *Asiatische Studien /*

Writing Support, Format, and Layout

Both "Laozi" manuscripts are made of a particularly fine, tightly woven silk fabric.[11] Manuscript A (MS.A) (plate 3)[12] takes the smaller, half-width (*bànfú* 半幅) format, that is, the text is written in 464 columns of 23.8 centimeters over a length of 318.2 centimeters.[13] This is by far the longest of all Mawangdui manuscripts. Manuscript B (MS.B) (plate 4) has a full-width (*zhěngfú* 整幅) format of approximately 48 centimeters and is about 166 centimeters long. The columns in MS.B are, as in MS.A, divided by thin red lines that were most probably drawn with a brush.[14] MS.B has at least one blank column at the beginning, followed by 252 columns with writing and a number of blank columns at the end. While MS.A uses the full width of the material, MS.B has upper and lower margins of approximately 1.6 centimeters. They are divided from the writing space by a thick black line. The full-width format probably represented a higher value, even if the overall length of the material was shorter. After all, its production required a loom double the size of that

---

Études Asiatiques 59.1 (2005): 169–207.

11. The silk manuscripts are generally referred to as *bóshū* 帛書. The excavation report describes the material as "yellowish-brown silk" (*huánghè sè sībó*" 黃褐色絲帛); He Jiejun, *Changsha Mawangdui*, 87. However, this particular type of silk, made of tightly woven very thin threads, is more properly called *juàn* 絹, as opposed to the coarser type of silk, *zēng* 繒; Cf. Chen Songchang, *Boshu shihua*, 5.
12. I provisionally use the neutral designation "manuscript A" (MS.A) to avoid the misleading customary appellation "Laozi A manuscript," which obscures the fact that the counterparts of the *Laozi* are only two of altogether six texts contained in this manuscript. I likewise refer to the "Laozi B manuscript" as "manuscript B" (MS.B).
13. I wish to thank Chen Songchang 陳松長, Yuelu Shuyuan 嶽麓書院, Changsha, former curator of the Mawangdui finds at the Hunan Sheng Bowuguan 湖南省博物館, for providing this information. The original length of the severely fragmented manuscripts may have differed by at least a few millimeters from the precise measurements given in the records of the museum. What I describe as width is sometimes also termed "height." However, it seems more appropriate to envisage a silk manuscript as positioned horizontally rather than vertically. This is certainly the case from the perspective of the weaving of the material and the process of writing on it as well as most probably with regard to the act of reading it. Hence, the length of a column (including margins) is the width of the manuscript.
14. It is not well understood how these remarkably straight and regular lines were drawn, nor do we know their motivation or significance. The most likely function seems to be visual guidance for the eyes of both writer and reader. There is no evidence to support the assumption that the lines were meant to allude to the form of "bamboo or wooden" (*cè* 冊/策) manuscripts.

used for the half-width format.

The two manuscripts are radically different in their text layouts, just as, in format, MS.A is the plainer and MS.B the more elaborate. Clearly, the design of MS.B followed not just the individual choice of the scribe but, at least to some degree, an underlying standard of production. Several manuscripts of the Mawangdui corpus share the same format (folded silk of 48 cm width) and, to some extent, the same layout (ruled lines, margins) and the same style of script. Apparently, they were produced in the same manufacture or scribal school. Besides MS.B., there are the *Zhou yi* manuscript (containing the texts <*Zhou yi* 周易>, <*Er san zi wen* 二三子問>), the *Xi ci* manuscript (containing the texts <*Xi ci* 繫辭>, <*Yi zhi yi* 易之義>, *Yao* 要, *Mou he* 繆和, and *Zhao li* 昭力), the *Xing de* B manuscript <刑德・乙>, the *Wu xing zhan* manuscript <五星占>, and the *Xiang ma jing* manuscript <相馬經>.[15] MS.B itself contains six texts, all titled and, moreover, furnished with character counts (see table 6.1).

Table 6.1 Individual texts of Manuscript B

Text	Title of text	Position (columns)	Length of text (in columns)
1	*Jing fa* 經法	1–77b	77; 9 titled chapters
2	*Shiliu jing* 十六經	78a–142b	65; 14 titled chapters + 1 untitled chapter
3	*Cheng* 稱	143a–167a	25; 52 untitled sections
4	*Dao yuan* 道原	168a–174a	7
5	*De* 德	175a–217b	43
6	*Dao* 道	218–252b	35

15. Only some of the titles of texts appear in the manuscript. Titles in brackets < > were given by the editors of the manuscripts. The format of the *Xiang ma jing* manuscript is slightly larger (49 cm), and that of the *Xing de* B manuscript is smaller (44 cm). Possibly, the *Zhou yi* and *Xi ci* were not two separate manuscripts but are parts of what was originally one physical manuscript. This would be an especially interesting case for further study, as they are written in different hands. The text *Xi ci* was possibly originally titled *Zhong* 衷, as is suggested by a fragment that probably belongs to this manuscript (Chen Songchang, personal communication, April 2007).

MS.A is one of only two Mawangdui silk manuscripts — the other one being the *Chunqiu shiyu* 春秋事語 — that were not folded but rolled and were stored together with some wooden and bamboo manuscripts in the long side compartment of the lacquer box that contained the entire cache of manuscripts. All other silk manuscripts were found in one of the middle compartments of this box. MS.A is commonly understood to contain six texts as well (see table 6.2).

Table 6.2 Individual texts of Manuscript A

Text	Title of text	Position (columns)	Length of text (in columns)
1	<*De* 德>	1–92	92
2	<*Dao* 道>	93–169	77
3a	<*Wu xing* 五行>	170–214 (*jing* 經)	182 (45+137)
3b		215–351 (*shuo* 說)	
4	<*Jiu zhu* 九主>	352–403	52
5	<*Ming jun* 明君>	404–451	48
6	<*De sheng* 德聖>	452–464	13

In both manuscripts, the division between the individual texts is clearly indicated by leaving the rest of the column blank after the end of a text and beginning the new text at the top of the next column preceded by a black dot (MS.A) or more conspicuously by blackening the whole width of the column in the margin (MS.B). MS.B even marks and titles the individual chapters of the first two texts, *Jing fa* and *Shiliu jing*. MS.A, however, gives no such clear indications; the texts in this manuscript are untitled, and the textual delineations are ambiguous. MS.A is today commonly understood to contain six individual texts (in Chinese scholarship termed *piān* 篇). However, within the borders of some of these six texts, several units are set off against one another in exactly the same manner as these six larger units ("texts") are, namely, by beginning a new column, leaving some of the preceding column blank, and placing a black dot before the first character.

In order to understand the impact that scribes and the act of writing can have on textual identity, it is necessary to distinguish between textual and codicological units: the parts into which a text is divided according to textual criteria, regardless of any physical representation of the text, are properly called textual units, whereas the divisions of the text that are governed by its physical representation (e.g., composition of writing support, layout, punctuation) are codicological units.[16] According to layout features, the text of MS.A is divided into twenty-six codicological units of very different length. Texts 1, 2, 4, and 6 each coincide exactly with one codicological unit, but the cases of the third (*Wu xing*) and the fifth (*Ming jun*) text are much less clear (see table 6.3).

The lack of disambiguation in the textual division shows that this manuscript — not just today but already at the time of its production — required of its users a certain degree of interpretive competence or at least familiarity with the texts. As for the first two texts, we can assume that they were known at the time — perhaps under the titles *De* and *Dao* as given in MS.B, which has basically the same text, differing only in very few, though important, points.[17] Possibly, the name of "Laozi" was

---

16. I owe the terminological distinction between textual and codicological units to Marc Kalinowski, although I use these categories differently. Kalinowski treats the entire manuscript as one codicological unit and treats the parts of texts that are marked off against each other visually as textual units: "Chaque recension fait partie d'un ensemble de textes différents copiés sur des laizes de soie formant des unités codicologiques (UC) autonomes. Dans ce qui suit, j'examinerai les caractéristiques matérielles des deux manuscrits et la manière dont les textes se distinguent les uns des autres au sein même de l'unité codicologique qui les contient. J'utiliserai le terme 'unité textuelle' (UT) pour désigner une portion de texte envisagée sous un angle purement formel et indépendamment de son contenu" [Each recension is part of an assemblage of different texts, copied onto panels of silk that form autonomous codicological units. In what follows, I shall examine the physical characteristics of the two manuscripts and the way in which the texts are distinguished from one another within the codicological unit that contains them. I shall use the term 'textual unit' to designate a portion of text considered from a vantage point that is purely formal and independent of its content]. See Marc Kalinowski, "La production des manuscrits dans la Chine ancienne: Une approche codicologique de la bibliothèque funéraire de Mawangdui," *Asiatische Studien / Études Asiatiques* 59.1 (2005): 145. I prefer to refer to the portions of text whose delineations are signaled by codicological — that is, visual, material — means (e.g., layout features and marks) as codicological units, in order to maintain a strict distinction between a text and its material representations. This distinction has been emphasized by Harold Roth, whose somewhat elusive but nonetheless helpful definition of text as "the unique complex and expression of ideas created by an author or authors" is based on Vinton Dearing; see Harold Roth, "Text and Edition in Early Chinese Philosophical Literature," *Journal of the American Oriental Society* 113 (1993): 215.
17. E.g., the MS.A counterpart of *Laozi* chapter 8 shows a marked ideological difference from both the MS.B and received versions. In fact, the MS.A text takes a view opposite to the received *Laozi*. For a discussion of this case, see Matthias Richter, "Der Alte und das Wasser: Lesarten von *Laozi* 8 im überlieferten Text und in den Manuskripten von Mawangdui," in *Han-Zeit: Festschrift für Hans Stumpfeldt aus Anlaß seines 65:*

Table 6.3 Texts vs. codicological units in Manuscript A

Text	Title of text	Codicological unit number(s)	Number of codicological units
1	<*De* 德>	1	1
2	<*Dao* 道>	2	1
3a	<*Wu xing jing*>	3	1
3b	<*Wu xing shuo*>	4–21	18
4	<*Jiu zhu* 九主>	22	1
5	<*Ming jun* 明君>	23–25	3
6	<*De sheng* 德聖>	26	1

already attached to these texts at that time.[18] In any case, the text was not unique to this manuscript but was probably widely known and already had a history of a certain duration. The three Guodian counterparts to the *Laozi* attest to the fact that a substantial amount of this text existed at least as early as around 300 B.C.E.[19] In comparing the two MS.A texts with the Guodian *Laozi* counterparts, it is interesting to note that the Guodian manuscripts to some extent still treat what are now known as *Laozi* chapters (*zhāng* 章) as individual texts, although not always with the same textual delineations. There is no indication in the three Guodian manuscripts called *Laozi* A, B, and C that the individual sections of each are to be understood as parts of one larger text, and there is even less reason to assume that all three manuscripts were understood as representing parts of the same text at the time of their production. MS.A occasionally marks divisions between chapters as separate codicological units, thus indicating subordinate textual units on a level below that of the first two texts of the manuscript (matching the texts *De* and *Dao* in MS.B).

Geburtstages, ed. Michael Friedrich, Reinhard Emmerich, and Hans van Ess (Wiesbaden: Harrassowitz, 2006), 261–71.

18. Assuming that the *Hanfeizi* chapters 20 ("Jie lao" 解老) and 21 ("Yu lao" 喻老) already bore their present titles by that time, this would even seem likely.

19. See the edition of these manuscripts in Jingmen Shi Bowuguan 荊門市博物館, ed., *Guodian Chu mu zhujian* 郭店楚墓竹簡 (Beijing: Wenwu Chubanshe, 1998), 1–10, 109–22.

Moreover, the textual sequence within both the *De* and *Dao* parts of the text in MS.A and MS.B is almost the same as in the received *Laozi*. Had such a textual hierarchy, not to mention the order of chapters, been established by the time the Guodian manuscripts were written, it would indeed seem surprising that these manuscripts, which are supposedly florilegia from an early *Laozi*, reflect so little of the *Laozi*'s textual order. The claim that a complete early *Laozi* existed at that time is far from being sufficiently founded.[20] It is far more likely that at this early formative stage, the textual material that later formed the eighty-one-chapter *Laozi* was not yet customarily collected in one compilation, no matter how much of it may already have existed as part of early Chinese textual culture.

The *Wu xing* text is the one with the most codicological units on the same level as that of the preceding two parts of the *Laozi*, that is, units beginning with a black dot on top of the first column and leaving the rest of the last column blank after the end of the unit. The first such unit extends over forty-four columns and comprises the entire *jing* 經 section of the text — that is to say, the extension of this codicological unit is identical with one main textual unit, if the following commentary is understood as a separate text. Given its status as a "guideline" (*jīng* 經) type of text, the reader could be expected to be familiar with the text of this particular unit. Moreover, just as in the case of the *Laozi* matches, a Guodian counterpart attests that the text already had a history reaching back to at least around 300 B.C.E. Its systematic logical structure also makes the textual delineations fairly clear. The following eighteen codicological units are much shorter; they take up a total of only thirty-six columns. Due to their clear reference to the preceding *jing* text, these codicological units could be expected to be recognized by the reader of the

---

20. The discussion of this sensitive issue has produced a plethora of articles and books. For an influential study of the Guodian *Laozi*, see Sarah Allan and Crispin Williams, eds., *The Guodian* Laozi: *Proceedings of the International Conference, Dartmouth College, May 1998*, Early China Special Monograph Series 5 (Berkeley, CA: The Society for the Study of Early China, 2000); with regard to textual history/formation, see esp. the article by Harold Roth, 71–88. For a view close to my own, see Boltz, "The Composite Nature." For a caution not to exclude the possibility of an early *Laozi*, as well as a brief survey of the discussion of the ideological implications of this issue, both within China and between Chinese and Western scholarship, see Edward L. Shaughnessy, "The Guodian Manuscripts and Their Place in Twentieth-Century Historiography on the *Laozi*," *Harvard Journal of Asiatic Studies* 65.2 (2005): 417–57. For a translation of the *Laozi* counterparts in the Guodian manuscripts, see Robert G. Henricks, *Lao Tzu's Tao Te Ching: A Translation of the Startling New Documents Found at Guodian* (New York: Columbia University Press, 2000).

manuscript as representing short textual units of a *subordinate* order and as belonging together to form one larger textual unit, that is, the commentary (*shuō* 說) to the preceding main textual unit *Wu xing*.

The delineations of the next text, *Jiu zhu*, can be inferred from its narrative structure. Here, as in the case of the first three texts of the manuscript, what we read as one textual unit coincides with the codicological unit as marked by a preceding black dot and by beginning in a new column and leaving a blank after the end of the preceding text.

It becomes even clearer in the last part of MS.A that the editorial act of choosing certain codicological units to present as one individual text is highly problematic: the remaining text after *Jiu zhu* is divided into four codicological units. The last of these was interpreted by the editors as a separate textual unit in the sense of *piān* 篇 (which is how the first four texts — *De*, *Dao*, *Wu xing*, and *Jiu zhu* — were defined as well) and titled *De sheng*. The motive for treating these severely fragmented last thirteen columns of the manuscript as separate from the preceding three codicological units rests in the judgment that this last unit is closely related in content to the *Wu xing* text and commentary. The remaining three codicological units are treated in the Wenwu edition as one text, titled *Ming jun* after a phrase in the opening sentence.

The intent here is not to question the soundness of these editorial decisions. The important point is that this particular division of the manuscript into six separate texts does not accord with the codicological divisions indicated in the manuscript itself. Rather, it is a matter of interpretive judgments and editorial decisions through which the manuscript was "translated" into a printed edition, which in turn set a new pattern of perception. When the manuscript text is discussed today in terms of these six (or if *De* and *Dao* are treated as one *Laozi*, five) texts, this division is usually taken for granted, and the degree to which this pattern is consistent with the perception of the texts at the time the manuscript was produced is not often reflected. By the same token, the material representation of the texts, also at that time, had an influence on how texts were understood individually and in their relation to one another and how they would continue to be transmitted. Ambiguity in textual arrangement would leave open the possibility of either splitting up one text and treating it as several, which would possibly be transmitted separately thereafter, or interpreting texts that were originally completely unrelated as one integral text and transmitting them as such. Both changes would fundamentally influence future interpretations of the respective texts. As long as the written text stays within its situational context, such as a certain school in which it is interpreted by teachers who thus hand it on to their students, it can dispense with further elaboration. Once it leaves its interpretive situational context, however, further disambiguation becomes necessary, if fixing the text in writing has the function of transmitting the text.[21]

The elaborate layout features in MS.B seem to bespeak such an effort to exert control over the transmission of the text. Ironically, this effort has not been able to prevent the authority of later textual traditions from superseding the design of the manuscript as an interpretive pattern. Bereft as the texts now are of their situational context — in the sense of any institution that could control its correct transmission, such as teachers of a certain intellectual lineage — Plato's skepticism proves to be true: texts, once put into writing, are out of control and available for all kinds of people to use as they please.[22]

Despite the explicit arrangement of six texts in MS.B, the manuscript is usually divided into two main parts. This convention is even reflected in the way the original is stored in the Hunan Provincial Museum: the fragments of the first four texts are mounted on individual sheets, like separate pages, with the upper and lower halves of the columns still divided, whereas the two texts *De* and *Dao* are mounted like a scroll on a continuous piece of material, the full width of 48 centimeters, with the upper and lower halves of the columns reassembled. The texts titled *De* and *Dao* are usually referred to as either *Laozi*, *De dao jing*, or even *Dao de jing*.[23] The close relation of these texts with the transmitted *Laozi* is

---

21. Another important aspect, which gets lost when a text leaves the sphere of oral communication and is fixed and transmitted in writing, is the illocutionary force, that is, the specification of the kind of communicative act as which the text was intended to function. David R. Olson reminds us that "writing readily represents the locutionary act, leaving the illocutionary force underspecified . . . the discovery and then the management of illocutionary force make up a fundamental part of the history of literacy." See David R. Olson, *The World on Paper: The Conceptual and Cognitive Implications of Writing and Reading* (Cambridge: Cambridge University Press, 1994), 93.
22. "When it has once been written down, every discourse rolls about everywhere, reaching indiscriminately those with understanding no less than those who have no business with it, and it doesn't know to whom it should speak and to whom it should not. And when it is faulted and attacked unfairly, it always needs its father's support; alone, it can neither defend itself nor come to its own support." Cf. *Phaidros* 275e, see *Plato: Phaedrus*, trans. Alexander Nehamas and Paul Woodruff (Indianapolis, Ind.: Hackett, 1995), 81.
23. The title *De dao jing* was used (and to my knowledge introduced) by Robert G. Henricks, *Te-tao Ching: A New Translation Based on the Recently Discovered Ma-wang-tui Texts* (New York: Ballantine Books, 1989).

undisputed and has been mentioned above, so *Laozi* may be a convenient designation for casual everyday usage. But a serious study of the manuscript will at least have to take into account that MS.B does not accord these two texts the status of a *jīng* — a term that does appear in the titles of two other texts of this manuscript, although only in the second one, the *Shiliu jing*, as a generic term.[24]

As for the first four texts of the manuscript, their materiality amply proves that the designers and manufacturers of this manuscript did not conceive of them as more closely related to one another than to the two texts they precede. It is the mere fact that the latter have transmitted counterparts, while these four texts do not, that has led scholars to see these four as belonging together in distinction from a *Laozi* text. Tang Lan's 唐蘭 suggestion to identify the four texts with the *Huangdi sijing*

---

24. The title *Shiliu jing* is controversial. The characters *liù* 六 'six' and *dà* 大 'major' look almost completely alike in the style of writing applied in this manuscript, and the text in question has only fourteen titled "chapters" plus an untitled one. Notwithstanding this discrepancy, the consistent layout standards throughout the manuscript make highly improbable Li Xueqin's 李學勤 suggestion that the first two characters should be read as 十大 'ten major' and understood to be the title of the fifteenth chapter, the title of the whole second text then being *jīng* 經 'guidelines'. It is much more likely that the copyist omitted a portion of the text titled *Shiliu jing* 十六經 or "Sixteen Guidelines" — probably, as Kalinowski assumes, the title of chapter 15 as well as chapter 16 along with its title; see Kalinowski, "La Production des Manuscrits," 151 n. 39. The readings 十大經 ("Ten major guidelines") or even 十四經 ("Fourteen major guidelines") are both implausible; see Gao Zheng 高正, "Boshu Shisi jing zhengming", 帛書十四經正名, in *Daojia wenhua yanjiu* 道家文化研究 3, ed. Chen Guying 陳鼓應 (Shanghai: Shanghai Guji, 1993), 283–84. Based on the impression created by the black-and-white reproductions of the manuscript in the 1980 Wenwu edition (*Mawangdui Han mu boshu*), Robin Yates has suggested that the manuscript is fragmented in column 142 immediately above 十六經 (or 十大經) and that originally another character may have preceded 十. However, the original manuscript shows unmistakably that the material is here intact and that there is no trace whatsoever of writing in the space before the title; moreover, at the end of text 1 (*Jing fa*), the difference between this title and the preceding title of the last section of the text is marked with extra spacing, while no such spacing occurs before the 經 in the title of the second text (see plate 5, a–b). The misleading impression of damage to the manuscript in this area is due to the fact that in the Wenwu edition the division of separate photos occurs just between columns 141 and 142 and the edge of the photo beginning with column 142 is of poor quality. For a different discussion of the title, including the arguments of Li Xueqin and Robin Yates, see Lin Qingyuan 林清源, *Jiandu boshu biaoti geshi yanjiu* 簡牘帛書標題格式研究 (Taipei: Yiwen, 2004), 153–84.

黃帝四經, a title transmitted in Ban Gu's 班固 Han bibliographical treatise under the heading *dàojiā* 道家, has meanwhile lost its influence.[25] Yet, despite Qiu Xigui's 裘錫圭 well-founded arguments against such a notion, the interpretive pattern still survives that sees the four as belonging to one philosophical lineage, related to but different from the *Laozi*.[26] It is indisputable that the texts *Jing fa* and *Shiliu jing* are indeed similar in genre and ideological orientation and even share some common textual material. These two are doubtless closely related, but the opposite is true of the third text, *Cheng*, which is a collection of apophthegms without any especially close connection to either the two preceding (*Jing fa* and *Shiliu jing*) or the three subsequent texts in the manuscript. The fourth text, *Dao yuan*, is again different. In terms of language and thought, it is much more closely related to the subsequent texts *De* and *Dao* than to any of the preceding texts. Thus, the perception of MS.B as consisting of two main parts, one being the *Laozi* and the other the *Huangdi sijing*, is a misconception founded on dubious interpretive habits and neglect of the codicological features of the manuscript.

Judging from the format and layout — including paratextual features such as titles and character counts — MS.A relies to a greater degree on the competence of the reader and is better suited for use within a certain situational context that could ensure the correct interpretation and transmission of its texts. As a scroll of half-width format, rolled around a wooden core, it was probably quite easy to use for the purpose of reading. MS.B shows more efforts, however unsuccessful, to exert control over the text and to make it independent of a situational context. Its full-width format made it more cumbersome to handle. It had to be folded to be stored away and needed to be unfolded and probably spread out on some supporting surface if one wanted to look at the text.

---

25. Cf. *Hanshu* ("Yiwen zhi" 藝文志), 30:1730. Tang Lan's suggestion first appeared in *Wenwu* 1974.9 and was reiterated in his article in the following issue of *Wenwu*. See Anonymous, "Zuotan Changsha Mawangdui Han mu boshu" 座談長沙馬王堆漢墓帛書, *Wenwu* 1974.9: 45–57; Tang Lan 唐蘭, "Huangdi sijing chutan" 黃帝四經初探, *Wenwu* 1974.10: 48–52.
26. Cf. Qiu Xigui 裘錫圭, "Mawangdui boshu *Laozi* yi ben juan qian gu yishu bing fei *Huangdi si jing*" 馬王堆帛書《老子》乙本卷前古佚書並非《黃帝四經》, in *Daojia wenhua yanjiu* 道家文化研究 3, ed. Chen Guying 陳鼓應 (Shanghai: Shanghai Guji Chubanshe, 1993), 249–55.

Style of Script and Orthography

MS.A is written in archaic clerical script and MS.B in Han clerical script.[27] The former is written in a neat and experienced yet somewhat casual hand, whereas the latter is written in extremely regular, almost printlike tiny characters (cf. plates 3 and 4). Each manuscript was apparently written by one scribe. The larger characters of MS.A are easier to read, whereas the small, neat ones of MS.B are perhaps of a higher representational value.

The orthography of both manuscripts does show irregularities but is on the whole much less irregular than is often assumed. An earlier study of the orthography in MS.A and MS.B found that MS.B generally shows the higher degree of regularity.[28] Usually one word is written with only one character, though not necessarily the same one as in modern orthography. An especially interesting inconsistency is not an orthographic one but one of word choice, influenced by different regional usages. As Ōnishi Katsuya has convincingly shown, the character 殹, frequently used in MS.B, does not stand for the sentence final particle yě < *la? (?) {也}[29] but for the word yì < *ʔə̂ih or *ʔîh (?) {殹} that was customary in the state of Qin and had the same function as yě. During the reign of the Qin dynasty and into the beginning of the Western Han, the use of the final particle yì was required for official or especially prestigious writings.[30] The scribe of MS.B copied a text that in all likelihood originally used not yì but yě, which was customary in Chu. At the beginning of his work, he complied with the requirement to exchange yě for yì, but after some time, he relapsed into writing the word to which he was accustomed and that

---

27. I follow Chen Songchang's classification of three types of script in the Mawangdui manuscripts: the oldest being "(hybrid) small seal / clerical" (zhuànlì 篆隸), followed by "archaic clerical" (gǔlì 古隸) and then by "Han clerical" (Hànlì 漢隸). Cf. Chen, Mawangdui boshu yishu, foreword, 4. Different types of script could, of course, be employed at the same point in time. In the case of Mawangdui, however, there are indications that at least in some examples, the types of script actually correspond with earlier or later dates of production of the manuscripts.
28. See Richter, "Towards a Profile of Graphic Variation," 169–207.
29. Following a convention of Qiu Xigui (Wenzixue gaiyao), characters in {}-shaped brackets identify words according to modern orthographic standard; they do not designate the original manuscript characters. The modern equivalents of manuscript characters are given without brackets.
30. Ōnishi Katsuya 大西克也, " 'I', 'ya' no kōtai: Rikkoku tōitsu zengo ni okeru shomen gengo no issokumen" 「殹」「也」の交替 — 六国統一前後に於ける書面言語の一側面, Chūgoku shutsudo shiryō kenkyū 中國出土資料研究 2 (1998): 4–24.

was, moreover, much easier to write.

A true orthographic variation that probably also reflects local influences is the word *lǐ* < *rə? {理}, which in both manuscripts is occasionally written as 李 but more often as 理. The way this word is written in the Baoshan 包山 manuscripts (i.e., 杢) suggests that there existed an orthographic convention in the Chu area according to which 李 (representing the word *lǐ* < *rə? {李} in modern orthography) or the historically discontinuous 杢 could be used to write the homophonous *lǐ* {理}.³¹ Perhaps this variant shows a regional influence on the written form of the text. A yet more interesting point is the distribution of 李 vis-à-vis 理 in MS.A: The word *lǐ* {理} is written as 理 only in the text *Wu xing*, whereas it is written as 李 in the subsequent two texts, *Jiu zhu* and *Ming jun*.³² This one example could well be a coincidence, but it accords with a number of other cases in which a word is written consistently in one way and the change to writing it differently occurs exactly at the point where a new text begins. The fact that the manuscript employs different orthographic conventions for different texts — among them trivial differences such as the use of abbreviated versus full forms of a character — can be explained only by assuming that the individual texts were copied from different models that had been produced after different conventions.³³ It appears that in the case of MS.A, a uniform orthography

---

31. 來 (originally devised to write the word *mài* < *mrˆək {麥}, later used for *lái* < *rˆə < *rˆək/? {來}) is a plausible phonophoric for *lǐ* < *rə? {李/理}, which makes the character 李 a likely simplification of the former 杢. Reconstructed old pronunciations follow Schuessler, *ABC Etymological Dictionary of Old Chinese*.
32. The word appears altogether eight times in the entire manuscript. The only two instances in the text *Wu xing* are written as 理. Of the remaining six, all written as 李, three occur in *Jiu zhu* and *Ming jun*, respectively.
33. For a detailed study of this phenomenon, see Richter, "Towards a Profile of Graphic Variation," 190–97. For example, in the same two texts, *Jiu zhu* and *Ming jun*, that write 李 for *lǐ* {理}, the word *tīng* {聽} is written as 耴, whereas all other texts of MS.A write the word as 聽, but it is not these two particular texts that differ in their orthography from all others. The word *cōng* {聰} occurs only in the text *Wu xing* and in the last text of the manuscript, *Jiu zhu*. In the latter and in the *jīng* section of *Wu xing*, it is written as 怱 (> 悤), but in the *shuō* section of the same text, the form 嚶 is used. The word *shēng* {聲} is written as 殸 in the text *Dao* and as 聲 in all other texts. The same manuscript writes *shèng* {聖} as 殸 in the text *Dao* of MS.A and as 耴 in all other texts, that is, in the text *Dao* a change of component 攴 versus 攵 is used to distinguish between {聲} and {聖}, while the other texts write the two words

was no great concern, because the manuscript was used within a circle of people who were fairly well acquainted with the texts. In MS.B, however, there is an effort to control and unify orthography. This effort, though not always successful, fits the assumption made above that this manuscript was meant to preserve and transmit the text beyond a narrowly defined circle. Not only did this mean that the graphic representation of the text as such had to be as reliable as possible (i.e., independent of information extrinsic to the manuscript), but once the manuscript became detached from its situational context, its text had to be represented in an unambiguous manner and its dignity and status expressed in its visual representation.

Punctuation and Other Marks

Another feature that potentially contains valuable information about both production and use of manuscripts is the punctuation and all other kinds of marks in the manuscripts. In addition to marks such as initiator dots at the beginning of new textual units or separator dots marking subdivisions within these units, there is yet another sort of mark present in both MS.A and MS.B: a small hook, placed not like the separator dots in the middle of the column but farther to the right and usually closer to the preceding character than to the subsequent one — in a position just like that of the short double dash that is used as either a repetition or ligature mark.

The default assumption about the function of such a mark is naturally that it should, more or less in the way a comma or a period does in modern orthography, divide the text into meaningful units, according to its logical and thus either grammatical or rhetorical structure, in order to clarify its contents.[34] No matter whether a text is punctuated according to its grammatical or its rhetorical structure, the reader expects some consistency in the representation of either structure. Upon closer inspection of MS.A,

---

with completely different characters.

34. The primary function of punctuation is commonly understood, as Malcolm Parkes describes, "to resolve structural uncertainties in a text, and to signal nuances of semantic significance." But Parkes also points out that "a text can be ordered into graphic units which represent metrical units . . . and punctuation can delineate rhetorical structure, so that the reader can be explicitly alerted to certain formal contrivances relevant to the communicative significances embodied in a text." See M. B. Parkes, *Pause and Effect: An Introduction to the History of Punctuation in the West* (Berkeley: University of California Press, 1993), 1.

however, it becomes apparent that the hook mark (henceforth transcribed as ∠) does not reflect the logical structure of the text in the grammatical or the rhetorical sense but often even goes counter to it — for example, in the well-known beginning of the text *Dao* in MS.A (col. 93, see plate 5c). The following examples present a transcription of the manuscript text, followed by its reading in modern orthography with modern punctuation added, and then an English translation:

道可道也∠非恆道也∠名可名也∠非恆名也无名萬物之始也∠有名萬物之母也

道可道也，非恆道也；名可名也，非恆名也。無名萬物之始也；有名萬物之母也。

The Way that can be spoken is not the lasting Way; the name that can be named is not the lasting name. The nameless is the beginning of the Myriad Beings; the named is the mother of the Myriad Beings.[35]

This passage naturally divides into two parts: the first consists of two parallel pairs of clauses; the second, beginning with 无, has two sentences. So the *main* caesura within the passage (between 也 and 无) is unmarked. Rather, there are four such marks in the places that we might call caesuras of second rank, that is, the three divisions between the first four clauses and the division between the two sentences of the second half of the passage. If the function of the hook mark had been to indicate caesuras, it would be difficult to explain why it is missing in the positions of the more prominent caesuras. It seems, therefore, more likely that this kind of mark served a *performative* function, that is, it signaled to the reader and the reciter points in the text that for some reason required special attention. In this case, probably the special combination of antithetical and parallel phrases needed to be highlighted by special rhetorical means in recitation. The position between 也 and 无, however, where the sentence structure and, with it, the rhythm changes anyway, required no special mark. In such places, the reader or declaimer cannot help making a caesura and need not be specially reminded to do so.

A similar case occurs in the next column (col. 94; see plate 5c):

---

35. Translations from the *Laozi* counterparts of the manuscript are chiefly based on D.C. Lau, trans., *Tao Te Ching* (Hong Kong: Chinese University Press, 1996 [1982]).

【故】恆无欲也以觀其眇∠恆有欲也以觀其所噭兩者同出異名同胃∠玄之有玄眾眇之【門】³⁶

故恆無欲也，以觀其眇；恆有欲也，以觀其所噭。兩者同出異名，同謂：玄之又玄，眾眇之門。

Thus, constantly without desire, one sees their (the Myriad Beings') subtleties, constantly with desire, one sees what they proclaim. The two have the same origin but different names. They are likewise called: the darker than dark, the gate to all subtleties.³⁷

It is not known whether there was any mark at the beginning of this passage, because the end of this column is lost. It probably contained the character 故, as in the MS.B counterpart and transmitted versions. The top of one stroke of this character is still discernible, and judging from the spacing, we may assume that there was no hook mark to signal the end of the previous passage. The first hook in the new passage is useful for making clear that the main syntactic divisions in this case do not coincide with the final particle *yě* 也, as is usual, but that instead 也 is in the middle of each of the first two sentences. Again, the main caesura of this passage — between 噭 and 兩 — need not be specially marked, as the change of rhythm automatically produces a caesura. The second hook is also a very useful signal to prevent a likely mistake in reciting the text. Since *wèi* 謂 is a most unusual conclusion of a clause, a reader who is not familiar with the text could be tempted to automatically read "... 同謂玄" and then after the caesura be confronted with "之有(又)玄 ... ," which is not the beginning of a clause. However we were to read this passage, a short pause must be made directly after 謂 and the new clause begun with 玄, and the hook was likely meant to remind the reader to do so.

The function of the hook mark in both MS.A and MS.B appears to be that of an attention mark — a device that is fundamentally different from the initiator and separator dots mentioned above. These latter dots mark off

---

36. Characters in bold brackets (e.g., 【門】) are virtually absent from the manuscript. They are conjectured by the editors mostly on grounds of context (including the corresponding transmitted text) rather than inferred from the often minute remaining fragments of brushstrokes of the missing character.
37. I read *miǎo* 眇 in the literal sense of 'minute, subtle' rather than the more abstract *miào* 妙 'mysterious'; likewise, I read *jiào* 噭 'to cry/shout out' rather than *jiào/ jiǎo* 徼 'pursuit'.

textual units according to the logical structure of the text insofar as they can be seen as a property of the material realization of a text on the same level as the characters that represent its words. The hook marks, however, do not form part of the direct visual representation of the text. They are a pragmatic device with a purely performative function and are of no importance for the transmission of the manuscript text. Attention marks also often occur in places where one would identify a caesura according to content; however, it is not their primary function to mark these divisions.

The placement of hook marks in the following passage (cols. 95–96; see plate 5c) is yet more peculiar than in the one presented above:

天下皆知美為美惡已∠皆知善訾不善∠矣∠有无之相生也難易之相成也長短之相刑也高下之相盈也∠意聲之相和也先後之相隋恒也是以聲人居无為之事....

Adapted to modern orthography and in a layout that brings out the textual structure, the passage looks as follows:

天下皆知美為美惡已∠
皆知善此不善∠矣∠

有無之相生也
難易之相成也
長短之相形也
高下之相盈也∠
音聲之相和也
先後之相隨恒也

是以聖人居無為之事[...]

Everyone in the world knows the beautiful as beautiful; this is just ugly. Everyone knows goodness; this is already not good. Forever, being and non-being generate each other; difficult and easy complement each other; long and short shape each other; high and low fill each other; tone and sound harmonize each other; before and after follow each other. Therefore, the sage abides in non-interfering service....

Leaving aside textual problems such as the puzzling fact that the first two sentences are not as neatly parallel as in the transmitted *Laozi*, the main caesuras are those after 矣 and before 是以. In the latter, no mark is added, and the former is complemented by a hook mark after 已, so that the first two, largely parallel statements at the beginning of the passage are marked off in the *same* way. The hook mark before 矣, however, appears to be entirely incongruous. The most natural assumption would be that the scribe wrote the mark too early and either he or a proofreader later added a mark in the correct position after 矣. If that were the case, there should be an extra wide space before 矣 and normal spacing after it, but the reverse is true. This leaves two possibilities: *either* the scribe accidentally wrote the mark too early, but immediately detected his mistake and thus left no extra room for the mark but did so after 矣, where he drew the mark slightly thicker than the erroneous one, *or* the marks were drawn by two different people who did not share the same opinion about the recitation of the text.

The mark after 盈也, placed after the fourth of six parallel sentences, would seem inappropriate at first sight, especially if we expect the marks to divide the text according to content into units of comparable weight. Taking into account that the first four verses are connected to one another by nasal rhyme (*srêŋ 生 – *geŋ 成 – *gôŋ 形 – *leŋ 盈) and that the following two rhyme as well, but differently (both *[g]wâih 和 and *s-wa/oi ? 隨 being open syllables), the mark does make sense. Whoever added the mark probably did so to draw the reader's attention to the different rhyme.[38] Such a change of rhyme is no obstacle at all for reading and comprehending the text in terms of recognizing its structure, especially given the uninterrupted succession of perfectly parallel sentences, but it could pose a problem in the performance of recitation. After reciting several sentences with particular stress on their nasal rhyme words, the reciter could easily stumble over the surprising open syllable at the end of the last two members of this catalogue of parallel sentences. The attention mark would not serve its purpose if it were placed after the word that carries the new rhyme. As it is not an explanatory mark intended to ensure the correct interpretation of the text after an initial reading, but

---

38. One might argue that in the last verse, 先後之相隨恒也, *héng* < *gôŋ 恒 is the rhyme word. However, this attribute refers to the entire catalogue beginning from 有無之相生 down to 先後之相隨, a fact that is somewhat obscured by the peculiar use of *yě* 也 in this passage. The actual rhyme pattern of the six members of this catalogue is AAAABB. The attribute 恒 that summarizes all six takes up the A rhyme again. The presence of this word *héng* is apparently one of the special features that indicate the close genetic relatedness of the two Mawangdui versions of the *Laozi*. It occurs neither in any received version nor in the Guodian counterpart.

rather a mark that facilitates the process of reading itself, it needs to precede the feature to which it draws attention.[39]

The following example (cols. 124–27; see plate 5d) shows another passage in MS.A in which subdivisions of text on a lower level are marked whereas the main divisions remain unmarked:

大上下知有之其次親譽之[40]其次畏之其下母之信不足案有不信【猶呵】其貴言也成功遂事∠而百眚[41]胃我自然∠故大道廢∠案有仁義知快出∠案有大偽六親不和∠[42]案有畜茲邦家亂∠案有貞臣絕聲棄知民利百負∠絕仁棄義民復畜茲∠絕巧棄利盜賊无有此三言也以為文未足∠故令之有所屬

If the purpose were to divide this counterpart of the transmitted *Laozi* chapters 17 and 18 according to contents, marks would be placed elsewhere. While the division between the main constituent units of this passage are unmarked (except for the hook mark after 然, which may serve some other function), divisions *within* these main units are marked:

大上下知有之
其次親譽之
其次畏之

---

39. In the Guodian counterpart (*Laozi* A, slip 16), there is an additional stroke at the bottom of the character *xiāng* 相 immediately preceding the new rhyme *hé* {和}. It is possible that this stroke, although seemingly a feature of the character itself, serves the function of an attention mark as well. None of the other five instances of *xiāng* 相 has this additional stroke. In order to assume this function for the additional stroke with any certainty, however, more similar cases would have to be found in the same corpus or at least in manuscripts of similar provenance.
40. There is some extra space between these two characters (*zhī* 之 and *qí* 其). Unfortunately, the material is damaged just in the place where a mark would be positioned. There is a tiny black spot next to where the underlying silk support, on which the manuscript fragments are mounted, shows through, but it is impossible to tell from the photos available to me whether it is ink or merely a discoloration of the torn silk threads. Such isolated small ink spots are often impressions made by another layer of the manuscript, regardless of whether it was folded or rolled. Some ink became detached and remains on the other layer.
41. The editors of the Wenwu edition mistook 眚 for 省; cf. *Mawangdui Han mu boshu*, 11.
42. This mark has not been noted in the Wenwu edition, but despite the vertical breakage in the silk along the middle of the character 和, leaving only distorted remnants of the 口 component, the left part of the hook mark is still clearly discernible.

其下侮之
信不足安有不信猶呵其貴言也
成功遂事∠而百姓謂我自然∠

故
大道廢∠ 安有仁義
智快出∠ 安有大偽
六親不和∠ 安有畜茲
邦家昏亂∠ 安有貞臣

絕聖棄智 民利百倍∠
絕仁棄義 民復畜茲∠
絕巧棄利 盜賊無有
此三言也以為文未足∠故令之有所屬

Of the greatest ruler his subjects merely know he exists; the next they love and praise, the next they fear, the lowest they insult. Where there is lack of trustworthiness, there will be distrust. Hesitant is he in how he cherishes words. He consummates his achievements and completes his work and the Hundred Clans will all say, "We are so of ourselves." Thus, when the Great Way is abandoned, there will be benevolence and righteousness. When clever smugness[43] emerges, there will be great pretense. When the six familial relations are not in harmony, there will be parental affection.[44] When state and (ruling) family are in turmoil, there will be loyal ministers. Break with sagacity, discard cleverness and the people will benefit a hundredfold. Break with benevolence, discard righteousness and the people will return to parental affection. Break with artifice, discard benefit and there will be no thieves and robbers.

The mark before *ān* {安} may have been considered necessary to show that this word is to be understood as an initial particle, not a final one.[45]

---

43. I follow William Boltz's reading *kuài* 快 but not his interpretation of the word as "quickness, quick-wittedness"; see William G. Boltz, "Textual Criticism and the Ma Wang tui *Lao tzu*," *Harvard Journal of Asiatic Studies* 44.1 (1984): 211–12.
44. The reading 畜茲 follows Boltz, "Textual Criticism," 211–12.
45. Both *ān* < *ʔân 安 and *yān* < *ʔan 焉 can be used interchangeably as interrogative initial particles. The former is a fusion of the likewise interrogative *wū* < *ʔâ 惡/烏 with a demonstrative element *-n; the latter is a fusion of *yú* < *ʔa 於 with the same element *-n. Of these four, only *ān* < *ʔân 安, *wū* < *ʔâ 惡/烏 and *yān* < *ʔan 焉 occur as interrogative particles, whereas *yú* < *ʔa 於 does not. Accordingly, *yān* < *ʔan 焉 frequently occurs in a non-interrogative sense that equals 於之 or 於是;

This is of no little consequence, as the final particle — usually *yān* {焉} — would allow only one (i.e., the above) interpretation. Reading the word as an initial particle, however, opens up two possibilities. The non-interrogative sense of 於是/乃/則 produces the same interpretation as in the case of a final particle, only with a greater stress on the cause-and-effect relation. Reading it as an interrogative particle would result in the reverse: "Thus when the Great Way is abandoned / How could there be benevolence and propriety?" The former interpretation accords with the transmitted text that makes a pointed argument against some of the most prominent social values, chiefly advocated by the Ru 儒.[46] In other words, this explicitly anti-"Confucian" passage belongs to the ideologically most specific parts of the transmitted *Laozi*. This is possibly one of several indications that suggest a transformation of the originally heterogeneous *Laozi* (containing an at least potentially interrogative particle between the clauses) toward greater ideological coherence over time.[47]

It is not always possible to determine with any certainty why the hook mark was employed just where it is found in the manuscripts. Vastly different circumstances apparently suggested the need for such a mark to those who produced or used the manuscripts. In several instances, the hook mark occurs in rhymed passages before a change of rhyme, and in others, it is placed before the last element of a catalogue of parallel sentences, probably alerting the reader that the next sentence is to be particularly stressed when reciting the text to an audience. Such rhetorical means are commonly employed to signal an audience that an integral passage is ending — the aural equivalent to paragraphs or other structuring devices in written texts designed for readers who are yet unfamiliar with it and thus wholly reliant on accessing it through its written form. The proposed term

---

however, we cannot rely on orthography to identify the word. The word *yān* {焉} in early manuscripts is often written with an equivalent of the character 安.

46. The Wang Bi version has 大道廢, 有仁義. 智慧出, 有大偽. 六親不和, 有孝慈. 國家昏亂, 有忠臣.

47. I have discussed this question in more detail on the basis of another example elsewhere; Richter, "Der Alte und das Wasser," 267–71. Similar observations have been made by Liu Xiaogan, who discusses this homogenization of the text as an improvement or refinement. See Liu Xiaogan, "From Bamboo Slips to Received Versions: Common Features in the Transformation of the *Laozi*," *Harvard Journal of Asiatic Studies* 63.2 (2003): 338–39, 381–82; Liu Xiaogan 劉笑敢, *Laozi gu jin: Wu zhong duikan yu xiping yinlun* 老子古今：五種對勘與析評引論, 2 vols.

"attention mark" seems the most appropriate general functional description of the hook mark in the two manuscripts under discussion — and probably in many others.

On the whole, punctuation is far less regular in early Chinese manuscripts than, for example, in modern English orthography. The use of the attention marks is more inconsistent than that of the various initiator, separator, and terminator marks, because the attention marks do not form part of the orthography of a text in the sense of a mere visual representation of its wording. Rather, they are an ancillary device for reading the text aloud. They belong to the level of interpretation needed to recover the "illocutionary force" (i.e., the communicative intention) that gets lost in the transition of a text from the oral to the written mode of communication.[48]

The vast differences in the use of attention marks in different manuscripts reflect their different uses. The hook mark occurs more than 400 times in MS.A but only 19 times in MS.B. This cannot be explained by the differences between the texts, especially since about one-third of the text in both manuscripts (i.e., the *Laozi* counterparts) is virtually identical and the use of marks in these identical parts differs, too. The text *De* in MS.B has 4 hook marks, as compared to 55 in its MS.A counterpart, the text *Dao* has 1 such mark, and its MS.A counterpart has 101. This difference corroborates the assumption made above about the different purposes of these manuscripts. In MS.A, which from the beginning was designed to be used for actual reading, the hook marks seem to have been added during the process of writing the text. In most of the cases, the spacing between characters appears to be larger where such a mark occurs. In MS.B, however, in the few places with hook marks, no additional space was left between the characters to accommodate the marks. They were probably added at some later time, when someone checked the text or used it for reading and decided that its correct transmission required further disambiguation.

Errors and Corrections

The types of errors and the way they were corrected or remained unnoticed reflects the same difference in usage between MS.A and MS.B as

---

48. For a detailed discussion of this problem, see Olson, *The World on Paper*, esp. chapters 5–7.

described above with regard to punctuation.

The silk manuscripts of Mawangdui offer a much wider variety of methods for correcting errors than described in earlier sources. The chapter on corrections in Chen Mengjia's classic study on Han manuscripts, based primarily on the Wuwei 武威 slips, mentions the method of scraping off mistaken character(s) (*shānxuē* 刪削 or *xuēchú* 削除) with the "scholar's knife" or "book knife" (the latter a somewhat mistaken rendering for *shūdāo* 書刀, a "writing knife") and later inserting the correct text.[49] Such corrections by the method of *xuēgǎi* 削改 are usually easily discerned, because the material of the writing support is thinner in these places and the inserted characters are often faded. If the scribe realized his mistake as soon as he had made it, he could correct it by wiping off the wrong character with some liquid (water or saliva) and then writing the correct one over it. This method is called *túgǎi* 塗改. A third very common method was simply to insert omitted characters in a smaller size beside or between characters (*tiānxiě* 添寫). Whereas the former two methods could hardly be used in silk manuscripts, the latter could.[50] So could another method that is mentioned in early Chinese transmitted texts, that is, deletion (*diǎn* 點) by covering the erroneous character with ink or some other substance.

MS.A has considerably fewer errors than MS.B. The most common type of error in MS.A is the omission of a character that is then added in smaller script between the two characters where it belongs, though slightly

---

49. The different forms of such corrections, according to Chen Mengjia, are (1) one character is replaced by the correct one; (2) several characters are replaced by same number of correct ones; (3) only a character component is replaced; (4) a passage is deleted in order to rewrite it and supplement the character that had first been omitted, the characters of the whole being somewhat smaller than the surrounding ones; and (5) superfluous characters are deleted (either leaving a blank or rewriting the passage with wider spacing). Cf. Chen Mengjia 陳夢家, *Han jian zhuishu* 漢簡綴述 (Beijing: Zhonghua Shuju, 1980), 303–4. On the "book knife" as an eraser, see also Tsien Tsuen-hsuin, *Written on Bamboo and Silk: The Beginnings of Chinese Books and Inscriptions*, 2nd ed. (Chicago: University of Chicago Press, 2004 [1962]), 194–98. On the Wuwei find, see Gansu Sheng Bowuguan 甘肅省博物館 and Zhongguo Kexueyuan Kaogu Yanjiusuo 中國科學院考古研究所, eds., *Wuwei Han jian* 武威漢簡 (Beijing: Wenwu Chubanshe, 2006 [1964]).
50. It is also possible that a character could be wiped away from a silk writing support, but this probably was possible only for an extremely short time after applying the ink. Although the fabric was specially treated to serve as a writing support (Chen Songchang, personal communication, April 2007), it surely absorbed the ink more quickly than a bamboo or wooden surface did.

shifted to the right or left side of the column, depending on where there was more space between the characters (see the example in plate 6a, in which the 中 in the phrase 予之中心 in col. 256 had been omitted). Other errors apparently remained undetected or at least uncorrected. In the phrase 是故同形共謀為一 in column 390, 共 was written twice (see plate 6b). The two 於 characters at the beginning of column 73 are a different case; here, the first 於 should be 大: 禍莫//大於无敵 (cols. 72–73, "//" indicates change of column; see plate 6c). A similar mistake was corrected, probably not by the scribe who wrote the manuscript but later by a proofreader, in the phrase 德(得)者同於德(得), 失者同於失 in column 139,[51] where the first 失 was miswritten 者; the wrong character was covered with cinnabar (zhūshā 朱砂), onto which the missing 失 was then written. The topmost layer of such corrections, that is, the correct character, has usually vanished and the erroneous character is again visible beneath the faded cinnabar.[52] In this case, only the ends of the two strokes at the bottom of the character 失 are preserved, because they reached beyond the cinnabar and were written directly on the silk (see plate 6d). It is highly unlikely that corrections of this type, requiring the use of cinnabar, were made during the act of writing. Rather, they were most probably part of a separate process, which was performed later either by the scribe himself or, more likely, by someone else who was responsible for proofreading the completed manuscript.

Very few such corrections were made in MS.A, but they are quite frequent in MS.B. These corrections usually occur at the beginning of the six main codicological units, whereas the number of uncorrected errors increases toward the end of these six texts. This suggests that the proofreader slackened in performing his task. In column 81, the scribe first erroneously wrote 命 but immediately realized this mistake and wrote the correct 名 directly afterward. Only later did a proofreader delete the superfluous character with cinnabar (see plate 7a). A similar mistake happened in column 83, where the scribe omitted the 四 in the phrase 四時, realized the mistake on the spot, and wrote the correct two characters

---

51. The two homophonous words dé {得} and dé {德} are written interchangeably with either the character 德 or 得 in MS.A.
52. The same phenomenon occurs also in other Mawangdui silk manuscripts. Apparently, the topmost layer of ink was repelled by the cinnabar, and most of the cinnabar was probably likewise repelled by the ink layer below, but the place where it had been applied retained at least a faint red color.

after the 時 that he had written too early; again, the superfluous character was deleted by a later proofreader (see plate 7b). While there was a practical need to delete the superfluous character in these two cases, a correction was also made with cinnabar in column 139, where the scribe had left unfinished the character 夜, which he had begun to write too early (see plate 7c). The unfinished character would surely not have been misread. In other cases, the scribe just left the character unfinished, and it was not deleted afterward (e.g. 可 in col. 71, 爭 in col. 108, 我 in col. 141, and 使 in col. 148) (see plate 7d). Leaving the character incomplete was less conspicuous than crossing it out.

Erroneous characters that had already been completed were in some cases left uncorrected, as with the probable graphic error 富 for 密 in column 8 (see plate 7e), perhaps because they were not detected, but such characters usually were canceled as inconspicuously as possible, either by crossing them out with one stroke across the entire character (as 人 in col. 226; see plate 7f) or a stroke across part of the character (as 聽 in col. 229; see plate 7g) or by "wrapping" them in additional strokes (e.g., 臣 in col. 23, 者 in col. 39, and 成 in col. 40; see plate 7h–j). This manner of correction shows an effort to make corrections in an inconspicuous way, in order to leave the overall impression of neatness as unspoiled as possible. At the same time, great care was taken to ensure the correctness of the text and prevent ambiguity. An error in column 11, for example, was deleted with two clearly separated halves of a black square instead of with a whole black square that could have been mistaken for a division mark like the initiator mark two columns earlier (see plate 7k).

The errors and corrections in the two manuscripts indicate — at least as strongly as the other features discussed above — that MS.A was designed for practical use in actually reading the texts written on it, probably with the view of later performing them orally, while MS.B was produced for the purpose of transmitting the texts it contains.

Conclusion

MS.A is written on a half-width silk scroll in a clear but not particularly neat hand. The types of errors and their distribution do not suggest any lack of competence on the part of the scribe but seem to be due to speedy work. The orthography of the manuscript is fairly regular within its individual texts. Apparently the different orthographic conventions of the different models from which the texts were copied were simply carried over into the copy. Not much importance was attached to orthographic detail. Readers were apparently expected to be familiar with the texts. The layout is somewhat ambiguous with regard to textual borders and likewise requires competence on the part of readers.

The full-width silk manuscript MS.B was produced in a very elaborate fashion with unambiguous layout features, from textual division and explicit titles down to character counts. The manuscript shows an effort to unify orthography throughout its texts: orthographic correctness was apparently considered essential for a satisfactory visual representation of the texts. The types of errors and their relative frequency indicate that the scribe was a well-trained professional with a high level of craftsmanship in calligraphy but not with a particularly high level of competence with regard to the manuscript's contents. This lack of textual competence does not make a scribe mediocre. If the visual appearance of the manuscript was of greater importance than the function of acquainting a reader with its text, the skill of writing beautifully may have been the primary qualification. The scribe took much care to correct the errors in as inconspicuous a manner as possible; however, a fair number of errors remained undetected by the scribe and were left for the later proofreader, who seems to have worked rather superficially and only on parts of the text, preferably the beginnings.

On the one hand, MS.B, greater in format and more elaborate, seems to have been designed to serve a mainly representational function, implying suitability for transmitting the text it was to bear. MS.A, on the other hand, was actually written for the practical purpose of reading — a kind of reading that probably did not so much serve to make the reader acquainted with the text. Rather, this manuscript could be referred to in order to check and refresh one's knowledge of its texts or to practice for recitation to an audience. In their different ways, both manuscripts thus played a role in the transmission of their texts: one relying chiefly on the oral mode of transmission, the other aiming to secure its texts and carry them over time in a state of independence from human conveyors. Even if, as in the case of MS.B, the written form of a text aims to make textual identity explicit (e.g., by adding titles, marking the borders between texts and the divisions within them, controlling orthography, and adding word counts), even then textual identity can be only partially represented and cannot be preserved with absolute reliability. The preservation of this identity requires not only that the materialized text (i.e., the manuscript) survive or be recovered but that the reading competence in the broader sense, that is, the competence to decode the meaning the producers entrusted to the material features of the manuscripts, be recovered as well. As there is no reason to assume that universal encoding standards existed, we must resist the temptation either to assume that no such standards existed at all or to generalize findings derived from the study of particular manuscripts. Instead, we must continue comprehensive studies of individual manuscripts, hoping for patterns to arise, once we have reached the stage of a statistically more representative basis.

PART III

Literacy and Social Contexts

CHAPTER 7

The Royal Audience and Its Reflections in Western Zhou Bronze Inscriptions

Lothar von Falkenhausen

The basic textual scheme in the bulk of the extant corpus of Western Zhou bronze inscriptions comprises three parts: an initial "announcement of merit," a central, grammatically and semantically pivotal "statement of dedication," and a prayer-like "statement of purpose" at the end.[1] This tripartite structure is most clearly apparent in long inscriptions, but it is also expressed, albeit in abbreviated form, by the short texts that constitute the vast majority of extant inscriptions. This chapter presents a new interpretation of the "announcements of merit" at the beginning of long inscriptions. That most of these passages record the conferral of privileges during audience ceremonies at the royal Zhou court is well known. How does the audience protocol manifest itself in the structure of the texts? Olivier Venture's useful deliberations on the role of orality in Shang and Zhou ritual[2] suggest that particular attention be paid to the relationship between what was *said* during the court audiences and what was *recorded*

This chapter originates in a paper titled "The Oral Subtexts of Zhou Bronze Inscriptions," presented at the Religion, Poetry, and Memory in Ancient and Early Medieval China conference at Princeton University on May 20–22, 2004. My thanks to Martin Kern for organizing this stimulating scholarly meeting. A Chinese version, translated by Lai Guolong 來國龍, was published as part of Luo Tai 羅泰 (Lothar von Falkenhausen), "Xi Zhou tongqi mingwen de xingzhi" 西周銅器銘文的性質, *Kaoguxue yanjiu* 考古學研究 6 [Festschrift for Professor Gao Ming] (2006): 343–74.

1. Lothar von Falkenhausen, "Issues in Western Zhou: A Review Article," *Early China* 18 (1993): 152–56.
2. Olivier Venture, "L'écriture et la communication avec les esprits en Chine ancienne," *Bulletin of the Museum of Far Eastern Antiquities* 74 (2002): 34–65.

in the inscriptions.

In an earlier study, I distinguished two main types of long announcements of merit: oral proclamations by the inscribed objects' donors[3] and renderings of official documents formulated in clerical language. A newly discovered inscription has led to the realization that these two types — then referred to as announcements of merit in the "subjective mode" and in the "documentary mode" — are not distinct but complementary: each relates to a specific segment in the court-audience protocol. This discovery sheds new light on the nature of long announcement texts.

Audience Dialogues in the Bronze Inscriptions

Announcements of merit in the form of an oral proclamation begin with the expression X *yuē* [某]曰 (X proclaimed),[4] X being the name of the donor.[5] The word *yuē* 曰 (which has a semantic range including "to say," "to state [as in a written document]," and "to be called") in such instances explicitly marks the following text as a transcribed oral utterance.[6] Where

---

3. I use the following terms to refer to the persons commonly appearing in bronze inscriptions: The "donor" (the closest English equivalent to "Stifter" used by Ulrich Unger) is the individual who commissioned a bronze object and who figures as the subject governing the crucial verb *zuò* 作 'to make' in the statement of dedication ("making" is here to be understood in the causative sense); see Ulrich Unger, *Hao-ku: Sinologische Rundbriefe* (Münster: samizdat, 1982–2004). I reserve the term "maker" for the artisans who actually produced the objects. The "patron" is the one who confers on the donor the right (and sometimes the funds) to have the bronze object made. (Sometimes another highly placed individual, the "subpatron," is ordered by a patron to bestow gifts on the donor.) The "dedicatee" is a deceased ancestor in whose cult the vessel is to be used. The "beneficiary" is a living person (usually female) for whom a vessel is produced and who usually appears in the inscription's dedicatory clause. The "sponsor" is the person (usually the beneficiary's father, brother, or husband) who commissions a vessel for a living beneficiary.
4. The notion that these were proclamations offered in a specific context and met with a specific response calls for a translation in the past tense.
5. Falkenhausen, "Issues in Western Zhou," 158–59.
6. Bernhard Karlgren apostrophizes *yuē* as a "common initial particle, untranslatable," but a perusal of occurrences in the early classics and in bronze inscriptions reveals that virtually all of them fall under the semantic headings here given. See Bernhard Karlgren, "Glosses on the Book of Documents," *Bulletin of the Museum of Far Eastern Antiquities* 20 (1948): 44. Unsurprisingly, therefore, Axel Schuessler does not include a meaning of "initial particle"; *A Dictionary of Early Zhou Chinese* (Honolulu: University of Hawai'i Press, 1987), 795, lemma *yue*. *Yuē* occurs in some 174 bronze

that utterance ends must be deduced from the context.

Earlier, I identified addressees of the proclamation as the ancestors of the inscribed object's donor. This now seems questionable in light of the inscription of the Qiu *pan* 逑盤 (XS: 757) (a.k.a. Lai *pan* 逨盤),[7] discovered in January 2003 as part of a hoard of twenty-seven bronze vessels at Yangjiacun 楊家村, Meixian 眉縣, in Shaanxi.[8] The Qiu *pan* is one of twenty-six vessels from this hoard that are linked by inscription to the well-known Shan 單 lineage. The *pan* dates to the reign of King Xuan 宣王 (r. 827–782 B.C.E.). Its long inscription has attracted much attention because of its unique reign-by-reign account of the achievements of various Shan lineage members in the service of the successive Zhou kings.[9] Here, however, the reader's attention is directed to the textual structure of the announcement of merit and to the marking of oral speech within it.[10]

Qiu *pan* 逑盤:

---

inscriptions of the corpus indexed in *Jinwen yinde* 金文引得, in some cases more than once; this sample includes roughly nine Shang and transitional Shang/Zhou instances, 131 from Western Zhou (16 early, 58 middle, and 57 late Western Zhou) and 34 from Eastern Zhou. See *Jinwen yinde* 金文引得, 2 vols. (Nanning: Guangxi Jiaoyu Chubanshe, 2001).

7. In transcribing the donor's name as "Qiu," I follow Qiu Xigui 裘錫圭, "Du Qiu qi mingwen zhaji sanze" 讀逑器銘文札記三則, *Wenwu* 2003.6: 74–77. The excavators and local scholars (see the works quoted in note 9) use Lai; Li Xueqin 李學勤 proposes Cou 逨; "Meixian Yangjiacun xinchu qingtongqi yanjiu" 眉縣楊家村新出青銅器研究, *Wenwu* 2003.6: 66–73.

8. The bronzes from this cache are published in Shaanxi Sheng Kaogu Yanjiusuo 陝西省考古研究所 et al., "Shaanxi Meixian Yangjiacun Xi Zhou qingtongqi jiaocang fajue jianbao" 陝西眉縣楊家村西周青銅器窖藏發掘簡報, *Wenwu* 2003.6: 4–42; Shaanxi Sheng Wenwuju 陝西省文物局 et al., *Shengshi jijin: Shaanxi Baoji Meixian qingtongqi jiaocang* 盛世吉金: 陝西眉縣楊家村西周青銅器窖藏 (Beijing: Beijing Chubanshe, 2003).

9. For an in-depth treatment of this text, including a complete translation, see Lothar von Falkenhausen, "The Inscribed Bronzes from Yangjiacun: New Evidence on Social Structure and Historical Consciousness in Late Western Zhou China (*c.* 800 bc)," *Proceedings of the British Academy* 139 (2006): 239–95.

10. The following translation is informed by Li Ling 李零, "Du Yangjiacun chutu de Yu Qiu zhuqi" 讀楊家村出土的虞逑諸器, *Zhongguo lishi wenwu* 2003.4: 16–27; Li Xueqin 李學勤, "Meixian Yangjiacun xinchu qingtongqi yanjiu" 眉縣楊家村新出青銅器研究, *Wenwu* 2003.6: 66–73; and Wang Hui 王輝, "Qiu pan mingwen qianshi" 逑盤銘文淺, *Kaogu yu wenwu* 2003.3: 81–91.

述曰：

I, Qiu, proclaimed:

不（丕）顯朕皇高且（祖）單公，趩趩克明恕（哲）ᔕ（厥）德，夾
鹽文王、武王達殷，䧹受天魯令（命），匍有四方，並宅ᔕ（厥）堇
疆土，用配上帝。

My greatly manifest august high ancestor Shangong was able to watch courageously over his virtue and thus aid and assist Kings Wen and Wu in battering Yin, accepting and receiving Heaven's excellent mandate, holding fast to the four directions, establishing their residence within the territories they had labored [to conquer], and thereby being a counterpart of God on High. . . .

The proclamation continues through another six generations of ancestors down to Qiu himself. It concludes as follows:

述肇㡰朕皇且（祖）考服虔夙夕敬朕死事。辪（肆）天子多錫（賜）
述休，天子其萬年無疆，耆黃考，保奠周邦，諫辭（乂）四方。

I, Qiu, diligently have been continuing my august ancestors' and deceased father's service; devotedly by day and by night I have been reverently attending to my affairs of death-earnestness. Hence the Son of Heaven has in manifold ways bestowed his munificence on me, Qiu. May the Son of Heaven [live for] a myriad years without end, attaining great longevity, preserve and secure the Zhou kingdom, making order and governing the four directions.

Now follows the royal response.

王若曰：

The king approvingly said:

述！不（丕）顯文武，䧹受大令（命），匍有四方，則緐隹乃先聖且
（祖）考夾鹽先王爵堇大令（命）。今余隹𢆶乃先聖且（祖）考，䚏景
（就）乃令（命），令（命）女（汝）疋（胥）榮兌䢖（並）嗣（司）
四方吳（虞）䔲（林），用宮御。易（賜）女（汝）赤市（韍）、幽
黃（璜）、攸勒。

Qiu! That the greatly manifest [Kings] Wen and Wu accepted and received the great mandate and held fast to the four directions is due precisely to the fact that your former saintly ancestors and deceased father aided and assisted the former kings in exerting themselves and laboring on behalf of the great mandate. Now I, by way of following [the precedents of] your saintly ancestors and deceased father, extend and confirm your mandate. I order you to assist Rong Dui in comprehensively managing the Inspectors of the Forests of the four directions so that the temple-palaces be supplied. I bestow on you a red pendant and a dark-polished *huáng* jade as well as bronze-studded bridle gear.

The rest of the inscription concerns the aftermath of the exchange between Qiu and the king. Qiu's expression of gratitude leads into the Statement of Dedication, in which, at a later point in time, Qiu dedicates the inscribed vessel for use in sacrifices to his ancestors.

述敢對天子不（丕）顯魯休揚，用乍（作）朕皇且（祖）考寶尊盤。
I, Qiu, made bold in response to extol the Son of Heaven's greatly manifest excellent munificence, and on account of it I make for my august ancestors and deceased father a precious venerable *pan* basin. . . .

The Qiu *pan*'s announcement of merit comprises two transcribed oral statements, the first uttered by the donor and the second by the king. Earlier, such a document would have been interpreted as combining two unconnected episodes. Inscriptions of such composite character do exist.[11] But in this case, the king's mandate is obviously given in direct response to Qiu's proclamation, some of which is in fact repeated verbatim in the king's speech. Qiu's proclamation must thus be addressed to the king, not to the ancestors. The recorded exchange of speeches between Qiu and the king almost certainly took place at a court audience. The audience protocol in use during Zhou times stipulates an exchange in exactly the order reproduced in the text: a report from the person received in audience preceded the response from the host. Moreover, the phrase initiating the royal response — *wáng ruò yuē* 王若曰, here rendered as "The king approvingly said" — derives its significance from precisely this context.

One wonders how representative such a situation is for "announcements of merit in the subjective mode" in general, for none of the other known inscriptions beginning with a proclamation by the donor renders the patron's response as a transcribed oral utterance preceded by the verb *yuē*. All these inscriptions do, however, record the gist of such a response. As an example, let us consider the abridged version of the Qiu *pan* inscription inscribed on the Qiu *zhong* 述鐘 (XS: 772–75), a set of

---

11. The Hu *ding* 曶鼎 inscription is an example; see JC: 2838.

bells recovered in 1985 from another cache at Yangjiacun.[12]

Qiu *zhong* 逑鐘:

逑曰：

I, Qiu, proclaimed:

不（丕）顯朕皇考，克㽞（燮）明又（厥）心，帥用又（厥）先且（祖）考政德，享辟先王。逑卸（御）又（厥）辟不敢㒸（墜），虔夙夕，敬又（厥）死事。

My greatly manifest august deceased father could attentively brighten his mind and thereby take as his model the virtue [displayed in the fulfillment of their] official duties by his former ancestors and deceased father in offering respect to and protecting the former kings. I, Qiu, have taken over his [charge of] protecting; I dare not be neglectful; devotedly by day and by night, I reverently attend to my affairs of death-earnestness.

天子巠先且（祖）服，多易（賜）逑休，令（命）𦀳（籍）嗣（司）四方吳（虞）䔲（林）。

The Son of Heaven, following [the precedents of my] former ancestors' service, in manifold ways bestowed his munificence on me, Qiu, and he ordered me to manage comprehensively the Inspectors of the Forests of the four directions.

逑敢對天子不（丕）顯魯休揚，用乍（作）朕皇考龔叔龢鐘。

I, Qiu, made bold in response to extol the Son of Heaven's greatly manifest excellent munificence, and on account of it make my August Deceased Father Gongshu's harmonizing bells.

This inscription happens to refer to exactly the same event as the Qiu *pan*: the court audience during which Qiu was appointed as assistant to the

---

12. Liu Huaijun 劉懷君, "Meixian chutu yipi Xi Zhou jiaocang qingtong yueqi" 眉縣出土一批西周窖藏青銅樂器, *Wenbo* 1987.2: 17–25. Of the eight bells that originally constituted this chime, four were stolen during excavation. One of these is in the Cleveland Museum (ex collection Robert H. Ellsworth), reproduced in Robert H. Ellsworth, *Later Chinese Painting and Calligraphy, 1800–1950* (New York: Random House, 1987), 3:2. Another is in the Katherine and George Fan collection; see Shouyang Studio, Shanghai Museum, and Art Museum, The Chinese University of Hong Kong, *Ancient Chinese Bronzes from the Shouyang Studio* (Shanghai: Shanghai Shiji Chuban Gufen Youxian Gongsi and Shanghai Guji Chubanshe, 2008), 121–23, which explicitly mentions the Yangjiacun provenance of these bells.

chief official in charge of supervising the Inspectors of Forests throughout the Zhou realm. It is in fact an abbreviated version of the same text.[13] An earlier translation, now obsolete, considered the phrase beginning with "The Son of Heaven, following [the precedents of] my Former Ancestors. . ." as part of the donor's proclamation, taken as being directed to his ancestors,[14] but the Qiu *pan* inscription now makes it clear that this phrase summarizes the king's response to Qiu's oral proclamation. This response, marked as oral in the longer version of the text on the Qiu *pan*, is compressed into indirect speech in the *zhong* inscription; it is now Qiu who reports the king's words. Such retailoring of text may well have been common scribal practice, for example, when the space available for inscription did not allow — as it did on the Qiu *pan* — for a more complete transcription of the audience ritual.

It therefore seems safe to suggest that the one dozen or so other Western Zhou period inscriptions beginning with a donor's proclamation of the type "X *yuē*" are likewise abbreviated renderings of oral exchanges between donor and patron in an audience situation.[15]

There are also a few inscriptions that begin with an oral proclamation by the king, starting with either *wáng yuē* 王曰 'the king said', or the already mentioned phrase *wáng ruò yuē*, and conferring privileges and gifts upon the donor of the inscribed vessel.[16] As Li Chaoyuan has

---

13. Curiously, the Qiu *zhong* inscription leaves out the fact, noted on the Qiu *pan*, that Qiu was to serve as an *assistant*; this does not document a promotion as one might argue based on precedents discussed by Li Feng, but simply a textual abbreviation; see Li Feng, "Succession and Promotion: Elite Mobility during the Western Zhou," *Monumenta Serica* 52 (2004): 1–35. Qiu's appointment as assistant is cited in the inscription of another vessel from the 2003 Yangjiashan hoard, the Forty-third Year Qiu *ding* 四十三年逑鼎 (XS: 745–56), in which Qiu is promoted, but not to the headship of his department; instead his charge is expanded to include overseeing laborers (*lìrén* 歷人).

14. Falkenhausen, "Issues in Western Zhou," 159; in that study, I mistranscribed the donor's name as Mai 邁.

15. This finding also applies to the following inscriptions: Middle Western Zhou, Dong II-*ding* 茲鼎 (JC: 2824), Meng *gui* 孟簋 (JC: 4162–64), and Shenzi Tuo *gui* 沈子它簋 (JC: 4330); late Western Zhou, Guoshu Lü *zhong* 虢叔旅鐘 (JC: 238–44), Liang Qi *zhong* 梁其鐘 (JC: 187–92), Shanbo Haosheng *zhong* 單伯昊生鐘 (JC: 82), Shu Xiangfu Yu *gui* 叔向父禹簋 (JC: 4242), Yu *ding* 禹鼎 (JC: 2833–34), Xing *zhong* 癲鐘 (second group) (JC: 251–59), Xing *gui* 癲簋 (JC: 4170–77), and Da Ke *ding* 大克鼎 (JC: 2836).

16. Examples include the early Western Zhou Taibao *he* 太保盉 (JL: 942) and Taibao *lei* 太保罍 (JL: 987) (Zhongguo Shehui Kexueyuan Kaogu Yanjiusuo 中國社會科學院

observed, *wáng* 王 'the king' in Western Zhou bronze inscriptions is always to be taken in the third person.¹⁷ That none of the texts starting with *wáng yuē* or *wáng ruò yuē* could possibly be proclamations in the first person (such as "I, the king, proclaimed . . .") is evident also from the fact that the king is never the donor of the vessels on which they occur; the donors are, instead, the addressees of the royal announcements.¹⁸ Delivered in an audience context, the royal speeches recorded in these inscriptions are very probably responses to a preceding proclamation by the addressee, which for some reason — perhaps merely lack of space — were omitted. The Qiu *pan* renders the dialogue with a rare degree of completeness.

The foregoing analysis may account for about two dozen inscriptions in the known corpus: inscriptions in which either the donor's proclamation or the royal response (or, as in the sole case of the Qiu *pan*, both) are marked by the verb *yuē* as transcribed oral speech. But in a far larger number of inscriptions with long announcements of merit, the account of the conferral of privileges and gifts is marked by the clerical conventions that characterize Zhou written official documents.¹⁹ In announcements of

---

考古研究所 et al., "Beijing Liulihe 1193 hao damu fajue jianbao" 北京琉璃河1193號大墓發掘簡報, *Kaogu* 1990.1: 24–25), the middle Western Zhou Heng *gui* 恆簋 (cover) (JC: 4199–4200), and the late Western Zhou Hu *gui* 㝬簋 (JC: 4317), Maogong *ding* 毛公鼎 (JC: 2841), Xun *gui* 詢簋 (JC: 4321), Shi Yuan *gui* 師𡩜簋 (JC: 4313–14), and Shi Ke *xu* 師克盨 (JC: 4467–68).

17. Li Chaoyuan 李朝遠, "Xi Zhou jinwen zhong de wang yu wangqi" 西周金文中的王與王器, *Wenwu* 2006.5: 74–79. The same is, incidentally, true of the oracle bone inscriptions' usage of *wáng*.

18. The donor of the Hu *gui* (JC: 4317) has traditionally been taken to be King Li 厲王 (r. 857–840, d. 828 B.C.E.), but Li Chaoyuan has questioned this identification; Li Chaoyuan, "Hu gui wei Li wang zhi qi shuo xianyi" 㝬簋為厲王之器說獻疑, *Guwenzi yanjiu* 24 (2002): 220–24, and "Xi Zhou jinwen zhong de wang," 78. Li's ideas seem confirmed by this chapter.

19. Falkenhausen, "Issues in Western Zhou," 156–58. On such documents, which Edward L. Shaughnessy regards as the standard for all Western Zhou bronze inscriptions, see Huang Ranwei 黃然偉, *Yin Zhou qingtongqi shangci mingwen yanjiu* 殷周青銅器賞賜銘文研究 (Hong Kong: Longmen Shuju, 1978); Wang Zhongwen 汪中文, *Xi Zhou ceming jinwen suojian guanzhi yanjiu* 西周冊命金文所見官制研究 (Taipei: Guoli Bianyiguan, 1999); and He Shuhuan 何樹環, *Xi Zhou ximing mingwen xinyan* 西周錫命銘文新研, Wenshizhe Daxi, vol. 220 (Taipei: Wenjin Chubanshe, 2007). See also Edward L. Shaughnessy, *Sources of Western Zhou History: Inscribed Bronze Vessels* (Berkeley and Los Angeles: University of California Press, 1991), 73–85. The number of instances is too large to warrant an exhaustive listing here.

merit of this type, the audience context is made explicit. The texts begin with the date, continue with a formulaic description of the investiture ceremony, and conclude with the words of the charge, which often includes a list of gifts.

The above analysis of the Qiu *pan* inscription suggests that the steps in the audience protocol recorded in such documents were preceded by a proclamation by the one on whom the charge and gifts were conferred, to which the royal charge and gifts constituted a response. That this applies also to announcements of merit mimicking the wording of written documents is attested by the Da Ke *ding* 大克鼎 (JC: 2836), a famous late Western Zhou vessel now owned by the Shanghai Museum. Its inscription is the only other known instance besides the Qiu *pan* to mark both parts of the dialogue between the donor and his royal patron explicitly as oral utterances. As in the Qiu *pan* inscription, the donor's self-presentation and the king's response are initiated by the verb *yuē*, but here the response is preceded by clerical verbiage, emphasizing the official nature of the transcript.

Da Ke *ding* 大克鼎:

克曰：

I, Ke, proclaimed:

穆穆朕文且（祖）師華父悤讋乙（厥）心，宖靜于猷，盄（淑）悊乙（厥）德，肆（肆）克龏保乙（厥）辟龏王，諫辥（乂）王家，惠于萬民，柔（柔）遠能𤞷（邇），肆（肆）克昚（友?）[20] 于皇天，現于上下，𢍜屯（純）亡敃（愍），賜釐無疆，永念于乙（厥）孫辟天子。

My reverent accomplished ancestor Shi Huafu made his mind intelligent and modest, was quiet and calm in exerting his leadership, and made his virtue benevolent and well considered; therefore he was able respectfully to preserve his lord King Gong in making order and governing the royal family, being gracious to the myriad people as well as mild to those who were far and kind to those who were near; thereby enabling him [*sc*. King Gong] to be a companion (?) to August Heaven and diligent toward above and below, obtaining unadulterated absence of grief, bestowing awards without limit, and forever being remembered by his descendant my lord the [present] Son of Heaven.

20. A damaged character; I follow Lau's tentative reading. My translation of the royal gifts also follows Lau.

天子明恣，親孝于申（神）巠念ㄟ（厥）聖保且（祖）師華父，勔克王服，出內（入）王令，多易（賜）寶休。不（丕）顯天子。天子其萬年無疆，保辥周邦，叡尹四方。

The Son of Heaven is bright and enlightened and practices filial piety toward the spirits. Following [precedent] and remembering his saintly protector, my ancestor Shi Huafu, he has employed me, Ke, in the royal service with taking out and bringing in royal mandates; he has many times bestowed his precious munificence on me. Greatly manifest is the Son of Heaven; may the Son of Heaven for a myriad years without end preserve and govern the Zhou kingdom and unwaveringly rule over the four directions!

王在宗周。旦，王各穆廟，即立（位）。䚢（申）季右（佑）膳夫克入門立中廷，北鄉（嚮）。王乎（呼）尹氏冊令膳夫克。

The king was in Zongzhou. At dawn, the king went into the ancestral temple of King Mu and ascended the throne. Shenji assisted me, the Master of Viands Ke, in entering the gate and taking his position in the center of the courtyard, facing north. The king called out to the Lord Superintendent to appoint me, the Master of Viands Ke, with a written mandate.

王若曰：

The King approvingly said:

克！昔余既令女（汝）出內（入）朕令。今余佳䚢（申）𥃧（就）乃令（命），易（賜）女（汝）叔（淑）巿（珮），參冋苹恩，易（賜）女（汝）田于埜，易（賜）女（汝）田于渒，易（賜）女（汝）井（邢）㽙（宇）索田于眈以ㄟ（厥）臣妾。易（賜）女（汝）田于康，易（賜）女（汝）田于匽，易（賜）女（汝）田于𣸣原，易（賜）女（汝）田于寒山。易（賜）女（汝）史小臣、霝侖、鼓鐘。易（賜）女（汝）井（邢）逯索人，𩰲（並）易（賜）女（汝）井（邢）人奔于𣎆（量）。敬夙夜，用事，勿灋（廢）朕令（命）！

Ke! In the past I already ordered you to take out and bring in my mandates. Now I, by way of extending and confirming your mandate, bestow on you a cinnabar-colored pendant and a set of body-covering jades (?); I bestow on you fields at Ye; I bestow on you fields at Bei; I bestow on you Suo's fields that have been annexed by Xing at Yun, together with their male and female retainers; I bestow on you fields at Kang; I bestow on you fields at Yan; I bestow on you fields at Puyuan; I bestow on you fields at Hanshan; I bestow on you young servitors as scribes as well as wind-instrument players and percussion-instrument players; I bestow on you the retainers and Suo's people led by (?) Xing; and jointly with this I bestow on you the Xing people who have escaped to Liang. Be reverent by day and by night, use them in performing your affairs, do not abandon my mandate!

克拜稽首，敢對揚天子不（丕）顯魯休，用乍（作）朕文且（祖）師華夫寶䵼彝。

I, Ke, bowed and touched my head to the ground; I made bold in response to extol the Son of Heaven's greatly manifest excellent munificence; on account of it I make my accomplished ancestor Shi Huafu's precious meat-offering *ding* tripod. . . .[21]

Whereas the formulation of the Qiu *pan* inscription unambiguously suggests an oral dialogue, interestingly, the inscription on the Da Ke *ding* includes indications both of written recording and oral delivery. The most straightforward way to make sense of this is to assume that the written record of the mandate initiated by clerical language is the official transcript of a royal speech. This resonates with Virginia C. Kane's contention that the written versions of the royal mandates cited in the bronze inscriptions were secondary in importance and sacredness to the words that had issued from the king's mouth.[22] That some form of writ was nevertheless on hand during the audience is apparent from the technical term *cèmìng* 冊命, here rendered, following Li Feng, as "to appoint (an official) with a written document."[23] The word *cè* 冊, here used verbally, refers to the use of inscribed wooden or bamboo strips. The Da Ke *ding* inscription might be read as stating that the Lord Superintendent took down the king's words in writing as they were delivered, but in a departure from conventional readings, Martin Kern has argued that *cèmìng* in bronze inscriptions means not "take down the

---

21. This inscription is extensively discussed in Ulrich Lau, *Quellenstudien zur Landvergabe und Bodenübertragung in der Westlichen Zhou-Dynastie (1045?–771 v. Chr.)*, Monumenta Serica Monograph Series, vol. 41 (Nettetal: Steyler Verlag, 1999), 233–55. My translation differs in some respects from Lau's. As in the Qiu *pan* inscription, I consider the initial part of Ke's announcement as a grammatically pivotal sentence, thus taking the king (and not Ke) as the one who makes order, governs the royal family, and so on. Not only is this grammatically preferable, but it also seems to make better semantic sense as these actions are royal ones and not those of a mere functionary. Readers may furthermore take note of my treatment of the particle *wéi* 隹, which is often translated as the copula but serves principally to subordinate a clause grammatically to the following clause.
22. Virginia C. Kane, "Aspects of Western Zhou Appointment Inscriptions: The Charge, the Gifts, and the Response," *Early China* 8 (1982–83): 20.
23. Li Feng, "'Offices' in Bronze Inscriptions and Western Zhou Government Administration," *Early China* 26–27 (2001–2): 15–16 and passim.

mandate in writing" but "read aloud the writ of the mandate."[24] If Kern is correct, the Da Ke *ding* inscription would have to be interpreted in the sense that the Lord Superintendent read out a previously prepared document recording the king's oral reaction to Ke's self-presentation. In any case, it was through its oral delivery during the court audience that the royal mandate acquired its validity. A copy of the written version was later given to the awardee as a memorandum.

The interlude of clerical language between the marked oral utterances of Ke and the king conveys a greater sense of separation between the two speeches exchanged during the audience ritual than in the Qiu *pan* inscription, suggesting, perhaps, that some time elapsed between them. This would be compatible with the royal audience protocol known through transmitted sources. There is nevertheless no doubt that the king's statement responds to Ke's, as it takes up some of the exact same wording. This suggests that the contextual understanding offered above for inscriptions starting with the donor's proclamation applies as well to announcements of merit formulated in the "documentary mode."

Furthermore, the Qiu *pan* and Da Ke *ding* inscriptions, though exceptionally detailed in some of their formulations, are representative for most or all appointment inscriptions in their rendering of the dynamics between the donor and his patron in an audience context. It is true that the vast majority of announcements of merit include only the account of the royal charge, omitting the preceding proclamation by the donor, but this is perhaps not surprising if one considers that the former has a closer connection than the latter to the inscribed object. It was, after all, the appointments and rewards issued by rulers that provided the donor with the occasion and, often, the economic means for commissioning the inscribed objects (though it should be stressed that the bronzes themselves were never awarded as gifts on such occasions). By contrast, the donor's self-presentation was further removed from the part of the audience leading to the acquisition of the bronzes. Where an inscription renders such a self-presentation, it also at least summarizes the royal response, as in the Qiu *zhong* inscription.

The nuances await further research. Under what circumstances did

---

24. Martin Kern, "The Performance of Writing in Western Zhou China," in *The Poetics of Grammar and the Metaphysics of Sound and Sign*, ed. Sergio La Porta and David Shulman (Leiden: E. J. Brill, 2007), 109–76. Li Feng has kindly informed me that the same understanding is intended in his translation of *cèmìng* (personal communication, 2008).

donors give pride of place either (rarely) to their own self-presentation or (far more frequently) to the royal response? Why did they choose either (rarely) to render the royal charge as a transcribed oral utterance or (far more frequently) to couch it in the clerical language of official court documents? Why are relatively complete accounts such as those inscribed on the Qiu *pan* and the Da Ke *ding* so rare? Space available for inscription may well not be the only factor. At the same time, we cannot be sure that subtle differences in formulations that are puzzling to us today were meant in each case to convey profound authorial intentions.

The Audience Ritual in Canonical Texts

For a more comprehensive idea of the audience protocol, one may turn to the Confucian classics. The "Greater Elegantiae" (Daya 大雅) section of the *Book of Poetry* (Shijing 詩經) preserves a poem — "Jiang Han" 江漢 (Ode 262) — that renders an audience narrative analogous to that seen in bronze inscriptions with long announcements of merit.[25] The following translation departs somewhat from the traditional understanding of the poem. The text begins with an evocation of a successful Zhou military campaign in the southern regions, led by one Hu of Shao 召虎,[26] who later in the poem is identified as a descendant of Shaogong 召公, one of the founding heroes of the Zhou dynasty. When the campaign is over, the victory is reported to the king, presumably at an audience.

> "Jiang Han," *Book of Poetry* (Greater Elegentiae):
>
> 江漢浮浮。武夫滔滔。匪安匪舒。淮夷來求。
> 既出我車。既設我旟。匪安匪舒。淮夷來鋪。
>
> The Jiang and the Han [rivers] were amply-flowing;
> The warriors formed a mighty flow.
> There was no rest, no recreation;

---

25. *Shisanjing zhushu*, 18.4:573–74. The translation given below follows Bernhard Karlgren, *The Book of Odes* (Stockholm: Museum of Far Eastern Antiquities, 1950), 232–34, but with considerable modifications.
26. According to Shirakawa Shizuka 白川靜, this individual may be identical to the donor of the Fifth Year Shaobo Hu *gui* 五年召伯虎簋 (JC: 4292) and the Sixth Year Shaobo Hu *gui* 六年召伯虎簋 (JC: 4293); "Kinbun tsūshaku" 金文通釋, *Hakutsuru Bijutsukanshi* 白鶴美術館誌 (Kobe: Hakutsuru Bijutsukan, 1962–86), 33.194–95: 831–54.

The Huai tribes were coming to rob [from us]!

We brought out our carriage;
We raised our falcon-banners.
There was no rest, no leisure;
The Huai tribes were coming to harass [us]!

江漢湯湯。武夫洸洸。經營四方。告成于王。
四方既平。王國庶定。時靡有爭。王心載寧。

The Jiang and the Han were large-flowing;
The warriors formed a rushing flood:
Having regulated and disposed [of the regions of] the four quarters,
We reported [our] victory to the king:

[The regions of] the four quarters have been pacified;
The king's polities have all been established;
There is no longer any strife;
May the king's heart be at peace.

The last four lines of this stanza are the beginning of a proclamation by Hu at a royal audience, equivalent to the donor's self-presentations in some bronze inscriptions. Hu's proclamation continues in the following stanza. The text should be understood as Hu repeating the language of the royal mandate he had received before departing on his campaign.

江漢之滸。王命召虎。式辟四方。徹我疆土。
匪疚匪棘。王國來極。于疆于理。至于南海。

On the banks of the Jiang and the Han,
The king had charged me, Hu of Shao:
Open up [the regions of] the four quarters,
Tax my territories and soil,

Without distressing, without pressing [the people].
May the royal polities [come to =] rally around the pivot,
In the frontier areas, in the [tax-paying] settlements,
As far as the southern sea.

It is implied that Hu has fulfilled this charge. The following stanzas render the royal response with the conferral of gifts. To this, Hu responds in the ceremonially appropriate form (often identically recorded in bronze inscriptions) and ends by singing the king's praises.

王命召虎。來旬來宣。文武受命。召公維翰。
無曰予小子。召公是似。肇敏戎公。用錫爾祉。

The king charged me, Hu of Shao,
When I came to tell, when I came to announce [my achievements]:
When [Kings] Wen and Wu received the appointment [of Heaven],
The prince of Shao was their support.

Do not say: I am only a small child;
The prince of Shao, you are like him.
You have been active in your warlike endeavors;
Therefore I give you blessings.

釐爾圭瓚。秬鬯一卣。告于文人。錫山土田。
于周受命。自召祖命。虎拜稽首。天子萬年。

I give you a jade *gui* tablet and ladle,
And a *you* vessel of aromatic wine from black millet,
So that you may report to [the accomplished men =] your ancestors.
I give you hills, lands, and fields;

From Zhou you receive a charge;
It continues the charge of your ancestors in Shao.
I, Hu, made obeisance and bowed my head,
[Wishing] the Son of Heaven a myriad years.

虎拜稽首。對揚王休。作召公考。天子萬壽。
明明天子。命聞不已。矢其文德。洽此四國。

I, Hu made obeisance and bowed my head;
In response I extolled the king's grace.
By elevating the prince of Shao and my deceased father,
May the Son of Heaven live a myriad years!

Bright is the Son of Heaven,
May his good fame never cease;
Let us spread his fine virtue
And thus unite these polities of the four quarters.

Ode 262 is thought to have been performed as a hymn at Hu of Shao's lineage temple, during ancestral sacrifices that very possibly involved the use of bronze vessels with inscriptions referring to the same events. Like a bronze inscription, the poem is highly formulaic.[27] The military campaign

---

27. Shaughnessy accepts an emendation suggested by Arthur Waley by which this poem actually comes to commemorate the casting of a bronze tureen, but this is uncertain;

it refers to probably took place during late Western Zhou times.[28] When the text was written down is unclear; conceivably, poems like this circulated originally in oral form, and the main mode of transmission is likely to have remained oral even after the texts of the "Daya" odes had been committed to writing. But the bronze inscriptions attest that texts with similar phraseology were being written down as early as Western Zhou times.

A far more detailed protocol of an audience at the royal court may be found in the "Jinli" 覲禮 chapter of the *Yili* 儀禮, one of the Three Compendia on Ritual in the Classical canon. This text is unlikely to have been codified before the middle of Eastern Zhou, and its present form undoubtedly reflects a certain amount of idealization.[29] In addition to systematizing current practices, or obsolete practices that were still remembered, the authors of the Three Compendia reconstructed Zhou rites from available textual accounts describing practices that had already disappeared. Some of the information incorporated in the "Jinli" chapter may in fact have been culled from the *Book of Poetry* ode just quoted. Perhaps reflecting the shifts in political balance that had taken place by this time, "Jinli" describes a visit to the royal court by the ruler of an outlying principality (referred to in the text as *hóushì* 侯氏 'lord marquis' and hereinafter simply as "visitor"), whereas Western Zhou bronze inscriptions and Ode 262 mostly relate audiences of officials in the central government.[30] Even so, the ceremonial sequence described in "Jinli" offers some highly relevant parallels to what we read in the bronze inscriptions, making explicit some points that are only implied in the latter and thus helping to develop a more complete understanding.

Sources of Western Zhou History, 73–74.
28. The Mao 毛 preface connects the poem to a campaign against the Huaiyi 淮夷 'Barbarians' during King Xuan's reign; *Shisanjing zhushu* 18.4:305. For additional information on this campaign, see Li Feng, *Landscape and Power in Early China: The Crisis and Fall of the Western Zhou 1045–771 bc* (Cambridge: Cambridge University Press, 2006), 135–37.
29. William G. Boltz pertinently remarks that the "Jinli" chapter is unique among the extant *Yili* chapters in describing ceremonies involving the king and members of his administration. All others describe rituals allegedly performed by lower-ranking members of the Zhou aristocracy; "I li," in *Early Chinese Texts: A Bibliographical Guide*, ed. Michael Loewe (Berkeley: Society for the Study of Early China and Institute of East Asian Studies, University of California, Berkeley, 1993), 235. In its origin and history of transmission, the "Jinli" may thus differ from the other *Yili* chapters.
30. Audiences involving outside rulers do occasionally occur in Western Zhou bronze inscriptions; see Li Feng, *Landscape and Power*, 185–87.

The following summary with key passages quoted verbatim highlights those places where oral pronouncements are made and written documents are issued.[31]

Summary of "Jinli" in *Yili*:

1. *Arrival of the Visitor*. The visitor is greeted outside the gate of the capital by a royal envoy, who, in the course of a preliminary sacrifice at a makeshift altar platform (presumably directed at the divinities of the place), reads out to him (*orally*) the king's (*written*) greetings. The royal envoy is given rich presents by the Visitor, who thereafter enters the capital.

2. *Summons to the Audience*. The visitor is assigned lodgings. The king sends a magnate (higher-ranking than the previous envoy) with an (*oral* [?]) message summoning him to the initial audience ritual on a specific day.

3. *Sacrifice to the Royal Ancestors*. Before being received by the king, the visitor first places offerings at the ancestral temple of the royal house. From here, he travels in a carriage to the royal residence. The audience proper can now begin.

4. *Greetings and Report*. The king takes his position in front of a screen adorned with battle-axes in the main hall of his residence. The visitor, through a royal official, conveys (*orally*) his request for an audience, which is granted (*orally*). Then,

侯氏入門右，坐奠圭，再拜稽首。擯者謁。侯氏坐取圭，升致命。

the visitor enters on the right side of the Great Gate, kneels [in the center of the courtyard in front of the audience hall], puts down his pentagonal jade tablet, and twice bows and touches his head to the ground. The officer in charge of visitors communicates to him the king's (*oral*) welcoming words. The visitor, still kneeling, takes his jade tablet, ascends [to the audience hall], and delivers (*orally*) his mandate.

"Delivering the mandate" probably refers to the visitor's reporting on his fulfillment of a royal mandate previously received, either by himself or by his predecessor. (This may be equivalent to Shao Hu's repeating the wording of his original mandate when reporting back to the king in Ode 262.) The mandate is symbolized by the jade *gui*.

---

31. For the complete text with commentaries, see *Shisanjing zhushu* 26.2:1091–94. The text is translated in Séraphin Couvreur, 儀禮 *Cérémonial*, new ed. (Paris: Cathasia, 1951), 373–83.

王受之玉。侯氏降。階東，北面，再拜稽首。擯者延之，曰："升。"
升。成拜乃出。

> The king receives the jade tablet. The visitor descends. At the east of the steps, facing north, he twice bows and touches his head to the ground. The officer in charge of visitors invites him, saying: "Ascend" (*orally*). He ascends and completes his prostrations. Then he exits.

5. *Presentation of Tribute*. The visitor now presents his tribute (local products from his territory) in the courtyard of the audience hall; this is done in three stages, each one involving the use of a jade *bì* 璧 disk placed on layers of silk. Following another round of prostrations, the king announces (*orally*) through the officer in charge of visitors that he will accept the tributes. After this, the visitor again "ascends and (*orally*) delivers his mandate." Then the tributes are formally handed over to the king's officers, and the visitor exits again.

6. *Confession*. Reentering the courtyard, the visitor humiliates himself before the king, demanding (*orally*, through the officer in charge of visitors) punishment for his failings; the king (also *orally*, through the officer) absolves him. The visitor exits.[32]

7. *Commendation*. The visitor reenters the courtyard, this time on the left side of the Grand Gate.

入門左，北面立。王勞之，再稽拜首。

> He takes his position, facing north. The king commends him for his labors (*orally*). He twice bows and touches his head to the ground.

Again he is invited to ascend to the hall, where he completes his prostrations before exiting again.

8. *Presentation of Royal Gifts*. As a material token of the king's commendation, the visitor is rewarded with precious presents (the text mentions chariots, horses, and silk robes); their number is not fixed, giving

---

32. I suspect that this passage is a late insertion. In Classical Chinese thought, as Rolf Trauzettel has pertinently observed, "The concept of atonement and repenting was not truly available. . . . [To the thinkers of Confucius's time] what mattered solely was to avoid all deviant conduct from the very start." (Der Begriff der Sühne und Reue war eigentlich nicht vorhanden. . . . [Den Denkern der Konfuziuszeit] kam es einzig darauf an, alles Fehlverhalten von vornherein zu vermeiden.) See Rolf Trauzettel, "Grundsätzliches zur altkonfuzianischen Morallehre," in *Und folge nun dem, was mein Herz begehrt: Festschrift für Ulrich Unger zum 70. Geburtstag*, Hamburger Sinologische Schriften 8, ed. Reinhard Emmerich, Hans Stumpfeldt, et al. (Hamburg: Hamburger Sinologische Gesellschaft, 2002), 153.

the king leeway to show his generosity. The presentation takes place outside the Outer Gate of the palace (according to some commentators, at the visitor's lodgings).

9. *Presentation of Mandate*. The presentation of the new mandate also takes place at the visitor's lodgings, in an architectural setting mimicking that of the royal audience hall, albeit on a smaller scale.

諸公奉篋服，加命書于其上。升自西階，東面。大史是右。侯氏升，西面立。大史述命。侯氏降，兩階之間。北面，再拜稽首。升成拜。大史加書于服上。侯氏受。

The royal ministers present a basket containing ceremonial robes, with the (*written*) mandate writ placed on top. They ascend by the western steps, facing east. The Grand Scribe accompanies them on the right. The visitor ascends and takes position, facing west. The Grand Scribe reads (*orally*) the mandate aloud. The visitor descends. Between the two flights of steps, facing north, he twice bows and touches his head to the ground. He ascends to complete the prostrations. The Grand Scribe places the writ on top of the clothes. The visitor receives it.

The envoys leave, escorted by the visitor, who gives them rich presents.

10. *Aftermath*. The king offers the visitor a banquet, at which additional gifts are presented. (This is a separate ceremony, falling outside the purview of the "Jinli.") Then the visitor returns to his home.

An audience at the Zhou royal court — even when the king's political power was on the wane — was a vast synesthetic experience that engaged multiple performance media to communicate its central message, or messages, in many different yet mutually reaffirming ways. The dazzling display of royal prestige and the skills exhibited by the professional personnel in attendance were designed to awe the visitor, for whom such performances were presumably less of a routine than for his hosts.

For both sides, especially for the visitor, the audience as described in the "Jinli" constitutes a liminal experience. The ritual process marks a nodal point in time — isolated from the unstructured flow of events — with the goal of validating the past and building a basis for the future. It thus serves to reaffirm and strengthen sociopolitical relationships. Such relationships were expressed in terms of the seniority-based hierarchy built into the Zhou lineage system. In Eastern Zhou times, rulers of outlying polities were (or were assimilated into) the king's agnatic or collateral relatives (the "Jinli" and its commentaries prescribe and explain the appropriate forms of address expressing these relationships); the same was true during Western Zhou of the members of the administrative elite who appear in the bronze inscriptions.[33] A visitor's legitimacy as a ruler in his polity and an officials' authority in exerting the power of his office were iteratively legitimized through the ritual performance and physically manifested in the writ of the royal mandate. Even when an individual protagonist was new to the process, his ties were conceptualized as enduring ones that were being renewed, not initiated, with the expectation that they would be renewed again at regular intervals in the future.

Several poems in the *Book of Poetry* evoke a banquet following a court ceremony.[34] Contrasting to the affirmation of hierarchical relationships during an audience, the ensuing banquet emphasizes the community of the ruler and his subordinates, establishing an esprit de corps among elite members of different ranks that were related by agnatic or collateral ties (whether real or fictive). As Victor Turner has pointed out, this alternation of emphasis on separation and the (temporary) effacement of boundaries constitutes two mutually complementary aspects of ritual that operate jointly in bringing about a state of social and psychological equilibrium.[35] It is no accident that the "Jinli" also mentions a concluding banquet, but, perhaps as a sign of the increasing impermeability of social boundaries in Eastern Zhou, the king is not a participant, and if protocols of banquets elsewhere in the *Yili* are any indication,[36] it may have been a rather staid affair compared to the raucous drunkenness of the banquets described in the *Book of Poetry*.

---

33. The visitor's performance, before the beginning of the court audience, of a sacrifice to the royal ancestors — which in many cases would also have been the visitor's own ancestors — expresses this situation. Significantly, many of the audiences described in Western Zhou bronze inscriptions took place in the ancestral temple complexes dedicated to specific former Zhou kings, attesting the close relationship between the ancestral cult and the negotiation of social relationships among the living. See Tang Lan 唐蘭, "Xi Zhou tongqi duandai zhong de 'Kanggong' wenti" 西周銅器斷代中的 '康宮' 問題, *Kaogu xuebao* 1962.1: 15–48.
34. See, in the "Lesser Elegantiae" (Xiaoya 小雅) section of the *Book of Poetry*, "Changdi" 常棣 and "Famu" 伐木; in the "Greater Elegantiae" section, "Xingwei" 行葦; *Shisanjing zhushu* 9.2:407–9, 9.3:410–12, and 17.2:534–35.
35. Victor Turner, *The Ritual Process* (Ithaca, N.Y.: Cornell University Press, 1969).
36. E.g., in the "Yanli" 燕禮, in *Yili*; see *Shisanjing zhushu* 14:1014–18; 15:1020–27.

Parallels and Differences

In spite of the difference in date, the structural similarity between the audience narratives in long Western Zhou bronze inscriptions, Ode 262, and the "Jinli" is surely not fortuitous. Setting aside preliminaries (sections 1–3) and aftermath (section 10), the audience as reported by the "Jinli" can be divided into two main stages. Sections 4–6 represent the formal completion of the previous mandate, underlined by the presentation of tribute, with the visitor as the principal agent. During this stage, he enters the king's courtyard on the right side of the gate. Sections 7–9 represent the issuance of a new (or renewed) mandate, underlined by the bestowal of gifts. Now the king takes the initiative, and the visitor enters the courtyard on the left side of the gate.

The two stages mark a twofold exchange of messages and goods based on the *do ut des* principle: the visitor, in presenting tribute, expects to be given royal rewards, and the king bestows the latter in the expectation of future tribute. As is usual with gift exchange at political occasions, both sides primarily express social reciprocity, confirming the rank difference between them. The economic transaction accompanying the ceremony is likely to have been characterized by an asymmetry mirroring this difference in rank, for considerations of "face" — as well as, possibly, a political need for the higher-ranking side to redistribute wealth ostentatiously in order to secure the continued recognition of its power — dictated that the royal gifts should be more generous than any tributes brought in from the outside. Hence participation in a court audience tended to be economically beneficial to the lower-ranking party. Indeed, the presentation of tribute could be a foil for highly lopsided commercial transactions.[37]

Embedded in this reaffirmation of hierarchical sociopolitical ties is an

---

37. Such commerce under the guise of tribute may have been, in fact, the major form of long-distance trade in pre-imperial China; see Kwang-chih Chang, "Ancient Trade as Economy or as Ecology," in *Ancient Civilization and Trade*, ed. C. C. Lamberg-Karlovsky and Jeremy Sabloff (Albuquerque: University of New Mexico Press, 1975), 211–24; see also Thomas J. Barfield, *The Perilous Frontier: Nomadic Empires and China* (Cambridge: Basil Blackwell, 1989). For related reflections, see Eugene Cooper, "The Potlatch in Ancient China," *History of Religions* 22.3 (1982): 103–28; Constance A. Cook, "Wealth and the Western Zhou," *Bulletin of the School of African and Oriental Studies* 60.2 (1997): 253–93; and Eric C. Mullis, "Toward a Confucian Ethic of the Gift," *Dao* 7.2 (2008): 175–94.

exchange of oral pronouncements.[38] The visitor "delivers his mandate" in sections 4 and 5; the king responds in section 7. By way of a confirmation, a written version of that response is issued later, in section 9. Both types of messages — the visitor's report and the royal response — have their parallels in the announcements of merit of long Western Zhou bronze inscriptions: the donor's proclamation corresponds to the stage in the audience ritual represented by sections 4–6, the royal response, whether rendered as an oral statement or as a written document, to sections 7–9. Here, as in the "Jinli," the donor begins by displaying his unwavering loyalty, in response to which the king expresses his willingness to continue the relationship.

The overall structural correspondence between the "Jinli" protocol and the audience narrative in the bronze inscriptions is supported by several telling details. For instance, in the clerical accounts of audiences preserved in Western Zhou bronze inscriptions, the visitor never enters the courtyard alone but is always accompanied by a court official.[39] A certain Shenji 申季 performs this role for Ke in the Da Ke *ding* inscription. The technical term for what he does is *yòu* 右/佑, which means both "help" and "accompany" and has the additional connotation of "right-hand side." There is a synonymous verb, *zuǒ* 左/佐, which connotes the left, but interestingly, the bronze inscriptions never use *zuǒ*, implying that the assisting functionary was positioned on the visitor's right and the visitor entered the courtyard on the left. Now, the "Jinli" meticulously notes that the visitor, when "delivering the mandate" in section 4, enters on the right side of the gate; during this part of the ceremony, his escort presumably would have been placed to the left. Conversely, in section 7, when the king utters his commendation, the visitor enters on the left, with his escort presumably on the right; he remains on the left for the rest of the ceremonial sequence. If such right-left alternation was indeed practiced at the Western Zhou court, one would be able to infer that the clerical

---

38. As to how these pronouncements, when made in the appropriate ritual context, effectively produced the realities they refer to, see J. L. Austin, *How to Do Things with Words* (Cambridge, Mass.: Harvard University Press, 1969); as interpreted by Stanley J. Tambiah, "A Performative Approach to Ritual," in *Culture, Thought, and Social Action* (Cambridge, Mass.: Harvard University Press 1987), 17–59; further discussion in Catherine Bell, *Ritual Theory, Ritual Practice* (New York and Oxford: Oxford University Press, 1992), 37–47.
39. On the social connection between the *yòuzhě* 右者 and the appointee in Western Zhou appointment inscriptions, see Li, "'Offices' in Bronze Inscriptions," 38.

accounts of audience protocol inscribed on Western Zhou sacrificial bronzes all pertain to the later stages in the audience, corresponding to sections 7–9 in the "Jinli" sequence.[40] This would match perfectly the contents of these texts, given that they describe royal appointments and gifts.

Another noteworthy parallel is that in both the "Jinli" and the bronze inscriptions, writing is handed down only from the top. In the "Jinli," writing appears twice: in section 1, when the king sends his welcome in the form of a written document, thereby initiating the audience proceedings; and in section 9, when a representative of the king takes to the visitor's lodgings the written version of the royal mandate that had been issued orally in section 8. Bronze inscriptions with audience records couched in clerical language — which, as discussed above, probably cite written official documents — undoubtedly refer to the second of these occasions. What deserves emphasis here is that in the bronze inscriptions such clerical language never occurs in connection with the donors' proclamations. This perhaps not accidentally corresponds to the "Jinli" record that the visitor "delivered his mandate" orally.

There are also differences of detail. For instance, the "Jinli" text says nothing about any oral expressions of gratitude on the part of the visitor in acknowledgment of the mandate and gifts received. By contrast, both Ode 262 and virtually all relevant bronze inscriptions, following the end of the superior's announcement (whether explicitly marked as oral speech or not), state that the donor bowed, touched his head to the ground, and extolled his patron's munificence. Some bronze inscriptions make it explicit that this response was an oral one. One example is the inscription on the Hu gui 虎簋 cover, excavated in 1996 at Xigoucun 西溝村, Danfeng 丹鳳, in Shaanxi, and probably dating to the transition from middle to late Western Zhou.[41]

Hu gui 虎簋 cover:

---

40. On "right" and "left" in Early China, see Marcel Granet, *Études sociologiques sur la Chine* (Paris: Presses Universitaires de France 1953), 261–77.
41. Wang Hanzhang 王翰章, Chen Lianghe 陳良和, and Li Baolin 李保林, "Hu guigai ming jianshi" 虎簋蓋銘簡釋, *Kaogu yu wenwu* 1997.3: 78–80, 75. Also translated by Edward L. Shaughnessy, "New Sources of Western Zhou History: Recent Discoveries of Inscribed Bronze Vessels," *Early China* 26–27 (2001–2): 95, and Li Feng, "Succession and Promotion," 5–6.

隹卅年四月初吉甲戌，王在周新宫各（格）于大室。密叔内（入）右（佑）虎即立（位）。王乎（呼）入（内）史曰：册令（命）虎。曰：𩛥（在）乃且（祖）考事先王，嗣（司）虎臣，今令（命）女（汝）曰：更乃且（祖）考足（疋）师戯嗣（司）走马馭人眔五邑走马馭人，女（汝）毋敢不善于乃政。易（赐）女（汝）䆒市（韍）、幽黄（璜）、玄衣、㴱屯（纯）、鑾旂五日，用事。

It being the *jiǎxū* day in the first quarter (first auspiciousness) of the fourth month of the thirtieth year, the king, in the New Palace at Zhou, ascended to the Grand Hall. Mishu assisted me, Hu, in taking position. The king called out to the Inner Scribe, saying: "Issue a written mandate to Hu." He said: "When your ancestors and deceased father served the former kings, they supervised the tiger braves. Now I command you, saying: Replace your ancestors and deceased father by supporting Shi Xi in supervising the horse drivers and charioteers as well as the horse drivers and charioteers of the Five Townships. Dare not be unreliable in [the fulfillment of] your official duties. I bestow on you a white jade pendant, a dark-polished *huáng* jade, a dark robe with wavy-patterned (?) collar and cuffs, and a banner fitted with bronze jingles and adorned with five suns. Use these to perform your service."

虎敢拜稽首，對揚天子不（丕）㔻（丕）鲁休。虎曰：不（丕）顯朕剌（烈）且（祖）考龏（䵼）明，克事先王。辥（肆）天子弗望（忘）𠦪（厥）孫子，付𠦪（厥）尚（賞）官，天子萬年㽙（申）玆命。

I, Hu, made bold to bow and touched my head to the ground and in response extolled the Son of Heaven's incomparably excellent munificence. I, Hu, proclaimed: "My greatly manifest resplendent ancestors and deceased Father were attentive and bright, and they were able to serve the former kings. Therefore the Son of Heaven has not forgotten their descendant and son, and entrusted him with their long-standing official position. May the Son of Heaven extend this mandate for a myriad years!"

虎用乍（作）文考日庚䵼簋，子孫其寶用，夙夕享于宗。

I, Hu, on this account make this venerable ritual vessel for my accomplished Deceased Father of the sacrificial day *gēng*. May sons and grandsons forever treasure and use it, by day and by night offering sacrifice at the ancestral temple.

The triple marking of oral speech in the announcement of merit is unusually explicit. The first time, the speaker is certainly the king; the second time, the unmarked subject is either still the king or the Inner Scribe; the third *yuē* initiates a quote within a quote. The donor's own expression of gratitude, as well, is marked as oral. Interestingly, it somewhat resembles a donor's proclamation, and it may in fact repeat part of what the donor had already said during an earlier stage of the audience, not included in this inscription.⁴² The oral dialogue between host and guest during an audience may thus have involved more than just two episodes, but the guest's report followed by the host's response indubitably constituted the core component of the ceremony.

The audience protocol outlined above suggests a place in a ritual sequence for most of the numerous announcements of merit in Western Zhou bronze inscriptions in which the patron bestows privileges and presents on the donor. It also furnishes a blueprint for understanding those announcements of merit in which the proclamations of the two sides are not explicitly marked as oral utterances; in such inscriptions, the readership of these documents took for granted that these passages were transcribed speeches, even when — as in the case of the Qiu *zhong* inscription discussed above — the editing process had condensed them to such a point that their oral immediacy was lost.⁴³

Even though audience situations are overwhelmingly predominant, other kinds of ritual contexts are also documented in the bronze inscriptions. Long announcements of merit of Western Zhou date explicitly rendering oral utterances in non-audience situations include a marriage alliance,⁴⁴ an archery ritual,⁴⁵ a tilling ceremony followed by an archery ritual,⁴⁶ a ritual announcement,⁴⁷ the issuance of military orders,⁴⁸

---

42. Similar oral expressions of gratitude appear on the middle Western Zhou Ban *gui* 班簋 (JC: 4341) and on the late Western Zhou Wuji *gui* 無㠱簋 (JC: 4225–28). A much-telescoped version of what might have been a similar statement appears in the middle Western Zhou Da Shi Shi *ding* 大矢始鼎 (JC: 2792). Oral pronouncements of gratitude also appear with female superiors on the Man [?] *ding* 䗑鼎 (JC: 2765) and the Neishi Ling X *ding* 內史令㝬鼎 (a.k.a. X *ding* 㝬鼎; JC: 2696). In the Xian Ji *gui* 縣改簋 inscription (JC: 4269), a female beneficiary orally thanks her male sponsor.
43. In the Ban *gui* inscription (see note 42), the king issues mandates to four individuals during what seems to be one and the same court audience (or at any rate parallel events), yet only one of the king's speeches — the fourth — is preceded by *yuē*. Rather than assuming a profound intention for the omission of *yuē* in the other three cases, I would interpret this as showing that the drafters cared little about whether or not the originally oral nature of the transcribed utterances was made explicit.
44. Xian Ji *gui* 縣改簋 (JC: 4269).
45. Kuang *you* 匡卣 (JC: 5423).
46. Ling *ding* 令鼎 (JC: 2803).
47. He *zun* 冋尊 (JC: 6014).
48. Duoyou *ding* 多友鼎 (JC: 2835), Chen Jian *gui* 臣諫簋 (JC: 4237).

legal disputes,⁴⁹ and oaths.⁵⁰ Analogously composed passages in Eastern Zhou inscriptions include an announcement to the dead in the netherworld⁵¹ and a discourse on political philosophy.⁵² In each of these situations, oral pronouncements were made (and recorded) according to the respective ritual procedures, but the court audience is the only instance for which the evidence at hand permits reconstructing the protocol.

The Expression of the King's Grace

The reconstruction of the audience context suggests a resolution to an age-old philological debate. In the lead-in clauses to a minority of patrons' speeches in the bronze inscriptions, the character *ruò* 若 is inserted between the subject and *yuē*, the most frequent combination being *wáng ruò yuē* 王若曰.⁵³ This phrase also occurs in some of the early chapters of the *Book of Documents* (Shangshu 尚書), where it initiates a royal proclamation.⁵⁴ There is no disagreement as to matters of grammar — *ruò* is used as an adverb, modifying *yuē* — but with regard to semantics, a panoply of ingenious interpretations has been proposed. The simplest reading is to take *ruò* in the sense that it most commonly has in Classical Chinese, "like this," yielding the meaning "Thus spoke the king" for *wáng*

---

49. Hu *ding* 曶鼎 (JC: 2838), Da *gui* 大簋 II (JC: 4298–99), Fifth Year Shaobo Hu *gui* (JC: 4292), Fifth Year Wei *ding* 五祀衛鼎 (JC: 2832), and Ninth Year Wei *ding* 九年衛鼎 (JC: 2831).
50. Sanshi *pan* 散氏盤 (JC: 10176), Guo Cong *gui* 虢从簋 (JC: 4278), Guo You Cong *ding* 虢攸从鼎 (JC: 2818), and Sheng *yi* 儕匜 (JC: 10285).
51. Ai Chengshu *ding* 哀成叔鼎 (JC: 2782).
52. Zhongshanwang Cuo *fanghu* 中山王𰻝方壺 (JC: 9735).
53. Aside from appearing on the Qiu *pan* and the Da Ke *ding*, this phrase occurs in inscriptions on the early Western Zhou period Da Yu *ding* 大盂鼎 (JC: 2837); the middle Western Zhou period Lubo Dong *gui* 彔伯㺇簋 (cover; JC: 4302), Mu *gui* 牧簋 (JC: 4343), and Shi Hu *gui* 師虎簋 (JC: 4316); and the late Western Zhou period Cai *gui* 蔡簋 (JC: 4340), Hu *ding* (JC: 2838), Haosheng *zhong* 昊生鐘 fragments (JC: 104–5), Maogong *ding* (JC: 2841), Shi Yuan *gui* 師寰簋 (JC: 4313–14), Shi Ke *xu* (JC: 4467–68), Shi Li *gui* 師釐簋 (JC: 4324–25), Shi Xun *gui* 師訇簋 (JC: 4342), Xun *gui* 訇簋 (JC: 4321), and Yang *gui* 揚簋 (JC: 4294–95). Its increasing frequency over the Western Zhou period may indicate developments in court ceremonial necessitating an explicit categorization of who was in the king's good graces.
54. For example, at the beginning of "Dagao" 大誥 and "Kanggao" 康誥 in the *Book of Documents*; *Shisanjing zhushu* 13:197; 14:202.

ruò yuē.⁵⁵ This may well be correct. But probing into a possible semantic difference between the phrases X *ruò yuē* and X *yuē*, commentators have additionally hypothesized that whenever *ruò* is used, the subject of the sentence — the patron making the speech — was not actually present at the scene or was not visible to the donor; that the pronouncement was made by someone else in his stead; that it was written down and then read; or that the superior's words were not exactly reproduced.⁵⁶ Another explanation is graphically based; embracing Luo Zhenyu's explanation of the character *ruò* as it appears in the oracle bone and bronze inscriptions as the figure of a kneeling human figure with disheveled hair and waving arms, K. C. Chang has suggested that phrases beginning with *wáng ruò yuē* were pronounced by the king during a shamanistic ritual in a state of trance.⁵⁷

The realization that the *ruò yuē* phrase always initiates a *response* — for example, the response to a supplicant's ritual discourse pronounced in an audience context (even though that discourse is not always included in the text) — suggests a different line of explanation. One should note, to

---

55. For example, Karlgren, "Glosses of the Book of Documents," 279; see also Lau, *Quellenstudien*, 233–55. Legge comments: "[*ruò yuē*] intimates that what follows is not all in the exact words of the king, but the substance of what he said. Others will have it that the [*ruò*] is appropriate in the mouth of a minister speaking in the name of the sovereign, as we shall find it several times in the [Zhou period chapters of the *Book of Documents* (Shangshu 尚書)]; but even there the [*ruò*] = 'substantially thus.' " See James Legge, *The Shoo King*, vol. 3 of *The Chinese Classics* (Oxford: Clarendon Press, 1865; repr., Taipei, Southern Materials Center, 1991), 225, and cf. also 363.
56. Dong Zuobin 董作賓, "Wang ruo yue guyi" 王若曰詁義, *Shuowen yuekan* 4 (1944): 335–40; Shirakawa, "Kinbun tsūshaku," 12.61:649; Yu Xingwu 于省吾, "Wang ruo yue shiyi" 王若曰釋義, *Zhongguo yuwen* 1966.2: 147–49, 136; Chen Mengjia 陳夢家, "Wang ruo yue kao" 王若曰考, in *Shangshu tonglun* 商書通論 (Beijing: Zhonghua Shuju, 1985), 146–70.
57. Kwang-chih Chang, "Shang Shamans," in *The Power of Culture: Studies in Chinese Cultural History*, ed. Willard J. Peterson, Andrew H. Plaks, and Ying-shih Yü (Hong Kong: Chinese University Press, 1994), 20; this point of view has been greatly elaborated upon by Wang Zhankui 王占奎, "'Wang ruo yue' budang jiezuo 'Wang ruci shuo'" '王若曰' 不當解做 '王如此說', in *Zhou Qin wenhua yanjiu* 周秦文化研究 (Xi'an: Shaanxi Renmin Chubanshe, 1998), 359–77. I suspect that the original meaning of the character *ruò* is contained in the *Shuowen* explanation as "pulling vegetables"; *Shuowen jiezi zhu* (Shanghai: Shanghai Guji Chubanshe, 1981), 43. Its usage as a grammatical particle "as if" — and also its early usage in the meaning of "to approve," later differentiated by the addition of another radical — exemplify the "rebus" principle; see "Literacy and the Emergence of Writing in China," by William G. Boltz, chapter 2 in this volume.

begin with, that (1) X *ruò yuē* never introduces a donor's self-presentation but only (and only on relatively rare occasions) introduces speeches made by a patron, almost always the king[58] and (2) whenever the patron's speech is broken up into a string of separate marked utterances, *ruò* is invariably found only in the first. The latter fact should have given pause to the advocates of some of the earlier explanations: it would be awkward to posit that the initial pronouncement, which is invariably the most important, is given in approximate terms, or through an intermediary, whereas later on during the same harangue, the king would have addressed the donor directly.[59]

Luo Zhenyu's phonetically unproblematic gloss of *ruò* (*njak) as *nuò* 諾 (*nak)[60] 'to approve' seems best to fit the audience situation in which the phrase *ruò yuē* has its place. In these contexts, *ruò yuē* — or rather, *nuò yuē* — clerically expresses that the patron is pleased with the speech the donor has delivered. Being in the good graces of one's superior may well have been an official mark of distinction.

The little-known inscription on the Fu Gong Zhong *gui* 復公仲簋 cover, made for a female beneficiary during the late Spring and Autumn period, seems to corroborate this understanding by appending a direct object to *ruò*.[61] The text, albeit brief, is somewhat obscure.

Fu Gong Zhong *gui* 復公仲簋 (JC: 4128) cover:

復公仲若我曰：其擇吉金，用作我子孟姆婦X尊媵簋，其萬年永壽用羞萬邦。

---

58. Very rarely, the phrase is used with the subject being a superior other than the king; examples include the Ni *zhong* 逆甬鐘 (JC: 60–63) and Shi Hui *gui* 師毀簋 (JC: 4311).
59. In the Maogong *ding* inscription, for instance, a pronouncement beginning with "*wáng ruò yuē* . . ." is succeeded by four pronouncements beginning with "*wáng yuē* . . ."; in the Da Yu *ding*, by three, and in the Mu *gui*, Shi Ke *xu*, and Shi Xun *gui*, by one each (for references, see note 53).
60. Luo Zhenyu 羅振玉, *Zengding Yinxu shuqi kaoshi* 增訂殷墟書契考釋 (privately published, 1914), 2:56a; followed by *Jishi*, 6:2051–57. Phonetic reconstructions as in Schuessler, *A Dictionary of Early Zhou Chinese*, lemma *yuē*.
61. The *gui* cover is in the collection of the Palace Museum, Beijing; no photograph has been published. The *Yin Zhou Jinwen Jicheng*, which published its inscription for the first time, dates it to the Late Spring and Autumn period. Although the connoisseurship of the *Yin Zhou Jinwen Jicheng* compilers is generally to be trusted, one should verify the authenticity of this inscription before building too much of an argument on it. Besides, caution is in order when using an Eastern Zhou inscription to solve a Western Zhou problem.

Fu Gong Zhong, approving of Wo,[62] said: "May auspicious metals be selected; with them I make for Wo's child Meng Mu (?) Fu X [damaged character] this venerable dowry-*gui* vessel. May she for a myriad years enjoy eternal longevity and with it present ceremonial gifts (?)[63] to the myriad polities."

Aside from this example, the use of *ruò/nuò* in the phrase "X *yuē*" ceased in the Eastern Zhou period, when the audience dialogue seems no longer to have been the main point of reference in announcements of merit, and the ritually framed dialogue between supplicant and ruler gave way to unilateral proclamations of rulers.[64] This development illustrates the sociopolitical changes that had taken place since Western Zhou times.

Preserving the Memory of the Audiences

How were these various oral pronouncements made during such audiences committed to writing? Neither the bronze inscriptions nor Ode 262 yields any direct information on this point. In the "Jinli," it is perhaps relevant to

---

62. *Wǒ* 我 in this instance is most likely the donor's personal name. A translation of *wǒ* as the first-person pronoun is also possible; it would run "Fu Gong, approving of me, said: 'May [you] select auspicious metals.' With them I make for my daughter...." But in such a case, aside from other awkwardnesses, the sponsor would fail to give his own name, referring to himself only by the first-person pronoun; this is unheard of. *Wǒ* does occur as a personal name in other bronze inscriptions, such as those of the late Shang Wo *fangding* 我方鼎 (JC: 2763) and the early Western Zhou Shu Wo *ding* 叔我鼎 (JC: 1930).
63. The character 丑, here provisionally rendered as *xiū* 羞, needs further study.
64. Nevertheless, proclamations prefaced by the expression "X *yuē*" (sometimes preceded by a date) continued to be inscribed. For an interpretation of some of them, see "Education and the Way of the Former Kings," by Constance A. Cook, chapter 9 in this volume. Examples include the Qingong *zhong*, *bo*, and *gui* 秦公鐘、鎛、簋 (JC: 262–70, 4315); the Jin Jiang *ding* 晉姜鼎 (JC: 2826), Jingong *dian* 晉公奠 (JC: 10342), Rongsheng *zhong* 戎生鐘 (Li Xueqin, "Rongsheng bianzhong lunshi" 戎生編鐘論釋, *Wenwu* 1999.9: 75–82), and Lü X *zhong* 呂驫鐘 (JC: 225–37); the Chen Fang *gui* 陳賆簋 (cover; JC: 4190), Chen Ni *hu* 陳逆瑚 (JC: 4629–30), and Chenhou Yinzi *dui* 陳侯因齊敦 (JC: 4649); and the Caihou Shen *bo* 蔡侯申鎛 (JC: 210–22), Jia'er *zhong* 遱兒鐘 (which also includes a prefatory account of the donor's descent; JC: 183–86), Zhachao *zhong* 黿巢鐘 (Feng Shi 馮時, "Zhachao zhong mingwen kaoshi" 黿巢鐘銘文考釋, *Kaogu* 2000.6: 73–78), and Pei'er-*goudiao* 配兒句鑃 (JC: 427).

note that the writ of the royal mandate is issued late in the ritual sequence, and at the visitor's lodgings rather than at the royal court; this indicates, perhaps, that documents had not been prepared in advance when the visitor showed up for his audience but instead were produced by the king's clerical staff during or after the oral proclamation of the royal mandate.

Whereas the royal mandates eventually took the form of written documents, the proclamations made by the visitor during an audience — whether at the initial "delivering of the Mandate" or at the concluding expression of thanks — appear not to have been scripted. They are, however, highly formulaic, similar to the appended prayers in the final statements of purpose of the bronze inscriptions, as well as, perhaps more importantly, to the ritual hymns of the *Book of Poetry*.[65] Their stilted, grandiloquent phraseology is likely to have differed greatly from everyday speech and should perhaps be considered as the reflection of a specialized ritual idiom, as exists in many places in the ethnographic present (e.g., in Southeast Asia).[66] Mastery of this ritual idiom may have been a precondition for being received in audience by one's superior, and the scribes charged with producing texts for inscription on ritual bronzes certainly were conversant in it.[67] During Eastern Zhou times, as the *Zuo zhuan* 左傳 and the *Tales of the States* (Guoyu 國語) amply report, the skillful manipulation of memorized verses in the *Book of Poetry* was the major criterion of success in court speeches. The handling of stock phrases from the Zhou ritual language as recorded in the bronze inscriptions may represent an early stage in the formation of this culture of sophisticated rhetoric.

The audience narratives in the bronze inscriptions testify to a custom, in existence since middle Western Zhou times at the latest, of transcribing and preserving oral utterances made in connection with governmental

---

65. Xu Zhongshu 徐中舒, "Jinwen guci shili" 金文嘏辭實例, *Zhongyang yanjiuyuan lishi yuyan* yanjiusuo *jikan* 6.1 (1936): 1–44.
66. Tambiah, *Culture, Thought, and Social Action*, 17–59, 123–66; James J. Fox, "Semantic Parallelism in Rotinese Ritual Language," *Bijdragen tot de Taal- Land-, en Volkenkunde* 127 (1971): 215–55.
67. Ching-hsien Wang proposed to interpret the *Book of Poetry* poems as improvised oral poetry with the categories established in mid-twentieth-century Homeric scholarship; *The Bell and the Drum: Shih ching as Formulaic Poetry in an Oral Tradition* (Berkeley: University of California Press, 1974). See also David Schaberg, *A Patterned Past: Form and Thought in Early Chinese Historiography* (Cambridge, Mass.: Harvard University Press, 2001), 72–80, 234–243, 315–324, et seq.

activity, for example, during audiences at the royal court. Such transcripts should be kept conceptually separate from the writs of the mandate issued to the appointee. Unlike the latter, these utterances could include both the supplicant's self-presentation and the superior's response. They must have been at the disposition of the scribes in charge of composing the bronze inscriptions. Since we do not have the transcripts themselves, but only those portions that were secondarily incorporated into bronze inscriptions, it is now impossible to know how closely they adhered to their oral subtexts, but the inscriptions discussed herein (and many others listed in the footnotes) amply allude to the originally oral conveyance of their contents.

The mechanics of the transformation of oral pronouncements into written text requires a separate study. Without going deeply into the issue, it seems safe to note that the task of producing and archiving the transcripts must have constituted a significant challenge to the literate personnel at the Zhou court. Over time, it necessitated an increase in the number of professionals able to handle writing, thus contributing to the spread of literacy as well as, indirectly, to the expansion of the scope of writing outside the ritual and administrative realms.[68] If the wording and grammar of the utterances made during audience ceremonies resembled what can now be read in the bronze inscriptions, it would follow that the above-mentioned specialized ritual idiom was actually used at the Zhou court. Alternatively, it is possible that the speeches were comprehensively rewritten in order to make them more "correct." Or, since it is unlikely that stenography existed at this early stage of literate practice in China, the present highly formalized appearance of the texts might result simply from the scribes' limited speed in taking down speeches as they were being delivered, causing them to record only the essential points and recompose them as stock phrases.

The custom of fixing in writing what was said at court must have been an important factor in the early transmission of documents that eventually found their way into the early Classical texts. It prefigured the textual practices that preserved the grand court speeches transmitted in the *Zuozhuan* and the *Tales of the States*,[69] and it is very probably ancestral to

---

68. For the later stages of these developments, see "Soldiers, Scribes, and Women: Literacy among the Lower Orders in Early China," by Robin D. S. Yates, chapter 10 in this volume; Mark Edward Lewis, *Writing and Authority in Early China* (Albany: State University of New York Press, 1999).
69. Schaberg, *A Patterned Past*; Yuri Pines, *Foundations of Confucian Thought:*

later literate practices, such as the keeping of the "veritable records" (*shílù* 實錄) at the courts of imperial China, Korea, and other East Asian countries.

Intellectual Life in the Chunqiu Period (Honolulu: University of Hawai'i Press, 2002).

CHAPTER 8

Literacy and the Social Contexts of Writing in the Western Zhou

Li Feng

The archaeological evidence suggests that the Western Zhou (1045–771 B.C.E.) was a crucial period in the expansion of literacy in China, or, broadly speaking, in East Asia. A good indication of this process is the discovery of Western Zhou bronze vessels and weapons inscribed with written texts all over North China and a part of South China,[1] posing a sharp contrast to the Shang period, for which evidence of literacy has been found in few sites outside Anyang.[2] In the three centuries following the

---

1. On the geography of Western Zhou bronze inscriptions, see Li Feng, *Landscape and Power*, 27–90, 300–346. There are strong signs that many of these inscriptions were cast locally, even in non-Zhou cultural contexts. On this point, see Li Feng, "Literacy Crossing Cultural Borders: Evidence from the Bronze Inscriptions of the Western Zhou Period (1045–771 B.C.)," *Bulletin of the Museum of Far Eastern Antiquities* 74 (2002): 210–421, esp. 237–39.
2. See "Literacy to the South and East of Anyang in Shang China: Zhengzhou and Daxinzhuang," by Ken-ichi Takashima, chapter 4 in this volume, 141-72. Inscribed bronzes of the Shang period have been found in more sites than the oracle bones and shells, but their inscriptions are limited to ancestral titles or clan signs, displaying no grammar or syntax (in contrast with longer inscriptions on the bronzes from Anyang, e.g., those of tomb no. 1713). In other words, they are not indicative of substantial local literacy. See, for instance, inscribed bronzes from Lingshi 靈石 in Shanxi and from Luoshan 羅山 in southern Henan; Shanxi Sheng Kaogu Yanjiusuo 山西省考古研究所 et al., "Lingshi Jingjiecun Shang mu" 靈石旌介村商墓, *Wenwu* 1986.11: 7; Henan Sheng Xinyang Diqu Wenguanhui 河南省信陽地區文管會 et al., "Luoshan Tianhu Shang Zhou mudi" 羅山天湖商周墓地, *Kaogu xuebao* 1986.2: 173. On tomb no. 1713, see Zhongguo Shehui Kexueyuan Kaogu Yanjiusuo Anyang Gongzuodui 中國社會科學院考古研究所安陽工作隊, "Anyang Yinxu xiqu 1713 hao mu de fajue" 安陽殷墟西區1713號墓的發掘, *Kaogu* 1986.8: 703–16.

Western Zhou collapse, even elites of the newly rising states in the southeastern coastal regions were fully adapted to the Zhou culture of writing and inscribing.[3] However, literacy did not merely expand across geographical space but also penetrated different realms of Western Zhou society. Although literacy admittedly remained in the possession of the social elites, whose number was by all accounts small, there were varying social contexts that involved the roles of the elites who needed the service of and appreciated the art of writing and reading.[4]

This chapter looks into the evidence of writing currently available from the Western Zhou period — the bronze inscriptions — for direct evidence that can help clarify a broad range of the social contexts of writing with a focus on written documents used for administrative purposes. The examination begins with evidence in the bronze inscriptions that indicates documents possibly of perishable media were produced, handled, or transmitted on particular occasions during the Western Zhou. Some of these documents were copied onto the bronzes and thus became part of the inscriptions, while many others might have remained on wooden or bamboo strips that did not survive.[5] This is followed by a new reading of the famously long and difficult inscription on the Sanshi *pan* 散氏盤 (JC: 10176), which suggests important insights into the circumstances under which the text was written, signed, and eventually transferred to bronze. The last part of the chapter discusses the meaning of the bronze inscriptions themselves as evidence of literacy in different social contexts in which the "metal texts" were presented, displayed, and understood by the Zhou elites.

Although writing was elite-oriented, its role in Western Zhou society was far more central than marginal or inconsequential. Particularly in the sphere of administration, writing was the indispensable means by which the Zhou government operated, and scribal activities constituted a constant path to political-administrative authority. On the social level, written documents were the bearers of social relations as well as guarantors of contracted economic transactions. The bronze inscriptions, being themselves hallmarks of an "elite literacy," provided a suitable arena for

---

3. See "Education and the Way of the Former Kings," by Constance A. Cook, chapter 9 in this volume, 302-36, particularly on the Yue inscription.
4. Edward L. Shaughnessy commented on the extent of writing during the Western Zhou in "Western Zhou History," in *The Cambridge History of Ancient China*, ed. Loewe and Shaughnessy, 297–99.
5. For scenarios of writing recorded in the transmitted texts, see Kern, "The Performance of Writing," 122–26, 155–57.

the cross-context presentation of their inscribed contents, channeling them to a much larger social circle of Western Zhou elites beyond their immediate owners. Thus, the sphere of "elite literacy" in Western Zhou society might have been meaningfully larger than what has been described as a "scribal literacy."[6]

Social Functions of Writing in the Western Zhou

A recent analysis of Shang writing posits, by pure reasoning, a series of social contexts in which writing "might have been" used, but it concludes that, because in such cases writing was executed on perishable materials, we do not have evidence of it.[7] Instead of trying to list all possible circumstances in which writing "might have been" employed during the Western Zhou, this chapter looks directly into the Western Zhou bronze inscriptions for records that describe the actual use of specific types of written documents or certificates in Western Zhou society.[8] Although the picture constructed on the basis of these inscriptions is far from complete, each case adds a concrete building block to our understanding of both the social functions of writing during the Western Zhou and the expansion of literacy in general.

Writing at the Zhou Central Court

So far, the best evidence for the use of written documents in the Zhou central administration comes from a group of six appointment inscriptions: the Song *ding* 頌鼎 (JC: 2829), the Forty-second Year Lai *ding* 四十二年逨鼎 (a.k.a. Qiu *ding* 逑鼎; XS: 745), the Forty-third Year Lai *ding* 四十三年逨鼎 (XS: 747), the Mian *gui* 免簋 (JC: 4240), the Yuan *pan* 裏

---

6. William Harris defined "scribal literacy" as a "literacy restricted to a specialized social group which used it for such purpose as maintaining palace records"; see Harris, *Ancient Literacy*, 7.
7. These include management of agriculture, muster rolls of troops, operation of bronze foundries, land survey, contracts, trade and other commerce, records of the king's activities, communication with outlaying polities and settlements, and so on; Bagley, "Anyang Writing," 190–261, esp. 223–24.
8. For a recent attempt to identify writing in administrative and economic contexts of the Western Zhou in comparison to Mesopotamia, see Wang, "Writing and the State," 215–34. Unfortunately, Wang's work, which lacks grounding in the scholarship of bronze inscriptions, has missed most of the evidence discussed here.

盤 (JC: 10172), and the Feng *ding* 趞鼎 (JC: 2815). These inscriptions mention a type of document called the "document of royal command" (*wángmìngshū* 王命書) and describe the specific circumstances of the court ritual of official appointment in which this pre-prepared written order was handled and transferred. The fullest presentation of such context is found in the inscription of the Song *ding*:

惟三年五月既死霸甲戌，王在周康邵宮。旦，王格太室，即位。宰弘右頌入門，立中庭。尹氏受王命書，王呼史虢生冊命頌。王曰："頌！命汝官嗣成周貯二十家，監嗣新造貯，用宮御。賜汝玄衣黹純，赤市，朱黃，鑾旗，攸勒，用事。"頌拜頓首，受命冊，佩以出。反入瑾璋。頌敢對揚天子丕顯魯休，用作朕皇考龏叔皇母龏姒寶尊鼎。用追孝，祈匄康䚻純佑，通祿永命。頌其萬年眉壽，畯臣天子。零終。子子孫孫寶用。

It was the third year, fifth month, after the dying brightness, *jiǎxū* (day 11). The king was in Kang Shao Gong in Zhou. At dawn, the king entered the grand chamber and assumed his position. Superintendent Hong accompanied Song to his right, entering the gate and standing in the center of the courtyard. The Chief (Interior Scribe) received the document of royal command, and the king called out to Scribe Guosheng to command Song with the written document. The king said: "Song! [I] command you to take office in charge of the storage of twenty households in Chengzhou,[9] and to inspect and supervise the newly constructed storage house, using palace attendants. [I] award you a black jacket with brocaded hem, red knee pads, a scarlet semi-circlet, a jingle-bell pennant, and a bridle with bit and cheek-pieces, with which to serve!" Song bowed with his head touching the ground, received the bamboo document of royal command, hung it [on his body], and came out [of the courtyard]. He then returned and brought in a jade tablet. Song dares in response to extol the Son of Heaven's illustriously fine beneficence, herewith making [for] my august deceased father Gongshu and august mother Gong Si [this] treasured sacrificial *ding*-vessel. [It] will be used to pursue filial piety, to pray for peaceful harmony, pure blessings, pervading wealth, and eternal mandate. May Song for ten thousand years enjoy abundant longevity, and serve the Son of Heaven, with no end. [May Song's] sons' sons and grandsons' grandsons treasure and use [it]!

---

9. The meaning of "twenty households" here is not very clear. In Ma Chengyuan's 馬承源 interpretation, it refers to an area equivalent to what might have been occupied by twenty households; *Shang Zhou qingtongqi mingwen xuan* 商周青銅器銘文選 (Beijing: Wenwu Chubanshe, 1988–90), 3:303.

Previous scholars, such as Huang Ranwei, have considered the appointment ceremony as described in the Song *ding* inscription to have involved the procedure of actually "writing out" the royal command witnessed by both the king and the appointees at the court. Such a reading involves grammatical errors that are evident when the relevant inscriptions are carefully compared.[10] A consistent reading of all inscriptions describing this process suggests that a document detailing the king's command must have been prepared prior to the appointment ceremony in which it was used, and there is good evidence to suggest that the writing was done in the king's inner court by secretarial officials under the Chief Document Maker (Zuòcè Yǐn 作冊尹) if not actually written by the Chief himself. During the ceremony, the written document (*wángmìngshū* 王命書) was first handed over by the king to the Chief (Yǐnshì 尹氏 in the Song *ding*) or another person, symbolizing that the command originated with the king. Then the king would call out another secretarial official (Scribe Guosheng 虢生 in the Song *ding*) to orally pronounce the command to the candidate.[11] A recent study suggests that the employment

---

10. Huang reads the phrase *yǐnshì shòu wángmìng shū* 尹氏受王命書 to mean "The Chief received the royal command to write" (*shū* 書 as a verb). This contradicts the line *wáng shòu Zuòcè Yǐn shū, bǐ cèmìng Miǎn* 王受作冊尹書，俾冊命免 (Mian *gui* 免簋 [JC: 4240]) which, in Huang's reading, would have to mean that the king was commanded by the Document Maker to do the writing — this is clearly wrong. See Huang Ranwei, *Yin Zhou qingtongqi*, 90, 95. As I have noted previously, in the Mian *gui* inscription, *shòu* 受 clearly stands for *shòu* 授, and the scenario can only be that the king gave the Chief Document Maker the document and asked him to announce it to Mian (in the Song *ding*, this latter role of announcer is played by Scribe Guosheng 虢生 rather than by the Chief). By the same principle, the Chief (Yǐnshì) in the Song *ding* must be the recipient of the *wángmìngshū* 王命書, which should be treated as one term. See Li Feng, "'Offices' in Bronze Inscriptions," 50 n. 143.
11. For a recent discussion on the handling of written documents during the appointment ceremony, see Kern, "The Performance of Writing," 140–50. Kern also thinks that the written document was preprepared, but, following Shirakawa, he reads the line 史留受王命書 in the Feng *ding* 趠鼎 (JC: 2815) to mean "Secretary Liu presented the king with the written order" (reading *shòu* 受 as *shòu* 授 in this context, too, and treating *mìngshū* 命書 as one term); ibid., 148. This is different from my reading. Shirakawa, while reading the Chief Document Maker in the Song *ding* as giver (and the king as recipient), conversely reads the king as giver and the Chief Document Maker as recipient in the Mian *gui*; "Kinbun tsūshaku," 24.137: 158–59; 29.177: 593. Ma Chengyuan, treating *wángmìngshū* 王命書 as one term, believes that in the Song *ding* the document passed directly from the Chief to Scribe Guosheng, without the king being involved in the transaction; *Shang Zhou*, 3:303.

of two officials to transmit the written command at the court is likely a late–Western Zhou invention, while in the mid–Western Zhou, the two roles were not differentiated and were performed by a single official, similar to the circumstances described by the inscription of the Mian *gui* 免簋 (JC: 4240): "The king gave the Chief Document Maker the document, and let him command Mian."[12]

The most interesting points here are two. First, appointment to administrative offices in the Western Zhou period was, after a court session of oral presentation by one of the king's secretaries or sometimes by the king himself (e.g., in the Hai *gui* 害簋 [JC: 4259]), clearly transmitted in writing on a bamboo or wooden carrier that assumed very much the same function of the modern day's "letter of appointment." There is actually a way to estimate the extent to which such appointment letters were used in the middle to late Western Zhou court. To date, as many as one hundred appointment inscriptions have been discovered, and their number far exceeds any other group of inscriptions relating to any particular area of government activity.[13] Considering that these inscriptions probably constitute only a fraction of all appointment inscriptions ever cast during the middle to late Western Zhou period, and that they are copies of documents originally issued on bamboo or wood, many of which may never have been cast in bronze, we are in a strong position to suggest that the writing of official appointments was the rule rather than the exception in the middle-to-late Western Zhou government.

Second, in all six inscriptions that provide detailed information on the use of written documents in the context of official appointments, the word *shū* 書 is clearly differentiable from *cè* 冊. In the context of the Song *ding*, for instance, it is the royal document first mentioned as *wángmìngshū* 王命書, and then, when it was handed over to the candidate, it was called *mìngcè* 命冊, which the candidate Song hung on his body

---

12. See Li Feng, *Bureaucracy and the State in Early China: Governing the Western Zhou* (Cambridge: Cambridge University Press, 2008), 109.
13. A multifaceted survey conducted by Musha Akira 武者章 yielded ninety-one appointment inscriptions known by the end of the 1970s; "Sei Shū satsumei kinbun bunrui no kokoromi" 西周冊命金文分類の試み, in Matsumaru Michio, ed., 248–49. An accurate account of appointment inscriptions discovered thereafter is not available, but even the most conservative estimate would suggest that the total number is more than one hundred pieces. Two most recently discovered appointment inscriptions are the Shi You *ding* 師酉鼎 and the Jingbo Lu *gui* 井伯䢅簋, currently housed in the Poly Museum and the National Museum of China in Beijing, respectively.

before walking out of the courtyard (*pèi yǐ chū* 佩以出).¹⁴ Very likely, in the language of the bronze inscriptions, *cè* 冊 refers to the material form, wooden or bamboo strips, that carries the written document; *shū* 書, on the other hand, refers to the text itself as literary composition independent of the media on which it was written. This suggests that when a bronze inscription says *cèmìng* 冊命, as in all appointment inscriptions, it means that whoever carried out the action actually had a material form of written document in his hand and announced the royal command from it. A *shū* document could be reproduced in multiple copies and could eventually, if the recipient considered it necessary for preservation or better presentation, be transferred onto bronze.¹⁵

One of the main functions of a bureaucratic government is to take in, process, and send out information. The Western Zhou government has been considered particularly capable of discharging this function.¹⁶ It has been inferred recently, based mainly on comparison with records from Mesopotamia, that the exact account of land and people presented in such Western Zhou inscriptions as the Yihou Ze *gui* 宜侯夨簋 (JC: 4320) and the Da Yu *ding* 大盂鼎 (JC: 2837) might have been based on a land survey and population census of some kind, for which the Zhou government would have kept records of land and lists of the various subgroups of the population in writing.¹⁷ The point is well taken, in spite of the inferential and conjectural nature of the argument. There is, however, one area of Western Zhou government for which the inscriptional evidence suggests a strong tradition of bookkeeping.

For a long time, scholars have discussed the meaning of *mièlì* 蔑曆, a term that frequently appears in the Western Zhou bronze inscriptions and possibly designates the practice of merit-recounting. There are a total of more than thirty Western Zhou bronze inscriptions that mention officials

---

14. Besides the Song *ding*, this expression is found also on the Forty-third Year Lai *ding* 四十三年逨鼎 and the Shanfu Shan *ding* 善夫山鼎 (JC: 2825), though the inscription on the latter bronze does not describe the handling of the document by the royal secretary.
15. On the transfer of written documents onto bronze media, see Falkenhausen, "Issues in Western Zhou," 145–46, 161–67; Li Feng, "Ancient Reproductions and Calligraphic Variations: Studies of Western Zhou Bronzes with Identical Inscriptions," *Early China* 22 (1997): 40–41.
16. Herrlee Creel, *The Origins of Statecraft in China*, vol. 1, *The Western Chou Empire* (Chicago: University of Chicago Press, 1970), 124–25.
17. See Wang, "Writing and the State," 222–25.

honored with a ritual performance of *mièlì*,[18] such as the Mian *zun* 免尊 (JC: 6006):

唯六月初吉，王在鄭。丁亥，王格太室，井叔右免。王蔑免曆。命史懋賜免䎽市，䋛黃。作嗣工。對揚王休，用作尊彝。免其萬年永寶用。

It was the sixth month, first auspiciousness; the king was in Zheng. On day *dīnghài* (day 24), the king entered the grand chamber; Jingshu accompanied Mian to his right. The king recounted Mian's merit (*mièlì* 蔑曆) and commanded Scribe Mao to award Mian dark knee pads and a jade-circlet, to be Supervisor of Construction. In response [Mian] extols the king's beneficence, herewith makes [this] sacrificial vessel. May Mian for ten thousand years eternally treasure and use it.

In general, it can be said that *mièlì* was an action that a person with superior authority performed to or for his subordinates or subjects and that it was associated with a deep sense of recognition and appreciation, as shown by the fact that recipients considered it an honor worth recording on their bronzes. This point is further confirmed by the fact that such performance was often followed by grants of material rewards to the officials for whom the *mièlì* ritual was conducted. It is likely that the action involved the oral expression and recording in writing of what the authorities considered meritorious and what amounted to an account of an official's history of service in the Zhou government. Tang Lan interpreted the character *lì* 曆 (歷), glossed as *shǔ* 數 (counting) in the *Erya* 爾雅, as referring to the accumulated merits of a person or a family.[19] As for *miè* 蔑, scholars have read it *fá* 伐 'to attack, to punish';[20] Tang Lan suggested further that *fá* 伐 has the meaning of *měi* 美 'to praise, to honor' (verbal sense). Thus, the term *mièlì* refers to a ritual session in which the superior recounts the accumulated merits of his subordinate based on some kind of presentable record — an interpretation widely

---

18. An early list drawn up by Yan Yiping 嚴一萍 gives thirty-five inscriptions by 1962; "Mieli guyi" 蔑曆古意, *Zhongguo wenzi* 中國文字 10 (1962): 1–5. Zhang Yachu's 張亞初 new index to bronze inscriptional terms lists thirty-one clear cases of *mièlì*; *Yin Zhou jinwen jicheng yinde* 殷周金文集成引得 (Beijing: Zhonghua Shuju, 2001), 1086.
19. See Tang Lan 唐蘭, "Mieli xingu" 蔑曆新詁, *Wenwu* 1979.5: 42.
20. See Shirakawa Shizuka, "Betsureki kai" 蔑曆解, *Kōkotsugaku* 甲骨學 4-5 (1959): 89–104; Yan Yiping, "Mieli guyi," 1–5; Tang Lan, "Mieli xingu," 36–42.

accepted among scholars.[21] In fact, Tang Lan and, earlier, Yan Yiping both identified *mièlì* as an early form of what came to be called *fáyuè* 伐閱 in the Han dynasty, referring to the process of recounting an official's curriculum vitae.[22]

The semantic link between *miè* 蔑 and *fá* 伐 is unproblematic; however, in all thirty-plus *mièlì* inscriptions, *miè* 蔑 was never replaced by *fá* 伐 or vice versa. This suggests that, although the two words might have been cognates by origin, they had already become conventionally differentiated in the Western Zhou period. As such, *miè* 蔑 appears in two line-statements of the hexagram *Bō* 剝 in the *Book of Changes* (Yijing), and there is strong evidence that it is the archaic form of *miè* 滅, a post–Western Zhou graph for writing the same word, that never appears in any Shang or Western Zhou inscriptions.[23] Besides its use in military contexts to mean "to vanquish" or "to destroy," *miè* 滅 also had the meaning of "to cover up" or "to fill up" (close to the word *mò* 沒). This new reading of *miè* 蔑, which is more straightforward than the previous reading of it as *fá* 伐, suggests that in Western Zhou inscriptions, the ritual of *mièlì* might have involved not only the oral declaration of an official's merits but also the actual recording of his merits in some kind of "merit-book" by his superior or the Zhou king. The relatively large number of inscriptions that record this ritual suggests that it was performed regularly in the Zhou central government.

---

21. For an English-language discussion of the *mièlì* ritual, see Constance A. Cook, "Wealth and the Western Zhou," 278–79. Note that Cook translates the term *lì* 曆 straightforwardly as "chronicle," implying a documentary record in perhaps the written form. See also Ma Chengyuan, *Shang Zhou*, 3:4; Shaughnessy, *Sources of Western Zhou*, 191.
22. See Yan Yiping, "Mieli guyi," 1–13. Both the *Shiji* and the *Houhan shu* offer examples of officials being inspected for their *fáyuè* 伐閱 or being required to send in their *fáyuè* for inspection, clearly a type of written statement similar to modern-day *lǚlì* 履歷 'curriculum vitae'. See *Shiji* (Beijing: Zhonghua Shuju, 1959), 977; *Houhan shu* (Beijing: Zhonghua Shuju, 1965), 133.
23. The pre-Qin Xiang 象 commentary interprets it as *miè* 滅; see *Zhouyi, Shisanjing zhushu* (Beijing: Zhonghua Shuju, 1980), 3.38. The Xun Shuang 荀爽 edition of *Zhouyi* cited in the Tang dynasty *Jingdian shiwen* 經典釋文 simply has *miè* 滅 instead of *miè* 蔑 in the line statements; see *Jingdian shiwen* 經典釋文 (Beijing: Zhonghua Shuju, 1983), 23. In two phrases in the *Tales of the States* (Guoyu), *miè* 蔑 is actually used as *miè* 滅; see *Guoyu* (Shanghai: Guji Chubanshe, 1988), 57, 111.

"Paperwork" Beyond the Royal Court

New evidence suggests that the use of official written records was not only an essential administrative process in the Zhou central court; writing was also used extensively in local administration beyond the central court, as indicated by the following inscription on the newly discovered Wu Hu *ding* 吳虎鼎 (JL: 364):

> 惟十又八年十又三月既生霸丙戌，王在周康宮夷宮。導入右吴虎，王命膳夫豐生、嗣工雍毅醽剌（厲）王令，付吴盨舊疆，付吴虎。厥北疆涵人眔疆，厥东疆官人眔疆，厥南疆畢人眔疆，厥西疆莽姜眔疆。厥俱履封：豐生、雍毅、伯導、芮嗣土寺桒。吴虎拜稽首，天子休。賓膳夫豐生璋、馬匹；賓嗣工雍毅璋、馬匹；賓芮嗣土寺桒璧。援書：尹友守史。迺賓史桒韋兩。虎拜手稽首，敢對扬天子丕顯鲁休，用作朕皇祖考庚孟尊鼎，其子子孫孫永寶。

> It was the eighteenth year, thirteenth month, after the growing brightness, *bǐngxū* (day 23), the king was at Yi Palace of Kang Palace in Zhou. Dao entered to accompany Wu Hu to his right; the king ordered Provisioner Fengsheng and Supervisor of Construction Yongyi to extend the command [previously issued by] King Li, giving the old territory of Wu Xu to Wu Hu. Its northern boundary reaches the boundary of the people of Han; its eastern boundary reaches the boundary of the people who belong to the government; its southern boundary reaches the boundary of the Bi people; and its western boundary reaches the boundary of Pang Jiang. Those who have completed the survey (i.e., the walk through the fields) and demarcation: Fengsheng, Yongyi, Bo Dao, and Supervisor of Land of Rui, Sihui. Wu Hu bowed with his head reaching the ground, [and he extolled] the beneficence of the Son of Heaven. [He] presented Provisioner Fengsheng a jade *zhāng*-tablet and one horse; [he] presented Supervisor of Construction Yongyi a jade *zhāng*-tablet and one horse; [he] presented the Supervisor of Land of Rui, Sihui, a jade *bì*-disk. The person who handed over the document (*shū* 書) is the Guarding Scribe who was an associate of the Chief [Interior Scribe]. Therefore, [Hu] presented Scribe Hui two sets of furs. Hu bowed with his head touching the ground and dared to extol the greatly illustrious felicitous beneficence of the Son of Heaven, with which [he] makes for my august grandfather and father, Geng and Meng, this sacrificial *ding*-vessel. May his sons' sons and grandsons' grandsons eternally treasure it![24]

---

24. See Mu Xiaojun 穆曉軍, "Shaanxi Chang'an xian chutu Xi Zhou Wu Hu *ding*" 陝西

This inscription records a land transaction involving Wu Hu 吳虎 originally approved by King Li, only to be reissued by the next king, King Xuan. The court official, Provisioner Fengsheng 豐生, and Supervisor of Construction Yongyi 雍毅, after announcing the royal command, actually took the beneficiary Wu Hu to the field and, together with Bo Dao, possibly a patron of Wu Hu (Bo Dao 伯導 can be identified with Dao 導, who accompanied Wu Hu to court), demarcated the borders of the land with the assistance of a local administrator, Supervisor of Land of Rui 芮 (probably the area affected by this transaction), whose name is Sihui. When this was done, the transaction was officially concluded with the handover of the written document (*shū* 書) to the recipient of the land by a scribe, who is described in the inscriptions as an associate of the Chief (Interior Scribe or Document Maker), the head of the interior secretarial body of the king during the middle-to-late Western Zhou. An interesting and quite unique aspect of this inscription is that Wu Hu expressed his gratitude twice, first to the officials who had actually executed the transaction and to whom sets of gifts were handed (officials from the central court were differentiated from the administrator of Rui by the items Wu Hu offered) and then, *separately and specially*, to the carrier of the written document (perhaps a royal land charter), Scribe Hui, who was presented with two furs. The appearance of the phrase *bàishǒu qǐshǒu* 拜手稽首 twice in the inscription makes this distinction very clearly and suggests a special emphasis on the administrative procedure of carrying the written document over to the new owner who received the land. The inscription suggests that in Western Zhou society, business such as land transactions was conducted through the use of written documents that granted the recipients of the land the right to use and possess such economic resources.

Moreover, the Wu Hu *ding* 吳虎鼎 also shows a very meaningful composition of officials: (1) Official of Inner Court (Provisioner), (2) Executive Official, (3) Secretarial Official (Scribe Hui), and (4) Local Official (here, Sihui). The Provisioner (1) played an active role as the king's personal representative during the late Western Zhou when the Wu Hu *ding* was cast, but he was not significant during the mid–Western Zhou. "Executive Official" refers to the Three Supervisors belonging to the Ministry (*Qīngshìliáo* 卿事寮), the main division of Zhou central

---

長安縣出土西周吳虎鼎, *Kaogu yu wenwu* 1998.3: 69–71.

administration.[25] The pattern of (2) + (3) + (4) recurs quite typically in mid–Western Zhou inscriptions that record transactions of land property. For instance, in the Fifth Year Qiu Wei *ding* 五年裘衛鼎 (JC: 2832), Interior Scribe You 內史友 accompanied the Three Supervisors to complete the transaction in which Qiu Wei acquired four fields. In the Yong *yu* 永盂 (JC: 10322), the same role was played by a secretarial official called the Minor Scribe (*yàshǐ* 啟史) in an administrative structure very similar to that recorded in the Wu Hu *ding*. Although these inscriptions do not offer direct mention of written documents, they suggest that the literary function of the Zhou government, represented by the scribes and exemplified in the inscriptions of the Wu Hu *ding*, might have been an indispensable part of the economic conduct organized or supervised by the central government.

Land Register Used by the Lineages

Another important piece of evidence for the use of written documents in economic activities comes from the inscription of the Sixth Year Zhousheng *gui* 六年琱生簋 (JC: 4293). This was not a charter or edict issued by the Zhou government but a land register delivered by one aristocratic lineage to another:

> 唯六年四月甲子，王才莽，豐（召）伯虎告曰："余告慶！"曰："公
> 厥稟貝，用獄訟為，伯又厎又成。亦我考幽伯幽姜，令余告慶。余以
> 邑訊有嗣，余典勿敢封。今余既訊有嗣，曰：'侯令！'今余既一名典，
> 獻伯氏。"則報璧。琱生對揚朕宗君其休，用作朕剌祖豐（召）公嘗簋，
> 其萬年子子孫孫寶用享于宗。[26]

It was the sixth year, fourth month, on *jiǎzǐ* (day 1), the king was in [Capital] Pang. Shaobo Hu (of the Shao lineage) announced, saying: "I am pleased to report good news!" [He] said: "The duke (someone closely related to Zhousheng) sent in cowries, for payment for the lawsuit. The Bo (refers to Zhousheng) you now have a settlement and accomplishment [on your case]. It is also my father, Youbo, and mother, You Jiang, who asked

---

25. On the roles of the officials mentioned here and the organization of the middle-to-late Western Zhou government, see Li Feng, *Bureaucracy and the State*, 63–93.
26. This transcription and the translation here largely follow Lin Yun 林澐, "Zhousheng *gui* xinshi" 琱生簋新釋, *Guwenzi yanjiu* 3 (1980): 120–35. For a discussion of the content of these inscriptions, see also Shirakawa, "Kinbun tsūshaku," 33.195: 860–73.

me to report the good news. I took [the register of] *yì*-settlements to consult the government officials; therefore, I documented (in writing) but did not dare to seal [the register]. Now I have already consulted the officials, and they said: 'Follow the order [of Youbo and You Jiang, head of the Shaos]!' Now I have recorded [their] names one after another in the document and contribute [it] to Boshi (Zhousheng)." [Boshi] thus offered [Shaobo] a jade *bì*-disk. I, Zhousheng, in response extol the beneficence of my lineage-head, hereby making [for] my august ancestor the Duke of Shao [this] food-offering *guì*-vessel. May [my] sons' sons and grandsons' grandsons for ten thousand years treasure and use it in offerings in the lineage temple!

It is well known that this is one of the two interrelated inscriptions (the other being the Fifth Year Zhousheng *gui* 五年琱生簋 [JC: 4292] in Yale University Art Gallery), and the recent discovery made in Wujun Xicun 五郡西村, Fufeng County,[27] has added yet another inscription to this series that is chronologically positioned between the two already known. The circumstances surrounding the casting of these inscriptions are too complicated to discuss here. Roughly speaking, they document a land dispute that Zhousheng 琱生, most likely a member of a minor branch of the prestigious Shao 召 lineage, incurred sometime during the late Western Zhou period. The head of the Shao 召 lineage, whom Zhousheng honored as *zōngjūn* 宗君 (head of the primary lineage), sent his oldest son, Shaobo Hu 召伯虎, to stand at court representing Zhousheng. The lawsuit seems to have gone on for more than a year and seems to have been settled eventually in favor of Zhousheng after his family paid the necessary legal fees. The Sixth Year Zhousheng *gui* 六年琱生簋 (JC: 4293) was cast at the time of the settlement, and it records the visit of Shaobo Hu to Zhousheng's family to report the good news.

There are two references in this inscription. First, it is recorded that Shaobo Hu composed an initial *register* of settlements in dispute on behalf of Zhousheng's family and submitted it to the government officials for inspection. Second, when this document was approved by officials at the Zhou court, probably adopting the proposal made by the Shao lineage, the same Shaobo Hu carefully finalized the initial *land register* (or prepared a new document based on it) with the names of all settlements detailed (*yì*

---

27. See Baoji Shi Kaogu Yanjiusuo 寶鷄市考古研究所 et al., "Shaanxi Fufeng Wujun Xicun Xi Zhou qingtongti jiaocang fajue jianbao" 陝西扶風五郡西村西周青銅器窖藏發掘簡報, *Wenwu* 2007.8: 4–27.

míng diǎn 一名典) and delivered it to Zhousheng's family on his visit to them. While this new register would serve as the legal documentation of the previously disputed land for Zhousheng's family, it is quite possible that copies of the initial document might have been kept by the Zhou court and probably also by the Shao lineage. The inscription suggests that in cases of land dispute brought before the Zhou court, the primary lineage had the responsibility to prepare proper written documentation on behalf of its minor families involved in the dispute, and such written documents had an important legal role in the economic life of Western Zhou society.

Contract Tally Used in Land Transaction

The Sixth Year Zhousheng *gui* is a good example of a land register submitted to the government for approval in a legal dispute and then delivered to the involved family for recordkeeping, but there is also a case in which a contract tally may have been used in a private land transaction that does not seem to have involved the central government. This is the inscription on the Pengsheng *gui* 倗生簋 (JC: 4262) from the mid–Western Zhou period:

> 唯正月初吉癸子，王在成周。格伯取良馬乘于倗生，厥貯卅田，則析。格伯遽。殹妊伋托厥從格伯灰（安）伋田：殷谷杜木，邊谷旅桑，涉東門。厥書史戠武立盄（甬）成塦（壘），鑄保（寶）簋，用典格伯田。其萬年子子孫孫永保（寶）用。囘。
>
> It was the first month, first auspiciousness [of the moon], *guǐsì* (day 30), the king was in Chengzhou. Gebo took four fine horses from Pengsheng, and he compensated [him] with thirty fields; hence [he] split the [contract into halves]. Gebo regretted. Yiren and Tuo followed Gebo to settle [the borders of] the land: from the birch-pear trees in the Yin stream to the mulberry trees in the Yu stream, crossing the eastern gate. His (Pengsheng) Document Scribes Shi and Wu shoveled earth to build up a mound and cast the treasured vessel, in order to document the transfer of fields from Gebo. May for ten thousand years (his) sons' sons and grandsons' grandsons eternally treasure and use it. Family emblem.[28]

---

28. Guo Moruo wrongly named this vessel Gebo *gui* 格伯簋; *Liang Zhou jinwen ci daxi tulu kaoshi* 兩周金文辭大系圖錄考釋 (Beijing: Kexue Chubanshe, 1958), 6:81–82. This was corrected by Ma Chengyuan who considered Pengsheng 倗生 the caster of

The inscription suggests that Gebo 格伯 took four fine horses from an individual called Pengsheng 佣生, whom he compensated by offering thirty fields (*zhú sānshí tián* 貯卅田).²⁹ As in a number of other inscriptions that document such land transactions, the thirty fields were carefully inspected by a group composed of Gebo himself and two officials, probably from Pengsheng's lineage. When the borders were determined, Pengsheng's secretarial officials (scribes) themselves labored to shovel up an earth mound (*lěi* 壘) as a landmark and subsequently cast the bronze to document in writing (*diǎn* 典, same usage as in the Sixth Year Zhousheng *gui* discussed above) the thirty fields that were transferred from Gebo to Pengsheng.³⁰ The inscription unambiguously describes the purpose for which the bronze was cast and inscribed. In this case, the word *diǎn* points directly to the *documentary purpose* of the inscription, that is, it was cast to preserve information about a significant economic deal, whether for the owner of the bronze himself to reflect upon or for a larger audience to view.

It is significant that a bronze was cast as "the document" of the land transfer to Pengsheng and not as a copy of a more conventional form of document that had already been written on perhaps a perishable material as far as we can tell from the content of the inscription, but this point will be discussed later with respect to the documentary function of bronze inscriptions. Of concern here is the phrase "henceforth split" (*zé xī* 則析) that appears in the third line of the inscription. All scholars who have studied this inscription have taken it to mean that a land contract was split into two halves, to be held by the recipient and the seller respectively, and Yang Shuda has explained this point based on textual records.³¹ Although in the inscription, the verb *xī* 析 is not followed by an object word, it certainly means "to split" and very possibly describes the action, in the context of this inscription, of splitting some kind of contract after the agreement was reached, a common practice in later periods.

---

    the bronze and recipient of the fields; *Shang Zhou*, 3:143–44.
29. The reading of the word *zhú* 貯 involves a major debate in the economic history of Western Zhou China. With respect to the Pengsheng *gui*, Ma Chengyuan considered that the thirty fields were transferred (sold) to Pengsheng, but Guo Moruo earlier thought that the fields were "leased" to Pengsheng.
30. This reading of the context of the inscription largely accepts Ma Chengyuan, *Shang Zhou*, 3:144.
31. Yang Shuda 楊樹達, *Jiweiju jinwen shuo* 積微居金文說, supplemented (Beijing: Zhonghua Shuju, 1997), 11.

Use of Writing in a Military Context

Another case of writing emerging from the settlement of legal disputes concerns a military campaign that took place during the early phase of the mid–Western Zhou, as recorded in the Shi Qi *ding* 師旂鼎 (JC: 2809):

唯三月丁卯，師旂眾僕不從王征于方雷，使厥友弘以告于伯懋父，在 䣜。伯懋父迺罰得古三百孚，今弗克厥罰。伯懋父令曰："義（宜）播。 叡！厥不從厥右征。今毋播，其有納于師旂。"弘以告中史，書。旂對 厥質于尊彝。

It was the third month, on *dīngmǎo* (day 4), the many servants of Shi Qi would not follow the king on campaign against Lei of the polity of Yu; (Shi Qi) sent his associate Hong to report it to Bo Maofu, at Nai. Bo Maofu thereupon fined (them) *gǔ*-metal at three hundred *lüè*,[32] which (they) were not able to submit until now. Bo Maofu ordered, saying: "I should appropriately banish (them). *Zhā*! They would not follow their captain to go on campaign. Now I would not banish (them); (instead) they must send the fine to Shi Qi." Hong took this to report to the Central Scribe, who wrote (the verdict down). Qi responds to his verdict (by casting it) on (this) sacrificial vessel.

Laura Skosey discussed this case as a mutiny that happened during a military campaign led by the Zhou king.[33] The disobedient soldiers were fined by Bo Maofu, who was the supreme commander of a number of campaigns that took place during the reign of King Mu. For whatever reasons, the fines were not paid, and Bo Maofu gave a second verdict and, while threatening the soldiers with banishment, ordered them to pay the fine to Shi Qi. Shi Qi's associate thus reported the verdict to the Central Scribe (Zhōngshǐ 中史), most likely a secretarial official in Bo Maofu's headquarters since the event seems to have occurred during a campaign in a place called Nai.[34] It is significant that, on the one hand, the inscription offers a strong piece of evidence that the Central Scribe actually produced

---

32. According to Matsumaru's new study, the amount of three hundred *lüè* was roughly equal to three hundred kilograms; "Sei Shū jidai no jōryō tan'i" 西周時代の重量單位, *Tōyō bunka kenkyūjo kiyō* 117 (1992): 47–56.
33. See Skosey, "The Legal System and Legal Tradition of the Western Zhou, circa 1045–771 B.C.E." (PhD diss., University of Chicago, 1996), 95–96.
34. Personal letters (*shūjiǎn* 書簡) sent to soldiers on campaign are recorded in the received texts, for instance, the poem "Chuche" 出車 (Mao 168); see *Shisanjing zhushu*, 9.4:415–16.

the written record. On the other hand, Shi Qi himself cast this bronze *ding*-vessel to document the verdict. Thus, a single legal case gave rise to two written documents, one made by a royal scribe presumably on wooden or bamboo strips and kept in the commander's headquarters and another, cast on bronze and kept in Shi Qi's family, that could be checked against the official record when necessary. The use of the term *zhì* 質 'verdict' in the inscription conveys a clear sense that this was proof on which Shi Qi could rely to demand payment from the fined soldiers.

Although these direct references to writing in the Western Zhou bronze inscriptions may not be sufficient to produce a generalization about the extent of literacy in the Western Zhou period, they give us concrete glimpses into the specific social circumstances in which written documents were produced or handled. The use of writing ranged across a number of social spheres such as routine government administration, recordkeeping for officials, land transactions, legal cases involving property ownership, private commodity exchanges, military administration, and so on. In all of these areas, writing played a very significant role.

Writing and Afterward: A Case Analysis of the Sanshi *Pan*

One of the longest inscriptions of the Western Zhou period, the Sanshi *pan* 散氏盤 (JC: 10176) (fig. 8.1), not only offers us direct references to written documents but also elucidates in a unique way how and why a document might have ended up on bronze. The center of the San 散 lineage that manufactured the bronze was located to the south of the Wei River in the Baoji 寶鷄 area during the late Western Zhou. The state of Ze 夨 was north of San, having a territory stretching from Longxian in the north to the Baoji area in the south along the Qian 汧 River, which flows into the Wei River at Baoji. While San was a lineage-level polity located in the periphery of the Zhou royal domain, Ze had its own kingship that placed it outside the Zhou political system but might have shared the same ancestry as the Zhou royal house.[35] For unknown reasons, the state of Ze attacked the settlements belonging to the lineage of San. This long

---

35. On the geography of San and Ze, see Lu Liancheng 盧連成, "Xi Zhou Ze guo shiji kaolue jiqi xiangguan wenti" 西周夨國史跡考略及其相關問題, in *Xi Zhou shi yanjiu* 西周史研究 (Xi'an: 1984), 232–48. On the political status of the lineage of San and the state of Ze, see Li Feng, *Landscape and Power*, 186–87.

Figure 8.1 The Sanshi *pan* and its inscription. Upper: inscription. From Zou An, *Zhou jinwen cun* (Shanghai: Cangsheng Mingzhi Daxue, 1915–21), 4.1. Lower: vessel. From Gugong Bowuyuan, *Gugong*, vol. 1 (Beiping: Gugong Bowuyuan, 1929), 1.

inscription of 349 characters records the "postwar" settlement, by which a new border between San and Ze was carefully demarcated:

用矢撲散邑，迺即散用田。履：自瀗涉以南，至于大沽，一封；以陟，二封；至于邊柳，復涉瀗。陟𩁹𢆶𤔲陵以西，封于播城楮木，封于芻逨，封于芻衞。內陟芻，登于厂湶，封剢𨸏，𨸏陵、剛𨸏，封于單道，封于原道，封于周道。以東封于棘東疆右。還，封于履道。以南封于𦉢逨道；以西至于堆莫。履井邑田：自根木道左至于井邑封；道以東一封；還以西一封，陟剛三封；降以南封于同道；陟州剛，登𨸏，降棫，二封。矢人有𤔲履田：鮮、且、微、武父、西宮襄、豆人虞丂、彔貞、師氏右眚、小門人䜌、原人虞荓、淮𤔲工虎、𦍩𠁁、豐父、唯人有𤔲井、丂，凡十又五夫。正履矢舍散田：𤔲土逆𡨄、𤔲馬單堒、邦人𤔲工𩡣君、宰德父、散人小子履田戎、微父、效㮰父、襄之有𤔲橐、州景、攸從䚶，凡散有𤔲十夫。唯王九月辰才乙卯，矢俾鮮、且、䵼、旅誓曰："我既付散氏田器，有爽，實余有散氏心賊，則爰千罰千，傳棄之！"鮮、且、䵼、旅則誓。迺卑西宮襄、武父誓曰："我既付散氏隰田、畛田，余又爽糴，爰千罰千！"西宮襄、武父則誓。厥為圖，矢王于豆新宮東廷。

厥左執𦁴史正，中農。

Because Ze attacked the settlements of San, [the officials of Ze] then arrived in San to use land [as compensation]. Surveying: Cross the Xian River to the south and arrive at the Great Pond, making the first tree-marker; ascend, making the second tree-marker; arrive at Bianliu, crossing the Xian River again. Climb the slope of Zha and Luo west, tree-marking near the paper mulberry tree of Bo Town, tree-marking at Zoulai, and tree-marking at Zou-Lane. Entering Zou and ascending, upon the Cliff-Spring, tree-mark at Zhu-Bank, Slope-Hill, and Ridge-Bank. Tree-marking at Shan-Road, tree-marking at Yuan-Road, and tree-marking at Zhou-Road; moving east, tree-marking to the right of the eastern border of Chuo. Returning, tree-marking at Li-Road. Moving south, tree-mark at Zhulai-Road; moving west, reach Weimo. Surveying the fields of the settlement of Jing: from the left of *Láng*-tree-Road to the Jing settlement, tree-marking. To the east of the Road, one tree-marker; returning to the west, one tree-marker; ascending the ridge, three tree-markers; descending to the south, tree-mark at Tong-Road; going up Zhou-Ridge, climbing the bank, and descending to the Yu-woods, two tree-markers. Those officials of the Ze people who have surveyed the land: Xian, Qie, Wei, Wufu, Xigong Xiang; Supervisor of Marshes of the Dou people Gai, Lu Zhen, Marshal You Sheng, Little Gate Official Yao; Supervisor of Marshes of the Yuan people Nai; Supervisor of Construction of Huai named Hu, Zi Lun,

Fengfu; the officials of the Wei people Jing and Gai — in all, fifteen men. Those [from San] who have verified and surveyed the land transferred by Ze: Supervisor of Land Ni Yin, Supervisor of Horses Shan Kun; Supervisor of Construction of the Bang people Jing Jun, Superintendent Defu; the Young Boys of the San people who have participated in the survey, Rong, Weifu, and Yao Qufu; officials of the Xiang people, Tuo, Zhou Jing, You Cong Guo — in all, officials of San, ten men. It was the [Zhou] king's ninth month, the time was *yǐmaǒ* (day 52), Ze had Xian, Qie, X, and Lü take the oath, saying: "We have already submitted the land and the utensils to the San-lineage, and if we overturn [the agreement], having the fact of plotting against the San-lineage, fine us a thousand *yuán* of metal, publicly denouncing us [throughout the Zhou state]." Xian, Qie, X, and Lü thus swore the oath. Then, asking Xigong Xiang and Wufu to swear the oath: "We have handed over to the San-lineage the marshy fields and the fields divided into grids and, if we overturn [the agreement], will be fined one thousand *yuán* of metal!" Xigong Xiang and Wufu thus took the oath. They made a map, in the Ze king's presence in the eastern court of the New Palace of Dou.

    Its (his) Left Contract-Keeping Scribe verified; (signed) Zhong Nong

According to the treaty, Ze had to compensate San with considerable territory (or territories), presumably pocketed along the Qian River (the Xian 潏 River mentioned in the inscription) to the north of Baoji. All portions of the new border on which "tree-markers" (*fēng* 封) were made, as well as other features of the landscape, are carefully documented in the inscription. This description was doubtless meant to be traceable on the real ground. The second half of the inscription provides a detailed account of officials from both polities involved in the process of land transaction, including fifteen from the state of Ze and ten from the polity of San, all enumerated by name. Interestingly, the officials from each polity comprised two groups: officials from the central management of the polity and officials from the local settlements that would be affected by the transaction.[36] This point is further supported by the fact that only those from the central management of Ze — Xian 鮮, Qie 且, X 鼻, and Lü 旅 — were put under oath and swore that if they were to break the agreement and conspire against San, they could incur a heavy fine of one thousand *yuán* of metal and would be publicly denounced in the Zhou domain.

---

36. See Li Feng, *Bureaucracy and the State*, 184–87.

Xigong Xiang 西宮襄 and Wufu 武父 swore in turn that they would be subject to the same penalty if they were to break the agreement. The date on which the oaths were taken was *yǐmaǒ* (day 52) of the ninth month in the Zhou royal calendar. And a map was made when the king of Ze (Zewang 夨王) was present at the new palace of the polity of Dou 豆, in the jurisdiction of the state of Ze (see below).

No doubt, a map documenting the land transaction would be as detailed as the inscription. Presumably, all the placements along the new border mentioned in the inscription were annotated in writing. In a broad sense, the use of territorial maps is already attested in early Western Zhou bronze inscriptions. The Yihou Ze *gui* 宜侯夨簋 (JC: 4320) mentions the transfer of the ruler of Yu 虞 to become the ruler of Yi 宜. This was announced in a formal "territory"-granting ceremony during which the Zhou king consulted maps in order to determine the location of the new state. For our purposes, however, the most critical point is still to come and has been often overlooked by previous scholars: the last line of the inscription has eight characters that read "Its (or His) Left Contract-Keeping Scribe verified; Zhong Nong." Unlike all other known inscriptions that have a line that ends halfway, the placement of these eight characters is not at the top of the column but at the bottom, discontinuous with the main text (see fig. 8.1). This makes it crystal-clear that it is not part of the text but the *signature line* of the Contract-Keeping Scribe who had apparently certified the written text that was cast on the bronze later. This point is important in two ways. First, it reinforces the judicial nature of the text as a treaty, the violation of which could result in serious legal consequences, as stated in the inscription. Second, the appearance of the signature line on the bronze suggests strongly that the metal inscription truthfully replicates the compositional features of the original text. Such an inscription certainly could not have been cast merely or primarily for ancestor worship, to be read by the imagined ancestors if they would deign to weary themselves with the details of the secular world. It is itself a token of an important territorial concession secured by the *signature* and by the detailed list of officials who could be held responsible based on this inscription. As such, the Sanshi *pan* is not only a good example of the use of long textual statement in legal cases but also an excellent demonstration of the important role the metal inscriptions themselves played in the legal system of Western Zhou society.[37]

---

37. For the use of writing in Zhou legal administration, see also Skosey, "The Legal

It is understandable that such a critical text needed to be placed on a bronze. A treaty on wooden or bamboo media could be destroyed by fire; on a durable material like bronze, not only could the text acquire greater "durability" but it could be easily exhibited to members of the San elites in suitable circumstances such as public gatherings. A bronze *pan*-basin like this would probably have been kept on display in the small court of the San polity, to be viewed by San officials and whoever was paying a visit to the head of the polity. The judicial nature of the inscriptional text offers the most logical explanation for casting a bronze vessel to carry it when an original document probably already existed on bamboo or silk. In this connection, it should be noted, too, that the Sanshi *pan* is a unique inscription in that it does not name any individual as its principal caster.[38] Therefore, it is very likely that there was a perceived community or public sponsorship attached to the vessel, known probably to all who used and saw it.

In this regard, another good example of a bronze cast to serve the purpose of documentary conservation is the Hu *ding* 曶鼎 (JC: 2838), which carries three separate texts cast onto its inner surface. Two of the texts are records of two totally unrelated legal cases that the caster Hu had experienced; neither is related in any way to the third text, which is a typical appointment inscription, cast on the same bronze. The Hu *ding* presents an interesting case in which the caster selected a group of mutually unrelated, but important, documents from his family archive and then cast them collectively onto a single bronze for the very purpose of preserving such records for the future. By so doing, Hu had acquired potential "publicity," as the bronze vessel would be displayed to a larger social circle both in domestic social gatherings and in ancestor worship, as suggested earlier, hence playing a more prominent and pervasive role in Western Zhou society.

A final point concerns a traditional debate about the ownership of the Sanshi *pan*. There have been scholars who considered the bronze basin to have been cast by the state of Ze, and if this is the case, it should be properly named the Zeren *pan* 矢人盤.[39] The bronze must have been cast

---

System," 126–27.
38. The caster's name is the most important element in all content-rich inscriptions. The exception is a small group of short inscriptions, usually saying "Makes sacrificial vessel" (*zuò bǎo zūn yí* 作寶尊彝).
39. See Wu Dacheng 吳大澂, *Kezhai jigu lu* 愙齋集古錄 (Shanghai: Hanfenlou, 1918), 16:4; Liu Xinyuan 劉心源, *Qigushi jijin wen shu* 奇觚室吉金文述 (1902), 8:21.

by the San polity, just as other legal inscriptions from the period were all cast by the parties in whose favor the inscribed legal cases were settled. Ze would have preferred not to cast an inscription recording its political disadvantage. However, there is no internal evidence that the text must have been composed by scribes of San; on the contrary, grammatically, the term *jué* 厥 that appears as the functional subject of mapmaking in the last line of the text and as a pronoun heading the *signature line* would suggest a closer relation to Ze, not San — that is to say, the scribe (Zhong Nong 中農) who signed the text was probably a secretarial official of the king of Ze (Zèwáng 夨王).[40] This suggestion is further supported by the fact that the treaty was concluded and signed in the Ze king's presence in the palace of Dou, witnessed by officials from both Ze and San; since the officials from Dou (including Supervisor of Marshes Gai 丂, Lu Zhen 彔貞, Marshal You Sheng 右眚, and Little Gate Official Yao 縣) are counted among the officials of Ze earlier in the inscription, there is no doubt that Dou was located within the jurisdiction of Ze.

Bringing all these points together, it appears very likely that the original text of the Sanshi *pan* inscription was drafted on bamboo or silk by Ze officials (who would know their territory better) and subsequently signed in front of the Ze king by his secretary, the event being witnessed by fifteen officials of Ze and ten officials from San. The signed text was then brought back by the San officials from the peace conference at Dou, in Ze territory, and was cast on the bronze. This new interpretation most logically explains the context of the writing of the text and its casting on the Sanshi *pan* and provides further evidence that the inscription was a legal document that recorded the conclusion of an interpolity dispute that San had won.

Broadening the Context: Bronze Inscriptions as Evidence of Literacy

The Sanshi *pan* not only offers significant information on what might have happened to cause the casting of a bronze vessel; it also raises a more general question about the social functions of the bronze inscriptions. It goes without saying that bronze inscriptions are evidence of writing and

---

40. On the grammatical functions of *jué* 厥, see Ken-ichi Takashima, "The So-Called 'Third'-Person Possessive Pronoun *jue* 厥 in Classical Chinese," *Journal of the American Oriental Society* 119.3 (1999): 405–20.

literacy, but exactly what kind of evidence are they? Are they evidence of a function-specific "scribal literacy" in the sense that the writing of words on the bronzes and the reading of those written words were restricted to one specially trained social group, the scribes, or are they evidence of a general literacy that can be traced across a broad range of social contexts? Since the bronze inscriptions constitute the predominant group of works of writing from the Western Zhou, these are crucial questions for understanding the condition of literacy during this important period.

Many scholars have long held that the bronze vessels were primarily ritual objects used for sacrificial offerings in the worship of ancestors.[41] The question about the social function of the bronze inscriptions is different, though inseparable, from the question about the purposes the bronze vessels themselves served. Past scholarship has emphasized the inscriptions' role in religious-ritual communication with ancestral spirits in the supernatural realm, who were therefore the intended audience of the inscriptions.[42] Others look at the multiple social contexts that provided causes for the casting of bronzes and their inscribed texts.[43] Each inscription has its specific purpose, which must be determined by carefully analyzing the content of the inscription, and there is no single theory that can or should explain the creation of all of them. The Pengsheng *gui* 倗生簋 (JC: 4262), discussed above, offers a typical case of an economic transaction leading to the casting of an inscription with the explicit purpose of documenting (*diǎn* 典) the transaction. The Sanshi *pan* 散氏盤 (JC: 10176), in contrast, suggests that a bronze could be cast to

---

41. For a clear statement of this point, see Rong Geng 容庚, *Shang Zhou yiqi tongkao* 商周彝器通攷 (Beiping: Yanjing Daxue, 1940), 1–2; K.C. Chang, *Art, Myth, and Ritual: The Path to Political Authority in Ancient China* (Cambridge, Mass.: Harvard University Press, 1983), 56–80.
42. This view was most systematically discussed in Falkenhausen, "Issues in Western Zhou," 146–47, 167; Luo Tai (Lothar von Falkenhausen), "Xi Zhou tongqi mingwen," 343–74. In K.C. Chang's view, not only inscriptions but also the zoomorphic designs on the bronze vessels were intended to facilitate communications with the ancestors; *Art, Myth, and Ritual*, 61–65, 88.
43. See Li Feng, *Landscape and Power*, 9–10. Drawing a convincing distinction between sacrificial vessels (*jìqì* 祭器) and ritual vessels (*lǐqì* 禮器) and admitting that the majority of the bronzes were cast as sacrificial vessels, Zhu Fenghan points out that ritual bronzes were cast for other non-sacrificial purposes including marriages, banquets, audiences, and interstate meetings or specially as commemorations of merit. See Zhu Fenghan 朱鳳瀚, *Gudai Zhongguo qingtongqi* 古代中國青銅器 (Tianjin: Nankai Baxue, 1995), 17–18.

replicate, merely and exactly, an important territorial treaty concluded between two polities. The social contexts that gave rise to these bronzes must have been very different from that of many primarily "sacrificial vessels."

Certainly, this is not to argue that the religious-ritual context of ancestor worship was not important. The largest group of inscribed bronzes was cast as sacrificial vessels (*zūnyí* 尊彝),[44] a term that suggests they were intended primarily for use in sacrificial offerings. A long mid–Western Zhou inscription on one food vessel, the Dong *gui* 栽簋 (JC: 4322), celebrates in a religious tone the spiritual protection the caster's deceased mother provided for him during a military campaign and dedicates the bronze to her.[45] There are also many long religious prayers embedded in the inscriptions on bronze bells.[46] Such inscriptions can probably be considered religious documents because they establish a link between the world of their casters and the supernatural world of the ancestors. The religious context of inscribed bronzes has been fully discussed by previous scholars, so this chapter will analyze inscriptional evidence to reveal other social contexts in which the inscribed bronzes were used and read (and hence are evidence of literacy in such contexts), most importantly in the domestic life of the Western Zhou elites.

The Wu *gui* 殳簋 (JC: 3827) offers a very interesting example:

殳作寶簋，用餗（饋）厥孫子，厥不（丕）吉其辭。

Wu makes [this] treasured *gui*-vessel, using [it] to serve food to his grandsons and sons, who will be greatly fortunate and may XX.

Although the last graph of this inscription cannot be deciphered, the

---

44. A recent study by Chen Chao-jung 陳昭容 offers insights into the relative proportion of sacrificial vessels: among the 641 bronze vessels cast for/by female elites, 122 are marked "sacrificial vessels"; "Liang Zhou qingtongqi de nüxing jieshouzhe yu nüxing zhizuozhe," 兩周青銅器的女性接受者與女性製作者, paper presented at the Columbia Early China Seminar on 8 March 2008.
45. The Dong *gui* records the caster Dong's experience in a battle against the Huaiyi 淮夷 in the south. In the battle, as Dong proclaims, his deceased mother guided his way, broadened his heart, protected his body from injury, and led him to the final victory. After the battle, Dong cast this bronze as a tribute to his mother. The inscription suggests a clear religious context as the reason for casting the bronze. For a reading of this inscription, see Ma Chengyuan, *Shang Zhou*, 3:115.
46. For an analysis of these religious prayers on the bells, see Falkenhausen, "Issues in Western Zhou," 139–226.

reading of the inscription is nevertheless clear, and it suggests that the bronze was to be used in serving food to the Wu family members in a domestic context. The reading of the graph 饙 with a *shí* 食 component as *fēn* 饙 in verbal form (not to be confused with *huì* 𢆶 'to entreat') is well supported by its use as a generic term designating "food-serving" vessels on other bronzes and is required by the grammatical structure of this particular inscription.[47] Thus, the Wu *gui* offers a meaningful example of a bronze self-identified as a feasting utensil for the living members of its owner's family.

Another case is the Cui *pan* 毳盤 (JC: 10119), cast by a Zhou prince for his royal mother:

毳作王母媿氏沬盤。媿氏其眉壽萬年用。[48]

Cui makes for [my] royal mother Kuishi [this] face/hair-washing *gui* vessel. May Kuishi have abundant age and for ten thousand years use [it].

The graph still has its remnant archaic form in the *Shuowen jiezi* 說文解字, and its reading as *mò* 沫 'face-washing' or *mù* 沐 'hair-washing' is generally accepted among paleographers.[49] The bronze was cast by Cui 毳 on behalf of his mother, Kuishi 媿氏, who was not a deceased ancestor to whom the bronze was dedicated but a living person

---

47. Examples are JC: 666, JC: 3838, JC: 10305. Chen Mengjia regarded the term *fēnyú* 饙盂 on the Yanhou *yu* 燕侯盂 (JC: 10305) as essentially the same as *fànyú* 飯盂 (food-serving *yu*-vessel); Chen Mengjia 陳夢家, "Xi Zhou tongqi duandai II" 西周銅器斷代, *Kaogu xuebao* 10 (1955): 99–100. For this reading, see also Ma Chengyuan, *Shang Zhou*, 3:29. Particularly in this case, it must be read as such because if read *huì* 𢆶, grandsons and sons (*sūnzǐ* 孫子) cannot be the recipients of an entreating ritual that is usually due to the ancestors. Certainly the inscription cannot be punctuated as *Jué sūnzǐ jué pī jí* 厥孫子厥丕吉 because this would require the second *jué* 厥 to function as a modal word similar to *qí* 其 ("may" or "will"), but *jué* has never been used in such a way in oracle bone and bronze inscriptions. I thank Professor Ken-ichi Takashima for confirming the last point in a recent communication (May 8, 2008). See also Takashima, "The So-Called 'Third'-Person," 404–31.
48. Cui also cast the Cui *yi* 毳匜 (JC: 10247), which was paired with the Cui *pan*, and four Cui *gui* 毳簋 (JC: 3931–3934), which are literally called *fēnguǐ* 饙簋 (food-serving *gui*-vessel), all intended for use by the royal mother, Kuishi 媿氏.
49. See *Shuowen jiezi* (Beijing: Zhonghua, 1963), 236–37. On the interpretation of the graph, see Zhou Fagao 周法高, *Jinwen gulin* 金文詁林 (Hong Kong: Chinese University of Hong Kong Press, 1975), 9:5464–73.

and the intended user of the vessel.⁵⁰ The same is true of the Lubo Yufu *pan* 魯伯愈父盤 (JC: 10113) and Lubo Yufu *yi* 魯伯愈父匜 (JC: 10244), described as *mòpán* 沫盤 (face-washing *pan*) and *mòyí* 沫匜 (face-washing *yi*), which were cast by an elite of the state of Lu 魯 as dowries for his daughter, who married into the state of Zhu 邾. There seems little doubt that these bronzes were intended for use in the private quarters of aristocratic ladies.⁵¹

The above examples convey a strong sense of intimacy between the inscribed "metal texts" and the everyday lives of the Western Zhou elites. They highlight the need to look into the domestic living space of the Western Zhou elites as one of the contexts in which bronze vessels were used and in which their inscribed texts were read and understood. Other bronzes were intended for use in banquets attended not only by the caster's family members but also by friends and colleagues in the caster's social circle. The Duoyou *ding* 多友鼎 (JC: 2835) states that the bronze was intended for use in "soliciting friends and colleagues" (*yòng péng yòng yǒu* 用朋用友). The recently published Shoushu Huanfu *xu* 獸叔奐父盨 says explicitly that the bronze was used to hold four different types of grains — rice, early rice, glutinous rice, and sorghum — to "offer as feast to the honored guests" (*jiābīn yòng xiǎng* 嘉賓用饗) and that with food served in abundance, its owner and guests will enjoy longevity of ten thousand years without limit.⁵² Sometimes the Zhou king was the honored guest at receptions in the residential compounds of his elite officials, as indicated by the highly formal expression "Use in feasting the king and welcoming his awards" (*yòng xiǎngwáng nìshòu* 用饗王逆逅[受]) that appears on a number of bronzes, including the Zhong Cheng *gui* 仲爯簋 (JC: 3747) and Bo Zhefu *gui* 伯者父簋 (JC: 3748).⁵³ The scenario

---

50. On this relation, see Li Chaoyuan 李朝遠, "Xi Zhou jinwen zhong de wang yu wangqi" 西周金文中的王與王器, *Wenwu* 2006.5: 74–79.
51. It is worth noting that very rarely does a *pan*-basin of a Western Zhou date have a line of ancestral dedication in its inscription. The conventional *pan*-plus-*he* set is purposely excluded from a list of sacrificial vessels (*zūnqì* 尊器) inscribed on the Han Huangfu *pan* 函皇父盤 (JC: 10164). This suggests that the primary social function of *pan* and *yi* might have been different from that of the sacrificial vessels.
52. See Li Qingli 李清莉, "Guoguo bowuguan shoucang de yijian tong xu" 虢國博物館收藏的一件銅盨, *Wenwu* 2004.4: 90.
53. On this reading of *nìshòu* 逆受, see Ma Chengyuan, *Shang Zhou*, 3:48. Another possible reading is *nìzào* 逆造 (to welcome the king's visit); see Guo Moruo, *Liang*

described by this line indeed dovetails well with the pattern of the administrative conduct of the Zhou king.[54]

Such social gatherings of the Western Zhou elites are also described in Zhou literature such as the poems "Luming" 鹿鳴 (Mao 161) and "Liuyue" 六月 (Mao 177) in the *Book of Poetry*, but particularly in "Famu" 伐木 (Mao 165):

> Seeing then that even a bird
> Searches for its mate's voice,
> How much the more must man
> Needs search out friends and kin.
>
> For the spirits are listening
> Whether we are all friendly and at peace.
> "Heave ho," cry the woodcutters.
> I have strained my wine so clear;
>
> I have got a fatted lamb,
> To which I invite all my fathers (paternal uncles).
> Even if they choose not to come,
> They cannot say I have neglected them.
>
> Spick-and-span I have sprinkled and swept;
> *I have set out the meats, the eight* gui-*vessels of grain.* [my italics]
> I have got a fatted ox,
> To which I invite all my uncles,
> And even if they choose not to come,
> They cannot hold me to blame.
>
> They are cutting wood on the bank.
> Of strained wine I have good store;
> The dishes and trays are all in rows.
> Elder brothers and younger brothers, do not stay afar!
>
> If people lose the virtue that is in them,
> It is a dry throat that has led them astray.
> When we have got wine, we strain it, we!
> When we have none, we buy it, we!
>
> Bang, bang, we drum, do we!

Zhou jinwen, 3, 42.
54. The inscriptions suggest that the Zhou king frequently traveled to various facilities, including those that were occupied by his administrative officials. On this point, see Li Feng, "'Offices' in Bronze Inscriptions," 45.

Nimbly step the dance, do we!
And take this opportunity
Of drinking clear wine.⁵⁵

Note that the solicitation of "friends and kin" is regarded as the quintessential virtue of the Zhou elites, comparable to the bird's seeking a mate. Here, in particular, eight *gui*-vessels are displayed in the banquet hosted by the Zhou elite for the purpose of entertaining his social connections. The poem "Liuyue," on the other hand, describes a family celebration banquet that friends and neighbors attend upon the return of Jifu 吉甫 from his long campaign against the Xianyun 獫狁, a scenario very similar to what is suggested by the Duoyou *ding* mentioned above.⁵⁶ Of course, such social gatherings and entertainment that took place in the residential quarters of the Zhou elites could proceed according to ritual rules. They could also have included procedures conducted in a religious manner. It is significant, however, that domestic social events had a special protocol that was meaningfully different from what might have regulated religious performances in the lineage ancestral temples; they had their unique sociopolitical roles in Western Zhou society. More important, they constituted a parallel social context that was as important as the religious context of ancestor worship for the use of bronze vessels and the appreciation of their metal texts.

The identification of this social context also explains why, after all, many long texts that commemorate significant historical events were cast on bronze vessels. As with the Sanshi *pan*, the durability of the documents was doubtless an important concern. But more importantly, the "publicity" provided by displaying the bronze vessels at such social events was the best vehicle for conveying the commemorative texts — originally written on perishable materials and kept perhaps in the family's private archive — to the larger social circle. Since these metal texts document the honors and accomplishments of the families that created them, displaying them in beautiful calligraphy on treasured vessels to relatives, friends, and colleagues at such social events would doubtless serve to promote the

---

55. Waley's translation (with minor revision), in Arthur Waley, trans., *The Book of Songs: The Ancient Chinese Classics of Poetry*, ed. Joseph R. Allen (New York: Grove Press, 1996), 137–38.
56. The Duoyun *ding* also describes a campaign against the Xianyun, and the inscription says that the bronze would be used in entertaining friends and colleagues. For an analysis of the Duoyou *ding* and the poem "Liuyue," see Li Feng, *Landscape and Power*, 147–53.

family's social prestige.[57] The inscriptions of the Shi Tian *gui* 史話簋 (JC: 4031), which commemorates a royal gift of cowries to Scribe Tian, state clearly that the honorable text was to be "observed every morning and evening" (*zhāoxī jiàn* 朝夕監) by Scribe Tian; perhaps included in its targeted readership was any person who paid a visit to the family.[58] When the Zhou king was among the honored guests at the kind of social events mentioned above, reading texts that commemorate honors regarded as originating in the king would have been very pleasant for the royal person; it could certainly contribute further to the favorable standing of the family in the royal view. In this way, literacy fulfilled its crucial sociopolitical role as the most explicit expression of social values, the way to facilitate political relations and form social groups among the Western Zhou elites.

Needless to say, the religious-ritual conduct of ancestor worship in the lineage temple certainly constituted another social context in which bronze vessels achieved *publicity* among the lineage members. At these events, the merits of the lineage ancestors inscribed on the bronzes were read and cherished, and the present-day accomplishments of the particular families were extolled and admired by their peer families of the same lineage group — all this could contribute greatly to the solidarity of the lineage. This also explains why many texts that commemorate significant historical events or personal administrative or military achievements of lineage members and whose contents show no direct link to the religious protocol of the lineage temple were placed on sacrificial vessels. However, although the need to communicate with the ancestors certainly led to the casting of some inscriptions, such as the Dong *gui* 㺝簋 (JC: 4322) mentioned above, in the majority of cases, the discontinuity of the content of the inscriptions from the spiritual world suggests that it was probably the social effect created by such religious service, and not the religious service itself, that led to the placement of the texts on the sacrificial vessels. Still, many long texts were cast on bronze vessels that cannot be considered sacrificial vessels.

---

57. Martin Kern has recently discussed at some length the *display function* of Western Zhou bronze inscriptions; Kern also noted how the accentuated use of calligraphy on middle and late Western Zhou bronzes reinforces their function in public display; "The Performance of Writing," 112–14, 167–71.
58. See Ma Chengyuan, *Shang Zhou*, 3:55.

Conclusion

Closing his survey of the social contexts of early Greek literacy in the seventh to sixth centuries B.C.E., William V. Harris notes that, although the extent of literacy and semiliteracy attained by the Greeks remains unclear, "at all events enough Greeks learned to read and write to permit a steady growth in the functions of literacy."[59] We cannot say any more about Western Zhou literacy than this, but perhaps by the late Western Zhou time, "enough" Zhou elites had learned to read and appreciate the written word to have made production of the large number of long texts necessary and meaningful. In all likelihood, literacy might have passed the stage of "scribal literacy," that is, an audience significantly larger than the small group of trained scribes read the texts on the bronzes. Of course, the great majority of the population remained illiterate.

Literacy had a routine place in the operation of the Zhou government, with writing serving as the essential instrument in official appointments, and perhaps also in the recording of merit for middle-to-late Western Zhou officials. Beyond the royal court, literacy was used in validating property transactions, territorial concessions, legal documentation, and military memory in a wide range of social functions. In all of its forms, literacy commanded an unequivocal sense of political and judicial power and authority, and it was the most explicit expression of political and socioeconomic relations. The meaning of bronze vessels for Western Zhou literacy rested on their access, because of the material and cultural values they carry, to various social contexts. Whether as utensils used by the Zhou elites in their everyday lives, or as religious objects used in lineage temples, the bronze vessels helped create a wide readership that was necessary for the maintenance and further expansion of literacy during the Western Zhou period. Literacy had a special meaning for the Zhou elites as both a path toward personal or family political and social prominence and a way to promote the proper functioning of the existing social system. Instead of "scribal literacy," the condition of Western Zhou literacy is thus better described as "elite literacy."

---

59. See Harris, *Ancient Literacy*, 64.

CHAPTER 9

Education and the Way of the Former Kings

Constance A. Cook

By the end of the Warring States period (481–221 B.C.E.), text production and consumption were clearly dominated by literati, who were composed primarily of elite sons. By that time, familiarity with a broad range of commonly known contemporary texts was an essential expression of power. Yet, pre-Qin bronze inscription evidence suggests that control over literacy was originally in the hands of a clan elder, who functioned as a teacher and advisor to the royal heir and who supervised a team of craftsmen, diviners, invocators, and archivists. This evidence also suggests that lineage narratives, memorized and adapted for performance at musical ceremonies by graduating youth, formed the early core of literary knowledge. Up through the Warring States period, bureaucratic expansion of this original Zhou-inspired educational structure — quite possibly inherited from the Shang — and reduplication of it in numerous local and competing state variations led to the spread of literacy among the elite throughout the Yellow and Yangzi River valleys.

The spread of lineage narratives and songs from court to court, as well as the spread of functional literacy by master teachers or refugee members of the original Zhou-style teams, can be attributed not only to official contacts during the Western Zhou period and exchanges between states after the fall of the Zhou but also to the numerous wars and internecine struggles that resulted in floods of refugees and the disenfranchisement of members of the original teams. This dispersal of ritual teachers and technicians contributed to the independent creation of texts of all types, examples of which can presently be dated only as far back as the Warring States period but which no doubt existed earlier. By the third century B.C.E., literacy at the highest levels was displayed not only in the ability to author lengthy texts but also in the ability to display knowledge of a vast array of popular political and religious theories.

Before the disintegration of the Zhou lineage network, general elite literacy was most likely limited to oral recitation of lineage historical narratives during key ceremonies, such as coming-of-age ceremonies, with specific higher-level skills reserved for a select few. In this system, an elder would tutor the lineage heir, who in turn would be responsible for leading his or her generation of youth. Bronze records of coming-of-age ceremonies suggest that training for these performances functioned as a crucible for text production among the elite.[1] Spring and Autumn period examples offer clear evidence of an active musical performance, which is reflected also in the transmitted *Book of Poetry* (Shijing) and *Book of Documents* (Shangshu), known popularly as the *Shi* 詩 and the *Shu* 書, that can be linked to sections of text originally rooted in tales of ancestral founders and kings, that is, lineage narratives.[2] By the end of this period, there is a shift away from displays of knowledge of lineage history to displays of common literary knowledge, suggesting the rise of oral- and text-based learning shared among the elites in all powerful courts of the time. The rhetoric reflecting the lively musical ceremonies of Spring and Autumn period regional cultures changed dramatically, which further suggests social disruption, lost histories, and the manipulation of text (lineage records, songs, and tales) for purposes of political suasion and debate.[3]

---

1. For example, the *Book of Rites* (Liji 禮記) ("Neize" 內則) notes that at the age of six, boys are taught numbers and vocabulary; at eight, they have to understand social rank; at nine, the calendar; at ten, they learn to write and perform certain rituals; at thirteen, they learn music, eulogies, songs, dance, and archery; and at twenty, when they are capped, they must perform grand dances. Girls were separated out at age seven and were directed down a different path of learning; at fifteen, their hair was pinned up, symbolizing marriageability; at twenty-three, they married. See *Shisanjing zhushu* 27:1461–65. For musical education, see also Yang Hua 楊華, *Xian Qin liyue wenhua* 先秦禮樂文化 (Hankou: Hubei Jiaoyu Chubanshe, 1997), 120–26.
2. See Yang Hua, *Xian Qin liyue,* 127–37, 179–208; Shaughnessy, *Before Confucius: Studies in the Creation of the Chinese Classics* (Albany, NY: SUNY, 1997), 165–95; Falkenhausen, "Issues in Western Zhou Studies," 156–70; Cook, "Wealth and the Western Zhou," 278–82; Martin Kern, "Bronze Inscriptions, the *Shijing* and the *Shangshu*: The Evolution of the Ancestral Sacrifice during the Western Zhou," in *Early Chinese Religion*, ed., J. Lagerwey and M. Kalinowski (Leiden: Brill, 2008), 143–200.
3. See Wai-yee Li's discussion on the formation and use of various *Chunqiu* style texts and the rise of an oral and written exegetical tradition during the Warring States period; *The Readability of the Past in Early Chinese Historiography* (Cambridge, Mass.: Harvard University Press, 2008), 29–84.

The early literati of the Eastern Zhou period for the most part were linked either directly or obliquely to the disintegrated network of clan-based alliances built originally by the Zhou and through which education of the youth or "learning" (*xué* 學) passed. By the time of Confucius, the effort to carry on high Zhou traditions had become a matter of creative rearticulation and perhaps led to the accumulation of texts — both oral and written — representing "lost words." During the fourth century B.C.E., powerful courts with long literary traditions tried to gather some of the most influential of the groups of migrating elite into academies, such as the Jixia 稷下 in Qi 齊, to provide an archive of contemporary knowledge and for the prestige for the royal house. Itinerant teachers, some followed by groups of disciples who no doubt manufactured bamboo texts as memory aids (perhaps carried about in woven grass quivers and stored in wall niches) gathered in such academies. These texts, like the bronze inscriptions, recorded methods of obtaining *dé* 德, a type of inner power or accumulated merit obtained from Heaven by following a prescribed plan of action on earth. During the Western Zhou period, ancestors connected to a founder king of a particular geographical region were required intermediaries for obtaining *dé*, but by the Warring States period, the literati had broken loose from this requirement and internalized the old rituals for purposes of individual self-enlightenment.[4]

Most notable among the Warring States period teachers for whom literacy and the practice of Zhou-style "ritual" *lǐ* 禮 to obtain *dé* were those Ru 儒 whose ancestral master was the fifth-century B.C.E. Confucius — a man who lived precisely at the time when education and elite text production had shifted away from the performance of lineage narratives at musical ceremonies and toward independent teachers and text generation by disenfranchised literati.[5] A minor member of an elite family in the northeastern state of Lu, he took as his own ancestral model the founding ancestor of the Lu state, Zhougong, who, according to legend, was the uncle, advisor, and teacher of the youthful Zhou king Cheng in late eleventh century B.C.E.,[6] an archetypical role of teacher as elder kin. This

---

4. This practice is documented in Michael Puett, *To Become a God: Cosmology, Sacrifice, and Self-Divinization in Early China* (Cambridge, Mass.: Harvard University Press, 2002), 80–121.
5. See Cho-yun Hsu, "The Spring and Autumn Period," in Loewe and Shaughnessy, eds., esp. 583–86.
6. See Robert Eno, "The Background of the Kong Family of Lu and the Origins of Ruism," *Early China* 28 (2003): 1–41; David Nivison, "The Classical Philosophical Writings,"

pedigree authorized the Ru to practice Zhou "ritual" and to preserve texts required for learning the Way (*dào* 道) through the imitation of the "ancients" (*gǔrén* 古人). Ru practices emerged out of the Western Zhou educational model for training youth for performances that took place during ancestor worship ceremonies.[7] According to the Ru formulation, "elite children" (*guózǐ* 國子), especially those in line to inherit power and wealth (*shìzǐ* 世子), must be trained in the Six Arts (*Liùyì* 六藝) inherited from the "ancients," which, according to the transmitted *Zhouli* ("Diguan situ" 地官司徒, 2), consisted of the performance of ritual (*lǐ* 禮), music (*yuè* 樂), archery (*shè* 射), driving (a chariot) (*yù* 御), writing (*shū* 書), and calculation (of calendars) (*shù* 數)[8] — all arts to which Zhou bronze inscriptions attest.

As some Warring States thinkers who did not derive from Zhou heritage states contested the Ru Way as irrelevant to solving contemporary social crises, a variety of ancient models were proposed that would affect education and text production. Oral debate over curriculum focused on recovering the "lost words of the former kings" (*xiānwáng zhī yíyán* 先王之遺言).[9] The great Ru scholar Xunzi 荀子 (circa 310–circa 210 B.C.E.), tried to clarify the relevance of the Ru path, and, as an acknowledgment of the spread of literacy beyond the courts — many of which he viewed as

---

in Loewe and Shaughnessy, eds., 753–54, 759. For Zhougong as founder ancestor, see Kominami Ichirō, "Rituals for the Earth," in Lagerwey and Kalinowski, eds., 221; Cook, "Ancestor Worship during the Eastern Zhou," in Lagerwey and Kalinowski, eds., 245.

7. See Rao Zongyi 饒宗頤, Peng Lin 彭林, Chen Wei 陳偉, and Gong Jianping 龔建平, in Wuhan Daxue Zhongguo Wenhua Yanjiuyuan, ed., *Guodian Chujian guoji xueshu yantaohui lunwenji* 郭店楚簡國際學術研討會論文集 (Wuhan: Hubei Renmin, 2000); Shen Pei 沈培, in *Disijie guoji Zhongguo guwenzixue yantaohui lunwen* 第四屆中國古文字學研討會論文, ed. Zhang Guangyu 張光裕 (Hong Kong: The Chinese University of Hong Kong, 2004), 217–31; Cook, "Wealth and the Western Zhou," 284; Cook, "Ancestor Worship," 237–62.

8. *Shisanjing zhushu*, 10:707. For dating the formation of the *Zhouli* text, see Peng Lin 彭林, *Zhouli zhuti sixiang yu chengshu niandai yanjiu* 周禮主體思想與成書年代研究 (Hebei: Zhongguo Shehui Kexue, 1991). For links between oral performance, text, and the Six Arts, see Martin Kern, "The Odes in Excavated Manuscripts," in *Text and Ritual in Early China* (Seattle: University of Washington Press, 2005), 148–93, esp. 180–82. Most useful is the notion of an "open text" (180) and the use of oral elements in "canonical teaching" (181). See also Kern, "The Performance of Writing," 109.

9. *Xunzi* ("Quanxue" 勸學), *Zhuzi jicheng* 諸子集成 edition (1986; reprint, Shanghai: Shanghai Shudian, 1991), 2:1–2.

corrupt — he advocated the establishment of merit-based schools for everyone, which at the time were most likely located in ancestral shrine buildings where clans also cared for their elderly.[10] Despite the array of "more ancient sages" (*shèngrén* 聖人) whom thinkers of his time followed, Xunzi, not surprisingly, claimed that the early Zhou kings and the ultimate teacher Zhougong[11] provided the true Way of the former kings (*xiānwáng zhī dào*) to be "traversed" (*xíng* 行).[12] It is no accident that, for the Ru, following this model involved ritual musical performance (*lǐyuè* 禮樂) and that the sign of achievement was observed in the practitioner's decorum or outer manifestation (*yí* 儀).[13] The rhetoric can be traced through bronze inscriptions, particularly those commemorating coming-of-age ceremonies, right back to the Western Zhou period. By Xunzi's time, the Ru curriculum included knowledge of oral and written versions of an ur-canon — the *Book of Documents* and the *Book of Poetry*,

---

10. J. Knoblock, *Xunzi: A Translation and Study of the Complete Works*, (Palo Alto, Calif.: Stanford University, 1994), 1:3–35; *Xunzi* ("Wangzhi" 王制), *Zhuzi jicheng* edition, 94. The establishment of schools in cities (*yì* 邑) and for non-elite boys is also mentioned in the *Liji* ("Wangzhi" 王制); see *Shisanjing zhushu*, 12:1338–39. It is also described as a means of transforming the people, mentioned in *Liji* ("Xueji" 學記); *Shisanjing zhushu*, 36:1521. Village clan-based schools (*xiāngxiào* 鄉校) may have existed as early as the Spring and Autumn period for the nurturing of loyalty and skillfulness in governing (*zhōngshàn*) 忠善, as mentioned in *Zuozhuan* (Xiang 襄, 31); *Shisanjing zhushu*, 40:2016. For ancestral shrines as schools, see *Liji* ("Wenwang shizi" 文王世子); *Shisanjing zhushu*, 20:1404–6. For the same shrines linked to different sages and earlier time periods, see *Liji* ("Neize" 內則 and "Mingtang wei" 明堂位); *Shisanjing zhushu*, 28:1467 and 31:1491. For *xiáng* 庠 (Zhou), *xù* 序 (Shang), *xué* 學, and *xiào* 校 (Xia) and for "nurturing (the elderly)" (*yǎng* 養), archery (*shè* 射), and teaching (*jiào* 教), see Yang Hua, *Xian Qin liyue*, 123–25. All *xué* taught proper human relations; see *Mengzi* 孟子 ("Teng Wengong: shang" 滕文公上), *Zhuzi jicheng* 諸子集成 edition (1986; reprint, Shanghai: Shanghai Shudian, 1991), 1:202.
11. See Knoblock's discussion; *Xunzi*, 2:28–31.
12. See Ke Heli (Constance A. Cook), "Xianwang zhi dao yu 'weiyi' de waihua biaoxian" 先王之道與"威儀"的外化表現, in *Chudi jianbo sixiang yanjiu* 楚地簡帛思想研究, ed. Ding Sixin 丁四新 (Wuhan: Hubei Jiaoyu, 2007), 3:270–83.
13. Mozi 墨子 described this as an "evil technique" (*xiéshù* 邪術), a play on the term "Ru technique" (*rúshù* 儒術]). For Mozi, the "expression of decorum" (*shìyí* 示儀) by a certain man named Kong, with all of its group singing, drumming, and dancing and their elaborate rituals of "rising and descending," was, like the entire the Ru system of "broad learning" (*bóxué* 博學), completely useless for ordinary people. See *Mozi* 墨子, *Zhuzi jicheng* edition (1986; reprint, Shanghai: Shanghai Shudian, 1991), 4:185.

the *Rites* (Li 禮) and the *Music* (Yue 樂), and the *Spring and Autumn Annals* (Chunqiu 春秋)[14] — texts that existed in multiple forms during Xunzi's time and may indeed have retained vestiges of Zhou narratives, as traditionally believed.

Education by the end of the Warring States period seems to have been a combination of traditional Zhou-style performance-based learning taught by hired "masters" (*shī* 師) and the reading and memorization of an array of texts that prepared students (*xuéshì* 學士 or *dìzǐ* 弟子) for debate (*shuō* 說, *jiǎng* 講, *lùn* 論, or *biàn* 辯).[15] By the time of archivist Sima Qian (circa 145–86 B.C.E.), however, "literary culture" (*wén* 文) had evolved away from a simple public display of literary knowledge through speeches to a more text-based learning. This cultural move away from what David Schaberg denotes as "an ideology of mimesis" represents the true loss of Zhou tradition.[16]

Elite Education in Western Zhou

Education and literacy developed within the context of ancestor worship, a fundamental organizing principle of ancient Chinese society. Late Shang records — which, like Zhou bronze inscriptions, represent a functional literacy — display the incorporation of oral literature into text and hence a

---

14. *Xunzi* ("Quanxue"), *Zhuzi jicheng* edition The *Spring and Autumn Annals* is not mentioned in the ("Wangzhi"); *Shisanjing zhushu*, 13:1342. For later editing and rewriting of early manuscripts, see Edward Shaughnessy, *Rewriting Early Chinese Texts* (Albany: State University of New York, 2006), 1–61.
15. According to the "Wangzhi" chapter of the *Liji*, the teaching of royal children took place in the left side of the southern section of the patriarch's hall (*gōng gōng nán zhī zuǒ* 公宮南之左), whereas older students were taught outside the city wall or in the suburbs (*jiāo* 郊); see *Shisanjing zhushu*, 12:1332. Evidence for the use of "learning" as a preparation for debate is strongest in the *Mozi* and *Xunzi* texts. Xunzi, who advocated the transformative power of learning the "lost words" of the former kings, notes that in order to gain "broad learning," one must chant when young and debate when grown; see *Xunzi*, *Zhuzi jicheng* edition, 2:335. Mozi deplored the chanting of the Way and words of the former kings for the sake of persuading the governing elite when people would do better by focusing their efforts on agriculture; see *Mozi*, *Zhuzi jicheng* edition, 287.
16. Stephen W. Durrant, *The Cloudy Mirror: Tension and Conflict in the Writings of Sima Qian* (Albany: State University of New York, 1995), xiv–xv. On the ritual signification of speech as *wén* in the formation of texts during the Warring States period, see Schaberg, *A Patterned Past*, 57–95.

higher level of literacy; they consist of military and ritual records of activities that would concern the ancestors, such as the welfare of their families, their descendants, and their lands. Records inscribed on bronze sacrificial vessels and bells were made as testimonies of satisfactory communication with the ancestors and as awards of their approval. For Zhou youth, "learning" focused on the military and ritual arts taught in "halls" (*gōng* 宮) or outside by clansmen who had achieved the rank of "master" (*shī* 師). The ritual arts that required the recounting of lineage narratives were the most likely forum for the transfer of literacy among the elite.

A study of the ritual rhetoric preserved on Western Zhou bronze inscriptions shows that the Way (or, really, the "ways") of the former kings so popular during the Eastern Zhou period developed out of the Western Zhou tradition of "following the model" (*shuàixíng* 帥型) of ancestral lineage founders by "youth" (*xiǎozǐ* 小子).[17] By the late tenth century B.C.E., music (*yuè* 樂) had clearly become integral to the ritual display of successful modeling during feasts and sacrifices, such as in the *dì* 禘 ceremony, when all the ancestral spirits were perceived as watching and adjustments were made in rank.[18] These ceremonies marked moments

---

17. Kimura Hideumi 木村秀海 reviewed hundreds of *xiǎozǐ* examples in 1981 and concluded that by the Western Zhou period, the term was a general term for "children, youth" or a special reference to the lineage heir; "Sei Shū kinbun ni mieru shōshi ni tsuite — Sei Shū no shihai kikō no ichimen" 西周金文に見える小子について — 西周の支配機構の一面, *Shirin* 64, no. 6 (1981): 62–82. It could also be a personal term of self-reference by the heir; see Lothar von Falkenhausen, *Chinese Society in the Age of Confucius (100–250 BC): The Archaeological Evidence* (Los Angeles: Cotsen Institute of Archaeology, University of California, 2006), 170. By the Warring States period, it was also pejorative or self-deprecatory.
18. See JC: 10175, 247–50, 4170–77, dated roughly to the time of the middle Western Zhou cultural shift away from the Shang model; see Falkenhausen, *Chinese Society*, 29–73. For feasting, see Constance A. Cook, "Ritual Feasting in Ancient China," in *Di'erjie guoji Zhongguo guwenzixue yantaohui lunwenji* 第二屆國際中國古文字學研討會論文集, ed. Chinese Department, The University of Hong Kong (Hong Kong: The Chinese University of Hong Kong, 1993), 469–87; Constance A. Cook, "Scribes, Cooks, and Artisans: Breaking Zhou Tradition," *Early China* 20 (1995–96): 241–69; Constance A. Cook, "Wealth and the Western Zhou," 264, 285–90; Constance A. Cook, "Moonshine and Millet: Feasting and Purification Rituals in Ancient China," in *Of Tripod and Palate: Food, Politics, and Religion in Traditional China*, ed. Roel Sterckx (New York: Palgrave Macmillan, 2005), 9–23; and Liu Yu 劉雨, *Jinwen lunji* 金文論集 (Beijing: Zijincheng Chubanshe, 2006), 61–73.

of completion in the cycles of "mortuary feasts" (xiǎng 享) and mourning for the deceased.[19] The ritual display, called "Awesome Decorum" (wēiyí 威儀), involved prescribed movements of "grasping" the ancestral dé (bǐngdé 秉德), a symbolic process perceived as "opening up the heart (or body)" (guǎngpì xīn/shēn 廣辟心/身) of the "youth" before he could successfully take up his inherited position.[20] The "awesome" wēi 威 or terrifying nature of the performance mimicked the way Heaven had appeared to the former kings (a process called "matching" [pèi 配] the sky pattern) and how the Zhou soldiers must appear in battle against non-Zhou peoples in the "four regions" (sìfāng 四方). Military training and a ritual mimesis of military success, likely musical performance, was a key aspect of Zhou education. Their authority required an ancestral link to the original Zhou event of "creating the nation" (zuòbāng 作邦). A display of successful training required proof of the perpetual reenactment of that event through continuous battles in order to "spread" (fū 敷) the Zhou mandate and ritual to peoples in the four regions. Literacy, too, was spread through this mechanism.

The Eastern Zhou Period

The traumatic loss of authority and voice suffered by the Zhou when they were forced to flee east, away from their ancestral burial grounds, in the eighth century B.C.E. was felt throughout the Chinese heartland. Zhou

---

19. See JC: 64, 145–48, 246, 4242, and 4326. The fact that the verb "to open up" the body was the same used to represent the settling of a new land after conquest suggests an early metaphor for micro- and macro-spaces and a parallel need to exorcise them both; see *Mozi, Zhuzi jicheng* edition, 272; Cook, "Wealth of the Western Zhou," 273–74. For a study of the journey of the deceased from the tomb to Heaven, see Constance A. Cook, *Death in Ancient China: The Tale of One Man's Journey* (Leiden: Brill, 2006), 19–42; Cook, "Ancestor Worship," 254, 271–75.
20. Michael Nylan notes that by the Qin period, the performances of wēiyí (which she translates as "Awesome Authority") were public displays of power involving banquets and the parade of a deceased emperor's remains "as they were conveyed from gravesite to temple"; "Toward an Archaeology of Writing," in Kern, ed., 23–24. Bronze examples are too numerous to list here and are the focus of another more detailed study. From the examples in the *Book of Poetry* (e.g., "Pan Shui" 泮水), the context is a martial dance; see *Shisanjing zhushu*, 20.1:610–12. Mozi rather disdainfully referred to the Ru wēiyí performance as "bowing, stretching, and going around in circles"; *Mozi, Zhuzi jicheng* edition, 103.

codes and lineage records lost their ceremonial connection to the ancestors, as lineages in the Zhou network of alliances were forced to break off into independent clan-run states and as non-Zhou states rose to power.[21] The Zhou family itself never recovered, although the gravitas of the Zhou model instigated a scramble for refugee masters of proper Zhou-style ritual among local patrons less familiar with Zhou arts.[22]

An examination of Spring and Autumn period inscriptions from the states of Qin 秦, Jin 晉, Chu 楚, Qi, and Yue 越 — dispersed over geography and time — reveals clear continuities with and radical differences from the Zhou-style rhetoric. First, there were structural changes. Many Western Zhou inscriptions reveal a statement-and-response structure of oral statements, with the statements or testimonies of the king or patriarch establishing the authority for the event followed by the awardee or "youth's" response (a eulogy or *duìyáng* 對揚, typically cast separately on a different vessel or bell). Only in Qi was a version of this original gift-giving structure retained. All other examples were modeled on the "response" only.[23] The lineage narrative was usually recited as an opening to the reward, but in some cases, including the Qi, it was reserved for the "response."

A major shift evident in all Spring and Autumn examples is the move away from the Zhou ancestral model to one involving either a pre-Zhou sage or none at all. Bronze inscriptions cast in the Zhou homeland and throughout its ancient network in the Yellow River region retained titular acknowledgment of the Zhou through the use of the title "patriarch" (*gōng* 公) instead of "king" (*wáng* 王) or through reference to the Zhou "reign

---

21. For a study of radical changes in the social ranking system, see Falkenhausen, *Chinese Society*, 326–99.
22. For tales from the *Zuozhuan*, see Cook, "Scribes, Cooks, and Artisans," 243, 256–60; Constance A. Cook, "The Ideology of the Chu Ruling Class: Ritual Rhetoric and Bronze Inscriptions," in *Defining Chu: Image and Reality in Ancient China*, ed. Constance A. Cook and John Steel Major (Honolulu: University of Hawai'i Press, 1999), 67–76.
23. For example, the Liang Qi *zhong* 梁其鐘 (JC: 187–92) inscription, translated in Constance A. Cook, "The Bell of Liang Qi," in *Chinese Religion*, ed. D. A. Sommer (Oxford: Oxford University Press, 1994), 15–16. For bell inscriptions in the "subjective mode" (i.e., inscriptions that do not mention a patron or gift-giver but only the gift recipient or vessel maker), see Lother von Falkenhausen, "Ritual Music in Bronze Age China: An Archaeological Perspective" (PhD diss., Harvard University, 1988), 646–61; see also Constance A. Cook, "Auspicious Metals," 94–161; Constance A. Cook, "Wealth of the Western Zhou," 255–60. These statements functioned as the recipient's response narrative to the award.

calendar" (*wángnián* 王年) in the dating formula.

Even in the southern tradition, which ignored many of the Zhou prerogatives, the emphasis on ritual music and performance flourished. Indeed, while it is clear that ritual music was important to the Zhou during the second half of the Western Zhou period, Spring and Autumn period inscriptions, particularly those from Qin, Jin, and Chu (the western and earlier end of the spectrum of examples studied here), reveal an active social setting, one that involved groups of dancing youths, tales of successful battles, eulogies of the former kings, and the display of "awesome decorum" (*wēiyí*) that corresponds in language to songs in the "Daya," "Xiaoya," and "Song" sections of the *Book of Poetry*.[24] The most salient evidence is the surge in use of reduplicated binoms. Attention to the type and distribution of these binoms reveals regions of mutual influence and the ancient paths used for the spread of literacy.

Reduplicated binoms consisted of two graphs representing a repeated descriptive modifier in the *Book of Poetry* and in the received textual tradition. In the inscriptions, the graphs themselves are not repeated but marked for repetition with a little sign for "two" underneath the graph in question. The oral nature of their function in the record is confirmed by their occurrence on some inscriptions marked by the oral cue *yuē* 曰 in prayer formulas. It is possible that originally their reduplication may not have represented repetition so much as a method of pronunciation — perhaps a lengthening of the syllable or a particular pitch followed by a breath, suggested by the use of the breath word *xī* 兮 in place of the second syllable in some later texts and where they are explained as expressions of *wēiyí* (e.g., "Thunderous! Glistening!" 赫兮烜兮) and linked to cultivation of the Dao and *dé*.[25] In the *Book of Poetry* and the inscriptions, they are used before nouns requiring respect, for example, the names of ancestors, rulers, or shrines, but also, particularly in later times, before styles of behavior or performance — even governing performance

---

24. For reduplicated binoms on inscriptions and in the *Book of Poetry* as indicators of ritual music performances at feasts for ancestors, see Falkenhausen, "Ritual Music," 676–94, 1370–71, table 44; *Suspended Music: Chime-bells in the Culture of Bronze Age China* (Berkeley: University of California Press, 1993), 23–32. For oral performance, see Martin Kern, "*Shi Jing* Songs as Performance Texts: A Case Study of the 'Chu Ci' (Thorny Caltrop)," *Early China* 25 (2000): 55–76; "Bronze Inscriptions," 143–88. For Western Zhou ancestor rituals, see Liu Yu, "Xi Zhou jinwen zhong de jizuli" 西周金文中的祭祖禮, *Kaogu xuebao* 1989.4: 499–522.

25. See similar uses in *Liji* ("Daxue") and *Erya*; *Shisanjing zhushu*, 60:1673, 4:2591.

— that were considered as enacted before the ancestors in sacred places. The trajectory of their frequency and use over time and geography, however, discloses that these oral formulas suffer a precipitous decline at the end of the Spring and Autumn period, particularly in inscriptions generated in the coastal region. This loss of an oral musical tradition coincides with the rise of independent textual production as symbolized by Confucius.

The Zhou ancestral model suffered a loss in the previously unquestioned superior status of its founder ancestors and hence precipitated a crisis over the very definition of spirits, human nature, and life. While local leaders scrambled to set up their own founder ancestors in positions of power,[26] new cosmic ideologies, promulgated at places like the Jixia academy, removed ancestral power entirely. Instead of conceiving of oneself as the privileged incarnation of ancestral *dé*, one was merely a coagulation of *qì*, the cosmic vapor that composed all material objects — *dé* was an accumulation of *qì* channeled through music;[27] however, for some time, the knowledge of the narrative literature and musical forms associated with various sets of former kings continued to be a source of power. Han editors of Warring States texts dealt with the cacophony of different Ways of different former kings by aligning texts in chapters and books, such as the *Book of Documents* (Shujing 書經), along an evolutionary model of the Three Dynasties.[28]

As the Zhou structure crumbled, musical performance of ancestral narratives continued to be an arena for the transfer of literary knowledge among the elite.[29] There was also local manipulation of the traditional Zhou format of statement and response between the gift giver or king and the awardee in order to account for the loss of Zhou authority. At the same time, local rulers were appealing to non-Zhou founder kings as sources of power, hence revealing versions of previously uninscribed lineage

---

26. See Cook, "Ancestor Worship," 241–50, 256–71; Constance A. Cook, "Ritual, Politics, and the Issue of *Feng* 封," in *Shi Quan xiansheng jiushi danchen jinian wenji* 石泉先生九十誕辰紀念文集, ed. Wuhan Daxue Lishi Dili Yanjiusuo (Wuhan: Hubei Renmin Chubanshe, 2007), 215–67.
27. See Erica Brindley, "The Cosmic Power of Sound in the Late Warring States and Han Periods," *Journal of Chinese Religions* 35 (2007): 29–63.
28. Constance A. Cook, "Xianwang zhi dao," 273, 726–83.
29. For a history of Qin's relations with the Zhou, see Li Feng, *Landscape and Power in Early China*, 262–78. For Chu, see Barry Blakeley, "The Geography of Chu," in Cook and Major, eds., 9–13. For a study of the Zhou culture's sweep east, see Falkenhausen, *Chinese Society*, 252–71.

EDUCATION AND THE WAY OF THE FORMER KINGS

narratives. During this era, literacy, which had already been transferred by the Zhou to the elite of local areas, took on new life and expanded even further.

The Qin

The Qin coming-of-age inscriptions were structured like Western Zhou "response" narratives, which begin with a "statement" or oral cue (*yuē*) by the lineage head, the patriarch. The bell inscription on the Qingong *zhong* is divided into two speeches followed by a general oath regarding the making of the bells,[30] their use, and the blessing he hopes to receive as a result. The tureen inscription on the Qingong *gui* is a single speech, which can be broken into three sections:[31] the first section, like the first speech on the bell, eulogizing his ancestors and reciting a lineage narrative; the second section, like the second speech on the bell, describing his own training and behavior; the third section, much like the one on the bell, describing his use of the vessel for sacrifices to the ancestral spirits and the blessings he would receive, including long life and extended political power.

In the first section of this tripartite "response" narrative, the patriarch addresses a general audience from the position in the ancestral shrine of the main lineage heir. He summons the ancestral spirits to the ceremony through his recitation of lineage empowerment and sacred authority.

The bell:

秦公曰：我先且（祖）受天命，商（賞）宅受或（域），烈烈卲（昭）文公、靜公、憲公，不墜于上，卲（昭）合皇天，以虩事蠻方。

The patriarch of Qin said: "My former ancestor received Heaven's mandate and was rewarded with a dwelling and territory. Blazing, so blazing! The illustrious Patriarch Wen, Patriarch Jing, and Patriarch Xian did not upset (the mandate) of those (spirits) up above. They summoned and joined brilliant Heaven to vigilantly deal with the Man-fang peoples."

The tureen:

---

30. JC: 262-64 (slightly different version on JC: 267–70); Falkenhausen, "Ritual Music," 1040–65; Gilbert Mattos, "Eastern Zhou Inscriptions," in E. Shaughnessy, ed., 111–20.
31. JC: 4315; Mattos, "Eastern Zhou," 114–17.

秦公曰：不（丕）顯朕皇且（祖）受天命，鼏（定）宅禹責（蹟），
十又二公才（在）帝之坏（坏），嚴龏（恭）夤天命，保業厥秦，虩
事蠻夏，

The patriarch of Qin said: "Greatly manifest are my brilliant ancestors who received the heavenly mandate to settle and reside in the tracks of Yu. The twelve patriarchs who reside on the lord's (Di's) flanks sternly paid their respects and revered Heaven's mandate. They protected the (Zhou) legacy for them in Qin and vigilantly dealt (with issues of) the Man and Xia peoples."

The use of the word "mandate" reveals the double meaning of this section. The "mandate" first of all references the original Zhou mandate as well as the Zhou authorization of the Qin house to function as a member of the Zhou tribute and trade network. This implies a contract of mutual protection strengthened though intermarriage.[32] The fact that the Zhou ancestral kings and their mandate were discredited adds a new level of interpretation to the word "mandate," that is, the Qin rulers could now establish their own rights to rule. Their lineage narrative begins not with the Zhou at all but with "the tracks" of sage-king Yu 禹, the legendary founder of the pre-Shang Xia dynasty. In the song tradition recorded in the *Book of Poetry*, the "tracks of Yu" actually refers to the Zhou homeland around the Feng River 豐水 area and, by extension, the entire protective network of allied states and territories set up by the Zhou, which included the ancient lands of Yu's reputed rule.[33] This independence was in fact not totally new but relied on an earlier minority tradition, already evident in the Western Zhou period, of the Yu founder king worship.[34]

In the second section, the patriarch extends the narrative to himself, providing testimony that he had accurately followed the ancestral model defined in the first section. From this section, we know that living elders were now being addressed.

The bell:

公及王姬曰：余小子，余夙夕虔敬朕祀，以受多福，克明又（有）厥

---

32. Li Feng, *Landscape and Power*, 270–76.
33. Song "Wenwang you sheng" 文王有聲, in "Daya"; *Shisanjing zhushu*, 16.5:526–27.
34. See Constance A. Cook, "The Bin Gong *xu* and Sage King Yu," in *The X Gong* Xu: *A Report and Papers fron the Dartmouth Workshop*, ed. Xing Wen (Hanover, N.H.: Dartmouth College, 2003), 23–28.

心，螯（戾）穌亂士，咸畜左右：藹藹允義（儀），翼受明德，以康奠協朕或（域），羨百蠻具即其服，

The patriarch approached the royal woman of the Ji clan (his widowed mother) and said: "As a youth, I presented offerings from dawn to dusk and paid my respects through (the performance of) my ancestral sacrifices so that I received multiple blessings of good fortune. I was then able to illuminate my heart completely so that I could put the next generation of educated men into order and harmony, nurturing them all for (positions) on the left and right (of me), so that they flocked (to court), perfecting (their) demeanors. Protected, (I) received the luminous inner power and made my territory peaceful, settled, and unified by bringing all the rebellious Man peoples into submission."

The tureen:

余雖小子，穆穆帥秉明德，烈烈桓桓，邁（萬）民是敕（利），咸畜亂士，藹藹文武，鎮（？）靜不廷，

"Even though I was (but) a youth, I gravely, so gravely, followed (the ancestors' model) and grasped (from them) the luminous inner power. Blazing, so blazing! Valiantly, so valiantly! The ten thousand peoples have benefited from this (grasped power) so that all the younger generation of men nurtured (in this tradition) flock (to court) and, acting like Wen and Wu in manner, (together) squash and pacify those who would not come to court."

The musical aspect of this section is apparent in the Qin use of reduplicative binoms. The Qin praise of the Wen and Wu style of ritual and military behavior (but not of the kings themselves) has more in common with *Book of Poetry* odes than with Western Zhou rhetorical models, which employed many fewer binoms. The binoms reveal aspects of the performance. First, there is the somber aspect of following in the ancestral footsteps using *mùmù* 穆穆, the most ancient Zhou term for introducing the "greatly manifest" (*pīxiǎn* 丕顯) ancestors, and a description of stone chime music in the *Book of Poetry*.[35] Then the dance speeds up into a light-filled and glorious display of "awesomeness."[36] In the ode "Juan E" 卷阿, *ǎiǎi* 藹藹 (flocking to court) describes elite

---

35. Mao no. 301; *Shisanjing zhushu*, 20.3:620–21.
36. The *Erya* defines *huánhuán lièliè* as "awesomeness" (*wēi* 威); *Shisanjing zhushu*, 4:2589.

youths (王多吉士/人) preparing for battle in the four regions. The "gathering" immediately follows the image of phoenixes turning as a group in flight, which suggests birdlike dance movements and even possible costume attributes. Yet, we still know from the similar use of binoms *jǐjǐ* 濟濟 or *qiàngqiàng* 蹌蹌 in the *Book of Poetry* that the dance was martial in nature and involved a group expression of "awesome decorum."[37]

Ritual expressions of battles for the Qin had to be matched by actual battles to suppress non-tribute-paying peoples. The Qin patriarch received "the luminous inner power" from his ancestors as a reward for his performance in both arenas. He then rose to the position of leader over his entire generation of men and successfully expanded the state.[38] This exact pattern, derived from the Western Zhou, was later repeated in Jin.

The third section of the inscriptions explains more about the celebration of his successful ascendance to his father's position followed by the Qin ruler's prescient prayer for control of the world. One step in gaining control was successful management of the lineage network. This was codified into the ancestral ritual code requiring the heir to "nurture" his male relatives in exchange for their protection, a pattern seen also in the Western Zhou. Literacy among this cohort may have been limited to the ability to memorize lineage narratives and dance patterns.

The bell:

乍（作）厥龢鐘，靈音鎗鎗（鍠鍠）雝雝，以匽（宴）皇公，以受大福，屯（純）魯多釐，大壽萬年，秦公其畯令才（在）立（位），膺受大命，眉壽無彊（疆），匍（敷）有四方，其康寶。

I make these harmonious bells so that their numinous tones (sing like birds) in harmony entertaining (during feasts) the brilliant patriarchs and handing us great blessings of good fortune, abundant wealth and many gifts, with a great long life of ten thousand years. May it be that I, the Qin patriarch, will control and command in (my) position (as ruler) taking on and receiving Heaven's mandate. (And may I) have extended long life without limit and be able to spread (the mandate) throughout the Four Regions. May I have peace and treasure (these bells).

---

37. Mao no. 252; *Shisanjing zhushu*, 17.4:547; *Erya*; *Shisanjing zhushu*, 4:2589.

38. The *shì* were like *shìzǐ* 世子 mentioned in later texts. Examples of *yìn* 胤 in the sense of lineage successors concerned with the preservation of *dé* and the writing of songs (*zuòshī* 作詩) are attested in the *Zuozhuan* (Yin 11, Xi 24, Cheng 13); *Shisanjing zhushu*, 4:1735–37, 15:1816–18, 27:1911–13.

The tureen:

虔敬朕祀，作尊（？）宗彞，以卲（昭）皇且（祖），其嚴遄（？）
各（格）， 以受屯（純）魯多釐，眉壽無疆，畯寏（傑/至）才（在）
立（位），高引又（有） 慶，造（誥） 囿（佑）四方宜。

I present my respects in my ancestral sacrifices and make this sacrificial vessel for expressing reverence in the ancestral shrine to summon the brilliant ancestors. May they sternly come and go so that (I) may receive abundant wealth and many gifts, extended long life without limit. (May I) control and bring (them to court) in (my) position (as ruler), elevating and guiding (the youths) with rewards, announcing their aid (to the throne) throughout the Four Regions, (so they) act with propriety.

The Qin version of the coming-of-age ceremony included a version of self-perfection practices performed for approval by the former patriarchs — these involved the production of "numinous tones" (*língyīn* 靈音) during a feast for the founder, the "brilliant patriarch" (*huánggōng* 皇公). A number of transmitted odes describe a similar ceremony, such as "Already Inebriated" (Ji zui 既醉), which describes a performance of "Awesome Decorum" during a feast. The performance by the "matched (in rank) aides, peer group" (*péngyǒu* 朋友) results in their successfully bringing down "bright and luminous" (*zhāomíng* 昭明) blessings, wealth, and promises of progeny from the ancestors.[39] In the bronze inscriptions, *péngyǒu*, written 佣友, indicates a group, who along with the main performer's father and brothers, relatives by marriage, and other allies participated in the sacrifices and musical feasting events in the lineage shrine.[40] This group (also referred to in the *Book of Poetry* as "the many aides" [*duōyǒu* or *zhūyǒu*]) included the elite sons of branch lineages who were charged with protecting the heirs and represented the Zhou-style politicized kinship network replete with military and economic obligations to the patriarch.[41]

The "numinous tones" are described by a set of reduplicated binoms

---

39. Mao no. 247; *Shisanjing zhushu*, 17.2:535–36.
40. For many early-through-middle Western Zhou period examples, see Zhang Yachu, *Yin Zhou jinwen*, 414–15. For their role in feasting, see Cook, "Ritual Feasting," 469–87. Qu Wanli 屈萬里 explains that the *péngyǒu* were a group of officials who helped with the sacrifice; *Shijing shiyi* 詩經釋義 (Taipei: Huagang, 1977), 226 n. 9.
41. See the late Western Zhou period Shi Xun *guǐ* 師詢簋 (JC: 4342), in which the awardee is charged to *yǒugān* 友干 'act as personal bodyguard' to the king.

that in the *Book of Poetry* can describe bell music or phoenixes calling (bells were often decorated with phoenixes), with extended meanings associated with ceremonial movements, such as the king arriving or the display of model behavior.[42] In a recent excavation in Gansu of a Qin sacrificial pit containing musical instruments, one inscription specifically describes the "tones" (*yīn* 音) of three *bó*-style hanging bells with this pair of binoms.[43] These binoms reinforce our understanding of the musical dance ceremony performed by the youth as well as the preeminence of bird imagery that had dominated bronze décor for centuries.

The Qin inscriptions reveal the clear continuity of a song or performance tradition popular in powerful families during the last hundred years of Zhou rule. Like the ninth-century B.C.E. Wei family (made famous with the discovery of the long lineage narrative on the Shi Qiang basin),[44] the Qin traced the origins of their power to an ancestral award, although, unlike the Wei family inscription, in which a Zhou connection is clearly defined, the giver of the original gift to Qin is unmentioned, perhaps even taboo: a need to hark back to the Xia founder. Nevertheless, Zhou influence on the Qin performance is just as obvious as the spread of this influence from Qin east into Jin in Shanxi and into northern Henan, the likely locus of the ancient Xia nation.[45] In the Jin inscriptions, cast many generations after the Qin examples and the Chu inscriptions a century after that, the spectrum of Zhou-style rhetoric reveals not only mutual influence among Qin, Jin, and Chu courts but also evidence of earlier independent connections to the Zhou. Even so, the application of what we are calling Zhou-style rhetoric in the different states reflects local customs. The Jin inscriptions show a shared literary tradition with Qin but also a clear

---

42. Mao nos. 34, 173, 240, 252, 282; *Shisanjing zhushu*, 2.2:302–3, 10.1:420, 16.3:515, 17.4:545, 19.3:595–96.
43. Zaoqi Qin Wenhua Lianhe Kaogudui 早期秦文化聯合考古隊, "2006 nian Gansu Lixian Dabaozishan 21 hao jianzhu jizhi fajue jianbao" 2006 年甘肅禮縣大堡子山建築基址發掘簡報, *Wenwu* 2008.9: 26–27. The first binom is transcribed in a number of conflicting ways, but a study of the graph's evolution over time confirms the Mao 252 transcription. I suspect the "Daya" odes were written in archaic forms not always understood by later scribes who may also have been confused by the regional use of variant graphs.
44. Shaughnessy, *Sources of Western Zhou*, 183–98.
45. K. C. Chang, *The Archaeology of Ancient China*, 4th ed. (New Haven, Conn.: Yale University Press, 1986), 370, map 309. See also on Qin's proclaimed Xia identity, Yuri Pines, "The Question of Interpretation: Qin History in Light of New Epigraphic Sources," *Early China* 29 (2004): 28–35.

EDUCATION AND THE WAY OF THE FORMER KINGS 319

exchange with the Chu elite, located south of the Yellow River valley, down along the Han River valley and into the middle Yangzi River valley.

The Jin

The style and rhetoric of the Jin record of the coming-of-age ceremony are so close to the Qin version that we can use the earlier Qin texts to fill in the undecipherable sections of the inscriptions by the patriarch of Jin on the Jingong *pen*.[46] The Jin elite and their scribes must have been trained by Qin masters. Nevertheless, Jin's need to negotiate with the rising power of the Chu polity in the Han River valley to the south influenced the flow of literacy between the north and south. The states of Chu and Jin were both in a stage of growth, rich in resources, and encompassing numerous tributary states and walled-city hubs. The historical relations of Jin with the Chu peoples — the battles and covenants — were the subject of numerous tales recorded in the *Zuozhuan*. The basin inscription recorded the patriarch's dedication of a dowry vessel for his eldest daughter upon her marriage to Chu. Instructions on her duties in the Chu lineage shrine indicate it was a politically important marriage. This inscription also reveals that women were trained for a coming-of-age ceremony, too.

This inscription, also structured in a "response" speech mode, is divided into three sections that parallel the divisions in rhetoric in the Qin inscriptions. The first consists of a typical Zhou dating formula followed by the patriarch's recitation of Jin's heroic lineage narrative, and the second consists of the patriarch's personal statement of worth. The first two sections, directed to the ancestors, are marked as speeches, but the third, directed to his daughter, is not. This structure confirms Schaberg's observations that public speech-making in religious contexts functioned to reaffirm social hierarchy, particularly during sacrifices when the spirit and human worlds intersect.[47]

The Jin lineage narrative, unlike that of the Qin, immediately acknowledges the Jin founder ancestor's connection to Zhou. His "Brilliant Ancestor Patriarch Tang" 皇且（祖）唐公 helped Zhou king Wu battle Man peoples — a euphemism for native peoples settled in the Chu area. The mandate was to "broadly supervise the four regions" 廣司四方 and, like the Qin mission, to force non-tribute-paying peoples to the Zhou

---

46. JC: 10342; Falkenhausen, "Ritual Music," 1063.
47. Schaberg, *A Patterned Past*, 125–30.

court. The text borrows many Qin expressions and specific graphic variants. The Jin lineage narrative then moves on, as with Western Zhou style, to the establishment of the Jin nation 晉邦. The reduplicated binoms once again provide clues to the ceremony.

As is the case with Qin, the binoms connect the Jin inscription with the *Book of Poetry* and the *Book of Documents* but also with a later Qi inscription. The phrase "thunderous up above" 虩虩（赫赫）才（在）上 represents the movement of the ancestors or their signals to descendants below.[48] The fact that "thunderous" is written in as *hèhè* 赫赫 in the transmitted *Book of Poetry* but as *xìxì* 虩虩 in the bamboo text versions of the odes suggests different dialects but common rhetoric in a Jin-Chu-Qi sphere of cultural interaction.[49] The equivalent line in the *Book of Poetry* recites a Zhou lineage narrative beginning with founder King Wen, whose spirit is "luminous (like a star) to those below and thunderous up above" 明明在下，赫赫在上, but the *Book of Documents* version of the line has "grave, so grave up above and luminous to those below" 穆穆在上，明明在下.[50] The binom *mùmù* 穆穆, like *xìxì*, could describe the sounds and signs of ancestral movement and mood, the dark and light days, inclement versus fair weather.[51]

In the second speech, the patriarch brings the narrative to his own qualifications: "Even though now I am only a youth, I dare to follow the model of the former kings, grasping the inner power" 余雖今小子，敢帥井（型）先王秉德. After this statement, he breaks into song with a binom found in Qin songs in the *Book of Poetry*, "repeated (sound), resoundingly" (*zhìzhì* 秩秩), the "tone" of one's inner power (*déyīn* 德音),[52] and perhaps an indication of ancestral response. The patriarch then swore to

---

48. The *guà* statement of the "Zhen" 震 hexagram in the *Book of Changes* describes the terrifying but auspicious sound of thunder.
49. See quotes from "Jie nanshan" 節南山 (Mao no. 191) and "Da Ming" 大明 (Mao no. 236) in the Guodian, Shanghai Museum, and Mawangdui manuscripts; Kern, *Text and Ritual*, 162, 171–72, 4–5.
50. "Da ming" (Mao no. 236); *Shisanjing zhushu*, 16. 2, 506. "Lü Xing" 呂刑; *Shisanjing zhushu*, 19:247–51.
51. Both binoms could refer to bell sounds, fame, and manifest power; see Mao no. 305; *Shisanjing zhushu*, 20.4:627.
52. "Xiao rong" 小戎 and "Jia le" 假樂 in the "Daya" section; *Shisanjing zhushu*, 6.3:369, 17.3:540. Elsewhere, it refers to people in rank or the Zhou plan, Mao no. 220; *Shisanjing zhushu*, 14.3:484; "Zhongni" 仲尼 in *Xunzi*; see *Xunzi* (*Zhuzi jicheng* edition), 2:67.

tame the Man peoples and to nurture all the men of his generation (*xiánchù yìnshì* 咸畜胤士) so as to protect the "king's state" (*wángguó* 王國) — evidence of Jin acceptance of Zhou authority, obviously a continued if old-fashioned source of political legitimacy.

In the final section, the patriarch directs his attention to the member of his lineage who is going through the coming-of-age ceremony, his daughter. He instructs her on proper mortuary ritual behavior and role in the main Chu ancestral shrine (*zōngfù Chǔ bāng* 宗婦楚邦).[53] In the shrine, she must "treat as kin the Hundred Ascendant Ones" 慎親百㞢（至）(i.e., the Chu pantheon). The patriarch charges her to display proper decorum — "Even though now you are but a youth, manage and govern your appearance" 雖今小子，整辥（乂）爾容 — so that she (and by extension Jin) would be without blame for ten thousand years, and in this way the (reputation of the) Jin nation would soar 烏（無）咎萬年，晉邦佳翰. The female *wēiyí* performance was described as a sashaying style of dance done with a radiant "numinous" expression on the face, while following in the footsteps of King Wu's mother (as described on another dowry vessel of the sixth century B.C.E.).[54]

Neither dowry vessel was a bell, yet words like "to soar" (*hàn* 翰) to describe both the use of the vessels in sacrifice and also the prestige gained through the proclamation of the patriarch's merit[55] tap right into a southern song tradition recorded on bells, particularly those belonging to the Chu system of state tribute.[56] This suggests that the Jin ritual masters in charge of composing these ceremonial records were not isolated from the masters of arts and divination who traveled in the south.

---

53. These women used ancestral shrine sacrificial vessels (*zōngyí* 宗彝) to bring down good fortune for the protection of the state (JC: 2683–89, 4076–87, 9698, 10152). They set up and cleared the food display and helped name the heirs (*Zuozhuan*, Huan 6); see *Shisanjing zhushu*, 6:1749–51.
54. The mothers of the founder kings, Wen and Wu, may have had goddess-like attributes and power over fertility for Ji-clan women. JC: 6010, 10171; see discussion in Cook, "Moonshine and Millet," 15; Cook, *Death in Ancient China*, 74; Cook, "Ancestor Worship," 260–61. The *Mozi* refers to a marriage ritual *wēiyí*; see *Mozi, Zhuzi jicheng* edition, 197. For a song preserved in the *Book of Poetry* dedicated to King Wen's mother, see "Si qi" 思齊 (Mao 240); *Shisanjing zhushu*, 16.3:516.
55. This is the connection between "name" (*míng* 名), "mandate (or gift, award)" (*mìng* 命), and "inscription" (*míng* 銘), described in a chapter of similar title in Cook, "Auspicious Metals," 212–59; also mentioned in Falkenhausen, "Issues in Western Zhou," 153.
56. See Blakeley, "The Geography of Chu," 9–20.

The Chu

Food vessel and bell inscriptions in the Yangzi River valley show clear linguistic affinities with the late Zhou peoples and the Qin and Jin courts and a shared culture of mimetic performances during musical feasts for the ancestors. Similarities in language in the heirs' testimonies are most obvious in the inscriptions from a sixth-century B.C.E. Chu burial ground in Xichuan, Henan — along the Han River, an intercultural conduit of travel between Chu and the Zhou homeland, Qin, and Jin.[57] The testimony by Yizhe (The One Remaining) of the lineage Royal Grandson (Wángsūn) was inscribed upon a bell, the preferred Chu medium for coming-of-age records. This bell, the Wangsun Yizhe *zhong* (discovered farther south in Yichang, Hubei) had more in common with other bell inscriptions cast in a network of small states north of the Yangzi and east to the Pacific coast.[58] Ritual teams who specialized in bronze inscriptions clearly traveled among these states and had contact with coastal political and trade networks.

Yizhe's record takes an unabashedly non-Zhou stand. Chu rulers were kings and not mere clan patriarchs. They made no mention of any links to the Zhou, their Heaven, or their mandate. They did however display their governmental *dé* through an Awesome Decorum performance, but their performance would not emphasize the suppression of non-Zhou peoples in the four regions. Governmental *dé* for the Chu was a sophisticated blend of military and civil deeds aimed at "harmony" among its peoples.

Connection to Zhou style is evident in the use of a popular late Western Zhou dating formula, the most auspicious for such events: "It was the first month, early auspicious phase of the month, *dinghai* (day 24)" 隹（唯）正月初吉丁亥. Without the oral cues of a "response" statement, the Chu descendant explains that the bell casting was of his own volition and not the result of a Zhou-style award ceremony: "I, Wangsun Yizhe, selected these auspicious metals and made for myself harmonious bells" 王孫遺者擇其吉金，自乍（作）龢鐘. Next, he describes in rhyme the function of the bell texts: "to endlessly let soar and to eulogize (the reputations of the

---

57. Cook, "Auspicious Metals," 375–410. Two of these inscriptions, originally translated by Cook, have been retranslated in Mattos, "Eastern Zhou," 97–104. For ritual rhetoric, see Cook, "Auspicious Metals," 239–59.
58. JC: 261; Cook, "Auspicious Metals," 411–19; Mattos, "Eastern Zhou," 88–91; Falkenhausen, "Ritual Music," 705–7, 1085, 1341, table 20. Compare to JC: 2811; Falkenhausen, "Ritual Music," 1076–1116; Cook, "Auspicious Metals," 241–47, 385–96.

ancestors) with primary sounds and resounding brilliance. I use (the bells when) presenting memorial feasts to express my piety to our Brilliant Ancestor and Accomplished Dead Father, and I use (them) to pray for extended long life" 中（終）翰且揚，元鳴孔皇，用享台（以）孝，于我皇且（祖）文考，用旂眉壽.

The lineage narrative is embedded in a prayer to the founder ancestor and Yizhe's deceased father but then restricts the praise of his own decorum to himself: "I behave with vast reverence and an even temper, and in awe and fear, I step carefully, acting serious and attentive, sagely and martial; I am benevolent with my governing power and good at my awesome decorum;[59] in strategies and plans, I am not lax" 余宏龏胡犀，畏忌翼翼，肅質（慎）聖武，惠于政德，淑于威義（儀），誨猷不飤.
The Chu expansion of decorum from the arena of ritual display into that of proper government was not new to bronze inscription rhetoric. It is found in late Western Zhou examples, such as the lengthy Maogong *ding* narrative.[60] However, the use of reduplicated binoms in this section and the next where the bell music is described as *jiǎnjiǎn* 簡簡 specifically reveal the influence of the musical ceremony. The dance descriptor *yìyì* 翼翼 (careful stepping) is found only in Chu inscriptions and probably descended from an older cultural layer that traces back to Shang shamanic performances.[61] The *Book of Poetry* versions of the expression, 異 written with "wings" 羽 instead of the "stepping" semantic 走 as in the archaic graph in the Chu inscriptions, describe repetitive movements or images performed with care,[62] such as in the Zhou Wan 萬 (Ten Thousand) dance in which the "many sirs" (*duōshì* 多士) acted out *wēiyí* modeled on King Wen's legendary "cautious" (*shèn* 慎) care of sacrifices to Shangdi.[63] The step was "slow paced" (*chìchì* 遲遲) and brought

---

59. Being *shūshèn* 淑慎 'good at and careful about' one's *yí* is seen in "Yi" 抑 (Mao no. 256) in the *Book of Poetry*; *Shisanjing zhushu*, 18.1:554–56. It is mirrored in the capping ceremony in the *Yili*; see *Shisanjing zhushu*, 3:957–59.
60. JC: 2841.
61. Elizabeth Childs-Johnson, The Meaning of the Graph Yi 異 and Its Implications for Shang Belief and Art (London: Saffron, 2008).
62. Mao nos. 167, 178, 209, 210, 235, 237, 305; *Shisanjing zhushu*, 9.3:414, 10.2:425, 13.2:467, 13.2:471, 16.1:504, 16.2, 20.4:628.
63. Mao nos. 226, 263, 260. *Mozi*, *Zhuzi jicheng* edition, 161; written as 奕奕, also found in the "Shang Song" ode "Na," Mao no. 301. Dallas McCurley, "Performing Patterns: Numinous Relations in Shang and Zhou China," *Drama Review* 49.3 (2005): 135–56;

"those above and below together in harmony."

The term for large expansive musical sounds, such as those emitted by a concert of bells, drums, and chimes, *jiǎnjiǎn* 簡簡 ("gong gong"), signaled contact with the spirits and the descent of blessings in the *Book of Poetry* during the performance of Awesome Decorum or the Wan dance.[64] After this sound, the Chu descendant testified to his preparedness in terms reminiscent of the Zhou ritual but expressed more as an internalized learning with the meaning of *dé* closer to that of *qì* than to any Zhou-style lineage narrative: "I embrace with my heart and extend forever my inner power, harmonizing the people and making them peaceful, I spread (it) throughout the kingdom" 余恁台心，延永余德，穌引民人，余專(敷)昀于國. The southern expression of embracing the inner power with his heart, while using different vocabulary, goes right back in meaning to the Western Zhou practice of "grasping *dé*" (*bǐngdé* 秉德) and "opening the heart" (*guǎngpì xīn* 廣辟心) to ancestral *dé*.[65] The participation of the ancestral spirits in this process is signaled by more words describing the bells, but both sound and light are indicated in a double binom: "flash and glitter" (*huánghuáng xīxī* 皇皇熙熙). The term *huánghuáng*, found on Chu bells and in the *Book of Poetry* and the *Book of Rites* (Liji 禮記), had both a brilliant and a solemn aspect. It might describe the feeling of the descendant at the burial of his father or the brilliance of flowers. Like *mùmù* 穆穆, it was used in prayers and, like *yìyì*, may have had a terrifying aspect as well.[66] The second aspect of the bells, *xīxī* (glistening), appears in prayers and in the *Zuozhuan* to describe the mellifluous harmonies of Daya songs in praise of King Wen's *dé*.[67] *Xīxī* may have been a local variant of the graphically similar *huánhuán* 桓桓 (Valiant! So valiant!) found on Qin and Yue inscriptions. A simplified version was written as 炬炬 (glistening, glorious) in the transmitted literature.

The sense is that the music acted as the medium for transferring the ancestral power and that many ancestral narratives and songs were retold

---

Yang Hua, *Xian Qin liyue*, esp. 143–46.
64. See "Zhijing" and "Shang Song," in *Shisanjing zhushu 19.2:589, 20.3:620*.
65. The word *rèn* 恁, read here as a loan for *niàn* 念, replaces the Western Zhou locution of "embracing" (*huái* 懷) the ancestral *dé*, an internal process.
66. *Liji, Shisanjing zhushu*, 6:1278; *Shijing*, Mao nos. 163, 249, 299, 300; *Shisanjing zhushu*, 9.2:407, 17.3:540, 20.1:612, 20.2:615.
67. JC: 9704; Cook, "Auspicious Metals," 107. See also JC: 153-54, 203. Xiang 29 in *Zuozhuan*; *Shisanjing zhushu*, 39:2008.

and transmitted through this medium to the next generation.[68] In this way, Chu elite shared a basic cultural similarity with the Yellow River valley elite, the performance of ancestral worship ceremonies to produce oral and eventually written texts.[69] Two centuries before there is evidence for bamboo tomb inventory texts, the Chu focus for literary production was ancestral worship, although it seems less preoccupied with history than was the Qin or Jin.

The Qi

The northeastern tradition of bell inscriptions contrasts sharply with the Chu tradition. From the coastal state of Qi comes one of the longest inscriptions of the Spring and Autumn period, the Shu Yi zhong, dating to Patriarch Ling 靈 of Qi's rule (581–554 B.C.E.).[70] The style of the inscription harks back to the second half of the Western Zhou era, when kings and patriarchs documented at length the accumulated merit of both a gift giver and a gift recipient, followed by the list of gifts or awards given for service and the recipient's formulaic statements of obeisance to his patron. As with the Chu and most inscribed vessels and bells, the text ends with prayers for long life, greater wealth, and numerous descendants.

Like several lengthy late Western Zhou inscriptions and typical of Yellow River tradition, the text recalls a lengthy lineage history through a series of speeches.[71] Unlike most Western Zhou examples, the Qi inscription includes both the award speeches and the response. Typical of Spring and Autumn inscriptions, lineage history was recited in the response section as part of a prayer to the ancestors, whereas in most older inscriptions, the lineage narrative would be recited by the gift giver, not the awardee. The most unusual feature of the Shu Yi inscription is the

---

68. Falkenhausen, *Suspended Music*, 25–32; Cook, "Auspicious Metals," 212–59; 1995, 242–50.
69. Li, The Readability of the Past, 118–47.
70. Ten Shu Yi 叔尸（夷）bells (JC: 272-9, 285), the remains of larger sets, were found near the ancient capital of Qi in 1123. There are slight differences in the *bó* 鎛 versus the *zhōng* 鐘 bell inscriptions. See Darrel P. Doty, "The Bronze Inscriptions of Ch'i" (PhD diss., University of Washington, 1982), 245–384.
71. For example, Maogong *ding* 毛公鼎 (JC: 2841) and Lai *pan* 逨盤; Li Xueqin 李學勤, "Meixian Yangjiacun xinchu qingtongqi yanjiu" 眉縣楊家村新出青銅器研究, *Wenwu* 2003.6: 66–73. Shaanxi archaeologists read the name as *lái*, Li as *zuǒ* 佐, and Qiu Xigui as *qiú* 逑.

"polyvocal structure" of award statements by the patriarch and recorded responses to each statement by the awardee.[72] In this way, the narrative structure is closer in format to the capping ceremony recorded in the *Yili* 儀禮[73] rather than to earlier inscriptions. Another communicative layer in this text must be the bells themselves, which, like the Chu bells, signaled ancestral approval in an onomatopoetic language of bright lights and thunderous sounds.[74]

A major difference between Western Zhou and Qi inscriptions is the lineage allegiances eulogized by Shu Yi. The Qi inscription mentions "the king" but only as part of the introductory dating formula. There, however, all mention of connection to the Zhou ends, despite Qi's long-term engagement with the Zhou and its early Spring and Autumn attempt to act as protector or "hegemon" (*bà* 霸) over the former Zhou tribute network.[75] Like Qin, the Qi linked their lineage histories to pre-Zhou founders, but unlike the Qin, the Qi eulogized the rise of Shang and the Shang founder's legendary, if not mythical, conquest of the Xia.

Key phrases used in the Qi inscription nevertheless reveal the spread of Zhou-style education and literacy and its local variation. The patriarch praised Shu Yi for "taking as model your Former Ancestor(s) so that since I have already spread (this model) to your heart, you act with caution and fear. You do not allow (the mandate) to fall (as you work) from dawn to dusk to serve (me) and manage governmental affairs" 余經乃先且（祖），余既尃（敷）乃心，女少（小）心畏忌，女（汝）不墜，夙夜宦執而政事. The inscription also expresses the Zhou imperative for continued martial merit. Shu Yi was put in charge of armies to complete the ruler's "governing power" 政德. In the Qi case, however, the battles were not against non-Zhou border peoples but against rebellious peoples within Qi itself.

After Shu Yi's expression of obedience to the patriarch's charge, the patriarch then gets more specific with his charge, explaining that Shu Yi (like the bodyguards of Zhou times) was responsible for the royal house but (unlike the guards) would be simultaneously responsible for managing

---

72. Martin Kern has noted this inherent feature in late Western Zhou bronze inscriptions and in sections of the *Shi*; "Bronze Inscriptions," 173–77.
73. *Shisanjing zhushu*, 3:957–59.
74. Falkenhausen, "Ritual Music," 683, 701–7; 1993, 25–32, 100–101; Cook, "Auspicious Metals," 226–35; Cook, "Scribes, Cooks, and Artisans," 242–50.
75. Cho-yun Hsu, "The Chunqiu Period," in Loewe and Shaughnessy, eds., 553–56.

his cohort of "traveling masters" (and their "armies") (*xíngshī* 行師) to suppress rebellion. This section also details specific urban communities and their associated ranked officers and soldiers that Shu Yi would command. Shu Yi's gratitude for the "mandate" (*mìng* 命) was then recorded, and the patriarch continued to praise Shu Yi for not avoiding warfare (thereby "spreading" [*fū* 敷] the mandate) by claiming he was but a "youth," a legitimate excuse if one had not finished mourning for one's father or was still in training.

In the next speech, the patriarch praises Shu Yi's capable management of his officers matched up (by rank) (*díliáo* 敵寮), in other words, his cohort of subordinate lineage relations, who with Shu Yi might challenge ("change" [*yì* 易]) the patriarch's mandate. He charged Shu Yi "to target (relevant cases) and spread the luminous model (ancestral law) in his management of the major affairs in the inner and outer spheres" 為大事執 (治) 命于外內之事, 中尃 (敷) 盟 (明) 井 (刑/型).[76] These affairs, besides protecting the ruler's person, involved taking charge of lineage ritual, the "luminous concerns" 盟 (明) 卹. The patriarch explained that the gifts he then awarded Shu Yi — horses, chariots, militia, and slaves — were specifically for use in warfare, a Zhou tradition.

The rest of the inscription consists of Shu Yi's "response," which, during the Western Zhou period, we would expect to be cast on a separate vessel. In the first section, he recites his lineage narrative, and in the second section, he prays to his ancestors for blessings and promises to properly instruct his progeny. Specifically in these two passages, we see evidence of the musical performance of Awesome Decorum by Shu Yi and his cohort:

尸 (夷) 用或敢再拜稽首, 膺受君公之易 (賜) 光, 余弗敢灋 (廢) 乃命, 尸 (夷) 典其先舊及其高祖, 虩虩 (赫赫) 成唐, 又敢才 (在) 帝所, 尃 (敷) 受天命, 削伐夏后, 敗厥靈師, 伊少臣隹 (唯) 輔, 咸有九州, 處禹之堵, 不 (丕) 顯穆公之孫, 其配襄公之姚, 而成公之女, 遳生叔尸, 是辟于齊侯之所, 是少 (小) 心恭疐, 靈力若虎, 堇 (勤) 裻

---

76. The expression *míngxíng*, but written 明刑, is found in the "Yi" ode in the *Book of Poetry* and is associated with following the way of the former kings; *Shisanjing zhushu*, 18.1:554. Elsewhere in the *Book of Poetry*, it is clear that the meaning of "model" is intended. This model, practiced with proper decorum (*yí* 儀) also functioned as customary law ("Wenwang" 文王 and "Wo Jiang" 我將); *Shisanjing zhushu* 16.1:502, 19.2:588.

(勞) 其政事，又共于桓武靈公之所，

I, Yi, take this opportunity to repeatedly clap my hands together and bump my head (on the ground) as I take on the responsibility of receiving the lord patriarch's awarded glory. I dare not discard your mandate as I, Yi, take as law those former old ones and that high ancestor — with thunderous sounds, so Cheng Tang dares to reside with the Lord (Di) — who, spreading and receiving Heaven's mandate, cut down Xia Hou, defeating his numinous army. With Young Minister Yin acting as aide, (Cheng Tang) occupied the entire nine continents and resided in Yu's capital. The grandson of the greatly manifest Patriarch Mu took as mate the niece of Patriarch Xiang and the daughter of Patriarch Cheng; she gave birth to me, Shu Yi. It is this (Shu Yi) who administers the residence of the Warlord of Qi and who cautiously steps forward with reverence and, with the numinous power of a tiger, diligently labors in his governmental service, expressing complete reverence at the residence of the majestic and martial Patriarch Ling.

Qi shared with the Zhou, Qin, and Jin the tradition of educating a special cadre of youth whose "mandates" of governance of "affairs" inside and outside the central court were the most likely vehicles for the transmission of literacy among the elite. The Qi description of the youth "prancing like tigers" — a phrase used to describe the Wan dance in the *Book of Poetry* — confirms the role of these cadres,[77] who in Western Zhou inscriptions were called "tiger servants" (*hǔchén* 虎臣), whose symbols of status included a tiger-skin chariot cover lined in pale red. Their first job was to protect the ruler; they ranked under the chief masters and teachers, the Shishi 師氏, but above the technical ministers (*yǐn* 尹), a group that included scribes.[78] Tiger servants (also called the "many sirs") are mentioned in a Lu song eulogizing the ruler's *wēiyí* and the ability of the "sirs" to suppress the Yi peoples. Just as described in Western Zhou inscriptions, these men were "able to broaden their hearts with *dé*" (*kè*

---

77. In the "Jian xi" 簡兮 song in the "Bei feng" 邶風 section, a "thunderous" 赫 performance with flutes in the left hand and feathers in the right precedes the patriarch announcing "awarding the ranks"; *Shisanjing zhushu* 2.3:308–9.
78. See the Shi Ke *xu* 師克盨 (JC: 4467-68) and Maogong *ding* 毛公鼎 (JC: 2841). The rank is apparent in Maogong *ding* and the "Guming" 顧命 chapter in the *Book of Documents* (in which a Maogong also happens to be mentioned, although this narrative purports to be the dying words of King Cheng and a record of the ascension ritual of his son who claims to be "but a *xiǎozi*" before going through the ritual in the main shrine in the company of the "various warrior lords" [*zhūhóu*]); *Shisanjing zhushu* 18:237–41.

guǎng déxīn 克廣德心) and thus perform the ancestral narrative.[79]

In the final section, Shu Yi dedicates the awarded bronze for use during mortuary feasts to his brilliant ancestor, brilliant ancestress, brilliant mother, and brilliant aged one (father) to pray for long life (用享于其皇祖、皇妣、皇母、皇考，用旂眉壽，靈命難老) but also so that the greatly manifest brilliant ancestors (不 [丕] 顯皇祖) would, through the medium of bell-and-drum music, bring specific blessings of longevity, wealth, and harmony to his affairs inside and outside the court, specifically to "their prime descendant" (其乍 [作] 福元孫，其萬福屯 [純] 魯，穌協而又事，卑 [俾] 若鐘鼓，外內剴辟). Then he breaks into song, and the young men perform:

鋯鋯 (喈喈) 譻譻 (與與)，達而儞臬，母 (毋) 或承類，女 (汝) 考壽萬年永保其身，卑 (俾) 百斯男而執 (設) 斯字 (子)，肅肅義政，齊侯左右，母 (毋) 疾母 (毋) 已，至于世，曰武靈成，子孫永保用享。

Harmonious! Respectful! (the bell sounds) reach (them) and your aides who are matched up (by rank) and all of whom offer up sacrifices so that your aged and long lived ones (will send down) ten thousand years (of life and riches), eternally protect their persons, and cause their males to number two hundred and their sons be set up (with ranks and lands). Somberly, so somberly, righteously governing, may they who are taking up (their) positions to the left and right of the Warrior Lord of Qi be without affliction and without stopping go on through the generations saying: "Martial! Numinous! Accomplished!" (May) sons and grandsons eternally protect (the bells) and use (them) in mortuary feasts.

Reduplicated binoms occur only in the final section, reserved for prayers and song. This minimal use of binoms may reflect a more conservative tradition preserved on the east coast. Archaic linguistic features in this inscription can be traced back hundreds of years to particular variations found on bronzes from the ancestral Zhou region: the use of "constant (pattern)" (*jīng* 經) for "model" (*xíng*), "death" (*sǐ* 死) for "corpse, take on the ancestor's role in life" (*shī* 尸), and a rare word meaning "to carry on (a position previously awarded)" that was popular in the Wei River valley during the latter half of the middle Western Zhou

---

79. "Pan shui" 泮水 in the "Lu Song" section of the *Book of Poetry*; *Shisanjing zhushu*, 20.1:610–12.

period.⁸⁰ This suggests that masters and their scribes connected to those ancient Zhou houses migrated east to Qi and influenced literary production.

Although the east coast may have served as a harbor for preserved Zhou language and rhetorical styles, it was also a crucible for change. The inscription mixed archaic rhetoric with a more colloquial style represented by longer sentences using more grammatical particles and words such as the causative *bǐ* 俾. This latter feature is shared with many songs in the *Book of Poetry* and Spring and Autumn period bronze inscriptions from the eastern coastal region. The changes apparent in this inscription occurred at the beginning of a time when "broad learning" (*bóxué* 博學) was consciously promulgated by itinerant scholars such as Confucius. It is also the time when ecstatic musical ceremonies, if they continued, gradually ceased to be recorded in bronze inscriptions.

The Yue

Like the Qi inscription, the fifth-century B.C.E. bell inscriptions by Zhediao 者汈 of the southeastern coastal state of Yue, the Zhediao *bo* and *zhong*, also had an "archaic ring."⁸¹ Yue, located at the end of the Yangzi River, was forced to interact with both the Qi and Chu trade and tribute networks, which provided access to the larger culture of shared knowledge and access to commonly known songs and tales now reflected in the transmitted *Book of Poetry* and *Zuozhuan*. Like the Qi, the Yue recorded a gift-giving ceremony, but, like the Chu, they focused more on the musical ceremony than on the historical narrative. Most significant, like the Chu leader, the Yue leader was a "king" not a "patriarch."

The Yue inscription is a single speech, but unlike those of Qin and Jin, it is an award narrative and not in "response" style. After a dating formula,

---

80. For "constant (pattern)" see Shi Ke *xu* 師克盨 (tureen) (JC: 4467-68), for "death" see Shi Hui *gui* 師毀簋 (JC: 4311). The archaic word for "to carry on" (possibly a form of *jiān* 兼) first appeared in the inscriptional record during the early middle Western Zhou period; see JC: 4326.

81. JC: 120–32; Falkenhausen, "Ritual Music," 449. He notes that originally Zhe Diao had likely made a number of bell sets with this inscription, of which only random bells survive. Rubbings and transcriptions are found in *Shiwen*, 1:85–100 (nos. 120–132.1); Ma Chengyuan, *Shang Zhou*, 4:372–75 (no. 552). Guo Moruo's 郭沫若 transcriptions and readings are found in *Shiwen* 1:100. See also, Dong Chuping 董楚平, *Wu Yue wenhua xintan* 吳越文化新探 (Zhejiang: Zhejiang Renmin, 1988), 345–47.

the king praises Zhediao's dutiful religious service to the spirits, culminating in his "grasping the greatly constant (ancestral) power" (*bǐng pījīng dé* 秉丕 [丕] 經德).[82] This could happen only because of the "gathered radiance" (*zǒng* [*jī*] *guāng* 總 [緝] 光) generated by his "obedient studies" (*sūn* [*shùn*] *xué* 愻 [順] 學). Then the king breaks into verse, crying, "How valiant!" (*huánhuán zāi* 桓桓哉), followed by a declaration of Zhediao's ritual and military merit, accumulated through protecting the royal residence, its spirits, and the king's position.

The king then turns to the preparation for the present coming-of-age ritual: "Now I with regard to them recall your services for those avoided ones (i.e., the dead), purifying, favoring, invoking, and completing, and so take this opportunity to extol (your) blazing adulthood, making it radiant through a (bell) display" 今余其念衛 (違) 乃有 [事] 齊 (齋) 休祝成。用再 (偁) 烈壯光之于 (聿) 肆.[83] This is followed by further instructions, first to use the bells to "open up (oneself)" 廣啟 and calm the ancestors with music. Then follows a warning similar to those found in the ode "Yi" 抑, in which an elder warns a youth not to slack off. In the Yue inscription, the youth is warned to keep up his "decorum" (*yì* [*yí*] 義 [儀]), not allowing for "change" (*gǎi* 改). It was through use of the bells, he made explicit, that this "inner power" would be "supremely called out" (*yuán míng* 元鳴), rhetoric common to most Chu-influenced inscriptions.[84]

The clue to unpacking the description of the ritual behavior of the newly "blazing adult" is found in the "Ji tong" chapter of the *Book of Rites*. Purification was done before entering the ancestral shrine. The word *xiū* 休 in bronze inscriptions traditionally referred to the "favor" of the award bestowed by a gift giver or patron on the awardee or gift recipient.[85] In a

---

82. The specific expression "constant power" (*jīngdé*) is also found on the early Warring States period Chen Man *fu* 陳曼簠 (JC: 4595–96) vessels from Qi.
83. Usually an ancestor's or deceased person's name follows the verb *niàn* in bronze inscriptions. For the reading of *wéi* 違, see the Cai Hou *pan* 蔡侯盤 (JC: 10171); Ma Chengyuan, *Shang Zhou*, 4:395 (no. 13). The phrase *nǎiyǒu* 乃有 is probably short for *nǎiyǒu shì* 乃有事 found on the Shu Yi bells.
84. From other southern bell inscriptions dating to the late Spring and Autumn period, we know that *yuán míng* 元鳴 referred to bells' ringing, for instance, on Yun'er *bo* 沇兒鎛 (JC: 203), Wangsun Yizhe *zhong* 王孫遺者鐘 (JC: 261), and Cai Hou *zhong* 蔡侯鐘 (JC: 210).
85. "Ji tong" 祭統; *Shisanjing zhushu*, 49:1602–8.

Wei inscription described in the same chapter, an awardee is praised as "favored" (*xiū*) for his untiring service to his ancestors. Invocation rites included a call for the spirits to descend and join the mortuary feast or announcements to the ancestors to enjoy the music.[86] "Completing" refers to the culmination of the musical performance typically called the "great completion" (*dàchéng* 大成).[87] The sense of "completing" may also symbolize the very notion of nurturing life itself for the Ru as mentioned in the *Analects* and the *Liji*, in which each life stage is marked by the strength of one's "blood and breath" (*xuèqì* 血氣), which peaks during the middle "adult" (*zhuàng* 壯) stage after "capping" (*guàn* 冠), when one marries and begins a family. It follows the stage of "being in one's minority" (*shào* 少), dedicated to "learning" (*xué*), and still "weak" (*ruò* 弱). The final stage was "being an elder" (*lǎo* 老).[88]

The Yue use of the term *xué* (to study, learn) is consistent with Zhou song tradition and with the formulaic language of contemporary bell inscriptions. This inscription documents the Yue king's commendation of an elite member of his house for his "obedient studies" (*shùnxué*). In pre-Qin texts, the word *shùn* 順 describes a youth who properly followed the legacy handed down from Heaven or Shangdi to his ancestors and his immediate elders — a pattern evident in the inscriptions and transmitted and excavated texts. A phrase from the "Huangyi" 皇矣, an old Zhou song praising King Wen's "luminous inner power" (*míngdé* 明德), preserved in the *Book of Poetry* and quoted throughout Warring States literature, explains that he, "innocent and unknowing, followed the rule of the Di" 不識不知，順帝之則.[89] The *Zuozhuan*, in describing events of 542 B.C.E., explains that in this song "following the rule" means to "copy" or "imitate" (*xiàng* 象).[90] It goes on to explain the context of the song's

---

86. For a discussion regarding how "joy" (*lè*) and "music" (*yuè*), represented by the same graph 樂, had a "conceptual unity," see Knoblock, *Xunzi*, 3:74–76; for his discussion of the Ru value of music and its effect on the emotions and body, see 76–80.
87. "Li yun" 禮運; *Shisanjing zhushu*, 21:1416–17.
88. "Jishi" 季氏, in *Lunyu* 16; *Shisanjing zhushu*, 16:2522; "Quli shang" 曲禮上, in *Liji*, see *Shisanjing zhushu*, 1:1232.
89. *Shisanjing zhushu*, 16.4:522. Quoted in the *Zuozhuan* and by Xunzi, Mozi, and Liezi. For Shangdi as a Sky god, see David Pankenier, "A Brief History of Beiji," 211–36; Sarah Allan, "On the Identity of Shang Di 上帝 and the Origin of the Concept of a Celestial Mandate (*tian ming* 天命)," *Early China* 31 (2007), 1–46.
90. *Zuozhuan* (Xiang 31); *Shisanjing zhushu*, 40:2016.

popularity: everyone (All Descended from Heaven 天下) eulogized (*sòng* 誦) King's Wen's merit (*gōng* 功) and his ability to terrify (*wèi* 畏) other peoples. The "movements of King Wen" (*Wénwáng zhī xíng* 文王之行) sung and danced were the "rules" or "patterns" (*zé* 則) imitated (*xiàng*) to display their "awesome decorum" (*wēiyí*). The term "studies" or "learning" (*xué*) is also mentioned in the Zhou song "Jing zhi" 敬之 in a phrase and context very similar to the those of the Yue inscription:[91]

> 敬之敬之，天維顯思。命不易哉！無曰：高高在上。陟降厥士，日監在茲。
>
> Pay respects to it, pay respects to it; Heaven is so manifest. Don't let the mandate change! Do not say "(those) high, high up above." Ascending and descending (to) their elite (descendants), (those up above) watch them every day in this (place).
>
> 維予小子，不聰敬止。日就月將，學有緝熙于光明。佛時仔肩，示我顯德行。
>
> It is I, the young child, who, not being enlightened, pay my respects to the end. Day by day as months go by, I learn from those radiant luminaries of gathered brilliance who aid this one's burden to reveal our manifest way of (inner) power.

It is clear that "obedient studies" refers to those rituals learned by a youth and performed under the gaze of his ancestors, a tradition with ancient roots throughout the early Chinese heartland. The Yue inscription shows the importance of displaying a broad knowledge of both contemporary literature and the transition of oral narratives into written texts.

Literacy in the Warring States Period

The education of the elite youth who were responsible for their peers and the transmission of literary narratives and songs evolved out of the Western Zhou traditions of *wēiyí* and the arts. This is explained by the

---

91. *Shijing*, Mao no. 288; *Shisanjing zhushu* 19.3:598–99. Kern notes that the near-rhyming binom *jīxī* 緝熙 is written with cognate graphs in the Guodian quotes of the line 於緝熙敬之 "Wenwang" (Mao no. 235) but in an abbreviated verse with entirely different graphs in the Shanghai version, 於幾義之, confirming oral transmission; *Text and Ritual*, 160–61.

Zuozhuan's gloss of the use of *wēiyí* in the *Shi*: "the way of the peer group requires mutual instruction in order to enact awesome decorum" 朋友之道必相教訓以威儀.[92] At the same time that the exclusive Zhou-style education was collapsing, there is archaeological evidence for a coincidental expression of functional literacy in a vast array of textual types including everything from inventory lists, covenants, administrative records, curses, prayers, sacrificial records, almanacs, and philosophical tracts to exercise manuals, divination manuals, medical manuals, and so forth. Given the range of fourth- and third-century texts preserved in Chu tombs by climatic and geographic happenstance, text production in Qi and its northeastern constellation of old Zhou-influenced states must have been substantial and diverse.

Recent discoveries of fourth- and third-century B.C.E. bamboo texts are proof that texts were circulated in multiple hand-copied versions — each bearing some idiosyncrasy marking the individual copy yet still providing no clue of the copyist's identity.[93] This confirms the idea that teachers were traditionally accompanied by teams of scribes, diviners, and others who all combined to spread functional as well as higher literacy. By tracing the cultural contexts of the word *xué* through time, we see that learning evolved away from the modeling of one's behavior on a historical or ancestral pattern and away from their performance. Learning became increasingly tied to the ability to articulate an ideological position and was measured by the ability to recite from the *Book of Poetry*, the *Book of Documents*, and the *Rites* — texts that preserved the songs, narratives, and dance instructions of the dying *wēiyí* practice. By the third century B.C.E., although the practice of music was lauded as essential for the "outer expression" (*yí* 儀) of inner power (*dé*), the actual expression of *wēiyí* was not a focus nor was the correct Dao of the former kings quite so intensely argued. Yet at the same time, musical modes remained closely linked to founder sages and kings. As Mozi exclaimed, if you want to know what Ru music was like, you must read the texts of the former kings.[94]

Although the spread of literacy was not tied to the spread of an ancestral "mandate" during the Warring States period, the use of bronze inscriptions to display knowledge to ancestors may have continued in

---

92. *Zuozhuan* (Xiang 31); *Shisanjing zhushu*, 40:2016.
93. The issue of anonymity and the placement of texts in tombs is explored by Cao Wei 曹瑋, *Zhouyuan yizhi yu Xi Zhou tongqi yanjiu* 周原遺址與西周銅器研究 (Beijing: Kexue, 2004), 262; see also Cook, *Death in Ancient China*, 8–13, 83–118.
94. *Mozi* ("Feiyue shang"), *Zhuzi jicheng* edition, 160–61

award rituals. Lengthy bronze inscriptions generally did not survive the interstate battles, but the unusually long inscriptions from the northeastern minority state of Zhongshan escaped destruction and testify to the perseverance of the old Zhou ceremony in some areas. In some respects, the bronze cast by King Cuo of Zhongshan in 316 B.C.E.[95] functioned as a eulogy for his teacher and senior advisor, the role likely also played by Shu Yi of Qi two centuries earlier and by the legendary Zhougong, whose tale was preserved in circulating texts. The rhetoric of the eulogy in the Zhongshan inscription affirms the continuity of the tradition of royal education, which involved modeling oneself on Heaven and one's ancestors albeit with some expected differences. The king lauded the "inner power" internally generated by his old advisor named Zhou, who ran the country for him while he was a child (but might not have been a relative), just as Zhougong had famously done for his nephew. This allusion legitimized as a noble act of state building the fortunate results of his advisor's presumptuous attack on the neighbor state of Yan and the capture of border lands. Unlike Zhougong — who, according to legend, after suppressing rebels, was awarded with the eastern lands that became the state of Lu — the Zhongshan Zhou was put to death for taking charge of the battle and essentially usurping the king's mandate. The inscription was cast as a eulogy for the advisor and a clear warning to the king's descendants.

The composer of this inscription was familiar with the literary jargon of Warring States rhetoric, which later scholars associated with Ruist,[96] Legalist, and even Daoist movements, such as concern with being humane, executing proper punishments and laws, and ritual "wandering." Links to song texts such as the *Book of Poetry* seem to represent less the musical modes and martial dances of mortuary feasts than common metaphors or popular expressions. The style of the inscription — for example, in its use of the expression "the altar of soil and millet" (*shèjì*) as a symbol of the state — has more in common with popular historical tales one might find in the *Zuozhuan* or *Tales of the States* than with earlier bronze records. This inscription shows the effects of the "broad learning" initiated during the Eastern Zhou period and the lingering effects of a strong Zhou tradition.

---

95. JC: 2840; Constance A. Cook, "Chung-shan Bronze Inscriptions: Introduction and Translation" (master's thesis, University of Washington, 1980), 43–53, 75–87; Mattos, "Eastern Zhou," 104–11.
96. See Mattos, "Eastern Zhou," 110.

Conclusion

Literacy among the elite evolved out of the study of the Six Arts by the heirs of royal lineages during the Western Zhou period. Using bronze inscriptions as a reflection of this evolution, we can trace the spread of cultural practices and rhetorical norms to regions and peoples previously on the periphery of the Zhou hegemony. In the rhetorical styles of these inscription, we see the paths of teachers and ritual masters as they dispersed throughout the ancient networks of tribute and trade beginning with the Western Zhou imperative to "spread" the Mandate throughout the four regions. By the end of the Warring States period, literacy, which had initially spilled out of a Zhou center, was now flowing back in from the edges of that imagined empire.

PART IV

The Extent of Literacy in the Early Empire

CHAPTER 10

Soldiers, Scribes, and Women: Literacy among the Lower Orders in Early China

Robin D. S. Yates

This chapter reviews the evidence for literacy among the lower orders, that is, those below the ninth rank in the Qin and early Han (third to early second centuries B.C.E.) system of meritocratic ranking.[1] The group

---

I would like to thank Li Feng, Anthony Barbieri-Low, Matthias Richter, and Endymion Wilkinson for their valuable comments, criticisms, and corrections on an earlier draft of this chapter. In addition, I would also like to thank Donald Harper for generously sharing his own translations of the "Statutes on Scribes" with me and much appreciate the feedback and comments I received from colleagues and students when I presented this chapter as a paper at the Early China Seminar, Columbia University, 7 April 2007, and at Rice University, 20 April 2007. A longer version of this chapter in Chinese has been published as Ye Shan 葉山 (Robin D. S. Yates), "Zu, shi yu nüxing: Zhanguo Qin Han shiqi xiaceng shehui de duxie nengli" 卒、史與女性：戰國秦漢時期下層社會的讀寫能力, *Jianbo* 簡帛 3 (2008): 361–86.

1. For an early study of this ranking system, see Michael Loewe, "The Orders of Aristocratic Rank of Han China," *T'oung Pao* 48.1-3 (1960): 97–174. Since the time Loewe wrote this article, much new information on the ranking system has been discovered, and Zhu Shaohou 朱紹侯 has devoted considerable attention to elucidating its complexities, especially as seen in early Han legal documents, such as those published in Zhangjiashan Ersiqi Hao Han Mu Zhujian Zhengli Xiaozu 張家山二四七號漢墓竹簡整理小組, ed., *Zhangjiashan Han mu zhujian (ersiqi hao mu)* 張家山漢墓竹簡（二四七號墓）(Beijing: Wenwu Chubanshe, 2001) (hereafter *ZJS*); *Zhangjiashan Han mu zhujian (ersiqi hao mu) (shiwen xiuding ben)* 張家山漢墓竹簡（二四七號墓）（釋文修訂本）(Beijing: Wenwu Chubanshe, 2006) hereafter *ZJS-XD*); Peng Hao 彭浩, Chen Wei 陳偉, and Kudō Motoo 工藤元男, eds., *Ernian lüling yu Zouyan shu: Zhangjiashan ersiqi hao Han mu chutu falü wenxian shidu* 二年律令與奏讞書：張家山二四七號漢墓出土法律文獻釋讀 (Shanghai: Shanghai Guji

includes commoners, meaning those without meritocratic rank, thus designated *shiwŭ* 士伍 (member of the rank and file).² Although the evidence is inadequate at present, or at least circumstantial, there is enough to justify some tentative conclusions concerning the need for members of the lower orders, including women, to gain mastery of a limited range of written words and to suggest that therefore literacy was a technology that had gradually diffused from the courts and the religious experts associated with ancestral cults of the competing states, where it apparently was first deployed.³ While there is no evidence to determine exactly what constituted "literacy" for the lower orders, in other words, whether or to what extent they possessed the ability to recognize and/or reproduce a certain number of written graphs,⁴ the contention here, contra Mark Edward Lewis, is that the power of writing was not just focused on the ruler, who "held himself attentive at the center and responded to what was presented to him, whether in the writings of his officials or in the signs offered by the world."⁵ Rather, or in addition, the state required the lower orders in late Warring States and early Han times to be functionally literate, meaning able to meet the state's demands for competency in reading and

---

Chubanshe, 2007) (hereafter *ENL)*; Zhu Honglin 朱紅林, *Zhangjiashan Han jian 'Ernian lüling' jishi* 張家山漢簡《二年律令》集釋 (Beijing: Shehui Kexue Chubanshe, 2005).

2. For commoner status, see Robin D. S. Yates, "Social Status in the Ch'in: Evidence from the Yün-meng Legal Documents, Part One: Commoners," *Harvard Journal of Asiatic Studies* 47.1 (1987): 197–237; and Liu Hainian 劉海年, "Qin Han 'shiwu' de shenfen yu jieji diwei" 秦漢士伍的身份與階級地位, *Wenwu* 文物 1978.2: 58–62, reprinted in *Zhanguo Qin dai fazhi guankui* 戰國秦代法制管窺 (Beijing: Falü Chubanshe, 2006), 313–21.
3. The scribes (*shǐ* 史) were probably primarily responsible for composing the inscriptions engraved on bronzes, and, earlier, on oracle bones, that were held in the royal archives and the archives of the ruling houses of the Zhou world. These bronzes were dedicated to ancestors and used in the ancestral cult, as many studies have demonstrated. The most recent book-length study of scribes in Early China is Xu Zhaochang 許兆昌, *Xian-Qin shiguan de zhidu yu wenhua* 先秦史官的制度與文化 (Harbin: Heilongjiang Renmin Chubanshe, 2006). Mark Edward Lewis argues that between the time of the early court and the period examined in this chapter, writing diffused into the scholarly traditions of the "masters," such as Confucius and Mo Di; see *Writing and Authority*, 53–97.
4. For a discussion on the difficulty of defining the term "literacy" in the Chinese context, see Rawski, *Education and Popular Literacy*, 1–23.
5. Lewis, *Writing and Authority*, 35. Cf. Christopher Leigh Connery, *The Empire of the Text: Writing and Authority in Early Imperial China* (Lanham, Md.: Rowman and Littlefield, 1998).

writing within specific domains, social formations, and ideologies, to observe the regulations promulgated by the state, to be incorporated into its ever-expanding administrative and economic system, and to be ever more legible to its officers.[6] This generated a multiplicity of nodes of resistance where writing could be manipulated and used as a source of power and self-definition, even though that self-definition was by no means as clearly articulated as it was for the upper echelons of society.[7]

The Evidence for Literacy in the *Mozi*

An intriguing passage in the *Mozi* 墨子 suggests that ordinary commoners and those performing military service as part of their tax obligations in late Warring States and early imperial China may have been more literate than we have previously imagined:

命必足畏、賞必足利、令必行、令出輒人隨、省其可行不行。號：夕有號、失號斷。為守備程而署之曰：某程。置署(街)*術、街、衢、階、若門。令往來者皆視而放。[8]

---

6. An individual's competency in recognizing graphs (reading) might be much greater than his or her ability to reproduce them and create grammatical sentences. People may deploy this technology for their own personal needs. In addition, literacy, once learned, is not a technology that remains for a lifetime. An individual can forget his functional literacy, if it is no longer required and deployed in his or her social environment. For an analysis of the "ideological" model of literacy against the "autonomous model" proposed by Jack Goody and his colleagues, see Brian V. Street, *Literacy in Theory and Practice* (Cambridge: Cambridge University Press, 1984), 19–125. There have been many studies analyzing functional literacy in modern complex societies, and obviously these modern criteria far exceed the requirements of the early Chinese state.
7. By this I mean as articulated by the highly literate philosophers who are the focus of most studies on Early China. See Lewis, *Writing and Authority*; Michael J. Puett, *To Become a God: Cosmology, Sacrifice, and Self-Divinization in Early China* (Cambridge, Mass.: Harvard University Asia Center for the Harvard-Yenching Institute, 2002), esp. 80–121; Mark Csikszentmihalyi, *Material Virtue: Ethics and the Body in Early China* (Leiden: Brill, 2004), esp. 80–121.
8. Robin D. S. Yates, "The City under Siege: A Reconstruction and Translation of the Military Chapters of *Mo-tzu*" (PhD diss., Harvard University, 1980), 466–67 (474–75); text taken from the Ming (1445) edition of the *Mozi* in the *Dao zang* 道藏, *juan* 845, *Wuqiubei zhai Mozi jicheng* 無求備齋墨子集成, vol. 1, ed. Yan Lingfeng 嚴靈峯 (Taipei: Chengwen, 1977); Sun Yirang 孫詒讓, *Mozi jiangu* 墨子閒詁, *Guoxue jiben congshu* ed. (Shanghai: Shangwu Yinshuguan, 1936), 367–68; Cen Zhongmian 岑仲勉, *Mozi chengshou gepian jianzhu* 墨子城守各篇簡注 (Beijing: Zhonghua Shuju, 1958), 532.

> Commands must be sufficiently awesome, rewards must be sufficiently beneficial, and orders must be obeyed. When orders are issued, people should immediately follow (them). Be alert to those (laws) that can be carried out and those that cannot.
>
> Verbal Commands: at night there are verbal commands. Those who disobey verbal commands are to be executed. Make regulations for the preparations of defense and set them up stating, *X Regulations*. Place them in the offices, roads, streets, crossroads, staircases, and gates. Order all those who are traveling back and forth to look at and follow them.

The types of regulations that may have been posted are scattered in various fragments preserved in chapter 15 of this same text. The authors of these passages, whoever they were, Mohists or other military strategists, presume that orders written and posted on boards at key locations throughout the city under siege could have been read, understood, and obeyed by a significant body of the inhabitants, soldiers and civilians alike, both men and women, for both were expected to take part in the defense and were assigned different tasks and were rewarded for success in different ways. They make no provision for those who could not read. Presumably, they never even thought of illiteracy as a valid excuse for failure to abide by the written regulations; they expected those who could not read to know someone who could decipher the instructions and to ask that person to enlighten them as to the purport of the instructions on the signboards.

In another passage, the authors presume that those who would be recruited for the defense as subordinate officers would be able to write their own names and hang them in the posts where they were assigned. And they assume that ordinary members of the population were perfectly capable of writing and circulating private letters. These letters could reveal details of the defense or might discuss the letter writers' own private matters — matters that could be of use to the enemy — could suborn other defenders, could focus attention away from the crucial issue at hand (the defense of the city), or could indicate how the correspondents might profit from the crisis situation. The authors are also very concerned that attackers outside the city might try to communicate with those inside. Thus they forbid city residents to pick up letters shot over the city wall attached to arrows and likewise prohibit those trapped inside from sending messages in a similar fashion to those outside. It is doubtful they would have issued these prohibitions if this tactic had not been attempted or proved successful in previous sieges, albeit there is no historical evidence from this period that describes precise details of such a tactic working. In fact, all of these instructions are given as though an adequate level of literacy could be presumed among the urban population at large.[9] Military regulations similar to those found in the Mohist corpus continued to be issued in later times, and examples are included in most military encyclopedias and manuals.[10]

Are these passages unique and merely wishful thinking on the part of experts dedicated to the defense of cities, written with the aim of impressing a ruler or lord from whom they were seeking employment guarding against the attacks that were so common in late Warring States times? This is unlikely, for in a similar fashion, the *Zhouli* 周禮 recommends that laws be exposed on the first day of the month "at the places dedicated for their exposure" and taken down on the tenth day.[11] Although the *Zhouli* does not represent actual bureaucratic practice in Warring States times, it is clear from several other sources, such as the *Book of Lord Shang* (*Shangjun shu* 商君書), that ordinary commoners were not denied the privilege of finding out what was contained in the laws, as was the rule in later imperial times; to the contrary, the people were expected to find out about the texts of the laws and legal officials were required to answer questions about the law posed to them by the general population.[12]

---

9. Given that the Mohists also urge depriving the enemy outside the town or city under attack of all matériel outside the walls, including even the local population, one could suggest that peasants brought in from the countryside might also have been expected to have some basic level of literacy. See Robin D. S. Yates, Joseph Needham, et al., *Science and Civilisation in China*, vol. 5, part 6: *Military Technology: Missiles and Sieges* (Cambridge: Cambridge University Press, 1994), 271–72.
10. See Robin D. S. Yates, "Law and the Military in Early China," in *Military Culture in Imperial China*, ed. Nicola Di Cosmo (Cambridge, Mass.: Harvard University Press, 2009), 23–44.
11. Sun Yirang, *Zhouli zhengyi* 周禮正義 ("Da sima" 大司馬), *Sibu beiyao* 四部備要 ed., 55.4:6b; Édouard Biot, *Le Tcheou-Li ou Rites des Tcheou*, vol. 2 (Paris: Imprimerie Nationale, 1851; repr., Taipei: Chengwen, 1967), 167.
12. In the "Fixing of Rights and Duties" (Dingfen 定分) chapter of the *Shangjun shu* 商君書; see Zhu Shiche 朱師轍, *Shangjun shu jiegu* 商君書解詁 (Hong Kong: Zhonghua Shuju, 1974), 92; J. J. L. Duyvendak, *The Book of Lord Shang* (London: Probsthain, 1928; rpt., Chicago: University of Chicago Press), 327–31. In the famous incident of the burning of the books in 213 B.C.E., following the suggestion of Li Si 李斯, the Qin required in an ordinance (*ling* 令) that the populace learn from the officials (*li* 吏) either about the laws and ordinances (*faling* 法令) (*Shiji*, 6.255) or, more generally, about the books on medicine, pharmaceutics, divination by bone-cracking and milfoil,

If, then, members of the lower orders were permitted access to the laws, and were expected to read and obey written instructions at such a crucial time as when a town or city was under siege, how did they acquire the basic literacy that enabled them to read such instructions? If there were not a significant number of literate members of the lower orders in the cities defended by the Mohists, how could the defenders (shǒu 守) in charge of protecting the towns and cities under siege expect the laws and orders they issued to be obeyed?

This skill was acquired in late Warring States, Qin, and Han times primarily in two ways. The first was through participation in the conscript armies in which only males served. These armies were increasingly managed by means of the written word.[13] The second was in response to the demands of the state, which sought to regulate the lives of the people, to monitor all goods and transactions, to require handicraft products to be marked, and to register the population. But exactly *how* basic literacy was acquired by the general population is not clear. Nor is it possible to determine the extent of literacy among the general population of the times — it is hardly possible even to calculate the size of the population. Nor is it possible to determine the level of literacy achieved by the ordinary population, or the extent to which literacy was gendered — in other words, the extent to which males and females were respectively literate — for there is only limited evidence at present for the existence of either private or government schools for such individuals, nor does it seem that private teachers who instructed budding high-level officials and philosophers stooped to pass basic instruction on to the general populace.[14] Recently

---

and arboriculture that were not proscribed; see *Shiji,* 87:2546. The former requirement is more likely, since it appears that Sima Qian is quoting the language of the ordinance directly in the chapter "Basic Annals of Qin Shihuangdi." See Derk Bodde, *China's First Unifier: A Study of the Ch'in Dynasty as Seen in the Life of Li Ssû* 李斯 *280?–208 B.C.* (Hong Kong: Hong Kong University Press, 1967), 24, 83.

13. See Yates, "Law and the Military in Early China," 25–42.
14. In his study, Jan L. Hagman concerns himself only with schools for the elite, not for the general populace; "Private and Government Schools in the Han Dynasty," in *Outstretched Leaves on His Bamboo Staff: Studies in Honour of Göran Malmqvist on his 70th Birthday,* ed. Joakim Enwall (Stockholm: The Association for Oriental Studies, 1994), 114–30. I am grateful to Griet Vankeerberghen for bringing this reference to my attention. The term "private school" or "private student" (sīxué 私學) first appears in the *Hanfeizi* 韓非子 and seems to mean those who studied outside the government schools. See Yu Zhenbo 于振波, *Zoumalou Wu jian chutan* 走馬樓吳簡初探 (Taipei: Wenjin Chubanshe, 2004), ch. 7: "Han Jin sixue kaoshu" 漢晉私學考述, 175–224. In

discovered evidence can help clarify the contexts of literacy among the lower orders, however, and, if not answer the questions posed above at least permit some productive speculation. The following review of the role of scribes (*shǐ* 史) in late Warring States, Qin, and early Han times and presentation of evidence from documents left behind by Han soldiers in the forts along the northwestern frontier serve as a starting point.

Scribes

In late Warring States times, scribes became essential components of the increasingly complex bureaucratic administration, and it was their skill that allowed the reach of higher state officials to penetrate into the towns and villages of the incipient empire. Through their efforts, the state was able to exploit the labor power of the population. At the same time, however, their technology required the participation and complicity of the population: it required the population to become basically proficient in the same technology — segments of the population became functionally literate and used that technology on occasion to resist the penetration of the state or at least tried to use it to their own advantage in the negotiation or practice of daily life.

Recent archaeological discoveries of the legal statutes and other rules issued by the state of Qin and early Han authorities have provided previously unimagined detail about the training of scribes (*shǐ* 史) and, in passing, allude to the ability to write among other members of the general population. The first group of legal documents that provide evidence are those found buried with an individual whose given name can be identified as Xi 喜 from a calendar of his life that was also deposited in his coffin.[15]

---

the late Han dynasty, Cui Shi 崔寔 (circa 103–circa 170) recommended in his *Monthly Ordinances for the Four Peoples* (*Simin yueling* 四民月令) that there be two types of schools for boys: one for older children, who would learn the five Confucian canons, and the other for younger children, who would learn "reading, writing, and arithmetic" during the agricultural slack seasons. See the translations of this text by Cho-yun Hsu, *Han Agriculture: The Formation of Early Chinese Agrarian Economy (206 B.C.–A.D. 220)* (Seattle: University of Washington Press, 1980), 216, 224, 226, and 227. I am grateful to Anthony Barbieri-Low for this reference.

15. Shuihudi Qin Mu Zhujian Zhengli Xiaozu 睡虎地秦墓竹簡整理小組, ed., *Shuihudi Qinmu zhujian* 睡虎地秦墓竹簡 (Beijing: Wenwu, 2001 [1990]; hereafter *SHD*). The statutes and other legal documents, but not the calendar, "The Way of Being an Official" 為吏之道, or the almanac texts also found in the tomb, are translated by A. F. P.

These documents were apparently consigned to the earth in 217 B.C.E. or shortly thereafter, probably immediately following his death, and they may have been used by him when he tried law cases in the fourth month of 235 B.C.E.[16] Here, the regulations titled "*Nei shi*: Miscellaneous" (*Nèishǐ zá* 內史雜), which the late expert on early Chinese law A. F. P. Hulsewé assumes to derive from the statutes (*lü* 律) of the Ministry of Finance (*Nèishǐ*) but are more likely to have come from the ordinances (*lìng* 令),[17] enunciate the following rule:

令敖史毋從事官府。非史子(殹)也毋敢學學室。犯令者有罪。[18]

[191] According to the Ordinances . . . scribes must not be made to work in government storehouses. If (persons) are not sons of scribes, they must not venture to study in the study-room. Those who transgress this Ordinance will have committed a crime.

The second graph of this rule is unknown, and the editors of the Shuihudi Qin legal documents suggest that it may be an alternate form of *shè* 赦 'amnestied'. In a note, Hulsewé rejects a Japanese scholar's suggestion that it is an alternate form of *áo* 敖 'proud, overbearing' but offers no solution. It is likely that the word designates a type of scribe and that the first word in the regulation should not be understood as "ordinance" (*lìng* 令), as Hulsewé does, but rather the first graph in the term *lìngshǐ* 令史,

---

Hulsewé, in *Remnants of Ch'in Law: An Annotated Translation of the Ch'in Legal and Administrative Rules of the 3rd Century b.c. Discovered in Yün-meng Prefecture, Hu-pei Province, in 1975* (Leiden: E. J. Brill, 1985).

16. Katrina C. D. McLeod and Robin D. S. Yates, "Forms of Ch'in Law: An Annotated Translation of the *Feng-chen shih*," *Harvard Journal of Asiatic Studies* 41.1 (1981): 121.
17. Ye Shan 葉山 (R. Yates), "Qin de falü yu shehui: Guanyu Zhangjiashan 'Ernian lüling' deng xin chutu wenxian de sikao" 秦的法律與社會：關於張家山《二年律令》等新出土文獻的思考, *Rujia wenhua yanjiu: Xin chu Chu jian yanjiu zhuanhao* 儒家文化研究：新出楚簡研究專號 1 (2007): 299–325.
18. *SHD*, 63, slip 191; Hulsewé, *Remnants of Ch'in Law*, 87–88. I have modified Hulsewé's translation of *shǐ* which he renders as "clerk." In a personal communication, Anthony Barbieri-Low offers the following comment on this translation: "Or why not, the X Shi are commanded not to engage in work in government storehouses. If we take the reading as Ao 'proud', then maybe these are pretentious but talented men who claim to be scribes but who do not have the lineage. This would fit better with the next section, where students of improper scribal lineage cannot enter the school. Even taking the original transcription of 'amnestied scribes' also fits this same sense and explains why they cannot work in government offices anymore."

such that the rule is referring to either of two different types of scribe, the *lìngshǐ* and the X-*shǐ*, or, more likely, that there was a special type of *lìngshǐ* called the *lìng* X-*shǐ*. These scribes were not permitted, for some unexplained reason, to work in Qin government storehouses. The *lìngshǐ* appears in many of the Shuihudi legal documents and also in the transmitted texts from the Han dynasty. The late Yu Haoliang 于豪亮 concludes that they were general service personnel,[19] whereas Hulsewé, translating the term as "prefectural clerk," follows Ikeda Yūichi 池田雄一 in viewing them as holding a relatively high position just subordinate to the assistant prefect (*chéng* 丞) (of a county [*xiàn* 縣]) and holding the same rank as the overseers (*sèfū* 嗇夫).[20] Hulsewé also notes that the term *xuéshì* 學室 is unknown and suggests that it must refer to some sort of school. This is undoubtedly correct, and it is clear from this rule that only sons of scribes were permitted to be trained in this school, which was specially designated for them.[21] In other words, the function of scribe in

---

19. Yu Haoliang 于豪亮, "Yunmeng Qin jian suojian zhiguan shulüe" 雲夢秦簡所見職官述略, in *Yu Haoliang xueshu wencun* 于豪亮學術文存 (Beijing: Zhonghua Shuju, 1985), 109.
20. Hulsewé, *Remnants of Ch'in Law*, 39, A 22, n. 4; Ikeda Yūichi 池田雄一, "Kohoku Unmei Suikochi Shin bo kanken" 湖北雲夢睡虎地秦墓管見, *Chūō daigaku bungakubu kiyō* 中央大學文學部紀要 100 (1981): 33–66.
21. Zhang Jinguang 張金光 believes that *zǐ* 'sons' also refers to scribes' apprentice disciples (*xuétú dìzǐ* 學徒弟子), in other words, their retainers, and that the Statutes concerning the Appointment of Retainers (*Chú dìzǐ lǜ* 除弟子律) also refers to these retainers or disciples; *Qin zhi yanjiu* 秦制研究 (Shanghai: Shanghai Guji, 2004), 710; see also, *SHD*, 130–31. Hulsewé translates this statute as follows:

當除弟子籍不得、置任不審、皆耐為侯(候)。使其弟子贏律、及治(笞)之、貲一甲。決革、二甲。

When (a person) is warranted to appoint retainers (but) the population register does not allow this, (or) when appointments are made carelessly, (such cases) are all punished by shaving off the beard [facial hair] and being made a *hòu* [watchman]. Employment of one's retainers in excess (of the norms established by) the Statutes, as well as beating them, is fined one suit of armour; if the skin is broken (the fine is) two suits of armour.

See *Remnants of Ch'in Law*, 104–5, C 4. The difficulty with Zhang's interpretation is that there is no evidence that lowly scribes had the legal right to make such appointments, nor is there evidence that scribes had retainers; retainers gathered around those much higher up on the social scale.

Qin was hereditary.²² Furthermore, two other rules from the same set of regulations of the Ministry of Finance specify that:

下吏能書者、毋敢從史之事。²³

Persons in detention who are able to write must not venture to engage in the work of scribes.

侯(候)、司寇及群下吏毋敢為官府佐、禁苑憲盜。²⁴

Watchmen, robber guards, and the multitude of persons in detention must not venture to act as assistants and scribes in government storehouses nor as guards of the Forbidden Parks.

The term *xiàlì* 下吏 appears to designate some type of low-status individual, but exactly what it meant in Qin times is unknown. Hulsewé follows the interpretation of the editors of *Shuihudi Qinmu zhujian* in taking it as "persons in detention;" this view seems doubtful. Perhaps the full publication of other recently discovered Qin documents will lead to a solution to this problem. Nevertheless, no matter which interpretation we accept, it is clear that the Qin state recognized the likelihood that persons of this status sometimes had the ability to write and, by this rule, was trying to prevent them from performing the function of scribes for government business. The Qin state may not always have succeeded in preventing this abuse, for in the Shuihudi statutes, it is (probably) prescribed that male and female bondservants (*lìchénqiè* 隸臣妾) are old and weak and are not to be entrusted with conveying government documents.²⁵ However, the Qin boards and slips from Liye reveal that it

---

22. See below for further evidence in support of this contention.
23. *SHD*, 63, slip 192; translation by Hulsewé, *Remnants of Ch'in Law*, 88, A 102 (slightly emended); Léon Vandermeersch, "Le développement de la procédure écrite dans l'administration chinoise à l'époque ancienne," in *State and Law in East Asia: Festschrift Karl Bünger*, ed. D. Eikemeier and H. Franke (Wiesbaden, Germany: Harrassowitz, 1981), 20.
24. *SHD*, 63, slip 193; translation by Hulsewé, *Remnants of Ch'in Law*, 88, A 103 (slightly emended).
25. For (Statutes) on the Forwarding of Documents (*Xíngshū* 行書), see Hulsewé, *Remnants of Ch'in Law*, 86, A96. The statute reads "Bond-servants and bond-women who are old and weak, as well as those who are not to be trusted, are not to be. . . ." (184). 隸臣妾老弱及不可誠仁者勿; *SHD*, 61, slip 184. The passage concludes at the end of the strip, and the editors then attached slip 185 to slip 184. The following passage on slip 185 reads 令書廷辟有曰報宜到不來者追之. The *SHD* editors joined the two slips together and then read the sentence as ending with the clause "are not to

was very common to entrust bondservants with such documents, although they might not have been "old and weak."[26] These documents provide excellent evidence for the actual day-to-day running of the Qin administrative system, and, once they all are published, we will be able to compare them with the ideal stipulations issued by the Qin court as statutes, ordinances, and other legal rules.

To return to the training of scribes and the matter of the (apparent) special school for the sons of scribes, another hoard of legal documents was discovered in tomb no. 247, Zhangjiashan, Hubei.[27] Included in this selection of early Han legal documents, which were probably buried in 186 B.C.E. or shortly thereafter, were at least eight regulations taken from the "Statutes on Scribes" (*Shilü* 史律). It would appear that these statutes represent late Qin or early Han laws and reflect Qin and early Han practice. Slip no. 474 specifies the following:

史、卜子年十七歲學。史、卜、祝學童學三歲，學佴將詣大史、大卜、大祝，郡史學童詣其守，皆會八月朔日試之。(474)[28]

Sons of scribes and diviners, when they are seventeen years (*suì* 歲) of age, are to go to school (to study). Student scribes, diviners, and invocators are to study three years; the school-masters are to pay formal visits to the Grand Scribe, the Grand Diviner, or Grand Invocator; the student scribes in commanderies are to pay formal visits to their (respective) Defenders (i.e., Governors); and in all cases they are to gather and be tested on the first day of the eighth month.

---

be ordered [to transport documents]" (*wùlìng* 勿令). Hulsewé rejects this interpretation and translates the passage "When written orders and summonses by the office say 'Report,' persons who should have arrived but who have not come should be traced," suggesting that, although the law may well have had the provision that such individuals were not to be ordered to deliver government documents, the two slips were independent of each other, and that *lìng* is to be understood as comparable to *mìng* 命 and joined with the next word *shū* to mean "written orders"; *Remnants of Ch'in Law*, 86 n. 4. Such an interpretation is certainly possible.

26. For a female bondservant by the name of Ran 冉 delivering a government document, see board J1 (8) 157, in Wang Huanlin 王煥林, *Liye Qin jian jiaogu* 里耶秦簡校詁 (Beijing: Zhongguo Wenlian Chubanshe, 2007), 51–55, and for a comment on the Qin statute and the practice of bond servants actually transporting government documents in the Liye hoard, see Li Li 李力, "*Lichenqie*" shenfen zai yanjiu "隸臣妾" 身份再研究 (Beijing: Zhongguo Falü Chubanshe, 2007), 389.
27. See note 1.
28. *ZJS*, 203; *ZJS-XD*, 80; *ENL*, 296–97; Zhu Honglin, *Zhangjiashan Han jian*, 280.

As Li Xueqin points out, in comparison with the Han "Statutes of the Commandant" (Weilü 尉律) quoted by Xu Shen 許慎 in his preface to the *Shuowen* 說文 dictionary of the early Eastern Han, in which there does not seem to be a similar restriction on access to the school for scribes, this statute indicates that the status of scribe was hereditary at this early stage of the empire and had probably been handed down from generation to generation for centuries.[29] According to Cao Lüning 曹旅寧, this statute indicates that the specialist functions of diviners and invocators, as well as scribes, were included in the general category of "scribe" at this time.[30] Thus, the system for recruitment of scribes must have changed during the course of the Han dynasty, although there is no record of when the previous restriction was lifted. This statute further implies that the early training of these specialist functionaries, scribes, diviners, and invocators would have taken place in their homes, before they commenced their studies under official teachers in officially sanctioned schools. It additionally indicates that there were such schools in the metropolitan or capital areas as well as at the commandery level. What was the curriculum? This is specified in other statutes:

[試]史學童以十五篇。能風(諷) 書五千字以上、能得為史。有(又)以八(體)試之，郡移其八(體)課大史，大史誦課，取取(最)一人以為其縣令(475)史，殿者勿以為史。三歲壹并課，取取(最)一人以為尚書卒史(476)

[Test] the student scribes on the *Fifteen Sections*. Those who are capable of

---

29. Duan Yucai 段玉裁, *Shuowen jiezi zhu* 說文解字注 (Shanghai: Shanghai Guji Chubanshe, 1986 [1981]), 15A.11b–12b, 758–59. Li Xueqin, "Shishuo Zhangjiashan jian 'Shi lü'" 試說張家山漢簡史律, *Wenwu* 2002.4: 69–72. Cf. A. F. P. Hulsewé, "The Shuo-wen Dictionary as a Source for Ancient Chinese Law," in *Studia Serica Bernhard Karlgren Dedicata*, ed. Søren Egerod and Else Glahn (Copenhagen: Munksgaard, 1959), 239–58; Zhang Zhenglang 張政烺, "*Shuowen jiezi xu* yin Wei lü kao" 說文解字序引尉律考, in *Zhang Zhenglang wenshi lunji* 張政烺文史論集 (Beijing: Zhonghua Shuju, 2004), 208–14; Cheng Shude 程樹德, *Jiuchao lü kao* 九朝律考 (Beijing: Zhonghua Shuju, 2006), 83–84.
30. Cao Lüning 曹旅寧, "Zhangjiashan Han jian 'Shi lü' kao" 張家山漢簡《史律》考, in *Zhangjiashan Han lü yanjiu* 張家山漢律研究 (Beijing: Zhonghua Shuju, 2005), 175. Scribes and invocators were also closely linked officials, with similar obligations in the state of Qi 齊, if we may judge from the story concerning the desire of Duke Jing to kill his highest-ranking scribe and invocator because the duke was suffering from a protracted illness. See Pu Maozuo's 濮茅左 transcription of "Jing gong nüe" 競(景)公瘧 in Ma Chengyuan 馬承源 ed., *Shanghai Bowuguan cang Zhanguo Chu zhushu* 上海博物館藏戰國楚竹書, vol. 7 (Shanghai: Shanghai Guji Chubanshe, 2007), 166.

reciting and writing more than five thousand graphs then get to be scribes. Furthermore, test them on the eight forms of writing; the commandery sends those (capable in the) eight forms of writing to be examined by the Grand Scribe; the Grand Scribe examines their reciting and selects the best individual(s) to become *lìngshĭ* at the county level. Those who are of poor quality are not to be made scribes. Every three years, they are to be examined together once. Take the best individual to be a *Shàngshū cuìshĭ* (scribe in the Imperial Secretariat).

The *Fifteen Sections* may possibly have been a version of the *Shi Zhou* 史籀, a work recorded in the "Yiwen zhi" 藝文志 chapter of the *Hanshu* 漢書 as having fifteen sections. The *Shi Zhou* is said to have been composed in large seal-script form by the Grand Scribe during the reign of King Xuan of Zhou 周宣王 and lost during the Jianwu 建武 era of the Han, the reign period established by Guangwudi 光武帝 at the beginning of the Eastern Han (starting 25).[31] The number of graphs the scribes were expected to be able to recite (five thousand) is slightly less than the graphs that were eventually included in the *Cangjie pian* 倉頡篇, said to have been produced by the First Emperor of Qin's prime minister, the infamous legalist Li Si 李斯;[32] in the later Han "Statutes of the Commandant," the number of graphs required in the Grand Scribe's examinations was set at nine thousand, but the number of forms of writing was only six.[33]

However, it should not be assumed that the figures of five thousand and nine thousand graphs refer to five thousand and nine thousand *different*

---

31. *Hanshu* 漢書 ("Yiwen zhi" 藝文志), 30:1719. See Wang Guowei 王國維, "Shi Zhou pian zhengxu" 史籀篇證序, in *Wang Guowei yishu* 王國維遺書 (Shanghai: Shanghai Guji Chubanshe, 1983), 1, 5:17a–20a. Zang Zhifei, however, doubts this identification; see Zang Zhifei 臧知非, " 'Shi lü' xinzheng" 《史律》新證, *Shixue yuekan* 史學月刊 2008.11: 20–26.
32. Fragments of the *Cangjie pian* have been discovered in Han forts along the northwestern frontier and also in an early Western Han tomb excavated in Fuyang, Anhui. See Roger Greatrex, "An Early Western Han Synonymicon: The Fuyang Copy of the *Cang jie pian*," in *Outstretched Leaves on His Bamboo Staff*, 97–113; Hu Pingsheng 胡平生, "Han jian 'Cangjie pian' xin ziliao de yanjiu" 漢簡《倉頡篇》新資料的研究, in *Hu Pingsheng jiandu wenwu lunji* 胡平生簡牘文物論集 (Taipei: Lantai, 2000), 45–69, and Hu Pingsheng, "Fuyang Han jian 'Cangjie pian' de chubu yanjiu" 阜陽漢簡《倉頡篇》的初步研究, in ibid., 278–93.
33. However, the *Jiuchao lü kao* quotes the *Kunxue jiwen* 困學紀聞 as saying that the preface to the *Shuowen* indicates that the number of forms of writing was eight. See Cheng Shude, *Jiuchao lü kao*, 84.

graphs. There is no indication in the statutes that this is what is meant. It is highly likely that the texts used to train scribes resembled the slips found in both the Shuihudi tomb now known as "The Way of Being a Good Official" (Wei li zhi dao 為吏之道)[34] and those containing the two versions of texts titled by the editors "Warnings for Officials" (Guan zhen 官箴), now held by the Yuelu Shuyuan, Hunan University, which probably were taken from the graves of two different Qin scribes.[35] Some of the passages in these two collections are either identical or very similar to each other. Indeed, some passages in "The Way of Being a Good Official" seem to be lists of different words that any scribe would need to know, but other passages are clauses that repeat words and grammatical particles.[36] Furthermore, it is quite possible that scribes were also trained in mathematics, as they were required to keep accurate and detailed records of all the various accounts under their purview, as Zang Zhifei argues,[37] so the mathematics texts found in both Zhangjiashan tomb no. 247 and the Yuelu Qin hoard may also have been used to train scribes and may have been included in the *Fifteen Sections*.[38] The training manuals may even have contained texts of selected statutes and ordinances themselves, as Wang Chong 王充 (27–89) laments that common students all rush to study "the books of the scribes, read the statutes, and intone the ordinances" 史書讀律諷令.[39] Finally, on the issue of how many *different* graphs *in total* a scribe would be expected not only to be familiar with but to be able to read and write in the Qin and early Han dynasties, before a satisfactory

---

34. *SHD*, 167–76. Cf. Liu Hainian 劉海年, "Cong Qin jian 'Wei li zhi dao' kan Qin de 'Zhi li' sixiang" 從秦簡《為吏之道》看秦的'治吏'思想, in *Zhanguo Qin dai fazhi guankui* 戰國秦代法制管窺 (Beijing: Falü Chubanshe, 2006), 364–77.
35. Chen Songchang 陳松長, "Yuelu shuyuan suocang Qin jian zongshu" 岳麓書院所藏秦簡綜述, *Wenwu* 2009.3: 79–83.
36. According to Zhang Shouzhong 張守中, the entire corpus of the Shuihudi texts is composed of approximately 1,555 slips with more than 37,000 total graphs, with 1,798 different graphs and 12 composite (double) graphs (*héwén* 合文), for a total of 1,810 different graphs; *Shuihudi Qin jian wenzi bian* 睡虎地秦簡文字編 (Beijing: Wenwu Chubanshe, 1993), 238–57 (figures based on author's count).
37. Zang Zhifei, " 'Shi lü' xinzheng," 23.
38. For an analysis and translation of the Zhangjiashan mathematics text, see Christopher Cullen, "The *Suàn shù shū* 算數書, 'Writings on Reckoning': Rewriting the History of Early Chinese Mathematics in the Light of an Excavated Manuscript," *Historia Mathematica* 34 (2007): 10–44.
39. Beijing Daxue Lishixi *Lunheng* Zhushi Xiaozu 北京大學歷史系《論衡》注釋小組, ed., *Lunheng zhushi* 論衡注釋 (Beijing: Zhonghua Shuju, 1979), 2:685.

conclusion can be drawn, it will be necessary to catalog all the different graphs in the recently discovered legal and administrative texts as well as those found in earlier excavations, at sites such as the Han fort at Juyan and related signal stations and posts in the northwestern desert. A significant number would be the names of administrative positions and place-names as well as personal names, graphs (words) that would necessarily be used only occasionally. Overall, therefore, a scribe was probably expected to be able to read and write approximately 2,500 to 3,500 different graphs. This figure may be taken as a rough approximation until further research clarifies the issue.

Historians of literacy and writing have been interested in determining when reading became silent, and this regulation brings up the question of whether or not these late Qin or early Han scribes were reading silently. Clearly, when being examined by the Grand Scribe, they were expected to chant (*sòng* 誦) the words, but what does the word *fěng* (風[諷]) imply? Xunzi 荀子 states:

少不諷[誦]、壯不論議; 雖可、未成也。[40]

If you do not recite and chant when still small and discuss and deliberate when a youth, then although you may try, you will never master them.

Thus, the literate commonly practiced the two ways of reading, *fěng* and *sòng*. The late Han commentator Zheng Xuan 鄭玄 (127–200), remarking on a passage in the *Zhouli,* notes that *fěng* means to "read it silently and not rely on humming" 謂闇讀之不依詠也, which the Tang scholar Jia Gongyan 賈公彥 (seventh century) explains further as reading silently without the help of humming to the accompaniment of a *qin* or *se* zither.[41] Whether this distinction between *fěng* and *sòng* held true in the period of the Qin-Han transition cannot as yet be reliably determined, but Zheng's remark is evidence that Chinese scholars could read silently by the second century.

In these early Han statutes, it is clear that scribes were expected to have command over a range of written graphs (*zì* 字) different from those required of either diviners or invocators, for students training to become

---

40. *Xunzi* 荀子 (*pian* 27, "Da lüe" 大略), *Sibu beiyao* ed. (Taipei: Zhonghua Shuju, 1970), 19:12a; translation in, Knoblock, *Xunzi*, 3.27:88, 228. The word *song* has been added to the text from a parallel in the *Da Dai Li ji* 大戴禮記.
41. *Zhouli*, "Chun guan" 春官 ("Gu meng" 瞽矇); see *Shisanjing zhushu*, 23:797b.

diviners were expected to master three thousand written graphs from the "scribe's text" (*shǐshū* 史書) and three thousand graphs from the "diviner's text" (*bǔshū* 卜書) and be capable of chanting (*sòng*) more than thirty thousand words (*yán* 言). If they were capable of that, then they could become government diviners.[42] The students attempting to become invocators, in contrast, were tested on an invocator text composed of fourteen sections (*zhù shísì zhāng* 祝十四章) and had to be capable of chanting more than seven thousand words (*yán*): again, they were not tested on written graphs (*zì*). They were obliged to provide five tours of duty (*gēng* 更).[43] The item in the statutes on slip 479 reads:

以祝十四章試祝學童，能誦七千言以上者，乃得為祝，五更。大祝試祝，善祝、明祠事者，以為冗祝，冗之。[44]

Test the student invocators on the *Fourteen Sections*. Those who are capable of chanting more than seven thousand words then get to be invocators and perform five tours of duty. The Grand Invocator tests the invocators. As for those who are excellent invocators and understand spiritual affairs, if they can be assigned for service (*rǒng* 冗)[45] as invocators, assign them.

A scribe, diviner, or invocator who, probably after passing the examination, failed to take up a position appropriate to his training was given the heavy fine of four *liǎng* of gold, and his teacher was fined half as much.

---

42. Slip 478 reads: [卜][學]童能風(諷)書史書三千字，誦卜書三千字，卜六發中一以上，乃得為卜，以為官□。其能誦三萬以上者，以為(477)卜，上計六更。缺，試脩法，以六發中三以上者補之。(*ZJS-XD*, 81; *ENL*, 299–301). Zhu Honglin incorrectly reads *zhēng* 征(證?) for *sòng* 誦; *Zhangjiashan Hanjian*, 282–83.
43. For tours of duty by rotation (*gēng* 更), see the discussion by Michael Loewe, who quotes and translates a passage from Ru Chun (transliterated as "Ju Chun" and "Ru Shun" in some previous Western scholarship) 如淳 (fl. 189–265), the early commentator on the *Hanshu*, on the various types of military service; appendix 2: "Texts concerning the Han System of Conscription," in *Records of Han Administration: Volume 1: Historical Assessment* (Cambridge: Cambridge University Press, 1967), 162–64.
44. *ZJS-XD*, 81; *ENL*, 301.
45. For the meaning of the term *rǒng* in the Shuihudi Qin legal documents, see Hulsewé, *Remnants of Ch'in Law*, 26–27, note 6 to A 7 (*SHD*, 39, slip 80). Anthony Barbieri-Low interprets *rǒng* as a kind of floating, non-specific appointment; "The Organization of Imperial Workshops during the Han Dynasty" (PhD diss., Princeton University, 2001), 327–28.

As with other officials, there were specific statutory regulations concerning these appointments: scribes had to receive their appointments from the Grand Scribe, and diviners from the Grand Diviner, and if there were insufficient numbers of scribes or diviners, an assistant (*zuǒ* 佐) could be appointed as a stopgap measure.[46] It would therefore seem that such assistants, who appear not infrequently in the Qin laws from Shuihudi, were of a lower status than the scribes or diviners and yet were sufficiently literate to perform the necessary tasks. They were apparently also subordinate to the Ministry of Finance (*Nèishǐ*), as one of the other regulations preserved at Shuihudi specifies that such assistants must be of adult age and not commoners (members of the rank and file) (*shìwǔ* 士伍) who had only been newly registered.[47] Other statutory regulations prohibited the schoolteachers from using the labor of all three types of students without specific authority; if they did, they would be fined four *liǎng* of gold.[48] Further statutory regulations specified that:

大史、大卜謹以吏員調官史、卜縣道官，官受除事，勿環。吏備(憊)罷、佐勞少者，毋敢亶(擅)史、卜。史、卜受調書大史、大卜而逋、(482) 留、及亶(擅)不視事盈三月，斥以為史、卜。吏壹弗除事者，與同罪；其非吏也，奪爵一級。史、人〈卜〉屬郡者，亦以從事。[49]

The Grand Scribe and Grand Diviner are to be careful when transferring official personnel and are to appoint government scribes and diviners to offices in the counties and circuits. When offices have received them and they are performing service, do not return them. When officials are decrepit or assistants' length of service is deficient,[50] do not venture on

---

46. The text of slip 481 reads □□, 大史官之；郡，郡守官之。卜，大卜官之。史、人〈卜〉不足，乃除佐；ZJS-XD, 81–82; ENL, 302.
47. SHD, 62, slip 190; Hulsewé, *Remnants of Ch'in Law*, 87, A 100.
48. The text reads □□學佴敢擅繇(徭)使史、卜祝學童者，罰金四兩 (Slip 484); ZJS-XD, 82; ENL, 303–4; Zhu Honglin, *Zhangjiashan Han jian*, 285.
49. Slip 483, ZJS-XD, 82; ENL, 302–3.
50. The legal documents (SHD, 63, slips 15–16), contain an item from the "Statutes on Reporting Years of Hardship" (Zhonglao lü 中勞律) which Hulsewé translates as "Persons who venture greatly to increase the number of their years of hardship are fined one suit of armour and the hardship is cancelled"; *Remnants of Ch'in Law*, 109. Hulsewé does not understand the use of the word *zhōng* in the title of the statute and leaves the word untranslated. It probably should be understood in the way that it appears in the "Chun guan" (Tian fu 天府) section of the *Zhouli* as reporting to higher authority a government registration document or list, according to Zheng Xuan's comment quoting Zheng Sinong 鄭司農, "*Zhìzhōng* means the essentials relating to

your own responsibility to make them scribes or diviners. When scribes and diviners receive a transfer in writing from the Grand Scribe or Grand Diviner and they flee or delay and on their own responsibility do not take up service for a full three months, upbraid/dismiss them and do not make them scribes or diviners. If officials similarly do not appoint them to serve, they share the same crime. Remove one degree of rank from those who are not officials. Scribes and diviners subordinate to the commanderies are also to perform service (in the same fashion).

謁任史、卜上計脩法。謁任卜學童令外學者，許之。□□學佴敢擅繇 (徭) 使史、卜學童者，罰金四兩。史、卜年五十六, (484) 佐為吏盈廿歲，年五十六，皆為八更；六十，為十二【更】。五百石以下至有秩為吏盈十歲，年當睆老者，為十二更，踐更□□。(485) 疇尸。菑御、杜主樂皆五更，屬大祝。祝年盈六十者，十二更，踐更大祝。(486)[51]

Receptionists (?)[52] are to guarantee that the scribes and diviners submit reports to higher authorities and prepare the laws. If the Receptionists guarantee to let student diviners study outside (the special school?), permit them. As for . . . , if the schoolmasters venture on their own responsibility to use the labor of student scribes, diviners, and invocators, they are fined four *liǎng* of gold. Scribes and diviners fifty-six years old, and assistants who have been officials for a full twenty years and are fifty-six years old, are all to be considered (to have done) eight tours of duty; those who are sixty, (to have done) twelve [tours of duty]. Those whose salary is five hundred *shí* (bushels of grain) on down to rank holders[53] who have been officials for a full ten years, and whose age warrants (their being considered) old men are to be considered (to have done) twelve tours of duty; (they pay a fee for) release from service[54] to. . . .[55] Hereditary impersonators (of gods, i.e., shamans), drinkers of wine offerings, Lord

---

the records and documents of their administration" 治中謂其治職簿書之要. See *Shisanjing zhushu*, 20:776a; Biot, *Le Tcheou-Li*, 1.481.

51. ZJS, 204; ZJS-XD, 82; ENL, 303–4; Zhu Honglin, *Zhangjiashan Han jian*, 285.
52. I am not sure of this translation. *Yèzhě* 謁者 were eunuch officials in the early Han, but the term *yè* here may refer to some other Qin or early Han functionary to whom the scribes reported directly and who was responsible for making legal decisions, for such an official appears in one of the cases reported to higher authorities ("Zouyan shu" 奏讞書) that are found in the Zhangjiashan tomb, where he renders a legal decision; see ZJS-XD, 97; ENL, 337.
53. For the term *yǒuzhì*, see Hulsewé, *Remnants of Ch'in Law*, 39 n. 3 on A 22; he observes that they normally received a salary of one hundred bushels per year and were locally appointed.
54. For the term *jiàn'gēng* 踐更, see Loewe, *Records of Han Administration*, 81 and n. 33.
55. Presumably the two indecipherable graphs are *Dàshǐ* 大史 (the Grand Scribe).

Dus, all are subordinate to the Grand Invocator.[56] When invocators are a full sixty years of age (they are considered to have done) twelve tours of duty, and they (pay a fee for) release from service to the Grand Invocator.

One example of a scribe's career can be deduced from excavated material. Xi, the owner of the tomb at Shuihudi, was evidently a scribe. According to the calendar placed in his tomb, he was born in the forty-fifth year of King Zhaoxiang of Qin (262 B.C.E.), was registered (fù 傅), presumably as a scribe, in the first year of King Zheng (246 B.C.E.). He then proceeded to be qualified as a scribe (shǐ), evidently having passed the scribal examinations after three years of study, in the third year of King Zheng (244 B.C.E.). He was appointed to be an yùshǐ 御史 at Anlu 安陸,[57] later was promoted to be a lìngshǐ 令史 there, and in the first month of the following year was transferred to Yan 鄢 in the same position. He tried cases at Yan in 235 B.C.E., and in 231 B.C.E., his father died and he registered himself and his property (zìzhān 自占).[58] He may have done this because he probably became the head of his household at this time. At no time did he reach any higher in the administrative hierarchy, which suggests that scribes played a fixed role in the Qin and early Han bureaucracy and were not permitted to be appointed to other types of positions, for example, assistant prefects (chéng) or prefects (xiànlìng 縣令 or xiànzhǎng 縣長). Nevertheless, Xi took a considerable amount of wealth with him into the afterlife and was buried in a fairly ostentatious

---

56. For identifications of these religious specialists, see the notes to ZJS-XD, 82. The drinkers of the offerings would have impersonated the spirits. Lord Dus were presumably religious experts who impersonated Lord Du, a minor deity worshipped at the Thatch Shrine of Yong. See Shiji 28:1378; Burton Watson, Records of the Grand Historian of China Translated from the "Shi chi" of Ssu-ma Ch'ien (New York: Columbia University Press, 1961), 2:29.
57. The graph above shǐ is obscure, and the SHD editors supply the graph yù 御 on the basis of the presence of this term in several texts, such as the Hanfeizi 韓非子 ("Nei chushuo shang" 內儲說上) and the Zhanguo ce 戰國策 ("Han ce" 韓策 3); see SHD, 6, slip 11.2, 10 n. 48. This was a low post and should not be confused with the high-level dignitary of the same name, the Imperial Prosecutor; for the rendering of this office, see Enno Giele, Imperial Decision-making and Communication in Early China: A Study of Cai Yong's Duduan (Wiesbaden, Germany: Otto Harrassowitz), 330.
58. See McLeod and Yates, "Forms of Ch'in Law," 117–20; Huang Shengzhang 黃盛璋, "Yunmeng Qin jian 'Biannianji' chubu yanjiu" 雲夢秦簡《編年記》初步研究, Kaogu xuebao 考古學報1977.1: 1–21; Huang Shengzhang, "Yunmeng Qin jian bianzheng" 雲夢秦簡辨正, Kaogu xuebao 1979.1: 1–24.

way, which suggests that a scribe who served only at the county level was able to accumulate a significant amount of property during his lifetime.[59]

Zhang Jinguang argues that Xi, following the Qin-promulgated regulation that officials become teachers, became an instructor for other scribes and aspiring trainees (*dìzǐ* 弟子), and the legal documents buried in his tomb were the texts he used to instruct his students.[60] Thus, presumably most, if not all, of the texts that accompanied him to the afterlife were those that he penned (brushed?) himself. Zhang argues that this explains the peculiar nature of the selection of statutes and other documents and suggests that some parts of the texts, such as the "Way of Being a Good Official" and the second part of the *Yu shu* 語書, were written by Xi himself to help instruct his disciples and students.[61] Zhang notes the similarities between the language in the "Way of Being a Good Official" and the *Yu shu* and that of the later, Han, abecedarium, *Jijiu pian* 急就篇, which was used as a manual for teaching aspiring scribes and students their basic written graphs.[62] This interpretation is quite possible, but Xi probably never became an instructor (*xuéěr* 學佴) in an official scribal school. If he had, this appointment would doubtless have been recorded in the calendar of his life.

What types of scribes were there, what kind of jobs did these scribes perform, and have any original records of their writings been found? The following types of scribes can be identified in the recently discovered documents: *yùshǐ* 獄史, *cuìshǐ* 卒史, *lìngshǐ* 令史, and *tíngshǐ* 庭史.

---

59. See McLeod and Yates, "Forms of Ch'in Law," 111–63.
60. Zhang Jinguang, *Qin zhi yanjiu*, 710 et seq.
61. For the *Yu shu*, see *SHD*, 13–16. The first part was a letter composed by Teng, governor of Nan Commandery 南郡騰, and sent down to all the subordinate officials in his jurisdiction who had recently been conquered by the Qin and who were evidently rather reluctant to enforce newly introduced Qin laws and follow Qin administrative procedures. Zhang contends that the section beginning on page 15 of *Bamboo Slips from the Qin Tomb at Shuihudi* (Shuihudi Qinmu zhujian), "In general, good officials make clear the laws, statutes, and ordinances . . ." 凡良吏明法律令, was composed by Xi himself. As another version of the "Way of Being a Good Official" has been recovered associated with the contents of another Qin scribe's tomb, it is actually most unlikely that Xi was the original author of the text in the Shuihudi hoard. It probably was another text circulated to lower functionaries by either the central Qin government in Xianyang or the commandery officials. Full publication of this important new Qin material should provide further information on this matter. See Zhang Jinguang, *Qin zhi yanjiu*, 724–27. For a preliminary report, see Chen Songchang, "Yuelu shuyuan," 79–83.
62. For parallels, see Zhang Jinguang, *Qin zhi yanjiu*, 735, table 1.

Their functions were multifarious at different levels of the bureaucratic hierarchy, and, without them, the entire Qin administration would have ceased to function as it was intended to.[63] Scribes were seconded to the lowest levels of the Qin administrative hierarchy in, for example, the out-of-way end of the lines of communication in far western Hunan, the small town of Qianling, modern Liye 里耶, and the numerous offices at the capital, where there were two "scribes of the court" (*tíngshǐ* 庭史) who were experts in legal affairs.[64]

One of the most important of the scribes' functions was to prepare the household registers (*hùjí* 戶籍) and the documents generated in legal cases. The earliest household registers discovered to date were found in a pit, designated K11, at the bottom of the northern moat outside the ancient city of Liye.[65] These are probably of Qin date, like the 36,000 boards and slips found in well no. 1.[66] The following is one example:

1 (K27)

> Line 1: "Nanyang householder Man Qiang, of Jing rank *bugeng*" 南陽戶人荊不更蠻強;
>
> Line 2: "Wife called Qian" 妻曰嗛;
>
> Line 3: "Son non-adult ... of *shangzao* rank" 子小...上造;
>
> Line 4: "Daughter non-adult Tuo" 子小女子駝;
>
> Line 5: "Slave called Ju" 臣曰聚
>
> "Head of the five-family unit" 伍長[67]

---

63. For example, the *cuìshǐ* was a scribe at the commandery level. In a note to *Shiji* ("Xiao xiangguo shijia" 蕭相國世家), Ru Chun states that according to the statutes, there were to be ten *cuìshǐ* and ten "assistant scribes" (*shūzuǒ* 書佐) per commandery. See *ZJS-XD*, 105 n. 1.

64. The *tíngshǐ* were officials of the six-hundred-bushel rank. See Wan Rong 萬榮, "Zhangjiashan Han jian 'Zouyan shu' jishi yu xiangguan wenti yanjiu" 張家山漢簡《奏讞書》集釋與相關問題研究 (PhD diss., Wuhan University, 2006), 101. I am grateful to Professor Chen Wei 陳偉 for sending me a copy of this dissertation.

65. Hunan Sheng Wenwu Kaogu Yanjiusuo 湖南省文物考古研究所, *Liye fajue baogao* 里耶發掘報告 (Changsha: Yuelu Shushe, 2006), 203–11.

66. Hunan sheng, *Liye fajue baogao*, esp. 179–217 and 234–36. There were fifty-one fragments, and the archaeologists were able to reconstruct ten slips completely, with fourteen more partially. Total length of the original slips was approximately 46 centimeters, and they were 0.9 to 3 millimeters thick.

67. Hunan Sheng, *Liye fajue baogao*, 203. The graphs *wǔzhǎng* are written in larger script.

Here, only a basic vocabulary would have been required, but obviously, for security purposes (so that no errors were made in the records), scribes would have composed these documents. Nevertheless, the information would have been provided by the individual head of household together with the lowest-ranking officials at the village level: the village head (*lǐzhèng/diǎn* 里正/典) and the head of the unit of five families, the *wǔzhǎng* 伍長. This is supported by an item in the Qin "Statutes on Enrollment" that specifies punishment for the village chief and elders if they fail to provide accurate reports of male adult members of their communities and those who were disabled,[68] and, according to the Zhangjiashan "Statutes on Households," the village heads were also to confirm the details of households that moved to their jurisdiction. The details were all written down in documents and sealed for transfer. It is hard to see how these village-level functionaries would have been able to carry out their duties without some basic competency in the writing and reading of graphs. It remains a mystery why these records from Nanyang were deposited in the moat outside ancient Qianling.[69]

Soldiers

It is probable that many ordinary individuals among the lower orders would have been able to write and read a simple set of words that could have been set down in the form of lists, as described in the texts quoted above. In many ways, they may have resembled the kind of lists often found in tombs that record the offerings consigned to the graves. Similar lists of materials have been found among the wooden boards and slips abandoned in Han forts in the northwestern desert. These lists could have been prepared by soldiers of limited literacy, familiar only with numbers, basic words for their equipment, and the amounts of various types of foodstuffs. They may have been obliged to learn how to write in order to satisfy their superior officers, and the central government, that they were doing their jobs. Li Tianhong 李天虹 has analyzed the various types of

---

68. *SHD*, 87, slip 32; Hulsewé, *Remnants of Ch'in Law*, 115, C 20; cf. Yates, "Social Status in the Ch'in," 197–236.
69. Of interest in these documents, too, is the use of the term *jīng* 荊 in front of the name of the rank *bùgēng* in the householders' names. This may mean that these men were of Chu origin, and, if these documents do date from Qin times, we might infer that Qin recognized Chu ranks after the conquest of Chu territory.

lists and registers left by the soldiers and divided them into the following ten categories: (1) officers, men, and other personnel; (2) salaries and cash; (3) foodstuffs and grain; (4) military equipment; (5) matters concerning daily life; (6) goods for purchase or sale and debts; (7) merit and lengths of service; (8) oxen, horses, and chariots; (9) exit and entry through the passes; and (10) other matters.[70]

To be sure, not all of these lists would have been prepared by those of limited writing skills, as scribes (*lingshi*) are mentioned in the documents (they would have written up the more important communications, lawsuits, and other matters for the senior officers), but the lists are generally standardized in format and the vocabulary is repetitive, such that they could have been written by those without specialized training. Indeed, it is clear from recovered slips and boards that at least some were written by those who were practicing how to write. For example, E.P.T. 58:118 (E.P.T. represents excavation trenches at Pochengzi 破城子, headquarters of Jiaqu Commandant), a broken slip, consists of six consecutive graphs of the word *bù* 不 'not',[71] while E.P.T. 56:370 consists of six consecutive graphs for *shí* 食 'food/grain rations', and E.P.T. 56:375 consists of four consecutive graphs for *zhì* 置 'place'.[72] And many more examples could be cited. What kinds of reports did the ordinary soldiers compose? They prepared reports of the days on which members of their units checked the glacis outside their stations for footprints of intruders, which required knowledge only of how to write the names of the soldiers, the name of the unit, and the days counted according to the sixty-day cycle. They were also obliged to check the credentials of those passing through the gates. Here again, only limited reading skills would have been required. E.P.T. 59:104 records the literacy skills of one soldier:

延城甲溝候官第三十隊長上造范尊中勞十月十柰日能書會計治官民頗

---

70. Li Tianhong 李天虹, *Juyan Han jian buji fenlei yanjiu* 居延漢簡簿籍分類研究 (Beijing: Kexue Chubanshe, 2003). For two lengthy studies of government documents in the Han and in the Juyan documents in particular, see Wang Guihai 汪桂海, *Han dai guan wenshu zhidu* 漢代官文書制度 (Nanning: Guangxi Jiaoyu Chubanshe, 1999), and Li Junming 李均明 and Liu Jun 劉軍, *Jiandu wenshu xue* 簡牘文書學 (Nanning: Guangxi Jiaoyu Chubanshe, 1999).
71. Gansu Sheng Wenwu Kaogu Yanjiusuo 甘肅省文物考古所 et al., *Juyan xinjian* 居延新簡 (Beijing: Wenwu Chubanshe, 1990), 357.
72. Gansu Sheng, *Juyan xinjian*, 332.

知律令丈年三十二歲長桼尺五寸 . . .⁷³

Leader of the thirtieth station of Jiagou *hòuguān*, of Yancheng, the *shàngzào* Fan Zun merits length of service of ten months, seventeen days. He is capable of writing reports to higher authorities and managing official (business) and people. He is somewhat familiar with the texts of the statutes and ordinances. He is thirty-two years (*suì*) old; 7 *chǐ* 5 *cùn* tall. . . .

In this case, a soldier of the second rank is being recognized for his ability to write reports to higher authorities but is described as being only "somewhat" knowledgeable of the statutes and ordinances, the two main types of legal documents that were used to control the troops guarding the western limes against the intrusions of Xiongnu horsemen. These texts were written in a much more complex technical language than what he would have used to write the records of day-to-day affairs that he composed for his superior officers. The more literate officers would have had to convey the content of these more sophisticated texts to the less literate soldiers by word of mouth.

Perhaps the most remarkable record of ordinary soldiers' ability to make use of the written medium was found in another Shuihudi Qin tomb: two letters, written on wooden boards by two brothers, Heifu 黑夫 and Jing 惊, who were fighting in the last stages of the Qin campaign against Chu in 224–223 B.C.E., apparently to their brother Zhong 中 (=衷), the occupant of the tomb. In the first, they ask for cash and for their mother to make spring clothing for them and bring it to the front. They also inquire about the health of their mother, about Jing's new wife and whether she is looking after Jing's father in a proper fashion, and about other friends and ask whether the rank they have won on the battlefield (presumably by cutting off enemy heads) has arrived. The second letter repeats the request for money and clothes, indicating that the situation was serious, and asks that the money be sent quickly. The brothers inquire whether their aunt's childbirth has been successful and worry about the security situation, with so many rebels (i.e., probably remnant Chu soldiers) on the prowl.⁷⁴

---

73. Gansu Sheng, *Juyan xinjian*, 366.
74. See Hubei Xiaogan Diqu Di Erqi Yigong Yinong Wenwu Kaogu Xunlian Ban 湖北孝感地區第二期亦工亦農文物考古訓練班, "Hubei Yunmeng Shuihudi shiyi zuo Qin mu fajue jianbao" 湖北雲夢睡虎地十一座秦墓發掘簡報, *Wenwu* 1976.9: 51–61 (the transcription of the letters is on p. 61); Huang Shengzhang 黃盛璋, "Yunmeng Qin mu chutu de liangfeng jiaxin yu lishi dili wenti" 雲夢秦墓出土的兩封家信與歷史地理問

These letters indicate that ordinary Qin soldiers in the field could consign their concerns to writing, that the postal system was sufficiently organized and operational, even in a time of war, and that written communications could be passed back and forth between soldiers at the front and people at home. These are truly remarkable, rare, and precious documents confirming that ordinary Qin soldiers were perfectly comfortable in communicating with their loved ones in a written medium and that the government tolerated this kind of communication by soldiers in their private capacity at the same time as it corrects some errors in Sima Qian's account of the final stages of the unification process. And one presumes that these letters were not unique, that many ordinary individuals had the ability to communicate by means of the written word to their loved ones far away.

It is, of course, quite possible that the two brothers solicited the help of a literate colleague to write these letters.[75] In the same way, it appears that a man by the name of Yuan 元 had the assistance of an amanuensis in writing a long letter on silk to another individual by the name of Zifang 子方 found among the Han period documents at Xuanquan.[76] The bulk of this letter, the longest (319 graphs including four reduplications) and most complete of all Han period private letters found to date, was obviously dictated by Yuan to an amanuensis, but he appended sixteen words (graphs) at the end, apparently in his own handwriting — he uses the phrase *zìshū* 自書 'written by myself' to introduce his closing remarks.[77] This letter demonstrates that even those who were literate sought the assistance of others with more advanced skills in composition for letters that were of importance to them.

In late imperial and early Republican times, publishers produced pulp

---

題, in *Lishi dili lunji* 歷史地理論集 (Beijing: Renmin Chubanshe, 1982), 545–55. I am very grateful to Anthony Barbieri-Low for sharing his translations of these letters with me.

75. Anthony Barbieri-Low raises the possibility that the soldiers sought the assistance of a professional scribe in a market near the army to write these letters. This is certainly possible, for such professional or semiprofessional scribes are known from later times. However, I know of no evidence at present that would suggest such a practice existed in pre-unification times.

76. I am grateful to Matthias Richter for bringing this important manuscript to my attention.

77. Hu Pingsheng and Zhang Defang 張德芳, *Dunhuang Xuanquan Han jian shicui* 敦煌懸泉漢簡釋粹 (Shanghai: Shanghai Guji Chubanshe, 2001), strip II 0114③: 611, on 187–91.

guidebooks to assist letter writers, suggesting not only general themes but precise wording for letters of various sorts to be sent to relatives, friends, and business partners and for all types of social and professional occasions. This type of popular manual has not been studied, nor is it clear when this genre of publication began, but it might have been as early as the late Ming or early Qing, or possibly even earlier.[78]

The Literacy of Women

Female members of the Han elite, especially those belonging to the Ban family — Ban Jieyu 班婕妤, remembered for her poetry, and her grandniece Ban Zhao 班昭, the coauthor with her brother Ban Gu 班固 of the *History of the Han Dynasty (Hanshu)* — are some of the most renowned women scholars in all of Chinese history.[79] In the Western Han, one of the most well-known stories about a literate woman concerned the youngest daughter, Tiying 緹縈, of Chunyu Yi 淳于意, a doctor born around 216 B.C.E. and holder of the position of *tàicāng* 太倉 in charge of the imperial granaries in Qi. Tiying saved her father from mutilation under Emperor Wen by writing a memorial begging to be enslaved in order to ransom her father from punishment, and her filial devotion won her a mention in Liu Xiang's 劉向 *Lienü zhuan* 列女傳. Emperor Wen is said have been so impressed with her written eloquence that he ordered the abolition of the system of mutilating punishments.[80] Another story tells about the daughter of Master Fu (Fu Sheng 伏生), who is said in the early Western Han to have interpreted her ninety-year-old father's incomprehensible mutterings on the *Book of Documents* (Shangshu 尚書),

---

78. These remarks are based on an analysis of one such manual in the author's private collection.
79. See, inter alia, Nancy Lee Swann, *The Biography of Empress Teng* (Montreal: McGill University Publications, 1931); Swann, *Pan Chao: Foremost Woman Scholar of China* (New York: Century, 1932; rpt., Ann Arbor, Mich.: Center for Chinese Studies, 2001).
80. *Shiji*, 105:2795; *Hanshu*, 23:1098; Clarence Martin Wilbur, *Slavery in China during the Former Han Dynasty 206 B.C.–A.D.25* (Chicago: Field Museum of Natural History, 1943), 286–87; Lisa Raphals, *Sharing the Light: Representations of Women and Virtue in Early China* (Albany: State University of New York Press, 1998), 133–36. It is possible that this story is somewhat fictionalized and that Tiying had a male friend compose the memorial; however, the fact remains that the writers of the story, and their readers, thought it perfectly possible for a young woman to have accomplished this task herself.

thus saving the text from oblivion.[81] These women all seem to have learned to read and write within their families, and their families seem to have had a tradition of training daughters as well as sons.

But what of women from the lower orders? Did they have any opportunities to learn how to read and write, or were they just trained from childhood to weave, sew, cook, and produce and rear children, all according to the social norms of morality?[82] Quite obviously, they were not recruited into the Han armies to serve as soldiers, so they did not have the opportunity, like their male kin, to gain some literacy training in military service, but some wives certainly did accompany their husbands to the military colonies in the northwest, as their names are preserved in records of passport examinations permitting them to travel together as families into the barren wastes of the Gobi desert.[83] The newly discovered documents also provide some clues as to their possible knowledge of letters.

First, the "Statutes on Households," the "Statutes on Enrollments" (Fu lü 傅律), and the "Statutes on Establishing Heirs" (Zhihou lü 置後律), the latter studied recently by Li Junming,[84] provide information on inheritance and household registration. Among the features of the early Han system relevant to the status of women, one statute clearly stipulates that a woman has a rank comparable to that of her husband and therefore, by implication, receives all the same benefits that come with the rank held by her husband.[85] The state gave a certain amount of land and a certain number of buildings or houses to individuals depending on their rank. Even those without rank received the means by which to survive. The

---

81. This version of events is recounted by the Han scholar Wei Hong 衛宏, but as her efforts to interpret her toothless father's Shandong accent are not recorded in either the *Records of the Grand Scribe* (Shiji 史記) or the *History of the Han Dynasty* (Hanshu 漢書), the veracity of the account has been challenged over the centuries.
82. The bibliography on the history of women's work and its symbolic and economic significance is enormous. See Francesca Bray, *Technology and Gender: Fabrics of Power in Late Imperial China* (Berkeley: University of California Press, 1997), and Robin D. S. Yates, *Women in China from Earliest Times to the Present: A Bibliography of Studies in Western Languages* (Leiden: Brill, 2009).
83. For example, two wives are recorded on two tallies as accompanying their husbands along with their daughters and sons and a secondary wife; see Li Tianhong, *Juyan Han jian buji*, 149.
84. Li Junming, "Zhangjiashan Han jian suojian guifan jicheng guanxi de falü" 張家山漢簡所見規範繼承關係的法律, *Zhongguo lishi wenwu* 中國歷史文物 2 (37) (2002): 26–32.
85. *ZJS-XD*, 59, slip 372; *ENL*, 236; Zhu Honglin, *Zhangjiashan Han jian*, 228.

exact amounts and numbers were specified in detail, and the size of the buildings and the size of the land were also specified. Registering as a separate household apparently entitled the head of the household to receive land and houses. While it is known that the Qin obliged adult sons to split their households from those of their fathers and brothers, and that the Han continued this legal requirement in some form, the new documents provide much information concerning the detailed regulations that applied to this procedure. For example, slips 342 and 343 of the "Statutes on Households" states:

寡夫、寡婦毋子及同居，若有子，子年未盈十四，及寡子年未盈十八，及夫妻皆癃(癃)病，及老年七十以上，毋 (342) 異其子；今毋它子，欲令歸戶入養，許之。(343)

Widowers and widows without children and co-residents, or if they have children and the children are not a full fourteen years old or orphan children who are not yet a full eighteen years old, and all husbands and wives suffering from infirmities and old people more than seventy years old, are not to separate from their children. Now if they have no other children and they desire to be allowed to return to their (original) households and enter (them) to be nourished, let them.[86]

Equally interesting is that the Han permitted women in certain circumstances to establish households,[87] although married women were not permitted to establish households separate from their husbands,[88] and that the authorities accepted the wills of the dying for the purpose of dividing the property.[89]

In light of these complex rules, it would seem that those women who were heads of households would have had the same obligations as their male counterparts to report the members of their households and the state of their financial holdings. Thus they would have been obliged to provide the authorities with the same type of documentation (zìzhān 自占)

---

86. ZJS, 179, slips 342–43; ZJS-XD, 55–56; ENL, 226.
87. For example, when a grandson who was a householder (i.e., the heir to his father) died, his mother was allowed to inherit and replace him as the head of household, although she was not permitted to drive away her late husband's parents (XDB, 55, slip 338; ENL, 225).
88. ZJS-XD, 56, slip 345; ENL, 227; Zhu Honglin, Zhangjiashan Han jian, 212.
89. For a Han dynasty will dated 5 C.E. that cites the dispositions a woman made of her real property among her offspring, see Bret Hinsch, "Women, Kinship, and Property as Seen in a Han Dynasty Will," T'oung Pao 84.1-3 (1998): 1–20.

referred to above.[90] With respect to whether women were involved in trade as merchants, this, too, is quite possible. Sima Qian recounts the business skill of a widow entrepreneur named Qing 清 who took over the family cinnabar mining business in Ba during the Qin. She became a very wealthy woman and was honored by the First Emperor.[91] It is hard to imagine that she would have been able to manage her business effectively if she had not been literate, given the detailed rules the Qin government forced merchants to operate under.

In short, although the evidence is somewhat circumstantial, there is enough to support the contention that at least some women of the lower orders possessed basic literacy skills at the beginning of the Chinese empires.[92] It is worth pointing out that, according to recently discovered documents, after the end of the Han, women could become heads of household and may also have been obliged to learn basic letters in order to respond to the administrative demands of the state.[93]

Conclusion

The evidence presented above suggests that ordinary members of the population in Qin and Han times could have possessed basic literacy skills, even though there is no clear record of schools for such individuals.[94] Basic literacy could have been learned at home or during apprenticeship in a trade. With all males required to perform military service in the armies of the late Warring States, men would have been required to write reports for

---

90. In the Qin, when an individual was charged with a crime, the local officials went to his or her house, made an inventory of the person's property, and "sealed" (*fēng* 封) it. See *SHD*, 139, slips 9–12; Hulsewé, *Remnants of Ch'in Law*, 184–85, E 3; McLeod and Yates, "Forms of Ch'in Law," 137–39.
91. *Shiji* 129:3260; Watson, *Records of the Grand Historian*, 2:483–84.
92. For the literacy of female lacquer workers in state factories, see "Craftsman's Literacy: Uses of Writing among Male and Female Artisans in Qin and Han China," by Anthony Barbieri-Low, chapter 11 in this volume.
93. See the documents from the Changsha commandery under the Wu regime of the Three Kingdoms time period discovered at Zoumalou, Changsha. Changsha Shi Wenwu Yanjiusuo 長沙市文物研究所 et al., *Changsha Zoumalou Wu guo jian, Jiahe limin tianjia* 長沙走馬樓吳簡嘉禾吏民田家 (Beijing: Wenwu Chubanshe, 1999). It is always possible that female heads of household asked male kin to write for them, but would this have always been the case?
94. As in late imperial times, schools were not absolutely necessary for acquiring functional literacy.

their superior officers, as in the Han, and they would have been obliged to read and comply with the written orders that organized their lives and by which they had to fight: the late Warring States military text *Weiliaozi* 尉繚子 (or *Yuliaozi*) mentions two military laws, the Law on Abandoning Positions and Fleeing (*Lidi duntao zhi fa* 離地遁逃之法) and the Law on Battlefield Executions (*Zhanzhu zhi fa* 戰誅之法).[95] Furthermore, not all written communications generated by the late Warring States armies were produced only for the officers and authorities at headquarters or in the capitals of their respective states. The letters from the ordinary Qin soldiers Heifu and Jing discussed above indicate that soldiers communicated with their families back home to inquire about both personal issues (family members' health and circumstances) and whether the Qin military system of ranks was functioning correctly to their personal benefit (the soldiers had cut off heads in battle, and that rank could be used to mitigate family members' crimes and secure other social and economic benefits). Thus, either they were literate themselves or there was someone within their military unit who was able to write on their behalf. In addition, by implication, merchants and others engaged in commercial enterprises were also obliged to gain some level of literacy in order to comply with the state's legal regulations that objects put on sale had to have prices on them. Artisans, too, had to be capable of marking their names on their products so that they could comply with the authorities' desire to monitor quality.

Finally, a few of the legal case records deposited in the Zhangjiashan and Shuihudi tombs indicate that ordinary members of the Qin population tried to use the system the Qin and Han imposed on them, to learn basic literacy skills and report their names and property to the authorities and to resist or subvert the aims of the state. For example, in one case recorded in the Zhangjiashan hoard, probably dated 197 B.C.E., a woman named Fu 符 illegally absconded (*wáng* 亡) from her home location where she had been registered and then lied to the authorities, saying she had not yet registered her name.[96] She duly registered her property and her name according to

---

95. "Orders for Binding the Squads of Five" (Shuwu ling 束伍令), in the *Weiliaozi* (pian 16). See Liu Yin 劉寅, *Wujing qishu zhijie* 武經七書直解 (Changsha: Yuelu Shushe, 1992), 327–28; *Zhongguo lidai bingshu jicheng* 中國歷代兵書集成, ed. Cheng Suhong 程素紅 (Beijing: Tuanjie Chubanshe, 1999), 1:132; Ralph D. Sawyer, trans., *Seven Military Classics of China* (Boulder, Colo.: Westview Press 1993), 265.
96. *ZJS-XD*, 94; *ENL*, 341–43; Wan Rong, "Zhangjiashan Han jian 'Zouyan shu jishi',"

the ordinances, presumably in the district to which she had fled, and claimed that she was a dependent (*lì* 隸) of a man called Ming 明, of *dàfū* 大夫 rank. Ming then married her off to a man, Jie 解, of *yǐnguān* 隱官 status, without revealing that she had, in fact, run away without legal permission from her local authorities, a clear violation of statutory law. The authorities were able to apprehend and prosecute her. She was obviously trying to use the legal system, with its requirement that she register her name, to her own advantage in order to marry herself off in another district. It is not stated why she chose to abandon her home district, but it is clear that she was able to write her name and register her property and had tried to get a fresh start. This case shows that ordinary members of the empire in its early stages were not all pawns and objects of the state's control and that some tried, as best they could, to use the legal system to their personal advantage. They resisted when they felt the need, in order to subvert the imposition of its power.

So as the state was inscribing and naming its subjects by registering them on its population lists, the objects of the state's gaze and control were given the technology to observe the state and, ultimately, could use it to further their own interests, which were not always in harmony with the state's aims. Literacy, however limited, acquired by the lower orders evidently gave its users some powers of resistance.

32–36. For a detailed analysis of the crime of abscondence in the Qin and Han periods, see Zhang Gong 張功, *Qin Han taowang fanzui yanjiu* 秦漢逃亡犯罪研究 (Wuhan: Hubei Renmin Chubanshe, 2006)..

CHAPTER 11

Craftsman's Literacy:
Uses of Writing by Male and Female Artisans in Qin and Han China

Anthony J. Barbieri-Low

In significant ways, this chapter is a complement to the preceding chapter, by Robin D. S. Yates, which considers the problem of how non-elites in Warring States, Qin, and Han society acquired functional literacy and to what ends they employed that literacy.[1] Yates argues that the body of literate persons was expanded because the bureaucratic state required people's semi-literacy in order to better control and exploit them. Compulsory military service and mandatory household registration initiated men into the realm of the written word, and even women, as widowed heads of household, were brought into this world. He further argues that even though the state originally required the literacy of commoners as a means of more tightly controlling them, people soon found ways to manipulate the skill of literacy to their own advantage and even use it as a node of resistance with which to "subvert the aims of the state."

One of the so-called lower orders not addressed by Yates is the artisan class of Early China. Artisans in early imperial China were compelled by the state to become functionally literate through regulations and processes similar to those described by Yates for soldiers and heads of household.

This chapter is an elaboration of the argument published in my book *Artisans in Early Imperial China* (Seattle: University of Washington Press, 2007), supplemented by further examples and a more detailed argument. Several extended passages are reproduced here, with permission.

1. See "Soldiers, Scribes, and Women: Literacy among the Lower Orders in Early China," by Robin D. S. Yates, chapter 10 in this volume, 339-69.

Artisans in government-sponsored and privately-run factories and workshops were often required to inscribe their names and other information on their finished products, as a method of assuming responsibility and to facilitate accounting. Some of these inscriptions present actual physical evidence for artisan writing, a demonstration of the implementation of the regulations laid out in legal and philosophical texts. Some artisans subsequently used that literacy, originally acquired by their class through compulsion, to their own advantage in the pursuit of maximum profit.

It is difficult to assess the general level of literacy in early imperial China and quite impossible to arrive at any valid numbers for the percentage of men or women of any class who could read and write. The written word was valued in traditional China more so than in almost any other traditional society. Eventually, literacy came to be considered a proper and desirable goal by more than just the professional scribal caste or the leisured aristocracy. Literary scholarship, focusing on the memorization and interpretation of Classical texts, ultimately came to be viewed as rigorous mental training for the gentleman and as a means to entering the official bureaucracy. By the Eastern Han, books were sold in the metropolitan marketplaces [2] and local governments sometimes maintained primary and secondary schools that taught reading and writing, often limited in duration to the agricultural slack seasons. Even so, the vast majority of peasants were probably not literate beyond recognizing their own names in written form. When commoners required binding contracts in the marketplace, the documents were usually drawn up by professional scribes and the contract text read to the transacting parties and witnesses for verification.

The level of literacy among those employed in government service seems to have been far higher than among the peasant population. The Qin and Han empires were run by massive, hierarchical bureaucracies that relied on the collation and dissemination of millions of pieces of written data for their smooth operation. Written census records were supposedly maintained at the local level for every household unit in the empire, and, theoretically, these files were updated annually. Records of grain in storage, land use figures, military and civilian labor conscription rolls, job performance evaluations, sighted omens and prodigies: all of these were

---

2. See reference in Sahara Yasuo 佐原康夫, "Kandai no ichi ni tsuite" 漢代の市について, *Shirin* 68.5 (1985): 33–71.

meticulously written down, copied, and disseminated throughout the bureaucracy. Nearly every civilian or military work unit employed at least one professional scribe (*shǐ* 史) for bureaucratic correspondence, and some employed hundreds. As Yates describes in chapter 10, during the Western Han period, scribes-in-training had to pass a written test for recognition, pronunciation, and reproduction of five thousand Chinese characters, after three years of study, in order to qualify for an actual post.[3] In 5 B.C.E., the government directly employed 130,285 officials, most of whom we may safely assume to have been either functionally or fully literate.[4] At least twice that many literate scribal assistants, copyists, and functionally literate runners were probably employed by local administrations for the labor-intensive tax and census collection activities.

What percentage of Qin and Han artisans were literate, and what was the nature of their literacy? Experts in the field of ancient literacy distinguish among many different levels and types of literacy, ranging from simple recognition and reproduction of one's name to the ability to understand and communicate profound thoughts through reading and writing.[5] Classicist William V. Harris has used the term "craftsman's

---

3. Yates, "Soldiers, Scribes, and Women," in this volume, 339-69.
4. Wang Xianqian 王先謙, *Hanshu buzhu* 漢書補注 (Taipei: Yiwen Yinshuguan, 1955), 19A:31a–b; *Hanshu,* 19A:743. The figure of 120,285 given in these two editions is emended to 130,285 by Bielenstein, *The Bureaucracy of Han Times* (Cambridge: Cambridge University Press, 1980), 156, 205–6 n. 1. Yates argues, in chapter 10 in this volume, that during the Warring States, Qin, and early Han, the position of scribe was a hereditary caste and that the men employed as scribes in government bureaus had to be the sons of scribes. Their superiors in the bureaucracy did not necessarily have to be literate, since they only had to approve or seal the final copied document. By the mid-Han, however, access to scribal training no longer appears to have been hereditary, and a greater proportion of the bureaucratic corps was presumably fully literate.
5. A Tang period will found at Dunhuang (Stein, no. 2199) displays an interesting range of literacy within one family. The will of the nun Linghui 靈惠 (15 November 865) found at cave 17 at Dunhuang is appended with a list of witnesses, several of whom attempted to "sign" the will. Linghui's niece, Shi'er-niang, apparently was illiterate and signed the will with an outline of her finger joints. This practice was fairly common in contract signing during the Tang. Her nephew, Kang Mao, was able to sign his name, but the first character was drawn unusually large and the second character was written incorrectly. Her other nephew, Fu Sheng, signed his name with a single character, which some scholars have read as *shè* 社 and others as *dù* 杜. The final signature on the document is that of her nephew, Sheng Xian. His level of literacy is so basic that he signs his name backward as Xian Sheng. The addition of a little flip mark next to the name signifies that he meant to invert those two characters. The will has been translated

literacy" to describe the situation in which a sizable proportion of skilled craftsmen gain and transmit literacy at a functional level that enables them to carry out their craft and its related business functions.[6] In classical Greece and Rome, and up until the nineteenth century in the West, a far greater percentage of craftsmen were functionally literate than were members of the general population. On a historical continuum, craftsman's literacy follows the more limited scribal literacy seen in the formative periods of Mesopotamia and Egypt, the Shang and Western Zhou period in China, and the Bronze Age on Crete and the Greek mainland. At the stage of scribal literacy, only a small group of palace and temple scribes or diviners has achieved literacy and transmits such knowledge as a guarded secret, often through lineages. Harris theorizes that the transition from scribal literacy to craftsman's literacy in the Near East and Mediterranean cultures after the Bronze Age (and again in Europe in the late Middle Ages) was stimulated in part by "administrative and business documents and the desire to make use of them."[7] The stage of craftsman's literacy also precedes any kind of mass literacy. Scholars of literacy in traditional societies agree that most societies cannot move from craftsman's literacy to mass literacy without a concerted, often state-sponsored effort promoting literacy, usually with compulsory education.[8]

There is abundant material evidence that many artisans in early imperial China possessed craftsman's literacy. The master of an artisan work crew in an imperial workshop was required by law to inscribe his name, work unit, and the year of manufacture on finished pieces in order to guarantee quality control and to enable accountants to track production quotas and materials. Master artisans in private workshops occasionally inscribed their names, auspicious slogans, or other information on bronze mirrors, lacquer vessels, iron tools, pottery, and textiles. The names inscribed on these articles are our chief source for the identity of common artisans, men and women whose names and lives would be lost to history were it not for their ability to write.

---

in Jacques Gernet, *Buddhism in Chinese Society: An Economic History from the Fifth to the Tenth Centuries*, trans. Fanciscus Verellen (New York: Columbia University Press, 1995), 81–82.
6. Harris, *Ancient Literacy*, 7–8, 13, 61–62. Harris extends the basic definition of the term to include both artisans and the elite stratum of society, who have obtained this same level of literacy.
7. Harris, *Ancient Literacy*, 61.
8. Harris, *Ancient Literacy*, 12–13.

Quality Control and Accounting Inscriptions

Methods of mass production, including fine division of labor (the assembly line), standardization of parts, multitiered management, complex accounting, and quality control procedures, were not solely products of the First Industrial Revolution in Europe; similar developments could be seen in early imperial China, especially in the imperial factory systems operated by the Qin and Han governments.[9] The "quality control and accounting inscription" was an integral part of this production system.[10]

According to current knowledge, Bronze Age inscriptions on manufactured objects (ritual bronzes, weapons, jades) never mention the craftsman who produced the piece. The typical Western Zhou bronze inscription might mention the name of a person who "caused a vessel to be made," or the vessel might be cast with the lineage emblem of the vessel's owner, but these have nothing to do with the actual producers. Bronze casters in Shang and Zhou times do seem to have belonged to a corporate group with some low level of official status, but they are never mentioned by name on the bronzes themselves.[11]

Late in the Spring and Autumn period and into the early Warring States period, heads of state or medium-level officials, often the Gongshi 工師 (Master of Artisans), began to take responsibility for production of a vessel

---

9. See Barbieri-Low, "The Organization of Imperial Workshops."
10. For examples of quality control and accounting inscriptions, see Li Xueqin 李學勤, "Zhanguo shidai de Qin guo tongqi" 戰國時代的秦國銅器, *Wenwu cankao ziliao* 1957.8: 38–40, 53; "Zhanguo timing gaishu (xia)" 戰國題銘概述（下）, *Wenwu* 1959.9: 58–61; Satō Taketoshi 佐藤武敏, *Chūgoku kodai kōgyōshi no kenkyū* 中国古代工業史の研究 (Tokyo: Yoshikawa Kōbunkan, 1962), 329–58; Sumiya Sadatoshi 角谷定俊, "Shin ni okeru seidō kōgyō no ikkōsatsu: kōkan o chūshin ni" 秦における青銅工業の一考察 — 工官を中心に *Sundai shigaku* 55 (1982): 52–86; Sahara Yasuo 佐原康夫, "Senkoku jidai no fu-ko ni tsuite" 戦国時代の府庫について, *Tōyōshi kenkyū* 43.1 (1984): 31–59; Yuan Zhongyi 袁仲一, "Qin zhongyang duzao de bingqi keci zongshu" 秦中央督造的兵器刻辭綜述, *Kaogu yu wenwu* 1984.5:101–12, 100; Huang Shengzhang 黃盛璋, "Qin bingqi fenguo, duandai yu youguan zhidu yanjiu" 秦兵器分國斷代與有關制度研究, *Guwenzi yanjiu* 21 (2001): 227–85.
11. For the status of artisans in Shang and Zhou times, see David N. Keightley, *Public Work in Ancient China: A Study of Forced Labor in the Shang and Western Chou* (PhD diss., Columbia University, 1969), esp. chapter 1.

or weapon. They are sometimes said to have *zào* 造 (made), *zhíjì* 執齊 (carried out the alloying [of]), or *zhù* 鑄 (cast) the piece. This type of inscription appears to have first developed in the state of Qi in the east (circa 600 B.C.E.) and then been taken up by the Jin-descended states of Han, Wei, and Zhao, from where it was probably transmitted to the state of Qin in the early- to mid-fourth century B.C.E. In fact, nearly every major state employed quality control inscriptions by the beginning of the third century B.C.E. Also, during the late Warring States period, there seems to have been a transition (in several states) from a middle-level or high official taking "name responsibility" for production, to a more complex roster mentioning both high officials and the commoner or convict-labor artisans who actually made the product. This is seen first in bronze vessel and weapons production and most prominently in Qin.

The philosophy behind quality control and accounting inscriptions appears decidedly "Legalist" in nature, emphasizing responsibility, standardization, and accountability, but it was employed universally by all states in the third century. The locus classicus promoting the practice is found in the "Almanac" section of the *Lüshi chunqiu* 呂氏春秋 and the corresponding "Monthly Ordinances" (Yueling 月令) chapter of the *Book of Rites* (Liji 禮記),[12] which states the following:

是月也，工師效功，陳祭器，按度程。無或作為淫巧，以蕩上心，必功致為上。 物勒工名，以考其誠。功有不當，必行其罪，以窮其情。

In this month, the Master of Artisans verifies that the various products accord with specifications. He organizes the sacrificial vessels and examines their proportions and patterns, so that in each product there is no innovation created out of licentious ingenuity, which might debauch the minds of superiors. He makes certain that each finished product is delivered to the superiors. Each article is to be inscribed with the artisan's

---

12. *Lüshi chunqiu* 呂氏春秋, *Ershi'er zi* 二十二子 ed. (Shanghai: Shanghai Guji Chubanshe, 1986), 10:656–57; Translation from John Knoblock and Jeffrey Riegel, *The Annals of Lü Buwei* (Stanford, Calif.: Stanford University Press, 2000), 225 (with modification). The "Monthly Ordinances" (Yueling) is a section in the current text of the *Liji*. For this passage, see *Shisanjing zhushu*, 17:1381. It is believed by most scholars that the "Yueling" was compiled from the *Lüshi chunqiu*, but the situation may be more complex than that. See the discussion in Knoblock and Riegel, *The Annals of Lü Buwei*, 27–43. Compare the translation of this quote in James Legge, *The Li Ki* (*Sacred Books of China*, vols. 3, 16, 27, 28, 39, 40 of *The Sacred Books of the East*), ed. F. Max Müller (Oxford: Clarendon Press, 1885), 27:299.

name, in order to ensure his honesty. When products of the artisans do not accord with the standards, then they must be punished in order to put an end to such a situation.

The first part of the regulation is not necessarily an exclusively "Legalist" idea. Nearly every philosophical school criticized elaborate decoration (or "licentious ingenuity") as a waste of resources or an invitation to moral dissipation. The latter part of the passage seems to be a more novel concept. Artisans were to inscribe their names on objects so that they could be punished if the goods were defective or "licentious." The requirement of quality control did not just grow out of an obsessive need to hold people accountable but addressed a real problem with defective products. Quality control procedures evolved simultaneously with methods of mass production. Once assembly-line production developed, and individual artisans were responsible for only one step in the process, quality control had to be introduced in order to ensure that the final product was of acceptable quality.

Procedures for quality control and accounting are best seen in the digest of Qin legal statutes from Shuihudi. The products and conduct of artisans in imperial factories were under constant scrutiny, and violations could result in significant fines or corporal punishment. For example, according to the Qin statutes, if the inspected products of an imperial workshop were judged *diàn* 殿 'poor', all the officials and artisans at the factory were to be fined on a sliding scale according to their position in the factory hierarchy. The factory head would be fined the value of one suit of armor; his assistant and the foreman of the individual workshop unit would each be fined the lesser value of one shield; and the producing artisans would be fined only the value of twenty sets of armor-plate laces. If their goods failed inspections for three straight years, the fines were more than doubled.[13] Officials, along with free and conscripted artisans, were monetarily fined for shoddy work, since presumably they had the means to pay such fines. Convict laborers who worked alongside the free artisans, however, were given fifty to one hundred strokes of the bamboo pole if their work failed inspections.[14]

---

13. *SHD* ("Qin lü zachao"), 83–84, slips 17–18; Hulsewé, *Remnants of Ch'in Law*, C11. For more examples, see also Hulsewé, *Remnants of Ch'in Law*, C12, C13, C14, and B22.
14. Hulsewé, *Remnants of Ch'in Law*, C12.

The inscriptions on vessels and other objects were also designed to facilitate accounting. According to the statutes, each object was to have a standardized name and dimensions and was to be recorded in the proper column of the account books.[15] These accounts would allow officials not only to calculate total output but also to track the use of materials and labor and discover if officials were siphoning off goods (including weapons) through corruption. Factories were to produce goods according to a written quota from the central government, and factory heads were fined for not meeting *or exceeding* the quota.[16]

The Qin institution (which the Han inherited) may have worked for a time as originally intended, but by the Eastern Han, the naming of artisans and officials on imperially produced products had become a hollow procedure. According to the critic Cui Shi 崔寔 (circa 150):

《月令》曰:"物刻工名,以覆其誠,功有不當,必行其罪,以窮其情。"今雖刻名之,而賞罰不能,又數有赦贖,主者輕翫,無所懲畏。夫兵革國之大事,宜特留意重其治罰,敢有巧詐輒行之輩,罪勿以赦贖除,則吏敬其職,工慎其業矣。

The "Monthly Ordinances" says, "Each article is to be inscribed with the artisan's name, in order to ensure his honesty. When products of the artisans do not accord with the standards, then they must be punished in order to put an end to such a situation." Nowadays, even though the goods are inscribed with the artisans' names, one is not able to reward or punish them. Also, there are so many amnesties proclaimed and redemptions allowed, and those in charge are so lax, that there is no punishment for the artisans to fear. Now, metal weapons and leather articles are of great concern to the state. It is thus fitting to give special attention to these matters and increase the penalties related to [weapons] manufacture. For those who dare to artfully make shoddy goods or engage in corrupt behavior, if they are guilty, do not let them get off with amnesties or redemption fines. Then, officials will indeed be respectful in their duties and artisans will be careful in their work.[17]

The system of quality control and accounting inscription appears to have been originally imposed only on government-sponsored production,

---

15. *SHD* ("Qin lü shiba zhong"), 43, slips 98–99; Hulsewé, *Remnants of Ch'in Law*, A52.
16. *SHD* ("Qin lü zachao"), 84, slip 18; Hulsewé, *Remnants of Ch'in Law*, C11.
17. Cui Shi 崔寔, "Zhenglun," in Yan Kejun 嚴可均, *Quan shanggu sandai Qin Han Sanguo Liuchao wen* 全上古三代秦漢三國六朝文 (*Quan Hou Han wen* 全後漢文) (Beijing: Zhonghua Shuju, 1965), 46:1:7a (translation by author).

but later the legal statutes extended the practice to privately-run workshops, especially those wishing to sell in the official marketplace, where products and standards could be more tightly regulated.

A fragment of the Jin dynasty law code, preserved in the *Taiping yulan* 太平御覽 sets out the legal requirements for those wishing to privately manufacture and sell lacquered objects in the marketplace.[18]

> 欲作漆器物賣者，各先移主吏者名乃得作，皆當淳漆著布骨，器成，以朱題年月姓名。

> For those who desire to make lacquer vessels and other lacquered objects and sell them [in the official marketplace], they must each first inform the responsible [marketplace] officials of their name; then they may proceed to make [lacquer vessels]. For all those finished articles consisting of solid lacquer, ramie- or hemp-cored lacquered objects, or bone-cored lacquer objects, the [artisan] must use vermilion [lacquer paint] to inscribe the year and month [of manufacture] and his or her surname and given name.

It is interesting that these privately produced lacquers are required to carry the *xing* 姓 'surname' and *ming* 名 'given name' of the lacquer producer, for imperial lacquer vessels never appear to carry the *xing* of the artisans or officials, only the *ming*, *zi* 字 'courtesy name', or shop name. This may have been related to the question of audience. The emperor and his wives personally ate off imperial lacquer tableware, and it would have been offensive for one of them to turn over the wine cup and see the surname of a commoner. Inscriptions on surviving lacquer objects from private workshops do not always contain the entire name of the artisan either, but they do often carry the family name of the maker, often appended by the word *shi* 氏 (lineage).

---

18. *Taiping yulan* 太平御覽 (Beijing: Zhonghua Shuju, 1960), 3354 (translation by author). This clause is quoted from the "Ordinance on Markets and Passes" (Guanshi ling 關市令) of the Jin dyansty. Both the Qin and Han law codes contain a major statute with a similar name, "Statute on Markets and Passes" (Guanshi lü 關市律), concerning issues of trade, customs, and marketplace. (*Tang liudian* 唐六典 says that the Jin article was a statute, not an ordinance.) I think it very likely that this Jin statute or ordinance was inherited from the earlier Han and Qin "Statute on Markets and Passes" and provides a glimpse of Qin and Han regulations mandating inscriptions on privately produced objects sold in official marketplaces.

The Terra-cotta Army of the First Emperor of Qin

The Qin system of accountability and quality control compelled certain members of the work crews that made the magnificent terra-cotta army for the First Emperor of Qin at Lintong, Shaanxi, to indicate their name, official affiliation if any, and sometimes their native place of registration. Some of these inscriptions were stamped onto the figures with seals, while others were incised into the wet clay with a stylus or similar instrument (see plate 8a). To date, eighty-seven different names have been found on the more than one thousand reconstructed human and equestrian figures.[19] These names can be broken down into two distinct categories of artisans.

The first group encompasses those state artisans employed by palace ceramic workshops. Their names are usually affixed to the figurine by means of stamp blocks, and the given names are generally prefixed by the word gōng 宮 'palace', which, according to Yuan Zhongyi 袁仲一, is likely an abbreviation of Gongshui 宮水 'Palace Water Factory', a Qin palace bureau in charge of making water pipes, hollow architectural bricks, and ceramic roof tiles.

The second group of names recorded on the terra-cotta warriors seems to have belonged to artisans normally employed in private ceramic workshops in Xianyang or the surrounding counties who were conscripted to work on the tomb project. Their names usually are inscribed with a stylus or other sharp implement into the clay of the figurine and are not affixed with official stamps, like those used by the palace artisans. Some of the given names of these artisans include Ye 野, Jing 敬, Zhong 重, and Yue 嫽 'Beautiful'. The last name mentioned is written with a graph that contains a female semantic classifier and is used only in phrases describing female beauty. Thus, the name possibly belonged to a functionally literate, female master potter.[20] The inscribed given names are occasionally prefixed by the county of residence of the master potter,

---

19. Rubbings and transcriptions of the inscribed texts and stamps are in Shaanxi Sheng Kaogu Yanjiusuo 陝西省考古研究所 et al., *Qin Shihuangling bingmayong keng: Yi hao keng fajue baogao 1974-1984* 秦始皇陵兵馬俑坑：一號坑發掘報告1974–84 (Beijing: Wenwu Chubanshe, 1988), 194–207, 433–43. The analysis given here follows the interpretation of Yuan Zhongyi 袁仲一, "Qin ling bingmayong de zuozhe" 秦陵兵馬俑的作者 *Wenbo* 1986.4: 52–62; *Qin bingmayong keng* 秦兵馬俑坑 (Beijing: Wenwu Chubanshe, 2003), 169–73.
20. For a table of these names, see Shaanxi Sheng Kaogu Yanjiusuo et al., *Qin Shihuangling bingmayong*, 1:203.

such as Xianyang 咸陽 (the Qin capital), Yueyang 櫟陽, Linjin 臨晉, or Anyi 安邑. These names clearly indicate artisans and not bureaucrats or some other non-craftsmen, because occasionally a person affixed the word *gōng* 工 'artisan' in front of his or her name instead of the standard place-name. In format, these inscriptions match closely those seen on contemporary lacquer vessels made in Xianyang and found in Hubei.

Both Yuan Zhongyi and Lothar Ledderose argue that the seal stamps and the incised inscriptions were made only by the foreman of the work crew, whom they identify as a "master" (*gōngshī* 工師). They estimate that at least ten potters would have worked under each master, leading to an estimated total workforce of about 850–1,000 men.[21] A professional scribe probably carved the seals, so the seal impressions do not offer much information about artisan literacy. The inscriptions incised with the stylus are more informative. They demonstrate that master potters from private workshops in the vicinity of Xianyang were capable of writing their given names and native places with a good degree of standard orthography (i.e., orthography similar to that employed by official scribes for administrative documents). The inscriptions all seem to have been written with a type of small seal script. One terra-cotta warrior (T2G1:33) bears an inscribed text that is eleven characters long.[22] It lists three different place-name–given-name pairs (Gao of Xianyang 咸陽高, Zhong of Yueyang 櫟陽重, Guai of Linjin 臨晉茦) and one place-name (Anyi 安邑) (with the given name missing on a damaged section) and appears to have been written in four different hands. All the given names mentioned, except perhaps the first, are unique to this figure, so they may represent the signatures of sub-foremen or regular artisans, for it is unlikely that one work crew had four foremen.

Numeracy and literacy are certainly related, and several members of the terra-cotta army work crew, not just the foreman, appear to have incised serial numbers on the figures as well. These are not serial numbers for the entire figure within the larger army but production serial numbers written by individual artisans recording their own output. These numbers do not

---

21. Lothar Ledderose, *Ten Thousand Things: Module and Mass Production in Chinese Art* (Princeton, N.J.: Princeton University Press, 2000), 70; Yuan, *Qin bingmayong keng*, 169.
22. Shaanxi Sheng Kaogu Yanjiusuo et al., *Qin Shihuangling bingmayong*, 1:201, fig. 116.1.

appear consistently on every piece, being found on only about 19 percent of excavated figures. Certain numbers, such as five and ten, occur more frequently than others, possibly indicating that only the lot-header figure was incised and that the warriors tended to be counted in groups of five and ten, just like commoners and soldiers in the real world.[23]

Lacquer Vessels from Shuihudi and Dafentou, Hubei

The dozens of inscribed lacquers found in the Qin and incipient Han tombs at Shuihudi and Dafentou 大墳頭 in Hubei reveal the Qin system of quality control inscriptions in operation in another medium.[24] Like the near contemporary terra-cotta army from Qin Shihuang's mausoleum, the lacquers from Shuihudi and Dafentou appear to have been made at both government-sponsored workshops and private workshops. Those pieces interpreted as having been made in privately-run workshops are occasionally incised with the name, native place, and age classification of at least one of the artisans involved in producing the lacquer. Judging by the names and titles mentioned in the inscriptions, the Hubei lacquers appear to have been made by male and female artisans, including both adults and minors. Since the names were incised at the very end of the production process, in the topmost layer of lacquer, the name arguably belonged to the design painter (or possibly the person who applied the top coat of lacquer to monochrome pieces). I strongly doubt that the names belonged exclusively to the foremen of work crews, given the presence of several minors (less than fifteen years of age) among the names.

If the surviving sample is in any way indicative, it would appear that adult female lacquer painters were more prevalent than either adult male painters or child painters. A couple of the male painters mention their rank in the Qin system of ranks (usually one of the lower ones). Most of the minor boys and girls usually just write *xiǎo nǚzǐ* 小女子 'minor girl' or

---

23. See Ledderose, *Ten Thousand Things*, 73.
24. For the Shuihudi lacquers, see Yunmeng Shuihudi Qinmu Bianxiezu 雲夢睡虎地秦墓編寫組, *Yunmeng Shuihudi Qin mu* 雲夢睡虎地秦墓 (Beijing: Wenwu Chubanshe, 1981); for the Dafentou lacquers, see Hubei Sheng Bowuguan 湖北省博物館, "Yunmeng Dafentou yihao Han mu" 雲夢大墳頭一號漢墓, *Wenwu ziliao congkan* 4 (1981): 1–28; for an analysis of Qin lacquer inscriptions from these sites, see especially Satō Taketoshi 佐藤武敏, "Shin Kan sho no shikki no seisan ni tsuite" 秦漢初の漆器の生産について, *Koshi shunjū* 4 (1987): 3–16.

xiǎo nánzǐ 小男子 'minor boy', without even giving a personal name. Adults were far more likely than minors to write their personal name.

There seems to have also been a distinction in the types of vessels decorated by adults as opposed to minors. Adult artisans were more likely to have painted the more complex bowls, toiletry boxes, and stacking cup sets, whereas the boys and girls were more likely to have painted the simply decorated or monochrome eared cups. It is possible that the minor artisans were either the children or apprentices of the adult artisans mentioned. Following the interpretation of Satō Taketoshi, it appears that some adult artisans worked most of the time in private workshops in the Xianyang area but were occasionally conscripted to work in government-sponsored workshops in Xianyang, supervised by marketplace officials. The fact that some pieces carry brands on the wooden cores that say *tíng* 亭 or *Xián tíng* 咸亭, which is taken as an abbreviation of the market official's pavilion of Xianyang, supports this contention.

One of the most versatile and prolific lacquer painters was a woman known only as Woman Ao (Dà Nǚzǐ Áo 大女子鶩). Judging by the full form of her workshop signature, her residential registration was in Huan Village, a hamlet probably located somewhere near the Qin capital of Xianyang (see plate 8b). Her given name, Ao 鶩, is not a common one among the known names for women in early imperial China and carries the connotations of "fine." Among the eighty-one lacquers found in tomb no. 1 at Dafentou, she signed at least twenty-three of them, including five different types of vessels.[25]

One simple, eared cup with geometric decoration from tomb no. 12 at Shuihudi is signed *xiǎo nánzǐ Gài* 小男子匃 'minor male, Gai'.[26] The given name Gai 匃 seems a little odd, (lit. "to pray, to ask for") but is seen in at least one other contemporary Qin text.[27] The little boy Gai could write his name and designation, with a needle no less, though one wonders if he could write anything beyond that.

Other examples of the artisan signatures from the Shuihudi tombs

---

25. Hubei Sheng Bowuguan, "Yunmeng Dafentou," 1–28.
26. For a drawing of the inscription, see Yunmeng Shuihudi, *Yunmeng Shuihudi Qin mu*, 132; for a photograph, see plate 49.5.
27. The same graph is seen as a personal name in the Qin boards from Liye. See especially board no. 157 from stratum 8 of well no. 1 (J1⑧157). See Hunan Sheng, *Liye fajue baogao*, 184, color plate 22.

include the following:[28]

錢里大女子 (M11:3) (*lian* box with other brands)
Adult female from Qian Village

左里漆界 (M13:22) (big eared cup, no brands)
Lacquerer Jie from Zuo Village

□ (? 閣) 里一八 (M13:5) (*ting* brand)
No. 18 from Ge Village

士五軍 (M11:19, M11:9, M11:18) (eared cups, with brands)
Member of the rank and file, Jun

上造載 (?) (M11:16) (bowl)
Shangzao-ranked male, Zai

大女子絲 (M6:5, M7:27, M8:7, M11:51, M11:28, M11:35) (painted cups and bowls)
Adult female Wan

大女子臧 (M11:29) (eared cup)
Adult female Zang

大女子小 (M34) (circular *lian* with painted decoration [color plate 56])
Adult Female Xiao

大女子 (M11:22, M11:17, M11:46)
Adult female (possibly more than one individual)

小女子甲 (M13:32) (eared cup)
Minor girl Jia

小女子 (M11:2, M11:21, M11:7, M11:49, M11:24) (eared cups)
Minor girl (possibly more than one individual)

These signatures offer some impression of the functional literacy of this group of artisans. In general, the artisan signatures from the Hubei lacquers indicate little more than that Qin and early Han lacquer artisans could inscribe their names, ranks, and native places when required. It is not very likely that they would fit the classic 1958 UNESCO (United Nations Educational, Scientific and Cultural Organization) definition of

---

28. See Yunmeng Shuihudi, *Yunmeng Shuihudi qin mu*, 131, plate 49.3 (M11:3); 135, plate 49.8 (M13:22); 135 (M13:5); 123 (M11:19, M11:9, M11:18); 132, plate 49.4 (M11:16).

literacy and "with understanding, both read and write a short simple statement on his or her everyday life,"[29] but perhaps they could read one another's names (to know who had made which pieces) and could recognize a few dozen place-names mentioned on the pieces. This seems to be a reasonable extension of functional literacy, at least.

The graphs of these inscriptions often appear rushed and abbreviated, with many missing or "non-standard" strokes. Much of this may be attributed to the minuscule size of the inscriptions and also to the nature of the tool used, which was probably a needle or sharp burin. Signatures of private-workshop foremen on the First Emperor of Qin's terra-cotta army provide a more favorable impression of the quality of artisan writing. Inscriptions written with a stylus on clay are much more legible than the needle-incised lacquer inscriptions from Shuihudi and Dafentou. Dorothy Ko has suggested that for the lacquer painters,[30] the process of learning to write their names and designations, with an ordered sequence of strokes, might have seemed very similar to learning the sequence of brushstrokes required for painting designs in lacquer.

The Hubei lacquers also carry a good number of marks or glyphs that are difficult to interpret. Some are simply cross-shaped in appearance, while others are more complex. Were these maker-marks written by some illiterate artisan on the work crew, or do they represent something else? In many cases, they are placed alongside or underneath the signatures of functionally literate artisans. Perhaps, they are merely "check-off" marks meant to indicate that the production process was complete and the piece was ready for sale. Possibly, they are accumulative graphs, and each person involved in a different stage of painting the final coating completed a portion of the glyph until the work was done. One mark that shows up frequently looks vaguely like the archaic form of the graph *háng* 行 (lane or intersection), a term that would be used in Tang times to indicate a merchants' association or guild. The Qin and Han legal statutes show that a group responsibility system resembling incipient guilds already existed in early imperial China, but the term *háng* was not yet used to refer to it.[31]

---

29. For a review of the evolving UNESCO definitions of literacy, see UNESCO Education Sector, "The Plurality of Literacy and Its Implications for Policies and Programmes," position paper (Paris: UNESCO, 2004).
30. Columbia Early China Seminar, September 22, 2007.
31. *ZJS* ("Ernian lüling"), 168–69, slip 260; a similar Qin statute is in *SHD* ("Qin lü shiba zhong"), 36–37, slip 68; Hulsewé, *Remnants of Ch'in Law*, A45.

Nevertheless, one could speculate that this mark might indicate an affiliation with a proto-guild of artisans who worked on the same "lane."[32]

Lacquer Vessels from Han Imperial Factories

The inscribed lacquer and bronze vessels from the Western Workshop of Shu Commandery 蜀郡西工 and the Guanghan Commandery Office of Workmen 廣漢郡工官 are special in that, more so than pieces from other imperial factories, they often list nearly all of the artisans involved in the production process. Western Workshop lacquer vessels from around the turn of the Common Era list as many as eight artisan names along with the names of up to seven foremen, officials, and inspectors on each piece. The names are incised with a needle-like instrument in minute graphs, only fractions of a centimeter in height, frequently in an unobtrusive location on the vessel.

It is apparent from examining these inscriptions that each was written by a single individual and was not collectively "signed" by the individual artisans and officials named. By around 3 B.C.E., these inscriptions no longer appeared in the rushed and haphazard graphs seen on the Hubei lacquers but were written in a very accomplished needle-drawn clerical script. Each of the eight artisans involved in the production of the piece did not inscribe his or her name upon completion of the vessel. If we had to guess who was responsible for the writing of these elaborate quality control and accounting inscriptions, we might assume it was the *lìngshǐ* 令史 (foreman clerk) mentioned in the inscriptions. This was the lead, professional scribe employed by the factory for official correspondence. Foreman clerks were trained and tested in official schools during the early Han, as described by Robin D. S. Yates in chapter 10. This assumption, however, turns out to be illogical and, upon examination, incorrect. Perhaps it was beneath the stipendiary position of foreman clerk to descend into the dusty and fume-filled workshop to squat on the floor, squint at the minute graphs, and turn out hundreds of detailed inscriptions.

It might be useful to look at the calligraphy of the inscriptions to see if consistent writing patterns can be associated with one or another of the officials or artisans named. Table 11.1 shows calligraphic samples from imperial lacquer inscriptions. Note the examples from 3–4 C.E.

---

32. The same glyph shows up on one terra-cotta warrior as well (T2:G3:98). See Shaanxi Sheng Kaogu Yanjiusuo et al., *Qin Shihuangling bingmayong*, 1, fig. 118.4.

Table 11.1 Selected graphs from Han imperial lacquers made at the Western Workshop of Shu Commandery, between 2 B.C.E. and 4 C.E.

Vessel nos.	2 B.C.E. a	1 C.E. b	3 C.E. c	3 C.E. d	4 C.E. e	4 C.E. f	4 C.E. g	4 C.E. h
Design painter	畫工？	畫工黃	畫工譚	畫工豐	畫工張	畫工岑	畫工孟	畫工定
Zhou-artisan	洀工豐		洀工戎	洀工宜	洀工戎	洀工戎	洀工豐	洀工豐
Touch-up artist	清工白		清工政	清工政	清工平	清工平	清工平	清工平
Master artisan	造工告	造工仁	造工宜	造工宜	造工宗	造工宗	造工宜	造工宗
蜀								
造								
史								
畫								

The calligraphy of the graphs 蜀, 造, 史 is fairly uniform across all the examples, but the graph *huà* 畫 is present in two distinct forms. On vessels e, f, and h, *huà* is drawn with ten strokes, while on vessels c, d, and g, it is drawn with only nine, lacking one horizontal stroke below the first three horizontals. On each of the nine-stroke pieces, the master artisan (foreman) was Yi 宜, and on each of the ten-stroke pieces, it was a person named Zong 宗. This orthographic variation does not correspond with any of the other artisan names on the vessels. Thus, judging from this admittedly limited sample, it seems that each master artisan, or at least a scribal assistant exclusively employed by him or her, was responsible for the final task of carving the quality control and accounting inscriptions on these imperial lacquer vessels.

Since the inscription was carved all at once, in a consistent hand, some sort of intermediate record must have been kept throughout the production process, perhaps a written record that traveled with each piece or, more likely, with an entire lot of pieces. As the lot moved to the next work station in the production process, the artisan who completed the previous step would have added his or her name or cipher to the production report. When the lot finally arrived at the master artisan's station, he or she could then transcribe the names of all seven or eight artisans who had worked on the piece.

There is one further note of interest concerning the lacquer inscriptions from the Western Workshop. In 85 B.C.E., the Western Workshop of Shu employed a woman called Mother Yi (Mu Yi 母夷) as a foreman clerk.[33] This was not an artisan position at all. Some foreman clerks in the civil bureaucracy had to pass an exam requiring knowledge of numerous Chinese characters. The position of foreman clerk usually carried no official bureaucratic rank but did merit a regular salary of around 480 coins per month in the years around 85 B.C.E.[34] In addition, the Yi in Mother Yi's name is a common graph, which could denote non-Han ethnic groups to the northeast and southwest of Han China.[35] Thus, it seems

---

33. Umehara Sueji 梅原末治, *Shina Kandai kinenmei shikki zusetsu* 支那漢代記年銘漆器図説 (Kyoto: Kuwana Bunseidō, 1943; repr., Kyoto: Dohōsha, 1984), Western Han no. 1.
34. Bielenstein, *Bureaucracy*, 9, 19.
35. There are other possible interpretations. The graph 夷 was used to write many words in Early China. The same graph was used in early texts to write words meaning "norm" or "level," with the extended meaning of "to pacify," as well as words meaning

doubly remarkable that a government factory not only would employ a woman in a scribal position of great responsibility but might select a non–ethnic Han woman at that. Possibly Mother Yi had been an artisan at the factory for a number of years and was eventually promoted to the foreman clerk position because of her long experience. Women were not allowed to become officials in the civilian bureaucracy, so it would have been impossible for Mother Yi to pursue her bureaucratic career outside the insulated world of her factory in Chengdu.

The Stonecarvers of Zhongshan and Rencheng

Two particular imperial family tombs of the first century of the Eastern Han stand out for their revelation of hundreds of masons' signatures. The first tomb was excavated by Chinese archaeologists in 1959 in Ding County, Hebei. It likely belonged to Liu Yan 劉焉, Prince Jian of Zhongshan 中山簡王 (r. 54–90), a junior son of Liu Xiu 劉秀, the founder of the Eastern Han.[36] The central brick chamber was reinforced with a wall composed of 4,000 sandstone blocks, each more than three hundred kilograms in weight. Thus far, 174 blocks have been found to display inscriptions written by the masons who finished the stone (see fig. 11.1a, b). The standard format of the inscriptions from Zhongshan mentions the source of the stone, the place of registration, and the surname and given name of the mason.[37] Most of the inscriptions were carved, but a few were written in black ink with a brush. Well over one hundred

---

"agricultural tool," "large," and many others. One principal reason I chose this interpretation was because of Mother Yi's presence in Chengdu, home to many of the indigenous Southwestern Yi (Xi'nan Yi 西南夷), discussed in Han texts. Even into modern times, indigenous women in Yunnan specialized in lacquer painting, while their men carved the wooden cores.

36. Hebei Sheng Wenhuaju Wenwu Gongzuodui 河北省文化局文物工作隊, "Hebei Ding Xian beizhuang Han mu fajue baogao" 河北定縣北莊漢墓發掘報告, *Kaogu xuebao* 1964.2: 127–94. Based on internal evidence from inscriptions, the tomb itself was most likely begun between 84 and 88, and expanded after Liu Yan's death in 90.

37. The ceramic bricks of the central chamber also carry some inscriptions by the work crew, sometimes referring to serial numbers of bricks or their proper placement in the tomb. One brushed in vermilion states, "the underlying three courses of bricks amount to 114." One artisan even painted a beautiful picture of a duck in lampblack on one brick.

different mason names can be detected on the Zhongshan stones. This information can be used to track the typical distance from which men were conscripted to work on Prince Jian's tomb.[38] Here are some examples of the Zhongshan inscriptions.

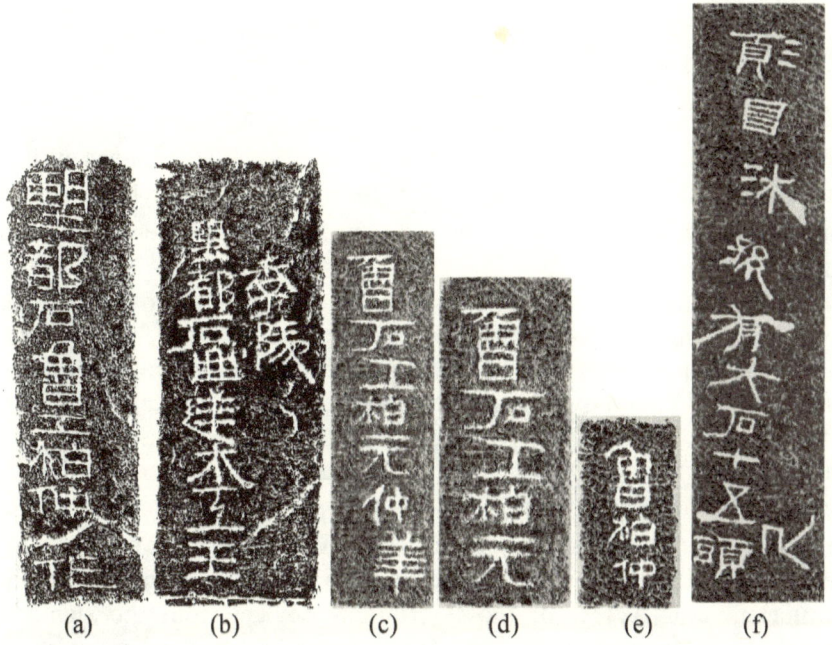

Figure 11.1 Mason signatures, Eastern Han period, circa 84–93 C.E. (a) "Stones from Wangdu. Made by artisan Bo Zhong from Lu"; (b) "Stones from Wangdu. Carpenter Wang Jiling from Quni County." From Hebei Sheng Wenhuaju, "Hebei Ding Xian beizhuang," *Kaogu xuebao* 1964.2: 188, rubbing 19; 189, rubbing 155. (c) "Lu Masons Bo Yuan, [Bo] Zhong, [Bo] Hua"; (d) "Lu Mason Bo Yuan"; (e) "Lu [Mason] Bo Zhong"; (f) rubbing from stone at the tomb of Prince Xiao of Rencheng (ink-on-paper rubbings, sizes vary, not reproduced to comparable scale. From Shandong Sheng Jining Shi Wenwuju, *Han Rencheng Wang mu keshi jingxuan*, 12, 118 (right and left), and 120 (upper left).

北平石，北新城，王文伯作。

Stone from Beiping County [in Zhongshan Princedom], made by Wang Wenbo from Beixincheng County, [Zhongshan].

---

38. Barbieri-Low, *Artisans in Early Imperial China*, 131–35.

望都石，曲逆，工<u>高巨</u>作。

Stone from Wangdu County [in Zhongshan Princedom], made by the artisan Gao Ju from Quni County, [Zhongshan].

望都石，魯國，文陽，石工<u>于魚</u>作。

Stone from Wangdu County [in Zhongshan Princedom], made by the mason Yu Yu from Wenyang County in Lu Princedom.

The other relevant tomb was excavated in 1992 near Jining City, Shandong. Nearly contemporary with Liu Yan's tomb at Zhongshan, this Shandong tomb likely belonged to Liu Shang 劉尚 (r. 84–101), Prince Xiao of Rencheng 任城孝王.[39] In fact, Liu Shang was a nephew of Liu Yan.

More than fifty different names of masons have been discovered on the stones from Prince Xiao's tomb at Rencheng. The standard format of the mason signatures from Prince Xiao's tomb lists the commandery or princedom and/or county of registration along with the surname and given name of the mason (fig. 11.1c–e).[40] This differs slightly from the Zhongshan format, in that the source of the stone is never mentioned. Occasionally, they also wrote their occupational title, *shizhì* 石治 (stone leveler) or *shigōng* 石工 (stone mason). These inscriptions are very clearly carved in enormous characters, sometimes as large as fifteen centimeters tall. A few of the inscriptions deviate from the standard formula and demonstrate an even higher level of literacy among some masons. The longest inscription from Rencheng (fig. 11.1f) contains eleven characters:

彭昌<u>沐孫</u>有大石十五頭。〔尺〕

---

39. Liu Shang's brief biography can be found in Fan Ye 范曄, *Hou Hanshu* 後漢書 (Beijing: Zhonghua Shuju, 1965), 42.1443. For a more complete publication of the stone inscriptions, see Shandong Sheng Jining Shi Wenwuju, *Han Rencheng wang mu keshi jingxuan* 漢任城王墓刻石精選 (Ji'nan: Shandong Meishu Chubanshe, 1998).
40. Most of these masons' names from Zhongshan and Rencheng list the full surname and given name of the artisan. This seems to be a new development on official government projects. I have rarely seen this on Qin or Western Han products. It is especially interesting in this case because these names are in direct contact with the everlasting palaces of princes of the imperial line. This phenomenon has also been helpful in establishing stonemason family connections based on the patterning of names from different locations.

Mu Sun from Xuchang county has [completed] fifteen large stones. One *chi* [in thickness].[41]

This is a complete sentence in Chinese, and Mu Sun even included a measure word for counting large stones, *tóu* 頭. *Shítóu* 石頭 would later become the standard bisyllabic word for "stone" in modern Chinese.[42] Also, even though Mu Sun endeavored to make his calligraphy handsome, especially the extended foot on his surname, Mu, he wrote the first graph of his home county's name in a "non-standard" form, switching the three strokes from the left to the right of the graph.[43] Overall, however, he writes in very handsome, standard orthography.

Stonemasons, at least master stonemasons and master draftsmen, may have been some of the most literate artisans during the Eastern Han because of their involvement in carving funerary epitaphs and stelae. The famous stelae appear to have been written first with brush calligraphy, possibly by a student or colleague of the deceased, and only then would the stonemasons engrave the calligraphy into the stone. Funerary epitaphs of lower- to middle-income persons would not receive such luxury treatment. These inscriptions appear to have been written by a member of the stonecarving crew, using boilerplate language, and likely required only minimal biographical input from the family. Compared to calligraphy on the stelae of scholars and high officials, the calligraphy of these inscriptions is rushed and inaccurate, and phonetic loans are more common.

From Compulsion to Promotion

Artisans in government-sponsored and private workshops during the Qin and Han periods demonstrated a functional level of literacy in compliance with government regulations requiring accountability for their work. Around the beginning of the Eastern Han period, certain private workshops began to modify the practice of quality control and accounting

---

41. Shandong Sheng Jining, *Han Rencheng wang*, plate 12.
42. *Tóu* 頭 was already used in the Han (or earlier) as a measure word for cattle, sheep, and sometimes people.
43. Xuchang County was in Dongping Princedom and was located about seventy kilometers from the tomb site. The county name appears in both forms on other stones from the Rencheng site, carved by at least three different masons. The variation was apparently acceptable to residents.

Figure 11.2 Lacquer tray, underside with inscription, Eastern Han period, dated 69; lacquer over fabric-reinforced wooden core, diam. 54 cm. From Harada and Tazawa, *Rakurō*, plate 56.

inscriptions in efforts to market their goods in a competitive environment.

In 1925, Japanese archaeologists excavated two large lacquer trays from the tomb of Wang Xu 王盱, a provincial official who served in the Han commandery of Lelang, located near present-day Pyongyang, North

Korea.[44] On the interior of one platter sits a marvelous polychrome miniature portrait of a deity seated on a raised platform, sheltered by a canopy, with a male kneeling in supplication. The iconography of the image clearly identifies the central figure as the Queen Mother of the West (Xiwangmu), the popular deity of the Han immortality cult. Her presence suggests that this platter may have been purchased specifically for burial.

On the underside of the platter, the lacquer artisans emblazoned their creation with a large inscription and surrounded it with leaping deer-like animals (see fig. 11.2). The text reads:

永平十二年，蜀郡西工，夾紵行三丸，治（值)千二百，盧氏作，宜子孫，牢。

The twelfth year of the Yongping era [69].
The Western Workshop of Shu Commandery.
Ramie cored and coated with several layers of mixed lacquer and ash [for strength]. It is worth twelve hundred coins.[45]
Made by the Lu family.
May it bring you sons and grandsons.
Very sturdy.

At first glance, this appears to be yet another imperial lacquer workshop inscription from the Western Workshop of Shu Commandery in Chengdu, and many scholars have indeed taken it for that. But something else is going on here.

After the date notation, and the claim to manufacture at the Western

---

44. See the original report in Harada Yoshito 原田淑人 and Tazawa Kingo 田沢金吾, *Rakurō* 楽浪 (Tokyo: Tōkō-shoin, 1930).

45. Though the two words sounded very similar during the Han, the substitution of *zhì* 治 (to make, to regulate) for *zhí* 值 (value) is not commonly seen as a phonetic loan in inscriptions dated to the Han period. GSR=Bernhard Karlgren, *Grammata Serica Recensa* (Stockholm: Museum of Far Eastern Antiquities, 1964); SE=Axel Schuessler, *ABC Etymological Dictionary of Old Chinese* (Honolulu: University of Hawaii Press, 2007).

治 GSR976z: *d'i̯əg > d̂'i > *chí* and *d'i̯əg > d̂'i- > *zhì* // SE:*d-ləh
值 GSR919h: *d'i̯əg > d̂'i- > *zhí* // SE:*drəkh

The equivalence is seen in texts like the *Shiming* 釋名. If taken literally, the graph *zhì* could make this passage translate as "made 1,200 pieces" or "underwent 1,200 manufacturing and inspection processes." Because of the common practice of listing the value (*zhí*) on bronze vessels at this time, I would still argue for the substitution.

Workshop, the inscription continues with some slightly exaggerated descriptions of the object's construction and monetary value. Then there is the peculiar mention of a Lu family as the manufacturers (not an individual), followed by the auspicious slogan *yí zǐsūn* 宜子孫 (may it bring you sons and grandsons) and the word *láo* 牢, which in this Han context probably means "sturdy."[46]

The style of decoration, as well as the content and context of the inscription, reveal clearly that this platter *was not made* at the Western Workshop of Shu. Surviving, genuine imperial pieces made at the Western Workshop during this time (circa 69) are largely undecorated, following Confucian-inspired declarations advocating the suppression of ornament at court. Nor does the decoration on this flashy piece correspond to the earlier heraldic style at the Western Workshop, which flourished from at least 30 B.C.E. to 14 C.E.[47]

The phrasing and placement of the inscription also preclude the possibility that this piece was really made at the Western Workshop. A legitimate Western Workshop inscription would mention the year and place of manufacture, detailed product specifications, and the names of artisans and supervisors responsible for the object's production, listed in order of precedence. This dry, detailed document would have been engraved with a sharp stylus in an unobtrusive location on the lacquer, using minute graphs, not flashy vermilion calligraphy (see fig. 11.2).

It appears that a private lacquer workshop in Chengdu, operated by the Lu family, borrowed from the tradition of quality-control inscriptions and modified it to suit more commercial purposes. Though the Lu family painter began his inscription conservatively enough with the year of manufacture and the factory name, he then proceeded to broach crass notions of monetary value and rattle off auspicious slogans concerning fertility. The phrases are broken up into three- and four-character units, following the traditions of popular verse and incantations meant to ward off evil. Such phrases never appear within quality-control inscriptions on genuine imperial products. They often appear, however, on privately produced pieces with no explicit claim to imperial provenance.

---

46. The word *láo* could also mean "diligent and careful," as in "carefully made by diligent artisans" or "carefully submitted."
47. For the stylistic history of Western Workshop lacquers, see Barbieri-Low, "The Organization of Imperial Workshops," ch. 3.

Speaking to inscriptional placement, private workshops would frequently move their enlarged inscriptions to a central location. The inscription on this platter was painted in brilliant vermilion lacquer. It was executed in a decorative clerical script, displaying dramatic thickening and thinning of line and a dashing, trailing flourish at the end of the final graph. The four leaping deer that seem to vault toward the inscription further highlight the text. The same four deer appear on the other Lu family–manufactured platter from Wang Xu's tomb and may have been the family's trademark.[48]

What were the Lus trying to accomplish here? Were they trying to make a high-quality counterfeit of an imperial lacquer platter? Were they trying to deceive their customers into thinking that their products were made at the Western Workshop of Shu? This seems unlikely. The upper levels of official society were well aware of the Western Workshop and its lacquerware, for many officials owned one or more examples of its products. In order to demonstrate his munificence, the emperor would often award presents of lacquer tableware to officials serving in the capital and provinces. Thus, the Lu family workshop's motivation for labeling its products with the name of the imperial lacquer factory was probably not deception. Most well-placed and knowledgeable people who might come across this piece in the marketplace would not be fooled into believing it was a genuine imperial piece. Nor was the Lu family platter intended to be an inexpensive, poor-quality knockoff. It is very well made, and the list price was almost two weeks' salary for a county magistrate during the Eastern Han.

It appears that the Lu family workshop borrowed the name of the Western Workshop to lend cachet to its products. According to literary descriptions, the Chengdu marketplace, where this platter was probably made, was filled with lacquer workshops, and competition for market share was apparently fierce. As an industrious proprietor, the Lu family sought to invest this lacquer platter with every conceivable selling point, namely, that it was well constructed, as fine as any piece made by the Western Workshop; that it was fashionable and beautiful; that it was valuable; and that it would bring good luck and male offspring.

Artisans like those of the Lu family workshop took advantage of the general public's familiarity with quality control and accounting inscriptions and borrowed some of that genre's language in order to create

---

48. For the other platter, see Harada and Tazawa, *Rakurō*, 43–44, plate 60.

a new form of marketing. Since the state no longer had the will to enforce the letter of the law regulating private production, people like the Lus modified the practice to suit their own ends.

During the Eastern Han, a growing number of artisans would begin to use their names to promote their businesses, not just to accord with the law. Families of bronze casters, iron casters, stonemasons, and lacquerers signed their names out of pride and in hopes of future business, not just out of fear of punishment. If it were not for this practice, research on artisans would be quite difficult. Occasionally, these inscriptions seem almost like modern commercial jingles, complete with rhyming doggerel verse and unreasonable promises of performance or value.

An amusing example comes from an unlikely source, a homely, iron axle bushing. In 1975, archaeologists recovered a hoard of Eastern Han iron parts and tools along with the molds for making them at a site near Zhenping in present-day Henan.[49] The items were all stuffed into a large ceramic jar, probably stowed for safekeeping during some emergency. The site itself does not appear to be part of a workshop but rather seems to be the remains of a habitation area for ironworkers. Among the iron objects in the hoard was a group of hexagonal axle bushings (*gāng*), used to reinforce the hubs of carriages and carts and to provide a smooth turning surface for the axle tree. Two of the bushings from the hoard were inscribed with the following rhyming couplet (note that the end rhyme was closer in antiquity than it sounds today in standard Chinese):[50]

王氏大牢工（釭）
Wángshì dà láo gāng

作真伲（輥）中。
zuò zhēn gǔn zhōng

---

49. Henan Sheng Wenwu Yanjiusuo and Zhenping Xian Wenhuaguan, "Henan Zhenping chutu de Handai jiaocang tiefan he tieqi" 河南鎮平出土的漢代窖藏鐵範和鐵器, *Kaogu* 1982.3: 243–51.
50. The two final graphs in the couplet, *gāng* 釭 (bushing) and *zhōng* 中 (middle), begin with different initials and end with different finals. Although 釭 belongs to the 東 rhyme group (Baxter 1992 *-ong) and 中 to the 冬 rhyme group (Baxter 1992 *-ung), for practical purposes, they rhyme. Leaving off the metal determinative on the final character of the first line may have also been an intentional pun, since the unadorned graph is just *gōng* 工 (artisan). Thus, the line could also be read as "The Wang family are big strong artisans."

Made by the Wangs — a bushing big and strong.

Bored straight and true — all the way through.

These advertisements were clumsily rhymed in doggerel verse and contain several phonetic loans for other more difficult graphs (including the word for "bushing"). They were designed to hype the quality of the product. In this case, the Wang family artisans claimed that their large bushings were sturdy and that the interior surfaces were perfectly straight and smooth, preventing undue wear on the axle. Ironically, all the Wang family–made bushings from the Zhenping hoard exhibit casting flaws and other defects. The inside sleeves of the bushings are riddled with air-bubble pockmarks and would have made terrible bushings for carriage hubs. Perhaps these bushings were rejects, destined to be melted down and recast. Otherwise, this is a perfect example of an advertising claim not living up to the product.

Conclusions

Scholars writing on the history of literacy have often portrayed literacy as a liberating and enlightening development, promoting culture and democracy, yet the early development of writing could hardly be characterized by such liberal notions. Claude Lévi-Strauss probes these darker roots of literacy in the following passage from his travel memoir, *Tristes Tropiques*:

> The one phenomenon [in human history] which has invariably accompanied [writing] is the formation of cities and empires: the integration into a political system, that is to say, of a considerable number of individuals, and the distribution of those individuals into a hierarchy of castes and classes. Such is, at any rate, the type of development we find, from Egypt right across to China, at the moment when writing makes its debut; it seems to favor rather the exploitation than the enlightenment of mankind. This exploitation made it possible to assemble workpeople by the thousand and set them tasks that taxed them to the limits of their strength: to this, surely, we must attribute the beginnings of architecture as we know it. *If my hypothesis is correct, the primary function of writing, as a means of communication, is to facilitate the enslavement of other human beings.* The use of writing for disinterested ends, and with a view to satisfactions of the mind the fields either of science or the arts, is a secondary result of

its invention — and may even be no more than a way of reinforcing, justifying, or dissimulating its primary function.[51]

In the Bronze Age of the Old World, writing was used to exert political, economic, and cultural hegemony. Politically, small ruling groups used writing to classify, conscript, and exploit lower-ranking groups in society. Economically, writing was used to tax the labor and produce of farmers, hoard and store commodities and luxury items, and facilitate the trade of raw materials and finished goods. Culturally, writing was used hegemonically by small groups of scribes, diviners, and priests to maintain privileged access to divine wisdom through oracles, revealed texts, and liturgies.

The state and empire of Qin relied on the written word to conquer and exploit the vast territory of early imperial China. Household registration, legal procedures, military reports, quality control and accounting inscriptions — the ruling elite used all of these in its exploitation of the peasant masses of China. The dukes and kings of Qin might have been able to conquer the vast territory of China without the written word, but they certainly would not have been able to administer it. The stable size of early empires was dependent not on military technology but on administrative technology. One could certainly conquer territory enough for a large empire if one were a fortunate and brilliant commander like Cyrus or Alexander, but without an efficient literate apparatus for controlling and exploiting it, such a vast empire could only be administered feudally, that is through satrapies or independent governors. If one wanted to control such an empire directly from the center, the only way to do so was through advances in communications technology such as a pony express, signal fire relays, and document processing. Thus, the Qin were able to control the largest, centrally administered empire the world had ever seen because it relied to the greatest extent on the tool of oppression par excellence, writing.

However, because the Qin required its citizens to acquire some skill in literacy, so that they could be more easily exploited, it also introduced a potential counterforce to its oppression. William V. Harris contends that writing is most efficiently used as a tool of oppression when a small elite is

---

51. Claude Lévi-Strauss, *Tristes Tropiques*, trans. John Russell (New York: Criterion, 1961), 292 (italics added).

literate and the mass of the population is not. When more and more of the masses learn the skill of reading and writing, they can begin to express their identity, contest the hegemony of the state, and even promote alternate political arrangements.[52] Such was the case in Early China, as the Qin and Han empires compelled artisans to become literate and take responsibility for their production. Once in possession of this skill, artisans used it to conduct their business and even to modify the oppressive format of the quality control and accounting inscription in order to promote their business interests.

---

52. Harris, *Ancient Literacy*, 332–34.

Abbreviations

Capital letters are used to prefix numbers of specific bones and inscriptions in the respective publications (e.g., HJ: 18946, JC: 4292, etc.). Abbreviations of works of oracle bones (in brackets) follow Keightley's 2000 list,[1] and abbreviations of bronze inscriptions and bamboo scripts follow accepted conventions.

BB (*Bingbian*): Zhang Bingquan 張秉權. *Xiaotun 2: Yinxu wenzi bingbian* 小屯第二本：殷墟文字丙編. 3 vols. Taipei: Zhongyang Yanjiuyuan Lishi Yuyan Yanjiusuo 中央研究院歷史語言研究所, 1965–72.

CB (*Cuibian*): Guo Moruo 郭沫若.*Yinqi cuibian* 殷契粹編. Tokyo: Bunkyūdō, 1937; revised, Beijing: Kexue, 1965; reprint, Beijing: Beijing Tushuguan Chubanshe 北京圖書館出版社, 2000.

ENL: Peng Hao 彭浩, Chen Wei 陳偉, and Kudō Motoo 工藤元男, eds. *Ernian lüling yu zouyanshu: Zhangjiashan ersiqi hao Han mu chutu falü wenxian shidu* 二年律令與秦讞書：張家山二四七號漢墓出土法律文獻釋讀. Shanghai: Shanghai Guji Chubanshe 上海古籍出版社, 2007.

GL (*Gulin*): Yu Xingwu 于省吾. *Jiagu wenzi gulin* 甲骨文字詁林. 4 vols. Edited by Yu Xingwu 于省吾. Beijing: Zhonghua Shuju 中華書局, 1996.

HB (*Hebu*): Peng Bangjoing 彭邦炯, Xie Ji 謝濟, and Ma Jifan 馬季凡. *Jiaguwen heji: Bubian* 甲骨文合集：補編. 7 vols. Beijing: Yuyan Chubanshe 語言出版社, 1999.

HD (*Huadong*): Zhongguo Shehuikexueyuan Kaogu Yanjiusuo 中國社會科學院考古研究所. *Yinxu Huayuanzhuang dong di jiagu* 殷墟花園莊東地甲骨. 6 vols. Kunming: Yunnan Renmin Chubanshe 雲南人民出版社, 2003.

HJ (*Heji*): Zhongguo Shehui Kexueyuan Lishi Yanjiusuo 中國社會科學院歷史研究所. Guo Moruo 郭沫若, general editor. *Jiaguwen heji* 甲骨文合集. 13 vols. Beijing: Zhonghua Shuju 中華書局, 1978–82.

---

1. David N. Keightley, *The Ancestral Landscape: Time, Space, and Community in Late Shang China (ca. 1200–1045 B.C.)* (Berkeley: Institute of East Asian Studies, University of California, 2000), 159–62.

JB (*Jiabian*): Dong Zuobin 董作賓. *Xiaotun 2: Yinxu wenzi jiabian* 小屯第二本：殷墟文字甲編. Nanjing: Zhongyang Yanjiuyuan Lishi Yuyan Yanjiusuo 中央研究院歷史語言研究所, 1948; reprint, Taipei, 1977.

JC (*Jicheng*): Zhonguo Shehui Kexueyuan Kaogu Yanjiusuo 中國社會科學院考古研究所. *Yin Zhou jinwen jicheng* 殷周金文集成. 18 vols. Beijing: Zhonghua Shuju, 1984–94.

JGWB: Sun Haibo 孫海波 (Zhongguo Shehui Kexueyuan Kaogu Yanjiusuo 中國社會科學院考古研究所). *Jiaguwen bian* 甲骨文編. Corrected version (改訂本). Beijing: Zhonghua Shuju, 1965.

Jishi: Li Xiaoding 李孝定. *Jiagu wenzi jishi* 甲骨文字集釋. 15 vols. Taipei: Zhongyang Yanjiuyuan Lishi Yuyan Yanjiusuo 中央研究院歷史語言研究所, 1965.

JL (*Jilu*): Liu Yu 劉雨 and Lu Yan 盧岩. *Jinchu Yin Zhou jinwen jilu* 近出殷周金文集錄. 4 vols. Beijing: Zhonghua Shuju, 2002.

JWB: Rong Geng 容庚. *Jinwenbian* 金文編. Beijing: Zhonghua Shuju, 1985.

JWGL: Zhou Fagao 周法高. *Jinwen gulin* 金文詁林. 14 vols. Hong Kong: Chinese University of Hong Kong Press, 1975.

Leizuan: Yao Xiaosui 姚孝遂 and Xiao Ding 蕭丁. *Yinxu jiagu keci leizuan* 殷墟刻辭類纂. 3 vols. Beijing: Zhonghua Shuju, 1989.

NH (*Ninghu*): Hu Houxuan 胡厚宣. *Zhanhou Ning Hu xinhuo jiaguji* 戰後寧滬新獲甲骨集. Shanghai: Laixunge, 1951.

SHD: Shuihudi Qinmu Zhujian Zhengli Xiaozu 睡虎地秦墓整理小組. *Shuihudi Qinmu zhujian* 睡虎地秦墓竹簡. Beijing: Wenwu Chubanshe, 1990.

Shiwen: Zhongguo Shehui Kexueyuan Kaogu Yanjiusuo. *Yin Zhou jinwen jicheng shiwen* 殷周金文集成釋文. 5 vols. Hong Kong: Chinese University of Hong Kong Press, 2001.

Sōrui: Shima Kunio 島邦男. *Inkyo bokuji sōrui* 殷墟卜辭綜類. Tokyo: Kyūko Shoin 汲古書院, 1971.

TN (*Tunnan*): Zhongguo Shehuikexueyuan Kaogu Yanjiusuo 中國社會科學院考古研究所. *Xiaotun nandi jiagu* 小屯南地甲骨. 2 vols. Beijing: Zhonghua Shuju, 1980–83.

XB (*Xubian*): Lu Zhenyu 羅振玉. *Yinxu shuqi xubian* 殷墟書契續編. 1933.

XS (*Xinshou*): Zhong Bosheng 鍾伯生, Chen Zhaorong 陳昭容, Huang Mingchong 黃銘崇, and Yuan Guohua 袁國華. *Xinshou Yin Zhou qingtongqi mingwen ji qiying huibian* 新收殷周青銅器銘文暨器影彙編. 3 vols. Taipei: Yiwen Yinshuguan 藝文印書館, 2006.

YB (*Yibian*): Dong Zuobin 董作賓. *Xiaotun 2: Yinxu wenzi yibian* 小屯第二本: 殷墟文字乙編. Zhongyang Yanjiuyuan Lishi Yuyan Yanjiusuo 中央研究院歷史語言研究所, 1948; reprint, Taipei, 1977.

YZ (*Yizhu*): Jin Zutong 金祖同. *Yinqi yizhu* 殷契遺珠. Shanghai: Zhongfa Wenhua, 1939; reprint, Taipei: Yinwen Yinshuguan, 1974.

ZJS: Zhangjiashan 247 Hao Mu Zhujian Zhengli Xiaozu 張家山二四七號漢墓竹簡整理小組. *Zhangjiashan Han mu zhujian* 張家山漢墓竹簡. Beijing: Wenwu Chubanshe 文物出版社, 2001.

ZJS-XD: Zhangjiashan Ersiqi Hao Han Mu Zhujian Zhengli Xiaozu 張家山二四七號漢墓竹簡整理小組. *Zhangjiashan Han mu zhujian (ersiqi hao mu) (shiwen xiuding ben)* 張家山漢墓竹簡（二十七號墓）（釋文修訂本）. Beijing: Wenwu Chubanshe, 2006.

Bibliography

Allan, Sarah. "On the Identity of Shang Di 上帝 and the Origin of the Concept of a Celestial Mandate (*tian ming* 天命)." *Early China* 31 (2007), 1-46.
Allan, Sarah, and Crispin Williams, eds. *The Guodian* Laozi: *Proceedings of the International Conference, Dartmouth College, May 1998* (Early China Special Monograph Series 5). Berkeley, Calif.: The Society for the Study of Early China, 2000.
Anonymous. "Zuotan Changsha Mawangdui Han mu boshu" 座談長沙馬王堆漢墓帛書 (An informal discussion about the silk manuscript from the Han tomb at Mawangdui in Changsha). *Wenwu* 1974.9: 45–57.
Austin, J. L. *How to Do Things with Words.* Cambridge, Mass.: Harvard University Press, 1967.
Bagley, Robert. "Anyang Writing and the Origin of the Chinese Writing System." In *The First Writing*, edited by Stephen D. Houston, 190–249. Cambridge: Cambridge University Press, 2004.
Baines, John. "Birth of Writing and Kingship. Introduction." In *Egypt at Its Origins 2*, edited by B. Midant-Reynes and Y. Tristant, 841–49. Louvain, Belgium: Peters, 2008.
———. "The Earliest Egyptian Writing: Development, Context, Purpose." In *The First Writing*, edited by Stephen D. Houston, 150–89. Cambridge: Cambridge University Press, 2004.
———. *Visual and Written Culture in Ancient Egypt.* Oxford: Oxford University Press, 2007.
Ban Dawei 班大爲. See David W. Pankenier.
Baoji Shi Kaogu Yanjiusuo 寶鷄市考古研究所 and Fufeng Xian Wenhuaguan 扶風縣文化館. "Shaanxi Fufeng Wujun Xicun Xi Zhou qingtongti jiaocang fajue jianbao" 陝西扶風五郡西村西周青銅器窖藏發掘簡報 (A short report on the excavation of a bronze vessel cache from the Western Zhou in Xicun, Wujun, Fufeng, Shaanxi). *Wenwu* 文物 2007.8: 4–27.
Barbieri-Low, Anthony. *Artisans in Early Imperial China.* Seattle: University of Washington Press, 2007.
———. *The Organization of Imperial Workshops during the Han Dynasty.* PhD diss., Princeton University, 2001.
Barfield, Thomas J. *The Perilous Frontier: Nomadic Empires and China.* Cambridge: Basil Blackwell, 1989.
Baxter, William H. *A Handbook of Old Chinese Phonology.* Berlin and New

York: Mouton de Gruyter, 1992.

Beijing Daxue Lishixi Kaogu Jiaoyanshi Shang Zhou Zu 北京大學歷史考古教研室商周組. *Shang Zhou kaogu* 商周考古 (Archaeology of the Shang and Zhou). Beijing: Wenwu Chubanshe 文物出版社, 1979.

Beijing Daxue Lishixi *Lunheng* Zhushi Xiaozu 北京大學歷史系《論衡》注釋小組, ed. *Lunheng zhushi* 論衡注釋 (Commentary on and explication of the *Lunheng*). Beijing: Zhonghua Shuju 中華書局, 1979.

Bell, Catherine. *Ritual Theory, Ritual Practice.* New York and Oxford: Oxford University Press, 1992.

Bielenstein, Hans. *The Bureaucracy of Han Times.* Cambridge: Cambridge University Press, 1980.

Biot, Édouard. *Le Tcheou-Li ou Rites des Tcheou.* Vol. 2. Paris: Imprimerie Nationale, 1851; reprint, Taipei: Chengwen, 1967.

Blakeley, Barry. "The Geography of Chu." In *Defining Chu*, edited by Cook and Major, 9–20.

Bodde, Derk. *China's First Unifier: A Study of the Ch'in Dynasty as Seen in the Life of Li Ssû* 李斯 *280?–208 B.C.* Hong Kong: Hong Kong University Press, 1967.

Boltz, William G. "The Composite Nature of Early Chinese Texts." In *Text and Ritual in Early China*, edited by Martin Kern, 50–78. Seattle: University of Washington Press, 2005.

———. "I li." In *Early Chinese Texts*, edited by Michael Loewe, 234–43. Berkeley: Society for the Study of Early China and Institute of East Asian Studies, University of California, Berkeley, 1993.

———. "Language and Writing." In *The Cambridge History of Ancient China*, edited by Michael Loewe and Edward L. Shaughnessy, 74–123.

———. "Notes on *Shuoh*." In *Dem Text ein Freund: Erkundungen des chinesischen Altertums, Robert H. Gassmann gewidmet*, edited by Roland Altenburger, Martin Lehnert, and Andrea Riemenschnitter, 39–56. Bern: Peter Lang, 2009.

———. *The Origin and Early Development of the Chinese Writing System.* New Haven: American Oriental Society, 1994; paperback edition, 2004.

———. "Pictographic Myths." *Bochumer Jahrbuch zur Ostasienforschung* Bd. 30 (2006): 39–54.

———. "Textual Criticism and the Ma Wang Tui *Lao tzu*." *Harvard Journal of Asiatic Studies* 44.1 (1984): 185–224.

———. "Three Footnotes on the *Ting* 鼎 'Tripod'." *Journal of the American Oriental Society* 110.1 (1990): 1–8.

Boodberg, Peter A. "The Chinese Script: An Essay on Nomenclature (the First Hecaton)." *Zhongyang yanjiuyuan lishi yuyan yanjiusuo jikan* 中央研究院歷史語言研究所集刊 29.1(1957): 113–20.

———. "'Ideography' or Iconolatry?" *T'oung pao* 35 (1940): 266–88.

———. "Some Proleptical Remarks on the Evolution of Archaic Chinese." *Harvard Journal of Asiatic Studies* 2 (1937): 329–72.
Boone, Elizabeth Hill. "Beyond Writing." In *The First Writing*, edited by Stephen D. Houston, 313–48.
Bottéro, Françoise. "Review of Boltz, *The Origin and Early Development of the Chinese Writing System*." *Journal of the American Oriental Society* 116.3 (1996): 574–77.
———. "Writing on Shell and Bone in Shang China." In *The First Writing*, edited by Stephen D. Houston, 252–54.
Branner, David Prager. *The Chinese Rime-tables: Linguistic Philosophy and Historical-Comparative Phonology*. Amsterdam: John Benjamins, 2006.
———. "Common Chinese and Early Chinese Morphology." *Journal of the American Oriental Society* 122.4 (2002): 706–21.
———. "Crypto-phonograms in Chinese and the Ideography Debate." Presented at the 213th Annual Meeting of the American Oriental Society, Nashville, 4 April 2003.
———. "A Gutyan Jongbao Dialect Notebook." In *The Yuen Ren Society Treasury of Chinese Dialect Data I* (March 1995): 243–338.
———. "The Linguistic Ideas of Edward Harper Parker." *Journal of the American Oriental Society* 119/1 (1999): 12–34.
———. "Loan-Graphs and the Sound of Written Chinese." Presented at the 218th Annual Meeting of the American Oriental Society, Chicago, 15 March 2008.
———. "On Early Chinese Morphology and Its Intellectual History." *Journal of the Royal Asiatic Society*, ser. 3, 15.1 (2003): 45–76.
———. "Portmanteau Characters in Chinese." To appear in the *Journal of the American Oriental Society* 131.1 (2012): 73-82.
———. *Problems in Comparative Chinese Dialectology: The Classification of Miin and Hakka*. Trends in Linguistics series, no. 123. Berlin: Mouton de Gruyter, 2000.
———. "'Red Cliffs' in Taiwanese *Hànbûn*." *CHINOPERL Papers* 24 (2002): 67–100.
Bray, Francesca. *Technology and Gender: Fabrics of Power in Late Imperial China*. Berkeley: University of California Press, 1997.
Brindley, Erica. "The Cosmic Power of Sound in the Late Warring States and Han Periods." *Journal of Chinese Religions* 35 (2007): 29–63.
Campbell, William. *A Dictionary of the Amoy Vernacular*. Tainan, Taiwan: Ho Tai Hong Print, 1913.
Cao Lüning 曹旅寧. "Zhangjiashan Han jian 'Shi lü' kao" 張家山漢簡《史律》考 (Textual studies on the *shǐ lǜ* "statutes pertaining to scribes" in the Han bamboo slips found at Zhangjiashan). In *Zhangjiashan Han lü yanjiu* 張家山漢律研究, 175–83. Beijing: Zhonghua Shuju, 2005.
Cao Wei 曹瑋. *Zhouyuan yizhi yu Xi Zhou tongqi yanjiu* 周原遺址與西周銅器研究 (Studies on the Zhouyuan ruins and Western Zhou Bronzes). Beijing:

Kexue Chubanshe 科學出版社, 2004.
Cen Zhongmian 岑仲勉. *Mozi chengshou gepian jianzhu* 墨子城守各篇簡注 (Brief commentary on the chapters of *Mozi* dealing with the defense of walled cities). Beijing: Zhonghua Shuju, 1958.
Chang, Kwang-chih (K.C.). "Ancient Trade as Economy or as Ecology." In *Ancient Civilization and Trade*, edited by C. C. Lamberg-Karlovsky and Jeremy Sabloff, 211–24. Albuquerque: University of New Mexico Press, 1975.
——. *The Archaeology of Ancient China*. 4th edition. New Haven, Conn.: Yale University Press, 1986.
——. *Art, Myth, and Ritual: The Path to Political Authority in Ancient China*. Cambridge, Mass.: Harvard University Press, 1983.
——. *Shang Civilization*. New Haven, Conn.: Yale University Press, 1980.
——. "Shang Shamans." In *The Power of Culture: Studies in Chinese Cultural History*, edited by Willard J. Peterson, Andrew H. Plaks, and Ying-shih Yü, 10–36. Hong Kong: Chinese University Press, 1994.
Chang Yuzhi 常玉芝. "Zhengzhou chutu de Shangdai niu leigu keci yu shesi yiji" 鄭州出土的商代牛肋骨刻辭與社祀遺蹟 (The Shang bovine rib inscriptions unearthed in Zhengzhou and the remains of altar rituals). *Zhongyuan wenwu* 中原文物 2007.5: 96–103.
Changsha Shi Wenwu Yanjiusuo 長沙市文物研究所 et al. *Changsha Zoumalou Wu guo jian, Jiahe limin tianjia* 長沙走馬樓吳國簡嘉禾吏民田家 (The officials and people of the farming households of Jiahe, in the bamboo slips from the State of Wu found at Zoumalou near Changsha). 2 vols. Beijing: Wenwu Chubanshe, 1999.
Chao, Yuen Ren. "A Note on an Early Logographic Theory of Chinese Writing." *Harvard Journal of Asiatic Studies* 5.2 (1940): 189–91.
Chen Jian 陳劍. "Shuo Huayuanzhang Dongdi jiagu buci de Ding" 說花園莊東地甲骨卜辭的丁 (Discussion of *dīng* 丁 in the oracle bone inscriptions of Huayuanzhuang Dongdi). *Gugong Bowuyuan Yuankan* 故宮博物院院刊 114 (2004.4): 51–63.
Chen Mengjia 陳夢家. *Han jian zhuishu* 漢簡綴述 (Collation and discussion of Han bamboo slips). Beijing: Zhonghua Shuju, 1980.
——. "Wang ruo yue kao" 王若曰考 (Investigation into the phrase "*wáng ruò yuē*"). In *Shangshu tonglun* 商書通論, by Chen Mengjia, 146–70. Beijing: Zhonghua Shuju, 1985.
——. "Xi Zhou tongqi duandai I–VI" 西周銅器斷代 (Periodization of Western Zhou bronzes I–VI). *Kaogu xuebao* 考古學報 9 (1955): 137–75; 10 (1955): 69–142; 1956.1: 65–114; 1956.2: 85–94; 1956.3: 105–278; 1956.4: 85–122.
——. *Yinxu buci zongshu* 殷虛卜辭綜述 (Comprehensive survey of the oracle-bone inscriptions from Yinxu). Beijing: Kexue Chubanshe, 1956.

Chen Pan 陳槃. *Chunqiu dashibiao lieguo juexing ji cunmiebiao zhuanyi* 春秋大事表列國爵姓及存滅表譔異 (Discussion of differences appearing in the table of major events and the table of aristocratic surnames, and of survival and destruction of the various states in the *Spring and Autumn Annals*). Taipei: Academia Sinica, 1969.

Chen Songchang 陳松長. *Boshu shihua* 帛書史話 (Historical remarks on the silk manuscripts). Beijing: Zhongguo Da Baike Quanshu Chubanshe 中國大百科全書出版社, 2000.

——. *Mawangdui boshu yishu* 馬王堆帛書藝術 (The art of the Mawangdui silk manuscript). Shanghai: Shanghai Shudian 上海書店, 1996.

——. "Yuelu shuyuan suocang Qin jian zongshu" 岳麓書院所藏秦簡綜述 (Summary of information about the Qin bamboo slips stored in the Yuelu Library). *Wenwu* 2009.3: 79–83.

Chen Xu 陳旭 and Xu Zhaofeng 徐昭峰. "Zhengzhou chutu Shangdai niu leigu keci shiwen louzi yuanyin tanjiu" 鄭州出土商代牛肋骨刻辭釋文漏字原因探究 (Probing the causes for the omission of characters in the transcription of the Shang bovine rib inscriptions unearthed in Zhengzhou). *Zhongyuan wenwu* 中原文物 2006.3: 58–96.

Cheng Shude 程樹德. *Jiuchao lü kao* 九朝律考 (Investigation into the laws of nine dynasties). 2 vols. Taipei: Taiwan Shangwu Yinshuguan, 1965; reprint, Beijing: Zhonghua Shuju, 2006.

Childs-Johnson, Elizabeth. *The Meaning of the Graph* 異 *and Its Implications for Shang Belief and Art*. East Asia Journal Monograph no. 1. London: Saffron, 2008.

Chua, Fook Kee 蔡福基. "Visual Perception of the Chinese Character: Configural or Separable Processing?" *Psychologia* 42.4 (1999): 209–21.

Connery, Christopher Leigh. *The Empire of the Text: Writing and Authority in Early Imperial China*. Lanham, Md.: Rowman and Littlefield, 1998.

Cook, Constance A. "Ancestor Worship During the Eastern Zhou." In *Early Chinese Religion: Part One: Shang through Han (1250 BC–220 AD)*, edited by Lagerwey and Kalinowski, 237–79. Leiden: E. J. Brill, 2009.

——. "Auspicious Metals and Southern Spirits: An Analysis of the Chu Bronze Inscriptions." PhD diss., University of California, Berkeley, 1990.

——. "The Bin Gong *xu* and Sage King Yu." In *The X Gong Xu: A Report and Papers from the Dartmouth Workshop*, a special issue of *International Research on Bamboo and Silk Documents: Newsletter*, edited by Xing Wen, 23–28. Hanover, N.H.: Dartmouth College, 2003.

——. "Chung-shan Bronze Inscriptions: Introduction and Translation." MA thesis, University of Washington, 1980.

——. *Death in Ancient China: The Tale of One Man's Journey*. Leiden: E. J. Brill, 2006.

——. "The Ideology of the Chu Ruling Class: Ritual Rhetoric and Bronze Inscriptions." In *Defining Chu*, edited by Cook and Major, 67–76.
——. "Moonshine and Millet: Feasting and Purification Rituals in Ancient China." In *Of Tripod and Palate: Food, Politics and Religion in Traditional China*, edited by Roel Sterckx, 9–23. New York: Palgrave Macmillan, 2005.
——. "Review of Boltz, *The Origin and Early Development of the Chinese Writing System*." *Bulletin of the School of Oriental and African Studies, University of London* 59.1 (1996): 403–5.
——. "Ritual Feasting in Ancient China." In *Di'erjie guoji Zhongguo guwenzixue yantaohui lunwenji* 第二屆國際中國古文字學研討會論文集, edited by Chinese Department, The University of Hong Kong, 469–87. Hong Kong: The Chinese University of Hong Kong, 1993.
——. "Ritual, Politics, and the Issue of *Feng* (封)." In *Shi Quan xiansheng jiushi danchen jinian wenji* 石泉先生九十誕辰紀念文集, edited by Wuhan Daxue Lishi Dili Yanjiusuo 武漢大學歷史地理研究所, 215–67. Wuhan: Hubei Renmin Chubanshe 湖北人民出版社, 2007.
——. "Scribes, Cooks, and Artisans: Breaking Zhou Tradition." *Early China* 20 (1995–96): 241–69.
——. "Wealth and the Western Zhou." *The Bulletin of the School of Oriental and African Studies* 60.2 (1997): 253–94.
——. "Xianwang zhi dao yu 'weiyi' de waihua biaoxian" 先王之道與'威儀'的外化表現 (The way of the former kings and the externalization of *wēiyí*) . In *Chudi jianbo sixiang yanjiu* 楚地簡帛思想研究, vol. 3, edited by Ding Sixin 丁四新, 270–83. Wuhan: Hubei Jiaoyu Chubanshe 武漢教育出版社, 2007.
Cook, Constance A., and John S. Major, eds. *Defining Chu: Image and Reality in Ancient China*. Honolulu: University of Hawai'i Press, 1999.
Cook, Richard S. "The Etymology of Chinese 辰 *Chén*." Monograph. *Linguistics of the Tibeto-Burman Area* 18.2 (1995).
Cooper, Eugene. "The Potlatch in Ancient China." *History of Religions* 22.3 (1982): 103–28.
Coss, John J. "The New Freshman Course in Columbia College." *Columbia University Quarterly* 21 (1919): 248. Cited in Timothy P. Cross, *An Oasis of Order: The Core Curriculum at Columbia College*. New York: Columbia University, Columbia College, 1995, 12.
Couvreur, Séraphin. 儀禮 *Cérémonial*. New edition. Paris: Cathasia, 1951.
Creel, Herrlee G. "Bronze Inscriptions of the Western Chou Dynasty as Historical Documents." *Journal of the American Oriental Society* 56.3 (1936): 335–49.
——. "On the Ideographic Element in Ancient Chinese." *T'oung pao* 34 (1938): 265–94.
——. "On the Nature of Chinese Ideography." *T'oung pao* 32 (1936): 85–161.
——. *The Origins of Statecraft in China*. Vol. 1, *The Western Chou Empire*.

Chicago: University of Chicago Press, 1970.
Cross, Timothy P. *An Oasis of Order: The Core Curriculum at Columbia College.* New York: Columbia University, Columbia College, 1995.
Csikszentmihalyi, Mark. *Material Virtue: Ethics and the Body in Early China.* Leiden: Brill, 2004.
Cullen, Christopher. "The *Suàn shù shū* 算數書, 'Writings on Reckoning': Rewriting the History of Early Chinese Mathematics in the Light of an Excavated Manuscript." *Historia Mathematica* 34 (2007): 10–44.
Damerow, Peter. "The Origins of Writing as a Problem of Historical Epistemology." *Cuneiform Digital Library Journal* 1 (2006): 1–10.
de Bary, William Theodore, and John W. Chaffee, eds. *Neo-Confucian Education: The Formative Stage.* Berkeley: University of California Press, 1989.
de Saussure, Léopold. *Les origines de l'astronomie chinoise.* Paris: Maisonneuve, 1930.
DeFrancis, John. *The Chinese Language: Fact and Fantasy.* Honolulu: University of Hawai'i Press, 1984.
——. *Visible Speech: The Diverse Oneness of Writing Systems.* Honolulu: University of Hawai'i Press, 1989.
Didier, John C., "In and Outside the Square: The Sky and the Power of Belief in Ancient China and the World of 4500-100 bc," *Sino-Platonic Papers* 192, 2009.
Ding, Guosheng, Danling Peng, and Marcus Taft. "The Nature of the Mental Representation of Radicals in Chinese: A Priming Study." *Journal of Experimental Psychology: Learning, Memory, and Cognition* 30.2 (2004): 530–39.
Ding Fubao 丁福保. *Shuowen jiezi gulin* 說文解字詁林 (A "forest" of glosses on the *Shuowen jiezi*). Shanghai: Yixue Shuju 醫學書局, 1930.
Donald, Merlin. *The Origins of the Modern Mind: Three Stages in the Evolution of Culture and Cognition.* Cambridge, Mass.: Harvard University Press, 1991.
Dong Chuping 董楚平. *Wu Yue wenhua xintan* 吳越文化新探 (A new investigation into the culture of Wu and Yue). Zhejiang: Zhejiang Renmin, 1988.
Dong Zuobin 董作賓. "Wang ruo yue guyi" 王若曰詁義 (A gloss on the phrase "*wáng ruò yuē*"). *Shuowen yuekan* 說文月刊 4 (1944): 335–340.
Doty, Darrel P. "The Bronze Inscriptions of Ch'i: An Interpretation." PhD diss., University of Washington, 1982.
Dreyer, Günter. *Umm el-Qaab I: Das prädynastische Königsgrab U-j und seine frühen Schriftzeugnisse.* Mainz: Phillipp von Zabern, 1998.
Duan Yucai 段玉裁. *Shuowen jiezi zhu* 說文解字注 (A commentary on the *Shuowen jiezi*). Jingyun Lou cangban 經均樓臧版, repr. Shanghai: Shanghai Guji Chubanshe 上海古籍出版社, 1986 [1981].

Duponceau, Peter S. *A Dissertation on the Nature and Character of the Chinese System of Writing*. Philadelphia: American Philosophical Society, 1838.
Durrant, S. W. *The Cloudy Mirror: Tension and Conflict in the Writings of Sima Qian*. Albany: State University of New York, 1995.
Duyvendak, J. J. L. *The Book of Lord Shang*. London: Probsthain, 1928; reprint, Chicago: University of Chicago Press, 1963.
Ellsworth, Robert H. *Later Chinese Painting and Calligraphy, 1800–1950*. New York: Random House, 1987.
Elman, Benjamin A., and Alexander Woodside, eds. *Education and Society in Late Imperial China, 1600–1900*. Berkeley: University of California Press, 1994.
Embree, Bernard L. M., et al. *A Dictionary of Southern Min*. Taipei: Taipei Language Institute, 1984.
Englund, Robert K. "Texts from the Late Uruk Period." In *Mesopotamien: Späturuk-Zeit und Frühdynastische Zeit*, ed. Josef Bauer, Robert K. Englund, and Manfred Krebernik, 15–233. Freiburg, Germany: Universitätsverlag, 1998.
Eno, Robert. "The Background of the Kong Family of Lu and the Origins of Ruism." *Early China* 28 (2003): 1–41.
Falkenhausen, Lothar von (Luo Tai 羅泰). *Chinese Society in the Age of Confucius (100–250 BC): The Archaeological Evidence*. Los Angeles: Cotsen Institute of Archaeology, University of California, Los Angeles, 2006.
———. "The Inscribed Bronzes from Yangjiacun: New Evidence on Social Structure and Historical Consciousness in Late Western Zhou China (c. 800 BC)." *Proceedings of the British Academy* 139 (2006): 239–95.
———. "Issues in Western Zhou Studies: A Review Article." *Early China* 18 (1993): 139–226.
———. "Ritual Music in Bronze Age China: An Archaeological Perspective." PhD diss., Harvard University, 1988.
———. *Suspended Music: Chime-Bells in the Culture of Bronze Age China*. Berkeley: University of California Press, 1993.
———. "Xi Zhou tongqi mingwen de xingzhi" 西周銅器銘文的性質 (The nature of the Western Zhou bronze inscriptions). In *Kaoguxue yanjiu* 考古學研究 6 (Festschrift for Professor Gao Ming), 343–74. Beijing: Kexue Chubanshe, 2006.
Fangyan 方言 (Regional words). By Yang Xiong 楊雄. *Congshu jicheng* 叢書集成 edition. Beijing: Zhonghua Shuju, 1985.
Feng Shi 馮時. "Shandong Dinggong Longshan shidai wenzi jiedu" 山東丁公龍山時代文字解讀 (An analytical reading of Longshan-era writing from Dinggong in Shandong). *Kaogu* 1994.1: 37–54.
———. "Zhachao zhong mingwen kaoshi" 戚巢鐘銘文考釋 (A philological study

of the inscription on the Zhachao *zhong*). *Kaogu* 2000.6: 73–78.

———. *Zhongguo tianwen kaoguxue* 中國天文考古學 (Archaeoastronomy in China). Beijing: Zhongguo shehui kexue chubanshe 中國社會科學出版社, 2007.

Ferguson, Charles A. "Diglossia." *Word* 15 (1959): 325–40.

Fox, James J. "Semantic Parallelism in Rotinese Ritual Language." *Bijdragen tot de Taal-, Land-, en Volkenkunde* 127 (1971): 215–55.

Galambos, Imre. *Orthography of Early Chinese Writing: Evidence from Newly Excavated Manuscripts*. Budapest: Department of East Asian Studies, Eötvös Loránd University, 2006.

Gansu Sheng Bowuguan 甘肅省博物館 and Zhongguo Kexueyuan Kaogu Yanjiusuo 中國科學院考古研究所. *Wuwei Han jian* 武威漢簡 (Han bamboo slips from Wuwei). Beijing: Wenwu Chubanshe, 2006 [1964].

Gansu Sheng Wenwu Kaogu Yanjiusuo 甘肅省文物考古研究所. *Dunhuang Han jian* 敦煌漢簡 (Han bamboo slips from Dunhuang). Beijing: Zhonghua Shuju, 1991.

Gansu Sheng Wenwu Kaogu Yanjiusuo et al. *Juyan xinjian* 居延新簡 (New bamboo slips from Juyan). Beijing: Wenwu Chubanshe, 1990.

Gao Zheng 高正. "Boshu Shisi jing zhengming" 帛書十四經正名 (On the correct name of the "fourteen texts" in the silk manuscripts). In *Daojia wenhua yanjiu* 道家文化研究 3, edited by Chen Guying 陳鼓應, 283–84. Shanghai: Shanghai Guji Chubanshe, 1993.

Gassmann, Robert H., and Wolfgang Behr. *Antikchinesisch—Ein Lehrbuch in drei Teilen*, Teil 1. Bern: Peter Lang, 2005.

Gelb, Ignace J. *A Study of Writing: The Foundations of Grammatology*. Chicago: University of Chicago Press, 1963 [1952].

Genette, Gérard. *Paratexts: Thresholds of Interpretation*. Translated by Jane E. Lewin. Cambridge: Cambridge University Press, 1997.

Gernet, Jacques. *Buddhism in Chinese Society: An Economic History from the Fifth to the Tenth Centuries*. Translated by Fanciscus Verellen. New York: Columbia University Press, 1995.

Giele, Enno. *Imperial Decision-Making and Communication in Early China: A Study of Cai Yong's Duduan*. Wiesbaden, Germany: Otto Harrassowitz, 2006.

Granet, Marcel. *Études Sociologiques sur la Chine*. Paris: Presses Universitaires de France, 1953.

Greatrex, Roger. "An Early Western Han Synonymicon: The Fuyang Copy of the *Cang jie pian*." In *Outstretched Leaves on His Bamboo Staff: Essays in Honor of Göran Malmqvist on his 70th Birthday*, edited by Joakim Envall, 97–113. Stockholm: Association of Oriental Studies, 1994.

Gu Yanwu 顧炎武. *Jinshi wenzi ji* 金石文字記 (Notes on graphs found in bronze and stone inscriptions). In *Zhihai congshu* 指海叢書, *Congshu jicheng chubian* 叢書集成初編 edition, vols. 1517–18. Shanghai: Shangwu Yinshuguan, 1935–40; reprint, Beijing: Zhonghua Shuju, 1991.

Guaman Poma de Ayala, Felipe. *El primer nueva corónica y buen gobierno* (1615/1616). Copenhagen: Det Kongelige Bibliotek, GKS 2232 4°.

Guanzi 管子 (The *Guanzi*). *Ershi'er zi* 二十二子 ed. Shanghai: Shanghai Guji Chubanshe, 1986.

Gugong Bowuyuan 故宮博物院. *Gugong* 故宮 (The Imperial Palace). Vol. 1. Beiping: Gugong Bowuyuan, 1929.

Guo Moruo 郭沫若. *Liang Zhou jinwen ci daxi tulu kaoshi* 兩周金文辭大系圖錄考釋 (A Chronology, catalog, and philological study of bronze inscriptions from the Western and Eastern Zhou). 8 vols. 1st edition, Tokyo: Bunkyūdō 文求堂, 1935. Beijing: Kexue Chubanshe, 1958.

———. "Shi zhigan" 釋支干 (An interpretation of the cyclical signs). In *Guo Moruo quanji* 郭沫若全集 (Complete works of Guo Moruo). Archaeology series, vol. 1. Beijing: Kexue Chubanshe, 1982.

Guojia Wenwuju Gu Wenxian Yanjiushi 國家文物局古文獻研究室. *Mawangdui Han mu boshu* 馬王堆漢墓帛書 (The silk manuscript from the Han tomb at Mawangdui). Vol. 1. Beijing: Wenwu Chubanshe, 1980.

Guoyu 國語 (The tales of the states). *Sibu beiyao* 四部備要 edition. Shanghai: Zhonghua Shuju, 1933; reprint, Taipei: Zhonghua Shuju, 1975. Shanghai: Shanghai Guji Chubanshe, 1988.

Hagman, Jan L. "Private and Government Schools in the Han Dynasty." In *Outstretched Leaves on His Bamboo Staff*, edited by Joakim Envall, 114–30.

Hanshu 漢書 (The history of the Han dynasty). By Ban Gu 班固). 12 vols. Beijing: Zhonghua Shuju, 1962; reprint, 1990.

Harada Yoshito 原田淑人 and Tazawa Kingo 田沢金吾. *Rakurō* 楽浪 (Lelang: The tomb of Wang Xu). Tokyo: Tōkō-shoin, 1930.

Harper, Donald. "The Textual Form of Knowledge: Occult Miscellanies in Ancient and Medieval Chinese Manuscripts, Fourth Century B.C. to Tenth Century A.D." In *Looking at It from Asia: The Process That Shaped the Sources of History of Science*, edited by Florence Bretelle and Christine Proust. Unpublished draft of April 2008.

Harris, William V. *Ancient Literacy*. Cambridge, Mass.: Harvard University Press, 1989; paperback ed., 1991.

He Jiejun 何介鈞. *Changsha Mawangdui er, san hao Han mu* 長沙馬王堆二、三號漢墓 (Han tombs 2 and 3 of Mawangdui near Changsha) Vol. 1. Beijing: Wenwu Chubanshe, 2004.

He Nu 何駑, "Taosi zhongqi xiaocheng daxing jianzhu jizhi IIFJT1 shidi moni guanxiang baogao" 陶寺中期小城大形建築基址IIFJT1實地模擬觀象報告 (A report on the onsite imitative solar observation at the building foundation IIFJT1 in the small wall-enclosure dating to the mid-Taosi period), *Gudai wenming yanjiu tongxun* 古代文明研究通訊 [Ancient Civilizations Review] 29 (2006): 3–14.

He Shuhuan 何樹環. *Xi Zhou ximing mingwen xinyan* 西周錫命銘文新研 (New research on the appointment inscriptions of the Western Zhou). Wenshizhe daxi, vol. 220. Taipei: Wenjin Chubanshe, 2007.

Hebei Sheng Wenhuaju Wenwu Gongzuodui 河北省文化局文物工作隊. "Hebei Dingxian beizhuang Han mu fajue baogao" 河北定縣北莊漢墓發掘報告 (Excavation report of the Han tomb at Beizhuang, Ding County, Hebei). *Kaogu xuebao* 1964.2: 127–94.

Henan Sheng Wenhuaju Wenwu Gongzuodui 河南省文化局文物工作隊. *Zhengzhou Erligang* 鄭州二里岡 (Erligang in Zhengzhou). Beijing: Kexue Chubanshe, 1959.

Henan Sheng Wenwu Yanjiusuo 河南省文物研究所. "Zhengzhou Dianli Xuexiao kaogu fajue baogao" 鄭州電力學校考古發掘報告 (Archaeological excavation reports from the Zhengzhou Electric Power School). In *Zhengzhou Shangcheng kaogu xifaxian yu yanjiu* 鄭州商城考古新發現與研究 1985–92, 162–83. Zhengzhou: Zhongzhou Guji Chubanshe 中州古籍出版社, 1993.

Henan Sheng Wenwu Yanjiusuo 河南省文物研究所 and Zhenping Xian Wenhuaguan 鎮平縣文化館. "Henan Zhenping chutu de Handai jiaocang tiefan he tieqi" 河南鎮平出土的漢代窖藏鐵範和鐵器 (Iron articles and molds for iron casting found in the Han-period hoard unearthed at Zhenping, Henan). *Kaogu* 1982.3: 243–51.

Henan Sheng Xinyang Diqu Wenguanhui 河南省信陽地區文管會 and Luoshan Xian Wenhuaguan 羅山山縣文化館. "Luoshan Tianhu Shang Zhou mudi" 羅山天湖商周墓地 (The Shang and Zhou cemetery at Tianhu in Luoshan). *Kaogu xuebao* 1986.2: 153–97.

Henricks, Robert G. *Lao Tzu's Tao Te Ching: A Translation of the Startling New Documents Found at Guodian*. New York: Columbia University Press, 2000.

———. *Te-tao Ching: A New Translation Based on the Recently Discovered Ma-wang-tui Texts*. New York: Ballantine Books, 1989.

Hinsch, Bret. "Women, Kinship, and Property as Seen in a Han Dynasty Will." *T'oung Pao* 84.1–3 (1998): 1–20.

Ho, Connie Suk-Han. "The Importance of Phonological Awareness and Verbal Short-term Memory to Children's Success in Learning to Read Chinese." *Psychologia* 40.4 (1997): 211–19.

Ho, Connie Suk-Han, and Peter Bryant. "Learning to Read Chinese beyond the Logographic Phase." *Reading Research Quarterly* 32.3 (1997): 276–89.

Holenstein, Elmar. "Double Articulation in Writing." In *Writing in Focus,* edited by Florian Coulmas and Konrad Ehlich, 45–62. Berlin: Mouton, 1983.

Hou Hanshu 後漢書 (The history of the later Han dynasty). By Fan Ye 范曄. 18

vols. Beijing: Zhonghua Shuju, 1965.
Houston, Stephen D., ed. *The First Writing: Script Invention as History and Process*. Cambridge: Cambridge University Press, 2004.
Hsu, Cho-yun. "The Chunqiu Period." In *The Cambridge History of Ancient China*, edited by Loewe and Shaughnessy, 545–86.
———. *Han Agriculture: The Formation of Early Chinese Agrarian Economy (206 B.C.–A.D.220)*. Seattle: University of Washington Press, 1980.
Hu Houxuan 胡厚宣. *Zhanhou Ning Hu xinhuo jiaguji* 戰後寧滬新獲甲骨集 (A collection of oracle bones newly obtained in Nanjing and Shanghai after the war). Shanghai: Laixunge, 1951.
Hu Pingsheng 胡平生. "Fuyang Han jian 'Cang jie pian' de chubu yanjiu" 阜陽漢簡《倉頡篇》的初步研究 (A preliminary study of the *Cangjie pian* in the Fuyang Han bamboo strips). In *Hu Pingsheng jiandu wenwu lunji*, 278–93.
———. "Han jian 'Cangjie pian' xin ziliao" 漢簡《倉頡篇》新資料的研究 (A study of new materials in Han bamboo strips pertaining to the *Cangjie pian*). In *Hu Pingsheng jiandu wenwu lunji* 胡平生簡牘文物論集, 45–69. Taipei: Lantai, 2000.
Hu Pingsheng and Zhang Defang 張德芳. *Dunhuang Xuanquan Han jian shicui* 敦煌懸泉漢簡釋粹 (A study of the best examples of Han bamboo slips from Xuanquan near Dunhuang). Shanghai: Shanghai Guji Chubanshe, 2001.
Huadong Shifan Daxue Zhongguo Wenzi Yanjiu yu Yingyong Zhongxin 華東師範大學中國文字研究與應用中心. *Jinwen yinde* 金文引得 (An index of bronze inscriptions). 2 vols. Nanning: Guangxi Jiaoyu Chubanshe, 2001–2.
Huang Ranwei 黃然伟 (Wong Yin-wai). *Yin Zhou qingtongqi shangci mingwen yanjiu* 殷周青銅器賞賜銘文研究 (A study of bestowal inscriptions on Shang and Zhou bronzes). Hong Kong: Lungmen Bookstore, 1978.
Huang Shengzhang 黃盛璋. "Qin bingqi fenguo, duandai, yu youguan zhidu yanjiu" 秦兵器分國斷代與有關制度研究 (A study of the periodization, geographic distribution, and other related rules and regulations concerning Qin weaponry). *Guwenzi yanjiu* 古文字研究 21 (2001): 227–85.
———. "Yunmeng Qin mu chutu de liangfeng jiaxin yu lishi dili wenti" 雲夢秦墓出土的兩封家信與歷史地理問題 (Two family letters unearthed in the Qin tomb at Yunmeng and issues of historical geography). In *Lishi dili lunji* 歷史地理論集, 545–55. Beijing: Renmin, 1982.
———. "Yunmeng Qin jian 'Biannianji' chubu yanjiu" 雲夢秦簡《編年記》初步研究 (A preliminary study of the "annals" in the Qin bamboo strips found at Yunmeng). *Kaogu xuebao* 考古學報 1977.1: 1–21.
———. "Yunmeng Qin jian bianzheng" 雲夢秦簡辨正 (Transcription and correction of the Qin bamboo strips found at Yunmeng). *Kaogu xuebao* 1979.1: 1–24.

Huang Tianshu 黃天樹. *Yinxu wangbuci de fenlei yu duandai* 殷墟王卜辭的分類與斷代 (Classification and periodization of royal oracle-bone inscriptions from Yinxu). Taipei: Wenjin Chubanshe 文津出版社, 1991.

Hubei Sheng Bowuguan 湖北省博物館. "Yunmeng Dafentou yihao Han mu" 雲夢大墳頭一號漢墓 (Han tomb no. 1 at Dafentou, Yunmeng). *Wenwu ziliao congkan* 文物資料叢刊 4 (1981): 1–28.

Hubei Xiaogan Diqu Di Erqi Yigong Yinong Wenwu Kaogu Xunlian Ban 湖北孝感地區第二期亦工亦農文物考古訓練班. "Hubei Yunmeng Shuihudi shiyi zuo Qin mu fajue jianbao" 湖北雲夢睡虎地十一座秦墓發掘簡報 (A short excavation report on eleven Qin tombs at Shuihudi in Yunmeng, Hubei). *Wenwu* 1976.9: 51–61.

Hue, Chih-Wei, and James R. Erickson. "Short-term Memory for Chinese Characters and Radicals." *Memory & Cognition* 16.3 (1988): 196–205.

Hulsewé, A. F. P. *Remnants of Ch'in Law: An Annotated Translation of the Ch'in Legal and Administrative Rules of the 3rd Century B.C., Discovered in Yün-Meng Prefecture, Hu-Pei Province, in 1975*. Leiden: E. J. Brill, 1985.

——. "The Shuo-wen Dictionary as a Source for Ancient Chinese Law." In *Studia Serica Bernhard Karlgren Dedicata*, edited by Søren Egerod and Else Glahn, 239–58. Copenhagen: Munksgaard, 1959.

Hunan Sheng Wenwu Kaogu Yanjiusuo 湖南省文物考古研究所. *Liye fajue baogao* 里耶發掘報告 (Excavation report from Liye). Changsha: Yuelu Shushe 岳麓書社, 2007.

Hwang, Ming-chorng. "Ming-tang: Cosmology, Political Order and Monuments in Early China." PhD diss., Harvard University, 1996.

Hyman, Malcolm. "Of Glyphs and Glottography." *Language & Communication* 26 (2006): 231–49.

Ikeda Yūichi 池田雄一. "Kohoku Unmei Suikochi Shin bo kanken" 湖北雲夢睡虎地秦墓管見 (My own view of the Qin tombs at Shuihudi in Yunmeng, Hubei). *Chūō daigaku bungakubu kiyō* 中央大學文學部紀要 100 (1981): 33–66.

Institute of Archaeology (Chinese Academy of Social Sciences): see Zhongguo Shehui Kexueyuan Kaogu Yanjiusuo.

Itō Michiharu 伊藤道治, and Takashima Ken-ichi 高嶋謙一. *Studies in Early Chinese Civilization: Religion, Society, Language and Palaeography*. 2 vols. Part I: "Religion and Society," by Itō (vol. 1, 1–178); Part II: "Language and Palaeography," by Takashima (vol. 1, 179–505). Osaka: Kansai Gaidai University Press, 1996.

Jakobson, Roman. "Quest for the Essence of Language." In *On Language*, edited by Linda R. Waugh and Monique Monville-Burston, 407–21. Cambridge, Mass.: Harvard University Press, 1990.

Jianbo shufa xuan bianji zu 簡帛書法選編輯組. *Guodian Chu mu zhujian: Tang*

Yu zhi dao 郭店楚墓竹簡：唐虞之道 (Bamboo slips from the Chu tomb at Guodian: "The way of Tang and Yu"). Beijing: Xinhua Shudian, 2002; *ibid., Xing zi ming chu* 性自命出 ("Human nature emerges from destiny").

Jiang Xiaoyuan 江曉原. *Tianxue zhenyuan* 天學真原 (The true origin of the study of the heavens). Shenyang: Liaoning Jiaoyu Chubanshe, 1991; revised edition, 2004.

Jin Zutong 金祖同. *Yinqi yizhu* 殷契遺珠 (Reliquary treasures of the Shang oracle bones). Shanghai: Zhongfa Wenhua, 1939; reprint, Taipei: Yinwen Yinshuguan, 1974.

Jingdian shiwen 經典釋文 (Explicating the texts of the canonical books). By Lu Deming 陸德明. Beijing: Zhonghua Shuju, 1983.

Jingmen Shi Bowuguan 荊門市博物館. *Guodian Chu mu zhujian* 郭店楚墓竹簡 (Bamboo strips from the Chu tomb at Guodian). Beijing: Wenwu Chubanshe, 1998.

Jinshu 晉書 (The history of the Jin dynasty). By Fang Xuanling 房玄齡 et al.. *Sibu beiyao* 四部備要 edition. Taipei: Zhonghua Shuju, 1965.

Jinwen yinde 金文引得. See bove, Huadong Shifan Daxue Zhongguo Wenzi Yanjiu yu Yingyong Zhongxin 華東師範大學中國文字研究與應用中心.

Johnson, George. "Place-names." In *The Educational Review Supplementary Readings*, edited by George Hay, 1898.4, 87–94. Saint John, New Brunswick, Canada: Barnes & Co., 1900.

Johnson, William A., and Holt N. Parker, eds. *Ancient Literacies: The Culture of Reading in Greece and Rome*. Oxford: Oxford University Press, 2009.

Kaiho, Hiroyuki 海保博之, and Hirofumi Saito 齋藤洋典. "Measuring Various Aspects of Kanji (Chinese Characters) and Its Psychological Implications." *Quantitative Linguistics* 39 (1989): 151–63.

Kalinowski, Marc. "La production des manuscrits dans la Chine ancienne: Une approche codicologique de la bibliothèque funéraire de Mawangdui." *Asiatische Studien / Études Asiatiques* 59.1 (2005): 131–68.

Kane, Virginia C. "Aspects of Western Zhou Appointment Inscriptions: The Charge, the Gifts, and the Response." *Early China* 8 (1982–83): 14–28.

Karlgren, Bernhard. *The Book of Odes*. Stockholm: Museum of Far Eastern Antiquities, 1950.

——. "Glosses on the Book of Documents." *Bulletin of the Museum of Far Eastern Antiquities* 20 (1948): 39–315.

Ke Heli 柯鶴立. See Constance A. Cook.

Keightley, David N. *The Ancestral Landscape: Time, Space, and Community in Late Shang China (ca. 1200–1045 B.C.)*. Berkeley: Institute of East Asian Studies, University of California, 2000.

——. "The Origins of Writing in China: Scripts and Cultural Contexts." In *The Origins of Writing*, edited by W. M. Senner, 171–202. Lincoln: University of Nebraska Press, 1989.

——. "Public Work in Ancient China: A Study of Forced Labor in the Shang and Western Chou." PhD diss., Columbia University, 1969.

——. *Sources of Shang History: The Oracle-Bone Inscriptions of Bronze Age China*. Berkeley: University of California Press, 1978.

Kennedy, George A. "The Butterfly Case (part I)." *Wenti* 8 (1955): 1–25. Reprinted in *Selected Works of George A. Kennedy*, edited by Tien-yi Li, 274–322. New Haven, Conn.: Yale University Press, 1964.

——. "The Monosyllabic Myth." *Journal of the American Oriental Society* 71.3 (1951): 161–66. Reprinted in *Selected Works of George A. Kennedy*, edited by Tien-yi Li, 104–18. New Haven, Conn.: Yale University Press, 1964.

Kern, Martin. "Bronze Inscriptions, the *Shijing* and the *Shangshu*: The Evolution of the Ancestral Sacrifice During the Western Zhou." In *Early Chinese Religion*, edited by Lagerwey and Kalinowski, 143–200.

——. "Methodological Reflections on the Analysis of Textual Variants and the Modes of Manuscript Production in Early China." *Journal of East Asian Archaeology* 4.1–4 (2002): 143–81.

——. "The *Odes* in Excavated Manuscripts." In *Text and Ritual in Early China*, edited by Martin Kern, 149–93.

——. "The Performance of Writing in Western Zhou China." In *The Poetics of Grammar and the Metaphysics of Sound and Sign*, edited by Sergio La Porta and David Shulman, 122–26, 155–57. Leiden: E. J. Brill, 2007.

——. "Shi Jing Songs as Performance Texts: A Case Study of 'Chu Ci' (Thorny Caltrop)." *Early China* 25 (2000): 49–111.

——. *The Stele Inscriptions of Ch'in Shih-huang: Text and Ritual in Early Chinese Imperial Representation*. New Haven, Conn.: American Oriental Society, 2000.

——, ed. *Text and Ritual in Early China*. Seattle: University of Washington Press, 2005.

Kimura Hideumi 木村秀海. "Sei Shū kinbun ni mieru shōshi ni tsuite: Sei Shū no shihai kikō no ichimen" 西周金文にえる見小子について — 西周の支配機構の一面 (On the *xiǎozǐ* appearing in Western Zhou bronze inscriptions: One aspect of the control mechanism of the Western Zhou). *Shirin* 史林64.6 (1981): 62–82.

Knoblock, John. *Xunzi: A Translation and Study of the Complete Works*. 3 vols. Palo Alto, Calif.: Stanford University Press, 1994.

Knoblock, John, and Jeffrey Riegel. *The Annals of Lü Buwei*. Stanford, Calif.: Stanford University Press, 2000.

Kramer, Samuel Noah. "Schooldays: A Sumerian Composition Relating to the Education of a Scribe." *Journal of the American Oriental Society* 69.4 (1949): 199–215.

Krumbacher, Karl. *Das Problem der neugriechischen Schriftsprache*. Munich: Königliche Bayerische Akademie, 1902.

Kryukov, Mikhail. " K probleme tsiklicheskikh znakov v Drevnem Kitae (Toward the problem of cyclical signs in Ancient China)." In *Drevnye sistemy pis'ma—etnicheskaja semiotika* (Archaic writing systems—ethnic semiotics), edited by Ju.V. Knorozov, 107–13. Moscow: Nauka, 1986.

Lagerwey, J., and M. Kalinowski, eds. *Early Chinese Religion*. 2 vols. Leiden: E. J. Brill, 2008.

Lau, D. C., trans. *Tao Te Ching*. Hong Kong: Chinese University Press, 1982 (1996).

Lau, Ulrich. *Quellenstudien zur Landvergabe und Bodenübertragung in der Westlichen Zhou-Dynastie (1045?–771 v. Chr.)*, Monumenta Serica Monograph Series, vol. 41. Nettetal, Germany: Steyler Verlag, 1999.

Laurencich Minelli, Laura, and Giulio Magli. "A Calendar *Quipu* of the Early 17th Century and Its Relationship with the Inca Astronomy." *History of Physics* 801 (*ArXiv e-prints*, January 2008; arXiv:0801.1577v1, Web version).

Ledderose, Lothar. *Ten Thousand Things: Module and Mass Production in Chinese Art*. Princeton, N.J.: Princeton University Press, 2000.

Lee, Thomas H. C. *Education in Traditional China: A History*. Leiden: E. J. Brill, 2000.

Legge, James, trans. *The Li Ki (Sacred Books of China)*. Vols. 3, 16, 27, 28, 39, and 40 of *The Sacred Books of the East*, edited by F. Max Müller. Oxford: Clarendon Press, 1885; reprint, Delhi: Motilal Banarsidass Publishers, 2001.

———, trans. *The Shoo King*. Vol. 3 of *The Chinese Classics*. Oxford: Clarendon Press, 1865; reprint, Taipei, Southern Materials Center, 1991.

Lévi-Strauss, Claude. *Tristes Tropiques* Translated by John Russell. New York: Criterion, 1961.

Lewis, Mark Edward. *Writing and Authority in Early China*. Albany: State University of New York Press, 1999.

Li, Fang-Kuei (F.K. Li) 李方桂. "Shanggu yin" 上古音 (Old Chinese phonology). *The Tsing Hua Journal of Chinese Studies* 清華學報, n.s. 9, nos. 1 and 2 (1971): 1–61. Reprinted as monograph, Beijing: Shangwu Yinshuguan 商務印書館, 1980.

Li, Feng. "Ancient Reproductions and Calligraphic Variations: Studies of Western Zhou Bronzes with Identical Inscriptions." *Early China* 22 (1997): 15–36.

———. *Bureaucracy and the State in Early China: Governing the Western Zhou*. Cambridge: Cambridge University Press, 2008.

———. *Landscape and Power in Early China: The Crisis and Fall of the Western Zhou, 1045–771 B.C.* Cambridge: Cambridge University Press, 2006.

———. "Literacy Crossing Cultural Borders: Evidence from the Bronze Inscriptions of the Western Zhou Period (1045–771 B.C.)." *Bulletin of the Museum of Far Eastern Antiquities* 74 (2002): 210–42.

———. "'Offices' in Bronze Inscriptions and Western Zhou Government Administration." *Early China* 26–27 (2001–2): 1–72.

———. "Succession and Promotion: Elite Mobility During the Western Zhou."

Monumenta Serica 52 (2004): 1–35.

Li, Min. *Conquest, Concord, and Consumption: Becoming Shang in Eastern China*. PhD diss., University of Michigan, 2008.

Li, Wai-yee. *The Readability of the Past in Early Chinese Historiography*. Cambridge, MA: Harvard University Press, 2007.

Li Chaoyuan 李朝遠. "Hu gui wei Li wang zhi qi xianyi" 㝬簋為厲王之器說獻疑 (Some doubts about the theory that the Hu *gui* is a vessel of King Li). *Guwenzi yanjiu* 24 (2002): 220–224.

——. "Xi Zhou jinwen zhong de wang yu wangqi" 西周金文中的王與王器 (*Wáng* "king" and *wángqì* "royal vessel" in the Western Zhou bronze inscriptions). *Wenwu* 2006.5: 74–79.

Li Junming 李均明. "Zhangjiashan Han jian suojian guifan jicheng guanxi de falü" 張家山漢簡所見規範繼承關係的法律 (The law on regulating inheritance relationships appearing in the Han bamboo slips from Zhangjiashan). *Zhongguo lishi wenwu* 中國歷史文物 2.37 (2002): 26–32.

Li Junming and Liu Jun 劉軍. *Jiandu wenshu xue* 簡牘文書學 (The study of correspondence and documents). Nanning: Guangxi Jiaoyu Chubanshe 廣西教育出版社, 1999.

Li Li 李力. *'Lichenqie' shenfen zai yanjiu* '隸臣妾' 身份再研究 (A further study of the status of *lìchénqiè* "male and female bondservants"). Beijing: Zhongguo Falü Chubanshe 中國法律出版社, 2007.

Li Ling 李零. "Du Yangjiacun chutu de Yu Qiu zhuqi" 讀楊家村出土的虞逑諸器 (Reading the Yu Qiu vessels unearthed at Yangjiacun). *Zhongguo lishi wenwu* 2003.4: 16–27.

Li Minling 李旼姈. *Jiagu wenli yanjiu* 甲骨文例研究 (Illustrative passages from the oracle bone inscriptions). Taipei: Taiwan Guji Chuban Youxian Gongsi 臺灣古籍出版有限公司, 2002.

Li Qingli 李清莉. "Guoguo bowuguan shoucang de yijian tong xu" 虢國博物館收藏的一件銅盨 (A bronze *xu*-vessel in the collection of the Guoguo Museum). *Wenwu* 2004.4: 90.

Li Tianhong 李天虹. *Juyan Han jian buji fenlei yanjiu* 居延漢簡簿籍分類研究 (A classified study of the accounting records in the Han bamboo slips from Juyuan). Beijing: Kexue Chubanshe, 2003.

Li Weiming 李維明. "Bo bian" 亳辨 (Identifying "Bo"). In *2004 nian Anyang Yin Shang wenming guoji xueshu yantaohui lunwenji*, edited by Wang Yuxin, Song Zhenhao, and Meng Xianwu, 404–10. Also in *Zhongyuan wenwu* 中原文物 2006.6: 39–45.

Li Xiaoding 李孝定. *Jiagu wenzi jishi* 甲骨文字集釋 (Collected decipherings of oracle bone characters). Zhongyang Yanjiuyuan Lishi Yuyan Yanjiusuo Zhuankan 中央研究院歷史語言研究所專刊 50. 14 vols. Taipei:

Zhongyang Yanjiuyuan Lishi Yuyan Yanjiusuo 中央研究院歷史語言研究所, 1970.

Li Xueqin 李學勤. "Daxinzhuang jiagu buci de chubu kaocha" 大辛莊甲骨卜辭的初步考察 (Preliminary examination of oracle bone inscriptions from Daxinzhuang). *Wenshizhe* 文史哲 2003.4: 7–8.

———. *Li Xueqin zaoqi wenji* 李學勤早期文集 (A collection of Li Xueqin's early works). Shijiazhuang: Hebei Jiaoyu Chubanshe 河北教育出版社, 2008.

———. "Meixian Yangjiacun xinchu qingtongqi yanjiu" 眉縣楊家村新出青銅器研究 (A study of the bronze vessels newly unearthed at Yangjiacun in Meixian). *Wenwu* 2003.6: 66–73.

———. "Rongsheng bianzhong lunshi" 戎生編鐘論釋 (Discussion and transcription of the inscriptions on the Rongsheng bell set). *Wenwu* 1999.9: 75–82.

———. "Shishuo Zhangjiashan jian 'Shi lü'" 試說張家山漢簡史律 (A tentative theory about the *shǐ lǜ* "statutes pertaining to scribes" in the Han bamboo slips from Zhangjiashan). *Wenwu* 2002.4: 69–72.

———. "Tan Anyang Xiaotun yiwai chutu de youzi jiagu" 談安陽小屯以外出土的有字甲骨 (Inscribed bones unearthed in places other than Anyang Xiaotun). *Wenwu cankao ziliao* 文物參考資料 1956.11: 16–17. Reprinted in *Li Xueqin zaoqi wenji*, by Li Xueqin, 33–37.

———. "Zhanguo shidai de Qin guo tongqi" 戰國時代的秦國銅器 (Qin bronzes from the Warring States period). *Wenwu cankao ziliao* 1957.8: 38–40, 53.

———. "Zhanguo timing gaishu" (xia) 戰國題銘概述（下）(General description of Warring States period inscriptions [second part]). *Wenwu* 1959.9: 58–61.

———. "Zhengzhou Erligang zigu de yanjiu" 鄭州二里岡字骨的研究 (Studies of the inscribed bones from Erligang in Zhengzhou). *Zhongguo shehui kexueyuan lishi yanjiusuo xuekan* 中國社會科學院歷史研究所學刊 2001.1: 1–5.

Li Xueqin and Yushang Peng 彭裕商. *Yinxu jiagu fenqi yanjiu* 殷墟甲骨分期研究 (Studies of periodization of the bone inscriptions from Yinxu). Shanghai: Shanghai Guji Chubanshe 上海古籍出版社, 1996.

Li Xueqin and Yuxin Wang 王宇信. "Zhouyuan buci xuanshi" 周原卜辭選釋 (Interpretations of the selected pieces of Zhouyuan oracle-bone inscriptions). *Guwenzi yanjiu* 古文字研究 4 (1980): 245–57.

Li Xueshan 李雪山. "Zhenren wei fengguo shouling laichao zhizhang zhanbu jisi zhi guan" 貞人爲封國首領來朝職掌占卜祭祀之官 (Diviners as the leaders of the local states serving as divination-ritual officers in the Shang court). In *Title TK*, edited by Wang Yuxin, Song Zhenhao, and Meng Xianwu, eds., 284–93.

Lin Qingyuan 林清源. *Jiandu boshu biaoti geshi yanjiu* 簡牘帛書標題格式研究 (A study of the form of the headings in wooden and silk manuscripts).

Taipei: Yiwen, 2004.

Lin Yun 林澐. "Zhousheng *gui* xinshi" 琱生簋新釋 (A new transcription of the Zhousheng *gui*). *Guwenzi yanjiu* 古文字研究 3 (1980): 120–35.

Liu, Ciyuan, Liu Xueshun, and Ma Liping. "A Chinese Observatory Site of 4,000 Year [*sic*] Ago." *Journal of Astronomical History and Heritage* 8.2 (2005): 129–30.

Liu Hainian 劉海年, "Qin Han 'shiwu' de shenfen yu jieji diwei" 秦漢士伍的身份與階級地位 (On the sataus and class position of *shìwǔ* in Qin and Han), *Wenwu* 文物 1978.2: 58–62. Reprinted in *Zhanguo Qin dai fazhi guankui* 戰國秦代法制管窺, 313–21. Beijing: Falü Chubanshe, 2006.

———. "Cong Qin jian 'Wei li zhi dao' kan Qin de 'Zhi li' sixiang" 從秦簡《為吏之道》看秦的'治吏'思想 (The Qin idea of "Controlling officials" as seen in the *Wei li zhi dao* of the Qin bamboo strips). In *Zhanguo Qin dai fazhi guankui* 戰國秦代法制管窺, 364–77. Beijing: Falü Chubanshe, 2006.

Liu Huaijun 劉懷君. "Meixian chutu yipi Xi Zhou jiaocang qingtong yueqi" 眉縣出土一批西周窖藏青銅樂器 (A set of bronze bells from a Western Zhou pit, unearthed in Meixian). *Wenbo* 1987.2: 17–25.

Liu Xiaogan 劉笑敢. "From Bamboo Slips to Received Versions: Common Features in the Transformation of the *Laozi*." *Harvard Journal of Asiatic Studies* 63.2 (2003): 337–82.

———. *Laozi gu jin: wu zhong duikan yu xiping yinlun* 老子古今：五種對勘與析評引論 (*Laozi* past and present: Five collations and a critical introduction). 2 vols. Beijing: Zhongguo Shehui Kexue Chubanshe, 2006.

Liu Xinyuan 劉心源. *Qigushi jijin wen shu* 奇觚室吉金文述 (An exposition of bronze vessels inscriptions of Qigushi). 1902.

Liu Yiman 劉一曼. "Yinxu shougu keci chutan" 殷墟獸骨刻辭初探 (Initial inquiry into the inscriptions on the animal bones from Yinxu). *Yinxu bowuyuan yuankan* 殷墟博物苑苑刊, Chuangkan hao 創刊號, 1989: 113–21.

Liu Yin 劉寅. *Wujing qishu zhijie* 武經七書直解 (A literal explication of the Seven Great Military Texts). Changsha: Yuelu Shushe, 1992.

Liu Yu 劉雨. *Jinwen lunji* 金文論集 (Palace Museum Academic Series). Beijing: Zijincheng Chubanshe 紫禁城出版社, 2006.

Loewe, Michael. *Records of Han Administration*. Cambridge: Cambridge University Press, 1967.

Loewe, Michael, and Edward L. Shaughnessy, eds. *The Cambridge History of Ancient China: From the Origins of Civilization to 221 B.C.* Cambridge: Cambridge University Press, 1999.

Lu Liancheng 盧連成. "Xi Zhou Ze guo shiji kaolue jiqi xiangguan wenti" 西周夨國史跡考略及其相關問題 (An investigation into the historical sites of the state of Ze in the Western Zhou and related questions). In *Xi Zhou shi yanjiu* 西周史研究 (Monograph series of *Renwen zazhi* 人文雜志叢刊, no. 2), 232–48. Xi'an: 1984.

Lu Shixian 魯實先. "Buci xingshi tongshi zhi yi" 卜辭姓氏通釋之一 (Comprehensive transcription of surnames in the oracle bone inscriptions: Part I). *Donghai xuebao* 東海學報 1.1 (1956): 1–44.

Lunheng 論衡 (On balance). By Wang Chong 王充. *Sibu beiyao* edition. Taipei: Zhonghua Shuju, 1965.

Luo Tai 羅泰. See Lothar von Falkenhausen.

Luo Zhenyu 羅振玉. *Yinxu shuqi xubian* 殷墟書契續編 (A further compilation of inscriptions from Yinxu). 1933.

——. *Zengding Yinxu shuqi kaoshi* 增訂殷虛書契考釋 (Philological study and transcription of the Yinxu inscriptions enlarged and revised). 1914; reprint, Taipei: Yiwen Yinshuguan 藝文印書館, 1969.

Lurie, David B. "Language, Writing, and Disciplinarity in the Critique of the 'Ideographic Myth': Some Proleptical Remarks." *Language & Communication* 26 (2006): 250–69.

"*Lüshi chunqiu*" *xin jiaozheng* 呂氏春秋新校証 (A new collation of the *Lüshi chunqiu*). Collated by Bi Yuan 畢沅. *Xinbian Zhuzi jicheng* 新編諸子集成 edition, vol. 7. Taipei: Shijie Shuju, 1974.

Ma Chengyuan 馬承源, ed. *Shang Zhou qingtongqi mingwenxuan* 商周青銅器銘文選 (Selected inscriptions from Shang and Zhou bronzes). 4 vols. Beijing: Wenwu Chubanshe, 1986–90.

——, ed. *Shanghai Bowuguan cang Zhanguo Chu zhushu* 上海博物館藏戰國楚竹書 (Warring States bamboo manuscripts in the collection of the Shanghai Museum). Vol. 7. Shanghai: Shanghai Guji Chubanshe, 2007.

Maier, Joseph. *Frank Tannenbaum: A Biographical Essay*. New York: University Seminars, Columbia University, 1974.

Mair, Victor H. "Language and Script: Biology, Archaeology, and (Pre)history." *International Review of Chinese Linguistics* 1.1 (1996): 33b of 31a–41b.

Major, John S. *Heaven and Earth in Early Han Thought*. Albany: State University of New York Press, 1993.

Mann, Charles C. "Cracking the *Khipu* Code." *Science* 300 (1650–51), 13 June 2003.

Martinet, André. *Elements of General Linguistics*. Translated by Elisabeth Palmer. Chicago: University of Chicago Press, 1964, 22–28. (Original, in French: *Éléments de linguistique générale*. Paris: Colin, 1960.)

Matsumaru Michio 松丸道雄. "Jieshao yipian sifang feng ming keci gu" 介紹一片四方風名刻辭骨 (Introducing an inscribed bone with the names of the winds of the four directions). In *Jinian Yinxu jiaguwen faxian yi bai zhou nian guoji xueshu yantao hui lunwenji* 紀念殷墟甲骨文發現一百周年國際

學術研討會, edited by Wang Yuxin 王宇信 and Song Zhenhao 宋鎮豪, 83–87. Beijing: Shehui Kexue Wenxian Chubanshe 社會科學文獻出版社, 2003.

———. "Kanji kigen mondai no shintenkai: Santō shō Suihei ken shutsudo no 'Teikō tōhen' o megutte" 漢字起源問題の新展開 — 山東省鄒平縣出土の「丁公陶片」をめぐって (A new development in the problem of the origin of Chinese characters: On the "Dinggong potsherd" unearthed in Zouping County, Shandong Province). In *Chūgoku kodai no moji to bunka* 中國古代の文字と文化, 3–29. Tokyo: Kyūko Shoin 汲古書院, 1999.

———. "Sei Shū jidai no jōryō tan'i" 西周時代の重量單位. *Tōyō bunka kenkyūjo kiyō* 117 (1992): 47–56.

———. "Sei Shū seidōki seisaku no haikei: Shū kinbun kenkyū, joshō" 西周青銅器製作の背景 — 周金文研究（序章）(The background of the manufacture of Western Zhou bronzes: A study of Zhou bronze inscriptions, preface). *Tōyō bunka kenkyūjo kiyō* 東洋研究所紀要 72 (1977): 1–128. Reprinted in *Sei Shū seidōki to sono kokka*, edited by Matsumaru Michio, 11–136.

Matsumaru Michio 松丸道雄 ed. *Sei Shū seidōki to sono kokka* 西周青銅器とその国家. Tokyo: Tōkyō daigaku 東京大學, 1980.

Matsumaru Michio 松丸道雄 and Takashima Kenichi 高嶋謙一. *Kōkotsu moji jishaku sōran* 甲骨文字字釈総覧 (An overview of oracle bone character-explanations). Tokyo: Tōkyō Daigaku, 1993.

Mattingly, Ignatius G., and Pai-ling Hsiao. "Are Phonetic Elements in Chinese Characters Drawn from a Syllabary?" *Psychologia* 42.4 (December 1999): 281–89. Department of Educational Psychology of the Faculty of Education, Kyoto University.

Mattingly, Ignatius G., and Yi Xu. "Word Superiority in Chinese." *Haskins Laboratories Status Report on Speech Research* 113 (1993): 145–51.

Mattos, Gilbert. "Eastern Zhou Inscriptions." In *New Sources of Early Chinese History*, edited by Edward L. Shaughnessy, 85–123.

McCurley, Dallas. "Performing Patterns: Numinous Relations in Shang and Zhou China." *Drama Review* 49.3 (2005): 135–56.

McLeod, Katrina C.D., and Robin D.S. Yates. "Forms of Ch'in Law: An Annotated Translation of the *Feng-chen shih*." *Harvard Journal of Asiatic Studies* 41.1 (1981): 121.

Meng, Xiangzhi, Hua Shu, and Xiaolin Zhou. "Children's Chinese Characters Structure Awareness in Character Output." *Psychological Science* (China) 23.3 (2000): 260–64.

Mengzi 孟子 (The Mencius). *Zhuzi jicheng* 諸子集成 edition, vol. 1. Shanghai: Shanghai Shudian, 1986; reprint, 1991.

Midant-Reynes, B., and Y. Tristant, eds. *Egypt at Its Origins 2*. Louvain, Belgium: Peeters, 2008.

Ministry of Education (PRC). "Ordinances for Eliminating Illiteracy." http://www.moe.edu.cn/edoas/website18/15/info3915.htm (accessed 5 January 2010).

Miranda, Noemi, et al. "Uncovering Seshat: New Insights at the Stretching of the Cord Ceremony," in *Archaeologia Baltica: Astronomy and Cosmology in Folk Traditions and Cultural Heritage*. Klaipeda, Lithuania: University of Klaipeda, 2008, 57–61.

Moore, Oliver. *Chinese*. Berkeley: University of California Press, 2000.

Mou, Lien-chong, and Nancy S. Anderson. "Graphemic and Phonemic Codings of Chinese Characters in Short-term Retention." *Bulletin of the Psychonomic Society* 17.6 (1981): 255–58.

Mozi 墨子 (The *Mozi*). *Zhuzi jicheng* 諸子集成 edition, vol. 4. 1986; reprint, Shanghai: Shanghai Shudian, 1991.

Mu Xiaojun 穆曉軍. "Shaanxi Chang'an xian chutu Xi Zhou Wu Hu *ding*" 陝西長安縣出土西周吳虎鼎 (The Wu Hu *ding* unearthed in Chang'an County, Shaanxi). *Kaogu yu wenwu* 1998.3: 69–71.

Mullis, Eric C. "Toward a Confucian Ethic of the Gift." *Dao* 7.2 (2008): 175–94.

Musha Akira 武者章. "Sei Shū satsumei kinbun bunrui no kokoromi" 西周冊命金文分類の試み (An attempt to classify the appointment bronze inscriptions of the Western Zhou). In *Sei Shū seidōki to sono kokka*, edited by Matsumaru Michio, 241–324.

Nguyễn, Đình-Hoà. *Essential English-Vietnamese Dictionary*. Boston: Tuttle Publishing, 1983.

Nissen, Hans J., Peter Damerow, and Robert K. Englund. *Archaic Bookkeeping: Writing and Techniques of Economic Administration in the Ancient Near East*. Chicago: University of Chicago Press, 1993.

Nivison, David S. "The Classical Philosophical Writings." In *The Cambridge History of Ancient China*, edited by Loewe and Shaughnessy, 745–812.

———. "The 'Question' Question." *Early China* 14 (1989): 115–25.

Norman, Jerry, and W. South Coblin. "A New Approach to Chinese Historical Linguistics." *Journal of the American Oriental Society* 115.4 (1995): 576–84.

Nylan, Michael. "Toward an Archaeology of Writing." In *Text and Ritual in Early China*, edited by Martin Kern, 3–49.

Okamura Hidenori 岡村秀典. *Chūgoku kodai ōken to saishi* 中國古代王權と祭祀 (The sovereignty and sacrifices in ancient China). Tokyo: Gakuseisha 學生社, 2005.

Olson, David R. *The World on Paper: The Conceptual and Cognitive Implications of Writing and Reading*. Cambridge: Cambridge University Press, 1994.

Ōnishi Katsuya 大西克也. "'I,' 'ya' no kōtai: Rikkoku tōitsu zengo ni okeru shomen gengo no issokumen"「殹」「也」の交替 ── 六国統一前後に於ける書面言語の一側面 (The alternation of *yì* and *yě*: a side aspect of written language around the unification of the Six States). *Chūgoku shutsudo shiryō kenkyū* 中國出土資料研究 2 (1998): 4–24.

Pankenier, David W. (Ban Dawei 班大為). "Astronomical Dates in Shang and Western Zhou." *Early China* 20 (1995): 121–76.

———. "Beiji de faxian yu yingyong" 北極的發現與應用 (The discovery and use of Northern Culmen). *Ziran kexueshi yanjiu* 自然科學史研究 (Studies in the history of natural sciences) 27.3 (2008): 281–300.

———. "A Brief History of Beiji 北極 (Northern Culmen), with an Excursus on the Origin of the Character *di* 帝." *Journal of the American Oriental Society* 124.2 (2004): 211–36.

———. *Bringing Heaven down to Earth: Astrological and Cosmological Foundations of Chinese Civilization*. New York: Cambridge University Press, forthcoming.

———. "Characteristics of Field Allocation (*fenye* 分野) Astrology in Early China." In *Current Studies in Archaeoastronomy: Conversations across Time and Space*, edited by J. W. Fountain and R. M. Sinclair, 499–513. Durham, N.C.: Carolina Academic Press, 2005.

———. "The Cosmo-Political Background of Heaven's Mandate." *Early China* 7 (1995): 2–37.

———. "Zai tan beiji jianshi yu di zi de qiyuan" 再談北極簡史與帝字的起源 (Another brief history of *beiji* 北極 [Northern Culmen] and the origin of the graph *di* 帝 [Supreme Lord]). In *Xi fang Zhongguo shi yanjiu luncong* 西方中國史研究論叢 (Western Research on China: Collected Essays), edited by Patricia Ebrey and Yao Ping. Vol. 1: *Gudai shi yanjiu* 古代史研究 (Research on Ancient History), edited by Chen Zhi. Shanghai: Shanghai Guji Chubanshe, in press.

Pankenier, David W., Liu Ciyuan, and Salvo de Meis. "The Xiangfen, Taosi Site: A Chinese Neolithic 'Observatory'?" In *Archaeologia Baltica: Astronomy and Cosmology in Folk Traditions and Cultural Heritage*, 45–55. Klaipeda, Lithuania: University of Klaipeda Press, 2009.

Parkes, M. B. *Pause and Effect: An Introduction to the History of Punctuation in the West*. Berkeley: University of California Press, 1993.

Pei Mingxiang 裴明相. "Lüe tan Zhengzhou Shangdai qianqi de guke wenzi" 略談鄭州商代前期的骨刻文字 (A short discussion of the Zhengzhou bone inscriptions of the early Shang period). In *Quanguo Shangshi xueshu taolunhui lunwenji* 全國商史學術討論會論文集 (Collected essays from a national scholarly symposium on the study of Shang history), edited by Hu Houxuan 胡厚宣 (*Yindu xuekan zengkan* 殷都學刊增刊), 251–53.

Peng Hao 彭浩, Chen Wei 陳偉, and Kudō Motoo 工藤元男, eds. *Ernian lüling yu zouyanshu: Zhangjiashan er si qi hao Han mu chutu falü wenxian shidu* 二年律令與奏讞書：張家山二四七號漢墓出土法律文獻釋讀 (The

Second-year Statutes and the memorial documents on legal decisions: Transcription and readings in statutory documents unearthed in Tomb 247 at Zhangjiashan). Shanghai: Shanghai Guji Chubanshe, 2007.

Peng Lin 彭林. *Zhouli zhuti sixiang yu chengshu niandai yanjiu* 周禮主體思想與成書年代研究 (A study of the principal thoughts and time of the formation of the *Zhouli*). Hebei: Zhongguo Shehui Kexue, 1991.

Pines, Yuri. *Foundations of Confucian Thought: Intellectual Life in the Chunqiu Period.* Honolulu: University of Hawai'i Press, 2002.

———. "History as a Guide to the Netherworld: Rethinking the *Chunqiu shiyu*." *Journal of Chinese Religions* 31 (2003): 101–26.

———. "The Question of Interpretation: Qin History in Light of New Epigraphic Sources." *Early China* 29 (2004): 1–44.

Plato: Phaedrus. Translated by Alexander Nehamas and Paul Woodruff. Indianapolis, Ind.: Hackett, 1995.

Pollatsek, Alexander, Tan Li Hai, and Rayner, Keith. "The Role of Phonological Codes in Integrating Information across Saccadic Eye Movements in Chinese Character Identification." *Journal of Experimental Psychology: Human Perception and Performance* 26.2 (2000): 607–33.

Postgate, Nicholas, Tao Wang, and Toby Wilkinson. "The Evidence for Early Writing: Utilitarian or Ceremonial?" *Antiquity* 69.264 (1995): 459–80.

Pound, Ezra. Appendix to *The Chinese Written Character as a Medium for Poetry*, by Ernest Francisco Fenollosa (written before 1908). San Francisco: City Lights Books, 1936.

Pu Maozuo 濮茅左, transcriber. "Jing gong nüe" 競（景）公瘧 (The Jing gong nüe). In *Shanghai bowuguan cang Zhanguo Chu zhushu* 上海博物館藏戰國楚竹書, edited by Ma Chengyuan 馬承源. Vol. 7. Shanghai: Shanghai Guji Chubanshe, 2007.

Puett, Michael. *To Become a God: Cosmology, Sacrifice, and Self-Divination in Early China*. Cambridge, Mass.: Harvard University Press, 2002.

Pulleyblank, Edwin G. "The *Ganzhi* as Phonograms and Their Application to the Calendar." *Early China* 24 (1991): 39–80.

Qi Wenxin 齊文心. "Shi du 'Zhi jia cheng ce' xiangguan buci" 釋讀 '㞢叚爯冊' 相關卜辭 (A transcription and reading of oracle bone inscriptions related to the phrase *zhi jia cheng ce*). In *2004 nian Anyang Yin Shang wenming guoji xueshu yantaohui lunwenji*, edited by Wang Yuxin, Song Zhenhao, and Meng Xianwu, 251–60.

Qiu Xigui 裘錫圭. *Chinese Writing*. Translated by Gilbert L. Mattos and Jerry Norman. Berkeley: Society for the Study of Early China and Institute of East Asian Studies, University of California, 2000.

———. "Du Qiu qi mingwen zhaji sanze" 讀逑器銘文札記三則 (Three reading notes on the inscription from the Qiu vessel). *Wenwu* 2003.6: 74–77.

——. "Jiujing shibushi wenzi: Tantan woguo xin shiqi shidai shiyong de fuhao" 究竟是不是文字: 談談我國新石器時代使用的符號 (Is it writing or not? A discussion of marks used in our country during the Neolithic). *Wenwu tiandi* 1993.2: 26–30.

——. "Lun Lizu buci de shidai" 論歷組卜辭的時代 (Discussion on the date of the Li-group oracle bone inscriptions). *Guwenzi yanjiu* 古文字研究 1981.6: 263–321.

——. "Mawangdui boshu *Laozi* yi ben juan qian gu yishu bing fei *Huangdi sijing*" 馬王堆帛書《老子》乙本卷前古佚書並非《黃帝四經》 (The unknown ancient texts at the head of *Laozi* MS. B are not the *Huangdi sijing*). In *Daojia wenhua yanjiu* 道家文化研究 3, edited by Chen Guying 陳鼓應, 249–55. Shanghai: Shanghai Guji Chubanshe, 1993.

——. *Wenzixue gaiyao* 文字學概要 (An outline of the study of the Chinese script). Beijing: Shangwu Yinshuguan, 2003 [1988]. Translated as *Chinese Writing*.

Qu Wanli 屈萬里. *Shijing shiyi* 詩經釋義 (Interpreting the *Shijing*). Taipei: Huagang Chubanshe, 1977.

Rawski, Evelyn Sakakida. *Education and Popular Literacy in Ch'ing China*. Ann Arbor: University of Michigan Press, 1979.

Regulski, Ilona. "The Origin of Writing in Relation to the Emergence of the Egyptian State." In *Egypt at Its Origins 2*, edited by B. Midant-Reyes and Y. Tristant, 985–1009.

Richter, Matthias. "Der Alte und das Wasser: Lesarten von *Laozi* 8 im überlieferten Text und in den Manuskripten von Mawangdui." In *Han-Zeit: Festschrift für Hans Stumpfeldt aus Anlaß seines 65: Geburtstages*, edited by Michael Friedrich, Reinhard Emmerich, and Hans van Ess, 253–73. Wiesbaden, Germany: Harrassowitz, 2006.

——. "Towards a Profile of Graphic Variation: On the Distribution of Graphic Variants within the Mawangdui *Laozi* Manuscripts." *Asiatische Studien / Études Asiatiques* 59.1 (2005): 169–207.

Rong Geng 容庚. *Jinwenbian* 金文編 (A compilation of bronze inscriptions). Beijing: Zhonghua Shuju, 1985.

——. *Shang Zhou yiqi tongkao* 商周彝器通攷 (General research on the ritual vessels of the Shang and Zhou). Beiping: Yanjing Daxue, 1940.

Roth, Harold D. *Original Tao: Inward Training (Nei-yeh) and the Foundations of Taoist Mysticism*. New York: Columbia University Press, 1999.

——. "Text and Edition in Early Chinese Philosophical Literature." *Journal of American Oriental Studies* 113 (1993): 214–27.

Ruggles, Clive L.N. "Whose Equinox?" *Archaeoastronomy* 22 (supplement to *Journal for the History of Astronomy* 28 [1997]): 545–50.

Sahara, Yasuo 佐原康夫. "Kandai no ichi ni tsuite" 漢代の市について (On Han-period markets). *Shirin* 史林 68.5 (1985): 33–71.

——. "Senkoku jidai no fuko ni tsuite" 戦国時代の府庫について (Treasuries and depots during the Warring States period). *Tōyōshi kenkyū* 43.1 (1984): 31–59.

Sakuma, Naoko, Itoh Motonobu, and Sasanuma Sumiko. "Recognition Units of Kanji Words: Priming Effects on Kanji Recognition." *Shinrigaku kenkyu* 心理学研究 (The Japanese journal of psychology) 60.1 (1989): 1–8.

Sampson, Geoffrey. *Writing Systems*. Stanford, Calif.: Stanford University Press, 1985.

Sarnat, Bernard G. "Gross Growth and Regrowth of Sutures: Reflections on Some Personal Research." *Journal of Craniofacial Surgery* 2003.14 (4): 438–44.

Sasanuma, Sumiko, Sakuma Naoko, and Kitano Kunitaka. "Reading Kanji without Semantics: Evidence from a Longitudinal Study of Dementia." *Cognitive Neuropsychology* (United Kingdom) 9.6 (1992): 465–86.

Satō Taketoshi 佐藤武敏. *Chūgoku kodai kōgyōshi no kenkyū* 中国古代工業史の研究 (A study of the history of Ancient Chinese craft industry). Tokyo: Yoshikawa Kōbunkan, 1962.

——. "Shin Kan sho no shikki no seisan ni tsuite" 秦漢初の漆器の生産について (Lacquer production in the Qin and early Han periods). *Koshi shunjū* 4 (1987): 3–16.

Sawyer, Ralph D., trans. *Seven Military Classics of China*. Boulder, Colo.: Westview Press, 1993.

Schaberg, David. *A Patterned Past: Form and Thought in Early Chinese Historiography*. Cambridge, Mass.: Harvard University Press, 2001.

Schiffman, Harold F. "Diglossia as a Sociolinguistic Situation." In *The Handbook of Sociolinguistics*, edited by Florian Coulmas. London: Basil Blackwell, 1997.

Schuessler, Axel. *ABC Etymological Dictionary of Old Chinese*. Honolulu: University of Hawai'i Press, 2007.

——. *A Dictionary of Early Zhou Chinese*. Honolulu: University of Hawai'i Press, 1987.

Serruys, Paul L-M. "Studies in the Language of the Shang Oracle Inscriptions." *T'oung Pao* 60.1-3 (1974): 12–120.

Shaanxi Sheng Kaogu Yanjiusuo 陝西省考古研究所, Baoji Shi Kaogu Gongzuodui 寶雞市考古工作隊, Mei Xian Wenhuaguan 眉縣文化館, and Yangjiacun Lianhe Kaogudui 楊家村聯合考古隊. "Shaanxi Mei Xian Yangjiacun Xi Zhou qingtongqi jiaocang fajue jianbao" 陝西眉縣楊家村西周情銅器窖藏發掘簡報 (A short excavation report on a pit of Western Zhou bronze vessels at Yangjiacun in Meixian, Shaanxi). *Wenwu* 2003.6: 4–42.

Shaanxi Sheng Kaogu Yanjiusuo 陝西省考古研究所 and Shihuangling Qin Yongkeng Kaogu Fajuedui 始皇陵俑坑考古發掘隊. *Qin Shihuangling bingmayong keng: Yi hao keng fajue baogao 1974–1984* 秦始皇陵兵馬俑坑：一號坑發掘報告 (The pits containing the terra-cotta army in the necropolis of the First Emperor of Qin: Excavation report on pit no. 1, 1974–1984). 2 vols. Beijing: Wenwu Chubanshe, 1988.

Shaanxi Sheng Wenwuju 陝西省文物局 and Zhonghua Shijitan Yishuguan 中華世紀壇藝術館. *Shengshi jijin: Shaanxi Baoji Mei Xian qingtongqi jiaocang* 盛世吉金：陝西眉縣楊家村西周情銅器窖藏 (Bronzes in an era of great prosperity: A pit of Western Zhou bronze vessels at Yangjiacun in Meixian, Shaanxi). Beijing: Beijing Chubanshe 北京出版社, 2003.

Shandong Sheng Jining Shi Wenwuju 山東省濟寧市文物局. *Han Rencheng Wang mu keshi jingxuan* 漢任城王墓刻石精選 (A selection of the finest stone carvings from the Han Prince of Rencheng's tomb). Ji'nan: Shandong Meishu Chubanshe 山東美術出版社, 1998.

Shanxi Sheng Kaogu Yanjiusuo 山西省考古研究所 and Lingshi Xian Wenhua Ju 靈石縣文化局. "Lingshi Jingjiecun Shang mu" 靈石旌介村商墓 (The Shang tomb at Jingjiecun, Lingshi). *Wenwu* 1986.11: 1–18.

Shaughnessy, Edward L. *Before Confucius: Studies in the Creation of the Chinese Classics*. Albany: State University of New York Press, 1997.

——. "The Guodian Manuscripts and Their Place in Twentieth-Century Historiography on the *Laozi*." *Harvard Journal of Asiatic Studies* 65.2 (2005): 417–57.

——. *Rewriting Early Chinese Texts*. Albany: State University of New York, 2006.

——. *Sources of Western Zhou History: Inscribed Bronze Vessels*. Berkeley and Los Angeles: University of California Press, 1991.

——. "Western Zhou History." In *The Cambridge History of Ancient China*, edited by Loewe and Shaughnessy, 292–351.

——, ed. *New Sources of Early Chinese History: An Introduction to the Reading of Inscriptions and Manuscripts*. Early China Special Monograph Series no. 3) Berkeley: University of California, Society for the Study of Early China, and Institute of East Asian Studies, 1997.

Shen Jianshi 沈兼士. *Guangyun shengxi* 廣韻聲系 (The system of phonetic elements in the characters of the *Guangyun*). Beijing, 1944; reprint, Taipei: Zhonghua Shuju, 1969.

Shen Pei 沈培. *Yinxu jiagu buci yuxu yanjiu* 殷墟甲骨卜辭語序研究 (Study of word order in the oracle bone inscriptions from Yinxu). Taipei: Wenjin Chubanshe 文津出版社, 1992.

Shi Zhangru 石璋如 and Gao Quxun 高去尋. *Jiagu kengceng zhi yi: Yi ci zhi jiu ci chutu jiagu* 甲骨坑層之一：一次至九次出土甲骨 (One of the pit strata of oracle bones: Oracle bones from the first through ninth excavations) (Zhongguo kaogu bagaoji zhi er - Xiaotun - Di yi ben: Yizhi de faxian yu fajue - Ding bian 中國考古報告之二 – 小屯 – 第一本: 遺址的發現與發掘 – 丁編). Taipei: Zhongyang Yanjiuyuan Lishi Yuyan Yanjiusuo 中央研究院歷史語言研究所, 1985–86.

Shiji 史記 (Records of the Grand Scribe). By Sima Qian 司馬遷. Beijing: Zhonghua Shuju, 1959.

Shijing 詩經 (The book of poetry). *Shisanjing zhushu* 十三經註疏 edition. 2 vols. Beijing: Zhonghua Shuju, 1979.

Shirakawa Shizuka 白川静. "Betsureki kai" 蔑曆解 (An explanation of *mièlì*). *Kōkotsugaku* 甲骨學 4–5 (1959): 89–104.

———. "Kinbun tsūshaku" 金文通釈 (A comprehensive transcription of the bronze inscriptions). 56 vols. *Hakutsuru bijutsukanshi* 白鶴美術館誌. Kobe, 1966–83.

Shisanjing zhushu 十三經注疏 (The Thirteen Classics with commentary and subcommentary). Edited by Ruan Yuan 阮元. 2 vols. Beijing: Zhonghua Shuju, 1980. (Cited by traditional chapter numbers, followed after *colon* by page numbers consecutive in the two volumes.)

Shouyang Studio, Shanghai Museum, and Art Museum, The Chinese University of Hong Kong. *Ancient Chinese Bronzes from the Shouyang Studio.* Shanghai: Shanghai Shiji Chuban Gufen Youxian Gongsi 上海世紀出版股份有限公司 and Shanghai Guji Chubanshe, 2008.

Shuihudi Qin Mu Zhujian Zhengli Xiaozu 睡虎地秦墓竹簡整理小組. *Shuihudi Qinmu zhujian* 睡虎地秦墓竹簡 (Bamboo slips from the Qin tomb at Shuihudi). Beijing: Wenwu Chubanshe, 1990.

Shuowen jiezi 說文解字 (Explaining simple and compound graphs). Beijing: Zhonghua Shuju, 1963; reprint, 1979.

Skosey, Laura. "The Legal System and Legal Tradition of the Western Zhou, ca. 1045–771 B.C.E." PhD diss., University of Chicago, 1996.

Smith, Adam D. "Writing at Anyang: The role of the divination record in the emergence of Chinese literacy." PhD diss., University of California, Los Angeles, 2008.

Song Guoding 宋國定. "Zhengzhou Xiaoshuangqiao yizhi chutu taoqi shang de zhushu" 鄭州小雙橋遺址出土陶器上的朱書 (Red writing on pottery unearthed at the Xiaoshuangqiao site in Zhengzhou). *Wenwu* 2003.5: 35–44.

Song Zhenhao 宋鎮豪. "Cong jiaguwen kaoshu Shang dai de xuexiao jiaoyu" 從甲骨文考述商代的學校教育 (School education in the Shang era as documented using oracle bone inscriptions). In *2004 nian Anyang Yin Shang wenming guoji xueshu yantaohui lunwenji*, edited by Wang Yuxin, Song Zhenhao, and Meng Xianwu, 220–30.

Sprinkle, Russell, et al. *Amoy-English Dictionary*. Taichung: Maryknoll Fathers, 1976.

Starostin, Sergey. "The Tower of Babel Project: Evolution of Human Language

Project; Sino-Tibetan Etymology." http://starling.rinet.ru/cgi-bin/query.cgi?basename=¥data¥sintib¥stibet&root=config&morpho=0 (accessed 4 October 2009).

Street, Brian V. *Literacy in Theory and Practice*. Cambridge: Cambridge University Press, 1984.

Sumiya Sadatoshi 角谷定俊. "Shin ni okeru seidō kōgyō no ikkōsatsu: kōkan o chūshin ni" 秦における青銅工業の一考察 — 工官を中心に (Investigation of Qin bronze production, focusing on the Office of Workmen). *Sundai shigaku* 55 (1982): 52–86.

Sun Haibo 孫海波 (Zhongguo Shehui Kexueyuan Kaogu Yanjiusuo 中國社會科學院考古研究所). *Jiaguwen bian* 甲骨文編 (A compilation of oracle bone inscriptions). Corrected version (改訂本). Beijing: Zhonghua Shuju, 1965.

Sun Yabing 孫亞冰. "Bainian lai jiaguwen cailiao zai tongji" 百年來甲骨文材料再統計 (A revised statistical study of the sources of the bone inscriptions from the last one hundred years). *Zhongguo wenwu bao* 中國文物報, 28 September 2003.

Sun Yabing 孫亞冰 and Song Zhenhao 宋鎮豪. "Ji'nanshi Daxinzhuang yizhi xinchu jiagu buci tanxi" 濟南市大辛莊遺址新出甲骨卜辭探析 (Exploratory analyses of the newly found oracle bone inscriptions in the Daxinzhuang site in Jinan city). *Kaogu* 考古 2004.2: 66–75.

Sun Yirang 孫詒讓. *"Mozi" jiangu* 墨子閒詁 (Glosses on the gaps in our understanding of the *Mozi*). *Guoxue jiben congshu* 國學基本叢書 ed. Shanghai: Shangwu Yinshuguan, 1936.

———. *Zhouli zhengyi* 周禮正義 (The authentic meaning of the *Zhouli*). *Sibu beiyao* 四部備要 edition. Shanghai: Zhonghua Shuju, 1936.

Swann, Nancy Lee. *The Biography of Empress Teng*. Montreal: McGill University Publications, 1931.

———. *Pan Chao: Foremost Woman Scholar of China*. New York: Century, 1932; reprint, Ann Arbor, Mich.: Center for Chinese Studies, 2001.

Taft, Marcus, and Xiaoping Zhu. "Submorphemic Processing in Reading Chinese." *Journal of Experimental Psychology: Learning, Memory, and Cognition* 23.3 (1997): 761–75.

Taiping yulan 太平御覽 (His Majesty's readings, from the Taiping era). 4 vols. Beijing: Zhonghua Shuju, 1960.

Takashima, Ken-ichi 高嶋謙一. *Studies of Fascicle Three of Inscriptions from the Yin Ruins*, Volume 1: *General Notes, Text and Translations* (up to plastron #259 translated by Paul L-M. Serruys); Volume 2: *New Palaeographical and Philological Commentaries*. Taipei: Institute of History and Philology, Academia Sinica, 2010.

———. "The Graph 曰 for the Word 'Time' in Shang Oracle-Bone Inscriptions."

Bulletin of Chinese Linguistics 1.1 (2006): 61–79.

——. "Settling the Cauldron in the Right Place: A Study of 鼎 in the Bone Inscriptions," in *Wang Li Memorial Volumes* (English volume), Hong Kong: Joint Publishing Company, 1987, 408–9.

———. "The So-Called 'Third'-Person Possessive Pronoun *jue* 厥 in Classical Chinese." *Journal of the American Oriental Society*, 119.3 (1999): 404–31.

——. *Yinxu wenzi bingbian tongjian* 殷虛文字丙編通檢 (A concordance to Fascicle Three of inscriptions from the Yin ruins). Taipei: Institute of History and Philology, Academia Sinica, 1985.

Takashima, Ken-ichi 高嶋謙一, and Anne O. Yue 余靄芹. "Evidence of Possible Dialect Mixture in Oracle-Bone Inscriptions." In *Memory of Professor Li Fang-Kuei: Essays of Linguistic Change and the Chinese Dialects*, edited by Ting Pang-Hsin 丁邦新 and Anne O. Yue 余靄芹, 1–52. Taipei: Institute of Linguistics, Academia Sinica, 2000.

Tambiah, Stanley J. *Culture, Thought, and Social Action*. Cambridge, Mass.: Harvard University Press, 1985.

Tan, Li-hai (譚力海), and Charles A. Perfetti. "Phonological Codes as Early Sources of Constraint in Chinese Word Identification: A Review of Current Discoveries and Theoretical Accounts." *Reading and Writing* 10.3-5 (1998): 165–200.

Tan Buyun 譚步雲. *Shangdai tongqi mingwen shidu de ruogan wenti* 商代銅器銘文釋讀的若干問題 (A few problems in the interpretation of Shang bronze inscriptions). *Zhongshan renwen xueshu luncong* 中山人文學術論叢 2005.5: 1–19.

Tang Lan 唐蘭. "Huangdi sijing chutan" 黃帝四經初探 (A preliminary exploration of the "Four classics of the Yellow Emperor"). *Wenwu* 221.10 (1974): 48–52.

——. "Mieli xingu" 蔑曆新詁 (A new gloss on *mièlì*). In *Tang Lan xiansheng jinwen lunji* 唐蘭先生金文論集, 224–35. Beijing: Zijingcheng Chubanshe 紫禁城出版社, 1995.

——. "Xi Zhou tongqi duandai zhong de 'Kanggong' wenti" 西周銅器斷代中的'康宮' 問題 (The issue of the *kānggōng* in periodization of Western Zhou bronze vessels). *Kaogu xuebao* 1964.1: 15–48.

Tannenbaum, Frank. "Origin, Growth, and Theory of the University Seminar Movement." In *Community of Scholars: The University Seminars at Columbia*, edited by Frank Tannenbaum, 3–45. New York: Praeger, 1965.

Thomas, Rosalind. "Writing, Reading, Public and Private 'Literacies': Functional Literacy and Democratic Literacy." In *Ancient Literacies: The Culture of Reading in Greece and Rome*, edited by William A. Johnson and Holt N. Parker, 13–45. Oxford: Oxford University Press, 2009.

Trauzettel, Rolf. "Grundsätzliches zur altkonfuzianischen Morallehre." In *Und folge nun dem, was mein Herz begehrt: Festschrift für Ulrich Unger zum 70: Geburtstag*, edited by Reinhard Emmerich, Hans Stumpfeldt, et al., 137–53. Hamburger Sinologische Schriften 8. Hamburg: Hamburger Sinologische Gesellschaft, 2002.

Trigger, Bruce. "Writing Systems: A Case Study in Cultural Evolution." In *The First Writing*, edited by Stephen D. Houston, 39–68.

Tsai, Jie-Li, Chia-Ying Lee, Ovid J.L. Tzeng, Daisy L. Hung, and Nai-Shing Yen. "Use of Phonological Codes for Chinese Characters: Evidence from Processing of Parafoveal Preview When Reading Sentences." *Brain and Language* 91.2 (2004): 235–44.

Tsien Tsuen-hsuin. *Written on Bamboo and Silk: The Beginnings of Chinese Books and Inscriptions*. 2nd edition. 1962; Chicago: University of Chicago Press, 2004.

Turner, Victor. *The Ritual Process*. Ithaca, N.Y.: Cornell University Press, 1969.

Umehara Sueji 梅原末治. *Shina Kandai kinenmei shikki zusetsu* 支那漢代記年銘漆器図説 (Illustrated catalog of dated Han lacquers). Kyoto: Kuwana Bunseidō, 1943; reprint, Kyoto: Dohōsha, 1984.

Unger, J. Marshall. *Ideogram: Chinese Characters and the Myth of Disembodied Meaning*. Honolulu: University of Hawai'i Press, 2004.

Unger, J. Marshall, and John DeFrancis. "Logographic and Semasiographic Writing Systems: A Critique of Sampson's Classification." In *Scripts and Literacy: Reading and Learning to Read Alphabets, Syllabaries and Characters*, edited by I. Taylor and D. R. Olson, 45–58. Dordrecht, Netherlands: Kluwer Academic Publishers, 1995.

Unger, Ulrich. *Hao-ku: Sinologische Rundbriefe*. Samizdat for limited circulation. Münster, 1982–2004.

Urton, Gray. "From Knots to Narratives: Reconstructing the Art of Historical Record Keeping in the Andes from Spanish Transcriptions of Inka *Khipus*." *Ethnohistory* 45.3 (1998): 409–38.

——. *Signs of the Inka Khipu*. Austin: University of Texas Press, 2003.

Vandermeersch, Léon. "Le développement de la procédure écrite dans l'administration chinoise à l'époque ancienne." In *State and Law in East Asia: Festschrift Karl Bünger*, edited by D. Eikemeier and H. Franke, 1–24. Wiesbaden, Germany: Harrassowitz, 1981.

Veldhuis, Niek. "Elementary Education at Nippur: The Lists of Trees and Wooden Objects." PhD diss., University of Gröningen, 1997.

——. "How Did They Learn Cuneiform? 'Tribute/Word List C' as an Elementary Exercise." In *Approaches to Sumerian Literature in Honour of Stip (H.L.J. Vanstiphout)*, edited by Piotr Michalowski and Niek Veldhuis, 181–200. Leiden: E. J. Brill, 2006.

Venture, Olivier. "Étude d'un emploi rituel de l'écrit dans la Chine archaïque (XIIIe–VIIIe siècle avant notre ère): Réflexion sur les matériaux épigraphiques des Shang et des Zhou occidentaux." PhD diss., Université

Paris, 2002.

———. "L'écriture et la communication avec les esprits en Chine ancienne." *Bulletin of the Museum of Far Eastern Antiquities* 74 (2002): 34–65.

Waley, Arthur, trans. *The Book of Songs: The Ancient Chinese Classics of Poetry.* Edited by Joseph R. Allen. New York: Grove Press, 1996.

Wan Rong 萬榮. "Zhangjiashan Han jian 'Zouyan shu' jishi yu xiangguan wenti yanjiu" 張家山漢簡《奏讞書》集釋與相關問題研究 (Collected transcriptions of the *Zouyan shu* in the Han bamboo strips from Zhangjiashan and a study of related issues). PhD diss., Wuhan University, 2006.

Wang, Haicheng. "Writing and the State in Early China in Comparative Perspectives." PhD diss., Princeton University, 2007.

Wang Guihai 汪桂海. *Han dai guan wenshu zhidu* 漢代官文書制度 (The official documentary system of Han dynasty). Nanning: Guangxi Jiaoyu Chubanshe, 1999.

Wang Guowei 王國維. "*Shi Zhou pian* zhengxu" 史籀篇證序 (Preface to "Evidence about the *Shi Zhou pian*"). In *Wang Guowei yishu* 王國維遺書. Shanghai: Shanghai Guji Chubanshe, 1983.

Wang Hanzhang 王翰章, Chen Lianghe 陳良和, and Li Baolin 李保林. "Hu guigai ming jianshi" 虎簋蓋銘簡釋 (A brief transcription of the inscription on the lid of the Hu *gui*). *Kaogu yu wenwu* 1997.3: 78–80, 75.

Wang Huanlin 王煥林. *Liye Qin jian jiaogu* 里耶秦簡校詁 (Collation and glosses on the Qin bamboo strips from Liye). Beijing: Zhongguo Wenlian, 2007.

Wang Hui 王輝. "Qiu pan mingwen qianshi" 逑盤銘文淺釋 (A superficial transcription of the Qiu *pan*). *Kaogu yu wenwu* 2003.3: 81–91.

Wang Ning 王寧. "Shi zhigan bianbu" 釋支干辯補 (Supplement to the debate on the transcription of the *ganzhi*). *Zhongguo xian Qin shi* 中國先秦史 (30 July 2006). Web version, http://www.zgxqs.cn/article/2006/0730/article_905.html (accessed 2 April 2009).

Wang Xianqian 王先謙. *Hanshu buzhu* 漢書補注 (History of the Former Han dynasty with corrections and annotations). 1900; reprint, Taipei: Yiwen Yinshuguan, 1955.

Wang Yuxin 王宇信. *Xi Zhou jiagu tanlun* 西周甲骨探論 (A tentative study of Western Zhou oracle bones). Beijing: Kexue Chubanshe, 1984.

Wang Yuxin 王宇信, Song Zhenhao 宋鎮豪, and Meng Xianwu 孟憲武, eds. *2004 nian Anyang Yin Shang wenming guoji xueshu yantaohui lunwenji* 年安陽殷商文明國際研討會論文集 (Collected essays from the 2004 International Conference on Shang Civilization at Anyang). Beijing: Shehui Kexue Wenxian Chubanshe 社會科學文獻出版社, 2004.

Wang Yuxin 王宇信 and Yang Shengnan 楊升南, eds. *Jiaguxue yi bai nian* 甲骨學一百年 (A hundred years of oracle bone studies). Beijing: Shehui Kexue Wenxian Chubanshe, 1999.

Wang Zhankui 王占奎. " 'Wang ruo yue' budang jiezuo 'Wang ruci shuo' " '王若曰' 不當解做 '王如此說' (*Wáng ruò yuē* should not be explained as "Thus spake the King"). In *Zhou Qin wenhua yanjiu* 周秦文化研究, 359–77. Xi'an: Shaanxi Renmin Chubanshe 陝西人民出版社, 1998.

Wang Zhongwen 汪中文. *Xi Zhou ceming jinwen suojian guanzhi yanjiu* 西周冊命金文所見官制研究 (A study of the bureaucratic system appearing in the appointment bronze inscriptions of the Western Zhou). Taipei: Guoli Bianyiguan 國立編譯局, 1999.

Watson, Burton. *Records of the Grand Historian of China Translated from the "Shih chi" of Ssu-ma Ch'ien*. New York: Columbia University Press, 1961.

Wengrow, David. "Limits of Decipherment: Object Biographies and the Invention of Writing." In *Egypt at Its Origins 2*, edited by B. Midant-Reynes and Y. Tristant, 1022–32.

Wilbur, Clarence Martin. *Slavery in China during the Former Han Dynasty, 206 B.C.–A.D. 25*. Chicago: Field Museum of Natural History, 1943.

Willems, Klaas, and Ludovic De Cuypere, eds. *Naturalness and Iconicity in Language*. Amsterdam: John Benjamins, 2008.

Wu Dacheng 吳大澂. *Kezhai jigu lu* 愙齋集古錄 (A catalogue of collected antiquities from Kezhai). 26 vols. Shanghai: Hanfenlou 涵芬樓, 1918 (preface, 1896).

Wu Jiabi 武家璧. "Zeng Hou Yi mu qixiang fang xing tukao" 曾侯乙墓漆箱房星圖考 (A study of the illustration of asterism Fang on a lacquer box from the tomb of Marquis Yi of Zeng). *Ziran kexue shi yanjiu* 自然科學史研究 (Studies on the history of the natural sciences) 20.1 (2001): 90–94.

Wu Jiabi 武家璧, Chen Meidong 陳美東, and Liu Ciyuan 劉次沅. "Taosi guanxiangtai yizhi de tianwen gongneng yu niandai" 陶寺觀象台遺址的天文功能與年代 (The astronomical function and date of the Taosi observatory site). *Science in China* 中國科學 (G: Physics and astronomy issue) 38.9 (2008): 1265–72.

Wu Jiabi and He Nu 何駑. "A Preliminary Study about the Astronomical Date of the Large Building IIFJT1 at Taosi." *Gudai wenming yanjiu tongxun* 古代文明研究通訊 (Ancient civilizations review) 8 (2005): 50–55.

Wuhan Daxue Zhongguo Wenhua Yanjiuyuan 武漢大學中國文化研究院, ed. *Guodian Chujian guoji xueshu yantaohui lunwenji* 郭店楚簡國際學術研討會論文集 (Collected essays from the International Scholarly Conference on the Chu Bamboo Slips from Guodian). Wuhan: Hubei Renmin Chubanshe 湖北人民出版社, 2000.

Wuqiubei Zhai "Mozi" jicheng 無求備齋墨子集成 (A *Mozi* compendium from the Studio of Not Seeking Completeness). Edited by Yan Lingfeng 嚴靈峯. Taipei: Chengwen, 1977.

Xu Baohua 許寶華 and Tao Huan 陶寰. *Shanghai fangyan cidian* 上海方言詞典 (Dictionary of the Shanghai dialect). Nanjing: Jiangsu Jiaoyu Chubanshe 江蘇教育出版社, 1997.

Xu Dali 徐大立. "Bangbu, Shuangdun yizhi kehua fuhao jianshu" 蚌埠雙墩遺址刻畫符號簡述 (A brief account of the inscribed signs from the Shuangdun site in Bangbu). *Zhongyuan kaogu* 中原文物 3 (2008): 75–79.

Xu Hong 許宏. "Erlitou yizhi kaogu xin faxian de xueshu yiyi" 二里頭遺址考古新發現的學術意義 (The scholarly significance of the new archaeological discoveries at the Erlitou site). *Zhongguo wenwu bao* 中國文物報 (China cultural relics daily), 17 September 2004; reprint, 19 December 2007 (http://www.kaogu.cn/cn/detail.asp?ProductID=8497, 2007-12-19).

Xu Hongxiu 徐鴻修. "Daxinzhuang jiaguwen kaoshi" 大辛莊甲骨文考釋 (Philological study and transcription of bone inscriptions from Daxinzhuang). *Wenshizhe* 文史哲 2003.3: 10–1.

Xu Xitai 徐錫台. "Zhouyuan chutu de jiaguwen suojian renming, guanming, fangguo, diming qianshi" 周原出土的甲骨文所見人名 官名方國地名淺釋 (A cursory interpretation of the names of persons, officials, statelets, and locations as appearing in the bone inscriptions unearthed in Zhouyuan). *Guwenzi yanjiu* 古文字研究 1 (1979): 184–202.

Xu Zhongshu 徐中舒. "Jinwen guci shili" 金文嘏辭實例 (Examples of *gǔcí* "blessings" in the bronze inscriptions). *Zhongyang yanjiuyuan, Lishi yuyan yanjiusuo jikan* 中央研究院歷史語言研究所集刊 6.1 (1936): 1–44.

Xunzi 荀子 (The *Xunzi*). *Sibu beiyao* edition. Taipei: Zhonghua Shuju, 1970.

Xunzi 荀子 (The *Xunzi*). *Zhuzi jicheng* edition, vol. 2. Shanghai: Shanghai Shudian, 1986; reprint, 1991.

Yan Kejun 嚴可均, ed. *Quan shanggu sandai Qin Han Sanguo Liuchao wen* 全上古三代秦漢三國六朝文 (Complete prose of high antiquity, the Three Dynasties, Qin, Han, Three Kingdoms, and Six Dynasties periods). 5 vols. Beijing: Zhonghua Shuju, 1965 [1836].

Yan Yiping 嚴一萍. "Mieli guyi" 蔑歷古意 (The ancient meaning of *mièlì*). *Zhongguo wenzi* 中國文字 10 (1962): 1–13.

Yang Hua 楊華. *Xian Qin liyue wenhua* 先秦禮樂文化 (The culture of ritual and music in the pre-Han era). Hankou: Hubei Jiaoyu Chubanshe 湖北教育出版社, 1997.

Yang Kuan 楊寬. *Xi Zhou shi* 西周史 (History of the Western Zhou). Shanghai: Shanghai Renmin Chubanshe 上海人民出版社, 2003.

Yang Shengnan 楊升南. *Shangdai jingji shi* 商代經濟史 (Economic history of the Shang period). Guiyang: Guizhou Renmin Chubanshe 貴州人民出版社, 1992.

Yang Shuda 楊樹達. *Jiweiju jinwen shuo* 積微居金文說 (Explanations on bronze inscriptions from Jiweiju). Supplemented. 1st edition, Beijing: Kexue, 1952. Beijing: Zhonghua Shuju, 1997.

Yang Yubin 楊育彬 and Yuan Guangkuo 袁廣濶. *20 shiji Henan kaogu faxian yu yanjiu* 20世紀河南考古發現與研究 (Archaeological discoveries and studies in Henan in the twentieth century). Zhengzhou: Zhongzhou Guji Chubanshe 中州古籍出版社, 1997.

Yao Xiaosui 姚孝遂 and Xiao Ding 蕭丁. *Xiaotun nandi jiagu kaoshi* 小屯南地甲骨考釋 (A philological study of the oracle bones at Xiaotun South). Beijing: Zhonghua Shuju, 1985.

———. *Yinxu jiagu keci leizuan* 殷墟刻辭類纂 (Classification and compilation of inscriptions from Yinxu). 3 vols. Beijing: Zhonghua Shuju, 1989.

Yao Xuan 姚萱. *Yinxu Huayuanzhuang dongdi jiagu buci de chubu yanjiu* 殷墟花園莊東地甲骨卜辭的初步研究 (A preliminary study of divination inscriptions on the oracle bones of Huayuan Dongdi at Yinxu). Beijing: Xianzhuang Shuju 綫裝書局, 2006.

Yates, Robin D. S. (Ye Shan 葉山). "The City under Siege: A Reconstruction and Translation of the Military Chapters of *Mo-tzu*," PhD diss., Harvard University, 1980.

———. "Law and the Military in Early China." In *Military Culture in Imperial China*, edited by Nicola Di Cosmo, 23–44. Cambridge, Mass.: Harvard University Press, 2009.

———. "Qin de falü yu shehui: Guanyu Zhangjiashan 'Ernian lüling' deng xin chutu wenxian de sikao" 秦的法律與社會: 關於張家山《二年律令》等新出土文獻的思考 (Law and society in Qin: Reflections on the Second-year Statutes from Zhangjiashan and other newly excavated documents). *Rujia wenhua yanjiu: Xin chu Chu jian yanjiu zhuanhao* 儒家文化研究: 新出楚簡研究專號 1 (2007): 299–325.

———. "Social Status in the Ch'in: Evidence from the Yün-meng Legal Documents, Part One: Commoners." *Harvard Journal of Asiatic Studies* 47.1 (1987): 197–236.

———. *Women in China from Earliest Times to the Present: A Bibliography of Studies in Western Languages*. Leiden: Brill, 2009.

———. "Zu, shi yu nüxing: Zhanguo Qin Han shiqi xiaceng shehui de duxie nengli" 卒、史與女性: 戰國秦漢時期下層社會的讀寫能力 (Soldiers, scribes, and women: Literacy among the lower orders in Early China). *Jianbo* 簡帛 3 (2008): 361–86.

Yates, Robin D. S., Joseph Needham, et al. *Science and Civilisation in China*. Vol.

5, part 6, *Military Technology: Missiles and Sieges*. Cambridge: Cambridge University Press, 1994.

Ye Shan 葉山. See Robin D. S. Yates.

Yu Haoliang 于豪亮. "Yunmeng Qin jian suojian zhiguan shulüe" 雲夢秦簡所見職官述略 (A brief account of official titles appearing in the Qin bamboo strips from Yunmeng). In *Yu Haoliang xueshu wencun* 于豪亮學術文存. Beijing: Zhonghua Shuju, 1985.

Yu Xingwu 于省吾, ed. *Jiagu wenzi gulin* 甲骨文字詁林 (Collected glosses for the oracle bone characters). 4 vols. Beijing: Zhonghua Shuju, 1996.

———. "Wang ruo yue shiyi" 王若曰釋義 (Interpreting the meaning of *wáng ruò yuē*) *Zhongguo yuwen* 1966.2: 136, 147–49.

Yu Zhenbo 于振波. *Zoumalou Wu jian chutan* 走馬樓吳簡初探 (Preliminary investigation of the Wu bamboo strips from Zoumalou). Taipei: Wenjin Chubanshe, 2004.

Yuan Jing 袁靖 and Tang Jigen 唐際根. "Henan Anyang shi Huanbei Huayuanzhuang yizhi chutu dongwu guge yanjiu baogao" 河南安陽市洹北花園莊遺址出土動物骨骼研究報告 (Research report on the animal bones unearthed in Huayuanzhuang in the north of the Huan River in Anyang, Henan). *Kaogu* 2000.11: 75–81.

Yuan Zhongyi 袁仲一. *Qin bingmayong keng* 秦兵馬俑坑 (Pits of the Qin terra-cotta warriors and horses). Beijing: Wenwu Chubanshe, 2003.

———. "Qin ling bingmayong de zuozhe" 秦陵兵馬俑的作者 (The makers of the terra-cotta army in the Qin necropolis). *Wenbo* 1986.4: 52–62.

———. "Qin zhongyang duzao de bingqi keci zongshu" 秦中央督造的兵器刻辭綜述 (Comprehensive discussion of the inscriptions on Qin weapons made under government-supervised production). *Kaogu yu wenwu* 1984.5: 100–12.

Yunmeng Shuihudi Qin Mu Bianxiezu 雲夢睡虎地秦墓編寫組. *Yunmeng Shuihudi Qin mu* 雲夢睡虎地秦墓 (The Qin tombs at Shuihudi, Yunmeng). Beijing: Wenwu Chubanshe, 1981.

Zang Zhifei 臧知非. "'Shi lü' xinzheng" 《史律》新證 (New evidence about the *shǐ lù* "statutes pertaining to scribes"). *Shixue yuekan* 史學月刊 2008.11: 20–26.

Zaoqi Qin Wenhua Lianhe Kaogudui 早期秦文化聯合考古隊. "2006 nian Gansu Lixian Dabaozishan 21 hao jianzhu jizhi fajue jianbao" 年甘肅禮縣大堡子山建築基址發掘簡報 (Short report on the 2006 excavation of building foundation number 21 at Dabaozishan, Lixian, in Gansu). *Wenwu* 2008.9: 4–13.

Zhang Bingquan 張秉權. *Xiaotun 2: Yinxu wenzi bingbian* 小屯第二本: 殷墟文字丙編 (Xiaotun, vol. 2: Yinxu characters, part B). 3 vols. Taipei:

Zhongyang Yanjiuyuan Lishi Yuyan Yanjiusuo 中央研究院歷史語言研究所, 1965–72.

Zhang Gong 張功. *Qin Han taowang fanzui yanjiu* 秦漢逃亡犯罪研究 (A study of escaped criminals in the Qin and Han). Wuhan: Hubei Renmin Chubanshe, 2006.

Zhang Guangyu 張光裕, ed. *Disijie guoji Zhongguo guwenzixue yantaohui lunwen* 第四屆中國古文字學研討會論文 (Essays from the Fourth Conference on the Ancient Chinese Script). Hong Kong: The Chinese University of Hong Kong, 2004.

Zhang Jinguang 張金光. *Qin zhi yanjiu* 秦制研究 (A study of Qin institutions). Shanghai: Shanghai Guji Chubanshe, 2004.

Zhang Shichao 張世超. *Yinxu jiagu ziji yanjiu: Shi zu buci pian* 殷墟甲骨字跡研究–師組卜辭篇 (A study of oracle bone writing from Yinxu: Inscriptions from the Shi diviner group). Changchun: Dongbei Shifan Daxue Chubanshe 東北師範大學出版社, 2002.

Zhang Shouzhong 張守中. *Shuihudi Qin jian wenzi bian* 睡虎地秦簡文字編 (A compilation of graphs from the Qin bamboo strips at Shuihudi). Beijing: Wenwu Chubanshe, 1993.

Zhang Shouzhong, Sun Xiaocang 孫小滄, and Hao Jianwen 郝建文. *Guodian Chu jian wenzibian* 郭店楚簡文字編 (A compilation of graphs from the Chu bamboo strips at Guodian). Beijing: Wenwu Chubanshe, 2000.

Zhang Yachu 張亞初. *"Yin Zhou jinwen jicheng" yinde* 殷周金文集成引得 (An index to the *Yin Zhou jinwen jicheng*). Beijing: Zhonghua Shuju, 2001.

Zhang Zhenglang 張政烺. "*Shuowen jiezi xu* yin Wei lü kao" 說文解字序引尉律考 (An examination of Statutes of the Commandant in the postface to the *Shuowen jiezi*). In *Zhang Zhenglang wenshi lunji* 張政烺文史論集, 208–14. Beijing: Zhonghua Shuju, 2004.

Zhangjiashan Ersiqi Hao Han Mu Zhujian Zhengli Xiaozu 張家山二四七號漢墓竹簡整理小組. *Zhangjiashan Han mu zhujian (ersiqi hao mu)* 張家山漢墓竹簡（二四七號墓）(Bamboo strips from the Han tomb at Zhangjiashan [tomb number 247]). Beijing: Wenwu Chubanshe, 2001.

Zhangjiashan Ersiqi Hao Han Mu Zhujian Zhengli Xiaozu 張家山二四七號漢墓竹簡整理小組. *Zhangjiashan Han mu zhujian (ersiqi hao mu) (shiwen xiuding ben)* 張家山漢墓竹簡（二四七號墓）（釋文；修訂本）(Bamboo strips from the Han tomb at Zhangjiashan [tomb number 247] [revised edition of the transcription and annotation]). Beijing: Wenwu Chubanshe, 2006.

Zheng Huisheng 鄭慧生. "Shangdai buci sifang shenming fengming yu houshi chun xia qiu dong sishi zhi guanxi" 商代卜辭四方神名、風名與後世春夏秋冬四時之關係 (The names of the gods and winds of the four directions in the Shang oracle bone inscriptions and their relationship to the names of the four seasons in later eras). *Shixue yuekan* 史學月刊 6 (1984): 7–12.

Zheng Qiao 鄭樵. *Tong zhi* 通志 (A general gazetteer). Edited by Wang Shumin 王樹民. Beijing: Zhonghua Shuju, 1995.

Zhongguo lidai bingshu jicheng 中國歷代兵書集成 (A compendium of Chinese historical military writings). Vol. 1, edited by Cheng Suhong 程素紅. Beijing: Tuanjie Chubanshe, 1999.

Zhongguo Shehui Kexueyuan Kaogu Yanjiusuo 中國社會科學院考古研究所. *Anyang Yinxu faxian chutu yuqi* 安陽殷墟出土玉器 (Jades from Yinxu). Beijing: Kexue Chubanshe, 2005.

——. *Xiaotun nandi jiagu* 小屯南地甲骨 (Oracle bones of Xiaotun South). 2 vols. Beijing: Zhonghua Shuju, 1980–83.

——. *Xin Zhongguo de kaogu faxian yu yanjiu* 新中國的考古發現與研究 (Archaeological discoveries and research in new China). Beijing: Wenwu Chubanshe, 1984.

——. *Yin Zhou jinwen jicheng* 殷周金文集成 (A compendium of Shang and Zhou bronze inscriptions). 18 vols. Beijing: Zhonghua Shuju, 1984–94.

——. *Yin Zhou jinwen jicheng shiwen* 殷周金文集成釋文 (A compendium of transcriptions of the Shang and Zhou bronze inscriptions). 5 vols. Hong Kong: Chinese University of Hong Kong Press, 2001.

——. *Zhongguo kaoguxue Xia Shang juan* 中國考古學夏商卷 (Chinese archaeology, volume on Xia and Shang). Beijing: Zhongguo Shehui Kexue Chubanshe, 2003.

Zhongguo Shehui Kexueyuan Kaogu Yanjiusuo 中國社會科學院考古研究所 et al. "Beijing Liulihe 1193 hao damu fajue jianbao" 北京琉璃河1193號大墓發掘簡報 (A brief excavation report on large tomb number 1193 at Liulihe in Beijing). *Kaogu* 1990.1: 20–31.

Zhongguo Shehui Kexueyuan Kaogu Yanjiusuo Anyang Gongzuodui 中國社會科學院考古研究所安陽工作隊. "Anyang Yinxu xiqu 1713 hao mu de fajue" 安陽殷墟西區1713號墓的發掘 (The excavation of tomb number 1713 in the western district of Yinxu, Anyang). *Kaogu* 1986.8: 703–16.

Zhongguo Shehui Kexueyuan Lishi Yanjiusuo 中國社會科學院歷史研究所, Guo Moruo 郭沫若, general editor. *Jiaguwen heji* 甲骨文合集 (A combined collection of oracle bone inscriptions). 13 vols. Beijing: Zhonghua Shuju, 1978–82.

Zhou, Xiaolin, Shu Hua, Bi Yanchao, and Shi Dongfang. "Is There Phonologically Mediated Access to Lexical Semantics in Reading Chinese?" In *Reading Chinese Script: A Cognitive Analysis*, edited by Wang Jian, Albrecht W. Inhoff, et al., 135–71. Mahwah, N.J.: Lawrence Erlbaum Associates, 1999.

Zhou, Xiaolin, and William Marslen-Wilson. "The Relative Time Course of

Semantic and Phonological Activation in Reading Chinese." *Journal of Experimental Psychology. Learning, Memory, and Cognition* 26.5 (2000): 1245–65.

Zhou Fagao 周法高. *Jinwen gulin* 金文詁林 (A "forest" of interpretations of bronze inscriptions). 14 vols. Hong Kong: Chinese University of Hong Kong Press, 1975.

Zhou Zumo 周祖謨. *Fangyan jiaojian* 方言校箋 (Collation and commentary on the *Fangyan*). Beijing: Kexue Chubanshe, 1950 [1956]; reprint, 1993.

Zhu Fenghan 朱鳳瀚. *Gudai Zhongguo qingtongqi* 古代中國青銅器 (Ancient Chinese bronze vessels). Tianjin: Nankai Baxue, 1995.

Zhu Honglin 朱紅林. *Zhangjiashan Han jian 'Ernian lüling' jishi* 張家山漢簡《二年律令》集釋 (Collected transcriptions of the Second-year Statutes in the Han slips from Zhangjiashan). Beijing: Shehui Kexue Chubanshe, 2005.

Zhu Shiche 朱師轍. *"Shangjun shu" jiegu* 商君書解詁 (Explanatory scholia on the *Shangjun shu*). Hong Kong: Zhonghua Shuju, 1974.

Zhuangzi 莊子 (The *Zhuangzi*). *Ershi'er zi* 二十二子 ed. Shanghai: Shanghai Guji Chubanshe, 1985.

Zou An 鄒安. *Zhou jinwen cun* 周金文存 (A collection of Zhou bronze inscriptions). Shanghai: Cangsheng Mingzhi Daxue, 1915–21.

Contributors

Anthony Barbieri-Low, Associate Professor of History at the University of California, Santa Barbara, is a specialist in the social, economic, legal, and material cultural history of Early China. He was trained at Harvard University and Princeton University (PhD, 2001). He was research co-curator for the exhibition *Recarving China's Past: The Art, Archaeology, and Architecture of the Wu Family Shrines* and is the author of *Artisans in Early Imperial China*, which won the 2009 Joseph Levenson Prize of the Association for Asian Studies.

In "Craftsman's Literacy: Uses of Writing by Male and Female Artisans in Qin and Han China" (chapter 11), Barbieri-Low suggests that before the late Warring States period, literacy in China was extremely limited, first to a small scribal caste and later to an expanded group of elites. With the project of state building in the Warring States period, the newly centralized state required greater literacy from lower-ranking members of society in order to better control and exploit their labor and material resources. For more efficient quality control and accounting in state-run workshops, the Qin and other states required artisans to inscribe their names and native places on the objects they produced. Later, this system was expanded to private workshops whose goods were sold in official marketplaces. Because of this, a large proportion of the artisan class acquired the functional level of literacy (craftsmen's literacy) they needed to carry out their assigned tasks or run their operations. During the Eastern Han, when state control of the economy relaxed, artisans began to use their literacy skills to market their products. Borrowing the names of state factories and modifying the idiom of quality control and accounting inscriptions, these artisan entrepreneurs were able to employ the same tools the state had used to coerce and exploit them to promote their businesses and thereby undermine the state's policy of suppressing commercial activity.

William G. Boltz is Professor of Classical Chinese at the University of Washington, Seattle. He received his undergraduate and graduate education in Oriental Languages at the University of California, Berkeley

(PhD, 1974). His research and teaching interests include all aspects of early Chinese language history and texts, with particular attention to the early writing system, textual criticism, and paleographic vagaries of early manuscripts.

"Literacy and the Emergence of Writing in China" (chapter 2) illustrates Boltz's interest in the nature of the early Chinese writing system, in particular the circumstances surrounding its first appearance. Absent archaeological evidence affirming exactly when, where, and how writing first emerged in China, the study of the origin of the Chinese script must proceed inferentially from evidence from the present archaeological record, the structure of the Chinese writing system when first attested, and the extent to which the first appearance of writing in other ancient societies offers a pattern that might pertain to the Chinese case. The evidence of the archaeological record indicates the earliest known time, place, and use of the Chinese script; the structure of the first-attested Chinese writing system provides a basis for a theoretical description of how the formative stage of the script might have developed; and the first appearance of writing in other ancient societies provides comparative models that may serve to suggest developmental parallels with and differences from these other early writing systems. Boltz maintains that literacy at the earliest stage is defined by the emergence of writing itself. There can be no question of *varieties* or *extent* of literacy, since there is nothing beyond the "first use" in which to be literate. Evidence from Mesopotamia and Egypt suggests that de novo writing systems may have arisen from preexisting non-writing graphic notational systems. This implies two kinds of literacy: (1) literacy as the ability to construct and use a pre-writing graphic notational system and (2) literacy as the comparable ability to use "writing proper." The emergence of "writing proper" out of a precursor graphic notational system then becomes a matter of development from one kind of literacy to another.

David Prager Branner is a sinologist and lexicographer of Chinese. He was trained in Chinese dialectology and historical phonology under Jerry Norman at the University of Washington and in linguistic field methods under Robert Austerlitz at Columbia University. Academically, his specialties are dialect classification and fieldwork (especially in rural western Fujian), the intellectual history of Chinese linguistics, and phonology in the service of literature and paleography. He founded and led the Yuen Ren Society for the Promotion of Chinese Dialect Fieldwork from 1990 until 2003, producing three volumes of dialect reports. His principal books are *Problems in Comparative Chinese Dialectology* and *The Chinese Rime Tables*. After a career as Associate Professor of Chinese at the University of Maryland, Branner has devoted himself full-time to Chinese lexicography and computer science, while remaining active in the American Oriental Society and teaching specialized courses at Columbia University. He served as co-chair of the Columbia Early China Seminar in 2004–11.

In "Phonology in the Chinese Script and Its Relationship to Early Chinese Literacy" (chapter 3), Branner examines the phonological content of the Chinese script and what it implies about the tradition of literacy in early China. The script represents a compromise between phoneticism and defectiveness (explicit vs. imperfect phonological representation); phoneticism aided cognitive factors in spreading literacy, while defectiveness aided social factors. Some evidence suggests that literacy has not been a continuous tradition from the earliest times in China and that only a very crude and functional notion of homophony was ever meant to be embodied in standardized phonograms. A great advantage of such a crude system would have been to narrow the gap between high- and low-register language, helping to unify spoken language on the model of its own internal phonological relationships.

Constance A. Cook is Professor of Chinese at Lehigh University and a scholar of early Chinese excavated texts. Her training in paleography began with Father Paul Serruys at the University of Washington and continued at the University of California, Berkeley, with David Keightley (PhD, 1990), at Beijing University with Gao Ming, and at the Chinese Academy of Social Sciences with Li Xueqin and Qi Wenxin. Her books include *Death in Ancient China* and *Defining Chu* (coedited with John Major). Cook is also interested in the effect of religious practices on writing, a result of her work with Michel Strickmann at Berkeley. She is currently coediting a textbook on bronze inscriptions with Paul Goldin.

"Education and the Way of the Former Kings" (chapter 9) continues Cook's pervasive approach to interpreting early Sinitic cultures and texts, transmitted or otherwise, from the perspective of material cultural remains, in this case, bronze inscriptions. Here, she examines how literacy among the elite evolved during the Zhou period out of the recitation of eulogistic lineage narratives in ancestor worship ceremonies. Parts of these narratives form a core section of bronze inscription records of coming-of-age ceremonies for young men and women (e.g., when a person takes up the position of an ancestor or through capping and marriage). The records reveal an active musical culture that spread these songs throughout the elite of the Yellow and Yangzi River valleys, providing a shared literacy with local cultural characteristics. Cook notes that education advocated by Warring States period Ru groups preserved aspects of these earlier performances through their promotion of the Six Arts for educating youth and in self-cultivation rituals.

Lothar von Falkenhausen is Professor of Chinese Archaeology and Art History at the University of California, Los Angeles, where he concurrently serves as Associate Director of the Cotsen Institute of Archaeology. He was educated at Bonn, Beijing, Kyoto, and Harvard Universities (PhD, 1988). His research interests comprise Chinese archaeology in its transasiatic contexts, with an emphasis on the Bronze Age, paleography, and the history of archaeology in East Asia. He is the author of *Suspended Music: Chime-Bells in the Culture of Bronze Age China* and *Chinese Society in the Age of Confucius (1000–250 BC): The Archaeological Evidence*, which received the 2009 book award of the Society of American Archaeology. Falkenhausen has served as the U.S. co–principal investigator for a collaborative archaeological field project on ancient salt production in the Upper Yangzi River Basin (1999–) and is currently collaborating with Professor Alain Schnapp (Paris) on a world history of antiquarianism.

In "The Royal Audience and Its Reflections in Western Zhou Bronze Inscriptions" (chapter 7), Falkenhausen discusses some long statements of past merit at the beginning of Western Zhou bronze inscriptions, which render a spoken dialogue between the person who had the inscribed bronze cast and his patron, usually the king. Falkenhausen argues that these dialogues are transcriptions of verbal exchanges that occurred during court audiences. He goes on to scrutinize classical sources concerning Zhou royal audience protocol for clues enabling an improved understanding of the contexts, meanings, and literary significance of the bronze inscriptions. His findings are intended to serve as a point of departure for a new reconstruction of the process by which the extant inscription texts were produced.

Li Feng is Associate Professor of Early Chinese History and Archaeology at Columbia University. He was trained in archaeology and paleography at the Institute of Archaeology of the Chinese Academy of Social Sciences and the University of Tokyo and in history at the University of Chicago (PhD, 2000). Although Li specializes in bronze inscriptions and Western Zhou history, his research interests extend to the organization of early states, the workings of ancient bureaucracies, and early writing. He is also an active field archaeologist. His works include *Landscape and Power in Early China* and *Bureaucracy and the State in Early China*; the latter won the 2010 Joseph Levenson Prize Honorable Mention of the Association for Asian Studies. He is currently preparing a report with colleagues in China on their three-year collaborative archaeological survey in Guicheng, Shandong. Li was chair of the Early China Seminar in 2002–3 and cochair in 2004–11.

In "Literacy and the Social Contexts of Writing in the Western Zhou" (chapter 8), Li discusses a series of Western Zhou bronze inscriptions that specifically describe the social circumstances in which written documents were produced or handled. The circumstances included routine government management, recordkeeping for civil and military officers, land administration, legal processes involving property ownership, private commodity transfer, and so on. In all of these areas, writing commanded an unequivocal sense of authority. The inscription of the Sanshi *pan* offers a specific case of transfer onto bronze of documents that were initially drafted and *signed* by officials during an interpolity conference and afterward cast onto the bronze that doubtless carried judicial power. Li further discusses the meaning of bronze inscriptions as evidence of literacy. Expanding from the use of bronzes in ancestral worship, he provides concrete evidence that they were used in such social contexts as domestic living quarters, family banquets, and other gatherings during which the inscribed texts were displayed, observed, and appreciated by a much wider readership. Thus, the Western Zhou elites as a whole can be said to have achieved a level of literacy that can be defined as "elite literacy."

David W. Pankenier is Professor of Chinese at Lehigh University. His formal studies in Sinology, begun at the University of Stockholm with Göran Malmqvist, were augmented by three years of private study in the Chinese Classics with Aisin-Gioro Yü-yün in Taiwan and graduate study at Stanford University (PhD, 1983). An intellectual historian and astronomy enthusiast, he is best known for research focusing on the connection between astronomical phenomena and epoch-making cultural developments in ancient China. Pankenier's current research interests focus on the history of ideas in ancient China, especially cultural astronomy. He has coauthored translations of ancient Chinese astronomical observations, *East Asian Archaeoastronomy*, and is the author of *Revealing the Secrets of Ancient Chinese History: Research in Archaeoastronomy* as well as numerous articles on ancient Chinese chronology, cosmology, astrology, and thought.

In "Getting 'Right' with Heaven and the Origins of Writing in China" (chapter 1), Pankenier argues that the cyclical signs were initially devised to respond to the conceptual and recordkeeping demands of the calendar. He suggests further that calendrical astronomy lent impetus to the development of writing and prefigured its application to other forms of recordkeeping, leading to the Shang oracle bone inscriptions. Pankenier suggests that the mnemonic use of rhyme may have prompted the notional linkage between the set of cyclical signs and the *idea* of glottographic writing and identifies a prominent example of just such a transformational graph — *dīng* 丁 — which links the calendar, astronomy, and the inspiration that led to the adoption of a square as the written form of the word. *Dīng* provides a crucial link between the celestial abode of Shang Di, the "right" or *zhèng* 正 month of the calendar, the idea of a supernaturally revealed standard of what is "right" and "true" both spatially and conceptually, and the realization that the nexus of these several meanings could be represented graphically as a square. Finally, Pankenier adduces evidence in support of the tradition that writing was in a sense "Heaven bestowed."

Matthias L. Richter is Assistant Professor of Chinese at the University of Colorado at Boulder. He was trained in sinology at the Ludwig Maximilians University in Munich, Beijing University, and the University of Hamburg (PhD, 2000). He specializes in the study of Early Chinese literature and philosophy with a focus on textual criticism and manuscript studies. Richter is the author of the monograph *Guan ren: Texte der altchinesischen Literatur zur Charakterkunde und Beamtenrekrutierung*.

In "Textual Identity and the Role of Literacy in the Transmission of Early Chinese Literature" (chapter 6), Richter explores the question of what the material features of manuscripts can reveal about the identity of their texts—that is, their extension, internal division, and possibly titles—as well as about their production and use. The chapter focuses on the two silk manuscripts from Mawangdui tomb no. 3 that each bear a version of the *Laozi* and several other texts not known from transmitted literature. Richter offers a comprehensive examination of the material features of these manuscripts, comprising format and layout, type of script and calligraphic quality, orthography, and punctuation as well as errors and corrections. He argues that on all of these levels the materiality of the two manuscripts suggests that only one of them was written primarily for the purpose of reading. This manuscript was probably used within a small circle of people who were familiar with the texts to some extent and used the manuscript to prepare for their successful recitation. The other manuscript was designed primarily to be a representational object and was probably also written with a view to transmitting the texts it bears.

Adam D. Smith is currently a member of the Society of Fellows at Columbia University and a lecturer in the Department of East Asian Languages and Cultures. His research concerns the emergence and evolution of Chinese literacy during the late second and first millennia B.C.E. He is interested in institutions for scribal training, the link between incipient literacy and the recording of divination, the beginnings of textual transmission, the cognitive consequences of the transition to literacy, and linguistic reconstruction of the early stages of the Chinese language. Smith has an undergraduate degree in Mathematics and Philosophy from Oxford and an MA in archaeology from Beijing University. He received his PhD degree from the archaeology program at the University of California, Los Angeles, in 2008.

"The Evidence for Scribal Training at Anyang" (chapter 5) presents the evidence for scribal training associated with the divination workshops at Anyang. These workshops are the only late-second-millennium B.C.E. institutions that provide evidence of the routine and intensive use of writing. They trained their own scribes, and the remains of that training process, including the so-called *xíkè* 習刻 (practice engraving) inscriptions, have been repeatedly found at Anyang since the earliest excavations. Several authors have concluded that the trainees were already fully literate and were learning only to engrave on bone. Smith surveys the evidence and concludes, to the contrary, that scribal trainees in the divination workshops were acquiring the rudiments of literacy for the first time. That conclusion, he suggests, is compatible with a model of late-second-millennium Chinese literacy that sees writing as confined largely to the activities of a small number of individuals in the immediate entourage of the Shang kings.

Ken-ichi Takashima is Professor Emeritus, University of British Columbia, Vancouver. He studied German and English with a minor in general phonetics and *kambun kundoku* at Jōchi University in Tokyo and Chinese linguistics and paleography at the University of Washington, Seattle (MA, 1967; PhD, 1973). His research interests are pre-classical Chinese as recorded on the oracle bones and ritual bronzes. Takashima has held visiting professorships at the Institute of Oriental Culture, Tokyo University (1988–90), East China Normal University, Shanghai (2001–2), and Anhui University, Hefei (2006–7). His books include *A Comprehensive Guide to the Interpretations of the Oracle-Bone Graphs*, *Studies in Early Chinese Civilization*, and *Studies of Fascicle Three of Inscriptions from the Yin Ruins*.

In "Literacy to the South and the East of Anyang in Shang China: Zhengzhou and Daxinzhuang" (chapter 4), Takashima examines how literacy revolved around the major urban area, quite possibly the ritual center or capital city, of late Shang China. It was impossible to point to any reliable evidence for the geographic scope of Shang literacy before the discovery in 1953 of the inscribed bovine rib and elbow bones in Zhengzhou 鄭州 and, in 2003, of several pieces of inscribed oracle bone plastrons in Daxinzhuang 大辛莊, Shandong. Scholars did not pay much attention to the former for nearly fifty years, having dismissed them as nothing more than "practice inscriptions"; however, two more pieces were found in Zhengzhou in 1989–90, and the discovery of the Daxinzhuang pieces spurred rigorous examination of the inscriptions and larger archaeological issues. Paleographic scrutiny of the Zhengzhou and Daxinzhuang inscriptions gives an inkling of the processes through which the high degree of literacy in Anyang might have been achieved and the role literacy played in the cultural dynamics in Shang China, especially divinatory, social, sacrificial, and ritual practices in these regions. The chapter also pays attention to the degree to which these inscriptions contributed to the generally superior level of writing in Anyang as well as how the latter influenced writing in Zhengzhou and Daxinzhuang.

Robin D. S. Yates, James McGill Professor of History and East Asian Studies, McGill University, specializes in Chinese history, concentrating on Early China and the history of science, technology, and women. Trained at Oxford University, the University of California, Berkeley, and Harvard University (PhD, 1980), and chair of the Society for the Study of

Early China (2003–10), he is the author of *Women in China from Earliest Times to the Present*, *Five Lost Classics*, and *Science and Civilisation in China*, vol. 5, part 6 (with Joseph Needham et al). He is collaborating with Anthony Barbieri-Low on a translation and analysis of the newly discovered early Han legal texts from Zhangjiashan.

In "Soldiers, Scribes, and Women: Literacy among the Lower Orders in Early China" (chapter 10), Yates studies the issue of literacy among the lower orders in the Late Warring States, Qin, and early Han times. Using both recently excavated legal texts and transmitted historical and other records, he argues that three groups—scribes, soldiers, and women—may have been able to gain some ability to read and write. Scribes, an occupational caste, were fully literate, capable of reading, writing, reproducing, and teaching graphs. They went at age seventeen for their final training in special schools reserved only for the sons of scribes, having already been trained for many years at home. They were assigned particular positions or roles in the bureaucratic administration, and they kept the huge volume of documents flowing, enabling the new imperial state to function. The other two groups may have been able to acquire only a limited level of literacy. Although the state mandated literacy for members of the lower orders so that it could exploit them, they deployed this newly acquired technology in their own interests to resist the state's demands.

Index

A/B-syllable distinction, 42, 133
abbreviated characters, 222, 222–23n33
abscond illegally, abscondence, 368–69, 368n96
Abydos (tomb), 70–73, 71f2.2. See also Egypt, Egyptology
Academia Sinica, Institute of History and Philology, 201n49
academies, 304
accompanying official, 260n39
accountants, accounting, 176–77, 373, 374–78
accumulated merit, 278–79, 279n21, 304, 325
achronical rising, 24
adults, 331, 382
affricate sibilant initials, 128n63
agricultural activities, societies, 24, 25, 26f1.2a, 39, 273n7
agriculture, 307n15
Ai Chengshu ding 哀成叔鼎 (JC 2782), 264n51
"Airs of Yong" ("Yong feng" 鄘風, Book of Poetry), 38
alignment, function of asterism Dìng, 39–41; of characters, 186
Allan, Sarah, 9
Allen, James P., 91n15
alloying (of bronze vessel), 375
"Almanac" (Lüshi chunqiu), 375
almanacs, 28, 334, 345n15
Alpha Pegasus, 46

alphabetic writing, 35, 60, 62, 161
"Already Inebriated" ("Ji zui" 既醉, Book of Poetry), 317
altar, 150n21; of the soil and millet, 335; of the spirit of Bo, 146n18; to the spirit of the soil, 146, 150, 150n21
amnesty (shè 赦), 346, 346n18
ān 安 (particle), 229n45
Analects (Lunyu 論語), 42n40, 125, 332
analog devices, 24–27
analytical composite graphs, 94–104, 102tt3.10–11, 111tt3.14–15. See also characters; pictographs, pictography
ancestor, 111, 112t3.16; worship of, 19, 291, 294–335
ancestral: cults, 340; law, 327; movement and mood, 320; narrative, 329; power, 324; shrines, tablets, 67, 111, 112t3.6, 166, 167–68n55, 306, 308, 313; spirits, 166–67; titles, 271n2
ancients, 305
Anhui 安徽, 11, 44n44, 351n32
animal bones. See bone inscriptions, bones; bovine joints
animals, 176–77; consumption of, 170; in Neolithic writing: systems, 11n17, 43n44; sacrificial animals, 169–70 (see also pig; sacrifice); wild animals, 170n63
Anlu 安陸, 357
"announcement of merit", 239–6
announcement to the dead in the netherworld, 264

INDEX 453

anonymity, 334n93
Antares in Scorpius, 36n28, 41
antiquity, European, 92
Anyang 安陽: viii, ix, 12, 14, 65–69, 141–72, *147t4.1*, *149t4.2*, 173–205, 271, 291
Anyi 安邑, 380
áo 敖 'proud', 'overbearing', 346, 346n18
"Appended Commentary" ("Xici zhuan 繫辭傳", *Book of Changes*), 24, 47, 49–50
appoint with a written document (*cèmìng* 冊命), 249, 250n24, 277
appointment inscriptions, 260n39, 273–77
apprentice disciples, 347, 347n21
arboriculture, 344n12
Archaeological Sites, Map of: ix
archaeologists: Chinese, 388, 396; Japanese, 392
archaic script, 22; clerical script (*gǔlì* 古隸), 221n27
archery, 263, 303n1, 305, 306, 306n10
architectural bricks, 379, 388, 388n37
architecture, beginnings of, 397
aristocracy: lineage, 282; literacy, 371; lower rank, 170n63, 254n29; private quarters of ladies, 297; ranking system 339n1
armies, 326, 327, 344
armor, 376
army. *See* soldiers; war, warfare
arrows, use for transmissions, 342
articulation, double, 58
artisans, 13, 370–99; names of, *Plate 8*, 368, 379–91, *386t11.1*, *389f11.1*; signatures, 382–84.
arts, 321, 333. *See also* Six Arts
ascension ritual, 328n78
aspirated stops (aspiration), 128n63, 129, 130; rogue aspiration, *129t3.32*
assembly line, 374
Assistant Prefect (*chéng* 丞), 347, 357
assistant scribe (*shūzuǒ* 書佐), 359n63. *See also* scribal groups

assonance, 33, 35
asterisms. *See* astronomy; lunar lodges
astrologers, Inka. *See* Inka
astronomy, asterisms, 10, 14, 19–50, 25n14; rising and setting points, 25n14; sighting rod, *26f1.2b*. *See also* stars
attention marks, 225–26, 231
audience: context, procedures, protocol, 247, 259–70, 294n43; dialogs in bronze inscriptions, 240–51; ritual in canonical texts, 251–58
awards (narratives, speeches), 331–32. *See also* gifts; speeches
Awesome Decorum. *See wēiyí* 威儀
axial alignment, north-south, 37–38
axle bushing, 396, 397
Aymara spelling, 10n16
azimuth, 45
Babylonian: astronomy, 36n28; origins of stems and branches, 29n21; scribal education, 176, 177
backward writing (in oracle bone inscriptions), 199
Bactrian camel humps, 25n14, *26f1.2a*
Bagley, Robert W., 20n3, 48nn51–52, 66n28, 68, 72n38, 174–76, 204
Baines, John, 54n6, 71n37, 72
bàishǒu qǐshǒu 拜手稽首 'to bow and touch one's head to the ground', 281
ballot law, Roman, 3
bamboo documents, manuscripts (*cè* 冊/策, *jiǎncè* 簡冊), 13, 68, 96, 99, 203, 204, 205, 209–10, 211n14, 213, 232n50, 249, 272, 276, 277, 287, 292, 293, 304, 320, 325, 334, 359–62, *392f11.2*; of royal command (*mìngcè* 命冊), 274, 275n11, 276–77. *See also* manuscripts)
bamboo poles (punishment), 376
Ban family, 364–65; Ban Gu 班固, 220, 364; Ban Jieyu 班婕妤 364; Ban Zhao, 班昭, 364
Ban *gui* 班簋 (JC 4341), 164a, 263nn42–43
bànfú 半幅 'half-width format (of a scroll)', 211–12, 220, 234

454 INDEX

banquets, 258, 294n43, 297, 309n20. *See also* feasts, feasting
Baoji 寶鷄, ix, 287, 290
Baoshan MSS, 222
Barbarians, 254n28, 295n45
Barbieri-Low, Anthony, 13, 206n[0], 339n[0], 345n14, 346n18, 354n45, 363nn74–75
barley, 222n31
"Basic Annals of Qin" (*Records of the Grand Scribe*), 50
Baxter, William H., 88n6, *90t3.7*, *110t3.13*, 114, 119, 119n53, 122, *119–22t3.23–30*, 133, 134, *135–37t3.34*, 396n50
beer, 69
beginning of Spring, 44
behavior (styles of), 311–12
beheading, 168
Behr, Wolfgang, 33n25, 51n[0], 60n19, 133
"Bei feng" 邶風 (*Book of Poetry*), 328n77
Beijing 北京: ix, 130n64, 141n2; Institute of Archaeology, 144; National Museum 276n13; Palace Museum 266n61; Poly Museum 276n13
Belknap, Robert L., 9
bell inscriptions, bells, 244, 308, 310n23, 313–18, 320n51, 321–32. *See also* music (musical ceremony, performance)
beneficiary (definition), 240n3
Bengbu 蚌埠, 44n44
bí 鼻 'nose', 115; *114t3.20*
bǐ 俾 (causative particle), 330; 比 'compare', 'form an alliance with', 147b
bì 璧 (kind of ceremonial jade disk), 256, 280, 282–83; 畀 (phonetic in *bí* 鼻), 115
biāo 彪 'tiger's stripes', *89t3.2*; 髟 'long hair', 89, *89t3.2*
"Bibliographic Treatise". *See* "Yiwen zhi" 藝文志
Bielenstein, Hans, 372n4
Big Dipper, 49n53

Bin 賓 diviner group inscriptions, 142nn4–5, *147t4.1*, *149t4.2*, 151–52, 154–55, 154n31, 157, 158, 161, 168, 196
bīn 賓 'guest', 'to treat as a guest', 'to host', 166, 167, 167n53, 195, 195n39
binary cyclical signs, 36
bǐng 丙 (*tiāngān* #3), *32t1.1*, *34t1.2*, 184, *184f5.1*, *185f5.2c*, 186
bǐngdé 秉德 'to grasp the inner power', 309, 324
bìnglì 並立 'to stand side by side', ligature for, 99, *100t3.8*
bǐngxíngqì 柄形器 'handle-shaped artifact', 166n52
binoms: reduplicated, 311–12, 315–20, 323–24, 329; rhyming, 99, 333n91
bird imagery, 318
birdlike dance movements, 316
bǐshì 筆勢 'stroke extension in a Chinese character', 157
bisyllabic words, 56n8
blessings, 317, 324
Bo 亳, 146n18
Bō 剝 (hexagram in *Book of Changes*), 279, 279n23
bó 鎛 (kind of bronze bell), 318, 325n70, 331n84, 375n70
Bo Dao 伯導, 280–81
Bo Maofu 伯懋父, 286
Bo Zhefu *gui* 伯者父簋 (JC 3748), 297
boards and slips. *See* bamboo documents; slips
bodyguards, 326
Boltz, William G., 5, 11n17, 48n52, 85n[0], 87, 91, 92, 92n19, 123, 124, 133, 216n20, 229nn43–44, 254n28
bondservants (*lìchénqiè* 隸臣妾), 348–49, 348–49n25, 349n26
bone inscriptions, bones, 67, 70, 141–74, 182, 197–204, 246n17; oracle bone inscriptions, 11, 20, 23, 30n23, 42n41, 43, 48–49nn51–53, 88, 265, 271n2,

340n3; Shang, 41, 48n53, 51–52n1; Xiaochen Qiang bone, 29n20. *See also* bovine joints; cattle, cows; diviners; divination; OBI; scapula (fragments)
bone-cored lacquer objects, 378
bone-cracking, divination by, 11, 343n12
Boodberg, Peter A., 87, 89, 90–91, 94, 101, 115n49
Book of Changes (*Yijing* 易經), 24, 45–50, 279, 320n48
Book of Documents (*Shujing* 書經, *Shangshu* 尚書, *Shu* 書), 42, 264, 303, 306, 312, 320, 334, 364–65
Book of Lord Shang (*Shangjun shu* 商君書), 343, 343n12
Book of Poetry (*Shijing* 詩經, *Shi* 詩), 125, 126, 268n67, 303, 306–7, 315–34, 326n72, 375
Book of Rites (*Liji* 禮記, *Li* 禮), 303n1, 306n10, 307, 307n15, 311n25, 324, 331, 332, 332n88, 334, 375, 375n12
bookkeeping, 177, 277
books: burning, 343n12; selling, 371
Boone, Elizabeth Hill, 53, 53n4, 54
Boshe 亳社 'altar of the spirit of Bo', 146n18
Boshi, 283
bóshū 帛書 'silk manuscript', 211n11
Bottéro, Françoise, 92, 93n20, 104–6
bovine joints, *156f4.2*, 158
bowls, 383; shallow bowls, *Plate 8b*
bowstring, 95
boxes, lacquer. *See* lacquer objects
bóxué 博學 'broad learning', 306n13, 330
boys and girls, 381–82
brain, 102–3
branch lineages, 283, 317
branches, stems and. *See gānzhī* 干支
Branner, David Prager, 9, 11, 12, 33n25, 134
bricks (architectural), 379, 388, 388n37
"Brilliant Ancestor Patriarch Tang" 皇祖唐公, 319–20

Bronze Age: divination record, 203; Greek, 373; literacy, 4, 14; marks, 66; ritual specialists in, 37; structure, 21; writing, 398
bronze inscriptions, 48n51, 65, 67, 88, 91n12, *93t3.5*, 108–13, *110–16tt3.13–23*, 141, 148e, 151n23, 152n25, 154, 164, 169–70n61, 239–70, 271–310, *283f8.1*, 322–30, 331, 331n83, 334–36, 340n3, 374, 375; inscriptions as evidence of literacy, 293–300. *See also* bronzes *and the names of individual vessels*
bronzes, Western Zhou, 158, 276, 277n14, 308, 309n20; casters, 292, 297, 374, 396; décor, 318; vessels 299, 385, 393n45; other objects (mirrors, weapons), 271, 373, 37. *See also* bronze inscriptions
brush-writing, brushes, 172n64, 203, 204, 211, 225n36, 384, 391. *See also* writing
brushes, hair. *See* hair brushes
BS- initial cluster, 115n49
bǔ 卜 'to divine', 'prognosticate by cracking', 11, 77, 78, *78f2.3*, 80, 164, 187; written for word *wài* 外, 11, 78–81. *See also* divination (divination crack)
bù 不 (negative particle), 116, *116t3.22*, 161, 165, 165n50, 166, 361; 步 'pace', 'footstep', 92n19, 165–66
Buck, Linda, 58n12
bùfēn kāihé 不分開合 'lip-rounding non-distinctive', 134–37
bùgēng 不更 (ancient rank), 359, 360n69
bùjiàn 部件 'character components or elements', 103n35
burial grounds. *See* tomb texts
burial platters, 393
burin (tool for incising graphs), 384
burning of the books, 343n12
burnt sacrifice (*liáo* 燎), 150
bushing, 396, 397
bùshǒu 部首 'dictionary section-heads', 103n35
bǔshū 卜書 'diviner's text', 354
bǔxī 卜夕 'to divine for the night', 197

bŭxún 卜旬 'to divine for the week ahead', 187–89, 197–99, 203
cacoform category (Lieti *lei* 劣體類), 142n4, 148
caesuras, 224, 225, 226
Cai *gui* 蔡簋 (JC 4340), 264n53
Caihou *pan* 蔡侯盤 (JC 10171), 321n54, 331n83
Caihou Shen *bo* 蔡侯申鎛 (JC 219–22), 267n64
Caihou *zhong* 蔡侯鐘, 331n84
Caihou *zun* 蔡侯尊 (JC 6010), 321n54
calendar, 20–37, *31fl.3*, 43–49, 303n1; calculation of, 305; notation, 21–28; priests, 23, 45–46; use of cyclical signs, 28–37
calf, 177
calligraphy, 29, 142, 235, 300n57, 385–91, *386t11.1, 389fl1.1, 392fl1.2*, 394. *See also* writing
calyx of a flower (*fū* 柎), 116, *116t3.22*
camel humps, Bactrian, 25n14, *26fl.2a*
Canaanite, 92n15
Cangjie pian 倉頡篇, 351
"Canon of Yao" ("Yaodian" 堯典, *Book of Documents*), 49, 202
canonical teaching, texts, 251–58, 305n8
Cantonese, 151n23, 154
Cao Lüning 曹旅寧, 350
capital county (Qin), 380
capitals and cities (time to build), 41
capping. *See guàn* 冠
captives (*fú* 孚/俘), *147t4.1*, 148c
cardinal directions, 201–2
cardinal stone niche, 167–68n55. *See also* ancestral: shrines
casters of metal, 292, 297, 374, 396
catalog of *xíkè* inscriptions, 180n22
cattle, cows, 169, 170n63, 391n42; bones, 141n1; rib, 143, 144n8. *See also* bone inscriptions, bones; divination
cè 冊/策 'bamboo or wooden manuscript'. *See* bamboo documents

celestial images (*xiàng* 象), 44, 44n44
Celestial Temple, *Plate 1*, *40fl.4*, 41–50
Celestial Thearch, 49, 50
cèmìng 冊命 'to appoint with a written document', 'to read aloud the writ of the mandate', 249, 250n24, 277
census, 371, 372
ceramics, 159, 379, 388
ceremonial function of graphs, 72n39
ceremonies at Zhou court, 239, 303–36
Chang, Kwang-chih (K.C.) 張光直, 21nn6–7, 294n42
Chang Yuzhi 常玉芝, 147b
Changjiang 長江. *See* Yangzi River
Changsha 長沙, 211n13; Commandery, 367n93
chanting, 307n15, 333, 353, 354, 354n42
Chao Yuen Ren 趙元任, 92n16
chapter (*zhāng* 章), 215
characters, Chinese, 94, 104, 232–34, 365, 372, 387. *See also bùjiàn* 部件; compound graphs; graphs; *hanja*; *hànzì*; *kanji*; letters: written characters; paleography; phonophores; radicals; writing
chariot, 305, 327, 328, 361
"check-off" marks, 384
chén 臣 'minister', 'official', 234; 辰 (asterism), (*dìzhī* #5), *32t1.1, 34t1.2*, 36n28, 181 (*see also* lunar lodges)
Chen Chao-jung 陳昭容, 295n44
Chen Fang *gui* 墬防簋 (cover; JC 4190), 267n64
Chen Jian *gui* 臣諫簋 (JC 4237), 263n48
Chen Man *fu* 陳曼簠 (JC 4595–96), 331n82
Chen Mengjia 陳夢家, 143, 144, 145, 169, 232, 296n47
Chen Ni *fu* 陳逆簠 (JC 4629–30), 267n64
Chen Pan 陳槃, 158n40
Chen Songchang 陳松長, 209nn6–7, 211n13, 212n15, 221n27, 232n50
Chen Wei 陳偉, 359n64
Chen Xu 陳旭, 145
Cheng 成 (king), 42n39, 304, 328, 328n78

Cheng 稱 (excavated text), *212t6.1*, 220
chéng 丞 'Assistant Prefect', 347, 357, 成, 227, 234
Cheng, Patriarch, 328
chēngcè 再冊 (phrase found on divination records), 204n59
Chengdu 成都: ix, 388, 388n53, 393–95
Chengzhou 成周, 274, 284
Chenhou Yinzi *dui* 陳侯因𩰫敦 (JC 4649), 267n64
chhàu hĩⁿ lâng 臭耳聾 (Taiwanese 'deaf'), 130n64
chief document maker (*zuòcè yǐn* 作冊尹), 275, 275nn10–11, 276, 281
children, 139, 179n20, 180, 199, 282, 305, 308, 308n17, 310, 311, 315–17, 318, 327, 328n78, 332, 333, 347n21, 381–82
children of the elite, 305, 316n38, 317
Childs-Johnson, Elizabeth, 9, 9n15
chimes. *See* bell inscriptions, bells
Chin Chi On 錢志安, 151n23
China, Early. *See* Early China
Chinese (Northern), 129–30, *131t3.33*
Chinese: archaeologists, 388, 396; Bronze Age, (*see* Bronze Age; bronze inscriptions); characters, (*see* characters; letters: written characters); scholars, scholarship, 106, 216n20; University of Hong Kong, 244n12
Chinois archaïque. *See* Karlgren, Bernhard
chóngwén hào 重文號 'doubling mark', 96–100, *100t3.8*
chǒu 丑 (*dìzhī* #3), *32t1.1*, *34t1.2*, 147a, *147t4.1*, *149t4.2*, 150, 184, 186
chronicle (*lì* 曆/歷), 279n21
Chú dìzǐ lǜ 除弟子律 (Statutes concerning the Appointment of Retainers), 347n21
Chu 楚, *149t4.2*, 154, 221, 222, 310, 311, 312n29, 310, 319, 320, 321, 322–25, 326, 330, 331, 334, 360, 362
chù 豕 'pig', 161, 162–65, 168–70
chuān 川 'river', 157

chuáng 爿 (phonophore), 108–10, 117–18, *118t3.24*; 牀 'bed', 'frame', 108–10; 疒 'sick abed', 109
"Chuche" 出車 (*Book of Poetry*), 286n34
chǔn 蠢 'stupid', 130n64
Chunqiu 春秋 (or *Chunqiu jing* 春秋經). *See Spring and Autumn Annals*
Chunqiu shiyu 春秋事語, 213
Chunyu Yi 淳于意, 364
Chuqiu 楚丘, 38n31
Church romanization system, 128
chūwén 初文 'protoform', 109, 164
cinnabar, 233–34, 367
cities: foundation of, 397; schools in, 306n10; time to build, 41
civilian labor, 371–72
clan: control over literacy, 302; insignia, bronze, 152n25; 271n2; clan-based schools, 306n10, 308
classes: lower, (*see* commoners); social, (*see* social class)
Classical Chinese thought, 256n32
Classical texts, 371
classification of script types, 221n27
classifiers. *See* measure word
clay, inscriptions in, *Plate 8a*, 48n51, 379, 384
clay pots, 44n44
clerical script, 221, 268
clerks, 346–47, 346n18, 351, 357, 358, 361, 385
Cleveland Museum, 244n12
cloth. *See* silk
coastal region inscriptions, 312
Coblin, W. South, 117n51
codas, 33, 120–22, *122t3.31*
codicological units, definition, 213–17, *215t6.3*, 233
cognate: graphs, 333n91; pairs, 119; words in Sino-Tibetan, 42n40
cognition and reading, 102-3
collapse, Western Zhou, 272
colonization, 108
Columbia University: Contemporary Civilization, 8n12; Early China Seminar, (*see* Early China Seminar)

coming-of-age (ceremony, records, ritual), 317, 319, 321, 322, 331
commands, laws, regulations, 335, 342–43. *See also* military: orders, strategy; *mìng* 命; ordinance(s)
Commemoration of Merit, 294n43
commerce: in pre-imperial China, 259n37; enterprises, writing in, 368
commodities, 177
common language (*tōngyǔ* 通語), 125–26
commoners, 170n63, 340, 344–45, 355, 375
complex pictographs, 94–104, *102tt3.10–11, 111tt3.14–15*. *See also* pictographs, pictography
component parts, 103n35
compound graphs, composite characters, 57, *57t2.1*, 86–104, *88–90tt3.1–4, 93t3.5, 97–98tt3.6–7, 100tt3.8–9, 105t3.11*, 352n36. *See also* graphs, graphemes
concept script, 92
conferral of privileges, 239
Confucianist (*Ru* 儒), 230, 304–6, 306n13, 364–67, 309n20, 332, 332n86, 334
Confucius, 42n40, 230, 251, 256n32, 304, 312, 330, 340n3, 345n14, 394
cōng 聰 (proposed identification of an ancient graph), 222–23n33
cóng 从 'follow', 147b
conscription, military and civilian, 344, 371–72
consonantal homorganicity, 115, 116
constellations. *See* astronomy
consumption of animals, 170
contact: between *-p/-t* in *rùshēng*, 119–20, *119t3.25, 120tt3.26–27*; between corresponding syllable-codas (*duìzhuǎn* 對轉) or separate rimes (*xiéyùn* 叶韻), 122
Contemporary Civilization, Columbia University, 8n12
continuity of literacy, 108–17
contract signing, 372n5

contract tally used in land transaction, 284–85
contractions, oral, 98, *98t3.7*, 99
convict-labor artisans, 375, 376
Cook, Constance A., 9, 13, 14, 279n21, 334n93
Cook, Richard S., 36n28, 45n46
copying, copyists, 191–96, 199, 202, 372. *See also* sight-copying of divination records
cords (knotted, knotting), 24, 25, 47
correspondence sets, 109n45
corruption, 377
cosmology of Inkas, 24–25
costume attributes, 316
Cotsen Institute of Archaeology, University of California, 174n[0]
counting, pebbles 24; as the basis of classifiers, 169, 278. See also *gānzhī* 干支; *shǔ* 數
court: audience, 239–40 (*see also* audience: context); officials, 281–82; scribes, 359. *See also* scribal groups
courtesy name (*zì* 字), 378
covenants, 334
cracks, crack-numbers, 80, 83, 197, 198, 198n46, 201. *See also* hollows
craftsmen, 13, 374; literacy of, 372–73
Creel, Herrlee, 90, 91, 91n12, 93–94
creolization, 108
Crete, 373
crime, 367n90
crypto-phonogram theory of Chinese character structure, 12, 87–94, *89t3.2, 90tt3.3–4*
Cui 毳, 296–97; Cui *gui* 毳簋 (JC 3931–34), 296n48; Cui *pan* 毳盤 (JC 10119), 296; Cui *yi* 毳匜 (JC 10247), 296n48
Cui Shi 崔寔, 345n16, 377
cuìshǐ 卒史 'scribe in the Imperial Secretariat', 351, 358, 359n63
cults, ancestral, 340
cùn 寸 modern 'inch', as ancient character component, 95

INDEX

cuneiform: studies, 76, 91, 176, 177; tradition, 176; writing in Mesopotamia, 69, 175–77. *See also* Uruk periods
Cuo 罌 of Zhongshan (king), 335
cups, 382, 383
curriculum in schools for scribes, 350–54
curriculum vitae, 278–79, 279n22
curses, 334
customs, 378n18
Cuzco (mountain ridges), 25n14
cyclical signs, stems and branches, 183–84, *185f5.2c*, 186; dates, 180; in the Chinese calendar. See *gānzhī* 干支
Da (?) 狄 (diviner's name), 197, 198
dà 大 'major', 219n24, 233
Da Dai Liji 大戴禮記, 169–70n61, 353n40
Da Ding 大丁, 78, 78n47
Da *gui* 大簋 (JC 4298–99), 264n49
Da Ke *ding* 大克鼎 (JC 2836), 245n15, 247–51, 260, 264n53
Dà Nǚzǐ Áo 大女子鼇, 382
Da Shi Shi *ding* 大矢始鼎 (JC 2792), 263n42
"Da sima" 大司馬 (*Zhouli*), 343n11
Da Wu 大戊, 78
Da Yu *ding* 大盂鼎 (JC 2837), 178, 264n53, 266n59, 277
dàchéng 大成 'great completion', 332
Dafentou 大墳頭, 381–85
"Dahuang jing" 大荒經 (*Shanhaijing*), 23n9
dàifū or *dàfū* 大夫 'grandee', *100t3.8*, 369
dàláo 大牢 'major livestock', 169–70n61
dàliánkēng 大連坑 'large joined trenches', 191, 197–99, 203n57
Dan Zhu 丹朱, 167–68n55
dance, dancing, 303n1, 306n13, 309n20, 311, 316, 318, 321, 323–24, 328, 333, 334, 335; dance *shāng* (*wǔ shāng* 舞商), 179–80
Danfeng 丹鳳, 261
Dao 道 (excavated text), *212t6.1, 213t6.2*, 214–20, *215t6.3*, 222–23n33, 224, 231

Dao (*dào* 道) 'way', 305, 308, 311, 334
Dao de jing 道德經, 218
Dao yuan 道原 (excavated text), 220, *212t6.1*
dàojiā 道家 'Daoist', 220
dark and light days, 320
Dàshǐ 大史 'the Grand Scribe', 356n55
Dasikongcun 大司空村, 159
Dassow, Eva von, 92n15
date tables, 180–87. *184f5.1, 185f5.2*
dating formula, 322–23
Dawenkou 大汶口, 66, 66n28
Daxinzhuang 大辛莊, *Plate 2*, ix, 12, 141–72, *162f4.3, 163t4.3f*; inscription, 160–71
dàxué 大學 'site of a ritual', 178
"Daya" 大雅 ("Greater Elegantiae", *Book of Poetry*), 251, 254, 311, 314n33, 318n32, 320n52, 324
days, epagomenal, 25
De 德 (excavated text), *212t6.1, 213t6.2*, 214–20, *215t6.3*, 222–23n33, 231
dé 得 'to obtain', 233n51; 德 'virtue', 233n51, 304, 309, 311, 312, 316n38, 322, 324, 328, 331, 334
De dao jing 道德經, 218
de Saussure, Léopold, 46n48
De sheng 德聖 (excavated text), *213t6.2, 215t6.3*, 217
the dead, 264n51; announcement to, 264
deaf, 130n64
Dearing, Vinton, 214n16
debate, 307
deceased, 309n19
decorum, 306, 321, 327n76, 331, 334
dedicated (definition), 240n3
dedication, statement of, 239, 243
deer, 44n44, 105, *105t3.11*, 198n47, *392f11.2*, 393, 395
definition of writing, 52–56
DeFrancis, John, 62n22, 91
deity, portrait of, 393
deletion of characters, 232
delivering the mandate, 255, 260, 261, 268
dental codas, 120. *See also* codas

dependent, 369
depictions on clay pots, 44n44
descent of blessings, 324
desert, 353, 360, 365
design painter, *386t11.1*
devil worship, 25
dewlap (*hú* 胡), 63–64
déyīn 德音 'the "tone" of one's inner power', 320
Di 帝 'lord', 314, 328, 332. See also *Shangdi*
Di 狄 (a people), 38n31
dí 滌 'to wash', 'rinse', 113, *113t3.18*
dǐ 底 'bottom', 'to reach', 44
dì 禘 (name of a ceremony), 308; 禘 (also written 帝; name of a sacrifice), 151
Di Xin 帝辛 (king), 159n43; period, 141n2
Di Yi 帝乙 (king), 148d, 159n43
dialect, 150, 151, 152; dialect mixture, 154, 154n29
dialogs, 175, 176
diǎn 典 'to document in writing', 285, 294; 點 'to delete characters', 232
diàn 殿 'poor in quality', 376
Diaosheng 琱生. See Zhousheng 琱生
dictionaries, 56n8, 86n1, 130n65; section-heads (*bùshǒu* 部首), 103n35
Didier, John, 49n53
diglossia, 123–32
digraphs, 59n17
"Diguan situ" 地官司徒 (*Zhouli*), 305
díliáo 敵寮 'to match up (officers) by rank', 327
dīng 丁 (*tiāngān* #4), 'fourth', 10, 21n7, *34t1.2*, 47–50, 48n51, 49n53, 184, *185t5.2b*
dǐng 鼎 'cauldron', 42n41, 43, 44, 49n53
Dìng 定 (asterism), 38–50, *40f1.4*, *47f1.5*, 49n53
dìng 定 'to fix (position)', 42–44, 42n39, 49n43
Ding County 定縣, Hebei, 388

"Dìng zhi fang zhong" 定之方中 (*Book of Poetry*), 38, 39, 43, 49n53
"Dingfen" 定分 (*Book of Lord Shang*), 343n12
Dinggong 丁公, Shandong: ix, 11n17
direct objects, 152n25, 153, 153n26
directions, cardinal, 201–2
the disabled, 360
disambiguate, 87
disciples, apprentices, 347, 347n21
disputes, legal, 264
distinctions, tonal. See tone categories
ditto marks, 99n29
divination, 42, 48, 51–52n1, 67, 150–72, 173–205, 174n3, 343n12; by bone cracking, 11, 343n12; divination crack, 78, *78f2.3*, 189 (see also *bǔ* 卜); workshop, 204, 334. See also bone inscriptions, bones; diviners; literacy
divining, 11, 77, 78, *78f2.3*, 80, 164, 187–89, 197–99, 203
diviners, 142, *147t4.1*, *149t4.2*, 150–72, 173–205, 174n3, 302, 321, 350–56, 373, 398; diviner's text (*bǔshū* 卜書), 354. See also divination; Grand Diviner; scribal groups. *For specific diviners see entries by name, e.g.*, Bin 賓; Da (?) 狄; He 何; Kou 口; Peng 彭; Zhu 宁
division of labor, 374
dìzhī 地支 ('earthly branches', 'twelve branches': cyclical signs), 33, *34t1.2*, 36, *185f5.2b*. See also *tiāngān dìzhī* 天干地支
dìzǐ 弟子 'student', 'trainee', 307, 358. See also students (trainees)
do ut des principle, 259
documents, written, 271–301, 308, 355–56n50, 360–64, 380; document of command (*mìngshū* 命書), 274, 275nn10–11, 276. See also legal: documents; record-keeping
domestic life of Western Zhou elites, 295–300
Donald, Merlin, 21n5, 24, 28n18, 47n50
Dong *gui* 㚇簋 (JC 4322), 295, 300

Dong II-*ding* 彧鼎 (JC 2824), 245n15
Dongbi 東壁 (asterism), 38, 39, 45
Dongping 東平 Princedom, 391n43
donors, 240n3, 250
dots, 113, 213, 216, 217, 223, 225–26
Dou 豆, 289, 290, 291, 293
double articulation, 58
double-object construction, 152–53
doubled initials, 33n25
doubling mark, 96–100, *100t3.8*
dragon, 46n48; constellation, 36n28, 41, 46
drumming, drums, 306n13, 324, 329
drunkenness, at banquets, 258
Du Ponceau, Peter. *See* Duponceau, Peter
Du Yu 杜預, 158n40
dual usage of words. *See* words (dual usage of)
duality of patterning, 58
Duan Yucai 段玉裁, 94, 94n21, 350n29
ductus, wedge-shaped, 69, *70f2.1*
duìyáng 對揚 'response-eulogy by the recipient of a eulogy', 310
duìzhēn 對貞 'paired divinations', 160, 164
duìzhuǎn 對轉 'contact between corresponding syllable-codas', 122. *See also* codas
dukes, 38n31, 350n30
Dunhuang 敦煌, 372n5
duōshì 多士 'many gentlemen, many sirs', 323, 328
Duoyou *ding* 多友鼎 (JC 2835), 263n48, 297, 299
duōyǒu 多友 'the many aides', 317
duōzǐ 多子 'Many Children', 179, 179n20
Duponceau, Peter, 92, 92n16
E *zun* 㓝尊 (JC 6014). *See* He *zun*
é-káu 啞狗 (Taiwanese 'mute'), 130n64
E.P.T. (excavation trench at Pochengzi 破城子), 361
Early China, 13–14, 85, 108, 259n37, 339–41, 370, 397–99; chronology, viii; right and left in, 261n40

Early China Seminar, Columbia University, 8–10, 49n53, 73n41, 85n[0], 174n[0], 295n44, 339
Early Chinese. *See* Old Chinese
Early Dynastic Period (Uruk), 177
earthly branches. *See* *dìzhī* 地支
East Asia, 271
Eastern Han dynasty. *See* Han dynasty: Eastern
Eastern Zhou Period, 309–33. *See also* Zhou dynasty: Eastern
"Eat Wheat" (*Shímài* 食麥, month of the Shang calendar), 30, 30n22, 49
echo noun, 169
eclipses, 25
economic transaction, 294
Edkins, Joseph, 132
education, 175, 176, 302–36, 373. *See also* girls' education; schools, schooling; teachers, teaching
Egypt, Egyptology: literacy, writing, 48n52, 52, 54n6, 69, 70–74, *71f2.2*, 76, 91, 92, 373, 393; ritual specialists, 37
elders, 360
elegant language (*yǎyán* 雅言), 124–27
Elegantiae. *See* "Greater Elegantiae"; "Lesser Elegantiae"
element of a Chinese character. *See* *bùjiàn* 部件; phonophores; radicals
elephant, 44n44, 113, 114n47
elites: ceremonies, 239, 303–36; chanting by, 307n15; children, youths, 305, 315–16, 317; education in Western Zhou, 307–9; practice of literacy, 10, 173, 336, 373n6
Ellsworth, Robert H., 244n12
employment, government, 371–72
English language, 59, 81n49, 231; influence of, 151n23
Englund, Robert K., 70n35, 176
engraving practice, 180–87, 199. *See also* bone inscriptions, bones
epagomenal days (in astronomy), 25
epitext (definition), 210n9
equinox, ancient, 36n28

Er san zi wen 二三子問 (Mawangdui MS), 212
Erligang 二里崗. *See* Zhengzhou: Erligang 鄭州二里崗
Erlitou 二里頭: ix
errors in writing. *See* writing: errors
Erya 爾雅, 38–39n33, 86, 88, 278, 315n36
eulogy, 303n1, 310, 333, 335
eunuch officials, 356n52
Europe: antiquity, 92; Middle Ages, 373
excavations, 91n12, 197, 209n6; trench at Pochengzi 破城子 (E.P.T.), 361
Executive Official, 281
exegetical tradition, 303n3
exorcism, 157, 309n19
extended use of a single character (phonetically based), 62, 63n25, 65, 76, 77n45
fá 伐 'attack punitively', 'human victim', 153, 278–79
factories, factory systems, 374–78, 385–88. *See also* imperial: factories; private: workshops; workshops
fǎlìng 法令 'laws and ordinances', 343n12
Falkenhausen, Lothar von, 13–14, 174n[0], 241n9, 294n42, 330n81
"Famu" 伐木 (*Book of Poetry*), 258n34, 298–99
Fan Sheng *gui* 番生簋 (JC 4326), 309n19
fànběn 範本 'model for learning to write', 181
Fang 房 (asterism), 36n28, 44–45, 45n46, 46. *See also* lunar lodges
Fang Hui 方輝, 160
Fangyan 方言, 126, 127
fànyú 飯盂 'vessel for serving food', 296n47
Farmer's Auspice (*Nóngxiáng* 農祥), 44, 45, 45n46, 46
Father Jia (Fu Jia 父甲), 191, 193
fáyuè 伐閱 'curriculum vitae', 279
feasts, feasting, 308–9, 311n24, 317n40, 335. *See also* banquets

fēi 朏 'to appear (new moon)', 99
fēi wáng bǔcí 非王卜辭 'non-royal oracle bone inscription', 142n4
"Feiyue shang" 非樂上 (*Mozi*), 334n94
females, 263n42, 295, 295nn44–45, 296, 321, 328, 344, 348, 349n26, 362, 364–67, 368–69, 370–99; literacy, (*see* literacy: women's). *See also* girls' education; women: category
fēn 饋 'to serve food', 295–96
Feng 封: ix
fēng 封 'tree-marker', 'to seal', 289–90, 367n90
fěng 諷/風 'to read silently', 353
Feng *ding* 趩鼎 (JC 2815), 273–74, 275n11
Feng River 豐水, 314
Fengchu 鳳雛, 141n2
Fengsheng 豐生, 280, 281
fēnguǐ 饋簋 '*guǐ* vessel for serving food', 296n48
fēnyú 饋盂 'vessel for serving food', 296n47
Ferguson, Charles A., 125
"field allocation" astrology, 50n56
Fifteen Sections (the *Shi Zhou* 史籀?), 350–52
Fifth Year Qiu Wei *ding* 五年裘衛鼎 (JC 2832), 264n49, 282
Fifth Year Shaobo Hu *gui* 五年召伯虎簋 (JC 4292), 251n26, 264n49, 283
Fifth Year Wei *ding* 五祀衛鼎 (JC 2832), 264n49, 282
Fifth Year Zhousheng *gui* 五年琱生簋 (JC 4292). *See* Fifth Year Shaobo Hu *gui* 五年召伯虎簋
fines, fining, 354, 376. *See also* punishments
Fire Star (Antares in Scorpius), 36n28, 41
First Emperor (Qin), 367, 379, 384. *See also* Qin
First Industrial Revolution (Europe), 374
five planets, 46, *47f1.5*, 50
"Fixing of Rights and Duties" (*Book of Lord Shang*), 343n12
floods, 157

INDEX

foreman (master artisan), 376, 380, 381, 384, 385, *386t11.1*, 387; foreman clerk, 385–88
format (of a scroll), 211–12, 220, 234
forts, 351n32, 353, 360
Forty-second Year Lai *ding* 四十二年逨鼎, 273–74
Forty-third Year Lai *ding* 四十三年逨鼎, 273–74, 277n14
Forty-third Year Qiu *ding* 四十三年逑鼎 (XS 745–56), 245n13
forwarding of documents, 348n25
four, fourth, 49
four quarters, 42, 201–2
four regions, 309, 316, 317
Fourmont, Étienne, 108, 124
French language, 59
fū 夫 'man', 99, *100t3.8*; 敷 'to spread (culture)', 309, 327; 柎 'drum-stand', 'calyx', 116, *116t3.22*
fú 俘/孚 'captive', *147t4.1*, 148c; 弗 (negative particle), 165, 165n50;
fù 傅 'to register', 357; 富 'wealthy', 234
Fu Hao 婦好, 194
Fu Jia 父甲 'Father Jia', 191, 193
"Fu lü" 傅律 ("Statutes on Enrollments"), 360, 365
Fu Sheng 伏生, 364, 372n5
Fu Yi 父乙, 166, 167
Fufeng 扶風 County, 283
Fugong Zhong *gui* 復公仲簋 (JC 4128), 266–67
full-width format (of a scroll), 211
functional homophony, 117–23
functional literacy. See literacy
funerary epitaphs, 391
Funü *lei* 婦女類 'the women category', 142n4, *149t4.2*, *163t4.3*, 161, 164c, 167, 171
Fuyang 阜陽, Anhui, 351n32
Gai 匄, 382
Galambos, Imre, 94–95n23, 123, 124

gān 干 (cyclical signs). See *tiāngān* 天干
gāng 釭 'iron axle bushing', 396–97
Gansu 甘肅, 318
gānzhī 干支 'cyclical signs in the Chinese calendar', 10–11, 19–37, *34t1.2*, 47–48, 73n41, 180–82, *185f5.2*, 186, 187, 189, 198, 202, 203; mnemonic phonology of 30–37; practicing the writing of 181–87, 203; astral correlates 29n21, 48–49. See also signs: cyclical; *dìzhī* 地支; *tiāngān* 天干; *and under individual names*
Gao of Xianyang 咸陽高, 38
Gassmann, Robert H., 60n19, 133
gē 戈 'halberd', 92, *93t3.5*
Gebo 格伯, 284–85; Gebo *gui* 格伯簋 (JC 4262), *see* Pengsheng *gui* 倗生簋
Gedao 閣道 ("Stepped Passageway", asterism), 50. See also lunar lodges
generic rhyming, 35. See also rhyming
Genette, Gérard, 210n9
gēng 庚 (*tiāngān* #7), *32t1.1*, *34t1.2*; 更 'tour of duty', 354, 354n43
German language, 59
gifts, 174, 177, 246–47, 256–57, 259, 310, 325, 330–32
girls' education, 303n1. See also females; schools, schooling
girls' ranking, 381–82
given name, 88, 345, 378, 380, 382, 388, 390n40
glottographic writing, 11, 27, 48, 48n52, 49, 54–56, 70–84. See also writing: systems
glyphs, 384
gnomon, 38
goat, *147t4.1*, 148a, *149t4.2*, 151, 153, 169–70n61, 170n63, 191, 197
Gobi desert. See desert
Goldin, Paul, 33n25, 35n27
gōng 公 'patriarch', 'lineage head', 310–30; 功 'merit', 333; 工 'artisan', 380, 396n50; 弓 'bow', 95; 共, 233
gōngshī 工師 'master artisan', 374–75, 380
Gongshui 宮水 'Palace Water Factory', 379
Gongsun Deng 公孫登, 167–68n55
Goody, Jack, 341n6

government: documents, 361n70 (*see also* documents: written); employment, service, 371–72; production: government sponsors, 377–78, 381, 382

Gragg, Gene, 91n15

grain (*hé* 禾), 11, 69, 77, 297, 335; bushels of (*shí* 石), 356, 361; rations, 361; records, storage of, 371; types of, 69, 297

grammar, 150–57; particles, see *ān* 安; *bǐ* 俾; *jué* 厥; *nǎi* 乃; *qí* 其; *qiě* 且; *wéi* 隹; *wū* 惡/烏; *yān* 焉; *yě* 也; *yì* 亦; *yì* 殹; *yǐ* 矣; *yú* 于; *yú* 於; *zhě* 者; *zhī* 之

granaries, 364

Grand Diviner, 355–56

Grand Invocator. *See* invocators

Grand Scribe (*Dàshǐ* 大史), 257, 351, 353, 355–56

grandsons and sons, 296n47, 394

graphs, graphemes, 5, 10, 11, 12, 19, 24, 27, 37, 48–49, 51–84, 87–124 *88–89tt5.1–2, 93t3.5n[0], 100t3.8, 103t3.11, 100–16tt3.13–23, 118–22tt3.24–30*, 132, 144–72, *147t4.1–2, 156f4.2*, 178–205, *185f5.2c*, 295–96, 311, 318n43, 323, 333n91, 340, 346–47, 350–54, 358–60, 361, 382n27, 384, 385–88, *386t11.1*. *See also* characters; compound graphs; inscriptions; phonemes; Shang dynasty: inscriptions

gratitude, oral expression of, 261, 263n42

graves. *See* tombs

Great Square of Pegasus, 39, *40f1.4*, 44, 44n46, 49n53, 50

"Greater Elegantiae" ("Daya" 大雅, *Book of Poetry*), 251

Greece, Greek language, 62n24, 301, 373

Gu 穀, 152n25, 154

gǔ 古 'antiquity', 60–65; kind of metal, 286

Gu Yanwu 顧炎武, 98n27

Guai of Linjin 臨晉恝, 380

guàn 冠 'to undergo the capping ceremony', 323n59, 326, 332

"Guan zhen" 官箴 (Warnings for Officials, MS), 352

Guanghan Commandery Office of Workmen 廣漢郡工官, 385

Guangwudi 光武帝, 351

Guangyun 廣韻, 98n27

Guanshi ling 關市令 ("Ordinance on Markets and Passes"), 378n18

"*Guanshi lü*" 關市律 ("Statute on Markets and Passes"), 378n18

Guanzi 管子, 40–41; *Guanzi* 管子, 41–42

guǐ 癸 (*tiāngān* #10), 21n7, *32t1.1, 34t1.2*

guì 劌/歲 'to cut (an animal) in sacrifice', 153, 168–69

guidebooks, manuals. *See* manuals

guideline text (*jīng* 經), 216, 219n24

guilds, 384–85

guǐsì 癸巳 (day 30), 29

guǐyǒu 癸酉 (day 10), 155

gǔlì 古隸 'archaic clerical script', 221n27

"Guming" 顧命 (*Book of Documents*), 328n78

gums, 95n24

Guo Cong *gui* 虢从簋 (JC 4278), 264n50

Guo Moruo 郭沫若, 29, 29nn20–21, 30, 36n28, 181, 182, 186–87, 284n28, 285n29, 330n81

Guo Pu 郭璞, 39n33

Guo You Cong *ding* 虢攸从鼎 (JC 2818), 264n50

Guodian 郭店: forms and manuscripts, 97, *97f3.1, 100t3.8*, 215, 216, 227n38, 228n39, 333n91; *Laozi*, (see *Laozi*); tomb no. 1, 210

Guosheng 虢生, 274, 275, 275nn10–11

Guoshu Lü *zhong* 虢叔旅鐘 (JC 238–44), 245n15

Guoyu 國語. See *Tales of the States*

guózǐ 國子 'children of the elite', 305

gǔrén 古人 'the ancients', 305

Hagman, Jan L., 344n14

hài 亥 (*dìzhī* #12), *32t1.1, 34t1.2, 185f5.2e*, 186

Hai *gui* 害簋 (JC 4259), 276

Hakka, 128n63

INDEX 465

halberd, 92, *93t3.5*
half-width format (of a scroll), 211–12, 220, 234
Han 韓, state of, 375
"Han ce" 韓策 (*Tales of the States*), 357n57
Han dynasty, 344, 345, 351; artisans, 13, 368, 370–99; bamboo manuscripts, 96 (*see also* bamboo); bibliography, 206n1; clerical script, 221, 221n27, 395; documents, manuscripts, 96, 363, 371, 382, 387; early, 124, 339–40, 345, 349, 357; Eastern, viii, 13, 350, 371, 377, 388–91, *392f11.2*, 396; editors of Warring States texts, 312; education 345n14; elite, 364; factory systems, 374, 377; forts, 331n32, 353, 360; *History of the Han Dynasty* (*Hanshu* 漢書), 364, 365n81; immortality cult, 393; language, 125–26, 127, 130, 132, 175, 176, 182, 279; legal documents, 343–69, 378n18, 384; military service, 367–68; scribes, 352, 353; territory, 280; texts, 388n35 (*see also* text writing); tomb murals, 38n33; Western, viii, 351n32, 364, 372, 390n40; women, 364–67, 387–88; writing, 370–99
Han Huangfu *pan* 函皇父盤 (JC 10164), 297n51
Han River 漢江, 251, 319, 322
handwriting, 180–81, 198–99. *See also* writing
Hanfeizi 韓非子, 315n18, 344n14, 357n57
háng 行 'lane', 'intersection', 384–85. *See also xíng* 行
hanja 漢字 'character of Chinese origin', 56
Hànlì 漢隸 'Han clerical script', 221n27
Hanshu 漢書 (*History of the Han Dynasty*), 351, 354n43, 364, 365n81
hànzì 漢字 'character of Chinese origin', 56
Haosheng *zhong* fragments 昊生殘鐘 (JC 104–5), 264n53
harelip, 130n64
Harper, Donald, 208n4, 339n[0]

Harris, William, 273n6, 301, 372–73
harvest, 11, 24, 30n22, 77; festival, 28
He 何 (diviner's name), 193–99; diviner group inscriptions, *147t4.1*, 148, *149t4.2*, 191–99
hé 和, as rhyme-word, 227, 228n39*hé*; 盉 (bronze vessel), 297n51; 禾 'grain', 'millet', 'rice', 11, 77, 80–81, 82. *See also* grain
He *zun* 何尊 (JC 6014), 263n47
head: five-family unit, 360, 360n67; primary lineage, 283
Heaven, 43, 49–50, 304, 309, 309n19, 313, 314, 316, 328, 322
Heavenly Quadriga, 45, 45n46
Heavenly River, *Plate 1*, 50
heavenly stems. *See tiāngān* 天干
Hebei 河北, 141n2, 173, 388
hékǒu 合口 'pronounced with lip-rounding', 134–37
hemp-cored lacquer objects, 378. *See also* lacquer objects
Henan 河南, 173, 271n2, 318, 322, 396
Heng *gui* 恆簋 (JC 4199–4200), 246n16
hereditary status of scribes, 347–48, 350, 372n4
héwén 合文 'ligatures', 'composite graphs', 96–101, *98t3.7, 100t3.8*, 101, 352n36
hexagrams (*guà* 卦), 320n48; *Bō* 剝, 279, 279n23; *Qián* 乾, 46, 46n48; *Zhèn* 震, 320n48
hieroglyphic writing, Egyptian, 69, 70, 92. *See also* proto-hieroglyphic writing
high-frequency characters, 104
high-register language, 125, 130
History of the Han Dynasty (*Hanshu* 漢書), 354n43, 364, 365n81
Holenstein, Elmar, 58n13
hollows, 164, 193–94, 201. *See also* cracks, crack-numbers
Homeric scholarship, 268n67
homophones, 113, 116, 128
homorganicity, consonantal, 115, 116
hook marks, 223–31
horizontal strokes (within graphs), 186–87

horses, 327, 361; celestial winged, 39. *See also* terra cotta warriors and horses
household register, 359, 365–66, 370
hóushì 侯氏 'lord marquis', 254
Houston, Stephen D., 29n19
hǔ 虎 'tiger', *89t3.2*, 328
Hu, Bo of Shao 召伯虎. *See* Shao Hu
Hu *ding* 曶鼎 (JC 2838), 243n11, 264n49, 264n53, 292
Hu *gui* 猷簋 (JC 4317), 246n16, 246n18
Hu *gui* 虎簋, 261–63
Hu Houxuan 胡厚宣, 201–2
huà 畫 'to draw', *386t11.1*, 387
Huadong Zi 花東子 (abbr. of Huayuanzhuang Dongdi Zi zu 花園莊東地子組) and diviner group, 142n4–5, *149t4.2*. *See also* Huayuanzhuang Dongdi
Huainanzi 淮南子, 9, 23n9
Huaiyi 淮夷 'Barbarians', 254n28, 295n45
Huaizhou 懷州, 158
Huan 桓, Duke, of Qi 齊, 38n31
Huan River 洹河, 170n63
Huang 黃 diviner group inscriptions, *147t4.1*, 148, *149t4.2*, 186
Huang Ranwei 黃然偉, 275
Huáng zǔ Tánggōng 皇祖唐公, 319–20
Huangdi sijing 黃帝四經, 219–20
huánggōng 皇公 'brilliant patriarch', 317
"Huangyi" 皇矣 (*Book of Poetry*), 332–33
Huayuanzhuang 花園莊, viii, 170n63; Huayuanzhuang Dongdi 花園莊東地, 67n31, 179, 182n25, 196, 203n55; corpus, 67n31; locus south, 170. *See also* Huadong Zi 花東子
Hubei 湖北, 322, 349, 380, 381–85
hǔchén 虎臣 'tiger servant', 328
huī 撝/麾 'to lead', 'to direct', 113, *113t3.19*
huì 蘽 'to entreat', 296, 296n47
huìyì 會意 'syssemantic graph', 88
hùjí 戶籍 'household register', 359, 365–66, 370

Hulsewé, A.F.P., 345n15, 346, 346n18, 347, 347n21, 348, 348–49n25, 355n50, 356n53
human victim, 153, 278–79
humming, 353
Hunan 湖南, 359; Sheng Bowuguan 湖南省博物館 (Hunan Provincial Museum), 211n13, 218; University, 352
Hungarian language, 59n17
hunting divinations, 189, 197
Hutchinson Cancer Center, 58n12
hybrid structure of writing, 71n37
Hyman, Malcolm, 54n5, 71n37
hymns, 175, 176, 268
icon (definition of graphic sign), 81
iconic images (*xiàng* 象), 44, 44n44
iconographs, iconic images, icons, 69–71, 75, 81–82
ideograph, 25, *26f1.2a*, 91, 101n31; ideographic writing, 11, 48–49, 92, 94. *See also huìyì* 會意
Ikeda Yūichi 池田雄一, 347
illiteracy, 301, 342
imminence, 166
imperial: factories, workshops, 373, 385, 390n40, 395; manuscripts, 206
Imperial Prosecutor, 357n57
implements, ritual, 174
Inca. *See* Inka
index (definition, graphic sign), indexicality, 11, 81–84
indirect objects, 152n25, 153, 153n26
Industrial Revolution (Europe), 374
information, recording of. *See* record-keeping
inheritance (women's), 365
initials, 133; affricate sibilant, 128n63; doubled initials, 33n25; initial types for *xiéshēng* groups, 132–37
initiator dots. *See* dots
ink transcriptions, writing, 203, 228n40, 232, 232n50, 233n52, 388–90, *389f11.1*
Inka, 10, 24–27, *26f1.2*, 28
inscriptions (*míng* 銘), 68n31, 99, 141–71, 191–99, 271n1, 308–13, 319–36, 321n55, 340n3, 374–91, *386t11.1*, *389f11.1*,

392f11.2; inscriptions that form a pair, 160, 164. *See also* bell inscriptions, bells; bone inscriptions, bones; bronze inscriptions; cattle, cows; diviners; graphs, graphemes; scapula: fragments; scribal groups; vessels
Institute of History and Philology, Academia Sinica, 201n49
instructors' models, 194, 195, 199–202
instruments (of factories and workshops), 385. *See also* factories, factory systems; workshops
Interior Scribe (*nèishǐ* 內史), 274, 280, 281, 282. *See also* scribal groups
intermarriage, 314
Internet, 130n65
interstate meetings, 294n43
invention of writing. *See* writing: invention of
inventory lists, 334; Shang court, 170
investiture ceremony, 247
invocators, 350, 354, 357
iron, 373, 396
issuance of military orders, 263
Itō Michiharu 伊藤道治, 67n30
jade, 141, 255–56, 262, 274, 278, 280, 283, 374
Japanese: kanji, 56, 101, 103 (*see also* characters); *kun*-readings, 117, *118t3.24*, 127; *on*-readings, 127; research, 346, 392; syllabic character, 102–3; words, 117–18, *118t3.24*
Ji 姬 clan, 315, 321n54
jí 及 'to get', 146, 147b, *147t4.1, 149t4.2*
jǐ 己 (*tiāngān* #6), 21n7, *32t1.1, 34t1.2*, 181
"Ji tong" 祭統 (*Book of Rites*), 331
"Ji zui" 既醉 (*Book of Poetry*), 317
jiǎ 甲 (*tiāngān* #1), *32t1.1, 34t1.2*
Jia Gongyan 賈公彥, 353
"Jia le" 假樂 (*Book of Poetry*), 320n52
Jiaguwen bian 甲骨文編, 106. Cited in text as JGWB

Jiaguwen heji 甲骨文合集, *93t3.5*, 153. Cited in text as HJ
jiǎjiè 假借 'loangraph usage', *jiǎjièzì* 假借字 'loan graph', 62n24, 111, 112, 117–18, 127, 324n65
Jian (Prince) of Zhongshan 中山簡王, 388, 389
jiān 兼 'to carry on (a position previously awarded)', 329, 330n80
"Jian xi" 簡兮 (*Book of Poetry*), 328n77
jiàn'gēng 踐更 'to be released from service', 356–57, 356n54
jiǎncè 簡冊 'wood or bamboo document', 204
Jiang 江 River, 251
jiǎng 講 'to debate', 307
"Jiang Han" 江漢 (*Book of Poetry*), 251–54, 267
Jiangling 江陵: ix
Jianwu 建武 reign period, 351
jiāo 郊 'suburbs', 307n15
jiǎo/jiào 徼 'pursuit', 225n37
jiào 嗷 'to cry out', 'to shout', 225, 225n37
jiǎxū 甲戌 (day 11), *185f5.2e*, 186
jiǎzǐ 甲子 (day 1), 29, 30, 36, 182, 282. *See also gānzhī* 干支
Jie 解, 369
"Jie lao" 解老 (*Hanfeizi*), 315n18
jiéqì 節氣 'solar period', 23
Jifu 吉甫, 299
Jijiu pian 急就篇, 182n26, 358
Jin 晉 (state), 311, 316, 318, 319–322, 325, 328, 330, 375
Jin 晉 dynasty, 378
jīn 今 'now', 120, 198, 198n46
Jin Jiang *ding* 晉姜鼎 (JC 2826), 267n64
Jin nation 晉邦, 320, 321
jīng 經 'guideline text', 216–19, 219n24; 經 'to arrange in order', 'constant pattern', 41–42, *213t6.2*, 219, 222–23n33, 329, 330n80; 荊 (possible marker of Chu origin), 360n69
Jing, Duke of Qi 齊景公, 350n30
Jing fa 經法 (excavated text): Plate 5b, *212t6.1*, 213, 219n24, 220

"Jing zhi" (*Book of Poetry*), 333
Jing Zhichun 荊志淳, 144n12, 172n64
Jingbo Lu *gui* 井伯親簋, 276n13
jīngdé 經德 'constant power', 331, 331n82
Jingong *dian* 晉公盦 (JC 10342), 267n64
Jingong *pen* 晉公盆 (JC 10342), 319
Jining 濟寧 City, 390
"Jinli" 覲禮 (*Yili*), 254–63, 268
Jinwen yinde 金文引得: 240–41n6
jìqì 祭器 'sacrificial vessels', 294n43
"Jishi" 季氏 (*Analects*), 332n88
jǐsì 己巳 (day 6), 30
Jiu zhu 九主 (excavated text), *213t6.2, 215t6.3*, 217, 222, 222–23n33
Jiuchao lükao 九朝律考, 351n33
Jixia 稷下, 304, 312
Johnson, Elizabeth Childs. *See* Childs-Johnson, Elizabeth
Johnson, George, 124n56
joint ritual, sacrifice, 167–71, 174, 177, 308, 313, 317n40, 319, 323, 334
juàn 絹 'silk made of tightly woven very thin threads', 211n11
"Juan E" 卷阿 (*Book of Poetry*), 315
judicial power of literacy, 301
jué 厥 (particle), 293, 293n40, 296n47
jūnzǐ 君子 'person of breeding', 96
Jupiter, *47f1.5*
Juyan 居延, ix, 353, 361n70
kāihé 開合 'lip-rounding (present or absent)', 134–37
kǎishū 楷書 'standard square script', 96
Kalinowski, Marc, 214n16, 219n24
kana 仮名 'Japanese syllabic character', 103
Kane, Virginia C., 249
Kang Ding 康丁 (king), 159n43, 193
kanji 漢字 'character of Chinese origin', 56, 101
Kaogu 考古, 160
Karlgren, Bernhard, 117, 123, 240n6, 251n25
Katherine and George Fan collection, 244n12

Kaye, Alan, 125n57
Ke 克, 260; Ke *ding* 克鼎, *see* Da Ke *ding* 大克鼎
kě 可 'able', 'permissible', 234
kè guǎng déxīn 克廣德心 'to be able to broaden one's heart with *dé*', 328–29
Keightley, David N., 20n4, 21n6, 29n20, 32–33n24, 191n37, 193n38
Kern, Martin, 99n28, 208n3, 239n[0], 249–50, 275n11, 300n57, 305n8, 326n72, 333n91
khia 奇 rime in Southern Min, 128, 128n63, *129t3.32*
khia-sò 奇數 (Taiwanese 'odd number'), 128–29, *129t3.32*
khipu 'knotted cords for recording', 10, 24–27, *26f1.2a*, 28
khipukamayuq 'knot-reader', 25, *26f1.2b*
kho 箍 (Taiwanese measure), 128, *129t3.32*
kings, 181, 246, 302–36, 340, 378; Cheng 成, 42n39, 304, 328, 328n78; Cuo 𰯼 of Zhongshan, 335; Di Xin 帝辛, 159n43; Di Yi 帝乙, 148d, 159n43; Kang Ding 康丁, 159n43, 193; Li 厲, 167–68n55, 246n18, 280, 281; Lin Xin 廩辛, 159n43, 193; Mu 穆, 152n25, 167–68n55, 248, 286, 328; Wen Ding 文丁 (Wen Wu Ding 文武丁), 159n43; Wu Yi 武乙, 159n43; Xuan 宣, 241, 254n28, 281, 351; Zewang 矢王, 287–93; Zhaoxiang 昭襄 (of Qin), 357; Zheng 政, 357; Zu Geng 祖庚, 159, 159n43; Zu Jia 祖甲, 159n43; Zu Xin 祖辛, 166, 167; Zu Yi 祖乙, 152, 166, 167, 169. *See also* Wen 文; Wu 武; Wu Ding 武丁; Zhou (kings)
kingship, 169
kinship, 179n18
kneeling figure (in inscriptions), 157, 265
knives: metal, 177; scholar's, 232
Knoblock, John, 375n12
knots (knotted strings, knotting cords), 24, 25, 47 (see also *khipu*); knot-reader, 25, *26f1.2b*)
Ko, Dorothy, 384

koinē, 126
Korea, 270, 392–93
Kou 口 (diviner's name), 197, 198
kǒu 口 'mouth', 90, *90t3.3–4*
Kramer, Samuel Noah, 175
Krumbacher, Karl, 125n57
Kuang *you* 匡卣 (JC 5423), 263n45
Kuishi 媿氏, 296–97, 296n48
kun 訓 -readings, 117, 118, *118t3.24*, 127
Kunxue jiwen 困學紀聞, 351n33
labials, 33, 35; codas, 120 (*see also* codas); labial-stop finals, 119n53
labor: and asterism Dìng, 41; civilian, 371–72; conscription rolls, 371–72; division of, 374
lacquer objects, vessels: *Plate 8*, 45, 213, 373, 378, 380, 381-88, *386t11.1*, 392–965, *392fl1.2*, 396. *See also* vessels
lacquer workers (female), 367n92
lái 來 (for *mài* 麥 'barley'), 222n31; 速, 325n71
Lai *ding* 速鼎. *See* Forty-second Year Lai *ding* 四十二年速鼎; Forty-third Year Lai *ding* 四十三年速鼎
Lai *pan* 速盤 (XS 757), 241, 325n71; *also known as* Qiu *pan* 逑盤, *q.v.*
Lai Yin Yung 賴彥融, 151n23
lampblack painting, 388n37
land, territory, *100t3.8*, *147t4.1*, *149t4.2*, 277, 280–91, 295, 301, 309n19, 365–66, 371; register used by the lineages, 282–84
language, recording of, 72
Lanzhou 蘭州, ix
láo 牢 'specially reared bovine', 'sturdy', 169–70n61, 394, 394n46
lǎo 老 'to be an elder', 332
Laozi 老子 MSS, 209–36
Larger Ke *ding* 大克鼎 (JC 2836). *See* Da Ke *ding* 大克鼎
Larger Yu *ding* 大盂鼎 (JC 2837). *See* Da Yu *ding* 大盂鼎
laryngeal types of initials, 134

Lau, Ulrich, 247n20, 249n21
Law on Abandoning Positions and Fleeing (*Lidi duntao zhi fa* 離地遁逃之法), 368
Law on Battlefield Executions (*Zhanzhu zhi fa* 戰誅之法), 368
laws, legal documents. *See* ancestral: law; commands, laws, regulations; legal: documents, rules; statutes
learning, oral- and text-based, 303–36
learning to engrave and write, 158n41, 183, 186–87, 189
Ledderose, Lothar, 380
left, 260, 261n41
legal: affairs, 335, 359, 398; disputes, 264; documents, rules, 293, 301, 343–69, 376, 378, 384
Legge, James, 265n55, 375n12
lěi 壘 'earth mound', 285
lèi 類. *See* Funü *lei*; Lieti *lei*; Yuanti *lei*
Lelang 樂浪, 392–93
"Lesser Annuary of Xia' (*Xia xiaozheng* 夏小正), 49
"Lesser Elegantiae" ("Xiaoya" 小雅, *Book of Poetry*), 258n34, 311
letters: epistles, 286n34, 342, 362–64, 368; of appointment, 276; written characters, 58–59, 58n12, 367
Lévi-Strauss, Claude, 397–98
Lewis, Mark Edward, 340, 340n3
lexical lists, texts, 176, 177n13
lexicalized tone change (irregular), *131t3.33*
lexicon, 148–50, 160, 164
Li 厲 (king), 167–68n55, 246n18, 280, 281
Li 禮. *See Book of Rites*
lǐ 李 'plum', 222, 222n31, 222–23n33; 禮 'ritual', 304, 305
lì 吏 'official', 343n12; 曆/歷 'accumulated merit', 'chronicle', 278–79, 279n21
Li, Fang-Kuei 李方桂, 115, 119, 121, 122, *122t3.31*, 146n18
Li, Feng. *See* Li Feng
Li, Min, 160
Li, Wai-yee, 303n3
Li Chaoyuan 李朝遠, 245–46, 246n18

470　　INDEX

Li 歷 diviner group inscriptions, 142nn4–5, 146, *147t4.1*, 148, *149t4.2*, 151–55, 157, 158, 161, *163t4.3*, 167–72, 196
Li Feng 李峰, 9, 12–13, 14, 206n[0], 245n13, 249, 250n24, 339n[0]
Li Junming 李均明, 365
Li Ling 李零, 241n10
Li Min. *See* Li, Min
Li Minling 李旼姈, 187n32
Li Si 李斯, 343n12, 351
Li Suting 李素婷, 156n35
Li Tianhong 李天虹, 360–61
Li Weiming 李維明, 146n18
Li Xueqin 李學勤, 144, 150–55, 158, 159, 219n24, 241n7, 325n71, 350
Li Xueshan 李雪山, 152n25, 155n32
"Li yun" 禮運 (*Book of Rites*), 332n87
liǎng 兩 'tael', 225, 354, 355, 356
Liang Qi *zhong* 梁其鐘 (JC 187–92), 245n15, 310n23
liáo 燎 'to conduct a burnt sacrifice', 150
lìchénqiè 隸臣妾 'male and female bondservants, 348–49, 349n26
Lìchūn 立春 ("Spring Begins"), 44
Lidi duntao zhi fa 離地遁逃之法 'Law on Abandoning Positions and Fleeing', 368
lǐdiǎn 里典 'village head', 360
liè 劣 'lesser', 99
Lienü zhuan 列女傳, 364
Lieti *lei* 劣體類 'cacoform category', 142n4, 148
Liezi 列子, 332n89
life, life stages, 312, 332
ligatures (*héwén* 合文), 96–101, *98t3.7*, *100t3.8*, 101, 352n36
Liji 禮記. *See Book of Rites*
Lin Xin 廩辛 (king), 159n43, 193
Lin Yun 林澐, 282n26
lineages, 378 (see also *shì* 氏); allegiances, 326–27; branch, 283, 317; head of, 310–30; narratives, 302, 303, 308, 308n17, 324, 325; ritual, 327; signs (*zúmíng* 族名), 66n28; successors (*yìn* 胤), 316n38. *See also* ancestral: shrines, San 散 lineage; Shan 單 lineage; Shao 召 lineage
Ling 靈, Patriarch of Qi, 325, 328
lìng 令 'ordinance', 343n12, 346, 348–49n25
Ling *ding* 令鼎 (JC 2803), 263n46
lìng X-shǐ 令 X 史 (kind of scribe), 347
Linghui 靈惠, 372n5
Lingshi 甼石, 271n2
lìngshǐ 令史 (kind of scribe), 346–47, 351, 357, 358, 361, 385. *See also* scribal groups
linguistic continuity, 115
língyīn 靈音 'numinous tones', 317–18
Linjin 臨晉, 380
Lintong 臨潼 County, 379; terra cotta warriors and horses, *Plate 8*
lip-rounding, 134–37
lǐqì 禮器 'ritual vessel', 294n43
lìrén 歷人 'to oversee laborers', 245n13
lists, registers, 360–61
literacy, 3–15, 51–84, 85–137, 141–72, 173–205, 206–236, 269, 271–301, 302–36, 339–69, 370–99; Anyang, (*see* Anyang); Bronze Age, 4, 302, 307; craftsmen's, 13, 372–73; definition, 3n3, 340n4; diglossia and, 123–32; diviners, 174n3; elites, 10, 13; functional, 13, 334, 384; levels and types of, 372–73; masons, 390–91; maximal hypotheses for in late Shang, 174; military, 360–64; models (autonomous or ideological), 341n6; professional, 13; scribal, 13, 273; spread of, in Early China, 12, 175n7, 302–36; uses of, 370–99; Warring States period, 333–36; writing and, 5–6; women's, 364–69; Zhou-style education and, 326. *See also* diviners; education; scribal groups; writing
Literacy Project, Columbia University, 8–10

literature, Sumerian, 175–76
Liu Shang 劉尚, 390, 390n39
Liu Xiang 劉向, 206, 206n1, 364
Liu Xiaogan 劉笑敢, 230n47
Liu Xin 劉歆, 206, 206n1
Liu Xiu 劉秀, 388
Liu Yan 劉焉, 388, 388n36, 390
Liu Yiman 劉一曼, 158n41
Liùyì 六藝 'the Six Arts', 305, 305n8, 336
"Liuyue" 六月 (*Book of Poetry*), 298, 299, 299n56
livestock, 69, 176; sacrifice of, 193, 204
lǐyuè 禮樂 'ritual musical performance', 306
lǐzhèng 里正 'village head', 360
loangraph. See *jiǎjiè* 假借
locally cast inscriptions, 271n1
Loewe, Michael, 339n1, 354n43
logogram, logographs, logographic writing type, 55n7, 56, 75, 101, 101n31, 117–18, 123, 128, 130
lóng 龍 'dragon', 46n48
Longqiuzhuang 龍虬莊: ix, 11n17
Longshan 龍山 (period): viii, 11n17
Longxian 隴縣, 287
Lu 魯, 38n31, 297, 304, 328, 335, 389fl1.1a/c/d/e
lǜ 律 'statute', 346. See also statutes
Lu Shixian 魯實先, 152n25, 154
"Lu songs" ("Lu sòng" 魯頌, *Book of Poetry*), 328, 329n79
Lü X zhong 邞 X 鐘 (JC 225–37), 267n64
Lubo Dong gui 彔伯戜簋 (JC 4302), 264n53
Lubo Yufu pan 魯伯愈父盤 (JC 10113), 297
Lubo Yufu yi 魯伯愈父匜 (JC 10244), 297
lüè 寽 (unit of weight), 286, 286n32
"Luming" 鹿鳴 (*Book of Poetry*), 298
lùn 論 'to debate', 307
lunar lodges, 36n28, 38, 44, 45, 46
Lunyu 論語. See *Analects*
Luo Zhenyu 羅振玉, 165, 265, 266
"Luogao" 洛誥 (*Book of Documents*), 42

Luoshan 羅山, 271n2
Luoyang 洛陽: viii, ix, *40f1.4*
Lurie, David, 91n12
Lüshi chunqiu 呂氏春秋, 41, 375
lustration ritual (*yù* 禦), 157, 161, 168, 169
*m-type negatives, 166
Ma Chengyuan 馬承源, 274n9, 275n11, 284–85n28, 285nn29–30
magic square, 50
Mai 邁 (for Qiu 逑), 244, 245n15
mài 麥 'barley', 222n31
Maier, Joseph, 8
maker-marks, 384–85
Man 蠻 peoples, 313–15, 319, 320
Man (?) ding 䖑鼎 (JC 2765), 263n42
Mandarin, 98, *98t3.7*, 107n42, 112n46, 114, 128–30; phonetic symbols (*zhùyīn fúhào* 注音符號), 103
mandate, 314, 321n55, 327. See also delivering the mandate; *mìng* 命; royalty: mandate
manuals, 334, 343n12, 352, 363–64, 371
manuscripts: bamboo, (see bamboo documents); imperial, 206; marks, 223–31; Mawangdui MS.A, *Plates 3, 5, 6, 14*, 211–36, *213t6.2, 215t6.3*; Mawangdui MS.B, *Plates 4, 5, 7, 14*, 211–36, *212t6.1*; production, 207–8, 209–10
Mao 毛 preface to the *Book of Poetry*, 39, 254n28
mǎo 卯 (*dìzhī* #4), *32t1.1, 34t1.2*, 181
Mao Heng 毛亨, 39
Maogong ding 毛公鼎 (JC 2841), 246n16, 264n53, 266n59, 323, 323n61, 325n71, 328n78
Map of Archaeological Sites: ix
mapmaking, 293
Markab (Alpha Pegasus), 46
marketplaces, 378, 378n18
marks: in manuscripts, 223–31; maker-marks, 384–85; tree-markers of territory, 291–91
Marquis Yi of Zeng 曾侯乙, 45
marriage: alliance, 263; ritual *wēiyí*, 321n54

marry and begin a family (a life stage), 332
Mars, *47f1.5*
martial, 92n19, *93t3.5* (*see also* war, warfare); dance, 309n20, 316, 335 (*see also* dance, dancing)
Martinet, André, 58
mass production, 374, 376
massing of planets, 46, *47f1.5*
master, 307, 308, 340n3; artisan, 374–75, 376, 380, 381, 384, 385, *386t11.1*, 387
Master Fu. *See* Fu Sheng 伏生
mathematics, 352, 352n38
Matsumaru Michio 松丸道雄, 180–81, 183n30, 200, 202, 286n32
Mattos, Gilbert L., 66n27, 85n[0], 86, 109
Mawangdui 馬王堆: ix, 227n38; MSS from, 14, 209–36. *See also the names of individual MSS*
May Fourth movement, 130
Maya, 76
meaning. *See* graphs, graphemes; semantic: value
measure words, 169. See also *khơ* 箍; *shǐshǐ* 豕豕, *tóu* 頭
medial semivowels, 133
medical books, 334, 343n12. *See also* manuals
medieval Chinese phonology, 89, 98n27, 109–127, *110t3.13*, *118t3.24*, 132–34, *135–37t3.34*, 182, 208n4; rime books, 96, 96n25, 98
Mediterranean cultures, 373
Meixian 眉縣, 241
Melchert, Craig, 91n15
member of the rank and file, 340, 355
memorization, 316
Mencius (*Mengzi* 孟子), 78
Meng *gui* 孟簋 (JC 4162–64), 245n15
Mengzi 孟子 (*Mencius*), 78
merchants: association of, 384–85; writing by, 27, 368
Mercury, *47f1.5*

merit. See *gōng* 功; see also *dé* 德; *lì* 曆/歷; *mièlì* 蔑曆
Mesoamerica, 69
Mesopotamia, 27, 36n28, 48n52, 52, 69, *70f2.1*, 72–73, 74, 175, 176, 176n11, 273n8, 277, 373
metal: inscriptions, 291; weapons, 377
meteorological events, 28
Mian *gui* 免簋 (JC 4240), 273–74, 275n10, 276
Mian *zun* 免尊 (JC 6006), 278
Miaopu 苗圃, 159
mid-autumn activities, 40
Middle Ages (Europe), 373
miè 滅 'to vanquish', 'to fill up', 278, 279, 279n23; 蔑, 279n23
mièlì 蔑曆 'recounting of meritorious acts', 277–79, 278n18, 279n21
miệng (Vietnamese 'mouth'), *miếng* (Vietnamese 'mouthful'), 114n47
migration, 108, 304
Miinnan dialect, 128
milfoil, 343n12
military: behavior, 315; campaign (Zhou), 251; conscription, 344, 371–72; context of writing, 286–87, 301; laws, 365–69; orders, strategy, 263, 342, 343 (*see also* commands); records, 308, *see also* documents: written; service, 354n43, 370; texts, 368; training, 309
militia, 327
milk, 177
Milky Way, *Plate 1*, 50
millet, 77
mimes, mimetic performances, 322
Min 閔, Duke of Lu 魯, 38n31
Min 閩 dialects, 128n63
Ming 明, 369
míng 冥 'night' (perhaps written 夕), 90, *90t3.3*; 名 'name', *90t3.3–4*, 114n47, 233, 321n55, 378; 銘 'inscription', 321n55; 鳴 'to sing', 'sound', *90t3.4*, 114n47
mìng 命 'command', 'mandate', *90t3.4*, 233, 321n55, 327, 348–49n25. See also

cèmìng 冊命; commands; wángmìngshū 王命書

Míng jun 明君 (excavated text), *213t6.2*, 214, *215t6.3*, 217, 222, 222–23n33

mìngcè 命冊 'bamboo document of royal command', 274, 275n11, 276–77

míngdé 明德 'luminous inner power', 315–16, 332

mìngshū 命書 'document of command', 274, 275nn10–11, 276. See also wángmìngshū 王命書

"Mingtang wei" 明堂位 (*Book of Rites*), 306n10

minimal hypothesis for literacy, 174

minister. See chén 臣; yǐn 尹

"Ministry" (qīngshìliáo 卿事寮), 281–82

minor, 381–82; to be in one's minority, 115, *115t3.21*, 332

minor livestock, 169–70n61

Miranda, Noemi, 37n29

mirrors, bronze, 373

missionaries, Spanish, 25

mò 沒 'to be submerged', 'buried', 279; 沬 'to wash (face)', 296

moat: at Anyang 安陽, 173; outside Qianling 乾陵, 360

modal negatives, 166

model: 308, 327, 327n76; for learning to write', 181; of literacy (autonomous or ideological), 341n6

Mohists, 342, 343, 343n9, 344. See also Mozi

monosyllabic words, 132

month: astronomical, 25, 36; regulation, 45

"Monthly Ordinances". See "Yueling" 月令, ordinance(s)

moon, 23–24, 25, 28, 32–33n24, 64, 76, 77, 81, 99, *147t4.1*, 148, *149t4.2*. See also *fěi* 朏; yuè 月

mòpán 沬盤 'face-washing basin', 297

Morohashi Tetsuji 諸橋轍次, 117

morphemes, 55, 56, 58n11, 59n13, 101, 109, 128, 130

morphology, 133

mortuary feast (xiǎng 享), 309, 329, 332, 335

Moshi editors, 194

mother, *121t3.29*; Four Mothers, 161, 168; Mother Yi (Mu Yi 母夷), 387–88; royal mother, 296, 296n48, 321n54; Queen Mother of the West, 393. See also women: category

Mou he 繆和 (text from Mawangdui), 212

mourning, 309, 327

mouth, 90, *90tt3.3–4*, 114n47

moving ancestral tablets, 167–68n55

mòyí 沬匜 'face-washing *yí*', 297

Mozi 墨子, 306n13, 307n15, 332n89, 334, 340n3 (see also Mohists); *Mozi* 墨子, 307n15, 321n54, 341–45, 341n8

MS. See manuscripts

Mu 穆 (king), 152n25, 167–68n55, 248, 286

mǔ 母 'mother', *121t3.29*

Mu gui 牧簋 (JC 4343), 264n53, 266n59

Mu Sun 沐孫, 390–91

Mu Yi 母夷, 387–88

Musha Akira 武者章, 276n13

music (musical ceremony, performance), 179–80, 302–22, 323–25, 327n77, 329, 330, 331, 332, 334. See also yuè 樂; bell inscriptions, bells

musical instruments, 248, 318

mute, 130n64

mutilation, 364

mutton, 30n22

myth, 50, 175, 176; of ideal character structure, 94–95n23

"Na" 那 (*Book of Poetry*), 323n63

nà 吶/訥 'halting of speech', *120t3.26*; 納 'to go in', 'to send in', 119, *120t3.26*; 軜 'inward-facing halter for outer horses on a team', *120t3.26*

nǎi 乃 (particle), 230

nǎiyǒu shì 乃有事 'your services' (also nǎiyǒu 乃有), 331n83

nameless group, *147t4.1*, 148

names, 68n31, 99, 141–71, 191–99, 271n1, 308–13, 319–36, 321n55, 340n3, 374–91, *386t11.1*, *392f11.2*; "Names of the Four Quarters and Winds", 201, 201n50; recognition and reproduction, 372; of artisans, Plate 8, 368, 379–91, *386t11.1*, *389f11.1*; of days and dates, 182n25

Nan 殷, 142–43n5, 151–52, 152n25, 154–55, 155nn31–32, 155n34, 171–72

nán 南 'south', 155

Nan Commandery 南郡, 358n61

Nan Geng 南庚, 155n34

Nanyang 南陽, 359–60

narrow view of writing, 52–53, 54

nasal: codas, 33, 122, *122t3.31* (see also codas); initials, 120; rhymes, 227. See also rhyming

nè or nà 訥 'halting of speech', 119, *120t3.26*

Near East, 48n52, 373

needle (tool for incising graphs), 384

negative particles. See bù 不; fú 弗; wù 勿; *m*-type negatives; *p*-type negatives; modal negatives

nèi 內 'within', *119t3.25*, *120t3.26*

"Nei chushuo shang" 內儲說上 (Hanfeizi), 357n57

Neishi 內史 'Ministry of Finance', 346–48, 355; Neishi Ling X ding 內史令X鼎 (JC 2696), 263n42; Nèishǐ zá 內史雜 ("Miscellaneous", excavated text from Shuihudi), 346

"Neiye" 內業 (Guanzi), 41, 41n38

"Neize" 內則 (Book of Rites), 303n1, 306n10

Neo-Platonism, 92

Neolithic: pictographs, 44n44; signs, 11, 20–21, 27; structure, 21; writing, 11n17; yard (measurement), 24. See also pictographs, pictography; potters, pottery

netherworld, 208–9n5, 264

Neugebauer, Otto, 24

Ni zhong 逆鐘 (JC 60–63), 266n58

nián 年 'harvest', 'year', 11, 77, 80–81

niàn 廿 'twenty', 98n27, *98t3.7*, 99; 念 'to recall', 98n27, *98t3.7*, 324n65, 331n83

Ninth Year Wei ding 九年衛鼎 (JC 2831), 264n49

nìshòu 逆受 'welcoming the king's awards', 297, 297n53

niú 牛 'ox', 'bovine', 'carabao', 170, 169–70n61, 170, 361. See also bovine joints; láo 牢

niú píqi 牛脾氣 'stubbornness', also niù píqi 拗脾氣, 130n65, *131t3.33*

Niucheng 牛城, 155

Nivison, David S., 42n43

nìzào 逆造 'to welcome the king's visit', 297n53

non-glottographic writing, 54, 55, 56, 72, 73, 74, 83

non-Han ethnic groups, 387

non-literacy, writing, 56, 177

non-modal negatives, 166

non-phonetic writing, 53–54, 66n28, 104, 124

non-Royal OBI, 142n4

non-vocalized elements, 101, 101n31

non-Zhou founders, 312

Nóngxiáng 農祥 'Farmer's Auspice', 44, 45, 45n46, 46

normalization: of complex pictographs, 95–96; of ancient graphs, *100t3.8*, 108–27

Norman, Jerry, 66n27, 86, 109, 114n47, 117n51, 123n55, 128n63

North Korea, 392–93

North Pole, 37–50

north-south axial alignment, 37–38

Northern Chinese, 129–30, *131t3.33*

nǚ 女 'woman', *121t3.29*, 161

numbers, 305; numeric ligatures, *98t3.7*

nuns, 372n5

nuò 諾 'to approve' (also written 若), 265n57, 266–67

nuò yuē 諾曰 'to say with approval'. See ruò yuē 若曰

Nylan, Michael, 309n20
oaths, 264
OBI (oracle bone inscriptions), 30n23, *93t3.5*, 95, *102t3.10, 105t3.11*, 106, 108, *110–13tt3.13–19*, *115–16tt3.21–23*, 142, 142n4, 143, 150, 151, 152n25, 153, 157, 159, 164, 170–71. *See also* bone inscriptions, bones
OBI periods: I, 148, 151, 153, 157, 159, 159n43, 160; II, 159, 159n43; III, 148, 159n43, 160; IV, 148, 159n43, 160; V, 151n23, 159n43
objects (grammatical). *See* direct objects; double-object construction; indirect objects; object-verb word order, verb-object word order
object-verb word order, 157
OC. *See* Old Chinese
"occasional texts" (Martin Kern), 208n3
O$_d$. *See* direct objects
odes, 317, 320, 323n63. See also *Book of Poetry*; songs
offices, 298n54
officials, 234, 343n12; in charge of imperial granaries, 364; service, 354, 354n45; status, 374–75; titles, 176–77; officials of courts, 281–82
O$_i$. *See* indirect objects
Okamura Hidenori 岡村秀典, 169, 169–70n61, 170n63
Old Babylonian. *See* Babylonian
Old Chinese, 4, 7, 132–34; phonology, 87–88n6, 128; reading, 109; rhyme and rhyming groups, 33n25, 47–48, 88n6, 94n21, 396n50; reconstruction, (*see* reconstructions of Old Chinese), 35, *122t3.31*, 133, 134, 146n18 (*see also* pronunciation)
Olson, David R., 218n21
omens and prodigies, 371
on-readings, Japanese, 127
Ōnishi Katsuya 大西克也, 221

open codas, 122, *122t3.31*
open text, 305n8
oracle bone inscriptions. *See* OBI
oral: contractions, 98, *98t3.7*, 99; cue, 313; expressions of gratitude, 261; performance, 305n8, 311n24, 312; segments in inscriptions, 14; transmission (orality), 235, 239–70, 276, 303, 333, 333n91
order of strokes (in graphs). *See* strokes: order
ordinance(s), 30, 41, 343n12, 346, 349n25, 375, 377, 378n18. *See also* commands, laws, regulations; *lìng* 令; *fǎlìng* 法令
origin of Chinese writing, 65–83
ornament (suppression of), 394
orthography, 207, 221–23, 235 (*see also* spelling); orthographic phonology, 133
ostracism (Greek practice of), 3
OV (object-verb) word order. *See* object-verb order
ox. See *niú* 牛
*-*p*/-*t* contact in *rùshēng*, 119–20, *119t3.25, 120tt3.26–27*
*p-type negatives, 165–66
"pagan devil worship" of Inkas, 25
painters (children as), 381, *386t11.1*
pairs: cognate, 119; rhyme, 33
palace, 38, 196, 308, 379
Palace Water Factory. *See* Gongshui 宮水
paleography, 7, 68n31, 121, 123, 141, 178n16. *See also* inscriptions; writing
pán 盤 'platter', 'basin', 116–17, *116t3.23*, 297n51
"Pan shui" 泮水 (*Book of Poetry*), 309n20, 328–29, 329n79
Pankenier, David W., 10–11, *22f1.1*, 50n56, 73n41, 133, 187n32
paratext (definition), 210n9
Parker, Malcolm, 223n34
paronomasia, 62n24
particles. *See* grammar: particles; measure words; negative particles; prosodic particles

patriarch, (*gōng* 公), 313, 320–21, 325, 326–27, 328, 328n77; Patriarch Ling 靈 of Qi, 325–26, 328
patron, definition of, 240n3
patterning (duality of), 58
peasant's literacy, 4n3, 371
pebbles, counting of, 125
peer group (*péngyǒu* 朋友), 317, 334
Pegasus (Great Square of), 39, *40fl.4*, 44, 45n46, 49n53, 50
pèi 配 'to match', 309
pèi jì 配祭 'joint sacrifice', 167
Pei Mingxiang 裴明相, 144–45, 159
pèi sì 配祀 'joint ritual', 167
Pei'er *goudiao* 配兒鉤鑃 (JC 427), 267n64
Peirce, Charles Sanders, 81, 82
pejoration, 130n64
Peking. *See* Beijing
pen-strokes. *See* strokes
pendants, cord, 24, 25, 47
Peng 彭 (diviner's name), 197, 198, 199, 199n48
Pengsheng 佣生, 284–85; Pengsheng *gui* 佣生簋 (JC 4262; a.k.a. Gebo *gui* 格伯簋), 284–85, 285n29, 294
péngyǒu 朋友/佣友 'peer group', 317, 334
penis, 111
percussion-instrument players, 245
perform the exorcism or lustration ritual, 157
performance: activities, 179–80; style of, 311–12
peritext (definition), 210n9
Persian, 92n15
personal names, use of, 382
pharmaceutics (books on), 343n12
philosophical tracts, 334
philosophy, political, 264
phoenixes, 316, 318
phonemes, 58–60, 62, 65. *See also* graphs, graphemes
phonetic: compounds, 87, 88n6, 96; determination, 77n45; loans, 115, 391, 393n45; reconstructions, 266n60; series, 61n22 (*see also* phonophoric series); *xiéshēng* 諧聲, 53–58, 66n28, 87, 92, 101–8, 132. *See also* Old Chinese: rhyme and rhyming groups; phonology; rhyming
phonograms. See *xiéshēng* 諧聲
phonology, 85–137; early (Old) Chinese, 87–88n6, 128. *See also* speech (spoken language)
phonophores, 87, 92–93, 94n21, 104, *107t3.12*, 115, 117, 124, 132
phonophoric series, 47, 61, *61t2.2*, 62, 63n25, 64. *See also* graphs, graphemes
pǐ 不, *106t3.22*
piān 篇 'separate textual unit', 213, 217
pictographs, pictography, 27n16, 44n44, 63n24, 65, 74–75, 94–104, *97t3.6*, 11, 113. *See also* complex pictographs; Neolithic: pictographs
pig, 44n44, 107, 161, 164, 168, 169, 170n63. See also *chù* 豖; *shǐ* 豕; *shǐshǐ* 豕豕; *zhì* 彘; *zhū* 豬
pillars, astronomical, 25n14, 27
Pines, Yuri, 208–9n5
píngshēng 平聲, 128n63
pinyin romanization, 103
pits, storage, 38, 170, 201, 359
place-names, 176–77, 353, 380, 384
planets, massing of, 46, *47fl.5*, 50
plastron pyromancy, 83
plastrons, turtle shells, *Plate 2*, 141n1, 158n41, 160, 178, 201, 203
Plato, 218
platters: lacquer trays, 393–95
play (sense of, in writing), 99
Pleiades rising, 25
Pochengzi 破城子. *See* E.P.T.
poems, poetry, 251–58, 268, 298–99, 364. See also *Book of Poetry*
polar "square", 49n53
Pole. *See* North Pole
political: philosophy, 264; power (suasion), 301, 303, 313; politico-philosophical literary texts, 208

Poly Museum, Beijing, 276n13
polyphony, 11, 76, 77, 81, 82, 83, 89, 115, 132
polysemy, 76n43
polyvocal structure of award statements, 326
Ponceau, Peter du. *See* Duponceau, Peter
porcine. *See* pig
portmanteaux graphs, 99–100, *100t3.9*
portrait of a deity, 393
postal system (Qin), 363
potters, pottery, 11n17, 44n44, 65–66, 70, 141, 172n64, 373, 379–81. *See also* brush-writing, brushes
Pound, Ezra, 101n31
power: displays of, 309n20; governing, 326
practice: bone divination, 11, 343n12; graphs (inscriptions, writing), 174–75, 180–87, 189–90, *200f5.6*, 201n49, 203n57; *jiǎzǐ*, 182; ritual, 126
prayers, 295, 311, 324, 325, 329, 334
pre-Anyang, 65, 66
pre-Columbian artifacts, 25
pre-Han, 85, 133
pre-literate societies, 25
pre-Qin, 125, 279n23, 302, 332
pre-Shang language, 49, 66
pre-writing notational systems, 11
pre-Wu Ding, 160
pre-Zhou, 326
prefect, 347, 357
prefectural clerk, 347
priests, priest-astronomers. *See* calendar: priests
primary grapheme, 62
Prince of Shao. *See* Shaogong
private: letters, (*see* letters: epistles); quarters, 297; school or student, 344n14; workshops, 373, 381, 391–99
privileges, conferral of, 239
proclamations, pronouncements (oral), 240. *See also* oral: transmission
prodigies, 371

production, government-sponsored. *See* government production
Professions List, 177n13, 200
progeny, promises of, 317
promotions, 245n13, 391–97
pronunciation, 63n25, 130, 311, 372
proper human relations, 306n10
prosodic particles. *See xī* 兮
proto-cuneiform texts, 69–70, *70f2.1*, 71–72, 177, 177n13
proto-hieroglyphic writing, 70, 71–72, *71f3.2*, 109
proto-*qùshēng* 去聲, 119
protoform, 109, 164; protoform hypothesis, 12, 109, 112–17, *111–16tt3.14–23*, 118
public displays of power, 309n20
Pulleyblank, Edwin G., 19, 33n26
pulp guidebooks, 363–64. *See also* manuals
punctuation, 207, 233n34; and other marks, 223–31
punishments, 335, 364, 376, 377. *See also* fines, fining
punning ligatures, 99, *100t3.8*
purification, 331
purpose, statement of 239
Pyongyang, North Korea, 392–93
pyromancy, plastron and scapula, 83
Qi 齊, 38n31, 304, 310, 320, 325–30, 331n82, 334, 335, 350n30, 364, 375
qī 七 'seven', *147t4.1, 149t4.2*
qí 其 (particle), 'may', 'will', 165, 228n40, 296n47
qì 氣 'cosmic vapor', 312, 324
Qian River 汧水, 287, 290
qiān 千 'thousand', 87
Qián 乾 (hexagram in *Book of Changes*), 46, 46n48
qiáng 牆 'wall', 109, *110t3.13*
Qianling 乾陵, 359, 360
Qie 且, 289, 290
qiě 且 (particle), 111, *112t3.16*
Qièyùn 切韻, 123, 132
Qijia 齊家, 141n2
Qin 秦 dynasty: *Plate 8*, viii, 6n10, 13, 88, 99, 124, 125, 127, 131, 221, 309n20,

339–69, 370–99; legal statutes, see Shuihudi: Qin legal documents; scribes, 352, 353; "Statutes on Enrollment", 360, 365

Qin 秦 state, 50, 50n54, 221, 310, 311, 312n29, 313–19, 322, 324–25, 326, 328, 330, 339

qín 琴 'zither', 353; 秜/矜 'spear handle', 120

"Qin benji" 秦本紀 (Records of the Grand Scribe), 50

"Qin feng" 秦風 ("Qin songs", Book of Poetry), 320

Qin Shihuang mausoleum, 381

Qing 清 period, 4, 7, 359, 364

Qingong bo 秦公鎛 (JC 262–70), 164a, 267n64, 313n30

Qingong gui 秦公簋 (JC 4315), 267n64, 313–18

Qingong zhong 秦公鐘 (JC 262–66), 267n64, 313n30

Qīngshìliáo 卿事寮 (administrative unit: "Ministry"), 281–82

Qishan 岐山, 141n2

qiú 逑 (also read zuǒ 佐, lái 逨), 325n71

Qiu ding 逑鼎. See Forty-third Year Qiu ding 四十三年逑鼎

Qiu pan 逑盤 (XS, 757), 241–51, 264n53; also known as Lai pan 逨盤

Qiu Wei 裘衛, 282; Qiu Wei ding 裘衛鼎, see Fifth Year Qiu Wei ding 五年裘衛鼎

Qiu Xigui 裘錫圭, 29n20, 66nn27–28, 154, 155, 220, 241n7, 325n71

Qiu zhong 逑鐘 (XS, 772–775), 243–45, 250, 253

"Qu li" 曲禮 (Book of Rites), 95n24, 332n88

Qu Wanli 屈萬里, 317n40

quadriga, 45, 45n46

quality control and accounting inscriptions, 374–78

quarters, four, 42, 201–2

Quechua spelling, 10n16

Queen Mother of the West, 393

quipu. See khipu

quiver (for arrows), 304

quotas, for production, 377

qùshēng 去聲, 119, 128n63

radicals, 103n35

ramie-cored lacquered objects, 378, 393

rammed earth structure, 21–22

Ran 冉, 349n26

rank, 308, 327, 339n1, 365, 381

Rawski, Evelyn, 6

reading: aloud (cèmìng 冊命), 249, 250n24, 277; process of, 87–108, 109, 235–36, 340, 341n6, 353, 371; silently, 353

rebellion, 326–27

rebus, 62–63n24, 74–75, 84, 265n57

recitation, 334

recognition, 104, 372

reconstructions of Old Chinese: of Baxter, (see Baxter, William H.); of Baxter-Sagart, 33n25; of Karlgren, (see Karlgren, Bernhard); of Li Fang Kuei, (see Li, Fang-Kuei)

record-keeping, recording information, records, 24, 25, 47, 183, 198, 279n21, 334; veritable (shílù 實錄), 270. See also documents

Records of the Grand Scribe (Shiji 史記), 99, 359n63, 365n81

recounting of an official or subject's meritorious acts (mièlì 蔑曆), 277–79, 278n18, 279n21

register of language, 130

regulations, (see commands, laws, regulations); regulation month, 45

reign: calendar, 310–11; period, 351

religious prayers, 295

rén 人 'person', 77, 81, 87, 88, 88t3.1, 234; 仁 'kernel', 87; 壬 (tiāngān #9), 32t1.1, 34t1.2

rèn 恁 (loangraph for niàn 念), 324n65

Renaissance, 92

Rencheng 任城, 388–91, 391n43; Prince Xiao of, 389fl1.1f, 390

Renmin Gongyuan 人民公園 phase, 144, 159
repetition of words, 99, 311
reproduction of Chinese characters, 372
response-eulogy by the recipient of a eulogy, 310
"response" narratives, 310, 313, 319, 330
retainers, 347n21
RG. See Renmin Gongyuan 人民公園
rhetoric, ritual. See rituals
rhyming, 48, 227–30, 396; binoms, see binoms: rhyming; generic, 35; nasal, 227; pairs, 33; Old Chinese, 33n25, 47–48, 88n6, 94n21, 396n50; phonetics, 33n25, 48, 88n6, 99, 133. See also rime: book
ribs:143, 144n8. See also bone inscriptions, bones
rice, 297
rìchén 日辰 'syzygy', 'sun's chronogram', 45
Richter, Matthias L., 14, 85n[0], 96n26, 214n17, 222–23n33, 339n[0], 363n76
Riegel, Jeffrey, 375n12
rime: book, 96, 96n25, 98; category (rime group), 87–88n6, 94n21, 96n25, 98, 98t3.7, 109, 115, 116, 117n51, 119n53, 119t3.25, 121, 122, 128n63, 133. See also rhyming
rìmíng 日名 'names of days and dates', 182n25
rising points, astronomical, 25n14
Rites (Liji 禮記, Li 禮). See Book of Rites
rituals, 157, 161, 168, 169, 178, 265, 315, 322n57, 328n78; bronzes, 263n47, 294n43, 374; function (implements, practice) of graphs, 72n39, 126, 157, 167, 168, 171, 174, 294, 311, 321; music, 306, 311; precincts (design of), 42, 43; sacrifice, 193, 204; vessel, 294n43; "wandering", 335
River Diagram (Hetu 河圖), 49, 50
rivers. See under individual names

Roberts, Moss, 9
rogue aspiration, 129t3.32
Roman ballot law, 3
Rome, literacy in, 373
rǒng 冗 (kind of official service), 354, 354n45
Rongsheng zhong 戎生鐘, 267n64
roof tiles (ceramic), 379
Roth, Harold, 214n16, 216n20
roundish-script category (Yuanti lei 圓體類), 142n4, 149t4.2
royalty, 239–70; ancestors (genealogy), 191n37, 195; education, 335 (see also education); gifts, (see gifts); house, 304, 326; mandate, 242–69; mother, 296, 296n48, 321n54; OBI (wáng bǔcí 王卜辭), 142n4; patron, 193
Ru 儒 'Confucianist', 'scholar', 230, 304–6, 364–67, 309n20, 332, 332n86, 334
rù 入 'to enter', 119t3.25, 120t3.26
Ru Chun 如淳, 354n43, 359n63
Ru technique (rúshù 儒術), 306n13
rubbings: from stones, 389fl1.1; of inscribed texts and stamps, 379n19
Ruggles, Clive L. N., 36n28
Rui 芮, 280, 281
Ruist, 335
rule, 293, 301, 333, 343–69, 376, 378, 384
rulers. See kings; royalty
runners, running, 157, 372
ruò 若 'like this', 'as if', 'substantially thus', (written for 諾 'to approve'), 243, 245, 246, 264–67, 265n57 (see also ruò yuē 若曰; wáng ruò yuē 王若曰)
ruò yuē 若曰 'to say thus' or 'to say approvingly', 265–66, 265n55. See also wáng ruò yuē 王若曰
rùshēng, 119–20, 119t3.25, 120tt3.26–27, 128n63
rúshù 儒術 'Ru technique', 306n13
rùxué 入學 'to enter the school', 178
sà 卅, contraction and ligature of sānshí 三十 'thirty', 98n27, 98t3.7, 99
sacrifice, (see guì 劌; láo 牢; liáo 燎; pèi jì 配祭); divinations, 197; of livestock, 193,

204; joint sacrifice, sacrificial terms, 167–71, 174, 177, 308, 313, 317n40, 319, 323, 334; vessel, 292n38, 294n43, 295, 297n51, 321n53 (see also vessels
Sagart, Laurent, 88n6, 133
sages, 42n40, 222–23n33, 226, 306
Sampson, Geoffrey, 54n5
San 散 lineage, 287–93
sandstone blocks, 388–89, 389fl1.1
Sanshi pan 散氏盤 (JC 10176), 264n50, 272, 287–95, 288f8.1, 299
Sanxingdui 三星堆, 155
Satō Taketoshi 佐藤武敏, 382
Saturn, 47f1.5
Saussure, Léopold de. See de Saussure
scapula: fragments, 142–43n5, 183–84, 184f5.1, 187–88, 188f5.3, 189, 191–203, 192f5.5, 200f5.6 (see also bone inscriptions, bones; inscriptions); pyromancy, 83
Schaberg, David, 307, 319
Schiffman, Harold F., 125n57
schools, schooling, 175–180, 302–9, 306n10, 344, 34n14, 347–51, 367, 371; Mesopotamian school life, 175. See also education; teachers, teaching
Schuessler, Axel, 240n6
Schwartz, Adam, 174n[0], 179n19
scorpion, 36n28
Scorpius, 41, 44
scrape off mistaken characters, 232
scribal groups, 10, 12–14, 48n51, 96, 141–43, 146n19, 150–62 163t4.3, 167n54, 173–239, 245, 268, 269, 275nn10–11, 278–91, 300, 301, 318n42, 328, 334, 340n3, 345–59, 361, 371–73, 380, 381–99. See also diviners; education; inscriptions; literacy
Scribe, Grand, 257, 351, 353, 355–56
scribe's text, 354
scribes. See shǐ 史; cuìshǐ 卒史; lìngshǐ 令史; tíngshǐ 庭史; see also shūzuǒ 書佐; yàshǐ 敔史; zhōngshǐ 中史

script: clerical, 385; concept, 92; first use of, 52, 84, 118, 177; normalization and standardization, 120, 127, 132, 385; square, 96; style of, 221–23. See also archaic script; 'Han dynasty: clerical script'; 'roundish-script category'; 'standard square script'
sè 瑟 'zither', 353
sealed inscriptions, stamps, Plate 8a, 379, 380
"Seasonal Rules" ("Shize" 時則, Lüshi chunqiu). See "Yueling" 月令
Secretarial Official, 275, 281, 285, 286, 293
sèfū 嗇夫 'overseer', 347
semantic: compounds, 87–89, 91, 94, 101, 101n31, 106–7; determinative, 63–65, 77n45; value, 54–55, 150, 151
semasiograph, 54n5
sense: determination and discrimination, 58–59, 60; of play, 99
sentences, formed by inscriptions, 155
separator dots. See dots
serial numbers of stonemasons, 380–81, 388n37
Serruys, Paul L.-M., 43n43, 146n17
servant, 328, 348–49, 348–49n25, 349n26
setting points, astronomical, 25n14
shā 沙 'sand', 115, 115n50, 115t3.2
Shaanxi 陝西, 141n2, 241, 261, 325n71, 379. See also Shanxi
shamans, 356; ritual, 265, 323
Shan 單 lineage, 241
shān 彡 'hair', 89, 89t3.2; 衫, 89
Shanbo Haosheng zhong 單伯昊生鐘 (JC 82), 245n15
Shandong 山東, 11n17, 173, 365n81, 390; Shandong accent, 365n81; Shandong Daxinzhuang inscription see Daxinzhuang
Shanfu Shan ding 善夫山鼎 (JC 2825), 277n14
Shang dynasty: 45, 65, 67, 170, 171, 173, 205, 326; calendar phases, divination, 32, 37–43, 45–49, 65, 67n31, 83, 159, 204;

elite, 150n21, 152n25, 170, 173–74, 308n18; gifts, 174, 177; inscriptions, 11, 29, 49n53, 51–52n1, 65, 67–80, *79–80ff2.4–5*, 83, 141–72, 173–205, 241n6, 271, 279, 302 (*see also* graphs, graphemes); late Shang, 20, 39, 67n31, 174, 182, 204, 241n6, 267n62, 307–8; "lineage sign", 66n28; rituals, 239; schools, 306n10; shamanic performances, 323; spiritual power, 49n53

shāng 商 'dance or musical performance'?, 179–80

Shang City 商城, 155–56

"Shang Sòng" 商頌 ("Shang Songs", *Book of Poetry*), 323n63

Shangdi 上帝 (name of divinity), 323, 332, 332n89

Shanghai 上海: ix, 98n27, 333n91; Museum, 244n12, 247

shǎngshēng 上聲, 128n63

Shanhaijing 山海經, 23n9, 202

Shanxi 山西, 21, 45, 141n2, 271n2, 318. *See also* Shaanxi

shānxuē 刪削 'to scrape off mistaken characters', 232

Shanyang 山陽, 158n40

Shao 召 lineage, 282–84

shǎo 少 'few', 115, *115t3.21*

shào 少 'young', 'in one's minority', 115, *115t3.21*, 332

Shao, Prince of. *See* Shaogong

Shao Hu 召虎 (Shaobo Hu 召伯虎), 251–53, 255, 282, 283; Shaobo Hu *gui* 召伯虎簋, *see* Fifth Year Shaobo Hu *gui* 五年召伯虎簋, Sixth Year Shaobo Hu *gui* 六年召伯虎簋

"Shaogao" 召誥 (*Book of Documents*), 42

Shaogong 召公, 251, 253

shǎoláo 少牢 'minor livestock', 169–70n61

shards, pottery. *See* potters, pottery

Shaughnessy, Edward L., 46n48, 216n20, 246n19, 253n27, 272n4

shé 蛇 'snake', 111, *111t3.15*

shè 射 'to shoot', 'archery', 95, 96n24, 198n47, 303n1, 305, 306n10; 攝 (grouping of medieval rimes), 134; 社 'altar to the spirit of the soil', 146, 150, 150n21; written 土 146, 151; 舍 'lodgings', 'habitations', 23n9; 赦 'to amnesty', 346; 韘 'archer's thumb-ring', *120t3.27*

sheep, *147t4.1*, 148a, *149t4.2*, 151, 153, 169–70n61, 170n63, 191, 197; (as initial) 135–36

shèjì 社稷 'altar of the soil and millet', 335. *See also* grain; millet

shells, writing on, 51–52n1, 67, 174, 180, 182, 197, 271n2. *See also* plastrons, turtle shells

shēn 申 (*dìzhī* #9), *32t1.1, 34t1.2*, 88, 181, 184; 身 'body', 88, 95, 95–96n24, *100t3.8*

shèn 慎 'cautious', 323

Shen Jianshi 沈兼士, 64n26, 76, 81, 83n51

Shen Pei 沈培, 153–54, 153n27

Sheng *yi* 媵匜 (JC 10285), 264n50

shēng 生, 227; 聲 'sound', 'voice', 222–23n33

shěng 省, 228n41; 眚, 228n41

shèng 聖 'sage', 222–23n33

shèngrén 聖人 'sage', 306

Shenzi Tuo *gui* 沈子它簋 (JC 4330), 245n15

Shi 詩. *See Book of Poetry*

Shi 師 diviner group inscriptions, 142n4, 146, *147t4.1*, 148, 148d, *149t4.2*, 151n23, 157n37, 161, *163t4.3*, 167, 171–72

shī 失, 233 'to lose'; 尸 'corpse', 'to take on the ancestor's role in life', 329 (*see also* Shu Yi bells); 師 'master', 307, 308, 340n3

shí 時 'time', 'season', 234; 石 'bushel of grain', 356, 356n53, 359n64, 361; 食 'to eat', 30n23, 361; as character component, 296 *shǐ* 使 'to send on a mission', 234; 史 'scribe', 340n3, 345, 346n18, 357, 372, *386t11.1*, 387; 矢 'arrow', 95; 弞 'to bare the gums', 95n24; 豕 'pig', 104–5, 105n40, *105t3.11*, 161, 162–64, 168–70, 169–70n61

shì 世 'generation', 119, *119t3.25*, *120t3.27*, 316n38; 士 'clerk', 'prefectural clerk', 'service personnel', 346n18, 347; 氏 'lineage', 378

Shi-Li 師歷 transition group inscriptions, 146, *147t4.1*, *149t4.2*, 151n23, 152, 153, 153n26, 154, 158, 161, *163t4.3*, 167

Shi Fu *zhong* 士父鐘 (JC 145–48), 309n19

Shi Hu *gui* 師虎簋 (JC 4316), 264n53

Shi Hui *gui* 師毀簋 (JC 4311), 266n58, 330n80

Shi Ke *xu* 師克盨 (JC 4467–68), 246n16, 264n53, 266n59, 328n78, 330n80

Shi Li *gui* 師聲 (釐) 簋 (JC 4324–25), 178, 264n53

Shi Qi 師旂, 286–87; Shi Qi *ding* 師旂鼎 (JC 2809), 286–87

Shi Qiang *pan* 史牆盤, 318

Shi Tian *gui* 史諎 (𧯄) 簋 (JC 4031), 300

Shi Xun *gui* 師訇 (詢) 簋 (JC 4342), 264n53, 266n59, 317n41

Shi You *ding* 師酉鼎, 276n13

Shi Yuan *gui* 師袁簋 (JC 4313–14), 246n16, 264n53

Shi Zhou 史籀, 351

Shiji 史記. See *Records of the Grand Scribe*

Shijing 詩經. See *Book of Poetry*

Shiliu jing 十六經 ("Sixteen Guidelines", excavated text): Plate 5, *212t6.1*, 213, 219, 219n24, 220

"*Shilü*" 史律. See "Statutes on Scribes"

shílù 實錄 'veritable records', 270

Shímài 食麥 (first month of the Shang calendar), 30, 30n22, 49

Shiming 釋名, 393n45

Shirakawa Shizuka 白川靜, 251n26, 275n11, 282n26

Shishi 師氏 (collective official title), 328

shǐshǐ 豕豕 'pigs (with classifier?)', 168–69

shǐshū 史書 'scribe's text', 354

"Shize" 時則 ("Seasonal Rules" or "Almanac", *Lüshi chunqiu*). See "Yueling" 月令

shìzǐ 世子 'children of the elite', 305, 316n38, 317

shooting, 95, 96n24, 198n47, 305, 306

shòu 受 'to receive', 148c, 275nn10–11); 授 'to hand over', 275nn10–11

Shoushu Huanfu *xu* 獸叔奐父盨, 297

Shouyang Studio 首陽齋, 244n12

shrines, 311, 321, 328n78

Shu 蜀, *386t11.1*, 387

Shu 書. See *Book of Documents*

shū 書 'to write', 'written document', 'written orders', 275n10, 276–77, 280, 281, 305, 348–49n25; 殳 (character component), 155n34, 222–23n33

shǔ 數 'to count', 278

shù 數 'numbers', 'calculation (of calendars)', 305

Shu Commandery 蜀郡, 385, *386t11.1*, 387, 393–95

Shu Wo *ding* 叔我鼎 (JC 1930), 267n62

Shu Xiangfu Yu *gui* 叔向父禹簋 (JC 4242), 245n15, 309n19

Shu Yi 叔尸 (夷), 326–29, 331n83, 335; Shu Yi *bo* 叔尸 (夷) 鎛 (JC 285), 325n70; Shu Yi *zhong* 叔尸 (夷) 鐘 (JC 272–79), 325–30, 331n83, 335

shuàixíng 帥型 'to follow the model', 308

Shuangdun 雙墩, 11, 44n44

shūdāo 書刀 'writing knife', 232, 232n49

shūguǎn 書館 'writing hall', 175

shuǐ 水 'water', 65, 115n50, 157n37

Shuihudi 睡虎地 archaeological site: ix; Qin legal documents, 346, 347, 348, 354n45, 355, 376; tomb, 352, 352n36, 357, 358n61, 362, 368, 381–85

shūjiǎn 書簡 'personal letter', 286n34

Shujing 書經. See *Book of Documents*

shùn 順 'obedient', 332

shùnkǒu liū 順口溜, also *shùnkǒu liú* 順口流, *shùnkǒu liù* 順口六 'doggerel or other rhymed saying', 130n65, *131t3.33*

shùnxué 順學 'obedient studies', 331–32, 333

shuō 說 'to explain', 'commentary', *213t6.2*, 217, 222–23n33, 307

shuò 朔 'first day of the new month', 76–77, 80

Shuowen jiezi 說文解字, 46n48, 85, 88, 94n21, 95n24, 99, *102t3.10*, 106, 108, 148e, 165, 265n57, 296, 350, 350n29, 351n33

shūshèn 淑慎 'good at and careful about', 323n59

Shuwu ling 束伍令 "Orders for Binding the Squads of Five", 368n95

shūzuǒ 書佐 'assistant scribe', 359n63

sǐ 死 'to die', 'death', 329, 330n80

"Si qi" 思齊 (*Book of Poetry*), 318n42, 321n54

sibilant initials, affricate, 128n63

sìfāng 四方 'the four regions', 309, 316, 317

sight-copying of divination records, 187–91

sighting rod, astronomical, *26f1.2b*

signatures of artisans, 382–84

signific, 87

signs: cyclical, 10, 19–21, 23, 28–37, *31f1.3, 34t1.2*, 47; Neolithic, 11, 20–21, 33; sign-pair sequence, 183; type, 75; of writing, 53–54, 56, 178n16, 182n25

silk: manuscripts, 209–35, 293, 365; measurement of silk manuscripts, 211n13; tightly woven silk, 211n11

Sima Qian 司馬遷, 307, 344n12, 363, 367

singing, 306n13, 333

single-graph piece, *156f4.2*, 158, 159

Sino-Tibetan, 42n40, 128

Six Arts (*Liùyì* 六藝), 305, 305n8, 336

six-hundred-bushel rank, 359n64

Sixth Year Shaobo Hu *gui* 六年召伯虎簋 (JC 4293), 251n26

Sixth Year Zhousheng *gui* 六年琱生簋 (JC 4293), 282–85

sixty signs, cycle of, 183–84, *185f5.2c*, 186

sixty-day cycle, 361

sīxué 私學 'private school', 'private student', 344n14

Skosey, Laura, 286

sky god, 332n89

slaves, 327, 364

slips, 348n25, 359, 360, 361

Smith, Adam, 12, 14, 59n16, 68n31

social class: control of, 24, 169–70; literacy of, 271–301, 339–69

social events, 298–300, 311

social functions: of bronze inscriptions, 294; of writing in Western Zhou, 273–79

social hierarchy, ranking systems, 310n21, 319

societies, agricultural. *See* agricultural activities, societies

Sogdian, 92n15

soldiers, 328, 360–64, 365, 368, 370, 379–81

solstices, 28; winter solstice, 41

Son of Heaven, references to, 242–53, 262, 274, 280

"Sòng" 頌 (*Book of Poetry*), 311

sòng 誦 'to chant', 'make a eulogy', 307n15, 333, 353, 354, 354n42

Song ceramic shards, 144

Song *ding* 頌鼎 (JC 2829), 273–77

Song Zhenhao 宋鎮豪, 179–80

songs, 303, 303n1, 311–12, 316n38, 318, 321, 321n54, 324, 328, 328n77, 329–34

sons of scribes, 347–48

south-north axial alignment, 37–38

Southeast Asia, 268

Southern Min, 128n63

spacing (in writing), 207

Spanish: Conquest, 24; language, 59; missionaries, 25

speech, spoken language, 28, 53, 54, 127–34, 307n16; sounds of language, 86, 87, 117. *See also* phonology

speeches, 266, 269, 319, 325–26, 330

spelling (Aymara and Quechua), 10n16. *See also* orthography

spirits, 165–67, 167–68n55, 308, 312, 313, 319, 324, 331, 332; altar of the spirit of Bo, 146n18; altar to the spirit of the soil, 146, 150, 150n21; of King Wen, 320

sponsor (definition), 240n3

Spring and Autumn Annals (*Chunqiu* 春秋, *Chunqiu jing* 春秋經), 76, 77, 83n51, 303n3, 307

Spring and Autumn period: viii, 40, 173, 306n10, 310, 311, 312, 325, 326, 330, 331n84, 374

"Spring Begins" (*Lìchūn* 立春), 44

square, 48, 49, 50; constellation, 49n53; in the sky, 48n51; square up, (see *zhèng* 正)

standard language, standardization, 96, 125, 126n60

standard square script, 96

Starostin, Sergey, 42n40

stars, 24, 39–50; charts, *40f1.4, 47f1.5*; Fire Star (Antares in Scorpius), 36n28, 41; Markab (Alpha Pegasus), 46. *See also* astronomy

statement of dedication, 239, 243

States, Warring. *See* Warring States

status of women, 365

statutes (*lǜ* 律), 346, 355–57, 359n63, 369; "Statutes concerning the Appointment of Retainers", 347n21; "Statutes of the Commandant", 350, 351; "Statutes on Enrollment", 360, 365; "Statutes on Establishing Heirs", 365; "Statutes on Households", 360, 365, 366; "Statutes on Scribes", 339n[0], 349, 354. *See also* legal documents, rules

stele inscriptions, 98n27, 99, 391

stems and branches. *See tiāngān dìzhī* 天干地支

Stifter (definition), 240n3

stilt-huts, depictions on clay pots, 44n44

stone: chimes, 315; inscriptions, 388–91

stonemasons, *Plate 8a-b*, 388–91, *389f11.1*; serial numbers of, 380–81, 388n37

stop (phonetics): codas, 122, *122t3.31*; glottal, 33, 33n25

storage pits. *See* pits, storage

storehouses, 348

Street, Brian V., 341n6

strings, knotted, 24, 25, 47

strokes (pen-strokes in a graph): extension in a Chinese character, 157; number of in Han lacquer graphs, *386t11.1*, 387; order, 186–87

strokes (punishment), 376

strontium analysis of bones, 172n64

structures, public, 178

students (trainees; *dìzǐ* 弟子, *xuéshì* 學士), 175–76, 307, 344n14, 354, 358; copying and writing, 191–96, 198, 199–205, *200f5.6*, 391. *See also* copying, copyists; education; scribal groups; writing

style: of behavior, performance, 311; of script and orthography, 221–23

stylus, 379 380, 384

subpatron (definition), 240n3

sucancas, 25n14, 27

suí 隨, 227

suì 歲 'year of age', 349

Sukhu, Gopal, 9

Sumerian literature, 175–76

sun, 21–25, 44; chronogram, 45; depictions of sun on clay pots), 44n44; shadow, 38

Sun Haibo 孫海波, 106

sūnzǐ 孫子 'grandsons and sons', 296n47

supernatural, 19–50

Supervisor of Construction, 280, 281

Supervisor of Land, 280, 281, 290

Supervisor of Marshes, 293

surname, 378, 390n40

syllabic writing, 56

syllable-final category, 96n25

syllables, 33n25, 123

syllabograph, 61

symbol (definition of graphic sign), 81

symbols, visual. *See* visuographic symbolism

syssemantic graph, 88
syzygy, 45
tā 它 'other', 111, *111t3.15*
tablets: ancestral, 111; Mesopotamian, 69, *70f2.1*, 175
tableware, 378
tael (*liǎng* 兩), 225, 354, 355, 356
tags, ivory, 70, *70f2.1*
Taibao *he* 太保盉 (JL 942), 245n16
Taibao *lei* 太保罍 (JL 987), 245n16
tàicāng 太倉 'official in charge of imperial granaries', 364
tàiláo 太牢 'major livestock', 169–70n61
Taiping yulan 太平御覽, 378, 378n18
Taiwanese language, 98n27, *98t3.7*, 128–29, *129t3.32*, 130
tàixué 大學 'major learning', 178
Takashima, Ken-ichi 高嶋謙一, 12, 14, 69n33, 85n[0], 146n17, 155n31, 174n[0], 296n47
tales, 303, 303n1
Tales of the States (*Guoyu* 國語), 40–41, 44, 45, 167–68n55, 268, 269, 279n43, 335
Tan Buyun 譚步雲, 151n23
Tang 唐 dynasty, 372n5, 384
Tang Jigen 唐際根, 170n63
Tang Lan 唐蘭, 219, 220n25, 278–79
Tang liudian 唐六典 (name of text), 378n18
Tannenbaum, Frank, 8
Taosi 陶寺 Neolithic Astronomical Observatory: ix, 10, 21, *22f1.1*, 27, 28, 44n44, 45–46
tautology, 94
tax, 341, 372
teachers (*xiānshēng* 先生), teaching, 181, 304, 305n8, 306n10, 307n15, 328, 334, 344, 358. *See also* education; schools, schooling
technical manuscript texts, 208n4
temple, 38, 38–39n33, 41; beneficiaries in proto-cuneiform texts, 72; compounds:166n52; of Zhougong, 141n2, 167–68n55. *See also* Celestial Temple

Teng, governor of Nan Commandery 南郡騰, 358n61
"Teng Wengong shang" 滕文公上 (*Mencius*), 306n10
terra cotta warriors and horses, *Plate 8*, 48n51, 379–81, 384
territory. *See* land
text writing, texts, 6, 52n13, 177, 181, *190f5.4*, 191, 194, 199–202, 206–36, 251–58, 268, 271–301, 302–35, 371, 387–88n35. *See also* writing
text-based learning, 303, 305
textiles, 373
texts: classical, 371; inscribed, 379n19; legal and administrative, 353, 358; military, 368; "texts with a history" (Martin Kern), 208n3; versus codicological units, 214, *215t6.3*
textual units (definition), 213–14
Thatch Shrine of Yong, 357n56
thián=khui 展開 (Taiwanese 'to unroll'), 128–29, *129t3.32*
thióng 冢 (Taiwanese 'grave'), 128, *129t3.32*
thoughts (understanding and communication of), 372–73
Three Dynasties, 312
Three Kingdoms period, 367n9
Three Supervisors (of the *Qīngshìliáo* 卿事寮), 281–82
thunder, 320n48; thunderous sounds, 326, 328
tiāngān 天干 ('heavenly stems', 'ten stems': cyclical signs), 184–86, *185f5.2*
tiāngān dìzhī 天干地支, 19, 73n41. *See also gānzhī* 干支
"Tianguan" 天官 (*Zhouli* 周禮), 169–70n61
"Tianguan shu" 天官書 (*Records of the Grand Scribe*), 36n28
Tiansi 天駟 ("Heavenly Quadriga", asterism), 45, 45n46. *See also* lunar lodges
tiānxiě 添寫 'to insert omitted characters', 232

Tibeto-Burman languages, 108
tiles (ceramic, roof), 379
tilling ceremony, 263
time (measurement, predicting), 24, 234
tīng 聽 'to hear', 222–23n33, 234
tíng 亭 'pavilion', 382–83
tíngshǐ 庭史 'scribe of the court', 358–59
titles: early texts, 207; official, 176–77
Tiying 緹縈, 364
tombs, 38, 38n33, 379–83, 388–91, 389f11.1. See also Abydos; Guodian: tomb no. 1; Shuihudi: tomb; Wang Xu tomb; Zhangjiashan: tomb no. 247
tomb texts, 208–9nn5–6, 325, 334, 334n93, 349, 351n32, 352, 360
tone categories, 122, *131t3.33*, 133
Tong Lu *zhong* 通祿鐘 (JC 64), 309n19
tōngyǔ 通語 'common language', 125–26
tools, 373, 384; tools of governance, 24
tóu 頭 (measure word and noun suffix), 391, 391n42
touch-up artist, *386t11.1*
trade: pre-imperial China, 259n37; Qin and Han law codes, 378n18
"tradition texts" (Matthias L. Richter), 208n3
trainee, 307, 358; date tables, 180–87. *184f5.1, 185f5.2*. See also copying, copyists; manuals; students
trance, king in state of, 265
transmission of literacy. See literacy: spread of
transport documents, 28n18, 348–49nn25–26
Trauzettel, Rolf, 256n32
traveling masters, 327
trenches, large joined, 191
tributary, *111t3.14*
tribute, 155, 256, 259, 259n37, 314, 321, 326, 330, 336
Trigger, Bruce, 60n18
tǔ 土 'land', *100t3.8, 147t4.1, 149t4.2*

tùchún 兔唇, also *tùchǔnr 兔蠢兒 'harelip', 130n64
túgǎi 塗改 'to wipe off a character', 232
tureen, 330n80
Turner, Victor, 258
turtle shells. See plastrons, turtle shells
twelve branches. See *dìzhī* 地支
"type A" syllables in Old Chinese, 33n25
U-j material, Egyptian, 70–74, *71f2.2*. See also Egypt, Egyptology
uncontracted numbers, *98t3.7*
UNESCO definition of literacy, 383–84
Unger, J. Marshall, 91
Unger, Ulrich, 240n3
unit characters, 57, *57t2.1*
unitary pictograph, 104
University Seminars, Columbia, 8
Ur III period, 177
urban planning, 47n50
Uruk periods, 69, 73, 176–77, 200, 202; tablets, *70f2.1*
Utz, David A., 92n15
Vankeerberghen, Griet, 344n14
vassalage, 152n25
velars, 33, 35, 134
Veldhuis, Niek, 176
Venture, Olivier, 239–40
Venus, *47f1.5*
verb-object word order, 157
verdict, 287
veritable records (*shílù* 實錄), 270
vermilion, 378
vertical strokes (of graphs), 51n1, 187
vessels, 176, 177n13, 240n3, 247, 271, 294n43, 295, 296, 296n48, 297n51, 299, 308, 317, 321, 321n53, 322, 331n82, 375, 377, 381–88; for serving food, (see *fànyú* 飯盂; *fēnguǐ* 饙簋; *fēnyú* 饙盂); maker, 310n23. See also lacquer objects
victim, human, 153. See also sacrifice
Vietnamese, 114n47, 123n55
visitors to court, 254–58
visuographic symbolism (visual symbols), 24, 28, 47n50

VO (verb-object) word order. *See* verb-object word order
vocalic assonance, 35
vocalization, 101n31
voi (Vietnamese 'elephant'), 114n47
Von Dassow, Eva. *See* Dassow
wài 外 'outer', external, written with character 卜, 11, 78–81, *80f2.5*, 83
Wai Bing 外丙, 78, *79f2.4*
Wai Ren 外壬, 78, *79f2.4*
Waley, Arthur, 253n27, 299n55
walled settlements, walls, 38, 41, 42
Wan 萬 dance, 323, 324, 328
"wandering" (ritual), 335
wáng 亡 'to abscond illegally', 'abscondence', 368–69, 368n96; 王 'king', 181, 246, 310, 330
wáng bǔcí 王卜辭 'royal oracle bone inscription', 142n4
Wang Ching-hsien 王敬獻, 268n67
Wang Chong 王充, 175, 352
Wang family 王氏 artisans, 396–97
wáng ruò yuē 王若曰 'the king approvingly said', 243, 245–46, 264–65, 266n59
Wang Xu 王盱 tomb, 392, 395
wáng yuē 王曰 'the king said', 245, 246, 266n59
Wang Yuxin 王宇信, 201n49
Wang, Haicheng, 176n11, 202–3
Wangdu County stone 望都石, *389f11.1*, 390
wángguó 王國 'the king's state', 321
wángmìngshū 王命書 'document of royal command', 274, 275, 275nn10–11, 276. *See also mìngshū* 命書
wángnián 王年 'reign calendar', 310–11
Wángsūn 王孫 'Royal Grandson', 322
Wangsun Yizhe 王孫遺者, 322–23; Wangsun Yizhe *zhong* 王孫遺者鐘 (JC 261), 322–24, 322n58, 331n84
wàngwén shēngyì 望文生義 'speculative etymology', 170–71

wǎngxué 往學 'to go to school', 178
"Wangzhi" 王制: (*Book of Rites*), 306n10, 307nn14–15; (*Xunzi*), 306n10, 307n14
Wangzi Wu *ding* 王子午鼎 (JC 2811), 322n58
war, warfare, *93t3.5*, 155, 316, 326–28. *See also wǔ* 武
Warring States period: viii, 45, 50n56, 96, 176, 206, 302–7, 308n17, 312, 331n82, 332, 333–36, 340–45, 367–68, 370, 372n4, 374, 375
warriors. *See* soldiers, terra cotta warriors and horses
water, 65, 115n50, 157n37; referring to Yingshi 營室, 41
water pipes, 379
Way (*dào* 道), 305, 308, 311, 334
weapons, 271, 374, 375, 377
weather, 320
weaving, 24, 211n13
wedge-shaped ductus, 69, *70f2.1*
week, ten-day. *See xún* 旬
Wei 尾 (asterism), 36n28. *See also* lunar lodges
Wei 衛. *See* Wey
wēi 威 'awesome', 309, 315n36
wéi 違 'to avoid', 331n83; 隹 (particle), 249n21; 為/爲 'to become', 'to take as', *113t3.19*
wèi 未 (*dìzhī* #8), *32t1.1*, *34t1.2*, 199; 畏 'to terrify', 333; 謂 'to be called', 225
Wei *ding* 衛鼎. *See* Fifth Year Wei *ding* 五祀衛鼎, Ninth Year Wei *ding* 九年衛鼎
Wei Hong 衛宏, 365n81
Wei River 渭河, 287, 329
Wei Zhao 韋昭, 43–44, 167–68n55
Weili zhi dao 為吏之道 (text, "The Way of Being a Good Official"), 345n15, 352, 358, 358n61
Weiliaozi 尉繚子 (or *Yuliaozi*), 368
"*Weilü*" 尉律 (text, "Statutes of the Commandant"), 350
wēiyí 威儀 'Awesome Decorum', 309, 311, 315, 315n36, 316, 317, 321, 321n54, 323, 328, 333–34

488 INDEX

welcoming the king's visit or awards, 297, 297n53
Wen 文: King, 242, 253, 313, 315, 320, 321n54, 323, 324, 327n76, 332–34 (*see also* "Wenwang" 文王); Duke of Wey 衛, 38n31; Emperor 文帝, 364
wēn 溫 'to heat up', 'warm', 'to prepare', 'cook', 164, 170–71
wén 文 'literary culture or knowledge', 303, 307
Wen Ding 文丁 (also Wen Wu Ding 文武丁, king), 159n43
Wen Wang 文王. *See* Wen 文 (king), "Wenwang" 文王
Wén Wáng zhī xíng 文王之行 'movements of King Wen', 333
Wen Wu Ding 文武丁 (king). *See* Wen Ding 文丁
"Wenwang" 文王 (*Book of Poetry*), 327n76. *See* Wen 文 (king), Wen Wang 文王
"Wenwang shizi" 文王世子 (*Book of Rites*), 306n10
"Wenwang you sheng" 文王有聲 (*Book of Poetry*), 314n33
Wenwu 文物, 228nn41–42
Western: alphabetic script, 55, 62; scholarship, 216n20
Western Han dynasty. *See* Han dynasty: Western
Western Workshop of Shu Commandery, 385, *386t11.1*, 387, 393–95
Western Zhou, (*see* Zhou dynasty: Western); bronzes, (*see* bronzes)
Wey [*Wèi*] 衛, 38n31
widows, widowers, 366, 370
wild animals, 170n63. *See also* animals
wills, 372–73n5
winter solstice, 41
wǒ 我 'I', 'me' (or name), 234, 267n62
Wo *fangding* 我方鼎 (JC 2763), 267n62
"Wo Jiang" 我將 (*Book of Poetry*), 327n76
Woman Ao (Dà Nǚzǐ Áo 大女子鷔), Plate 8, 382

women: Chu and Jin lineage, 319, 321nn53–54; category, *see* Funü *lei* 婦女類; Han dynasty, 364–67, 370; status, 365
wooden or bamboo document. *See* bamboo documents, manuscripts
words: dual usage of, 76, 77–81; families, 91; lost, 304, 305, 307n15; lost words of the former kings, 305); morphemes, (*see* morphemes); order, 151–53, 157; repetition, 99, 311; wording in early Chinese texts, 207. See also *yán* 言
workshops, 203, 373, 378, 381, 385–88. *See also* factories, factory systems
worm, 93n20
woven patterns (depictions on clay pots), 44n44. *See also* weaving
writing, 33, 34, *34t1.2*, 60n19, *61t2.2*, 69, 92, 98n27, *135–37t3.34*; analysis, definition, importance of, 4–6, 27n16, 271–301, 339–69, 371; and reading of graphs, 360; as literacy, 4–5; backward, 199; development, invention of, 10–13, 19–50, 51–84, 158n41, 173–205, 273, 371, 397–99; errors, 180–88, *184–85ff5.1–2*, 202, 235; forms of, 351–52; knife (*shūdāo* 書刀), 232, 232n49; legal writing, 291n37; maturity of, 99; modern Chinese writing, 55, 67, 127–30, 151n23, 264, 391; Neolithic, 11n17; pottery brush-writing, (*see* brush-writing, brushes; potters, pottery); systems, 11, 27–29, 57–84, 85–137, 275; tools, 202–8; transmission, 261; writing hall (*shūguǎn* 書館), 175. *See also* bone inscriptions, bones; brush-writing, brushes; calligraphy; diviners; glottographic writing; handwriting; ink inscriptions; literacy; manuscripts; pre-writing; scribal groups; silk manuscripts; students; text writing
written documents. *See* documents
Wu 武 (king), 242, 253, 319, 321
wū 惡/烏 (particle), 229n45

wǔ 午 (*dìzhī* #7), *32t1.1*, 33, *34t1.2*, 181; 武 'war', 'martial', 92n19, *93t3.5*
wù 勿 (negative particle), 156n35, 161, 166, 171; 戊 (*tiāngān* #5), *32t1.1, 34t1.2*, 186
Wu dialects, 98n27
Wu Ding 武丁 (king), 28, 48n52, 67, 69, 144, 151, 159, 159n43, 160, 167, 174, 177, 178, 180, 193, 196, 201
Wu diviner group inscriptions, *149t4.2; 157*
Wu *gui* 敔簋 (JC 3827), 295–96
Wu Hu 吳虎, 280–81; Wu Hu *ding* 吳虎鼎 (JL, 364), 280–82
Wu Jiabi 武家壁, 45n46
wǔ shāng 舞商 'to dance *shāng*', 179–80
Wu Wang 武王. *See* Wu 武 (king)
Wu xing 五行 (excavated text), 210, *213t6.2*, 214, *215t6.3*, 216–17, 222, 222–23n33
Wu xing zhan 五星占 (Mawangdui MS), 212
Wu Yi 武乙 (king), 159n43
Wucheng 吳城, 155
Wufu 武父, 289, 290, 291
Wuhan 武漢: ix
Wuji *gui* 無㠱簋 (JC 4225–28), 263n42
Wujun Xicun 五郡西村, 283
wùlìng 勿令 'not to be ordered', 348–49n25
Wuwei 武威 MSS, 232
wùxū 戊戌 (day 35; miswritten for *jiǎxū* 甲戌), *185f5.2e*, 186
wǔzhǎng 伍長 'head of a five-family unit', 360, 360n67
Wuzi Jiang Zhui *bo* 鄔子䤾自鎛 (JC 153–54), 324n67
X Hu *gui* X 虎簋 (JC 3838), 296n47
X-*shǐ* (general form of titles for specialized scribes), 347
Xi 喜, 345–46, 357–58, 358n61
xī 兮 (prosodic particle), 311; 夕 'night': written for *yuè* 'moon', 81; written for *míng* 'night' 90, *90t3.3*; 析 'to split', 285
xǐ 徙 'to move to', 'relocate', 160–61, *163t4.3*, 164–67, 171

xì 卅 'forty', 98n27, *98t3.7*;
Xi Jia *pan* 兮甲盤 (JC 10175), 308n18
xí jiǎzǐ 習甲子 'to practice one's *jiǎzǐ*', 182
Xi'an 西安: ix
Xi'nan Yi 西南夷, 388n35
Xia 夏 dynasty: viii, 20, 27–38, 45, 318, 318n45, 326
Xia Nai 夏鼐, 144
"Xia xiaozheng" 夏小正 ("Lesser Annuary of Xia", *Da Dai Liji*), 49
xiàlì 下吏 'low-status person', 348
xiàn 縣 'county', 347
Xian Qi *gui* 縣改簋 (JC 4269), 263n44
Xián tíng 咸亭 'pavilion in Xianyang', 382
Xianbei 鮮卑 (name of a people), 127
xiánchù yìnshì 咸畜胤士 'to nurture all the men of one's generation', 321
"Xiang" 象 commentary of the *Book of Changes*, 279n23
xiāng 相 'mutually', 228n39
xiáng 庠 'school', 306n10
xiǎng 享 'mortuary feast', 309, 329, 332, 335
xiàng 象 'image' 44, 44n44, 332–33
"Xiang dang" 鄉黨 (*Analects*), 42n40
Xiang ma jing 相馬經 MS, 212, 212n15
Xiangfen 襄汾, 21
xiāngxiào 鄉校 'village clan-based school', 306n10
xiànlìng 縣令 'county prefect', 357
xiānshēng 先生 'teacher', 181
xiānwáng zhī yíyán 先王之遺言 'the lost words of the former kings', 305
Xianyang 咸陽, 50, 358n61, 379, 380, 382
Xianyun 獫狁 (people), 299, 299n56
xiànzhǎng 縣長 'county prefect', 357
xiǎo 小 'small', 115, *115t3.21*
Xiao, Prince of Rencheng 任城孝王, *389f11.1f*, 390
xiǎo nánzǐ 小男子 'minor boy', 381–82
xiǎo nǚzǐ 小女子 'minor girl', 381–82
"Xiao rong" 小戎 (*Book of Poetry*), 320n52
"Xiao xiangguo shijia" 蕭相國世家 (*Records of the Historian*), 359n63
Xiao Yi 小乙, 167

Xiaochen Qiang 小臣牆 bone, 29n20
Xiaoshuangqiao 小雙橋, 172n64
Xiaotun 小屯, 144n8, 196; South 小屯南地 *xíkè* inscriptions, 180n22, 203n57
"Xiaoya" 小雅 ("Lesser Elegantiae", *Book of Poetry*), 258n34, 311
xiǎozǐ 小子 'youth', 'child', 308, 308n17, 310, 311, 315–16, 318, 327, 328n78, 332, 333
Xibo *gui* 戲伯簋 (JC 666), 296n47
Xichuan 淅川, 322
Xici 繫辭 (Mawangdui MS), 212, 212n15
"Xici zhuan" 繫辭傳 ("Appended Commentary", *Book of Changes*), 24, 47, 49–50
xiè 泄 'to spread', 'to leak', 'garrulous', *120t3.27*
xiéshēng 諧聲, type of character structure, 61–62n22, 63n25, 64, 85n[0], 86–109, 87–88n6, *93t3.5, 97t3.6, 105t3.11, 107t3.12, 110t3.13, 118–22t3.24–30*, 116, 117, 117n51, 118–37
xiéshù 邪術 'evil technique', 306n13
xiéyùn 叶韻 'contact between separate rimes', 122
Xigong Xiang 西宮襄, 289–91
Xigoucun 西溝村, 261
xíkè 習刻 'practice inscriptions', 174–75, 180–87, 194, 201n49, 203n57
Xin 心 (asterism), 36n28. *See also* lunar lodges
xīn 辛 (*tiāngān* #8), 21n7, *32t1.1, 34t1.2*, 181
xìn 信 'trust', 'sincere', 87–88, *88t3.1*, 101n31, 106
Xin, Female Ancestor 妣辛, 194
Xing de B 刑德 · 乙 MS, 212, 212n15
Xing *gui* 癲簋 (JC 4170–77), 245n15, 308n18
Xing *zhong* 癲鐘 (JC 246–59), 245n15, 308n18, 309n19
xíng 形, 227; 行 'to traverse', 'to walk', 'to perambulate', 306 (see also *háng* 行)

xǐng 省, 228n41
xìng 姓 'surname', 378, 390n40
xíngshēng 形聲 (*xíngshēngzì* 形聲字), type of character structure. *See xiéshēng* 諧聲
xíngshī 行師 'to send out the armies', 327
Xíngshū 行書 'forwarding of documents', 348n25
Xiongnu 匈奴 (people), 362
xīshuài 蟋蟀 'cricket', 56–57n8
xiū 休 'favored', 331–32; 羞 'to present ceremonial gifts', 267n63
Xiuwu of Huaizhou 懷州修武, 158n40
Xiwangmu 西王母 (deity), 393
xízì 習字 'to practice writing', 181
xū 戌 (*dìzhī* #11), *32t1.1*, 33, *34t1.2*
xù 序 'school', 306n10
Xu Hong 許宏, 47n50
Xu Hongxiu 徐鴻修, 169
Xu Kai 徐鍇, 108–9
Xu Shen 許慎, 350
Xu Zhaochang 許兆昌, 340n3
Xu Zhaofeng 徐昭峰, 145
Xuan 宣 (king), 241, 254n28, 281, 351
Xuanquan 懸泉 ix, 363
xuānxuān 烜烜 'glistening', 'glorious', 324
Xuchang 許昌, 391, 391n43
xué 學 'school', 'to learn', 'to practice', 178–80, 179n19, 180, 304, 306n10, 332–34
xué'ěr 學佴 'instructor', 358
xuēchú 削除 'to scrape off mistaken characters', 232
xuēgǎi 削改 'to correct by scraping off mistaken characters', 232
"Xueji" 學記 (*Book of Rites*), 306n10
xuékè 學刻 'to learn to carve', 181
xuèqì 血氣 'blood and breath', 332
xuéshì 學士 'student', 307; 學室 'school', 347
xuétú dìzǐ 學徒弟子 'apprentice disciples', 347, 347n21
xún 旬 'ten-day week', 29, 36, *185f5.2a*, 186
Xun *gui* 旬 (詢) 簋 (JC 4321), 246n16, 264n53

Xunzi 荀子, 305–7, 307n15, 332n89, 353
yà or yǎ 亞 (title), 152n25, 155n32, 189
Yan 鄢, 248, 335, 357
yān 焉 (particle), 229n45, 230
yán 延/征 'to continue', 165; 言 'to speak', 'to say', 'word', 88t3.1, 122t3.30, 354
yán zòu shāng 延奏商 'to continue to perform shāng', 179–80
Yan'er bo 沇兒鎛 (JC 203). See Yun'er bo
Yan Kejun 嚴可均, 206n1
Yan Yiping 嚴一萍, 278n18, 279
yáng 羊 'sheep', 'goat', 147t4.1, 148a, 149t4.2, 151, 153, 169–70n61, 170n63, 191, 197; (as initial) 135–36
Yang gui 揚簋 (JC 4294–95, also Yang Pang gui 揚旁簋), 264n53
Yang Shengnan 楊升南, 201n49
Yang Shuda 楊樹達, 285
Yang Yubin 楊育彬, 145
Yangjiacun 楊家村: ix, 241, 244
Yangjiashan 楊家山, 245n13
Yangshao 仰韶: viii
Yangzi River, ix, 13, 126, 302, 319, 322, 330
Yanhou yu 匽侯盂 (JC 10305), 296n47
Yao 繇, Little Gate Official, 289, 293
Yao 要 (Mawangdui MS), 212
Yao Xuan 姚萱, 68n31, 80f2.5, 179n20, 203n55
"Yaodian" 堯典 ("Canon of Yao", Book of Documents), 49, 202
yard (Neolithic measurement), 24
yàshǐ 亞史 'minor scribe', 282
Yates, Robin D. S., 13, 175n7, 219n24, 269n68, 370, 372, 372n4, 385
yǎyán 雅言 'elegant language', 124–27
yě 也 (particle), 221, 224, 225, 227n38; protoform of shé 蛇 111, 111t3.15
yè 夜 'night', 234; 枼/葉 'leaf', 119t3.25, 120t3.27; 腋 (also yì) 'armpit', 112, 112n46, 112t3.17
year (nián 年), 11, 77, 80–81; kinds of, 32n24; of age (suì 歲), 349; solar year, 25

Yellow River (Hé 河): ix, 49, 50n56, 143, 159, 197; valley, region, 302, 310, 319, 325
yèzhě 謁者 'receptionist', 356, 356n52
Yi 宜, 291, 387
Yi 夷 peoples, 328
"Yi" 抑 (Book of Poetry), 323n59, 327n76, 331
yí 儀 'school', 'decorum', 'outer manifestation', 'outer expression' (also written 義), 306, 321, 327n76, 331, 334
yǐ 乙 (tiāngān #2), 21n7, 32t1.1, 34t1.2, 147t4.1, 149t4.2, 185f5.2c, 186; 已 'to end', 226; 矣 (particle), 226, 227
yì 亦 (particle), 112, 112n46, 112t3.17; 易 'to change', 327; 殹 (particle), 221; 疫 'pestilence', 'to exhaustion', 179, 179n19; 腋 (also yè) 'armpit', 122; 迻 'to move', 'relocate', 165; 邑 'city', 306n10
yī míng diǎn 一名典 'register with names listed singly', 283–84
Yi of Xianyang City: Plate 8a
"Yi zhi yi" 易之義 (Mawangdui text), 212
Yi Zhou shu 逸周書, 30, 49
yí zǐsūn 宜子孫 'May it bring you sons and grandsons!', 394
Yichang 宜昌, 322
Yihou Ze gui 宜侯夨簋 (JC 4320), 277, 291
Yijing 易經. See Book of Changes
Yili 儀禮, 169–70n61, 254–58, 323n59, 326
yǐmǎo 乙卯 (day 52), 290, 291
Yin 殷 dynasty, 67n30, 144. See also Shang dynasty
yīn 音 'to make music', 'tone of a bell', 122t3.30, 318
yín 寅 (dìzhī #3), 32t1.1, 34t1.2, 184, 186
yǐn 尹 'technical minister', 328
yìn 胤 'lineage successor', 316n38
Yin Zhou jinwen jicheng 殷周金文集成, 93t3.5n[0], 266n61. Cited in text as JC
yíng 營 'delimit', 'delineate', 42
Ying Palace (Yinggong 營宮, asterism), 40, 41, 44. See also lunar lodges
Yingshi 營室 (asterism). See Dìng 定
yǐnguān 隱官 (rank), 369

yínqiǎo 淫巧 'licentious ingenuity', 376
yǐnshì 尹氏 (rank), 275, 275n10
Yinxu 殷墟, 144, 169; Dasikongcun 大司空村, 159; Huayuanzhuang Dongdi 花園莊東地, see Huayuanzhuang Dongdi; period, 20, 144, 159, 160, 169, 172n64
"Yiwen zhi" 藝文志 ("Bibliographic Treatise", *Hanshu*), 206n1, 220n25, 351, 351n31
yǒng 永 'eternally', 110–11; *111t3.14*; 泳 'to swim', 110–11; *111t3.14*
"Yong feng" 鄘風 ("Airs of Yong", *Book of Poetry*), 38
yòng péng yòng yǒu 用朋用友 'to solicit friends and colleagues', 297
Yong *yu* 永盂 (JC 10322), 282
Yongbo *ding* 雍伯鼎 (JC 2531), 158
Yongyi 雍毅, 280–81
yōu 攸 'smoothly and swiftly', as protoform of *dí* 滌 'to wash', 'rinse', 113, *113t3.18*
yóu 尤, 198n46
yǒu 酉 (*dìzhī* #10), *32t1.1*, *34t1.2*, 161, 162–63, 184–86, *185f5.2b*
yòu 又/侑 'to offer', 'to give', *147t4.1*, *149t4.2*, 150–55, 158; 右 'right (side)', 260; 右/佑 'to help', 'accompany', 260
You Sheng 右眚, 289, 293
yǒugān 友干 'to act as personal bodyguard', 317n41
yòuzhě 右者 'accompanying official', 260n39
yǒuzhì 有秩 'rank-holder', 356n53
yú 于 (particle), 151; 於 (particle), 229n45, 233
yù 御 'to drive (a chariot)', 305, 357n57; 浴 'to bathe', 170–71; 禦 'lustration ritual', 157, 161, 168, 169. See also ritual
Yu *ding* 禹鼎 (JC 2833–34), 245n15
Yu Haoliang 于豪亮, 347
"Yu lao" 喻老 (*Hanfeizi*), 215n18
Yu Mai Jia'er *zhong* 余購逨兒鐘 (JC 183–86), 267n64

Yu shu 語書 (excavated text), 358
yuán 爰 (unit for metal), 290
Yuan Guangkuo 袁廣濶, 145
Yuan Jing 袁靖, 170n63
yuán míng 元鳴 'to be supremely called out (inner power)', 'to ring (bells)', 331, 331n84
Yuan *pan* 裒盤 (JC 10172), 273–74
Yuan Zhongyi 袁仲一, 379, 380
Yuanti *lei* 圓體類 'roundish-script category', 142n4, *149t4.2*
Yue 越 (people), 310, 330–33
Yue 樂 (*Music*), 307
yuē 曰 'to say', 'to be called', 'to state', 240, 243, 245, 246, 247, 262, 263n43, 264–67, 311, 313. See also *nuò yuē* 諾曰; *ruò yuē* 若曰; *wáng ruò yuē* 王若曰; *wáng yuē* 王曰
yuè 月 'moon', 23–24, 25, 28, 32–33n24, 64, 76, 77, 81, *147t4.1*, 148, *149t4.2*; 樂 'music', 305, 308, 332n86. See also *fēi* 朏; *lǐyuè* 禮樂
Yue inscription, 272n3, 324, 333
yuè yī zhèng 月一正 'month one regular', 32
"Yueling" 月令 (*Yi Zhou shu*), 30, 30n22; (*Lüshi chunqiu*), 41; (*Book of Rites*), 365n12, 375, 377
Yuelu Shuyuan 嶽麓書院, 211n13, 352
Yueyang 櫟陽, 380
Yuliaozi 尉繚子 (or *Weiliaozi*), 368
yǔn 允 'surely', 161, 164a, 165
Yun'er *bo* 沇兒鎛 (JC 203), 324n67, 331n84
Yunnan 雲南, 388n35
yùnshū 韻書 'rime book', 96, 96n25, 98
yùshǐ 御史 (rank), 357, 358
Zang Zhifei 臧知非, 351n31, 352
zào 造 'to make', 375, *386t11.1*, 387
Ze 夨, 287–93
zé 則 'rule', 'pattern', 333
zēng 繒 'coarse silk', 211n11
Zeng, Marquis Yi of 曾侯乙, 45
"Zengzi tianyuan" 曾子天圓 (*Da Dai Liji*), 169–70n61
Zeren *pan* 夨人盤 (Sanshi *pan* 散氏盤), 292–93

Zewang 矢王 (king of Ze), 287–93
Zhachao zhong 罩巢鐘, 267n64
Zhang Jinguang 張金光, 347n21, 358
Zhang Shichao 張世超, 182
Zhang Shouzhong 張守中, 352n36
Zhangjiapo 張家坡: viii, ix
Zhangjiashan 張家山: ix, 349, 360; tomb no. 247, 352, 356n52, 368
Zhanguo ce 戰國策, 357n57
zhǎnkai 展開. See thián=khui
Zhanzhu zhi fa 戰誅之法 (Law on Battlefield Executions), 368
Zhao 趙, 375
Zhao (Duke) 昭公, 167–68n55
Zhao li 昭力 (Mawangdui MS), 212
Zhaoxiang 昭襄 (king of Qin), 357
zhě 者, 233, 234
Zhediao 者汈, 330, 330n81, 331; Zhediao bo and zhong 者汈鎛 and 鐘 (JC 120–32), 330n81
zhēn 貞 (introduces the charge in divination formula), 'test', 42, 42n41, 43, 43n43, 44, 49n53, 146n17, 147t4.1, 149t4.2, 150, 164. See also duìzhēn
Zhèn 震 (hexagram in Book of Changes), 320n48
Zheng 爭, 142–43n5, 151–52, 155n31
Zheng 政 (king of Qin 秦), 357
zhēng 征 'journey', 48n51, 354n42; 爭 'strife', 234
zhèng 正 'regular', 'to align', 39, 39n33, 41, 41n38, 42–45, 42n40, 48n51, 49, 49n53; 證, 354n42
Zheng Huisheng 鄭慧生, 201n50
Zheng Qiao 鄭樵, 109
Zheng Sinong 鄭司農, 355n50
Zheng Xuan 鄭玄, 169–70n61, 353, 355n50
zhèngdé 政德 'governing power', 323, 326
zhěngfú 整幅 'full-width format (of a scroll)', 211
Zhengzhou 鄭州: ix, 12, 141, 143–72; Dianli Xuexiao 鄭州電力學校 (archaeological site), 156n35; Erligang 鄭州二里崗, 143n7, 159; expansion, 172n64; period, viii, 144, 159; inscriptions, 143–60; Shang City 鄭州商城 work station, 155–56; Water-Conservancy Works Office No. 1, 156
Zhenping 鎮平, 396, 397
zhēnrén 貞人 'diviner', 174n3
zhī 之 (particle), 228n40; 支 (cyclical signs) (see dìzhī 地支)
zhí 值 'value', 393n45
zhǐ 止 'foot', 'to stop', 92–93, 92n19, 93t3.5, 105t3.11, 106, 106n41, 107, 191
zhì 彘 'pig', 161, 163t4.3, 164, 168; 治 'to make', 'to regulate', 393n45; 置 'to place', 361; 質 'verdict', 287
"Zhihou lü" 置後律 ("Statutes on Establishing Heirs"), 365
zhíjì 執齊 'to alloy', 375
zhìzhōng 治中 'details of central importance in administration', 155–56n50
Zhong 衷, possible original name of Xici zhuan, 212n15
zhōng 中 'middle', 233, 396n50
zhǒng 冢. See thióng 冢
Zhong Cheng gui 仲爯簋 (JC 3747), 297
Zhong Ding 中丁, 78
Zhong Nong 中農, 290, 291–93
Zhong of Yueyang 櫟陽重, 380
"Zhonglao lü" 中勞律, 355n50
Zhongshan 中山, 335, 388–91; Cuo, King of 中山王䰜, 335; Jian, Prince of 中山簡王, 388; stones 388–91; Zhongshan Wang Cuo ding 中山王䰜鼎 (JC 2840), 335n95; Zhongshan Wang Cuo fanghu 中山王䰜方壺 (JC 9735), 264n52, 335
zhōngshàn 忠善 'loyalty and skillfulness at governing', 306n10
zhōngshǐ 中史 'central scribe', 286
Zhongzhoulu 中州路: viii, ix, 40f1.4
Zhou, temple of, 141n2, 167–68n55
Zhou artisan, 386t11.1
Zhou dynasty, 37–38, 39, 43, 44, 45; Eastern, 13, 241n6, 254, 257, 264,

266n61, 267, 268, 302–6, 308, 309–33, 335; Western, viii, 12–13, 14, 35, 39, 96, 141n2, 142–43n5, 158, 173, 239–70, 271–301, 304, 305, 307–9, 310–36, 340n3, 373, 374
Zhou kings, 241, 253, 254n28, 281, 283–84; court, 286, 287, 290, 297–98, 300, 304, 310, 335, 351
Zhou military campaign, 251
Zhou Mu Wang 周穆王, 152n25, 167–68n55, 248, 286
"Zhou songs" ("Zhou sòng" 周頌, *Book of Poetry*), 332–33
Zhou yi 周易 MSS, 212, 212n15
Zhou Zumo 周祖謨, 126n60
Zhougong 周公, 304, 306, 335; temple of, 141n2, 167–68n55
Zhouli 周禮, 169–70n61, 305, 343, 353, 355n50
Zhousheng 瑪生, 282, 283, 284; Zhousheng *gui* 瑪生簋, *see* Fifth and Sixth Year Zhousheng *gui* 五/六年瑪生簋
"Zhouyu" 周語 (*Tales of the States*), 40
Zhouyuan 周原: ix, 141n2
Zhu 宁 (diviner's name), 193, 195, 196
Zhu 邾, 297
zhū 豬 'pig', 105, 105n40, *105t3.11*
zhú 貯 'to sell, lease', 285n29; 逐 'to chase', 104–7, *105t3.11*
zhǔ 煮 'to boil (a person)', 171
zhù 鑄 'to cast (a metal object)', 375
Zhu Fenghan 朱鳳瀚, 294n32
Zhu Honglin 朱紅林, 354n42
zhú sānshí tián 貯卅田 'to offer thirty fields', 285
Zhu Shaohou 朱紹侯, 339n1
zhuànlì 篆隸 'hybrid small seal/clerical script', 221n27
zhūhóu 諸侯 'various warrior lords', 328n78
zhūshā 朱砂 'cinnabar', 233–34, 367
zhùyīn fúhào 注音符號 'Mandarin phonetic symbols', 103
zǐ 子 'child', 'son', (*dìzhī* #1), *32t1.1, 34t1.2*, 97, *97f3.1*, 179n20, 347n21

zì 字 'written graph', 'courtesy name', 340, 353, 354, 378; 自 'from', 'nose', 'oneself', *114t3.20*, 115
Zichan 子產, 167–68n55
Zifang 子方, 363
Zijingshan lu 紫荊山路, 156
zither, 353
zìzhān 自占, 357, 366–67
zoa-entomoid semantic component, 56n8
zodiograph (definition), 27
zōngjūn 宗君 'head of primary lineage', 283
zōngyí 宗彝 'sacrificial vessel', 321n53
zoomorphic designs, 294n42
zǒu 走 'to step' as character component, 323
Zoumalou 走馬樓, 367n93
zòuyàn shū 奏讞書 'case reported to the higher authorities', 356n52
zǔ 俎 'block' *and* 祖 'ancestor', 111, *112t3.16*
Zu Geng 祖庚 (king), 159, 159n43
Zu Jia 祖甲 (king), 159n43
Zu Xin 祖辛 (king), 166, 167
Zu Yi 祖乙 (king), 152, 166, 167, 169
zúmíng 族名 'lineage sign', 66n28
zūnqì 尊器 'sacrificial vessel', 297n51
zūnyí 尊彝 'sacrificial vessel', 295
zuǒ 佐 'to assist', 'assistant', 260, 325n71, 355; 左 'left', 260
zuò 作 'to make', 240n3; 坐 'to seat', 'to put (some spirit) in situ', 166, 167, 167n53
zuò bǎo zūn yí 作寶尊彝 'to make a sacrificial vessel', 292n38
zuò xué 作學 'to build a school', 178
zuòbāng 作邦 'to create the nation', 309
zuòcè yǐn 作冊尹 'chief document maker', 275, 275nn10–11, 276, 281. *See also* scribal groups
zuòshī 作詩 'to write songs', 316n38
Zuozhuan 左傳, 40, 88, 158n40, 167–68n55, 268, 269, 310n21, 316n38, 319, 321n53, 324, 330, 332, 332n89, 334, 335

www.ingramcontent.com/pod-product-compliance
Lightning Source LLC
Chambersburg PA
CBHW030559230426
43661CB00053B/1775